Reconceptualizing New Media and Intercultural Communication in a Networked Society

Nurhayat Bilge
Florida International University, USA

María Inés Marino
Florida International University, USA

A volume in the Advances in Linguistics and Communication Studies (ALCS) Book Series

IGI Global
DISSEMINATOR OF KNOWLEDGE

Published in the United States of America by
IGI Global
Information Science Reference (an imprint of IGI Global)
701 E. Chocolate Avenue
Hershey PA, USA 17033
Tel: 717-533-8845
Fax: 717-533-8661
E-mail: cust@igi-global.com
Web site: http://www.igi-global.com

Library of Congress Cataloging-in-Publication Data

Names: Bilge, Nurhayat, 1976- editor. | Marino, Maria Ines, 1974- editor.
Title: Reconceptualizing new media and intercultural communication in a networked society / Nurhayat Bilge and Maria Ines Marino, editors.
Description: Hershey, PA : Information Science Reference, [2018] | Includes bibliographical references.
Identifiers: LCCN 2017022529| ISBN 9781522537847 (hardcover) | ISBN 9781522537854 (ebook)
Subjects: LCSH: Intercultural communication. | Digital media. | Social media.
Classification: LCC HM1211 .R444 2018 | DDC 303.48/2--dc23 LC record available at https://lccn.loc.gov/2017022529

This book is published in the IGI Global book series Advances in Linguistics and Communication Studies (ALCS) (ISSN: 2372-109X; eISSN: 2372-1111)

British Cataloguing in Publication Data
A Cataloguing in Publication record for this book is available from the British Library.

All work contributed to this book is new, previously-unpublished material.
The views expressed in this book are those of the authors, but not necessarily of the publisher.

For electronic access to this publication, please contact: eresources@igi-global.com.

Advances in Linguistics and Communication Studies (ALCS) Book Series

ISSN:2372-109X
EISSN:2372-1111

Editor-in-Chief: Abigail G. Scheg, Western Governors University, USA

MISSION

The scope of language and communication is constantly changing as society evolves, new modes of communication are developed through technological advancement, and novel words enter our lexicon as the result of cultural change. Understanding how we communicate and use language is crucial in all industries and updated research is necessary in order to promote further knowledge in this field.

The **Advances in Linguistics and Communication Studies (ALCS)** book series presents the latest research in diverse topics relating to language and communication. Interdisciplinary in its coverage, ALCS presents comprehensive research on the use of language and communication in various industries including business, education, government, and healthcare.

COVERAGE

- Language Acquisition
- Youth Language
- Discourse Analysis
- Dialectology
- Media and Public Communications
- Computational linguistics
- Graphic Communications
- Interpersonal Communication
- Semantics
- Language in the Media

IGI Global is currently accepting manuscripts for publication within this series. To submit a proposal for a volume in this series, please contact our Acquisition Editors at Acquisitions@igi-global.com or visit: http://www.igi-global.com/publish/.

The Advances in Linguistics and Communication Studies (ALCS) Book Series (ISSN 2372-109X) is published by IGI Global, 701 E. Chocolate Avenue, Hershey, PA 17033-1240, USA, www.igi-global.com. This series is composed of titles available for purchase individually; each title is edited to be contextually exclusive from any other title within the series. For pricing and ordering information please visit http://www.igi-global.com/book-series/advances-linguistics-communication-studies/78950. Postmaster: Send all address changes to above address.

Titles in this Series

For a list of additional titles in this series, please visit:
https://www.igi-global.com/book-series/advances-linguistics-communication-studies/78950

Establishing and Evaluating Digital Ethos and Online Credibility
Moe Folk (Kutztown University of Pennsylvania, USA) and Shawn Apostel (Bellarmine Universit, USA)
Information Science Reference • ©2017 • 400pp • H/C (ISBN: 9781522510727) • US $200.00

Computational and Cognitive Approaches to Narratology
Takashi Ogata (Iwate Prefectural University, Japan) and Taisuke Akimoto (The University of Electoro-Communications,Japan)
Information Science Reference • ©2016 • 467pp • H/C (ISBN: 9781522504320) • US $215.00

Analyzing Language and Humor in Online Communication
Rotimi Taiwo (Obafemi Awolowo University, Nigeria) Akinola Odebunmi (University of Ibadan, Nigeria) and Akin Adetunji (Emmanuel Alayande College of Education, Nigeria)
Information Science Reference • ©2016 • 324pp • H/C (ISBN: 9781522503385) • US $185.00

Discourse Analysis as a Tool for Understanding Gender Identity, Representation, and...
Nazmunnessa Mahtab (University of Dhaka, Bangladesh) Sara Parker (John Moores University, UK) Farah Kabir (Action Aid, Bangladesh) Tania Haque (University of Dhaka, Bangladesh) Aditi Sabur (University of Dhaka, Bangladesh) and Abu Saleh Mohammad Sowad (University of Dhaka, Bangladesh)
Information Science Reference • ©2016 • 323pp • H/C (ISBN: 9781522502258) • US $185.00

Revealing Gender Inequalities and Perceptions in South Asian Countries through...
Nazmunnessa Mahtab (University of Dhaka, Bangladesh) Sara Parker (John Moores University, UK) Farah Kabir (Action Aid, Bangladesh) Tania Haque (University of Dhaka, Bangladesh) Aditi Sabur (University of Dhaka, Bangladesh) and Abu Saleh Mohammad Sowad (University of Dhaka, Bangladesh)
Information Science Reference • ©2016 • 286pp • H/C (ISBN: 9781522502791) • US $185.00

For an entire list of titles in this series, please visit:
https://www.igi-global.com/book-series/advances-linguistics-communication-studies/78950

IGI Global
DISSEMINATOR OF KNOWLEDGE

701 East Chocolate Avenue, Hershey, PA 17033, USA
Tel: 717-533-8845 x100 • Fax: 717-533-8661
E-Mail: cust@igi-global.com • www.igi-global.com

Editorial Advisory Board

Table of Contents

Detailed Table of Contents

This chapter focuses on how culture and the new media shape one's identity. While culture and one's family initially shape one's identity, the new media provide new ideas and lifestyles that influence one's identity. One's identity changes throughout one's lifespan, and the new media presents more information and alternative lifestyle choices for individuals. Identity itself is a complex concept and the self is viewed as the continuing, consistent narrative that one presents over one's lifetime and over different contexts. The new media enable people to develop online identities, and such identities may be authentic or inauthentic when compared to one's real life identity. The new media present different venues for developing and expressing one's self. The new media also enable individuals to maintain cultural and identity links with their home culture although they may have located elsewhere in the world.

Following the sociocultural traditions of communication, the authors explore the commonalities between Latané's dynamic social impact theory (DSIT), and the concepts of homophily and heterophily, and find that the markers of DSIT appear quite strikingly similar to the concepts similarity espoused by homophily (i.e., clustering, correlation, and consolidation), while the continuing diversity in DSIT is very similar to heterophily, which exists in groups and cultures. The authors test these concepts by analyzing two different blog conversations and find support to the above propositions. In the process, the authors suggest that social media should be retitled sociocultural media as this media aids in the creation and maintenance of cultures that coexist with those of differing viewpoints.

Since the term intercultural communication was first used by Edward T. Hall in 1959, more than half a century has passed, and the context of intercultural communication has gone through dramatic changes. With the advent of the internet and the digital media technologies, instructors can offer students computer-mediated intercultural

way broadcasting media or as audiencing participants in social media marketing. Potentially more interactive communication exists within a closed community, especially because Facebook has defining cultural, psychological, and psychosocial characteristics. Conflict message interactions facilitate studying the intersection of culture and conflict within a new media setting. This chapter focuses on conflict within the cultural context of Facebook closed communities, theorizes about this relationship, and tests its application.

Groupthink puts pressure on individuals to conform to social norms, but anonymity has been found to reduce or lessen such influence. Apart from anonymity, the significance of the topic and self-censorship may or may not contribute to the influence of groupthink. Groupthink has been studied in the context of social media using various approaches, but to date it remains unclear how much and to what extent it influences the conflict among users within this cultural context. This chapter describes approaches to studying the influence of groupthink on the users of an open social media platform (e.g., Twitter) and proposes a methodology for conducting a study. Using data from a selected hashtag, it reports on the application of theory to research, considers the role and influence of groupthink, and discusses the implications of the findings for reconceptualizing approaches to the study of new media.

This section presents chapters exploring the connection between culture and politics using new media, specifically focusing on political identities, political conflict, and communication of politics in the new media platform.

To study political identity construction, a thematic analysis is used to explore online reviews of the book Beating Obamacare. Themes that emerged construct four political identities relevant to the construction Obamacare, the American public, President

Obama and politicians, and those in opposition to Obamacare. The construction of these identities contributes to group vitality. This process is facilitated by the juxtaposition of the construction of the American public with those who oppose Obamacare versus politicians. Notably, this construction is accomplished with the near absence of reference to political party affiliation creating a realignment of political identity in a way that provides stronger group vitality than would be achieved across traditional partisan lines. This chapter has implications for understanding how identity is constructed online to demonstrate group vitality in ways that facilitate intracultural and intercultural communication.

Ping Yang, Millersville University, USA
Mito Ogawa, Millersville University, USA

New media studies have attracted increasing scholarly attention as communication technologies become integrated into our everyday lives. New media provide unique contexts to share, record, and extend civic life and motivate civic commitment in the digital era. This chapter addresses the intersection of new media, culture, and political communication by exploring youths' civic engagement in China and Japan through individual voluntarism, civic participation, and political activism. It interrogates the civic use of social network sites in the digital age so as to increase our understanding of intercultural online interactions. Through the case studies of China and Japan, this research adds to the knowledge of intercultural communication in the networked society, with its potential to promote more democratic forms of engagement between citizens and states in the contexts of new media.

Wei Sun, Howard University, USA

Political communication in the digital age has brought new insights and challenges to American citizens across parties, genders, and ethnicity. The 2016 Presidential election has drawn global attention just as previous US presidential campaigns. Moreover, with two opposing and controversial candidates for the presidency, voters are divided across a wide range of issues. This chapter is interested in various minority women for Trump campaigns on social media sites, in the time frame when Trump's lewd comments about women were made headlines before the third Presidential Debate until Election Day. Selective and sampled posts from Facebook, Twitter, and Instagram are analyzed. How did minority women position themselves in Trump's campaign on social media discourse? How did minority women make decisions

Preface

WHY THE NEED?

During the past two decades, two major events have revolutionized our cultures and our communication: Globalization and New Media. Both events call for a deeper global view and an exhaustive and revolutionary analyses of the transformation we have been gestating and developing, as a culture, as individuals, and as citizens.

First, globalization, culture, and communication intermingle and are interconnected, altering each other (Chen & Dai, 2014). Globalization has impacted communication in significant and complex ways through the opening of ever-changing channels of information that expand and reinvent without limits through new media. At the same time, communication has driven and facilitated globalization while transforming cultural identities, establishing governmental structures through mass media, and individual identities (Chen, 2012; Başaran Ince, 2014; Bouvier, 2012; Giddens, 1990, 1991, 2000; Haslett, 2014). These changes brought about by the on-going transformative way of communicating through new media call for a compromise with a deeper understanding of the shapes of fresh reality that affects the development and maintenance of culture and identity. A profound analysis of the dynamics of how these changes influence the way we act is necessary (Foti & Ring. 2000). There is a need to rewire and revolutionize our views to think and act as global citizens.

Second, new media shapes the vital dynamics of everyday interactions within the political, interpersonal, and cultural contexts (Thumim, 2012; Zhang & Prosser, 2012), in positive and negative ways. The new features have helped to mingle the private and the public within co-existing spaces through a combination of mass media with tools of personal social media, and consequently modify the processes of socializing and display of identity (Gunn & Thumim, 2012; Ksiazek et al, 2010). The impact of new media continuously brings questions of credibility and balance on the power of information, evolutionary structures of culture and cultural identity, emergence of new paradigms and challenges in communication, and the ability and capacity to enhance and advance intercultural communication (Chen, 2012; Başaran Ince, 2014; Giddens, 2000; Pflug, 2011; Shuter, 2012).

This book is a production of the discipline of intercultural communication which aims to bridge intercultural communication research with emerging new media studies. The intent is to address an existing gap in knowledge. Even though new media has significantly and continuously impacted our lives in general, and specifically in the way we communicate, relate to others, and build our individual and cultural identities, there are scattered studies on the connection between new media and the implications for intercultural communication (Cheong, Martin, & MacFadyen, 2012; Pflug, 2011; Shuter, 2012). Researchers have called attention to the need for an emphasis on "intercultural new media research that takes a socio-cultural perspective" (Shuter, 2010, p. 231).

The design of each chapter comprises current research on challenges of new media supported by top-notch scholarly studies and theories related to each covered context, by exploring the real causes and effects of new media and how it impinges on culture and intercultural communication. The topics address the need to reconceptualize perspectives to expand and advance thought towards the creation of intercultural environments that inclusively support and advance interactions within new media paradigms. In addition, recommendations and solutions will be offered.

Finally, this book is significant because it will facilitate deep root analysis, providing the necessary power to research the relationships between culture and new media through a positive, effective, and transformational analysis that brings both fields together. While this book touches upon various areas of new media and intercultural communication, our book has a unique focus, which highlights identity and conflict while providing a comprehensive examination of intercultural interactions and conflict in different contexts.

Herein we address a national and global need for furthering a scientific understanding of complex connections among culture, identity, and new media.

NEW MEDIA AND COMMUNICATION

Communication focuses on social interactions and how people use messages to generate and share meaning across contexts, cultures, media, and channels (Samovar et al., 2010). Due to the diverse cultural backgrounds and challenges represented by the new media environments, globalization adds to the debate about how current research informs our experiences to provide more inclusive and integrative approaches that address the needs of the present constantly-transforming context. In new media, globalization conveys culture as a main source of diversity, bringing to the communication process contrasting worldviews that can be compared, contrasted, and aligned. This dialectic interaction involves negotiation meaning and dissonance as strong skills to advance our experiences through by processing other cultural perspectives, immersing them in deeper critical thinking. This then leads to the advancement of knowledge and cognitive flexibility (Chan & Chan, 2011; Knutson, 2003; Kreijns, 2003; Scardamalia, 2003).

First, new media has changed the dynamics, the structure, and the goals of how we communicate and interact, from how we have changed our face-to-face behavior in everyday interactions to how political debates are conceived. Addressing the changes and challenges that new media imposes has become a primary need and alleviates the boundaries imposed by the medium. For example, the private and public communicative contexts intermingle through new media, transforming the communication process and its functioning. The medium is crucial in the functioning of the communication process (Başaran Ince, 2014). Its structure, components, and effects define and redirect the construction of meaning and perceptions built from the interactions and experiences arising from the interchangeability of contextual cues, cultural backgrounds, and social expectations.

Second, new media revolutionizes communication by opening channels to immediately connect to other cultures. Consequently, participants are automatically incorporated into new cultural paradigms, expectations, and norms. This reshapes the fundamental and distinct characteristics of the modern communication process into a postmodern process characterized by interactivity, connectiveness, instantaneity, mobility, recurrence, and flexibility. The use of global communications enables the ability to build a new layer in how we communicate and engage in interactions (Basaran Ince, 2014; Castells, 2004). New media self-expands the communication process by adding complexity and constantly recombines adjourned and recurrent styles with new and constantly changing possibilities, options, views (Castells, 2004).

Third, according to researchers, new media combines transmission links and artificial memories with the capability of empowering users as active content producers instead of passive recipients of information, transforming communication by the absence of time and space limitations (Bruns, 2005; Başaran Ince, 2014; Castells, 2010; Dijk, 2012; Jenkins, 2007; Lister, 2006, Manovich 2001; Aitchison & Lewis 2006; Logan, 2010). Researchers refer to new media as rootless due to the absence of time and space. This enables social media to function at its fullest in a way which allows users to constantly reinvent and mediate communication between traditional and new media horizons (Başaran Ince, 2014; Candau, 1998; Castells, 2016). This also generates new questions about how identity is formed and maintained by and within culture and the effects of openness, flexibility, and the mutating nature of new media.

Fourth, researchers point out the need to consider accessibility limitations. New media has not reached all societies at the same level of access, and therefore, it is essential to question how the imbalance of global access to information (Başaran Ince, 2014; Wunnava & Leiter, 2009) affects communication. Questioning, analyzing, and interpreting new media among different cultures is essential to understanding how information is distributed for control and power effects over the communication process.

Fifth, researchers focus on how twenty-first century changes in technology have impacted all aspects of our culture and societies (Devran, 2010). Overall, the constant nature of evolving, changing, and redefining of new media helps to develop a discussion of intercultural communication as the basis for socializing and building identity from the debate of being versus existence (Başaran Ince, 2014; Castells, 2016).

Finally, intercultural communication is a well-established discipline exploring the delicate relationship between culture and communication. Culture is a learned process of perceptions, values, and behavior. Communication is key to the process of culture, since the way we communicate and how we understand communication exists hand-in-hand with contextual and cultural factors (Hall, 1973, 1977, 1990; Jaldemark, 2008; Yang et al., 2010). In other words, our culture teaches us how to communicate with others, what to pay attention to, and how to interpret messages when we communicate. Consequently, cultural differences have an impact on the way people participate in society in various contexts, contemporarily in new media spheres. These differences could create unique opportunities and challenges, becoming even more important given the impact of new media in today's increasingly globalized society.

Given the complexity of the challenges brought about by the alliance between new media and intercultural communication, there is a challenge to embrace new structures of engagement, involvement, and responsibility. Each topic is equipped with the most updated research to enhance understanding of today's communicative challenges imposed by the transformative aspects of new media, and by providing the necessary information as guidance to engage, participate in, and interact in ways that are more meaningful to each cultural profile while helping them develop success in new media environments (Scardamalia & Bereiter, 1993, 1996, 2003).

In sum, new media, as the transformative actor of intercultural communication, imposes critical questions that aim to analyze the connection between intercultural communication and new media. The intent is to adequately determine and explain intercultural communication patterns and variations, challenges, and limitations in cultural identity formation and conflict resolution.

NEW MEDIA AND CULTURE

In 2012, Robert Shuter proposed "a new field of inquiry called Intercultural New Media Studies (INMS)" (Shuter, 2012, p. 220), through which the author expressed a need for intercultural communication research to explore new media. This field represents not only an additional aspect of contemporary communication, but an organic and dynamic component of culture and communication, which presents the symbiotic influence of both. According to Shuter (2012, p. 230) "culture and new media are conjoined. Not only does culture affect the social uses of new media, but new media appears to change culture."

In his proposal, Shuter (2012) points out that intercultural communication, as a field, needs to examine the way culture impacts social media, and concurrently questions the way social media affects culture. Moreover, the author identifies five key intercultural communication concepts as areas of interest for Intercultural New Media Studies. These concepts, or areas of study, are: cultural identity, intercultural dialogue, third culture, acculturation, and intercultural competence (Shuter, 2012, p. 212). Many scholars followed Shuter's initiative and research exploring the mutual influence and affect between culture and new media has grown extensively since.

Culture is a socially constructed process, which consists of a set of values, beliefs, and practices that are shared by its members (Applegate & Sypher, 1988). Culture "emerges in social interaction" (Hecht, Collier & Ribeau, 2003, p. 29) and through this interaction presents a unique identity (Orbe & Harris, 2001). As members of cultural groups, we all communicate through a cultural lens and perform our cultural identities accordingly. Hence, our communicative practices reflect our cultural groups. Furthermore, as our culture alters through time and interaction with different cultural groups, so do our communicative practices. As Shuter, Cheong, & Chen (2016, p. 172) explain "cultural values are foundational to communicative behavior," which consequently impacts communication and behavior, including that in the new media platform.

Furthermore, the mutual influence of culture and new media, as scholars articulate, indicates a reverse effect in the connection between culture and communication. As our communicative practices alter, they also help shape the culture in new ways. As Chen (2012) explains:

New media not only influences the form and content of information/messages, but it also affects how people understand each other in the process of human communication, especially for those from different cultural or ethnic groups. (p. 2)

Thus, media is a cultural product. But it also helps shape culture and our communication. Wu and Li (2016) state that, as new media progresses and becomes a more integral part of our cultural configuration, it alters our core communication practices. We increasingly live in a networked society, which impacts "the overall dimension of human relations including the production relations, consumption, reproduction and power" (Basaran Ince, 2014, p. 13), influencing the very nature of our cultural structure. As a result, people rely on new media for more than an information exchange; they also utilize it for forming and performing their identities. Therefore, new media establishes new communicative practices, such as texting, social media use, and virtual communication. Yet, more importantly, new media also shapes "unheralded methods of identity, community, and culture formation" (Loehwing & Motter, 2012, p. 36). As Wu and Li (2016) argue:

People rely heavily on new media to share information and feelings, to construct and present identities, to build and maintain social relationships and form speech communities, which all point to the need and significance of further exploration and advancement in new media communication across cultures. (p. 25)

Research regarding media and culture has been prominent for decades. But early research focused on technology as a medium for communication and progressed in time to include the relationship between culture and media. Shuter (2012) presented a new and focused direction to scholarship regarding new media and culture. Scholars, such as Chen (2012), Croucher (2011), Ingraham and Reeves (2016), and Loehwing and Motter (2012) enhanced our understanding of new media and culture through their work.

New media empowers people by empowering reachability and inclusivity (Chen, 2012). Through new media, more people take part in creating and disseminating messages, which used to be "a privilege possessed only by church, state, and government" (Chen, 2012, p. 1). Power is a central concept for communication scholarship (Loehwing & Motter, 2012). Through new media, there is more empowerment and equalization of power, which influences not only power dynamics but also how power is perceived within the society (Loehwing & Motter, 2012). Marginalized groups, immigrants and/or refugees, minorities, and social outliers have an opportunity to participate in message construction and dissemination; therefore, these groups have an opportunity to change the discourse and shape cultural perceptions. New media was utilized for political discourse for various polarizing issues, such as the Arab Spring, which resulted in political change in various North African and Middle Eastern countries. Other areas where social media played a prominent role included the Black Lives Matter movement, which aimed to reduce the imbalance of power and racism against African Americans, and the Me Too campaign, which focused on raising awareness regarding sexual assault and harassment.

Concurrently, we need to consider new social dynamics that result in a shift in power and social practices. Ingraham and Reeves (2016, p. 456) explored the effects of public panic and public shaming in the new media age. Shaming individuals or groups, according to the authors, is easier than ever as a result of new media, more specifically social media. On the one hand, the ease of information dissemination and access to this information helps empower victims, raise awareness, and evoke change. Instead of state officials and corporate mass media being the authorities "once needed to produce and prosecute moral panics, citizens today have acquired an unprecedented capacity to independently investigate, judge, and punish their peers for moral infractions." On the other hand, ease of information dissemination is accompanied by ease of misinformation and bias. Therefore, in terms of power, who disseminates information and to what extent, are still relevant questions that need further exploration.

Shifting power dynamics and cultural identification impacts intercultural communication for both in-group and cross-cultural interactions. In terms of in-group communication, new media presents ways of reinforcing cultural identities and establishing strong ties between cultural group members, which also influences individuals' communication cross-culturally. Croucher (2011) explored this phenomenon further by examining cultural adaptation and new media. The author explained the significant impact social networking has on cultural adaptation of immigrants. According to Croucher, social network utilization directly influences immigrants' perception of the host culture, and consequently, it also influences communication by newcomers with members of the host culture. Furthermore, the author explains that, as immigrants adapt to their new cultural surroundings, social media becomes a way to reconnect with their original culture, reinforce their identity, and "retro-acculturate" (p. 262). As a result, Croucher offers two propositions:

P1: During cultural adaptation, the use of social networking sites affects immigrants' interactions with the dominant culture (Croucher, 2011, p. 261)

P2: During cultural adaptation, the use of social networking sites will affect immigrants' in-group communication (Croucher, 2011, p. 262)

The propositions put forth by Croucher (2011) and the focus areas offered by Shuter (2012) all demonstrate the significance of furthering scholarship on the mutual influence of culture and new media. Communication is not only a tool, but represents the process through which both culture and new media are established, shaped, and renegotiated. Hence all three concepts, communication, culture, and new media, are intertwined and interconnected. As Shuter (2012) explains, there is an immense need to explore these concepts and their connections to one another from a socio-cultural perspective. More specifically, the author identifies the need to:

Develop, refine or extend cultural theories of new media communication including, but not limited to, cultural values and the social uses of new media, co-cultural theory and new media behavior, and socio-cultural factors and cultural preferences of new media platforms (Shuter, 2012, p. 231)

This book is aimed at building upon the work of the aforementioned scholars and their call for a cultural perspective to study new media and communication. Our approach to communication, culture, and new media aims to explore the connection between these concepts in four distinct, yet related, areas: community, identity, conflict, and politics.

RECONCEPTUALIZING NEW MEDIA AND INTERCULTURAL COMMUNICATION IN A NETWORKED SOCIETY

This book offers a collection of contributions, which explored the connection between culture and new media from an intercultural communication perspective. A common thread is interwoven through these chapters, thanks to our authors from different countries with varied expertise. The authors provide a variety of contexts and frameworks which allowed us to present a rich and thorough compilation of perspectives.

As explained above, the book is divided into four sections. The first section – New Media, Culture, and Community – presents chapters exploring the connection between culture and community using new media, specifically focusing on establishing communities, maintaining communities and communal identities in the new media platform. Nurhayat Bilge examines the influence of social media on ethnic identity preservation, focusing on displaced communities. Kevin Wang explores online media consumption among Asian Americans, focusing on acculturation and enculturation. Sean Sadri offers insight into the millennial culture by examining the group's media habits and questioning the concept of media credibility.

The second section – New Media, Culture, and Identity – deals with the connection between culture and identity using new media, specifically focusing on identity negotiation, construction/reconstruction of identity, and communicating identities in the new media platform. Beth Haslett offers an extensive, in-depth exploration of the connection between identity, culture, and new media through the very foundation of theories upon which intercultural new media scholarship is built. Binod Sundararajan and Elizabeth Tetzlaff examine dynamic social impact theory in connection with heterophily and homophily within the new media platform. Sachiyo Shearman and Mariko Eguchi explore the connection between culture and new media through the use of new media in intercultural communication classes. Additionally, Anna Klyueva examines the concept of "saving face" within the contemporary communication practices of new media.

The third section – New Media, Culture, and Conflict – presents chapters exploring the connection between culture and conflict using new media, specifically focusing on conflict formation, conflict management, and conflict resolution. Amy Janan Johnson, Sun Kyong Lee, Iona A. Cionia, and Zachary B. Massey initiate the section with their thought-provoking work examining the benefits and challenges of new media on intercultural conflict. Godfrey Steele's solo-authored chapter explores culture and conflict in new media by focusing on Facebook communication. Additionally his chapter, co-authored with Niekitta Zephyrine, offers further insight into culture and conflict through the concept of groupthink in Twitter.

The fourth and final section – New Media, Culture, and Politics and Policies – presents chapters exploring the connection between culture and politics using new media, specifically focusing on political identities, political conflict, and communication of politics in the new media platform. The section starts with Anastacia Kurylo's work examining culture and political identity, where the author collates concepts of culture, community, and identity in connection with political perspectives. Ping Yang follows with her work exploring civic engagement of youth in China through social networks. Wei Sun examines political campaigns on social media, focusing on the group "Minority Women for Trump." The final chapter of the section, and the book, by Maria Elena Villar and Elizabeth Marsh, demonstrate unique challenges and benefits of new media, focusing on perceptions and policies regarding infectious diseases.

Our contributors offer diverse perceptions and approaches to exploring new media and culture from an intercultural communication perspective. We rely on research pioneered by scholars, who shaped this area of study. New media and culture are intertwined concepts. Our aim is to explore their mutual influence and help further scholarly understanding, upon which future studies can build.

Nurhayat Bilge
Florida International University, USA

Maria Ines Marino
Florida International University, USA

REFERENCES

Aitchison, J., & Lewis, D. (Eds.). (2006). New Media Language. London: Routledge.

Applegate, J. L., & Sypher, H. E. (1988). A constructivist theory of communication and culture. In Y. Y. Kim & W. B. Gudykunst (Eds.), *Theories in intercultural communication* (pp. 41–65). Newbury Park, CA: Sage.

Baron, N. S., & Segerstad, Y. A. F. (2010). Cross-cultural patterns in mobile-phone use: Public space and reachability in Sweden, the USA and Japan. *New Media & Society*, *12*(1), 13–34. doi:10.1177/1461444809355111

Basaran Ince, G. (2014). Digital Culture, New Media, and The Transformation of Collective Memory. *Iletisim*, *21*, 9–29.

Bouvier, G. (2012). How Facebook users select identity categories for self-presentation. *Journal of Multicultural Discourses*, *7*(1), 37–57. doi:10.1080/17447143.2011.652781

Bruns, A. (2005). *Gatewatching. Collaborative Online News Production*. New York: Peter Lang Publishing.

Campbell, S. W. (2007). A cross-cultural comparison of perceptions and uses of mobile telephony. *New Media & Society*, *9*(2), 343–363. doi:10.1177/1461444807075016

Candau, J. (1998). *Mémoire et Identité*. Paris: Presses Universtaires de France.

Castells, M. (2004). Informationalism, Networks and the Network Society: A Theoretical Blueprint. In The Network Society, A Cross-cultural Perspective. Edward Elgar Publishing. doi:10.4337/9781845421663.00010

Castells, M. (2010). *The Rise of the Network Society*. Wiley Blackwell Publishing.

Chang, T., & Lim, J. (2002). Cross-cultural communication and social presence in asynchronous learning processes. *e-Service Journal*, *1*(3), 83–105.

Chen, G. M. (2012). The impact of new media on intercultural communication in global context. *China Media Research*, *8*(2), 1–10.

Chen, G. M., & Dai, X.-d. (2014). New media and asymmetry in cultural identity negotiation. In P. H. Cheong, J. N. Martin, & L. Macfadyen (Eds.), *New media and intercultural communication: Identity, community and politics* (pp. 123–138). New York, NY: Peter Lang.

Cheong, P. H. Martin. J. N., & Macfadyen, L. (Eds.). (2012). New media and intercultural communication: Identity, community and politics. New York, NY: Peter Lang.

Clothier, I. M. (2005). Created identities: Hybrid cultures and the internet. *Convergence (London), 11*(4), 44–59. doi:10.1177//1354856505061053

Croucher, S. M. (2011). Social networking and cultural adaptation: A theoretical model. *Journal of International and Intercultural Communication, 4*(4), 259–264. doi:10.1080/17513057.2011.598046

Dijk, J. V. (2007). *Mediated Memories in the Digital Age*. Stanford University Press.

Dijk, J. V. (2012). *The Network Society*. London: Sage Publications.

Foti, S., & Ring, G. (2000). Portfolios: Beyond Assessment. *Teaching and Learning: The Journal of Natural Inquiry, 14*(2), 18–22.

Ganesh, S., & Holmes, P. (2011). Positioning intercultural dialogue – theories, pragmatics, and an agenda. *Journal of International and Intercultural Communication, 4*(2), 81–86. doi:10.1080/17513057.2011.557482

Giddens, A. (1990). *The consequences of modernity*. Cambridge, MA: Polity Press.

Giddens, A. (1991). *Modernity and self-identity: Self and society in the late modern age*. Cambridge, UK: Polity Press.

Giddens, A. (2003). *The runaway world*. New York, NY: Routledge.

Gunn, S.E. & Thumim, N. (2012). Socializing and self-representation online: Exploring Facebook. *Observatorio Journal, 6*(1), 87-105. doi: 1646-5954/ERC123483/2012 087

Hall, E. (1973). *The silent language*. Garden City, NY: Doubleday.

Hall, E. (1977). *Beyond culture*. Garden City, NY: Doubleday.

Hall, E. (1990). *Understanding cultural differences: Germans, French, and Americans*. Yarmouth, ME: Intercultural Press.

Haslett, B. (2014). Social media, communication and culture. In C. Litang & M. Prosser (Eds.), *Social media in Asia*. Lake Oswego, OR: Dignity Press.

Hecht, M. L., Collier, M. J., & Ribeau, S. A. (2003). *African American Communication: Exploring Identity and Culture*. Mahwah, NJ: Lawrence Erlbaum Associates.

Ingraham, C., & Reeves, J. (2016). New media, new panics. *Critical Studies in Media Communication, 33*(5), 455–467. doi:10.1080/15295036.2016.1227863

Jaldemark, J. (2008). Participation and genres of communication in online settings of higher education. *Education and Information Technologies, 13*(2), 129–146. doi:10.1007/s10639-008-9057-9

Jenkins, H. (2006). *Convergence Culture: Where Old and new media Collide*. New York: New York University Press.

Knutson, T., Komolsevin, R., Chatiketu, P., & Smith, V. (2003). A cross-cultural comparison of Thai and US American rhetorical sensitivity: Implications for intercultural communication effectiveness. *International Journal of Intercultural Relations*, *27*(1), 63–78. doi:10.1016/S0147-1767(02)00060-3

Koc, M. (2006). Cultural identity crisis in the age of globalization and technology. *The Turkish Online Journal of Educational Technology*, *5*, 37–43.

Kreijns, K., Kirschner, P., & Jochems, W. (2003). Identifying the pitfalls for social interaction in computer-supported collaborative learning environments: A review of the research. *Computers in Human Behavior*, *19*(3), 335–353. doi:10.1016/S0747-5632(02)00057-2

Ksiazek, T. B., Malthouse, E. C., & Webster, J. G. (2010). News-seekers and Avoiders: Exploring Patterns of Total News Consumption Across Media and the Relationship to Civic Participation. *Journal of Broadcasting & Electronic Media*, *54*(4), 551–568. doi:10.1080/08838151.2010.519808

Lin, J., Peng, W., Kim, M., Kim, S., & LaRose, R. (2012). Social networking and adjustments among international students. *New Media & Society*, *14*(3), 421–440. doi:10.1177/1461444811418627

M. Lister, J. Dovey, S. Giddings, I. Grant, & K. Kelly (Eds.). (2009). *New Media: A Critical Introduction* (2nd ed.). London: Routledge.

Loehwing, M., & Motter, J. (2012). Utilizing co-cultures & counterpublics in Intercultural new media research. *China Media Research*, *8*, 29–38.

Logan, R. K. (2010). *Understanding New Media, Extending Marshall McLuhan*. Peter Lang Publishing.

Manovich, L. (2001). *The Language of New Media*. London: The MIT Press.

Neagu, A. a., Pavaloiu, B. k., & Mateescu, L. M. (2017). Social media and virtual platforms facilitators for intercultural dialogue. *E-learning & Software for Education, 2,* 502-508. doi:10.12753/2066-026X-17-156

Orbe, M., & Harris, T. M. (2001). *Interracial communication: Theory into practice*. Belmont, CA: Wadsworth.

Pflug, J. (2011). Contextuality and computer-mediated communication: A cross cultural comparison. *Computers in Human Behavior*, *27*(1), 131–137. doi:10.1016/j.chb.2009.10.008

Scardamalia, M., & Bereiter, C. (2003). Knowledge building. In J. W. Guthrie (Ed.), *Encyclopedia of education* (pp. 1370–1373). New York: McMillan.

Scardamalia, M., & Bereiter, C. (2010). A brief history of knowledge building. *Canadian Journal of Learning and Technology*, *36*(1), 1–16. doi:10.21432/T2859M

Schroeder, R. (2010). Mobile phones and the inexorable advance of multimodal connectedness. *New Media & Society*, *12*(1), 75–90. doi:10.1177/1461444809355114

Shuter, R. (2011). Introduction: New media across cultures—prospect and promise. *Journal of International and Intercultural Communication*, *4*(4), 241–245. doi:10.1080/17513057.2011.598041

Shuter, R. (2012a). When Indian women text message: Culture, identity, and emerging interpersonal norms of new media. In P. H. Cheong, J. N. Martin, & L. Macfadyen (Eds.), *New media and intercultural communication: Identity, community and politics* (pp. 209–222). New York, NY: Peter Lang.

Shuter, R. (2012b). Intercultural New Media Studies: The Next Frontier in Intercultural Communication. *Journal of Intercultural Communication Research*, *41*(3), 219–237. doi:10.1080/17475759.2012.728761

Shuter, R., Cheong, P., & Chen, Y. (2016). The influence of cultural values on U.S. and Danish students' digital behavior: Exploring culture, new media, and social context. *Journal of International and Intercultural Communication*, *9*(2), 161–178. doi:10.1080/17513057.2016.1154183

Singh, C. (2010). New media and cultural identity. *China Media Research*, *6*(1), 86–90.

Thumim, N. (2012). Socializing and self-representation online: Exploring Facebook. *Observatorio Journal*, *6*(1), 087-105. doi: 1646-5954/ERC123483/2012087

Wu, D. D., & Li, C. (2016). Sociolinguistic approaches for intercultural new media studies. *Intercultural Communication Studies*, *21*, 14–31.

Wunnava, P. V., & Leiter, D. B. (2009). Determinants of Intercountry Internet Diffusion Rates. *American Journal of Economics and Sociology*, *68*(2), 413–426. doi:10.1111/j.1536-7150.2009.00634.x

Yang, D., Olesova, L., & Richardson, J. (2010). Impact of cultural differences on students' participation, communication, and learning in an online environment. *Journal of Educational Computing Research*, *43*(2), 165–182. doi:10.2190/EC.43.2.b

Zhang, S., & Prosser, M. (2012). Globalization, Asian modernity, values and Chinese civil society. *Chinese Media Research*, *8*, 18–25.

Acknowledgment

The editors would like to acknowledge the help of all the people involved in this project and, more specifically, to the authors and reviewers that took part in the review process. Without their support, this book would not have become a reality.

First, the editors would like to thank each one of the authors for their contributions. Our sincere gratitude goes to the chapter's authors who contributed their time and expertise to this book.

Second, the editors wish to acknowledge the valuable contributions of the reviewers regarding the improvement of quality, coherence, and content presentation of chapters. Most of the authors also served as referees; we highly appreciate their double task.

Nurhayat Bilge
Florida International University, USA

Maria Ines Marino
Florida International University, USA

Introduction

CONTESTATIONS AND CHALLENGES FOR CULTURE AND COMMUNICATION IN THE DIGITAL ERA

Scholars see new communications media and technologies as contentious topics embodying various layers of power[1] that can influence society and culture in diverse ways. New media and technology are thought to empower users (Benkler, 2006; Negroponte, 1996), enable more freedom and liberate people from various forms of oppression (Jones, 1998), as well as allow users to take power away from media and other institutions (Rezabakhsh et al., 2006; Shapiro, 1999). Facebook CEO Mark Zuckerberg recently envisioned new media as being able to lift the world out of poverty (Garcia, 2015). Others see new media and technology as unable to transcend traditional inequities and class-relations (Schiller, 1995, 2014; Turow, 2011), and instead reinforce preexisting power-related imbalances (Turow, 2011). In other words, new media and technology are likely to be subordinated under political and economic systems (Dyer-Witheford, 1999), and therefore exist within the political economy's chief developmental process (Schiller, 2014). With information rapidly becoming the currency of the digital era, Mayer-Schonberger (2009, p. 107) wonders if the redistribution of information power "from the powerless to the powerful" within this system will enable governments and private entities to further advance their own interests.

This essay explores several connections and contentions between 'new media'[2] and culture through the lens of power. It identifies antagonisms within four areas that present challenges for communication and culture scholarship during the digital era. Specifically, it focuses on how power intersects with the ownership of new media-related technologies, personal identity, political culture, and the culture and creative industries (CCI).[3] While there are many other areas that contribute to understanding new media technologies and power, these four areas have particular importance due to their influence on self-expression, the cultivation of ideas and the creation of a vibrant public commons essential to the maintenance of participatory democracy.

Ownership

The 1996 U.S. Telecommunications Act, largely written by industry, helped develop telecommunications, internet access and information services in the U.S., while serving as a model for liberalizing telecommunication markets worldwide (Winseck, 2016). The result of private ownership over new media technologies and the internet has had several consequences. While it has helped users share information and more easily create cultural goods, it has also established an extremely concentrated and in many cases, uncompetitive commercial structure. This structure has also evolved into creating one of the most effective surveillance apparatuses in the history of the world that anoints owners with the power to accept or censor online content. Connecting the cultural and interpersonal implications of this structure poses significant challenge.

Private ownership of new technologies and the internet have enabled users to communicate and share diverse information and creative productions mostly for free through social media. This has allowed many people to express themselves online in ways never thought before, as well as enabled many individuals and small businesses to enter online entrepreneurship arrangements. These aspects are important and beneficial at a time when the quality and quantity of journalism coming from news organizations has been challenged, partially as a result of the disruptive nature of new technologies and the financial market drop of 2009.

However, in the internet's relatively short lifespan, new media and technology companies soon reached levels of concentration not seen since the Guilded Age (McChesney, 2013). The Big 5 new tech corporations: Alphabet Inc, Amazon, Ebay, Facebook and Apple exist in monopolistic or oligopolistic markets, and are worth a collective $2.9 trillion. They also earned a combined $555 billion in revenue during 2016 (Desjardins, 2017). For comparative purposes, if the Big 5 companies were a country, that country would have the 10th largest revenue in the world, right behind Canada. Alphabet Inc, which owns Google, controls 70% of the search engine market and 97% of the mobile search market. Amazon sells the vast majority of online books, while Microsoft continues to be used on 90% of all computers. Ebay and Facebook have monopolistic power while the many Apple products like iTunes and the iPad dominate their markets (McChesney, 2013). Apple and Microsoft, like other new technology firms are spending significant money acquiring patents from other companies, litigation and lobbying than on research and development, which suggests their main goal is to lock down their domination by preventing competition (Reich, 2015). They have become quite successful at this. This Telecommunications, Media and Technology (TMT) sector has enriched forty-six out of the 200 wealthiest people in the world, with half of them in the top 10, while thirteen of the top-thirty U.S. corporations are also from digital or internet related industries (Information

Observatory, 2016; McChesney, 2013). Their goal is to keep power and control over the online world. A lack of competition creates a disproportionate economic and market advantage that can create barriers of entry for new companies, slow innovation, as well as increase prices for consumers.

Control over access to culture and information through the internet is also contested. The small contingency of website owners like Youtube and Facebook who surveil users, as well as decide what is and is not appropriate to express online questions constitutional values of privacy and free expression (Slobogin, 2011; Wu, 2011). For example, Facebook recently censored the following items: a Pulitzer price-winning Vietnam war image titled "Napalm Girl," a photo showing an Italian public statue of the Roman sea god Neptune, as well as the sale of Christmas cards featuring a robin redbreast bird (Bennett, 2017). The collusion between government pressure to censor information and private ownership over search engines like Google and websites like Youtube has given more power to these companies over privacy and free speech than presidents and kings (Rosen, 2011). Towards the end of 2017, U.S. Republicans and communications companies were working to further empower their ability to control the internet by eliminating the digital common carriage regulation of Net Neutrality during the Trump administration. If this is accomplished, corporate owners will be able filter out content they disagree with, as well as slow down site speeds of their choosing without consequences. These groups are rarely if ever interested in expanding public media and are more keen on consolidating corporate media than in diversifying media ownership.

Private ownership of the internet has also established the largest surveillance system in history. While not driven by public decision-making processes, the overarching goal the online infrastructure is to gather consumer data in order to further enable the sales effort (McChesney, 2013). The purpose of many of these companies is not to democratize communications and allow grassroots culture to flourish, but to extract as much capital as possible either by the capturing and selling of online user data through surveillance, or by the sale of electronic items that allow the capture of this information. In addition, online surveillance, data collection and pricing seem to function most efficiently under monopolistic and oligopolistic conditions. The incredibly profitable new industry in data mining has as its main purpose the goal to better persuade and influence individual online purchase decisions (Turow, 2011). At this stage, U.S. law does not enable citizens with the ability find out what companies know about them, meaning companies do not have to legally disclose this information (Ball, 2012).

Individualized Content, Political and Interpersonal Communication

There is a need to further examine the relationship between the individualized nature of the internet, political communication and interpersonal communication. Data mining, individualized content and online advertising have the ability to influence perspectives and can be used to manipulate information outside of commercial causes. Scholars suggest the individualized nature of the internet can result in the creation of idea cocoons, or internet filter bubbles, where online users are fragmented in their understanding of the world and largely stuck in their own information perspectives (Pariser, 2012). This individualized system is thought to limit exposure to different world views while creating less empathy and understanding for people of different cultures, races and perspectives (Kolko & Reid, 1998; Sunstein, 2001; Turow, 1997). This fragmentation can harm the creation of a potential online public sphere, which requires interpersonal communication with diverse users as an underlying tenant of democracy (Splichal, 2009).

Moreover, new media technologies, especially social media, have propagated individualized content much more efficiently than traditional mass media. Social media can easily be manipulated with political misinformation. Messages can be repeated from multiple users, a small number of users can create the majority of messages about an issue, while many messages can come from people and/or areas that aren't even experiencing the issue (Fisher, 2010). In addition, governments or individuals can also influence online public opinion by paying people to post, tweet and/or blog positively framed topics about political subjects or government perspectives (MacKinnon, 2013). One recent report that analyzed the costs of swaying public opinion through online misinformation found it's possible to potentially manipulate public opinion, and even elections, by spending as little as $400,000 on fake news and propaganda (Levin, 2017). For example, $6,000 can help gain 40,000 "high-quality" social media likes, $5,000 can get 20,000 online comments, $2,700 a false story, and $10,000 can promote a protest on social media. In addition, people can buy retweets as well as place videos on YouTube that help stories go viral (Levin, 2017). Moreover, online user data can easily be used by a campaign to individualize messages to Klu Klux Klan members, while simultaneously send a different message to African American groups in support of their needs. It's likely neither group would know they received different messages from the same source as they are unlikely to be in communication. In short, social media and the internet are vulnerable to manipulation and perception management.

How individualized content and politically oriented (mis)information in the digital era impacts interpersonal communication is of more importance now than ever because fruitful cultures of deliberation are needed to sustain democratic governance.

Political structures and (mis)information in the digital age often push people into camps and impact the manner in which interpersonal communication is conducted. This is particularly evident with climate change. Studies of media have found that discussions between accepters and skeptics are often characterized by mutual labeling and unfriendly language, with most of the latter emanating from skeptics (Elgesem, Steskal & Diakopoulos, 2015; Koteyko, Jaspal & Nehrich, 2012). Understanding how and why communication occurs within discussions of climate change and other challenges is important because many topics are considered collective action problems, which require an informed public conversation to facilitate policy change.

Identity

How new media technologies influence identity and self-expression is also an understudied and undertheorized area within the communications field. While extremely diverse and contested, as media, culture and identity are often sites of multiple meanings, the question of power and control is still relevant here. For example, new media technologies can enhance the ability to capture and express oneself more easily. In this sense, they appear to empower users. Access to media production equipment is easier now compared to any other time in history, while the ability to publish one's expression online is also simple, easy and in many cases appears free. Many independent people make a living from their expression through online markets and websites.

At the same time, the relationship between identity and new communication technologies is challenged as the power over, and use of these technologies creates significant points of contention. These antagonisms can hinder self-expression, thereby repressing online speech, especially through social media. This can occur when authority figures and employers request access to social media as a sort of acceptability test. Entry into a country, or access to employment can rest on their assessments. For many online users, their ability to sustain life may depend on what they have on their social media accounts. Authority figures can base movement in or out of a country, as well as access to employment on these profiles.

From war zones, to U.S. visa applicants, to seeking a job washing dishes at a nearby restaurant increasingly forces social media users to expose their online self-expression. For example, passing military road blocks in Syria often requires travelers to provide social media user names and passwords (Dredge, 2014). For visa seekers and tourists, passing U.S. boarders can also mean providing mobile phone contacts, social media passwords and online usernames for entry (Smith, 2017: Torbati, 2017). In addition, applying for more and more jobs means passing a social media test, where employers determine if applicants are hirable or not based on their posts. Studies note that up-to 90 percent of recruiters and hiring managers visit potential candidates' social network profiles as part of screening processes, with 63-69 percent rejecting a candidate based on the candidates' profile content (Davis, 2007; Reppler, 2011).

Ultimately, the power and control over online information can determine one's fortune or fate. This control of information power can deter or advance interests (Mayer-Schonberger, 2009). While these developments question online self-expression (Park, 2016), they should also be considered discriminatory because they can easily violate civil rights acts, which are designed to protect citizens from discrimination against, race, sex religion, age and disability. Moreover, if online social networking site expression always conforms with employer and/or government interests, then the diversity of voices needed for a robust democracy becomes limited (De la Llama et al., 2012).

Culture and Creative Industries (CCI)

Studying where and how culture fits within the privatized system of digital ownership and distribution is a demanding challenge, as new media ownership, technologies and policies change on a frequent basis. Ascertaining what these trends mean for consumers, culture and access is perhaps the most challenging part of studying the culture and creative industries.

The culture and creative industries exist within and are a part of commercial digital distribution networks. They are also contested. In one sense, these companies create products that people often enjoy. The surveillance system can also follow how online users produce and consume culture. Industries can then analyze these developments to assist movie, television or music companies where to invest. They can also observe grassroots online cultural expression and incorporate it into larger and better promoted corporate structures perhaps enabling artists with increased revenues. In addition, for those who prefer to create culture outside of the market or corporate structures, and there plenty of people who prefer this, the internet also enables users to share this content, as well as copyrighted content, albeit sometimes illegally depending on their copyright.

While the technologies of the digital era have clearly enabled a greater capacity to create, access and share different kinds of cultural forms, the industries and technologies also appear to exploit and limit the development of more inclusive markets for culture. The cultural and creative industries help drive online economies and contributed $200 billion in global sales, while the sales of digital devices that play their content grew to $530 billion in 2013 (UNESCO, 2015). While digital cultural industry profits are increasing, one must ask if they are being spread evenly among a diverse group of artists, or if a small number of carefully groomed commercially-oriented artists generate the bulk of revenue? The later is clearly the case for the music industry, as it has significantly downsized its rosters during the past decade (Park, 2009; Rogers, 2013). New media and technology companies also create subscriptions, exclusive content, digital locks and keys, as well as agreements between individual companies in efforts to control access and further monetize culture. In addition, publishing royalties and synchronization revenue from advertising and movies is increasing, which means scholars may want to examine the linkages between ownership and horizontal integration within commercial culture. The ramifications of these industry trends can clearly affect the ideas, images and sounds people encounter, as well as influence the desires, motivations, dreams and aspirations among fans.

Conclusion and Call for Public Participation

New communications media and technology embody various layers of power that influence society and culture in numerous contexts. Communications media, new technology, ownership and control influence culture, and present significant challenges for communications and culture scholarship in the digital era. As communications technologies are being more widely applied, there is increasing evidence that the economies of technologically advanced countries are becoming information and communications based economies, where the driving force is the generation and application of knowledge. The developments discussed in this essay point to a number of concerns regarding the asymmetric role of power relations generated by the digital era. These inequities can often challenge democratic participation. As Melody (2006) argues, there needs to be a clear set of public information needs in addition to the creation of a rich public commons essential to the maintenance of participatory democracy. How the digital era will impact these challenges is ultimately a political question, and one that also rests on the influence of power in society.

David J. Park
Florida International University, USA

REFERENCES

Ball, J. (2012, April 22). Me and my data: How much do the Internet giants really know? *The Guardian*. Retrieved from: http://www.theguardian.com/technology/2012/apr/22/me-and-my-data-Internet-giants

Benkler, Y. (2006). *The wealth of networks: How social production transforms markets and freedom*. New Haven, CT: Yale University Press.

Bennett, I. (2017, Nov 12). Artist's 'sexual' robin redbreast Christmas cards banned by Facebook. *The Guardian.* Retrieved from: https://www.theguardian.com/technology/2017/nov/12/artists-sexual-robin-redbreast-christmas-cards-banned-by-facebook

Davis, D. C. (2007). My Space Isn't Your Space: Expanding the Fair Credit Reporting Act to Ensure Accountability and Fairness in Employer Searches of Online Social Networking Services. *The Kansas Journal of Law & Public Policy, 16*, 237–256.

De la Llama, V., Barreto, C., Trueba, I., Voges, C., & Park, D. (2012). At Face(book) value: Uses of Facebook in hiring processes and the role of identity in social networks. *International Journal of Work Innovation, 1*(1), 114–136. doi:10.1504/IJWI.2012.047984

Desjardins, F. (2017). Chart: Here's how 5 tech giants make their billions. *Virtual Capitalist.* Retrieved from: http://www.visualcapitalist.com/chart-5-tech-giants-make- billions/

Dredge, S. (2014, March 7). Eric Schmidt to dictators: 'You don't turn off the Internet: you infiltrate it'. *The Guardian.* Retrieved from http://www.theguardian.com/technology/2014/mar/07/google-eric-schmidt-jared-cohen

Dyer-Witheford, N. (1999). Cyber-Marx: Cycles and circuits of struggle in high-technology capitalism. Chicago: University of Illinois Press.

Elgesem, D., Steskal, L., & Diakopoulos, N. (2015). Structure and content of the discourse on climate change in the blogosphere: The big picture. *Environmental Communication, 9*(2), 169–188. doi:10.1080/17524032.2014.983536

Fisher, A. (2009). Bullets with butterfly wings: Tweets, protest networks, and the Iranian election. In Y. R. Kamalipour (Ed.), *Media, power, and politics in the digital age* (pp. 105–118). Rowman & Littlefield.

Garcia, A. (2015, Sept. 27). Mark Zuckerberg: Internet access can eradicate extreme poverty. *CNN.com.* Retrieved from: http://money.cnn.com/2015/09/26/news/mark-zuckerberg-united-nations-poverty-internet/index.html

Information Observatory. (2016). Billionaires who owe their wealth to information. *Information Observatory.* Retrieved from: http://informationobservatory.info/2016/05/01/billionaires-who-owe-their-wealth-to-information/

Jones, S. (1998). *Cybersociety 2.0 revisiting computer-mediated communication and community.* Sage.

Kolko, B., & Reid, E. (1998). Dissolution and fragmentation: Problems in on-line communities. In S. Jones (Ed.), *Cybersociety 2.0 revisiting computer-mediated communication and community* (pp. 129–158). Sage. doi:10.4135/9781452243689.n8

Koteyko, N., Jaspal, R., & Nerlich, B. (2013). Climate change and 'climategate' in online reader comments: A mixed methods study. *The Geographical Journal*, *179*(1), 74–86. doi:10.1111/j.1475-4959.2012.00479.x

Levin, S. (2017, June 13). Pay to sway: Report reveals how easy it is to manipulate elections with fake news. *The Guardian*. Retrieved from: https://www.theguardian.com/media/2017/jun/13/fake-news-manipulate-elections-paid-propaganda

MacKinnon, R. (2013). *Consent of the networked: The worldwide struggle for Internet freedom*. Basic Books.

Mayer-Schonberger, V. (2009). *Delete: The virtue of forgetting in the digital age*. Princeton, NJ: Princeton University Press.

McChesney, R. W. (2013). *Digital disconnect: How capitalism is turning the internet against democracy*. New York, NY: New Press.

Melody, W. (2006). Markets and policies in new knowledge economies. *LIRNE.NET*. Retrieved from: https://idl-bnc-idrc.dspacedirect.org/bitstream/handle/10625/41875/129520.pdf?sequence=1

Negroponte, N. (1996). *Being digital*. New York, NY: Vintage Books.

Pariser, E. (2012). *The filter bubble: How the new personalized web is changing what we read and how we think (reprint edition)*. New York, NY: Penguin Books. doi:10.3139/9783446431164

Park, D. (2009). *Conglomerate rock: The music industry's quest to divide music and conquer wallets*. Lanham, MD: Lexington Books.

Park, D. (2016). The battle over SNS privacy for United States employees and job applicants: An analysis of 2012-2013 state legislation. *Information Communication and Society*. doi:10.1080/1369118X.2016.1202303

Reich, R. (2015, Sept 30). Bernie Sanders tells the truth: Former Clinton Labor Secretary Robert Reich on his surging campaign. *Democracynow!* Retrieved from: http://www.democracynow.org/2015/9/30/bernie_sanders_tells_the_truth_former?autostart=true&get_clicky_key=suggested_next_story

Reppler.com. (2011). Job Screening with Social Networks. *Reppler.com*. Retrieved from http://blog.reppler.com/2011/09/27/managing-your-online-image-across-social-networks/

Rezabakhsh, B., Bornemann, D., Hansen, U., & Schrader, U. (2006). Consumer power: A comparison of the old economy and the internet. *Journal of Consumer Policy*, *29*(1), 3–36. doi:10.1007/s10603-005-3307-7

Rogers, J. (2013). *The Death & Life of the Music Industry in the Digital Age*. New York: Bloomsbury Academic.

Rosen, J. (2011). The Deciders: Facebook, Google, and the Future of Privacy and Free Speech. In Constitution 3.0: Freedom and Technological Change. Washington, DC: Brookings Institution Press.

Schiller, D. (1996). *Theorizing communication: A history*. New York: Oxford University Press.

Schiller, D. (2014). Digital depression: Information technology and economic crisis. Urbana, IL: University of Illinois Press.

Shapiro, A. (1999). *The control revolution: How the internet is putting individuals in charge and changing the world we know*. New York, NY: Public Affairs.

Slobogin, C. (2011). Is the Fourth Amendment Relevant in a Technological Age? In Constitution 3.0: Freedom and Technological Change. Washington, DC: Brookings Institution Press. doi:10.2139/ssrn.1734755

Smith, D. (2017). *'Extreme vetting' would require visitors to US to share contacts andpasswords*. Retrieved from: https://www.theguardian.com/us-news/2017/apr/04/trump-extreme-vetting-visitors-to-us-share-contacts-passwords

Splichal, S. (2009). 'New' media, 'old' theories: Does the (national) public melt into the air of global governance? *European Journal of Communication*, *24*(4), 391–405. doi:10.1177/0267323109345522

Sunstein, C. (2001). *Republic.com*. Princeton, NJ: Princeton University Press.

Torbati, Y. (2017). Donald Trump administration approves social media checks for U.S. visa applicants. *Globalnews.ca*. Retrieved from: https://globalnews.ca/news/3498115/u-s-visa-social-media-checks/

Turow, J. (1997). Breaking up America: Advertisers and the new media world. Chicago: University of Chicago Press. doi:10.7208/chicago/9780226817514.001.0001

Turow, J. (2011). *The daily you: How the new advertising industry is defining your identity and your worth.* New Haven, CT: Yale University Press.

UNESCO. (2007). *Statistics on cultural industries: Framework for the Elaboration of National Data Capacity Building Projects.* Bangkok: UNESCO Bangkok. Retrieved from: http://unesdoc.unesco.org/images/0015/001549/154956e.pdf

UNESCO. (2015). Cultural times: The first global map of cultural and creative industries. *UNESCO.* Retrieved from: http://en.unesco.org/creativity/sites/creativity/files/cultural_times._the_first_global_map_of_cultural_and_creative_industries.pdf

Winseck, D. (2016). Reconstructing the political economy of communication for the digital media age. *The Political Economy of Communication, 4*(2), 73–114.

Wu, T. (2011). Is Filtering Censorship? The Second Free Speech Tradition. In Constitution 3.0: Freedom and Technological Change. Washington, DC: Brookings Institution Press.

ENDNOTES

1 This paper defines power as originating from the means of production. However, not everything falls under that category, especially with culture. Culture can exist inside and outside of the market and mode of production.

2 What was once considered 'new media,' like the internet, really are not that new anymore. They have been around for decades and many utopian scholar predictions have yet to turn into reality.

3 According to UNESCO (2007), The culture and creative industries constitute: "advertising; architecture; crafts and designer furniture; fashion clothing; film, video and other audiovisual production; graphic design; educational and leisure software; live and recorded music; performing arts and entertainment; television, radio and internet broadcasting; visual arts and antiques; publishing, press, and literature" (p. 11).

Section 1

New Media, Culture and Community

This section presents chapters exploring the connection between culture and community using new media, specifically focusing on establishing communities, maintaining communities and communal identities in the new media platform.

Chapter 1
Cultural Identity Preservation Through Social Media:
Refugees and Community

Nurhayat Bilge
Florida International University, USA

ABSTRACT

This chapter explores cultural identity negotiation on social media for a specific refugee group. Previous research indicates the importance of a sense of community and cultural preservation in regards to establishing and maintaining a cultural identity for this specific group. The group, Meskhetian Turks, is an example of ethnic identity and an established ethnicity through shared history and struggle. This chapter focuses on the virtual implications of the group's identity in social media. More specifically, it explores how social media platforms serve as a cultural unifier, where cultural identity is maintained and perpetuated in the face of an unattainable physical homeland.

INTRODUCTION

Social media is a part of everyday life for many people around the world. People use social media sites, such as Facebook, Instagram, and Twitter to express opinions, connect with people, share life events, and perform identities. Ease of reach and global connectivity make social media immensely influential socially, politically, and culturally for many cultural groups of nationalities, social and economic classes, races, sexualities, and ethnicities. The last group, ethnicities, is the focus of this chapter.

DOI: 10.4018/978-1-5225-3784-7.ch001

More specifically, the chapter aims to explore how refugee groups utilize social media for purposes of ethnic identity establishment and maintenance. To achieve this goal, one specific ethnic group's social media utilization is analyzed. The group, called Meskhetian Turks, are refugees, who are scattered in nine countries. Hence, without any physical borders or political systems to unite them, the group's social media utilization provides an example of ethnic identity's visibility and strength. To this end, the chapter first provides a framework for ethnicity and ethnic identity, then examines literature regarding ethnicity and ethnic identity in social media, after which two studies regarding Meskhetian Turks are explored. The main objective of the chapter is to examine the influence of social media on ethnic identity formation and preservation, which helps further research on both ethnic identities and intercultural new media.

BACKGROUND

Defining Ethnicity

Culture is a social construct (Applegate & Sypher, 1988) established and maintained through communication (Samovar, Porter, & McDaniel, 2007). It is a continually changing learned process of norms, values, beliefs, and perspectives (Sarbaugh, 1988). These shared cultural components (Martin & Nakayama, 1999) emerge as a bond that "forges a group's identity and assists in its survival" (Orbe & Harris, 2001, p.6). Each cultural group creates its own unique identity, as a result of which, culture is subjective (Samovar et al., 2007). Cultural group members establish and maintain their identity through traditions, rituals, practices, and artifacts (Fong, 2004), thus, culture is, first and foremost, a communicative process.

Communication is how people, as "active interpreters" (Applegate & Sypher, 1988, p. 42), learn and make sense of the cultural context (Samovar et al., 2007). Moreover, cultural group members perform their identity through communication (Collier & Thomas, 1988; Fong, 2004) by taking part in the traditions, rituals, and practices. Hence, communication and culture are inseparable.

Culture and the consequent identity it creates are terms "employed broadly to include related concepts such as subcultural, national, ethnolinguistic, and racial identity" (Kim, 2007, p. 238). There are numerous cultural groups such as nationality, race, ethnicity, gender, sexuality, and religion. These groups are not independent from one another and exist through a mutual influence on each other. Nonetheless, they all present a unique identity for their respective members.

This chapter focuses on one of these concepts: ethnicity. Ethnicity is a problematic and complex term (Volkan, 1999). It is often conflated with other terms, such as nationality, race, religion, or language spoken. Ethnic groups may have overlapping components with different groups defined by race, religion, language, and such; nonetheless, ethnicity is a unique designation, which establishes a distinct cultural identity. Ndhlovu (2007) states "ethnicity or ethnic identity refers to common descent and common cultural or linguistic heritage that is shared because of kinship relationship" (p.131). Kinship is the crucial term in this statement. Ethnicity is a self-categorization of its members for the purpose of negotiating an identity (Wilkinson, 2011). Its borders are more transparent compared to other cultural groups. These transparent borders may be the reason why ethnicity is often conflated or used interchangeably with other terms, such as nationality or race. However, ethnicity is a unique identifier, separate from other cultural identifiers. It is important to make the distinction, because ethnicity creates a unique communicative identity. Conflation of ethnic identity with other group identities, such as nationality or race, results in negligence of cultural distinctions.

Nationality, for instance, refers to citizenship within political borders (Anderson, 1991). Nations have a physicality to them (Anderson, 1991) and are defined by borders. There are political and economic aspects associated with belonging to a nation. Nationality, consequently, provides tangible symbols, such as flags, anthems, constitutions, and historical places (Anderson, 1991). Overall, national identities are visible through these symbols and representations.

Race, however socially constructed it is, refers to skin color. Skin color by itself cannot create a cultural identity. Similar to ethnicity, shared experiences and a sense of belonging is what creates a cultural group based on race (Orbe & Harris, 2001). Nonetheless, racial identity signifies a separate social construct than ethnicity. There is, for instance, a crucial difference between culturally identifying as "Black" and "African-American." Black refers to race regardless of nationality or ethnicity. People all around the globe, in relation to various national, religious, and ethnic cultural contexts can identify with belonging to the racial group of Black. African American, on the other hand, is an ethnicity, which emerges from and in return signifies, a shared history and shared struggles which, consequently creates a shared identity that is unique. A person can be a Black immigrant in the United States, however their ethnic identity will be different than one who identifies with the African-American ethnicity with its unique history and social experiences.

Ethnicity, evidently, has intangible borders. According to Orbe and Harris (2001) ethnicity has both a historical and a psychological component. The authors define ethnicity as "a cultural marker that indicates shared traditions, heritage, and ancestral origins; ethnicity is defined psychologically and historically" (p. 7). Shared history, language, religion provide the necessary components for an ethnic identity to emerge, but they are not enough to create an ethnic consciousness, independently or collectively; there is a need for a sense of belonging for an ethnicity to emerge

(Romanucci-Ross, 2006). Thus, ethnic borders are defined by each group's members through shared cultural components which lead to a kinship relationship as Ndhlovu (2007) claims.

Though shared symbols and cultural elements, such as language and religion, are necessary for an ethnicity to emerge, they are not sufficient to create an ethnicity or an ethnic identity. Ultimately, what creates an ethnicity is the need to establish ethnic boundaries, usually as a result of common "historical events," "political struggles," or simply a "common fate" (Fong, 2007, p. 44). Hence, ethnicity is derived from a shared history and shared struggles resulting in marginalization of a group (Volkan, 1999; Gilliland, 2006). Marginalization leads to a need for self-identification, which creates an ethnic identity that is "related basically to pride in a positive way, or to shame and degradation in a negative way" (De Vos & Romanucci-Ross, 2006, p. 396). Ethnicity is "subjective, symbolic" and "emblematic" (De Vos, 2006, p. 11), and a group's ethnic identity is "perceived separate origin and continuity, in order to differentiate themselves from other groups" (De Vos, 2006, p. 11). Ethnic identities emerge and strengthen when there is a threat to the group as a result of their cultural commonalities (Volkan, 2003). People unite against the threat and their ethnic identity becomes a unifying commonality (Volkan, 1999).

History presents abundant examples of common threat and marginalization resulting in established ethnic identities (Gilliland, 2006; Volkan, 1999), for instance, in conflict areas such as former Soviet Union, Sudan, and Rwanda. One recent example, according to Gilliland (2006), can be found in the European countries such as Bosnia, Serbia, Croatia, Kosovo, and Herzegovina. The author articulates that until the war of 1990s in the former Yugoslavia, ethnic identities were shadowed by a much stronger national identity. The war in 1990s highlighted differences, which led to strong ethnic identifications. As a result, ethnicities emerged and strengthened to the point of establishing independent counties respective of these ethnicities.

Thus, ethnicity is a cultural identification that is strengthened and even formed by a common threat to identity. Furthermore, these shared struggles (Volkan, 1999) help maintain the identity of the ethnic group for generations to come (Steinberg, 2001). The establishment and maintenance of ethnicities and ethnic identities transpire through communication. Shared histories or struggles are communicated within the group through generations, which is how ethnicities and ethnic identities are established and maintained (De Vos, 2006).

All cultural groups are social constructs. Yet, discussed above, some have relatively more tangible borders to define them. Ethnicity possesses more transparent borders which depend on each group's self-identification. Hence, ethnicity is utterly a communicative process. Unique identities associated with each ethnic group are products of communication. Not only are they established, but they are reinforced and redefined constantly through communication. Communication is more than a tool for ethnic identities; it is the foundation upon which ethnic identities are formed, shaped, and maintained.

Ethnicity and Ethnic Identity in Social Media

Since ethnicity has transparent borders, social media offers an opportunity to create and define borders for ethnic groups. Ethnic groups, as discussed above, is a "form of social identity" that involves "the identification of ethnic membership, knowledge of the ethnic culture, and a sense of feelings and belonging to the ethnic group" (Ju & Lcc, 2015, p. 335). Cultural groups maintain a distinct group identity by establishing boundaries that define their culture and by strengthening their connection to each other. As Croucher (2011) says:

One way many immigrant groups have established boundaries and defended their group identity is through the Internet. Many scholars have found immigrant populations in various nations use the Internet to reconnect with their homeland, strengthen community ties, retro-acculturate, culturally adapt, and find intimate partners (p. 262)

New media, especially social network sites, allow ethnic group members to create communities and share a sense of identity cross traditional borders (Gunduz & Erdem, 2017; Zhejiang, Jia, & Shoham, 2016). According to Gunduz and Erdem (2017) "a community identity serves as a coherent bonding for all community members, which also helps them discriminate themselves from other people outside the community" (p. 21). Facebook, for instance, "facilitate richer community experience not only by making community identities more concrete in tangible social interactions, but also by extending new opportunities to new identities" (Zhang, Jiang, & Carroll, 2010, p. 73). Morley and Robins (1995) state that "identity is a question of memory, and memories of 'home' in particular" (p. 91). Basaran Ince (2014) calls this a "cultural-communicative memory" (p. 19), instead of lasting a lifespan of an individual, this collective memory lasts a generation. One way of establishing and maintaining cultural identity for ethnic groups is to reinforce and provide continuity for the collective memory. Cultural memory, according to the author, is more powerful and has a wider reach through new media, because it is "global, digital, and mobile" (p. 20), which helps preserve and maintain the cultural identity. New media, including social media, exists within various aspects of everyday life, providing a far and convenient reach for many people. As Marlowe, Bartley, and Collins (2017) explain:

rather than existing in a separate 'virtual' sphere, technological developments including the internet, mobile phones and social media are integrated with the everyday 'real world' through their 'hard' infrastructural supports, capacity to link people and places and through the mediation of social spaces by digital information. (p. 85-86)

Consequently, new media provides ethnic groups; such as immigrants, refugees, and other minorities; with an ease of access and "unprecedented opportunities" (Marlowe, Bartley, & Collins, 2017, p. 87) to cross boundaries; geographical, social, or political; form and maintain connections, which aid in establishing a sense of community and preserving a cultural identity. According to Marlowe, Bartley, and Collins (2017) utilization of new media, especially social media, offers a communal sense of belonging, which leads to a "culture of connectivity" (p. 88).

A culture of connectivity is particularly significant for ethnic groups, who are displaced and/or forced to endure geographical separation. New media, by empowering otherwise silenced groups, provide a space for members of these groups to connect, form communities to "retain and reinforce their cultural identities" (Shuter, 2012, p. 222). What scholars deem as "ethnic media" (Ju & Lee, 2015, p. 327) has been assisting ethnic groups' identity maintenance and reinforcement. As Ju and Lee (2015) explain:

ethnic media for various diaspora subjects are the major source of information about their origin of country; therefore, ethnic media provide them with common reference points to socialize with people back home or with other diaspora members (p. 327)

Ethnic media, as the authors explain, existed in all forms of media, from print to visual; and in the contemporary world it translates into new media, including, if not most significantly, into social media. Ethnic groups utilize social media in various facets. First of all, social media, as explained before, helps create connections between group members, which then aids in the establishment, reinforcement, and maintenance of an ethnic identity. Additionally, social media is a resource, where ethnic group members support each other, which creates a sense of community. Finally, social media becomes a platform, where ethnic groups, such as refugees, immigrants, and other minority groups, can have a voice.

Authors, Kok and Rogers (2017) explain that through new media helps connect "diaspora networks, civil society actors and policymakers" (p. 28). By doing so, new media empowers politically under-privileged groups, such as groups enduring diaspora. The authors explain that, in addition to establishing and maintaining a cultural identity, "diasporas often use social media to build an online diasporic public sphere in support of integration, or to help fill in the social void experienced when migrating to a different country" (p. 28).

Thus, research points to new media, especially social media to be a crucial platform for ethnic groups, specifically displaced persons, refugees, and diasporas. Next, the chapter will test these assumptions by examining a particular ethnic group and their utilization of social media.

MAIN FOCUS OF THE CHAPTER

Meskhetian (Ahiska) Turks

Meskhetian Turks, or Ahiska Turks[1], is an ethnic group with a long and complicated history. The group is originally from a region called Ahiska or Meskheti, which is currently within the borders of Georgia. Historically the area was ruled under the Russian Empire, Ottoman Empire, and Soviet Union. In 1944, Meskhetian Turks were forced into exile from their homeland and as of 2017 they are prevented from returning to Ahiska (Meskheti) by the current Georgian government. Decades following the first exile left the group scattered in countries such as Azerbaijan, Kazakhstan, Kirgizstan, Ukraine, Uzbekistan, and Russia. Some Meskhetian Turks managed to immigrate to Turkey, and more are still trying to do the same; and a very small number, approximately 500 in the first count, managed to return to Georgia. In 2005, approximately 15,000 Meskhetian Turks from Russia were granted refugee status in the United States.

Meskhetian Turks present an example of an ethnic group. Members of the group possess a distinct cultural identity, which is not confined to any specific borders, language, or even religion. Meskhetian Turks are Muslims, speak Turkish as their first language, and originate from Ahiska (Meskheti); however, none of these cultural components create the collective identity for the group. These components are cultural commonalities, yet, the cultural identification of being a Meskhetian Turk stem from a shared history and shared struggle as a result of this history. The past; which is marked by forced relocation, oppression, discrimination, and enduring violence; and a shared connection to this past is what creates the cultural identity (Trier & Khanzihn, 2007).

According to scholars, such as Aydingun (2007) and Trier and Khanzihn (2007), a significant Meskhetian Turkish identity emerged in the first place as a result of the first exile in 1944. Despite the fact that Meskhetian Turks are scattered in 9 countries, and have been removed from their original homeland by 2 even 3 generations, there is still a prominent Meskhetian Turkish identity. Media, and especially the increasing availability and convenience of new media, present an opportunity for the group to maintain and preserve a cultural identity. In the next sections, the chapter outlines Meskhetian Turkish ethnic identity and how social media is utilized as a cultural unifier for the group.

Previous Research Results

This chapter continues research conducted on Meskhetian Turkish ethnic identity in a previous study (Bilge, 2017). Previous research comprised of narrative interviews and ethnographic field work, which explored Meskhetian Turkish cultural identity. The study guiding this chapter builds upon the previous work by examining the manifestation of Meskhetian Turkish ethnic identity on social media. As discussed above, Meskhetian Turkish identity is an ethnic identity, whose members are interconnected through a shared history and shared struggle. The first study revealed that Meskhetian Turkish identity comprised of a self-definition through self-proclaimed Meskhetian Turkish cultural traits and an ownership of connection to Turkey and the perceived Turkish culture for members of the group.

The first aspect of self-proclaimed cultural traits presented three themes (Table 1). These themes are cultural unifiers, cultural preservation, and a sense of community. Cultural unifiers are a collective longing for the lost/ unattainable homeland (Meksheti), and an ownership and pride in a common Turkish heritage. The longing for the unattainable homeland refers to Ahiska (Meskheti), where the group is prevented from returning since 1944. Homeland is almost a promised land, where all members profess a desire to return. Turkish heritage that provokes an ownership for the group comprises cultural traits such as Turkish language, religion, and certain values and traditions that are perceived to be Turkish. Cultural preservation refers to preservation of these cultural traits as a way to maintain a Meskhetian Turkish identity. The study demonstrated that there is a collective consciousness regarding the significance of cultural preservation and the importance of bequeathing these cultural traits onto next generations, which is entangled with the last theme that emerged: a sense of community. Being part of the community and participating in the Meskhetian Turkish culture are essential to the group's cultural identity. These

Table 1. Meskhetian Turkish ethnic identity

Meskhetian Turkish Ethnic Identity		
Cultural Unifiers	**Cultural Preservation**	**Sense of Community**
o Turkish heritage o Unattainable homeland	o Language o Religion o Family o Cultural Traditions	o Maintaining a community o Cultural bequest for next generations

themes are all inter-connected. Members of the community are mindful of cultural traits and cultural identifiers, moreover, preservation and maintenance of these traits are perceived to be crucial aspects of the community.

Additionally, the study revealed a strong connection between Meskhetian Turkish identity and Turkey, both the land and its people (Table 2). Connection to the land demonstrated an image of Turkey as a surrogate homeland, furthermore the interviewees professed an expectation of responsibility from the Turkish government, such as assistance with the political issues preventing their rights to return to Ahiska (Meskheti) and citizenship for Meskhetian Turks around the world, which indicates a sense of belonging to Turkey. Connection to the Turkish people revealed strong ties to Turks. These ties demonstrate a perception of Turks being an extended community for Meskhetian Turks, especially those who are refugees in the United States. Common cultural traits are further indications of cultural unification between two communities, from the Meskhetian Turkish perspective. Nonetheless, interviewees articulated differences, which signified the presence of a distinct Meskhetian Turkish identity, separate from what is perceived to be the general Turkish identity.

THE CURRENT STUDY: QUESTIONS, ISSUES, AND RESULTS

Building upon these results, the current study raised the question: how does social media influence refugee identities? Hence, the study aimed to explore how this particular refugee group, Meskhetian Turks, utilized social media, whether the cultural identifiers in social media are similar to previous results, and which new themes, in terms of the group's cultural identity, emerge in the social media platform. As literature suggests new media, particularly social media, is often utilized to reinforce, reshape, and communicate cultural identities. Examining Meskhetian Turkish identity on social media allowed for an analysis, which displayed ways members of the group perform their cultural identity on social media, while questioning whether their group identity performance is altered comparatively.

Table 2. Meskhetian Turks' connection to Turkey

Meskhetian Turks' Connection to Turkey	
The Land	**The People**
o Turkey as a surrogate homeland o Turkish government as a unifying authority	o Turks as an extended community o Turkish cultural traits as unifiers o Differences that signify a distinct Meskhetian Turkish identity

Data for the study was gathered using three Facebook pages devoted to Meskhetian Turkish communities globally. The official names of these groups are: The World Union of Ahiska Turks (Dunya Ahiska Turkleri Birligi- DATUB), Ajans Ahiska[2], and Ahiskali Gencler Birligi (AGB)[3]. These groups were chosen as the research site because they present the largest number of members among Facebook group pages devoted to Meskhetian Turks. Membership numbers, as of November 30, 2017, are: DATUB: 45,385; Ajans Ahiska: 15,955; and AGB: 6,179. All three pages have members from the 9 countries, where Meskhetian Turks reside: Turkey, Azerbaijan, Kazakhstan, Kirgizstan, Ukraine, Uzbekistan, Russia, and United States.

Data was collected by examining posts between September 1st, 2016 and September 1st 2017. The analysis was conducted by coding the posts for common themes. The posts were grouped in two categories, both of which contain three themes.

As the results demonstrate, there are a number of common themes between Meskhetian Turkish identity defined by its members in interviews and the identity presented on social media. These themes are grouped under "cultural discourse." Concurrently, there are new themes, grouped under "political discourse" articulate the group's additional utilization of social media. Connection between these themes, commonalities between the previous study and this one, and implications of political utilization provide an insight furthering knowledge on both Meskhetian Turks, as a refugee group with a distinct ethnic identity, and cultural identity representations on social media.

DISCUSSION AND RECOMMENDATIONS

As explained in the previous section, the study produced two distinct categories of posts, each consisting of three themes. This section focuses on the implications of these results, especially in terms of utilization of social media by this ethnic group. Building upon literature regarding ethnic identity, social media, and the connection between the two concepts, the implications can be organized into three points: social

Table 3. Categories of discourse

Cultural Discourse	Political Discourse
• Self-Identification • Sense of Community: o within Meskhetian Turkish community o with Turkey o with the larger Turkic community • Cultural Preservation	• Building a stronger community • Turkish citizenship • Return to Homeland

media as an ethnic unifier, social media as ethnic identity maintenance, and social media as a reclaim of a collective voice.

Social Media as an Ethnic Unifier

The goal of the DATUB GROUP on Facebook is to inform the world about the [ongoing] tragedy of Ahiska Turks, who have been fighting for their homeland for 73 years.

[We aim] to create unity and a community among Meskhetians (Ahiskalilar), who are scattered around many counties in the world, and [we aim] to continue our struggle to RETURN TO HOMELAND"[4] (DATUB, 2017)

These words greet people on the "about" section of The World Union of Ahiska Turks (Dunya Ahiska Turkleri Birligi- DATUB) group page on Facebook. Evidently, the group's aims are twofold: unify the community (cultural) and work toward regaining rights to their homeland (political). The cultural aim articulated by the group is in accordance with results from the previous study. Interviewees of the study, unequivocally, talked about a sense of community as a cultural identifier for Meskhetian Turks. Social media utilization of the group supports this notion. In all three group pages, there are frequent posts regarding creating a community, unifying, and establishing a sense of identity. The unification posts, though have the same underlying message, take different forms. First of all, on all three Facebook group pages there is a strong presence of recruitment for purposes of establishing a larger and stronger online community. Second, calls for unification translates into calls for support of community members. News about business owned by Meskhetian Turks are announced, encouraging members to unify outside social media as well.

Besides in-group unification, social media is also utilized for unification with Turks, Turkey, and the Turkish government. This notion is present in commemoration of Turkish holidays and official days, such as the Republic Day (October, 29), appreciation for the government, and extending community membership to Turkish people by invitations of participation into the online community. Similarly, there is an attempt of unification with the Turkic world at large (through posts regarding news from Turkic countries) and solidarity with the Muslim communities all around the world (through support for Muslims in Chechnya, and outcry for Muslims in China).

These findings support literature stating importance of social media as an ethnic unifier. Through the three Facebook group pages, members utilize social media to create a community, establish a sense of identity, and unify with larger communities, such as Turks, Turkic people, and Muslims.

Social Media as Ethnic Identity Maintenance

Concurrent to utilizing social media to establish a community, Meskhetian Turks also employ social media for ethnic identity maintenance and cultural preservation. First indication of identity maintenance and cultural preservation can be found in explicit calls for and statements about preserving cultural characteristics such as language, religion, customs, traditions, and rituals. These statements are accompanied by posts portraying news, photos, and videos of norms, traditions, and rituals being carried out: weddings, food preparations, dance, performances, and celebrations as a community. Additionally, all three sites depict videos and images such as historical movies, historical documents, photos of Ahiska (Meskheti), and documentaries about Meskhetian Turks (particularly about the exile and displacement).

The study, once again, support literature (Croucher, 2011; Shuter, 2012) articulating that ethnic groups utilize social media to reinforce and maintain a collective identity. New media, particularly social media, provides ethnic groups, such as minorities, immigrants, and in this case refugees, with opportunities of connectivity, which provides preservation of culture and cultural identity for these groups (Ju & Lee, 2015; Kok & Rogers, 2017).

Social Media as a Reclaim of a Collective Voice

So far, results of the current study echoes results from the previous study with Meskhetian Turks. However, social media platform offers an additional dimension of Meskhetian Turkish ethnic identity, which is a claim to a collective voice. The urge for gaining a voice and regaining their rights to Ahiska (Meskheti) was prominent in the first study as well. The significance of this study is that social media offers a platform where Meskhetian Turks can reclaim a collective voice and labor to gain/regain political rights.

These assertions are evident in posts expressing political expectations regarding (a) Turkish citizenship and (b) regaining rights in Ahiska (Meskheti). Political expectations regarding Turkish citizenship are evident in outcry to the Turkish government for action, and shared news about Turkish citizenship, such as laws and regulations specific to aiding Meskhetian Turks in obtaining Turkish citizenship. Political expectations regarding regaining rights in Ahiska (Meskheti) are in the form of posts expressing a call of action and intervention from Turkish government, Georgian government, and international entities. Raising awareness of Meskhetian Turkish history of diaspora, loss of rights, and endured violence and oppression are prominent among social media users of these sites, and members are using these platforms to reclaim a voice for their community.

Expectations regarding Turkish citizenship and regained rights were also professed by interviewees of the previous study. This study additionally found that social media offers an opportunity for Meskhetian Turks voice these expectations in a public forum and continue discussions with a larger audience. Thus, the study supports assertions of scholars, such as Kok and Rogers (2017) and Shuter (2012) who argue that social media empowers otherwise silenced or marginalized groups by providing a unique space for their members to claim or reclaim a collective voice.

FUTURE RESEARCH DIRECTIONS

Meskhetian Turks provide a clear example of an ethnic group. A collective Meskhetian identity is established and strengthened through a shared history and shared struggles. Since 1944 Meskhetian Turks have been scattered through many countries and adapted to co-exist in a number of cultural contexts. Yet, there is still a distinct Meskhetian ethnic identity. Results of this study support previous research regarding ethnic identities and ethnic group utilization of social media. Still, studies focusing on different ethnic groups, for instance those who do not share a past as tormented as Meskhetian Turks. As Volkan (1999) states, oppression and discrimination endured as a result of an ethnic identity results in strengthening that very identity. Therefore, other ethnic groups may utilize social media in very different ways.

Additionally, studies focusing on other cultural groups, identifying through unifiers such as nationality, race, and religion need to be studied to determine how these groups differ in their utilization of social media regarding their collective identity. Richer body of research in these matters can help scholars understand the mutual influence between culture and social media further.

CONCLUSION

The guiding question of the chapter was: how do ethnic groups utilize social media in regards to their cultural identity? The chapter answered this question by reporting a study concerning one particular ethnic group, and comparing the results to a previous study conducted on the same refugee group examining their ethnic identity. As a result, the chapter offers three distinct, yet inter-connected, ways members of Meskhetian Turkish community utilize social media: social media as an ethnic unifier, social media as ethnic identity maintenance, and social media as a reclaim of a collective voice. Thus, in addition to ethnic identity establishment and preservation, the findings reveal that social media empowers Meskhetian Turks, who reclaim a collective voice for their community. Hence, the study demonstrates support for research regarding ethnic identity and social media utilization.

REFERENCES

Anderson, B. (1991). *Imagined Communities*. New York, NY: Verso.

Applegate, J. L., & Sypher, H. E. (1988). A constructivist theory of communication and culture. In Y. Y. Kim & W. B. Gudykunst (Eds.), *Theories in intercultural communication* (pp. 41–65). Newbury Park, CA: Sage.

Aydıngün, A. (2007). Resettlement and belonging among cultural and ethnic kin: The Meskhetian Turks in Turkey. In T. Trier & A. Khanzihn (Eds.), *Meskhetian Turks at a crossroads: Integration, reparation or resettlement?* (pp. 340–377). Berlin, Germany: Lit Verlag.

Basaran Ince, G. (2014). Digital Culture, New Media and The Transformation of Collective Memory. *Iletisim*, *21*, 9–29.

Bilge, N. (2017). Secondary Cultures and Their Impact as Intermediaries on Refugee Adaptation to Host Cultures: Connections of Community. *Journal of Intercultural Communication Research*, *46*(2), 130–146. doi:10.1080/17475759.2016.1275029

Collier, M. J., & Thomas, M. (1988). Cultural identity: An interpretive perspective. In Y. Y. Kim & W. B. Gudykunst (Eds.), *Theories in intercultural communication* (pp. 99–122). Newbury Park, CA: Sage.

Croucher, S. M. (2011). Social networking and cultural adaptation: A theoretical model. *Journal of International and Intercultural Communication*, *4*(4), 259–264. doi:10.1080/17513057.2011.598046

DATUB. (2017). Retrieved from https://fr-fr.facebook.com/groups/datubburhanozkosar/about/

De Vos, G. A. (2006). Introduction: Ethnic pluralism: Conflict and accomodation. In L. Romanucci-Ross, G. A. De Vos, & T. Tsuda (Eds.), *Ethnic identity* (pp. 1–36). Oxford, UK: AltaMira.

De Vos, G. A., & Romanucci-Ross, L. (2006). Conclusion: Ethnic identity: A psychocultural perspective. In L. Romanucci-Ross, G. A. De Vos, & T. Tsuda (Eds.), *Ethnic identity* (pp. 375–401). Oxford, UK: AltaMira.

Fong, M. (2004). Identity and speech community. In M. Fong & R. Chuang (Eds.), *Communicating ethnic and cultural identity* (pp. 3–19). Lanham, MD: Rowman & Littlefield.

Gilliland, M. K. (2006). Ethnic nationality in the former Yugoslavia: Ethnogenesis, ethnic cleansing, and present-day identities among Croats, Serbs, and Bosniacs. In L. Romanucci-Ross, G. A. De Vos, & T. Tsuda (Eds.), *Ethnic identity* (pp. 88–118). Oxford, UK: AltaMira.

Gunduz, U., & Erdem, B. K. (2017). The concept of virtual nationalism in the digital age: Social media perspectives of Turkey. *Communication Today*, *8*, 18–28.

Ju, H., & Lee, S. (2015). The Korean Wave and Asian Americans: The ethnic meanings of transnational Korean pop culture in the USA. *Journal of Media & Cultural Studies*, *29*(3), 323–338. doi:10.1080/10304312.2014.986059

Kim, Y. Y. (2007). Ideology, identity, and intercultural communication: An analysis of differing academic conceptions of cultural identity. *Journal of Intercultural Communication Research*, *36*(3), 237–253. doi:10.1080/17475750701737181

Kok, S., & Rogers, R. (2017). Rethinking migration in the digital age: Transglocalization and the Somali diaspora. *Global Networks*, *17*(1), 23–46. doi:10.1111/glob.12127

Marlowe, J. M., Bartley, A., & Collins, F. (2017). Digital belongings: The intersections of social cohesion, connectivity and digital media. *Ethnicities*, *17*(1), 85–102. doi:10.1177/1468796816654174

Martin, J., & Nakayama, T. (1999). Thinking dialectically about culture and communication. *Communication Theory*, *9*(1), 1–25. doi:10.1111/j.1468-2885.1999.tb00160.x

Ndhlovu, F. (2007). The Role of Discourse in Identity Formation and the Manufacture of Ethnic Minorities in Zimbabwe. *Journal of Multicultural Discourses*, *2*(2), 131–147. doi:10.2167/md073.0

Orbe, M., & Harris, T. M. (2001). *Interracial communication: Theory into practice*. Belmont, CA: Wadsworth.

Romanucci-Ross, L. (2006). Matrices of an Italian identity: Past as prologue. In L. Romanucci-Ross, G. A. De Vos, & T. Tsuda (Eds.), *Ethnic identity*. Oxford, UK: AltaMira.

Samovar, L. A., Porter, R. E., & McDaniel, E. R. (2007). *Communication between cultures*. Belmont, CA: Thomson.

Sarbaugh, L. E. (1988). A taxonomic approach to intercultural communication. In Y. Y. Kim & W. B. Gudykunst (Eds.), *Theories in intercultural communication* (pp. 22–40). Newbury Park, CA: Sage.

Shuter, R. (2012b). Intercultural New Media Studies: The Next Frontier in Intercultural Communication. *Journal of Intercultural Communication Research*, *41*(3), 219–237. doi:10.1080/17475759.2012.728761

Steinberg, S. (2001). *The Ethnic Myth: Race, Ethnicity and Class in America*. Boston, MA: Beacon Press.

Trier, T., & Khanzihn, A. (2007). Introduction. In T. Trier & A. Khanzihn (Eds.), *Meskhetian Turks at a crossroads: Integration, reparation or resettlement?* (pp. 1–42). Berlin, Germany: Lit Verlag.

Volkan, V. (1999). *Bloodlines: From Ethnic Pride to Ethnic Terrorism*. Boulder, CO: Westview Press.

Volkan, V. (2003). The re-libidinalization of the internal world of a refugee family. *Group Analysis*, *36*(4), 555–570. doi:10.1177/0533316403364012

Wilkinson, S. (2011). Constructing ethnicity statistics in talk-in-interaction: Producing the 'White European.'. *Discourse & Society*, *22*(3), 343–361. doi:10.1177/0957926510395446

Zhang, S., Jiang, H., & Carroll, J. M. (2010). Social Identity in Facebook Community Life. *International Journal of Virtual Communities and Social Networking*, *2*(4), 64–76. doi:10.4018/jvcsn.2010100105

Zhejiang, R. J., Jia, M., & Shoham, M. (2016). Online social connection: Exploring international students' use of new media in their adaptation process. *China Media Research*, *12*, 76–89.

KEY TERMS AND DEFINITIONS

Cultural Preservation: The need and goal for cultural groups to maintain their shared set of values, norms, and traditions to maintain cultural continuity.

Ethnicity: A cultural group with a distinct identity, which is established through shared history and struggle.

Homeland: For ethnic groups, it is the point of origin; the land/nation for which group members feel a shared affiliation.

Meskhetian Turks: An ethnic group, originating in Meskheti, which is today within the borders of Georgia.

Online Community: Virtual communities created and maintained on social media, where members feel a sense of cultural belonging.

Refugee Identity: The cultural identification people have as a result of becoming refugees.

Social Media: New media sites, such as Facebook, Instagram, and Twitter, where people share written and/or visual messages.

ENDNOTES

1. Ahiska is the Turkish name for Meskhetian. Members of the group prefer using the Turkish name "Ahiska Turks" primarily, or in conjunction with Meskhetian Turks.
2. Ajans Ahiska denotatively translates as Agency Ahiska, and connotatively translates as Ahiska News.
3. Ahiskali Gencler Birligi translates as: Association of Meskhetian Youths.
4. The original text reads: "Facebook'taki DATUB GRUBU'nun Amaci 73 yildir vatan mucadelesi veren Ahiska Turklerinin davasini sosyal medya araciligi ile dunyaya duyurmaktir.
   Dunyanin bir cok ulkesine dagitilmis olan Ahiskalilarin birlik ve beraberligini saglamak ve VATANA DONUS DAVAMIZDAKI mucadeleyi surdurmektir."

Chapter 2
Online Ethnic Media Consumption, Acculturation, and Enculturation Among Asian Americans

Kevin Y. Wang
Butler University, USA

ABSTRACT

This chapter discusses a study that examines the extent to which Asian American individuals' acculturation, enculturation, and demographic background contribute to their use of online ethnic media, as well as the extent to which Asian American individuals with different ethnic self-identities may differ in their online ethnic media consumption. Data for this study is drawn from a survey questionnaire (N = 574) conducted 2015, with respondents representing different immigrant generational status from multiple Asian ethnic groups in the United States. Results broadly highlight the influence role of acculturation and enculturation behind online ethnic media consumption and contribute to a greater understanding of the Asian American experience in the digital and globalized media environment. Implications and recommendations for future studies are discussed.

INTRODUCTION

The term "Asian American" generally refers to any individual of Asian descent who resides in the United States on a permanent or long-term basis, regardless of citizenship or other legal status (Lien, Conway, & Wong, 2004). At 17 million strong, the Asian American population consists of 23 distinct ethnic groups identified by the

DOI: 10.4018/978-1-5225-3784-7.ch002

U.S. Census in 2010, with the six largest ethnic groups being Chinese, Asian Indians, Filipinos, Vietnamese, Korean, and Japanese (Hoeffel, Rastogi, Kim, & Hasan, 2012). In the United States, nearly three-quarters (74%) of Asian-American adults were born abroad (Pew Research Center, 2012). Many first- and second-generation Asian Americans continue to be actively involved with the social and political life in their country of heritage/cultural origin (e.g., Lien et al., 2004), particularly through the consumption of ethnic media products on the Internet. As the nation's "highest-income, best-educated, and fastest-growing racial group" (Pew Research Center, 2012, para. 2), Asian Americans and their media consumption experience are research areas with rising significance.

Attempts to understand media consumption among Asian Americans and other ethnic groups have traditionally emerged out of disciplines such as culture studies, media studies, and ethnic studies, with considerable attention paid to important issues such as identity formation, spatialities, hybridity, and transnationalism. With the advent of information communication technologies (ICTs) in recent years, scholars have turned their attention to the ways in which digital technologies (e.g., websites, social media, mobile devices) could influence the manifestation of these concepts (e.g., Alonso & Oiarzabal, 2010; Brinkerhoff, 2009). As ICTs continue to expand into every facet of contemporary life, calls for interdisciplinary research to provide a deeper understanding of the relationship between culture and new media have also steadily appeared (e.g., Chen, 2012; Smith Pfister & Soliz, 2011).

Heeding the need for new scholarship, this chapter draws on the literature from communication, ethnic studies, and psychology to explore the relationships among acculturation, enculturation, online ethnic media consumption, and ethnic identity in Asian Americans. Specifically, the study applies the Asian American acculturation and enculturation measures by Zhang and Moradi (2013) to analyze online ethnic media consumption through a national survey (N = 574) conducted in 2015, with respondents representing different generational statuses from multiple Asian ethnic groups in the United States. By examining this topic through an interdisciplinary lens, the author hopes to contribute to the ongoing conversations about this evolving field of research.

BACKGROUND

Constructing Ethnic Identities

The notion that self-identity is a fluid, mutable, and evolving concept embedded in multiple layers of social, cultural, and political processes has long been argued by many scholars (e.g., Anderson, 2006; Giddens, 1991; Goffman, 1978; Mead, 1934). In the construct of Hall (1990), identity is formed and transformed continuously in relation to the ways we are represented in the systems and ideologies that surround us—and therefore the production of identity is about "becoming" as well as "being," both of which are tied to the past, present, and future. In the realm of *ethnic* identity, such a constructionist perspective suggests that individuals, regardless of their racial/ethnic backgrounds, engage in a "dialectical process" involving their ethnic self-identification and how others perceive them (Nagel, 1994).

Consequently, individuals may form multiple dimensions of ethnic identities (Espiritu, 1993; Fong & Chuang 2004; Padilla 1985; Romero & Roberts, 1998) that they reveal or change according to the situations and audiences they encounter. This phenomenon is most pronounced among marginalized racial/ethnic individuals as they go about their daily lives in the mainstream society. In the United States, for example, African Americans, Latino Americans, or Asian Americans who were born and raised in the United States may juxtapose their ethnic identities as ways to navigate around the complex and sometimes contentious racial relationships in American society (e.g., Renn, 2000; Shelton & Sellers, 2000). For recent immigrants, refugees, or members of a diaspora community who may be permanently displaced from their ancestral homeland, the need to integrate into the new host society while staying connected, whether emotionally or culturally, to their previous homes makes the composition and construction of their ethnic identities more multifaceted and dynamic.

Taken together, one can conclude that individuals with immigrant or diasporic backgrounds often possess a sense of multiple belongings (Georgiou, 2006; Karim, 2003) and a multidirectional gaze that looks forward in the new home and back to the old homeland (Sreberny, 2000). Ethnic identities among these individuals can be understood as the ways in which they position and locate themselves within the broader mainstream American culture, as a consequence of their experiences of racialization (Gillespie, 2000), and as a function of their relationships with their homeland or heritage culture. More specifically, the formation, maintenance, and transformation of ethnic identities among diasporic individuals may be shaped by a combination of internal and external forces, such as individuals' perceptions of themselves and sense of belonging in the ethnic group (Kibria, 2003; Phinney & Chavira, 1992), their attitudes toward the collective ethnic group (Espiritu, 1993; Masuoka, 2006; Okamoto, 2003), or how members and other racial/ethnic groups perceive them (Ma, 2000; Oyserman & Sakamoto, 1997), as well as the ethnic groups' positions and competitions with other groups within the larger social structure of the time (Belanger & Pinard, 1991; Nielsen, 1985; Olzak, 1994). Additionally, these factors interact with individuals' demographic characteristics such as age, gender, education, socioeconomic status, geographic location, immigration generational status, etc. (Espiritu, 1994) to create a complex and dynamic process of ethnic identity formation and maintenance.

Transnational Media Use and the Impact of Digital Technologies

One of the many channels in which the aforementioned issues are manifested is the realm of mass media. The manners in which culture and race are expressed, contested, and transformed through films, television shows, and literature in the United States have been a vital part of communication research. Beyond American media and American popular culture, communication scholars have also examined the consumption of *transnational media* among diasporic individuals. Transnational media can be broadly defined as media content or product that crosses borders (e.g., Ang, 1990; Chalaby, 2005), and they represent a rich symbolic space for these individuals to connect with families and cultures of the homeland (Georgiou, 2001; Lee, 2003). Previous studies have found that diasporic individuals utilize these resources to connect with people and communities both in the host country and in their previous homelands (Thompson, 2002; Thussu, 2006), to practice rituals (Shi, 2005) and find shared meanings for themselves and for their communities (Cunningham, 2001), or to express individual or group voices—either socially or politically (Newland, 2010). Transnational media are therefore important resources for diasporic individuals (Oh, 2015), as they help them construct hybrid meanings about themselves or about the diaspora (de Block & Buckingham, 2007; Gillespie, 2000; Oh, 2015), and the consumption of transnational media contributes to their ethnic identities.

In the era of traditional electronic and print media, the physical format (i.e., VHS tapes, DVDs, CDs, and books) of transnational media products (e.g., films, music, literature) represented a problem of access, as consumption of these media largely depended on the availability of distribution channels to disseminate the physical products. With the rapid growth and diffusion of the Internet and digital media technologies over the past two decades, scholars have noted that these new media tools have become an ever more powerful and effective medium for diasporic individuals. These online avenues, including social networking sites (e.g., Facebook), blogs, micro-blogging applications (e.g., Twitter), and video-streaming and sharing sites (e.g., YouTube) allow users to engage in the transnational media practices mentioned above with a much greater level of immediacy and convenience.

The emergence of these digital media has led to a growing body of literature that examines the variety of ways in which ICTs are incorporated by diasporic individuals in different parts of the world. For example, it has been found that immigrant families engage in a variety of transnational media practices through ICTs to connect with faraway relatives (Benitez, 2012; Bernal, 2006; Hiller & Franz, 2004), to become socially and politically active (Chen, Ping, & Chen, 2015; Kissau, 2012), or to define and construct a new family structure (Katz, 2010; Nedelcu, 2012) and translocal space (Conradson & McKay, 2007; Hepp, 2009). Taken together, as global migration and digitization continues to expand their reach, new media technologies represent an increasingly dynamic and diverse digital public sphere that benefits the global diaspora. As Appadurai (1996) observed, digital media "increasingly link producers and audiences across national boundaries, and as these audiences themselves start new conversations between those who move and those who stay, we find a growing number of diasporic public spheres" (p. 22). Accordingly, the production and consumption of content distributed by these online media is an emerging subject worthy of additional scholarly exploration.

Acculturation and Enculturation: Conceptual Definitions

As discussed previously, consumption of transnational media is related to diasporic individuals' ethnic identities. A key factor that may play an influencing role in this dynamic process of media consumption and identity formation is the psychological mechanism of acculturation and enculturation. Broadly speaking, acculturation refers to the change in an individual's attitudes, values, and identity after being in contact with a dominant culture (Graves, 1967; Kim, 2007). In the United States, scholars (e.g., Schwartz, Unger, Zamboanga, & Szapocznik, 2010) have noted that members of ethnic minority groups are likely to adapt and adhere to the mainstream American culture. Therefore, acculturation is often observed among individuals with immigrant backgrounds, or American-born individuals raised in immigrant households.

Because acculturation theory describes the experience of adjustment and assimilation for many immigrants, it is a common framework used in previous cross-culture communication research. For example, Kim (1988; 2001) has provided an integrative model that connects diasporic individuals' social communication, mass media use, and cultural adaptation. With the rapid rise of social, mobile, and emerging media, Shuter (2012) cautioned that there are "scant data on new media and acculturation" (p. 227). Scholars have since noted the void, and a steady stream of studies (e.g., Croucher & Rahmani, 2015; Forbush & Foucault-Welles, 2016; Hendrickson & Rosen, 2017; Kim, 2015; Seifert, 2015) has emerged in recent years to provide a variety of empirical and theoretical analyses on the issue. While acculturation is a useful framework to study individuals with immigrant backgrounds, Lien et al. (2004), however, argued that acculturation provides only a partial view of the Asian American experience, as acculturation signifies a one-way adoption of mainstream cultural values, which does not reflect the experience of many Asian

Americans who remain strongly connected to the language and cultural heritage of their country of origins.

To account for this perspective, the notion of "enculturation" should be considered. According to Herskovits (1948), enculturation refers to the process of socialization and maintenance of the norms of one's indigenous culture. Kim (2007) argued that enculturation is a more accurate term to describe the Asian American experience, because while many of them are socialized into their ethnic groups' cultural norms and practices due to their immigrant backgrounds, they also fully embrace the mainstream American culture. In a critique of Berry's (1980) model of acculturation, Weinreich (2009) noted that acculturation theory builds on the assumption that "both the dominant and heritage cultures are benign and congenial, without racism, intolerance of difference and forms of oppression" (p. 125), which is not reflective of the realities in many communities. He then suggested that the concept of enculturation might be a more appropriate term that captures the process through which individuals actively and selectively acquire or retain elements of different cultures—whether of their own heritage culture, the dominant mainstream culture, or a third culture within a multicultural environment.

In sum, using both acculturation and enculturation as conceptual frameworks to examine members of the Asian American community thus recognizes the existence of such duality in identity construction and maintenance—as it places an equal emphasis on the process of retaining one's indigenous cultural roots and the process of adaptation or acquiring new cultural norms and practices.

Measuring Acculturation and Enculturation

Though the concept of acculturation—and to a lesser extent enculturation—is examined by communication scholars as constructs of interest in cross-cultural communication studies, the development of acculturation and enculturation measures as valid and reliable psychometrics has largely stemmed from the field of psychology. As psychological research into racial and ethnic groups has developed over time, the conceptualization and operationalization of acculturation and enculturation have evolved. For instance, early studies depicted both concepts as a *unilinear* process that positions acculturation and enculturation at opposite ends of a spectrum (Schwartz et al., 2010), which implies that acculturation and enculturation are mutually exclusive.

Berry (1980) introduced a bilinear perspective that suggests the possibility of individuals possessing and practicing multiple cultural values and norms simultaneously. The bilinear approach focuses on the degrees of adoption and reconciliation between one's heritage culture and of the host culture, as well as the changing beliefs, attitudes, and behaviors associated with conforming to these cultures (e.g., Cuéllar, Arnold, & Maldonado, 1995; Ryder, Alden, & Paulhus, 2000).

This perspective served as the foundation that informed many Asian American acculturation/enculturation research studies (e.g., Lee, Yoon, & Liu-Tom, 2006; Miller, 2007). In recent years, newer studies have updated Berry's concept of bilinearity and advanced acculturation and enculturation research by treating it not only as a global domain, but as a construct comprising multiple *dimensionalities* (Kim & Abreu, 2001; Schwartz et al., 2010; Zhang & Moradi, 2013) that encompass different aspects such as behaviors, values, knowledge, and cultural identity. Accordingly, the present study builds on this bilinear and multidimensional perspective of acculturation and enculturation to explore its relationship with online ethnic media consumption. Specifically, the study utilizes the measures provided by Zhang and Moradi (2013), who tested and consolidated their scales from previous Asian American acculturation and enculturation psychometrics.

MAIN FOCUS OF THE CHAPTER

Research Questions

Based on the literature review above, one can conclude that ethnic media consumption—especially *online* ethnic media use—is of rising scholarly significance today as it may influence diasporic individuals in the context of cultural adaptation and identity formation. As the contemporary media environment continues to empower consumers with greater levels of choice and control over their media diets, what motivates Asian Americans to engage with online ethnic media? More specifically, if we accept that acculturation and enculturation are key psychological mechanisms that could lead to different behaviors, then what are the particular *dimensions* of acculturation and enculturation as specified by Zhang and Moradi (2013) that could play a role in individuals' online media consumption? To explore this issue, the following research question is proposed:

RQ 1: What is the relationship between Asian American individuals' use of online ethnic media, demographic backgrounds, and the dimensions of acculturation and enculturation?

Further, while past studies have indicated that individuals with diasporic or immigrant backgrounds often possess multiple ethnic identities that they reveal to different audiences or situations, it is less clear whether the differences in ethnic identities may also reflect the ways Asian American individuals consume ethnic media on the Internet. Thus, the following research question is proposed:

RQ 2: To what extent does Asian American individuals' online ethnic media consumption differ according to their ethnic identity?

Methods and Participants

To explore the research questions, an online survey was conducted in 2015. Online survey is an appropriate method for this study because the sample is more likely to be digitally active, which fits well with the research focus on online media consumption. As noted by scholars (e.g., Aoki & Takeda, 2008; Kalsbeek, 2003), random sampling is often a challenging and expensive endeavor when it comes to reaching ethnic minorities. One approach to address this issue is through the use of a purposive sampling method (Stacks, 2016), which provides a cost-efficient way of recruiting participants with specific characteristics and was the sampling method used in this study. Respondents (N = 574) were recruited from a national online panel provided by SurveyMonkey Audience, which reaches more than 30 million people with diverse demographic backgrounds in the United States.

In order to participate in the study, respondents had to self-identify as adult individuals of Asian descent who legally reside in the United States. Respondents were asked to complete an 84-item questionnaire and received point-rewards from SurveyMonkey as compensation. The age of the respondents ranged from 18 to 66 years old (M = 37.38, SD = 11.99, Mdn = 36.50), with roughly 39% of the sample self-identified as male, 60% as female, and 1% as transgender or queer individuals. In terms of educational attainment, 40.2% of the respondents had a college degree, 23% had some college or technical school education, 20.7% had a professional or graduate degree, 9.1% completed no education beyond high school, 6.1% had some professional or graduate education, and .9% received less than a high school-level education. Respondents reported residing in 43 states, with most respondents from California (30%), New York (8.5%), Texas (7%), Illinois (5.7%), Hawaii (4.4%), Pennsylvania (4%), Florida (3.7%), and New Jersey (3.5%).

Among all 574 respondents, 263 were born in the United States, while 311 were born abroad. Respondents also represented a wide range of immigrant generational status, with most reporting that they were second-generation Asian Americans (31%), followed by first-generation (25.4%), non-US citizens (18.6%), 1.5-generation (11%), third-generation (7.7%), fourth-generation (2.8%), first-generation adoptee (2.1%), and fifth-generation or beyond (1.4%). In terms of ethnicity, respondents reported as Chinese (24.2%), Filipino (17.2%), Indian (14.6%), Japanese (13.2%), Korean (8.2%), Asian with more than one ethnic/racial background (5.1%), Vietnamese (4.0%), Taiwanese (3.8%), Pakistani (2.6%), Pacific Islander (1.7%), Cambodian (1.4%), Thai (1.2%), Laotian (1.0%), Malaysian (1.0%), and Hmong (.5%).

Measures

Measures for the survey included the Asian American acculturation and enculturation scale developed by Zhang and Moradi (2013), which consists of 22 acculturation and 18 enculturation items that examine three dimensions: language-related behavior, which addresses an individual's acquisition of the host culture language and/or retention of the mother tongue; cultural and sociopolitical knowledge, which refers to an individual's level of civic, political, and historical knowledge of the host culture and/or of the heritage culture; and pride and cultural group association, which deals with an individual's sense of pride associated with the host culture and/or with the heritage culture. The operationalization of the acculturation and enculturation subscales is included in the Appendix (Table 5).

Online ethnic media use items were adapted from a media usage survey (Wang, Atkin, & Lau, 2014), which included questions that examined general Internet access (e.g., type and speed of access) as well as the level and frequency of online ethnic media consumption for news/information and entertainment purposes. Ethnic self-identity was measured by asking respondents whether they think of themselves as the following: American; Asian American; Asian; (heritage cultural group) American (e.g., Filipino American or Chinese American); or simply as (heritage cultural group), such as Filipino or Chinese. Finally, demographic information including age, gender, ethnicity, generational status (e.g., non-US citizen, 1st generation, 1.5 generation, 2nd generation, 3rd generation, 4th generation, and 5th generation), languages spoken, years living in the United States, education, income, employment status, and geographic location were collected.

SOLUTIONS AND RECOMMENDATIONS

Factors Predicting Online Ethnic Media Use

In order to address the research questions, statistical analyses were performed using SPSS (version 22). To begin the analysis, the following measures were combined into index variables as individual items within the construct sharing high reliability: language-related behavior acculturation (7 items; $\alpha = .922$), cultural and sociopolitical knowledge acculturation (7 items; $\alpha = .936$), pride and cultural group association acculturation (7 items; $\alpha = .945$), language-related behavior enculturation (6 items; $\alpha = .934$), cultural and sociopolitical knowledge enculturation (5 items; $\alpha = .918$), pride and cultural group association enculturation (7 items; $\alpha = .920$), and online ethnic media use (3 items; $\alpha = .944$). In addition, the means and standard deviations of the key variables of interests were calculated and are shown in Table 1.

Table 1. Mean and standard deviation of variables

Measure	Mean and Standard Deviation
(ACC_B) Language-related Behavior Acculturation	(M = 3.64, SD = .49)
(ACC_K) Cultural and Sociopolitical Knowledge Acculturation	(M = 3.17, SD = .60)
(ACC_C) Pride and Cultural Group Association Acculturation	(M = 3.15, SD = .64)
(ENC_B) Language-related Behavior Enculturation	(M = 2.58, SD = .86)
(ENC_K) Cultural and Sociopolitical Knowledge Enculturation	(M = 2.79, SD = .73)
(ENC_C) Pride and Cultural Group Association Enculturation	(M = 2.99, SD = .60)
Online Ethnic Media Use	(M = 2.68, SD = 1.25)
Age	(M = 37.38, SD = 11.99)
Income	(M = 4.86, SD = 1.77)
Education	(M = 5.03, SD = .1.27)
Generational status	(M = 3.51, SD = 1.89)

To address RQ 1, bivariate correlation analysis was first conducted to explore the relationship between online ethnic media use, acculturation, enculturation, and various demographic variables including age, education, income, and generational status. As shown in Table 2, all three dimensions of acculturation showed statistically significant negative correlation with online ethnic media use. On the other hand, language-related behavior enculturation had the strongest correlation (r = .77, p <.01), followed by cultural and sociopolitical knowledge enculturation (r = .67, p <.01) and pride and cultural group association enculturation (r = .44, p <.01). Among the demographic variables, generational status had a moderately negative correlation with online ethnic media use (r = -.32, p <.01), followed by age (r = -.11, p <.01) and income (r = -.10, p <.05).

This result is not surprising, as it suggests that Asian American individuals who are more enculturated in all three dimensions of their heritage cultures are more likely to consume ethnic media online. In regard to demographics, newer immigrants (e.g., non-US citizens, first-generation Asian Americans, et al.) as well as younger individuals who naturally have lower income were more likely to use ethnic media online.

To further examine the relationship between these variables, multiple linear regressions were conducted using online ethnic media as the dependent variable, and the acculturation, enculturation, and demographic measures as the predictors. A multicollinearity diagnostic was first computed, and the tolerance measures for all predictor variables were well above the commonly accepted .20 threshold (Menard, 1995) and VIF measures were well below the boundary established by scholars (e.g., Mason, Gunst, & Hess, 1989), indicating that there were no multicollinearity issues.

Table 2. Correlation between acculturation, enculturation, demographic factors, and online ethnic media use

		ACC_B	ACC_C	ACC_K	ENC_B	ENC_K	ENC_C	Age	Education	Income	Generational Status	Online Ethnic Media Use
ACC_B	Pearson Correlation	1	.538**	.496**	-.343**	-.233**	-.022	.011	.036	.128**	.363**	-.309**
	Sig. (2-tailed)		.000	.000	.000	.000	.599	.800	.396	.002	.000	.000
	N	574	574	574	574	574	574	574	574	574	574	574
ACC_C	Pearson Correlation	.538**	1	.667**	-.280**	-.228**	-.106*	.160**	.010	.111**	.340**	-.254**
	Sig. (2-tailed)	.000		.000	.000	.000	.011	.000	.812	.008	.000	.000
	N	574	574	574	574	574	574	574	574	574	574	574
ACC_K	Pearson Correlation	.496**	.667**	1	-.249**	-.120**	-.007	.091*	.070	.170**	.373**	-.222**
	Sig. (2-tailed)	.000	.000		.000	.004	.866	.030	.094	.000	.000	.000
	N	574	574	574	574	574	574	574	574	574	574	574
ENC_B	Pearson Correlation	-.343**	-.280**	-.249**	1	.795**	.546**	-.067	.046	-.086*	-.379**	.769**
	Sig. (2-tailed)	.000	.000	.000		.000	.000	.110	.274	.040	.000	.000
	N	574	574	574	574	574	574	574	574	574	574	574
ENC_K	Pearson Correlation	-.233**	-.228**	-.120**	.795**	1	.608**	-.044	.129**	-.048	-.284**	.668**
	Sig. (2-tailed)	.000	.000	.004	.000		.000	.294	.002	.253	.000	.000
	N	574	574	574	574	574	574	574	574	574	574	574
ENC_C	Pearson Correlation	-.022	-.106*	-.007	.546**	.608**	1	-.134**	.033	.046	-.051	.443**
	Sig. (2-tailed)	.599	.011	.866	.000	.000		.001	.425	.268	.226	.000
	N	574	574	574	574	574	574	574	574	574	574	574
Age	Pearson Correlation	.011	.160**	.091*	-.067	-.044	-.134**	1	.160**	.136**	-.060	-.109**
	Sig. (2-tailed)	.800	.000	.030	.110	.294	.001		.000	.001	.152	.009
	N	574	574	574	574	574	574	574	574	574	574	574
Education	Pearson Correlation	.036	.010	.070	.046	.129**	.033	.160**	1	.346**	-.077	.075
	Sig. (2-tailed)	.396	.812	.094	.274	.002	.425	.000		.000	.064	.071
	N	574	574	574	574	574	574	574	574	574	574	574
Annual_Income	Pearson Correlation	.128**	.111**	.170**	-.086*	-.048	.046	.136**	.346**	1	.058	-.097*
	Sig. (2-tailed)	.002	.008	.000	.040	.253	.268	.001	.000		.163	.020
	N	574	574	574	574	574	574	574	574	574	574	574
Generational_Status	Pearson Correlation	.363**	.340**	.373**	-.379**	-.284**	-.051	-.060	-.077	.058	1	-.318**
	Sig. (2-tailed)	.000	.000	.000	.000	.000	.226	.152	.064	.163		.000
	N	574	574	574	574	574	574	574	574	574	574	574
HerMedia	Pearson Correlation	-.309**	-.254**	-.222**	.769**	.668**	.443**	-.109**	.075	-.097*	-.318**	1
	Sig. (2-tailed)	.000	.000	.000	.000	.000	.000	.009	.071	.020	.000	
	N	574	574	574	574	574	574	574	574	574	574	574

As shown in Table 3, results from the multiple regression model indicate that the predictors collectively accounted for 61% of the variance in Asian American individuals' online ethnic media consumption ($R^2 = .610$, $F (10, 563) = 87.99$, $p < .01$). The three major predictors were: language-related behavior enculturation ($\beta = .605$, $t = 12.719$, $p < .001$), cultural and sociopolitical knowledge enculturation ($\beta = .152$, $t = 3.201$, $p < .01$), and age ($\beta = -.065$, $t = -2.346$, $p < .05$), while the other predictors were not statistically significant.

Online Ethnic Media Use and Ethnic Identities

In regard to RQ 2, which explores the level of ethnic media usage among Asian individuals with different ethnic self-identities, descriptive statistics were first calculated. Among the participants, those who identified as Asian had the highest level of ethnic media use (M = 3.30, SD = 1.06), followed by those who defined themselves as their ethnicity, such as simply Chinese or Filipino (M = 3.19, SD =

Table 3. Regression coefficients (online ethnic media use)

	Unstandardized Coefficients		Standardized Coefficients	t	
	B	Std. Error	Beta		Sig.
(Constant)	.329	.362		.910	.363
ACC_B	-.134	.086	-.052	-1.557	.120
ACC_C	.028	.075	.014	.374	.708
ACC_K	-.042	.078	-.020	-.538	.591
ENC_B	.878	.069	.605	12.719	.000**
ENC_K	.259	.081	.152	3.201	.001**
ENC_C	.022	.073	.010	.296	.768
Age	-.007	.003	-.065	-2.346	.019*
Generational status	-.014	.020	-.021	-.691	.490
Education	.052	.028	.053	1.833	.067
Income	-.027	.020	-.039	-1.336	.182

Dependent Variable: Online ethnic media use
* p<.05
** p<.01
(ACC_B) Language-related Behavior Acculturation
(ACC_K) Cultural and Sociopolitical Knowledge Acculturation
(ACC_C) Pride and Cultural Group Association Acculturation
(ENC_B) Language-related Behavior Enculturation
(ENC_K) Cultural and Sociopolitical Knowledge Enculturation
(ENC_C) Pride and Cultural Group Association Enculturation

1.28), as Asian American (*M* = 2.48, *SD* = 1.19), as ethnic (e.g., Chinese or Filipino) American (*M* = 2.38, *SD* = 1.25), and simply as American (*M* = 2.20, *SD* = 1.29).

To compare whether the differences were meaningful, one-way ANOVA was to be performed. However, since the normality assumption could not be established according to the diagnostic results of the Shapiro-Wilk test, a rank-based nonparametric Kruskal-Wallis H test was used instead. The Kruskal-Wallis H test revealed that there was a statistically significant difference in online ethnic media consumption among the five groups of participants who embraced different types of ethnic self-identities, $\chi 2(4) = 62.194$, $p < 0.001$. Table 4 shows the post-hoc pairwise comparison using the Dunn-Bonferroni method, which indicated that there were essentially two groups: individuals who identified as Asian or by their Asian ethnicity belonged in one camp, while individuals who identified as Asian American, ethnic American, or simply American belonged to another—and the differences within each group were negligible.

Table 4. Difference in online ethnic media consumption among individuals with different self-identity

Group 1- Group 2	Test Statistics	Std. Error	Std. Test Statistics	Sig.	Adj. Sig.
American-Asian	-148.239	23.700	-6.255	.000	.000*
Asian American-Asian	-107.457	16.940	-6.344	.000	.000*
Ethnic American-Asian	119.575	25.868	4.622	.000	.000*
American-Ethnic	-130.216	34.596	-3.764	.000	.002*
Asian American-Ethnic	-89.434	30.367	-2.945	.003	.032*
Ethnic American-Ethnic	-101.552	36.116	-2.812	.005	.049*
American-Asian American	-40.782	21.854	-1.866	.062	.620
Ethnic American-Asian American	12.119	24.189	.501	.616	1.000
American-Ethnic American	-28.664	29.323	-.978	.328	1.000
Ethnic-Asian	18.023	31.721	.568	.570	1.000

Each row tests the null hypothesis that Group 1 and Group 2 distributions are the same.
Asymptotic significances (2-sided tests) are displayed. * p<.05
American = respondents who self-identified as American
Asian = respondents who self-identified as Asian
Asian American = respondents who self-identified as Asian American
Ethnic American = respondents who self-identified as Ethnic American (e.g., Chinese American)
Ethnic = respondents who self-identified by their ethnicity (e.g., Chinese)

This result goes hand in hand with findings from RQ 1. Individuals who perceived themselves as Asian or by their Asian ethnicity also tended to be more enculturated. Additionally, the test also confirmed that there was a statistically significant difference in language-related behavior enculturation ($\chi 2(4) = 78.289$, $p < 0.001$), cultural and sociopolitical knowledge enculturation ($\chi 2(4) = 58.857$, $p < 0.001$), and pride and cultural group association enculturation ($\chi 2(4) = 27.074$, $p < 0.001$). It is interesting to note that pride and culture group association, with the smallest chi-square value of the three, was the dimension of enculturation that varied the least among Asian individuals with different ethnic identities. The implication of this finding will be addressed further in the sections below.

FUTURE RESEARCH DIRECTIONS

This chapter describes a study that explores the relationship between acculturation, enculturation, self-identities, and demographic factors, and online ethnic media use among Asian Americans. Results suggest that online ethnic media consumption is negatively correlated with all three dimensions of acculturation and individuals' age, income, and generational status. In contrast, it is negatively correlated with all three dimensions of enculturation. In terms of predictive power, the variables identified by this study collectively accounted for a considerable amount of variance in online ethnic media use. Particularly, Asian Americans—especially those who are younger in age and are highly enculturated in their heritage culture on the dimensions of language-related behavior and cultural and sociopolitical knowledge—would be more likely to utilize online ethnic media in their day-to-day lives. Finally, in the context of self-identity and group membership, individuals who see themselves as Asian or by their Asian ethnicity are also more likely to consume online ethnic media than individuals who consider themselves to be Asian American, ethnic American, or simply American.

Findings from this research are in line with previous studies of ethnic media consumption, in that strongly enculturated individuals will use media as a resource to stay in connected with their homelands. In other words, the consumption patterns and functions of traditional ethnic media that scholars have observed previously may be replicated *online*. It is important to note that considering the technical nature of various online, mobile, and emerging media, *age* is found to be a predictor for online ethnic media use, as younger individuals are more tech-savvy and more likely to gravitate toward digital technologies than older generations.

Given the interdisciplinary nature of the study, the abovementioned findings can be considered and interpreted through different disciplinary lenses. In the space below, the author will discuss the contributions and limitations of this study from the perspective of communication, psychology, and ethnic studies research and point out possible directions for future studies.

Transnational Media Use in the Digital Era

First, in the context of communication research, this study contributes to a growing body of literature on transnational media that highlights the rising significance of digital technologies for immigrants and diasporas by offering an account of the Asian American case through a quantitative approach. There is ample empirical evidence (e.g., Bonfadelli, Bucher, & Piga, 2007; d'Haenens, Van Summeren, Kokhuis, & Beentjes, 2002; Treviño, Webster, & Stein, 2000) that ICTs are complementing traditional media to become a central part of people's media diets today. Accordingly, as ICTs continue to shape the lives of contemporary media consumers, an important question for scholars to consider at the individual level is the particular reasoning and motivation behind online ethnic media consumption and the specific application or utilization of technologies.

For instance, the current study notes that language-related behavior enculturation and cultural and sociopolitical knowledge enculturation are important factors behind online ethnic media consumption—but what specifically about language-related behavior and sociopolitical knowledge is important to immigrants and diasporic individuals, and why? Is it to maintain family relationships? To construct or express individual identities? Or something else entirely? Though the current study is limited by its methodological choice in its ability to fully address these questions, they are issues that many qualitative studies of transnational media use have examined, and future researchers of these topics should be cognizant of the methodological choices and take into consideration the benefits offered by mixed-method research (Creswell & Clark, 2011).

Further, in examining the intersection between ICTs and transnational media practices, it could be valuable to incorporate theoretical frameworks and perspectives from other sub-disciplines within the field of communication. For example, useful concepts in intercultural communication research, such as the distinction between low-context and high-context culture categorized by Hall (1989) and the cultural dimensions catalogued by Hofstede (2003), may influence how people behave online. In media effects research, scholars (e.g., Ruggiero, 2000; Stafford, Stafford, & Schkade, 2004) have also noted the value of uses-and-gratifications theory (Katz, Haas, & Gurevitch, 1973) in understanding the active audience in the high choice/control era of digital media. Both of these perspectives could offer additional insights into online ethnic media use by different immigrant groups and diasporic individuals.

Networked Individuals and Social Capital

At the macro level, findings from this study can be connected to the broader discourse about networked individuals living in an information society (e.g., Castells, 1996; Webster, 1995; Wellman et al., 2003). As our social and economic environment has become increasingly shaped and organized by digital technologies and information networks over the past few decades, scholars have debated the extent to which these social changes would undermine, transform, or facilitate individual and community life. While some have cautioned that the technological evolution would create isolated individuals and lead to an erosion of a sense of community and social capital (e.g., Edwards & Foley, 1998; Landholt & Portes, 1996), others were more optimistic about the positive long-term effects of the Internet on social ties (e.g., Benkler, 2006). To understand this social impact of the Internet, many scholars have turned to the notion of "bridging" and "bonding" social capital (Putnam, 2001), which refers to social networks that bring different (i.e., bridging) or similar (i.e., bonding) people together.

The question of bridging and bonding social capital is an interesting one in the context of online ethnic media consumption. As described previously, items in the questionnaire used by this study focused on the extent to which participants used online ethnic media to consume news, information, and entertainment from their heritage country. Therefore, findings from this research highlight the bonding function of the Internet because online ethnic media can help provide immigrants or diasporic individuals to establish and maintain relations *within* the group itself. However, another limitation of the present study is that it did not examine online ethnic media that produce content *about* their new home country. That is, for example, whether Asian American individuals use online ethnic media to learn about the sociocultural happenings in the United States—which could be considered as the bridging function of the Internet. As a key aspect in the lives of many immigrants and diasporic individuals is to become integrated into the mainstream society, online ethnic media may represent an effective means for individuals to acquire an understanding of current events, which could facilitate their integration process. Several studies (e.g., Elias, 2013; Lazzari, 2012; Parker & Song, 2006; Peeters & d'Haenens, 2005) have explored this issue of bridging/bonding social capital among immigrants, and future studies may seek to further explore this phenomenon in depth.

Acculturation and Enculturation in Communication Research

As noted in the literature review, while intercultural communication scholar have considered acculturation as a latent construct, the operationalization, development, and validation of acculturation and enculturation psychometrics are often conducted by psychologists, who then apply these scales to study issues related to mental health and psychological well-being, such as depressive symptoms (e.g., Rahman & Rollock, 2004) or acculturative stress (e.g., Hwang & Ting, 2008). Thus, few psychology research studies have extended the measures of acculturation and enculturation to behavioral outcomes in communication. To that end, the present study applied a newly developed Asian American acculturation and enculturation measure to studies of intercultural communication and media use.

Further, acculturation has received more consideration in intercultural communication research, as scholars (e.g., Dalisay, 2012; Lee & Tse, 1994; Moon & Park, 2007; Viswanath & Arora, 2000; Yang, Wu, Zhu, & Southwell, 2004) have applied the concept to study how immigrants and diasporic individuals utilize mainstream media in their new homeland as a part of their assimilation process. In contrast, the concept of enculturation has received less scholarly attention. This study broadly highlights *enculturation* as a psychological mechanism in predicting ethnic media consumption on the Internet. As scholars in psychology continue to refine ways to measure acculturation and enculturation, future communication research should continue to monitor such evolution and explore the roles that these constructs may play in the context of intercultural or interpersonal communication.

Asian American Ethnic Identities vs. Cultural Identities

As described in the results section, pride and culture group association is a dimension of enculturation that varies the least among Asian individuals with different ethnic self-identities. This is an interesting finding worthy of further consideration because it may be related to the ongoing debate over the conceptual difference between cultural and ethnic identity, as well as the appropriate operationalization of these measures. Cultural identity has been argued by some scholars to be a construct that focuses more on one's attitudes—such as preference for one's cultural practices or feelings toward his or her heritage group (Kim, 2007), while ethnic identity is described as a more relational construct, such as a sense of belonging to one's heritage group and/or how individuals relate to their own group as a subgroup in relation to the larger society (Fischer & Moradi, 2001; Phinney & Ong, 2007). Agreement has not yet been found on whether these constructs are related but different concepts, or are in fact one concept with multiple dimensions.

In the context of the present research, though the multidimensional enculturation items used in the study were comprehensive and captured individuals' feelings, attitudes, and relational identification with their heritage culture/groups, the way that self-identity was measured (see Methods section for detail) leaned more toward the definition of ethnic identity described above. This may explain the decreased variability for pride and culture group association enculturation among Asian individuals with different ethnic self-identities. However, this result also highlights the fact that the distinction between cultural and ethnic identity remains an issue to be examined in future studies on race and ethnicity.

CONCLUSION

In sum, this chapter presents an empirical study that illustrates the factors that contribute to Asian American individuals' use of ethnic media on the Internet, as well as how such consumption may differ among individuals with different ethnic self-identities. This study may open the door for future research described above. As the Asian American population continues to grow, so does its significance in the United States—as consumers, voters, and candidates. The evolution and diffusion of ICTs in the coming years will also empower the Asian diaspora in the United States to stay ever more connected with their country of cultural and ethnic origins with ease and convenience. A greater level of understanding of the Asian American experience in the digital and globalized media environment is therefore needed. To that end, this study offers empirical evidence from an interdisciplinary perspective that will contribute to this growing area of scholarship.

ACKNOWLEDGMENT

This research was supported by a Butler University Holcomb Awards Committee (HAC) Research Grant.

REFERENCES

Alonso, A., & Oiarzabal, P. J. (2010). *Diasporas in the new media age: Identity, politics, and community*. Reno, NV: University of Nevada Press.

Anderson, B. (2006). *Imagined communities: Reflections on the origin and spread of nationalism*. London: Verso Books.

Ang, I. (1990). The nature of the audience. In J. D. H. Downing, A. Mohammadi, & A. Sreberny (Eds.), *Questioning the media: A critical introduction* (pp. 155–165). Thousand Oaks, CA: Sage Publications.

Aoki, A., & Takeda, O. (2008). *Asian American Politics* (Vol. 1). Cambridge, UK: Polity Press.

Appadurai, A. (1996). *Modernity at large: Cultural dimensions of globalization*. Minneapolis, MN: University of Minnesota Press.

Belanger, S., & Pinard, M. (1991). Ethnic movements and the competition model: Some missing links. *American Sociological Review*, *56*(4), 446–457. doi:10.2307/2096267

Benítez, J. L. (2012). Salvadoran transnational families: ICT and communication practices in the network society. *Journal of Ethnic and Migration Studies*, *38*(9), 1439–1449. doi:10.1080/1369183X.2012.698214

Benkler, Y. (2006). *The wealth of networks: How social production transforms markets and freedom*. New Haven, CT: Yale University Press.

Bernal, V. (2006). Diaspora, cyberspace and political imagination: The Eritrean diaspora online. *Global Networks*, *6*(2), 161–179. doi:10.1111/j.1471-0374.2006.00139.x

Berry, J. W. (1980). Acculturation as varieties of adaptation. In A. M. Padilla (Ed.), *Acculturation: Theory, models, and some new findings* (pp. 9–25). Boulder, CO: Westview Press.

Bonfadelli, H., Bucher, P., & Piga, A. (2007). Use of old and new media by ethnic minority youth in Europe with a special emphasis on Switzerland. *Communications*, *32*(2), 141–170. doi:10.1515/COMMUN.2007.010

Brinkerhoff, J. M. (2009). *Digital diasporas: Identity and transnational engagement*. Cambridge, UK: Cambridge University Press. doi:10.1017/CBO9780511805158

Castells, M. (1996). *The network society* (Vol. 469). Oxford, UK: Blackwell.

Chalaby, J. K. (2005). From internationalization to transnationalization. *Global Media and Communication*, *1*(1), 28–33. doi:10.1177/174276650500100107

Chen, G. M. (2012). The impact of new media on intercultural communication in global context. *China Media Research*, *8*(2), 1–10.

Chen, H. T., Ping, S., & Chen, G. (2015). Far from reach but near at hand: The role of social media for cross-national mobilization. *Computers in Human Behavior*, *53*, 443–451. doi:10.1016/j.chb.2015.05.052

Conradson, D., & McKay, D. (2007). Translocal subjectivities: Mobility, connection, emotion. *Mobilities*, *2*(2), 167–174. doi:10.1080/17450100701381524

Creswell, J. W., & Clark, V. L. P. (2011). *Designing and conducting mixed methods research*. Thousand Oaks, CA: Sage Publications.

Croucher, S. M., & Rahmani, D. (2015). A longitudinal test of the effects of Facebook on cultural adaptation. *Journal of International and Intercultural Communication*, *8*(4), 330–345. doi:10.1080/17513057.2015.1087093

Cuéllar, I., Arnold, B., & Maldonado, R. (1995). Acculturation Rating Scale for Mexican Americans-II: A revision of the original ARSMA Scale. *Hispanic Journal of Behavioral Sciences*, *17*(3), 275–304. doi:10.1177/07399863950173001

Cunningham, S. (2001). Popular media as public "sphericules" for diasporic communities. *International Journal of Cultural Studies*, *4*(2), 131–147. doi:10.1177/136787790100400201

d'Haenens, L., Van Summeren, C., Kokhuis, M., & Beentjes, J. W. (2002). Ownership and use of old and new media among ethnic minority youth in the Netherlands: The role of the ethno-cultural position. *Communications*, *27*(3), 365–393. doi:10.1515/comm.27.3.365

Dalisay, F. (2012). Media use and acculturation of new immigrants in the United States. *Communication Research Reports*, *29*(2), 148–160. doi:10.1080/08824096.2012.667774

de Block, L., & Buckingham, D. (2007). *Global children, global media: Migration, media and childhood*. New York: Palgrave Macmillan. doi:10.1057/9780230591646

Edwards, B., & Foley, M. W. (1998). Civil society and social capital beyond Putnam. *The American Behavioral Scientist*, *42*(1), 124–139. doi:10.1177/0002764298042001010

Elias, N. (2013). Immigrant children and media. *The Routledge international handbook on children and media*, 336–343.

Espiritu, Y. L. (1993). *Asian American panethnicity: Bridging institutions and identities*. Philadelphia: Temple University Press.

Espiritu, Y. L. (1994). The intersection of race, ethnicity, and class: The multiple identities of second generation Filipinos. *Identities (Yverdon)*, *1*(2–3), 249–273. doi:10.1080/1070289X.1994.9962507

Fischer, A. R., & Moradi, B. (2001). Racial and ethnic identity: Recent development and needed directions. In J. G. Ponterotto, J. M. Casas, L. Suzuki, & C. M. Alexander (Eds.), *Handbook of multicultural counseling* (2nd ed.; pp. 341–370). Thousand Oaks, CA: Sage Publications.

Fong, M., & Chuang, R. (2004). *Communicating ethnic and cultural identity*. Lanham, MD: Rowman & Littlefield.

Forbush, E., & Foucault-Welles, B. (2016). Social media use and adaptation among Chinese students beginning to study in the United States. *International Journal of Intercultural Relations*, *50*, 1–12. doi:10.1016/j.ijintrel.2015.10.007

Georgiou, M. (2001). Crossing the boundaries of the ethnic home: Media consumption and ethnic identity construction in the public space: The case of the Cypriot Community Centre in North London. *Gazette*, *63*(4), 311–329. doi:10.1177/0016549201063004003

Georgiou, M. (2006). *Diaspora, identity and the media: Diasporic transnationalism and mediated spatialities*. New York: Hampton Press.

Giddens, A. (1991). *Modernity and self-identity: Self and society in the late modern age*. Redwood City, CA: Stanford University Press.

Gillespie, M. (2000). Transnational communications and diaspora communities. *Ethnic minorities and the media*, 164–178.

Goffman, E. (1978). *The presentation of self in everyday life* (p. 56). Harmondsworth, UK: Penguin Books.

Graves, T. D. (1967). Acculturation, access, and alcohol in a tri-ethnic community. *American Anthropologist*, *69*(3–4), 306–321. doi:10.1525/aa.1967.69.3-4.02a00030

Hall, E. T. (1989). *Beyond culture*. New York: Anchor Books.

Hall, S. (1990). Cultural identity and diaspora. In J. Rutherford (Ed.), *Identity: Community, Culture, Difference* (pp. 222–237). London: Lawrence & Wishart.

Hendrickson, B., & Rosen, D. (2017). Insights into new media use by international students: Implications for cross-cultural adaptation theory. *Social Networking*, *6*(02), 81–106. doi:10.4236/sn.2017.62006

Hepp, A. (2009). Localities of diasporic communicative spaces: Material aspects of translocal mediated networking. *Communication Review*, *12*(4), 327–348. doi:10.1080/10714420903344451

Herskovits, M. J. (1948). *Man and his works: The science of cultural anthropology*. New York: Knopf.

Hiller, H. H., & Franz, T. M. (2004). New ties, old ties and lost ties: The use of the internet in diaspora. *New Media & Society*, *6*(6), 731–752. doi:10.1177/146144804044327

Hoeffel, E. M., Rastogi, S., Kim, M. O., & Hasan, S. (2012). *The Asian Population: 2010*. US Department of Commerce, Economics and Statistics Administration, US Census Bureau. Retrieved from: http://www.census.gov/prod/cen2010/briefs/c2010br-11.pdf

Hofstede, G. (2003). *Culture's consequences: Comparing values, behaviors, institutions and organizations across nations*. Thousand Oaks, CA: Sage Publications.

Hwang, W. C., & Ting, J. Y. (2008). Disaggregating the effects of acculturation and acculturative stress on the mental health of Asian Americans. *Cultural Diversity & Ethnic Minority Psychology*, *14*(2), 147–154. doi:10.1037/1099-9809.14.2.147 PMID:18426287

Kalsbeek, W. D. (2003). Sampling minority groups in health surveys. *Statistics in Medicine*, *22*(9), 1527–1549. doi:10.1002/sim.1510 PMID:12704614

Karim, K. H. (2003). *The media of diaspora* (Vol. 7). New York: Routledge.

Katz, E., Haas, H., & Gurevitch, M. (1973). On the use of the mass media for important things. *American Sociological Review*, *38*(2), 164–181. doi:10.2307/2094393

Katz, V. S. (2010). How children of immigrants use media to connect their families to the community: The case of Latinos in South Los Angeles. *Journal of Children and Media*, *4*(3), 298–315. doi:10.1080/17482798.2010.486136

Kibria, N. (2003). *Becoming Asian American: Second-generation Chinese and Korean American identities*. Baltimore, MD: Johns Hopkins University Press.

Kim, B. S. K. (2007). Acculturation and enculturation. In F. T. L. Leong, A. G. Inman, A. Ebreo, L. H. Yang, L. M. Kinoshita, & M. Fu (Eds.), *Handbook of Asian American psychology* (2nd ed., pp. 141–158). Thousand Oaks, CA: Sage Publications.

Kim, B. S. K., & Abreu, J. M. (2001). Acculturation measurement: Theory, current instruments, and future directions. In J. G. Ponterotto, J. M. Casas, L. Suzuki, & C. M. Alexander (Eds.), *Handbook of multicultural counseling* (2nd ed.; pp. 394–424). Thousand Oaks, CA: Sage Publications.

Kim, Y. Y. (1988). *Communication and cross-cultural adaptation: An integrative theory*. Philadelphia: Multilingual Matters.

Kim, Y. Y. (2001). *Becoming intercultural: An integrative theory of communication and cross-cultural adaptation*. Thousand Oaks, CA: Sage Publications.

Kim, Y. Y. (2015). Finding a "home" beyond culture: The emergence of intercultural personhood in the globalizing world. *International Journal of Intercultural Relations*, *46*, 3–12. doi:10.1016/j.ijintrel.2015.03.018

Kissau, K. (2012). Structuring migrants' political activities on the internet: A two-dimensional approach. *Journal of Ethnic and Migration Studies*, *38*(9), 1381–1403. doi:10.1080/1369183X.2012.698207

Landolt, P., & Portes, A. (1996). The downside of social capital. *The American Prospect*, *26*, 18–21.

Lazzari, M. (2012, July). The role of social networking services to shape the double virtual citizenship of young immigrants in Italy. In *IADIS International Conference ICT, Society and Human Beings* (pp. 11–18). IADIS.

Lee, R. M. (2003). Do ethnic identity and other-group orientation protect against discrimination for Asian Americans? *Journal of Counseling Psychology*, *50*(2), 133–141. doi:10.1037/0022-0167.50.2.133

Lee, R. M., Yoon, E., & Liu-Tom, H. T. (2006). Structure and measurement of acculturation/enculturation for Asian Americans using the ARSMA-II. *Measurement & Evaluation in Counseling & Development*, *39*(1), 42–55. doi:10.1080/07481756.2006.11909789

Lee, W. N., & Tse, D. K. (1994). Changing media consumption in a new home: Acculturation patterns among Hong Kong immigrants to Canada. *Journal of Advertising*, *23*(1), 57–70. doi:10.1080/00913367.1994.10673431

Lien, P. T., Conway, M. M., & Wong, J. (2004). *The politics of Asian Americans: Diversity and community*. New York: Routledge.

Ma, S. M. (2000). *The deathly embrace: Orientalism and Asian American identity*. Minneapolis, MN: University of Minnesota Press.

Mason, R. L., Gunst, R. F., & Hess, J. L. (1989). *Statistical design and analysis of experiments: With applications to engineering and science*. New York: Wiley.

Masuoka, N. (2006). Together they become one: Examining the predictors of panethnic group consciousness among Asian Americans and Latinos. *Social Science Quarterly*, *87*(5), 993–1011. doi:10.1111/j.1540-6237.2006.00412.x

Mead, G. H. (1934). *Mind, self and society* (Vol. 111). Chicago: University of Chicago Press.

Menard, S. (1995). *Applied logistic regression analysis*. Thousand Oaks, CA: Sage Publications.

Miller, M. J. (2007). A bilinear multidimensional measurement model of Asian American acculturation and enculturation: Implications for counseling interventions. *Journal of Counseling Psychology*, *54*(2), 118–131. doi:10.1037/0022-0167.54.2.118

Moon, S. J., & Park, C. Y. (2007). Media effects on acculturation and biculturalism: A case study of Korean immigrants in Los Angeles' Koreatown. *Mass Communication & Society*, *10*(3), 319–343. doi:10.1080/15205430701407330

Nagel, J. (1994). Constructing ethnicity: Creating and recreating ethnic identity and culture. *Social Problems*, *41*(1), 152–176. doi:10.2307/3096847

Nedelcu, M. (2012). Migrants' new transnational habitus: Rethinking migration through a cosmopolitan lens in the digital age. *Journal of Ethnic and Migration Studies*, *38*(9), 1339–1356. doi:10.1080/1369183X.2012.698203

Newland, K. (2010). *Voice after exit: Diaspora advocacy*. Migration Policy Institute.

Nielsen, F. (1985). Toward a theory of ethnic solidarity in modern societies. *American Sociological Review*, *50*(2), 133–149. doi:10.2307/2095405

Oh, D. C. (2015). *Second-generation Korean Americans and transnational media: Diasporic identifications*. Lanham, MD: Lexington Books.

Okamoto, D. G. (2003). Toward a theory of panethnicity: Explaining Asian American collective action. *American Sociological Review*, *68*(6), 811–842. doi:10.2307/1519747

Olzak, S. (1994). *The dynamics of ethnic competition and conflict*. Redwood City, CA: Stanford University Press.

Oyserman, D., & Sakamoto, I. (1997). Being Asian American: Identity, cultural constructs, and stereotype perception. *The Journal of Applied Behavioral Science*, *33*(4), 435–453. doi:10.1177/0021886397334002

Padilla, F. M. (1985). *Latino ethnic consciousness: The case of Mexican Americans and Puerto Ricans in Chicago*. Notre Dame, IN: University of Notre Dame Press.

Parker, D., & Song, M. (2006). Ethnicity, social capital and the Internet: British Chinese websites. *Ethnicities*, *6*(2), 178–202. doi:10.1177/1468796806063751

Peeters, A. L., & d'Haenens, L. (2005). Bridging or bonding? Relationships between integration and media use among ethnic minorities in the Netherlands. *Communications*, *30*(2), 201–231. doi:10.1515/comm.2005.30.2.201

Pew Research Center. (2012). *The Rise of Asian Americans*. Retrieved from: http://www.pewsocialtrends.org/2012/06/19/the-rise-of-asian-americans/

Phinney, J. S., & Chavira, V. (1992). Ethnic identity and self-esteem: An exploratory longitudinal study. *Journal of Adolescence*, *15*(3), 271–281. doi:10.1016/0140-1971(92)90030-9 PMID:1447413

Phinney, J. S., & Ong, A. D. (2007). Conceptualization and measurement of ethnic identity: Current status and future directions. *Journal of Counseling Psychology*, *54*(3), 271–281. doi:10.1037/0022-0167.54.3.271

Putnam, R. D. (2001). *Bowling alone: The collapse and revival of American community*. New York: Simon and Schuster.

Rahman, O., & Rollock, D. (2004). Acculturation, competence, and mental health among South Asian students in the United States. *Journal of Multicultural Counseling and Development*, *32*(3), 130–142. doi:10.1002/j.2161-1912.2004.tb00366.x

Renn, K. A. (2000). Patterns of situational identity among biracial and multiracial college students. *The Review of Higher Education*, *23*(4), 399–420. doi:10.1353/rhe.2000.0019

Romero, A. J., & Roberts, R. E. (1998). Perception of discrimination and ethnocultural variables in a diverse group of adolescents. *Journal of Adolescence*, *21*(6), 641–656. doi:10.1006/jado.1998.0185 PMID:9971722

Ruggiero, T. E. (2000). Uses and gratifications theory in the 21st century. *Mass Communication & Society*, *3*(1), 3–37. doi:10.1207/S15327825MCS0301_02

Ryder, A. G., Alden, L. E., & Paulhus, D. L. (2000). Is acculturation unidimensional or bidimensional? A head-to-head comparison in the prediction of personality, self-identity, and adjustment. *Journal of Personality and Social Psychology*, *79*(1), 49–65. doi:10.1037/0022-3514.79.1.49 PMID:10909877

Schwartz, S. J., Unger, J. B., Zamboanga, B. L., & Szapocznik, J. (2010). Rethinking the concept of acculturation: Implications for theory and research. *The American Psychologist*, *65*(4), 237–251. doi:10.1037/a0019330 PMID:20455618

Seifert, J. L. (2015). A Culture of Survivors: SlutWalk, Third Culture, and New Media Communication. *International Journal of Interactive Communication Systems and Technologies*, *5*(1), 1–13. doi:10.4018/IJICST.2015010101

Shelton, J. N., & Sellers, R. M. (2000). Situational stability and variability in African American racial identity. *The Journal of Black Psychology*, *26*(1), 27–50. doi:10.1177/0095798400026001002

Shi, Y. (2005). Identity construction of the Chinese diaspora, ethnic media use, community formation, and the possibility of social activism. *Continuum*, *19*(1), 55–72. doi:10.1080/1030431052000336298

Shuter, R. (2012). Intercultural new media studies: The next frontier in intercultural communication. *Journal of Intercultural Communication Research*, *41*(3), 219–237. doi:10.1080/17475759.2012.728761

Smith Pfister, D., & Soliz, J. (2011). (Re)conceptualizing intercultural communication in a networked society. *Journal of International and Intercultural Communication*, *4*(4), 246–251. doi:10.1080/17513057.2011.598043

Sreberny, A. (2000). Media and diasporic consciousness: An exploration among Iranians in London. In S. Cottle, S. (Ed.), Ethnic Minorities and the Media: Changing Cultural Boundaries (pp. 179-196). Maidenhead, UK: Open University Press.

Stacks, D. W. (2016). *Primer of public relations research*. New York: Guilford Publications.

Stafford, T. F., Stafford, M. R., & Schkade, L. L. (2004). Determining uses and gratifications for the internet. *Decision Sciences*, *35*(2), 259–288. doi:10.1111/j.00117315.2004.02524.x

Thompson, K. (2002). Border crossings and diasporic identities: Media use and leisure practices of an ethnic minority. *Qualitative Sociology*, *25*(3), 409–418. doi:10.1023/A:1016038114625

Thussu, D. K. (2006). *Media on the move: global flow and contra-flow*. London, New York: Routledge.

Treviño, L. K., Webster, J., & Stein, E. W. (2000). Making connections: Complementary influences on communication media choices, attitudes, and use. *Organization Science*, *11*(2), 163–182. doi:10.1287/orsc.11.2.163.12510

Viswanath, K., & Arora, P. (2000). Ethnic media in the United States: An essay on their role in integration, assimilation, and social control. *Mass Communication & Society*, *3*(1), 39–56. doi:10.1207/S15327825MCS0301_03

Wang, K. Y., Atkin, D. J., & Lau, T. Y. (2014). Media versus individual frames and horizontal knowledge gaps: A study of the 2010 health care reform debate online. *Electronic News*, *8*(1), 30–48. doi:10.1177/1931243114524419

Webster, F. (1995). *Theories of the information society*. New York: Routledge.

Weinreich, P. (2009). "Enculturation", not "acculturation": Conceptualising and assessing identity processes in migrant communities. *International Journal of Intercultural Relations*, *33*(2), 124–139. doi:10.1016/j.ijintrel.2008.12.006

Wellman, B., Quan-Haase, A., Boase, J., Chen, W., Hampton, K., Díaz, I., & Miyata, K. (2003). The social affordances of the internet for networked individualism. *Journal of Computer-Mediated Communication, 8*(3).

Yang, C., Wu, H., Zhu, M., & Southwell, B. G. (2004). Tuning in to fit in? Acculturation and media use among Chinese students in the United States. *Asian Journal of Communication*, *14*(1), 81–94. doi:10.1080/01292980420001951512

Zhang, S., & Moradi, B. (2013). Asian American acculturation and enculturation: Construct clarification and measurement consolidation. *The Counseling Psychologist*, *41*(5), 750–790. doi:10.1177/0011000012456882

ADDITIONAL READING

Chen, W. (2010). Internet-usage patterns of immigrants in the process of intercultural adaptation. *Cyberpsychology, Behavior, and Social Networking*, *13*(4), 387–399. doi:10.1089/cyber.2009.0249 PMID:20712497

Dalisay, F. (2012). Media use and acculturation of new immigrants in the United States. *Communication Research Reports*, *29*(2), 148–160. doi:10.1080/08824096.2012.667774

Kim, Y. Y. (2001). *Becoming intercultural: An integrative theory of communication and cross-cultural adaptation*. Thousand Oaks, CA: Sage Publications.

Reece, D., & Palmgreen, P. (2000). Coming to America: Need for acculturation and media use motives among Indian sojourners in the US. *International Journal of Intercultural Relations*, *24*(6), 807–824. doi:10.1016/S0147-1767(00)00033-X

Rudmin, F. (2009). Constructs, measurements and models of acculturation and acculturative stress. *International Journal of Intercultural Relations*, *33*(2), 106–123. doi:10.1016/j.ijintrel.2008.12.001

Schwartz, S. J., Unger, J. B., Zamboanga, B. L., & Szapocznik, J. (2010). Rethinking the concept of acculturation: Implications for theory and research. *The American Psychologist*, *65*(4), 237–251. doi:10.1037/a0019330 PMID:20455618

Shuter, R. (2012). Intercultural new media studies: The next frontier in intercultural communication. *Journal of Intercultural Communication Research*, *41*(3), 219–237. doi:10.1080/17475759.2012.728761

Yang, C., Wu, H., Zhu, M., Brian, G., & Southwell, . (2004). Tuning in to fit in? Acculturation and media use among Chinese students in the United States. *Asian Journal of Communication*, *14*(1), 81–94. doi:10.1080/01292980420001951512

KEY TERMS AND DEFINITIONS

Acculturation: The change in an individual's attitudes, values, and identity after being in contact with a dominant culture.

Asian Americans: Any individual of Asian descent who resides in the United States on a permanent or long-term basis, regardless of citizenship or other legal status.

Enculturation: The process of socialization and maintenance of the norms of one's indigenous culture.

Information Communication Technologies: An umbrella term that describes all technologies for the communication of information.

APPENDIX

Table 5. Zhang and Moradi's (2013) Asian American Acculturation and Enculturation Scale

Acculturation Items
Language-related Behavior
Items:
I speak English well. I often write in English (e.g., letters). I enjoy speaking English. My thinking is often done in English. I feel comfortable speaking English. I enjoy reading in English (e.g., books). I enjoy watching TV in English.
Cultural and Sociopolitical Knowledge
I know the history of mainstream Americans well. I know popular mainstream American newspapers and magazines well. I know mainstream American current affairs well. I know the national heroes of mainstream America well. I know mainstream American literature well. I know mainstream American social norms and customs well. I am knowledgeable about mainstream American culture and traditions.
Pride and Cultural Group Association
I like to identify myself as mainstream American. I am proud to be a part of mainstream Americans. My friends now are mainstream Americans. I feel I have a lot in common with mainstream Americans. I like to interact and associate with mainstream Americans. I relate to my partner or spouse in a way that is similar to mainstream Americans. I identify with mainstream Americans. I feel connected with mainstream American culture.
Enculturation Items
Language-related Behavior
I enjoy watching TV in the language of my heritage culture. I enjoy reading in the language of my heritage culture (e.g., books). I often write in the language of my heritage culture (e.g., letters). I speak the language of my heritage culture well. I enjoy watching TV in the language of my heritage culture. I enjoy reading in the language of my heritage culture (e.g., books). I often write in the language of my heritage culture (e.g., letters). I speak the language of my heritage culture well. My thinking is often done in the language of my heritage culture. I read and write well in the language of my heritage culture.

continued on following page

Table 5. Continued

Cultural and Sociopolitical Knowledge
I know history of my heritage cultural group well. I am knowledgeable about the culture and traditions of my heritage culture. I know current affairs of my heritage cultural group well. I know national heroes from my heritage cultural group well. I know political leaders from my heritage cultural group well.
Pride and Cultural Group Association
I like to interact and associate with people from the same heritage culture as myself. I am proud to be a part of my heritage cultural group. I often interact and associate with people from the same heritage culture as myself. I feel I have a lot in common with people from the same heritage culture as myself. I go to places where people are from the same heritage culture as myself. I associate with my heritage cultural group. I identify with my heritage cultural group.

Chapter 3
Millennial Culture and Its Reluctant Acceptance of Modern News Media:
Examining Millennial Media Habits and Media Credibility in the Age of Listicles

Sean R. Sadri
Old Dominion University, USA

ABSTRACT

The growth of new media has caused dramatic changes in the types of news stories millennials are consuming. A new media phenomenon that has become ubiquitous throughout the media landscape are listicles (or articles that are simply lists and offer arguably less journalistic value than traditional articles). Millennial culture has embraced listicles and made BuzzFeed one of the most popular websites on the internet. This chapter examines millennial media habits and ways news credibility is evolving with the preferences of this digital native generation. Using a sample population of millennials, the author's own study sought to better understand their information-seeking behavior and the online and offline media sources millennials use regularly. Additionally, an experiment was conducted to determine which online article format is considered more credible to millennials: traditional articles or listicles. Analysis revealed that article format was an important factor in credibility ratings as participants found the listicle to be significantly more credible than the traditional article.

DOI: 10.4018/978-1-5225-3784-7.ch003

INTRODUCTION

New media and the online environment are vital aspects of daily life for individuals in the digital age. The limits of the Internet are seemingly boundless, and people use it every day to communicate with others, purchase goods and services, find their way around town, and even decide where to eat. People of all ages are reliant on new media in some way, and as technology advances, this reliance on smartphones, computers, and the Internet will only continue to grow. While most individuals see new media as essential, millennials have an even deeper, more profound connection to all aspects of media. Millennials are digital natives who were raised with computers and understand the complexities of mediated communication (Gottfried & Shearer, 2016; Serazio, 2015). They also exhibit a "networked hypersociality" where advanced online networks are paramount to their social media-based culture (Serazio, 2015, p. 599). Millennials also engage in "participatory exhibitionism" in which every aspect of their daily life is broadcast to followers online, which range from close friends and family to complete strangers (Serazio, 2015, p. 599).

Millennials are characterized as a generation of young adults born between the early 1980s and the late 1990s, and have a connection to media that is so ingrained in their daily lives that it can be characterized as a "perceived technological intimacy" (Serazio, 2015, pg. 600). Generations that immediately preceded millennials were reliant on a more constrained media environment of mass broadcasting in which news and information were delivered via traditional channels (Serazio, 2013). Conversely, the media ecosystem has since evolved to be more inclusive with user-generated content, social networking, and a collaborative culture built around community. Gumpert and Cathcart (1985) suggest that the value system, and even the way each generation comprehends information, is determined by that era's established media ecosystem. For example, the newspaper and print media ecosystem made people process reality in a way that was logically ordered, linear, and continuous. Heavily influenced by radio and television, the subsequent generation established an electronic reality in which logic was visual and auditory. The authors conclude that "different world perspectives and human relationships are as much a matter of media gaps as they are generation gaps" (Gumpert & Cathcart, 1985, p. 23). Thus, the digital age has brought forth a new age of media that has profoundly changed the way millennials think, behave, and process information.

Modern media organizations have had to progress to stay in line with advancements in technology as well as changes in audience preference (Kasiazek, Malthouse, & Webster, 2010). A new wave of media storytelling has formed from a hybrid media system in which traditional media and new media coexist (Chadwick, 2013). Unlike previous generations which dedicated large blocks of their day to consuming news (such as watching an evening broadcast or reading the morning paper), millennials ingest news throughout the day in a constant stream on a bevy of web-connected devices (Gottfried & Shearer, 2016; Kasiazek et al., 2010). Twitter and Facebook have sparked a mobile news environment in which users prefer stories that have a profound aesthetic appeal and are easy to read (Mitchell & Holcomb, 2016). While a 24-hour news cycle would suggest a more active investment from millennial news consumers, audiences are actually becoming more passive. 63% of Instagram users, 62% of Facebook users, and 58% of YouTube users report hearing of news stories during casual online browsing, not while actively searching for news (Gottfried & Shearer, 2016).

Despite growing passivity from its audience, technology companies and media organizations have established a symbiotic relationship that has taken news storytelling to a new level. Specific news outlets (including *The New York Times*) are experimenting with immersive reality journalism in which the news can be "experienced" firsthand (Mitchell & Holcomb, 2016). The *Washington Post* has introduced "chatbots" which provide personalized headlines and news content through mobile messaging services, such as Facebook Messenger. The growth of mobile news apps suggests that media companies are pouring efforts into new media to appeal to a younger, more mobile demographic (Mitchell & Holcomb, 2016).

The growth of new media has also spawned a news trend in which reality is logically ordered and linear (perhaps an homage to the print generation). Listicles are a new media phenomenon that has been adopted by virtually every news organization and are articles that are simply lists or rankings. They often have headlines that elicit thousands of clicks and shares on social media (i.e. "24 Ways to Get Siri to Bring Out Her True Sassiness"), and the presence of listicles has become ubiquitous throughout the Internet. Traditional journalists have been heavily critical of listicles since their inception (Holic, 2013; Steiger, 2010). Listicles carry a stigma for journalists who suggest that they are "sloppily researched and lazily written" as well as "brimming with regressive gender and racial stereotypes" (Steiger, 2010, p. 15).

Millennial culture has a profound connection to new media, and the present chapter outlines an experiment designed by the author to better understand that culture in our modern media ecosystem. This chapter examines the modern phenomenon of listicles and attempts to determine how credible they are to millennials. The popularity of listicles continues to grow as consumer preferences shift and now favor information presented concisely, quickly, and easy to digest (Denning, 2014). Popular websites, such as BuzzFeed, have made listicles the primary draw for their millennial readers, so their popularity seems poised to reach even greater heights. The study also seeks to examine the information seeking behavior of millennials with an emphasis on understanding their use of new media. Additionally, the study outlined in this chapter seeks to understand their motivations for reading listicles by comparing their credibility ratings and determine if those credibility perceptions are significantly different from traditional online articles. By examining the appeal of listicles, media organizations and media scholars can gain insight into the direction that news may be going for the next generation of news consumers. Ultimately, this chapter aims to provide a better understanding of the new media preferences of millennial news readers and provide suggestions on ways to enhance the perceived credibility of online news.

BACKGROUND

Millennial Culture in the Media Ecosystem

Defining a generation of individuals is a social construction that attempts to normalize perceptions and bring order (Edmunds & Turner, 2002). Mannheim (1952) suggests that a collective consciousness forms among an age group when experiencing important historical events from a singular chronological perspective. Serazio (2015) argues that "each generation is supposedly equipped with certain media grammars and literacies in its youth; these are influenced by that era's media ecology and reflected in the values and habits—and ways of thinking—of a given cohort" (p. 602). Although defining a generation is a social construct, those established definitions are a fluid, negotiated process (Alanen, 2001). Because millennials are so connected to technology, the ever-evolving nature of digital ecosystems makes it difficult to define millennials into a singular category. Millennials grew into adulthood during the digital age and are both empowered and hyperconnected to new media, so trying to understand millennial culture remains fluid (Goodstein, 2007; Serazio, 2015). While previous generations have a more passive relationship with mass media, technology has become "a liberating force for youth" (Serazio, 2015, p. 603). Millennials now have the means to engage with new forms of communication and establish a greater sense of belonging and community. Ito (2008) suggests that younger generations derive pleasure from the ability to "publicize and distribute their work to online audiences and to gain new forms of visibility and reputation" (p. 1).

The millennial connection to online media also extends to news. A 2016 Pew Research Center study found that 81 percent of Americans receive their news online either through websites, apps, or social networking sites (Mitchell, Gottfried, Barthel, & Shearer, 2016). The authors assert that the digital news era is still in its adolescence, and the role of friends and family continues to intensify as people share more news with peers. In a related survey, millennial news consumers were found to be considerably more tied to news on social media than older readers (Barthel, Shearer, Gottfried, & Mitchell, 2015). Half the participants in this age group identified

Facebook and Twitter as the most important way or an important way they receive news, compared to only 31 percent of those 35 and older (Barthel et al., 2015).

Millennials want news that is accessible at anytime and anywhere as well as an ability to search, share, comment, and contribute to the news ecosystem (Poindexter, 2012). Poindexter (2012) even argues that "coolness may re-define what news is, and expectations of it" (p. 28). Even the way millennials are exposed to news is starkly different than years past. One study found that millennials are exposed to news through incidental consumption (i.e. news that appears on social media), routine surveillance (i.e. checking for news on digital devices), and directed consumption (i.e. gathering supplemental information about a news story after incidental consumption or routine surveillance) (Antunovic, Parsons, & Cooke, 2016). Incidental consumption to news stories also has some additional benefits as the amount of time college students spend on social media has a positive correlation with the amount of news they consume (Ha et al., 2016).

Millennials may be getting their news primarily online, but they do not believe everything they read. Only one in ten 18-29 year olds admits to placing a lot of trust in the information they receive from national news organizations (Mitchell et al., 2016). However, looking at stories written by traditional versus citizen journalists, Swasy, Tandoc, Bhandari, and Davis (2015) found that millennial study participants rated the stories they thought were written by traditional journalists as significantly more credible than those indicated to have been written by citizen journalists. The authors also found that stories written as straight news were perceived as more credible than articles with an identifiable opinion. Netzley and Hemmer's (2012) study had contradictory results, and found no difference in how millennials rated the credibility of an article said to have been written by a professional journalist or a citizen journalist. Ultimately, journalism is at a crossroads with millennial news consumers. Although they are exposed to news daily on social media, they still question the information itself, even from established media organizations (Mitchell et al., 2016). Understanding the news preferences of this generation is necessary for media professionals to craft better stories and heighten their credibility with younger audiences.

Listicles and the BuzzFeed Generation

Despite claims of limited credibility and little public value (Steiger, 2010), listicles have not stalled as a force in the modern media environment (Reider, 2015). The meteoric rise of listicles in popular culture mirrors the rise of BuzzFeed among millennials. BuzzFeed is a prominent online media company focusing on social news, entertainment, and viral content. The website made its mark online with its reliance on listicles and the "shareability" of its content. In 2015, this unlikely media model paid dividends for the company when BuzzFeed received a $200 million investment from NBCUniversal in an effort to reach digital-native millennial readers (Spangler, 2015).

Millennials are drawn to viral content, and BuzzFeed is unique in its precision at predicting what videos, images, or stories will go viral (O'Leary, 2014). Virality is defined as something timely, interesting, important, gossip-worthy, and funny (O'Leary, 2014). As the website grows in readership, BuzzFeed is making a more concerted effort to incorporate traditional news coverage with original reporting on a wide array of serious topics. Interestingly, BuzzFeed is quickly becoming a respected media outlet for meaningful journalism with a 400-person news staff, including two Pulitzer Prize winners (Robischon, 2016). The media company has 16 global correspondents spread out over 12 different countries, rivaling that of the *Washington Post* which was 21 correspondents in 13 countries (Robischon, 2016). The juxtaposition of serious and silly news is what makes BuzzFeed so attractive to millennials (O'Leary, 2014). Their culture has deemed it acceptable to read a serious news report and jump to a celebrity gossip listicle without guilt. BuzzFeed's readership demographics also reflect a significant millennial audience with more than half of the website's 200 million unique visitors being between 18 and 34 years old (Maza, 2015).

While listicles have grown to prominence in the last decade, they predate television and have been appearing in American news since the late-1800s (Bungey, 2014). For nearly fifty years (1880-1930), articles that resembled what we now refer to as listicles were common in American and British newspapers (Bungey, 2014; Matheson, 2000). Prominent newspapers including the *New York Times* would routinely run stories with lists of facts on generic topics with titles like "Some Facts About Applause" or "Some Facts About Birds." These stories were ultimately phased out by journalists who believed that the newspaper industry should serve its citizens as an interpreter of what information was the most significant and act as the preeminent gatekeeper of vital information. A uniform prose style was adopted by journalists and news written in the "inverted pyramid" style became the norm (Bungey, 2014; Matheson, 2000). According to Bungey (2014), the uniform nature of television news and newspapers may have triggered the listicle resurgence with the millennial generation's desire to consume and share tidbits of information. Through listicles, the public has "a flawless delivery system of endless enumerated trifles" (Bungey, 2014, para. 45).

Despite the ubiquitous nature of listicles throughout modern media, there is a dearth of research from media scholars specifically on listicles. Some scholars have argued that people engage in list-making daily to help organize and structure ideas in the digital age (Booth, 2015; Couldry, 2003). Okrent (2014) argues that despite some listicles serving as merely "clickbait" on media websites, many impart important content to readers. While news stories can have a bevy of facts or anecdotes, lists can allow those facts to be broken up and easily understood. Lists are, thus, tools that help readers make order out of disorder (Booth, 2015). Because listicles are generally catered to millennial readers, the study outlined in this chapter is focused primarily on how millennials rate the credibility of these articles in comparison to traditional online articles. A review of previous literature found no studies focused on listicle credibility, so this chapter will focus its attention on credibility studies within the broader context of print and online news.

Online Credibility

Online news has evolved to meet the demands of consumers as more readers are exposed to news stories on their smart phones and on social media (Mitchell, 2015). In a recent Pew Research Center study, 39 of the top 50 digital news websites have more traffic on their websites from mobile devices than on desktop computers, signifying a shift in how online readers are consuming news (Mitchell, 2015). Nearly half of web-connected adults also report receiving political news in the past week from Facebook, where newsfeed influence is mainly driven by algorithms and the preferences of friends (Mitchell, 2015). Essentially, modern news consumers are exposed to news in a constant stream throughout the day from a multitude of sources, which may or may not be credible. Traditional print media carries an established level of credibility, but online news has developed a refinement in presentation, can link to related information, and has a seemingly unparalleled aesthetic (Gunter, Campbell, Touri & Gibson, 2009). Despite these strengths, scholars suggest that online information often fails to reach sufficient levels of factual information, and some online media outlets apply no pressure to present unbiased facts (Cassidy, 2007; Johnson & Kaye, 2010). The prevalence of fake news and the downward trend in media literacy has made it difficult for millennials to properly determine reliable online resources and credible news articles (McManus, 2017).

News credibility can be defined as a perceived quality in reported information based on several factors including trustworthiness, accuracy, and believability (Chung, Nam, & Stefanone, 2012; Metzger, Flanagin, Eyal, Lemus, & Mccann, 2003; Sternadori & Thorson, 2009). Scholars have found the reputation of the media organization (Metzger et al., 2003) and neutrality to be key components in the credibility perceptions of news consumers (Hasnat, 2014). Medium has also been shown to impact credibility in which an online news source was perceived as more credible than a printed news source when the online organization has both a positive reputation and a brand name known for meeting journalistic ethical standards (Hasnat, 2014). Choi, Watt, and Lynch (2006) assert that news credibility is reliant on both the subjective perception of the audience and the innate quality of the news story itself. Ultimately, the quality of online news ethics and integrity may remain at an established standard for journalists, but credibility perceptions from the audience are changing for readers with advancements in technology (Choi et al., 2006; Gunter et al., 2009).

Before computer algorithms could aggregate large amounts of information, credibility was a top-down concept in which individuals would defer to experts on a given topic, such as professors, librarians, movie critics, film critics, etc. (Metzger, Flanagin, & Medders, 2010). In the modern technological marketplace, bottom-up assessments of information quality have established a new standard in credibility with the collective efforts of millions of online reviews (i.e. Yelp! restaurant reviews and Amazon star ratings). For millennials, social recommendation from peers can make a strong impact on the credibility of an online article (Xu, 2013). Looking at the news aggregate website Digg, Xu (2013) determined that social recommendation (such as the specific number of diggs for an individual article) was the primary factor influencing an individual's click likelihood and the perceived source credibility of the story. This furthers the assumption that collective social efforts (either from friends on social media or anonymous online reviewers) can heighten perceived online credibility. 75 percent of BuzzFeed's online traffic comes from sharing on social media (Smith, 2016), so most stories already carry an increased level of credibility from the social efforts of friends, family, and coworkers.

For online news websites, a media source's reputation can also have a significant impact on credibility. Chung, Kim, and Kim (2010) examined the perceived credibility of online news and determined that there are three distinct categories: mainstream, independent, and index. The mainstream news website, such as usatoday.com, received the highest ratings on most credibility items, but the index website (a news aggregator website like Digg or Google News) received the highest scores in creativeness, attractiveness, and interesting items. The independent news site was rated as the least credible overall and had the lowest reported scores of attractiveness, expertise, and trustworthiness. Additionally, news brands established offline that migrate online generally command more trust from news consumers than news brands that exist solely online (Gunter, 2006).

The omnipresence of newsfeeds on Facebook, Twitter, and Instagram has made social media a one-stop shop for news and information (Hasnat, 2014). However, the absence of an information vetting process on social media has raised questions about credibility among online journalists. Hasnat (2014) surveyed working journalists who suggest that social media's growth potential is limitless as a platform for news, if credibility and transparency of information can be ensured. Additionally, journalists typically rate the credibility of their own medium higher than that of another (Cassidy, 2007). Online journalists place higher trust in web-based news than traditional news for source accuracy, fairness, and overall credibility. Conversely, print journalists regard newspapers as the most credible news source, but still regard online news sources as having credibility (Cassidy, 2007).

The profound impact of social media in the news industry is personified in Johnson and Kaye's (2015) online credibility study, which unsurprisingly found that traditional media organizations were rated as more credible than social media websites. Despite lower credibility, users reported higher gratification with social media websites and indicated they are willing to trade credibility for need satisfaction. An acceptance of lower credibility indicates that news needs to advance with new technology to better suit the preferences of the audience. The authors view the Internet as more than another news "medium;" it has become the *primary source* of news content provided by a vast number of suppliers (Johnson & Kaye, 2015). Ultimately, a number of factors influence the perceived credibility of a news article. While news consumers are exposed to dozens of articles every day on social media, they are more empowered by the articles they deem worthy of their clicks and their time.

STUDY DESIGN AND METHODOLOGY

For the present study, an online experiment was conducted to draw conclusions about the perceived credibility of listicles among millennials and compare those credibility assessments to traditional news articles. The study was also designed to examine the information seeking behavior of millennials to better understand their media preferences. The experiment was designed to examine online news articles, so the experiment was administered on the web to reflect the experience of reading an online article from a reputable news source. A convenience sample of college students was used based on accessibility to a sample population at a large public university in the Mid-Atlantic region of the United States.

363 participants were recruited from undergraduate social science classes, and extra credit was offered as an incentive for participation. The majority of participants were female ($N = 250$) and the mean age was 23.68 years old (Table 1). Although this study was not focused on gender, approximately two-thirds of the participants identified themselves as female, so additional data analysis to examine potential differences between the two genders was conducted. As outlined in Table 1, a univariate ANOVA was conducted to determine if a significant difference existed between male and female participants for the variable being studied. The scores on

Table 1. Profile of sample population

Total (N = 363)		
Gender	**Total**	**Percentage**
Female	250	68.9
Male	113	31.1
	Mean	**SD**
Age	23.68	6.18
Credibility Score	**Mean**	**SD**
Female	4.40	1.57
Male	4.31	1.52

Sternadori and Thorson's (2009) credibility scale were not significantly different between the genders ($F(1, 361) = .120, p = .729$). Because credibility scores were nearly identical for male and female participants, it can be determined that the uneven gender distribution in the experiment did not significantly influence the study findings.

The study outlined in this chapter was a two-group posttest-only experimental design, and participants were randomly assigned to read one of two news articles (either a traditional article or a listicle). The article was adapted by the author of this chapter from information found in four different BuzzFeed News articles about the 2015-2016 California drought (Dalrymple, 2015a; 2015b; 2015c; 2015d). This specific topic was chosen because the large majority of participants had no first-hand knowledge of it (considering they live and attend college on the U.S. East Coast). The article detailed different aspects of California's drought providing statistics about California's dwindling water supply and the state government's attempts to combat the problem (including placing restrictions on water usage and fining citizens who do not comply with those usage standards). The article title, author name, date and article information were identical in both stimuli. Participants also saw the same four pictures in each article that showed the devastating effects of the drought in California (such as dead crops on farms and completely dry rivers).

Although almost all features of each article were virtually identical, there were two differences between the stimuli. The listicle was indicated to have originated from *BuzzFeed News* and was designed to look like a listicle. For example, there was an introductory paragraph, followed by a numbered list of ten short facts regarding California's drought. The traditional article was indicated to have originated from *USA Today* and resembled the look of a standard online article (i.e. paragraphs). All of the information (including the introductory paragraph) was exactly the same in each article, and participants were randomly assigned to read one of the two stimuli midway through the experiment.

Before seeing the article, the experiment asked participants to answer questions about their information seeking behavior. The first four questions were adapted from Zhang and Zhang's (2013) study on the online information seeking behavior of individuals for Internet news. These four questions were open-ended questions in which participants were asked to indicate: 1) hours spent on the Internet per week; 2) hours spent reading Internet news stories per week; 3) number of different news websites accessed per week; 4) hours spent on social media (i.e. Facebook or Twitter) per week. Participants were then asked to indicate which primary sources of news they use on an average day: local television news, cable television news, newspapers, printed news magazines (such as *Time* or *Newsweek*), online, cell phone apps, or other. Participants were also asked to indicate their primary sources for news *online* on an average day: online newspaper websites, online television news websites, online-only news media websites (such as BuzzFeed), blogs, Twitter, Facebook, YouTube, Snapchat, and other. Additionally, participants were asked three demographic questions about their age, gender, and field of study.

After answering those questions, participants received instructions telling them that they will be shown a news article on the following page. The instructions also asked the participants to read everything they see on the following page and that they will be asked to answer additional questions regarding the article they just read. Participants were then randomly assigned to one of two stimuli, and read the traditional article or listicle.

After reading the news article, participants were asked to answer 13 questions about their judgements of the credibility of the article. The perceived credibility scale was developed from Sternadori and Thorson's (2009) study on news article credibility. Participants were asked to indicate how each of the following statements best describes their feelings about the article on a 7-point Likert scale: 1) The story was fair; 2) The story was complete; 3) The story was accurate; 4) I trust the information in this story; 5) I trust the sources quoted in this story; 6) The story was believable; 7) The story was credible; 8) The story was informative; 9) The story explored the issue in-depth; 10) The story was interesting; 11) I liked this story; 12) The story was well written; 13) The story was important. Sternadori and Thorson's (2009) scale was shown to be highly reliable for the present study (Cronbach's $\alpha =$ .915). After answering the perceived credibility questions, participants were shown a final debrief screen that thanked them for their participation and asked them not to discuss the study with others while data was being collected.

ARTICLE CREDIBILITY AND MILLENNIAL CULTURE: EXAMINING THE STUDY FINDINGS

Millennial News Consumption and Information Seeking Behavior

Millennial-targeted websites (such as BuzzFeed) have experienced massive growth since the turn of the century, and listicles signify a return to a journalistic style that was prominent a century ago (Bungey, 2014; Okrent, 2014; O'Leary, 2014). The digital native millennial generation has an unparalleled connection to new media that has shaped their value system and overall way of thinking (Goodstein, 2007; Serazio, 2015). Because millennials are hyperconnected to new media, the present study sought to examine the amount of online media and online news that millennials consume weekly. Using a sample population of millennials (N = 363), the study participants indicated they spend about 26 hours per week on the Internet (M = 25.89, SD = 21.19) and about 15 hours per week on social media (M = 15.22, SD = 17.31). Essentially, millennials spend more than three hours on the Internet and two hours on social media every day, which exemplifies the astounding amount of online media millennials consume daily. These findings suggest that millennials ingest news in a continual stream at times throughout the day.

A quick browse of Facebook, Twitter, and Instagram can elicit dozens of international, national, and local news stories juxtaposed with a friend's vacation selfies and one-minute cooking videos. The prevalence of news stories on social media indicates that millennials are frequently exposed to useful information, whether they are intentionally seeking it out or not. Participants also indicated they spend about 6.5 hours per week reading Internet news stories (M = 6.43, SD = 8.63) as well as access about four different news websites per week (M = 4.38, SD = 5.10). These results suggest that millennials are more than simply passive observers whose relationship with news is mainly predicated on incidental exposure (Antunovic et al., 2016; Ha et al., 2016). Millennials are spending about one hour each day reading online news, which is encouraging for online media companies who are looking to tap in to this younger demographic. Based on this data, they want to be informed and actively seek out several media outlets for that information.

Additionally, this study sought to determine the most prominent sources that millennials access for news across all media. The most popular primary source of news was online (90.4%), which was followed by cell phone apps (68%), local television news (44.6%), cable television news (36.9%), newspapers (15.4%), and printed news magazines (8%) (Table 2). Looking specifically at online news sources, Facebook (63.9%), online newspaper websites (60.3%), online TV news websites

(58.1%), online-only news media websites (such as BuzzFeed) (39.1%), and Twitter (38.8%) were shown to be the most popular among the participants (Table 2).

Interestingly, the only primary sources used by more than half the participants were online and cell phone apps. This signifies a strong reliance on online resources for millennials as smartphone apps are also dependent on an Internet connection. Apps are especially useful for individuals looking to stay informed throughout the day with push notifications and newsfeeds allowing information to update in real time. A study on millennial behaviors found that smartphone apps play a vital role in their daily lives because they significantly reduce social isolation and improve the personal lives of users (Cho, 2015). With significant customization and minimal effort needed, smartphone apps and online resources allow users to be informed on issues that specifically interest them. Speed, comfort, and overall satisfaction are potentially all reasons that make these sources so popular among millennials. Moreover, less than half the participants indicated using television and print news outlets which signifies that those media have seemingly lost power with millennials. Cable news providers have experienced a major wave of cord-cutting in households, which has resulted in a decline in television audiences overall (Steel & Marsh, 2015). Smartphones have essentially consolidated all the different media into one item that can be used like a television, newspaper, and a computer, rendering most traditional media obsolete for millennials.

Table 2. Primary sources for news offline and online

Source	Total (N = 363)	Percentage*
Primary News Sources		
Online	328	90.4
Cell Phone Apps	247	68.0
Local Television News	162	44.6
Cable Television News	134	36.9
Newspapers	56	15.4
Printed News Magazines	29	8.0
Other	18	5.0
Online News Sources		
Facebook	232	63.9
Online Newspaper Websites	219	60.3
Online TV News Websites	211	58.1
Online-only news media websites (ex. BuzzFeed)	142	39.1
Twitter	141	38.8
Snapchat	81	22.3
YouTube	74	20.4
Blogs	60	16.5
Other	33	9.1

*Note: Percentage totals exceed 100% because participants were asked to mark all applicable responses

The experiment also asked participants to indicate their primary sources for online news, and shockingly, none of the sources are used by a large majority of individuals. More than half the participants mentioned Facebook, online newspaper websites, and online TV news websites as online sources they use regularly. However, none of these sources are used by even two-thirds of the participants. Perhaps this is due to the sheer number of sources available online with useful information. It is worth noting that two of the three most popular online news sources are actually online versions of traditional media organizations. Thus, established offline media organizations still remain relevant with millennials audiences, but the online site may be more popular with this audience than their traditional news outlet. Additionally, less than 40 percent of participants indicated receiving news from Twitter, Snapchat, YouTube, and online-only media websites (such as BuzzFeed). All of those media companies launched in the 2000s, and have had less time to build brand loyalty and credibility as news organizations. Their brand credibility may eventually reach that of *CNN* or the *Washington Post*, but millennials are currently looking for their information from established media outlets.

Listicle Credibility

Listicles have experienced massive growth on media websites and their popularity remains unrivaled among millennials (Booth, 2015; Maza, 2015), so this study sought to determine whether millennial participants would find a listicle more credible than a traditional article. Participants rated the listicle ($M = 4.59$, $SD = 1.07$) higher on the credibility scale than the traditional article ($M = 4.26$, $SD = 1.07$). A univariate analysis of variance (ANOVA) of the credibility scores found that there was a significant difference ($F(1, 361) = 8.82$, $p = .003$), so the listicle was rated as significantly more credible than the traditional article. These findings suggest that younger readers are more inclined to believe the facts in and attribute more credibility to a listicle than a standard news article. Contradicting many of the established standards of newswriting (Bungey, 2014; Matheson, 2000), the inverted pyramid style of storytelling may be obsolete in the eyes of millennials.

The higher level of credibility may be connected to the simplicity associated with listicles and the scannable nature of the text. Some studies have found that people prefer scannable text as well as facts that are easily discernable (Chambers, 2006; Ruth, Monica, & Forbes, 2003). With listicles, there is no need to decipher a convoluted message because the facts are shown to the reader one at a time in a specific order. Conversely, traditional news articles put the onus on the reader to uncover the facts in a story that is meant to flow together from beginning to end.

Although listicles lack that storytelling aspect, millennials may only want the facts. More transparent facts and the absence of a fully formed story may be preferable to millennial news consumers, and may explain why they find them more credible.

Unlike traditional articles which make little effort to connect to readers, listicle credibility may be tied to a heightened level of personal connection. A listicle can have all the same facts as a traditional online article, but listicle titles often provide specific reasons readers should care about the information. For example, a traditional online article about the Syrian refugee crisis may have a generic title, such as "How different countries have responded to the Syrian refugee crisis." However, a listicle with similar information will have a title that specifically connects to the reader and can elicit more page views, such as "The top 12 reasons the Syrian refugee crisis is a world problem *you* should care about." Similar to social media in which individuals work daily to maintain connections with peers, this personal connection to the audience may be another reason listicle credibility remains high and listicles remain a prominent fixture in the modern media ecosystem.

Study Limitations

As outlined earlier, the uneven gender distribution of study participants was a noteworthy limitation of the study. Participants were recruited from undergraduate social science classes with the assumption that the number of male and female participants would be similar. Despite this assumption, twice as many female participants completed the study, so a gender bias may exist. However, because both genders had statistically similar scores on the variable being examined (perceived credibility), it can be determined that the study results have validity, and the gender inequities did not have a profound impact on the study findings.

Another limitation of the study was the use of a convenience sample of college students as participants. Although using a convenience sample can lower external validity, it has been used in other studies that examined media credibility (Bates, Romina, Ahmed & Hopson, 2006; Cho, Shah, Nah & Brossard, 2009; Shade, Kornfield & Oliver, 2015) and was particularly useful for targeting a sample population of millennials. College students may also be less representative of the general millennial population because they may be more educated or socially aware than average millennials and may be more inclined to follow the news closely. Although a convenience sample can make study results less generalizable to a larger population, college students were a viable option for this experiment because most listicles are specifically targeted at informed, college-aged individuals.

Future Studies

Based on the findings of the present study, several future studies could expand on the results of this experiment and examine different demographic groups. The present study focused specifically on millennial audiences, but another study could sample from an older demographic of the US population to determine if listicles carry the same level of perceived credibility among all adults. Listicles are targeted primarily at millennials, so another study that examines their credibility among individuals with much less exposure to this article format could offer different results.

An additional study could survey a representative sample of the US population to better understand information seeking behavior. Millennial participants indicated that online and cell phone apps were their primary sources for news, but the primary news sources for a general population could skew more towards traditional media outlets, such as newspapers or cable and local television news. Facebook was also the preferred online news source for millennials, so another study could be designed to determine whether an article on the social media site would carry more credibility than an article on a website for an established news brand (such as cnn.com or nytimes.com).

CONCLUSION

Unlike the generations that preceded them, millennials are digital natives who are both hyperconnected and empowered by new media (Goodstein, 2007; Serazio, 2015). Millennials spend hours a day on the Internet and are particularly engaged with social media. Based on the present study, millennials spend about an hour each day reading online news, so media organizations have enormous potential for growth when targeting the younger generation of news consumers. Modern journalists need to find new and innovative ways of hooking millennial audiences that are no longer reliant on traditional media (i.e. print, radio, and television) for news content. Listicles carry an established level of popularity and aesthetic appeal (as well as a newly recognized level of credibility) that make them a viable storytelling option for journalists. BuzzFeed's 200 million unique visitors per month (Maza, 2015) prove that listicles are an advantageous way for media companies to both attract readers to their brand and remain credible to those readers. Ultimately, media organizations and journalists who are willing to think beyond the inverted pyramid style of newswriting and adapt to the tastes of their audience will thrive in the modern media environment.

REFERENCES

Alanen, L. (2001). Explorations in Generational Analysis. In L. Alanen & B. Mayall (Eds.), *Conceptualizing Child-Adult Relations* (pp. 11–22). London: Routledge.

Antunovic, D., Parsons, P., & Cooke, T. R. (2016). 'Checking' and googling: Stages of news consumption among young adults. *Journalism*, 1–17.

Barthel, M., Shearer, E., Gottfried, J., & Mitchell, A. (2015, July 14). *The Evolving Role of News on Twitter and Facebook*. Retrieved from http://www.journalism.org/2015/07/14/the-evolving-role-of-news-on-twitter-and-facebook/

Bates, B. R., Romina, S., Ahmed, R., & Hopson, D. (2006). The effect of source credibility on consumers' perceptions of the quality of health information on the Internet. *Medical Informatics and the Internet in Medicine*, *31*(1), 45–52. doi:10.1080/14639230600552601 PMID:16754366

Booth, P. (2015). Fans' list-making: Memory, influence, and argument in the "event" of fandom. *MATRIZes*, *9*(2), 85–107. doi:10.11606/issn.1982-8160.v9i2p85-107

Bungey, S. (2014, September 30). Some Facts About the Listicle. *The Morning News*. Retrieved from http://www.themorningnews.org/article/some-facts-about-the-listicle

Cassidy, W. P. (2007). Online news credibility: An examination of the perceptions of newspaper journalists. *Journal of Computer-Mediated Communication*, *12*(2), 478–498. doi:10.1111/j.1083-6101.2007.00334.x

Chadwick, A. (2013). *The Hybrid Media System: Politics and power*. Oxford, UK: Oxford University Press. doi:10.1093/acprof:oso/9780199759477.001.0001

Chambers, C. W. (2006). Writing Patient Education Content for the Web. *AMWA Journal: American Medical Writers Association Journal*, *21*(3), 108–109.

Cho, J. (2015). Roles of Smartphone App Use in Improving Social Capital and Reducing Social Isolation. *Cyberpsychology, Behavior, and Social Networking*, *18*(6), 350–355. doi:10.1089/cyber.2014.0657 PMID:26075923

Cho, J., Shah, D. V., Nah, S., & Brossard, D. (2009). "Split Screens" and "Spin Rooms": Debate Modality, Post-Debate Coverage, and the New Videomalaise. *Journal of Broadcasting & Electronic Media*, *53*(2), 242–261. doi:10.1080/08838150902907827

Choi, J. H., Watt, J. H., & Lynch, M. (2006). Perceptions of News Credibility about the War in Iraq: Why War Opponents Perceived the Internet as the Most Credible Medium. *Journal of Computer-Mediated Communication*, *12*(1), 209–229. doi:10.1111/j.1083-6101.2006.00322.x

Chung, C. J., Kim, H., & Kim, J. H. (2010). An anatomy of the credibility of online newspapers. *Online Information Review*, *34*(5), 669–685. doi:10.1108/14684521011084564

Chung, C. J., Nam, Y., & Stefanone, M. A. (2012). Exploring Online News Credibility: The Relative Influence of Traditional and Technological Factors. *Journal of Computer-Mediated Communication*, *17*(2), 171–186. doi:10.1111/j.1083-6101.2011.01565.x

Couldry, N. (2003). *Media rituals: a critical approach*. London: Routledge.

Dalrymple, J. (2015a, April 2). Here's How California Will Enforce Its First-Ever Statewide Water Restrictions. *BuzzFeed News*. Retrieved from https://www.buzzfeed.com/jimdalrympleii/heres-how-california-will-enforce-its-first-ever-statewide-w?utm_term=.byn8eaoEOY#.mnJ3yMYR7b

Dalrymple, J. (2015b, April 16). How Severe Is California's Drought Really? *BuzzFeed News*. Retrieved from https://www.buzzfeed.com/jimdalrympleii/how-severe-is-californias-drought-really?utm_term=.knddvqPbAm#.olZOGBxXj2

Dalrymple, J. (2015c, May 7). Extreme Drought Prompts Starbucks To End California Water Bottling. *BuzzFeed News*. Retrieved from https://www.buzzfeed.com/jimdalrympleii/starbucks-ends-water-bottling-operations-in-california-citin?utm_term=.aud1dq5pnE#.ea072Vz3KY

Dalrymple, J. (2015d, August 3). Thousands of Water Wasters In California Hit With Fines. *BuzzFeed News*. Retrieved from https://www.buzzfeed.com/jimdalrympleii/california-cities-are-handing-out-thousands-of-fines-for-ove?utm_term=.jr9XKY6jRm#.lcpDq5l72a

Denning, S. (2014, August 29). Five Reasons Why Millennials Love Listicles. *Forbes*. Retrieved from http://www.forbes.com/sites/stevedenning/2014/08/29/five-reasons-why-millennials-love-listicles/#ea901f851aad

Edmunds, J., & Turner, B. S. (2002). *Generations, Culture, and Society*. Philadelphia: Open University Press.

Goodstein, A. (2007). *Totally Wired*. New York: St. Martin's Press.

Gottfried, J., & Shearer, E. (2016, May 26). News Use Across Social Media Platforms 2016. *Pew Research Center*. Retrieved from http://www.journalism.org/2016/05/26/news-use-across-social-media-platforms-2016/?utm_content=bufferae870&utm_medium=social&utm_source=twitter.com&utm_campaign=buffer

Gumpert, G., & Cathcart, R. (1985). Media Grammars, Generations, and Media Gaps. *Critical Studies in Mass Communication*, *2*(1), 23–35. doi:10.1080/15295038509360059

Gunter, B. (2006). Who do online news consumers trust? *Library and Information Update*, *5*(9), 40–41.

Gunter, B., Campbell, V., Touri, M., & Gibson, R. (2009). Blogs, news and credibility. *Aslib Proceedings*, *61*(2), 185–204. doi:10.1108/00012530910946929

Ha, L., Xu, Y., Yang, C., Wang, F., Yang, L., Abuljadail, M., ... Gabay, I. (2016). Decline in news content engagement or news medium engagement? A longitudinal analysis of news engagement since the rise of social and mobile media 2009–2012. *Journalism*, 1–22.

Hasnat, M. O. (2014). Credibility of Social Online Media: In the Eyes of Finnish Professional Journalists. *Communicacao e Sociedade*, *25*(0), 220–235. doi:10.17231/comsoc.25(2014).1870

Holic, N. (2014, January 23). An Open Letter to List Articles. *Huffington Post.* Retrieved from http://www.huffingtonpost.com/the-university-of-central-florida-forum/an-open-letter-to-list-articles_b_4268725.html

Ito, M. (2008). *Living and Learning with New Media*. Cambridge, MA: MIT Press.

Johnson, T., & Kaye, B. (2010). Choosing is believing? How web gratifications and reliance affect Internet credibility among politically interested users. *Atlantic Journal of Communication*, *18*(1), 1–21. doi:10.1080/15456870903340431

Johnson, T. J., & Kaye, B. K. (2015). Reasons to believe: Influence of credibility on motivations for using social networks. *Computers in Human Behavior*, *50*, 544–555. doi:10.1016/j.chb.2015.04.002

Ksiazek, T. B., Malthouse, E. C., & Webster, J. G. (2010). News-seekers and Avoiders: Exploring Patterns of Total News Consumption Across Media and the Relationship to Civic Participation. *Journal of Broadcasting & Electronic Media*, *54*(4), 551–568. doi:10.1080/08838151.2010.519808

Mannheim, K. (1952). The Problem of Generations. In P. Kecskemeti (Ed.), *Essays on the Sociology of Knowledge* (pp. 276–320). London: Routledge.

Matheson, D. (2000). The Birth of News Discourse: Changes in News Language in British Newspapers, 1880-1930. *Media Culture & Society*, *20*(5), 557–573. doi:10.1177/016344300022005002

Maza, C. (2015, August 18). NBC Universal invests $200 million in BuzzFeed: Can it win over Millennials? *Christian Science Monitor*. Retrieved from http://www.csmonitor.com/Business/2015/0818/NBC-Universal-invests-200-million-in-BuzzFeed-Can-it-win-over-Millennials

McManus, A. M. (2017). What's in a Name Revisited. *Reference and User Services Quarterly*, *56*(3), 156–157. doi:10.5860/rusq.56n3.156

Metzger, M. J., Flanagin, A. J., Eyal, K., Lemus, D. R., & Mccann, R. M. (2003). Credibility for the 21st century: Integrating perspectives on source, message, and media credibility in the contemporary media environment. *Communication Yearbook*, *27*(1), 293–335. doi:10.1207/s15567419cy2701_10

Metzger, M. J., Flanagin, A. J., & Medders, R. B. (2010). Social and Heuristic Approaches to Credibility Evaluation Online. *Journal of Communication*, *60*(3), 413–439. doi:10.1111/j.1460-2466.2010.01488.x

Mitchell, A. (2015, April 29). State of the News Media 2015. *Pew Research Center.* Retrieved from http://www.journalism.org/files/2015/04/FINAL-STATE-OF-THE-NEWS-MEDIA1.pdf

Mitchell, A., Gottfried, J., Barthel, M., & Shearer, E. (2016, July 7). The Modern News Consumer: News attitudes and practices in the digital era. *Pew Research Center.* Retrieved from http://www.journalism.org/2016/07/07/the-modern-news-consumer/

Mitchell, A., & Holcomb, J. (2016, June 15). State of the News Media 2016. *Pew Research Center*. Retrieved from http://www.journalism.org/2016/06/15/state-of-the-news-media-2016/

Netzley, S., & Hemmer, M. (2012). Citizen journalism just as credible as stories by pros, students say. *Newspaper Research Journal*, *33*(3), 49–61. doi:10.1177/073953291203300304

O'Leary, M. (2014). BuzzFeed and the New Virality. *Information Today*, *31*(3), 20–21.

Okrent, A. (2014). The listicle as literary form. *The University of Chicago Magazine*. Retrieved from http://mag.uchicago.edu/arts-humanities/listicle-literary-form

Poindexter, P. (2012). *Millennials, news, and social media: Is news engagement a thing of the past?* New York: Peter Lang.

Rieder, R. (2015, June 16). Rieder: BuzzFeed a burgeoning journalistic force. *USA Today*. Retrieved from http://www.usatoday.com/story/money/columnist/rieder/2015/06/15/buzzfeed-expands-as-journalism-force/71250444/

Robischon, N. (2016, February 22). BuzzFeed's Quest for Impact in the Viral News Era. *Fast Company*. Retrieved from https://www.fastcompany.com/3056365/buzzfeeds-quest-for-impact-in-the-viral-news-era

Ruth, W., Monica, L., & Forbes, G. (2003). The WEB Book experiments in electronic textbook design. *The Journal of Documentation*, *59*(4), 454–477. doi:10.1108/00220410310485721

Serazio, M. (2013). *Your Ad Here: The Cool Sell of Guerrilla Marketing*. New York: New York University Press.

Serazio, M. (2015). Selling (Digital) Millennials. *Television & New Media*, *16*(7), 599–615. doi:10.1177/1527476413491015

Shade, D. D., Kornfield, S., & Oliver, M. B. (2015). The Uses and Gratifications of Media Migration: Investigating the Activities, Motivations, and Predictors of Migration Behaviors Originating in Entertainment Television. *Journal of Broadcasting & Electronic Media*, *59*(2), 318–341. doi:10.1080/08838151.2015.1029121

Smith, C. (2016, July 14). By the Numbers: 28 Amazing BuzzFeed Statistics. *DMR*. Retrieved from http://expandedramblings.com/index.php/buzzfeed-statistics/

Spangler, T. (2015, August 18). NBCUniversal Invests $200 Million in BuzzFeed. *Variety*. Retrieved from http://variety.com/2015/digital/news/nbcuniversal-invests-200-million-in-buzzfeed-1201572244/

Steel, E., & Marsh, B. (2015, October 3). Millennials and Cutting the Cord. *The New York Times*. Retrieved from https://www.nytimes.com/interactive/2015/10/03/business/media/changing-media-consumption-millenials-cord-cutters.html?_r=0

Steiger, K. (2010). 99 PROBLEMS. *Bitch Magazine: Feminist Response To Pop Culture*, (49), 15-16.

Sternadori, M. M., & Thorson, E. (2009). Anonymous Sources Harm Credibility of All Stories. *Newspaper Research Journal*, *30*(4), 54–66. doi:10.1177/073953290903000405

Swasy, A., Tandoc, E., Bhandari, M., & Davis, R. (2015). Traditional Reporting More Credible than Citizen News. *Newspaper Research Journal*, *36*(2), 225–236. doi:10.1177/0739532915587298

Xu, Q. (2013). Social Recommendation, Source Credibility, and Recency: Effects of News Cues in a Social Bookmarking Website. *Journalism & Mass Communication Quarterly*, *90*(4), 757–775. doi:10.1177/1077699013503158

KEY TERMS AND DEFINITIONS

BuzzFeed: A prominent American internet media company focusing on social news, entertainment, and viral content, and a catalyst for the rise of online listicles in American culture.

Inverted Pyramid Style: A journalistic style of writing in which news stories prioritize the most pertinent information at the top and other material follows in order of diminishing importance.

Listicle: A written article or story that is presented partly or wholly as a list.

Media Credibility: The objective and subjective components of the believability and trustworthiness of a single media source, media organization, or the media as a whole.

Millennial: A demographic distinction for individuals born between the early 1980s to the late 1990s. Individuals in this age group are marked by having a strong familiarity with media, digital communication, technology, and the internet.

News Consumer: An individual who regularly consumes news through one or more media.

Newsfeed: A continuous stream of data on a website, usually consisting of news updates from different sources.

Virality: The tendency of an important, timely, interesting, or funny image, video, or story to be circulated quickly and widely throughout the internet.

Section 2

New Media, Culture and Identity

This section presents chapters exploring the connection between culture and identity using new media, specifically focusing on identity negotiation, construction/ reconstruction of identity, and communicating identities in the new media platform.

Chapter 4
Who Am I?
Identity, Culture, and the New Media

Beth Bonniwell Haslett
University of Delaware, USA

ABSTRACT

This chapter focuses on how culture and the new media shape one's identity. While culture and one's family initially shape one's identity, the new media provide new ideas and lifestyles that influence one's identity. One's identity changes throughout one's lifespan, and the new media presents more information and alternative lifestyle choices for individuals. Identity itself is a complex concept and the self is viewed as the continuing, consistent narrative that one presents over one's lifetime and over different contexts. The new media enable people to develop online identities, and such identities may be authentic or inauthentic when compared to one's real life identity. The new media present different venues for developing and expressing one's self. The new media also enable individuals to maintain cultural and identity links with their home culture although they may have located elsewhere in the world.

INTRODUCTION

Through modernity and globalization, the world is more interconnected now than ever before. Giddens' structuration theory (ST) explains how both transportation and telecommunication systems enable modern, interdependent economies and how this, in turn, has led to political, cultural and social changes (Giddens, 1990, 1991, 2003). These changes have fundamentally altered cultures, identities and the nature of interaction itself. This chapter will focus on the changes in communication and its influence on culture and identity. Identity and culture matter because they provide the fundamental bases upon which we engage others.

DOI: 10.4018/978-1-5225-3784-7.ch004

Structuration theory (ST) argues that social systems, like cultures, reflect both social structures and agency. Agency, viewed as social action and interaction, creates social structures, such as educational, legal, political and judicial structures. Through daily interaction, individuals create, support or change social practices. ST relies on the interaction order (Goffman, 1955, 1981) to characterize daily interactional practices, such as using face and alignment strategies. These interactions create, maintain and alter varied social structures, such as family structures, group patterns, organizations and cultures.

In addition, such interactions provide the means through which one establishes, maintains and alters one's identities.

Communication and culture are mutually interwoven and ST helps articulate these interconnections. Communication is needed to create the shared knowledge and values that form the basis for cultures: Cultures, in turn, shape communicative practices and individual identities. Communication can also introduce new information and ideas that challenge existing social structures and cultural patterns. Telecommunication systems, such as media, new media and social media platforms, introduce individuals to more information and from a more diverse set of sources previously available. This information may facilitate both cultural convergence and cultural divergence, and there is evidence to support both effects (Bauman, 2001; Giddens, 2003).

Modernization and access to many new sources of information have challenged our concepts of culture and relationships, providing new ways to interact and live our lives. We exist, as Ng (2004, p. 257) pointed out, in a "media landscape in which the roles of cultural producer, consumer, and citizen are merging and media content flows across a range of platforms and devices." Giddens' structuration theory plays an important role in illuminating the context in which communication, culture and identity influence one another.

Cultural patterns influence the manner in which we interact with one another, and thus provide a significant basis for our identities. Initially, families and cultures are the primary context in which we develop our identities—however, family models and cultures themselves are evolving. Media provide many competing models for parenting and childrearing as well as competing sources for identification. With new information and ideas from both intracultural and intercultural sources, new media alters the way in which we think about ourselves. More understanding of these interrelationships will help us unpack the various influences upon our own identity and how others in different cultures develop their identities. Understanding the complexity of identity will hopefully make us more effective cross-cultural and intercultural communicators through our increased knowledge of ourselves as well as others. We now turn to a more detailed analysis of the ways in which modern telecommunication processes have influenced culture and identity.

MAIN FOCUS OF THE CHAPTER

The Sociohistoric Context: Dynamic Change in Culture and Communication

Structuration Theory and Modernity

In modernity, Giddens argues, the pace of change is so rapid and global that it is "discontinuous" with prior changes in history (1990, 1991). Three sources of these dynamic changes are *distancation*, in which time and space are "emptied" and are no longer connected to a physical place. Thus, computer mediated communication (CMC) enables us to be both 'here and there' as in watching Olympic games from our homes or speaking with someone else in a different time zone. A second force for change is *disembedding* whereby CMC lifts social interaction and relationships out of local contexts. For example, we can purchase goods and services from other countries and locales. As Barnes (2008, p. 29) notes:

Networking technologies reach beyond national borders to enable people to self-organize around local or global political interests. People must now perceive the contexts andspaces in which they communicate instead ofseeing the physical location

Finally, the *reflexivity* of modernity encourages flexibility and change. With reflexivity, "In conditions of modernity, social practices are constantly examined and reformed in terms of novel information about their nature—in a process which has no intrinsic end-point" (Giddens, 1990. 306-307). These conditions, of course, heighten uncertainty and risk, with knowledge being questioned and subject to increasing human reflexivity (Bauman, 2000; Giddens, 1991, 2003). As Giddens suggests, telecommunication systems have produced distanciation, disembedding and reflexivity with an unprecedented scope and speed of change.

Cultures (social systems) can be viewed as characterizing nation-states, as well as being features of social groups and virtual communities categorized by age, gender, religion, education, and so forth. The focus of this chapter is on cultures as nation-states. For Giddens (1991, p. 32), in globalization, time and space are not anchored to place, such that for "the first time in human history, 'self' and 'society' are interrelated in a global milieu." Relationships may be disembedded from a given physical and/or social context, and exist in both geospace and cyberspace. Reflexivity in modern life is greatly enhanced by communication technologies, and trust, in others and in institutions, is balanced against risk as a part of modern life (Bauman, 2000; Giddens,1990).

All human action is performed within, and at least partly predetermined by, the context of a pre-existing set of social structures (culture). Such structures, roles and rules are sustained and modified over time through reflexive feedback and interaction. Giddens argues that cultures are systems of shared communication (language) and values, with control over an identified territory and a common group identity—this implies a view of culture as a nation-state. In addition, Giddens notes that modern telecommunication systems have been essential in forming and maintaining cultural commitments. And cultures have different social practices regarding computer mediated communication.

Identification with and commitment to a social group is an essential component of culture, but such commitments may extend beyond nation-state boundaries. As Morley (2006) points out, globalization allows us to imagine other worlds and regions, and influences how we see ourselves and others. In particular, the processes of distanciation and disembedding enable us to transcend time and space and place ourselves in new relationships.

With transnational flows of information, goods and people, cultural boundaries and cultures themselves are in dynamic, continuous flux, with globalization influencing different local contexts and regions unevenly and with different effects (i.e., adaptation, divergence or resistance). Clearly, with immigration, diasporas and travel, many people may experience multiple cultural connections and identify with different cultures. Through increased, expanded interconnections with others, our lives are transformed by new knowledge and awareness of alternative lifestyle choices. Giddens' theory of structuration enhances our understanding of the global as well as local processes that influence our lives and identities, and their interactions.

Goffman's Interaction Order

Giddens relies on Goffman's concept of the interaction order (1974, 1983) to describe the interactional patterns that sustain social order. These interactional patterns, both on a macro-level (e.g., within and across groups) and micro-level interactions (e.g., person to person) provide a foundation for the creation, maintenance, and extension of social systems such as institutions (like legal or educational institutions) and cultures. Cultures and groups, as macro-level structures, influence micro-level, individual patterns of communication. For example, high-context cultures tend to emphasize subtle, indirect interpersonal communication because much of the meaning being conveyed is embedded in the context. Both Giddens and Goffman link cultural institutions to daily communicative actions—through these repeated interactions, cultural patterns are built up, modified and/or sustained. Although his work primarily examined face-to-face interactions, scholars have usefully applied Goffman's theories in mediated contexts (Rettie, 2009).

The increasing range of lifestyle choices, more open and multiple contexts of action, and varied sources of authority provide agents (both individuals and groups) with complex daily choices for constructing identity (Giddens, 1991). Bargiela-Chiappini (2006, p. 4) argues that "glocalised identities are a fact of everyday life" and that language is an important component of identity. Hybridity is a term that reflects cultures in transnational movement shaped by flows of people, goods, communication, ideas, technologies, and finance (Lee, Kim & Min, 2009). Hybridity is also "inextricably linked to an engagement with one's own and other people's memories, perception, and worldviews" (Kramsch & Uryu, 2012, p. 219).

However, increasing transnational movements can also create divergence and increased cultural resistance to social change (Sorrels, 2013). The presence of a global digital divide between nation-states also creates an uneven flow of information which frequently disadvantages less developed countries (Hargiatti & Hsieh, 2013). Thus, increasing engagement across cultures can be both facilitate growth but also alienation and resistance (Giddens, 2003; Sorrels, 2013).

The Impact of Computer Mediated Communication (CMC)

For Giddens, globalization is directly related to mediated experience and increased dependence on other people, being that "we are constantly in communication with them all" (Interview with Giddens as cited in Rantanen, 2005, p. 73). Mediated communication enables a wider range of interactions both within and across cultures. As Giddens noted, "communications has become the driving force of successive waves of transformation of human society" ((Interview with Giddens as cited in Rantanen, 2005, p. 73). And media and communication have made possible many of the institutions associated with globalization (Giddens, 2003). Tomlinson (1997, p. 123) noted that because many of our experiences are mediated, it is important "to appreciate the subtleties and complexities of different modes of experience available" and to be cognizant of differences in experiences across different types of mediation. Giddens' work (1984, 2000) has been instrumental in highlighting the role of mediated communication in the reflexive evolution of culture.

With this understanding of culture and the changes fostered by communicative processes, especially mediated communication, we now turn to more fully discuss culture, identity and the new media. These complex interactions among culture, communication, new media and identity are significant and evolving. In what follows, conceptualizations of culture, communication and new media will be developed and their interactions discussed. Then, subsequently, culture, communication and new media will be examined in light of their influence on the development of identity over the lifespan.

Identity is assumed to be multiple, changing and developing over one's lifespan, and particular attention will be given to cultural identity. While identity develops and is negotiated in many different contexts, such as conflict (Ting-Toomey, 2005; Ting-Toomey, Yee-Jing, Chapiro, Garcia, Wright & Oetzel, 2000), our emphasis will be on new media's impact on identity. We now turn to a more detailed discussion of the concepts of culture, identity and new media.

INTEGRATING CULTURE, COMMUNICATION AND NEW MEDIA

Conceptualizing Culture and Communication

Communication and culture have always been significantly interwoven (Haslett, 1987, 2012, 2014a, 2014b). Culture generally rests upon a shared set of practices and beliefs among a group, and such shared knowledge depends upon communication. As such, communication is central to the development and maintenance of culture: Culture, in turn, shapes communication, including verbal, nonverbal and mediated forms of communication (Haslett, 1987, 2012).

Hofstede

Individualism and Collectivism

Hofstede (2001) has analyzed culture along four dimensions: individualism/ collectivism, masculinity/femininity, power distance, uncertainty avoidance and time orientation (long-term versus short-term). These dimensions have been verified cross-culturally and across multiple contexts. Although Hofstede's research has been criticized for being a static, over-generalized model of culture, nevertheless it remains one of the most widely used in examining cultures and cultural differences.

Hofstede's individualism/collectivism appears to represent attachment to groups. Individuals may be somewhat autonomous (individualism) or view themselves in terms of their positions within a group (collectivism). Collectivist cultures make sharper distinctions between in-groups and out-groups than do individualistic cultures. Individualistic cultures tend to use low-context communication in which the message content is direct. Collectivistic cultures tend to use high-context communication which relies on indirect communication because much of the meaning is built into the situation (Gudykunst & Kim, 2003).

Triandis (1995) argued that individualism/collectivism can be distinguished by whether individual relationships are horizontal or vertical. In horizontal cultures, people perceive themselves and others as equals whereas people in vertical cultures see themselves as different and unequal. Individuals in vertical, collective cultures, such as India or Japan, do not emphasize freedom or equality. In vertical, individualistic cultures, like the United States, people act individually and value standing out from others: Freedom is emphasized, but not equality. In horizontal, individualist cultures, like Norway, people act as individuals but do not try to stand out: both freedom and equality are highly valued. In horizontal, collectivist cultures people value equality but not freedom. Individualistic cultures tend to be universalistic in applying values to groups but collectivist cultures tend to be particularistic and assign different values to in-groups and out-groups. All cultures have aspects of individualism and collectivism, but one orientation tends to be dominant (Gudykunst & Kim, 2003).

Masculinity and Femininity

Masculinity/femininity appears to characterize how gender roles are defined in a culture. Cultures that are high in femininity value quality of life, nurturance and service to others while highly masculine cultures emphasize assertiveness, power and material objects.

Power Distance

Power distance reflects the relationships between people of different status. In high power distance cultures, individuals with high status possess more authority and receive the most respect and obedience from others. Hierarchy and formality are valued in high power distance cultures. Low power distance cultures respect individuals and equality more than high power distance cultures. Both power orientations are present in cultures, but one orientation tends to predominate.

Uncertainty Avoidance

Uncertainity avoidance reflects a culture's tendency to avoid ambiguity and uncertainty. Cultures high in uncertainty avoidance (UA) value formal rules and clear structures which reduce anxiety and stress for individuals and also tend to resist change and take fewer risks. In contrast, cultures low in UA have more tolerance for ambiguity and find differences to be matters of curiosity rather than fear. Later work by Hofstede emphasizes culture as a collective mental programming shared by a group (Hofstede & Hofstede, 2005).

Time Orientation

Cultures with a short-term orientation tend to focus on quick results and value social and status obligations. In contrast, cultures with long-term orientations value patience, willingness to change and can work toward results that may take a long time to develop.

Schwartz Cultural Values

Schwartz and his colleagues have developed a set of values that capture the range of values across cultures. These values collapse into four broad value dimensions: Self-enhancement, openness to change, self-transcendence and conservatism (Schwartz & Bardi, 2001). Self-enhancement represents power, achievement and hedonism while openness to change reflects novelty and stimulation. The values of universalism and benevolence reflect self-transcendence while conservatism reflects values of conformity, tradition and security. Across student and teacher samples in 54 cultures, benevolence, self-direction and universalism were consistently most highly valued while power, tradition and stimulation were least important. Cultures vary in the importance they place on these values and individuals within a given culture will vary in their identification with particular cultural values.

Other ways of viewing culture include the contrast between high-context cultures that rely heavily on the context and nonverbal cues for interpreting messages—much of this style of communication is implicit and indirect. In contrast, low-context cultures rely on explicit, direct communication of information and intent (Hall, 1976). Rather than essentializing culture into sets of characteristics, Oyserman and Lee (2008) view culture as "mental habits" that characterize the ways in which a group thinks.

Over time, cultural expectations of appropriate behaviors in a given context change, and "the assumptions that different cultures hold about similar context-related behaviors can create problems" (St. Amant, 2014, p. 77). A prime example of differing assumptions is the contrast between high-context and low-context cultures which vary in terms of how much information needs to be directly expressed as opposed to being tacitly understood as part of the communicative context (Hall, 1989).

As the concept of culture evolves, wider more inclusive viewpoints have developed, in particular moving away from static conceptions of culture. Scholars are increasingly recognizing the fallacy of over-generalizing cultural values and not recognizing intracultural diversity, especially the cultural orientations of indigenous people (Bhawuk, 2008). Globalization and flows of information worldwide can be sources for both adaptation and resistance.

Transnational cultures emerge when cultures are exposed to each other, and their intersection results in the "transformation of an existing cultural artifact and the creation of a new style. Something new is produced by mixing the foreign and the local" (Iwabuchi, 2010, p. 421). As he notes, what is adopted or adapted to a culture is *always negotiated with the local* [emphasis mine]. Iwabuchi also noted that spatial proximity among cultures has been underestimated as a factor in transnational cultures—increasing interregional flows of goods and services may reduce cultural distance and lead to increasing influence by proximal nations (e.g., flow of Korean music, Japanese technology and so forth to other Asian nations).

McEwan and Denton (2011) argue that CMC enables people to increase their social and cultural capital through hybrid cultures and the transnational flow of information (see also Bruggemann & Wessler, 2014, on different strategies explaining the use of globalized CMC). Sobre-Denton (2016, p. 1) further argues that social media "facilitates a global-local orientation to the world that allows individuals to engage in virtual community-building and participate in communication to build global citizenship." It is important to note, however, that globalization and the transnational flow of information may create resistance and divergence across cultures as well (Bhawuk, 2008; Sorrels, 2013).

Hybridization thus occurs on many levels across different cultures, rather than just reflecting the flow of modernization from Western countries to other non-Western countries. Shuter observed that intercultural research includes "myriad cultures, both within and across geo-political boundaries, as well as hybridized cultures that have developed transnationally due to migration, diaspora, and time and space reconfigurations in a digital age" (2012, p. 230). (See Croucher, 2011, for discussions of migration).

With the internet, we also have virtual cultures, groups formed on the basis of common interests, which are not bound by space or time: These virtual cultures may challenge or support traditional (organic) cultures (Singh, 2010). However, Shuter (2012, p. 222) questions whether "hybrid cultural identities are, indeed, possible and whether identity co-creation and negotiation can truly occur in virtual communities consisting of disparate, unrelated individuals."

With increasing interconnections among cultures, there may be points of convergence and divergence among values across individuals.

As this brief overview has shown, the conceptualization of culture is being transformed from earlier, static models of culture fixed in both time and space to more fluid models of culture reflecting the movement of people in time and space, in which their interconnections are made possible by travel and the internet. Giddens' structuration theory helps unpack some of these social and economic forces for change, and the role communication and travel have played in these changes. And Goffman's interaction order helps us link daily individual interactions to the formation and change in social structures.

Transnational and hybrid cultures also are being constructed via the flow of people worldwide. For our purposes, cultures reflect shared beliefs, values and ways of life, typically connected to a territory (although this last point about territoriality may not necessarily apply). CMC appears to play a vital role in maintaining cultural identity, irrespective of definitions of culture itself. While we can generally discuss computer mediated communication, it is important to look at how the media has evolved and to make distinctions among various media formats.

Culture, Communication and New Media

Mass communication systems, sometimes referred to as traditional media, are characterized by media, such as print media, radio broadcasting and television, which are centralized and have scripted messages sent to a largely mass audience (DeFluer & Dennis, 2010). In contrast, new media refers to communication/computer technologies (Web 2.0) that are interactive, decentralized, and allow individuals to connect with others directly, to form online communities, and to create new lifestyles (Manovich, 2001). New media depend upon user participation and feedback (Baym, 2010; Schorr, 2003). Neuman (1991) argues that new media reduce geophysical distance, increase communication, permit faster communication, provide more opportunities for interaction and integrate different forms of communication. Giddens' structuration theory also emphasizes the importance of digital communication, especially its ability to free one from space and time (via distanciation and disembedding) and its increased scope and speed.

Chen (2012) argues that new media and intercultural communication influence one another in multiple ways: culture influences the development of new media and new media, in turn, influence cultural/social identity and intercultural communication. The worldwide Web created a global community as well as varied independent, interconnected virtual communities: "new media simultaneously shape globalization into a process of differentiation and homogenization" (Chen & Dai, 2014, p. 124). Chen and Zhang (2010) suggest that new media enable a highly connected, complex interaction between humans and society: The convergence of new media and globalization helps create cultural identity and cultural hybridity. High-tech societies, such as those in East Asia, the U.S. and Europe, rely heavily on new media in their international and intercultural communication (Zhang & Prosser, 2012). As noted previously, cultural divergence may occur as a response to new media and globalization (Bhawuk, 2008). Additionally, Yuan (2013) points out that conceptions of both new media and intercultural communication are contentious and continuously evolving.

Lagerkvist (2013, p. 35) points out that the views that we form of other cultures and places are influenced by "broad and significant exposure to certain media representations through a variety of outlets over time." And increasingly, some of those images are via new media and varied platforms, with some being produced by individuals' personal representations (e.g., Facebook, blogging). Castells (2000, p. 1-2) envisions a networked society as a culture constructed through "pervasive, interconnected, and diversified media systems."

Mediatization

Mediatization refers to the way in which multiple forms of media have become a taken-for-granted, "invisible" aspect of modern life (Waisbord, 2013). We may arrange our life style around media, from scheduling times to watch our favorite shows to staying in contact with family and friends to conducting tasks or work to being informed about worldwide news events. As Rybas (2014, p. 94) suggests "Similar to other media, commodities, and technologies, online social networks merge with everyday reality and become invisible and taken for granted." Social interactions are mediated by technologies and those technologies are increasingly embedded in social relations.

Social Media

Evidence confirms that traditional media, like radio, television and magazines, have been supplemented by new media, rather than being replaced by them (Baym, 2010). Social media, a subset of new media, primarily refers to media technologies that connect users in very individual, unique manners Some common features of social media are interactive Web 2.0 internet applications, such as Facebook and Pinterest, user produced content, specific profiles, and formation of online social networks (Kaplan & Haenlein, 2010; Obar & Wildman, 2015). Boyd and Ellison (2008) defined SNSs (social network sites) as web-based services through which people can construct their own profiles, list others they wish to connect with, and view their connections and those of others in the platform. As Barnes (2008, p. 21) observed, "Simply stated, social media is software that enables people to interact with each other and build social networks that increase social capita.l" She notes that social networking has already altered social, political and personal communication across both individuals and organizations in the U.S. (Barnes, 2008, p. 22).

Social media websites are "essential ways in which people stay in touch" around the world (Mussell, 2012). New media, fueled by the vast expansion of the Internet worldwide, now reach over 50 percent of the world's population (Internet World Statistics, 2017). Web 2.0 heralded the development of prosumers, individuals who both produce and consume new media. The variety of social media includes blogging, micro-blogging, mobile chat rooms and instant messaging, online music, online trade, professional and corporate SNSs, wikis and platforms for sharing photos and videos (Ogilvy, 2010). P2P (peer-to-peer) media connectivity forms interpersonal relationships and online communities in unique and unpredictable ways (Barnes, 2008). In addition, internet sites have now evolved into popular internet platforms across different cultures, such as WeChat, Renren and Weibo in China, Cyworld in South Korea, Mixi in Japan and of course, the worldwide reach of Facebook, YouTube, Instagram and Twitter. Mobile phones are also a significant source of social and internet connectivity (Qui, 2010).

As we have seen, mediated communication has become a significant tool for receiving information, and for developing and expressing oneself. With new media technologies available, people express themselves in many different ways across varied media platforms such as Facebook, Snapchat and SinaWeibo: Their popularity and use is a worldwide phenomenon. New platforms are being developed continuously in different cultures and new media are thus complex and evolving. Through new sources of information and inspiration available via the internet, people have a wide range of options for expressing their identities. Within and across cultures, people shape and manage their online identities and try to establish trusted online identities. Online identities may, of course, clash with real life identities or they may be authentic. Identity, too, has become more complex with both online and offline identities available, and the lines blurring between the two.

With overviews of culture and new media having been developed, we now turn to discussing their influences on identity. New media provide new, challenging sources of information and lifestyles that may impact one's identity. We now turn to a more detailed discussion of identity, and then turn to discuss the influence of culture and new media on identity.

CULTURE, NEW MEDIA AND THEIR INFLUENCE ON IDENTITY

Perspectives on Identity

Identity has been studied for decades, and its importance for personal development and social belonging is well-documented (Gergen, 1991; Giddens, 1991). Simon (2004, p. 66-67) suggests three significant functions of identity: belonging, self-respect and self-esteem, and a sense of one's position in the social world. On the personal level, "self-identity is understood here as an individual's perception of who he or she is, linked to self-assessment and, arguable, continuous re-evaluation" (Bouvier, 2012. 43). Giddens (1991) argues that the self is a continuing narrative of consistency, across identities and contexts, that extends throughout one's lifespan. One's self-concept is a construal of one's beliefs about her/himself and memories about the self; selfhood is key to one's individual identity (Hecht et al., 2005; Spencer-Oatey, 2007).

Giddens (1990) suggests that the range of life style choices presented by new media enable individuals to construct a narrative of identity which reflect the various positions they hold over their life span (e.g., child, parent). A social position specifies a "definite 'identity' within a network of social relations, that identity, however, being a 'category' to which a particular range of normative sanctions is relevant" (Giddens, 1984. 83). Both Gergen and Giddens argue that identities are multiple and that technology expands the alternatives for developing identities. Giddens also points out that in modernity, with media and transportation, we are called upon to project identities in ever changing contexts—as Bouvier (2012, p. 44) observes, "we are called to identify who we are, and in an increasingly globasized and decontextualized setting." Rybas (2014, p. 95) also notes that identity is always "being multiplied and constructed across different, often competing and complementing, discourses and practices."

How to conceptualize identity has challenged scholars. Alternative theories of identity have been proposed and we now turn to review some of the major theories of identity.

Face Negotiation Theory

Ting-Toomey (2005) argues that all people try to maintain face which represents respect for one's identity. Emotions are attached to our identity and self-worth. Face needs reflect identity needs for autonomy, inclusion, status, reliability, competence and moral face (integrity and honor). Facework reflects the verbal and nonverbal behaviors we use to uphold, maintain and/or restore face so that interactions take place smoothly. The cultural dimensions of individualism/collectivism, and power distance influence the facework strategies people use in interaction. People from individualistic cultures value their own (self) face over the face of others: collectivists, in contrast, value mutual-face or other-face over self-face. The cultural dimension of power distance also influences face. In high power distance cultures, peoples' facework honors the face of the highest status individual over their self-face. Facework strategies differ as a function of culture, the individual (self-construal) and the situation.

Ting-Toomey's face negotiation theory also emphasizes the negotiation of identity in everyday conflict interactions. Research by Ting-Toomey and her colleagues (Ting-Toomey, Yee-Jung, Shapiro, Garcia, Wright & Oetzel, 2000) found that the saliency of both ethnic identity and cultural identity influenced conflict styles. Individuals with a strong cultural identity used more integrating, compromising and emotionally expressive styles than did those having a weak cultural identity. Those with a strong ethnic identity used an integrating style more than did those with a weak ethnic identity.

Social Identity Theory

This theory focuses on the social categorization of identity (Hogg, Abrams, Otten & Hinkle, 2004; Tajfel & Turner, 1985). Categories such as gender and ethnicity are produced by groups and identity forms on the basis of membership in these groups. Social identity is defined as the individual's awareness that she/he belongs to particular social groups and reflects their emotional attachment to those groups. These social identities connect individuals to society via group memberships that influence their beliefs and values. This approach investigates group membership and behavior in both large and small groups, interactive and non-interactive groups, task-oriented groups, and both intra-and intergroup phenomena. Hogg et al. (2004) suggest that one important research question is whether multiple groups can be simultaneously salient? Roccas and Brewer (2002) found that membership in many different groups (multiple social identities) facilitated social identity complexity. This complexity subsequently enhanced the possibility of a global identity, a superordinate social identity. This complexity may, in fact, may be a way in which people integrate their multiple identities when interacting with others.

Identity categories have been provided by governments and institutions (Bouvier, 2012). Identities may characterize what one does (functionally, such as a policewoman); identification (culturally who one is, such as Irish), a relational identity (such as brother or friend), and physical identification (e.g., hair, skin color). Machin and Van Leeuwen, (2008) discuss identities as constructed by nation-states (where you are from); lifestyle (consumer choices and values), and cultural or ethnic group (essentializing group characteristics, such as 'Caribbean identity') (Hall, 1989). Identity has also been analyzed on the individual level, relational level and group level.

The Communication Theory of Identity

From this perspective, identity develops and is expressed during interaction with others (Hecht, Warren, Jung & Krieger, 2005). The Communication Theory of Identity (CTI) builds upon social identity theory as well as Identity theory. Four layers of identity, the personal, enactment (communication), relational and communal (group), interpenetrate one another (Hecht, Collier & Ribeau, 1993). As such, identities have individual, social and group properties; have both content and relational levels of interpretation, are emergent and changing, and provide a source of motivation and expectations.

In their overview of identity, Vignoles, Schwarz and Luychx (2011, p. 5) conclude that "identities are inescapably both personal and social not only in their content, but also in the processes by which they are formed, maintained, and changed over time." Some of these processes are conscious choices while other processes, such as nationhood, might be taken-for-granted and natural; both explicit and implicit processes need to be studied (Vignoles, Schwarz & Luychx, 2011, p. 5). Although there are disciplinary and methodological divisions in studying identity, they contend that:

Identity is simultaneously a personal, relational and collective phenomenon; it is stable in some ways and fluid in others; and identity is formed and revised throughout the lifespans of individuals and the histories of social groups and categories, through an interplay of processes of self-discovery, personal construction, and social construction, some of which are relatively deliberate and explicit, whereas others are more automatic and implicit (Vignoles, Schwarz & Luychx, 2011, p.8).

However, fundamental differences in Eastern versus Western views of the self must be acknowledged as influencing identity: Western views of the self locate the self as an independent individual whereas Eastern views acknowledge the self as embedded in relationships (Yin, 2017). The Kemetic and Confucian traditions center the self in a transformational process of moral cultivation (e.g., sensitivity) and through connections with others (ibid.). Ideas such as identity being multiple and changing may apply to either view of the self.

Given these complex alternative approaches to identity, some unifying themes can be discerned across them. All theories allow for multiple identities on differing levels such as the personal, group or relational levels. Identities are viewed as evolving, enduring and changing over one's lifespan. Social categorization, social positions and roles are important sources of identity, and the social context of interaction influences the identity one emphases. Identity processes may include both conscious or unconscious processes, and identities are important and negotiated as well as defended. Face represents the respect one gives to oneself and to others, and reflects different needs such as autonomy and inclusion. Our identities develop and mature in interaction: We negotiate our identity via interactions with others.

With this overview of different levels and conceptualizations of identity, we next turn to cultural identity and the role of new media in developing, negotiating and expressing identity. Cultural identity is complex because of intracultural and intercultural variation worldwide; increasingly we may form commitments to virtual communities and to communities moving across the world and establishing new homelands.

Cultural Identity

Cultural identity is shaped by both self-identity and attachment to groups, and unites the social and personal aspects of our lives (Kim, 2007). Because new media brings new exposure to others and to different experiences as well as collapses time and space, cultural identity is dynamic and evolving (Chen & Dai, 2014; Giddens, 1990; Haslett, 2012, 2014a, 2014b). Dervin (2012, p. 183) argues that "cultural identity is what we construct whenever we are in contact with other human beings—regardless of the fact that they are from the same 'environment.'" As such, identity is multiple, dependent on context, and reflects different identities in differing contexts.

Cultural identity, according to Chen and Dai (2014, p. 125), needs the coherence and consistency provide by temporality, territoriality and interactionality. Temporality means that cultural identity is developed in a given sociohistoric time, with others who share values and community, and shifts over a variety of position-places (Giddens, 1991). Through distanciation (the compression and lifting out of time/space from a localized setting), new communities and interconnections can be formed (ibid). And territoriality is viewed as both virtual and organic (traditional) (Chen & Dai, 2014).

Many have argued that the Western views of modernity have dominated cultural identities. Chen and Dai (2014, p. 128). suggest that this dominance has produced a digital divide, advantageous of the West in terms of cultural hybridization, and which challenges non-Western societies in terms of change and identity. They note that hybridization is not a "power-free space" and that non-Western countries have less opportunity to define themselves: "to incorporate modern Western ideas denotes both empowerment and marginalization" (Chen & Dai, 2014, p.130). While power is asymmetrical, this overlooks the fact that globalizing forces are adapted to local settings, and thus global and local merge as glocalization. Such adaptation to globalizing forces is also uneven and a function of local, environmental conditions within countries. And groups may resist change and organize resistance to change (Sorrels, 2013). As such, cultural identity evolves and may reflect intracultural and intercultural differences in identity.

Culture, as a collective identity, develops on multiple levels (cognitive, symbolic and emotional) and rests upon shared interpretations of the world, common values and mutual solidarity as well as hierarchical and horizontal communication (Coretti & Pica, 2015; Giddens, 1984, 1991). There is disagreement among scholars as to whether collective identity is an individual's connection to a broader community or if collective identity needs to be viewed as developed within a given social environment and influenced by the subjectivity of the collective actor (see Coretti & Pica, 2015; and Ruelle & Peverelli, 2016, for a fuller discussion of these issues).

Reflecting these different views of collective identity, Yum (2007, p. 248) contrasts two approaches to cultural identity: One approach recognizes "the premise of the primacy of individual identity, a universalized vision of citizenship, and mutual accommodation" while a second approach recognizes "the primacy of group identity as a basic and profound right of individuals" (Yum, 2007, p. 248). She concluded that five themes characterized perspectives on identity: as adaptive, evolving; as flexible and negotiable, as a discrete, selected category, as a distinct, communal system of communicative practices and as a non-negotiable group right (Yum, 2007, p. 237).

Collier's theory of cultural identity views cultural identity as "socially constructed and negotiated in intercultural relationships" in the context of sociohistorical influences and public discourses (Collier, 2009). Collier's cultural identity theory (Collier, 2000) posits that cultural identity is always grounded in self-perception, both avowed by the individual and ascribed to by others. Cultural identities have core symbols and exist on the affective, cognitive and behavioral levels. This identity is expressed on the individual, relational and communal levels and incorporates both content and relational aspects. These identities are multiple, constantly changing, located in specific times and places, and contradictory as well as paradoxical. Collier also notes that cultural identity may be initially unexamined, then people may investigate and question those identities, and finally accept their cultural identities.

Belay (1996) argues that cultural identity categories may be sociological, occupational, geobasic (racial or ethnic), and/or national (having civil rights and obligations as citizens of a nation-state). Each cultural identity is characterized by temporality, territoriality, contrastivity (contrasting collectivities), interactivity and multiplicity. To maintain cohesivenss, people must have shared memories and lifestyles as well as a shared sociohistory. To provide continuity, cultural identity requires a shared geographic space. It may be that this last requirement of continuity may also be provided by shared cyberspace.

An insightful review of cross-cultural perspectives on identity by Smith (2011) displays the complexity of analyzing identity. Individualist nations were said to be those in which one's identity is defined by one's individual attributes and goals. Collectivist nations are those in which one's identity is more strongly defined in terms of long lasting group memberships. Individualistic respondents employed many more trait-like self/descriptions, whereas East Asians referred more frequently to social categories. Persons within collectivist cultures report more short-term variation in their experienced identities as they move across different social contexts. The effect of context is much greater among respondents from collectivistic cultures. Cultural identification was significantly associated with personal support of values typically associated with that culture (Wan et al., 2007).

The position taken here is that identities are socially enacted, maintained and changed over one's lifespan, and that collective identities may become part of an individual's multiplicity of identities, appearing and disappearing at varying times over one's lifespan as social positions change (Giddens, 1990). The self is the core of identity and is anchored in real life as we live, work and form relationships in a particular real life locale that may shift over time. While new media can and does provide new information and ideas, this information is "localized" and integrated, if relevant, to real life in particular locales. However, this local-global connection is complex as the local "undergoes profound changes due to the interactivity, mobility and multimedia capabilities of information and media technologies—existing and forthcoming" (Kraidy & Murphy, 2008, p. 350).

How do cultural values link to individuals? The concept of self-construal links culture to individuals by arguing that individuals' value certain aspects of culture more than others. Self-construal reflects those cultural values and beliefs most important to individual members of a culture, and this helps explain intracultural variability in groups. We now turn to a more detailed discussion of self-construal.

Self-Construal

Cultural identity may characterize general qualities of a given culture, but it is an individual's own self-construal that links that individual to a particular set of cultural values. Markus and Kitayama (1991) developed the concept of self-construal to explain that linkage; these self-construals reflect how individuals view themselves, and their relationships with others. They suggested that individualistic cultures tend to foster independent self-construal. North Americans focus on the self and exploring their unique qualities whereas Japanese, as members of a collectivist culture, emphasize their connections with others. These basic self-construals influence people's cognitions, emotional states and motivation. Independent self-construals emphasize self-face and use dominating, competing styles in interaction. In contrast, collectivist cultures emphasize interdependent self-construals with individuals respecting the others' face needs and using strategies of avoiding conflict, obliging and compromising (Jetten, Potmes & McAuliffe, 2002).

Church et al. (2006) found that self-construals also predicted whether personality traits (independent self-construal) or social context (interdependent self-construals) predicted behaviors. Individuals, of course, will vary in the strength and saliency of their links to particular cultural values and there is considerable variation within cultures. Individualism and collectivism can characterize nations, but independence/ interdependence is best used to describe individual self-construals (Smith, 2011).

In their meta-analysis of studies using the Singelis' self-construal scales, Oyserman, Coon and Kemmelmeter (2007) found that European Americans were more individualistic and more collectivist than Japanese and Koreans, but less collectivistic than Chinese. However, Smith (2011) noted that these findings might not be valid because of respondents' tendency to acquiesce in their responses: much of the self-construal research might be biased by acquiescent responses.

Smith (2011) reviewed four more dimensions of self-construal. A focus on *hierarchy* characterizes the importance of equality (horizontal relationships) or hierarchy (vertical relationships) when interacting with others. Smith (2011) concluded that collectivist cultures tend to be hierarchical in their relationships. Hofstede (2001) found that high power distance (emphasizing hierarchy) and collectivism are strongly correlated at the national level.

A focus on *relatedness* concerns the priority given to the quality of interpersonal relationships. Brewer and Gardener (1996) argued that relatedness needed to be distinguished from collectivism and advocated distinguishing among personal, relational and collective identity. Yamagishi and Yamagishi (1998) found that Japanese were focused upon their in-group relationships whereas U.S. respondents were more focused on the relationship between their group and other groups (see also Takemura, Yuki & Ohtsubo, 2010).

The Del Prado et al. (2007) survey on identity separated personal, relational, social (reputation) and collective (ethnicity) identities. They found that in individualistic cultures, independence predicted personal and relational identities while interdependence predicted social and collective identities. Smith (2011, p. 258) concluded that "clear separation between measures of personal identity and relational identity in differing cultural contexts has not yet been achieved." However, because the self emerges in the context of social interaction, a clear separation between personal and relational identities may not be possible.

A focus on *category inclusiveness* explored the degree of involvement in four different levels of social inclusiveness (personal, relational, collective [viewed as a category in which you are an interchangeable element, like a student] and humanity-as-a-whole) (Harb & Smith, 2008). Cultural differences were found among UK, Jordanian, Syrian and Lebanese students. As Smith (2011) notes, the validity of these more differentiated measures depends upon having good research exemplars for each dimension.

A final focus is on *agency*. Kagitcibasi (2005) argues that independence/interdependence includes two different self-construal dimensions (interpersonal distance incorporating separation vs. relatedness, and agency incorporating autonomy vs. heteronomy) Heteronomy is characterized as reliance on others for guidance. She suggests that autonomous-relational self-construal characterizes collectivist, urban areas while heteronomous-relational self-construal characterizes rural populations in collectivist cultures.

In summary, various dimensions of culture have been linked to specific orientations for identity. Cultural variables, such as individualism and collectivism, influence one's self-construal. Self-construal is influenced as well by context, the degree of inclusivity of social groups, and the priority placed on relationships, whether ones of equality or hierarchy. Eastern and Western cultural differences tend to locate the self either as relatively autonomous (Western perspective) as opposed to locating the self within one's ingroups (Eastern perspective). Contrasting individualistic with collectivist cultures supports the view that individualistic cultures foster independent personal and relational identities as opposed to interdependent identities reflected in social and collective identities. Context is more significant for identity in collectivist cultures, perhaps because much of meaning is contained with the social context. Ingroup identities are also critical for collectivists and much less significant for individualists.

Although not explicitly researched, the dimension of power distance would suggest that identity is closely linked to status in high power distance cultures and less important in low power distance cultures. The masculine/feminine cultural dimension would suggest that identities are more fluid in feminine cultures which are characterized by supportiveness and nurturing. Schwartz's value dimension of self-transcendence would suggest that one might strive for achievement beyond established standards and openness to change would encourage identity exploration. In contrast, the value of conservatism would tend to support well-established identity traditions. Future research could explore some of the connections between cultural dimensions and identity.

Smith (2011) points out that these more specific aspects of independence/interdependence enrich our understanding of self-construal and identity. However, theoretical and methodological weaknesses remain challenges to such research. The basis for comparison anchors remain elusive across studies in addition to the difficulty posed by acquiescent responses. Smith suggests that research on bilinguals raises the intriguing question as to the variety and depth of their identities, and generally, in terms of the saliency of cultural identity itself as a construct.

Thus far, we have examined the complexity of culture in an age of modernization and globalization. In addition, we have investigated the complexity of identity itself, and how culture influences identity. CMC (computer mediated communication) has expanded our interactional world, and increased our engagement with other cultures. Despite criticisms of using the nation-state as a measure of culture it remains a basis for comparing culture. Increasingly, social categories, such as age, gender, education and religion, are viewed as cultural categories that impact communication and intercultural communication, in mediated as well as face-to-face encounters (see for example, Lee & Choi, 2005; Ess, Kawbata & Kurosaki, 2007).

While face-to-face interaction is a significant context for developing identity, and provides the major research context for identity, the influence of mediated communication in daily life provides significant opportunities for new ideas to influence personal and cultural identity and for new opportunities for self-expression. For example, online self-presentation gives users control over their self-images by editing and putting forth a positive impression, concealing problematic issues, and deciding when and how to disclose information about age, gender and so forth (Barnes, 2008). Other factors influencing cultural identity online include whether one is known or anonymous, and the impact of alternative platforms on social network sites like Facebook, blogging or working over a virtual network. Increasingly the lines between our online and offline identities have become blurred. In what follows, we examine how new media has influenced identity. Although there is a voluminous literature on CMC, immigration and cultural adjustment, that literature is beyond the scope of this chapter and will not be discussed (see Croucher, 2011, and others on those issues).

CULTURE, NEW MEDIA AND IDENTITY

Cultures vary in their access to new media and this limits the possibilities for identity development. In addition, characteristics of social media platforms directly influence the negotiation, management and expression of identity. Finally, individual users vary in how they express and manage their online identities. This complex of influences—culture, social media and users—interact and provide online identity. Serious concerns are emerging around issues of trust, privacy and the degree to which online and offline identities are blurring. In what follows, some of the research on cultural variation in the development, maintenance and negotiation of identity will be discussed. However, the research literature is already extensive, and our coverage here will be limited and focus on some of the emerging themes from research on cultural influences on online identity.

Social information processing (SIP, Walther, 1992) argues that available cues in mediated communication support identity development online: Users can edit their online persona and present highly desirable self-impressions. User-generated media, like YouTube or blogging, will be used for information, entertainment and self-presentation (establishing identities) (Barnes, 2008; Shao, 2009).

Agency represents the user's ability to control and navigate a website. Goffman (1971) suggests that agency is critical for interactants. Sundar discusses technological choices in terms of what best supports the self-agency of users (self-as-source) in presenting their self-images online. In his model of agency as customization, he argues that sources of content rely on the technology platform (its interactivity, modality [its sensory richness and self-representation options], and navigability [its individualized exploration and ease in the nature of interaction] (Sundar, 2008, p. 69). Content effects thus reflect a user's involvement, identity and control. Sundar argues that self-as-source imbues the user with a greater sense of agency as well as involvement and control over one's identity. Online presentations of self provide "an unprecedented range of choices" in content and representation: "the greater personal agency afforded by self-as-source can impact behaviors by offering users a greater sense of control in the interaction" (Sundar, 2008, p. 71). The focus of Sundar's model is on the manner "in which aspects of communication technologies promote the sense of 'self as source'" (Sundar, 2008, p. 71).

Social information processing and agency are important aspects of new media irrespective of culture, and thus they are mentioned here. These approaches provide a general context for the more detailed discussion of cultural differences, identity and new media. Cultural variation in online identity is analyzed in two sections: one focusing on cultural variation in online usage and the second focusing on cultural variation in platform features.

Cultural Variation in Online Usage

Self-Presentation Online

In anonymous websites, such as MUDs, users developed alternative selves and may demonstrate negative attitudes (Turkle, 2011). When scholars studied nonymous online environments, such as dating sites, users tend to make more direct identity statements. Zhao, Grasmuck and Martin (2008, p. 1816) found that Facebook users claimed their identity implicitly and "stressed group and consumer identities over personally narrated ones." This appears to represent the lifestyle regime of identity previously noted. As they suggest, this was an important finding because online self-presentations vary as a function of the online setting (i.e., nonymous versus anonymous context). Marwick and Boyd (2010) point out that in sites such as Facebook and Twitter users address social contexts that are part of a network; as such, self-presentation may be authentic but also reflect concerns about privacy. As they note, "Individuals learn how to manage tensions between public and private, insider and outsider, and frontstage and backstage performances (Marwick & Boyd, 2010, p. 130).

Relational Orientation

How we relate to others, whether as independent individuals or as an interdependent self, reflects an important orientation in one's identity (Smith, 2011). Such differences are reflected in online relationships and identity. Asian Americans showed greater variability in how they described themselves in differing relationships (English & Chen, 2007). Hwang (2005) found that Chinese tend to express a relational self in contrast to the individualistic orientation found in individualistic cultures.

Sundar (2008) also suggests that self-as-source is more appealing to individualistic (independent) rather than collectivist cultures (interdependent) where the desire is to belong and fit in with the group. Evidence demonstrates that users prefer internet platforms and representations that reflect their own cultures and Sundar's model may enhance our understanding of those preferences.

Idealized Online Selves

Bouvier's study of Facebook identification by students found that identity performance online is more reflective, more idealized, assumes a familiar audience, and refers to a community of interests (for example, being a football fan). Consumer related identities (using product images, for example) and nationalistic identities were prominent forms of identity on Facebook. Bouvier (2012, p. 54) concluded that "While social media contain all the potential for global interactions they appear to foster more specialist interactions."

Tufecki (2008), relying on Goffman's presentation of the self, found that users of SNS (social network sites) distinguished between expressive uses of the internet (such as social monitoring and self-presentation) and instrumental uses (information seeking). Users of SNSs were influenced by their interest in social grooming (i.e., small talk, general social information about themselves and others) as well by privacy concerns. Users differed in their use of the expressive dimension but not in their use of the instrumental dimension of the internet. Baym and Boyd (2012) conclude that media users must balance the complex interactions among platform affordances, the communicative context, multiple audiences and privacy/self-disclosures in their media use.

An intriguing study, integrating face-to-face interaction with the presentation of a digital self, found that participants developed a "social, rich and ambiguous content" to present themselves online (Kyto & McGookin, 2017). Content from existing social media accounts was utilized as well as content from other sources: Participants shared digital selves through Smartwatches with private Head Mounted Displays. Discussing the digital self gave participants a good entre into a conversation, and a way to control self-disclosure. Such studies may provide linkages between offline and online identities.

Trust, Disclosure and Privacy

For South Koreans, minihompies (private sections on one's website that have access controlled by the site creator) function as "another me." A minihomphy provided a place/space for expressing private thoughts, self-revelation and emotions without the tension of face-to-face interaction (Kim & Yun, 2008). Information released online may depend on expectations for credible communication within a particular context, such as comfort level with and knowledge of other participants (Marcus & Krishnamurthi, 2009) and accountability (Chapman & Lahav, 2008).

Trust is also critical and may depend on recommendations from third parties before information is exchanged (Guo & Yu, 2009). Differences in the degree of self-disclosure online influences the trust placed in a relationship with more self-disclosure positively influencing U.S. respondents while Koreans trusted less, and it was a non-factor for Japanese (Yum & Hara, 2006). They concluded that when high and low-context cultures interact, more attention to face (identity) concerns may help prevent misunderstanding. Tokunga (2009) found that self-disclosure was significantly less in depth and breadth in online as opposed to face-to-face interactions, and that difference was greater for collectivistic cultures than for individualistic cultures. Self-disclosure is regarded as an important factor in constructing one's identity. And trust issues would likely be greater when media users engage with others from different cultures or outside their specific social groups.

Protecting one's privacy and depth of self-disclosure also varied across cultures. Liang, Shen and Fu (2016) found that privacy settings encouraged more self-disclosure in collectivist societies but there was no direct connection between cultural values and self-disclosure. Greater internet penetration in countries significantly influenced the adoption of privacy settings and self-disclosure with more options available with greater internet access. They argue that there is tension between the need to protect privacy against the interest in presenting a unique online identity.

Cultural and Ethnic Heritage

Self-presentations also serve to profile and elaborate users' cultural and ethnic heritage. Facebook profiles by Native Americans, African Americans, Vietnamese and Latinos produced narratives and images that emphasized their cultural roots (Grasmuck, Martin & Shanyang, 2009). French Muslims also maintained their Muslim connections and identity through using social media (Croucher & Cronn-Mills, 2011).

Greeks used Pathfinder, a popular SNS, to construct their identities using profile pages, colors, images, quotes and music to uniquely present themselves online (Georgalou, 2010). Using discourse analysis, Georgalou (2010, p. 55) found users relying on "allusions, irony, modality, pronouns, intertextuality and interdiscursivity along with a visual panoply of symbolic images and meticulous layout choices in color and typeface" to promote a polished self-image online.

Online expressions of interests (taste performances of identity) are used to represent identity and may convey prestige, authenticity, differentiation from others and a theatrical persona—Liu (2007) refers to such statements as "taste interests" and argued that cultural interests are expressed as taste statements. Users also negotiate tensions online between authenticity and positive impression management (Utz, 2010; Ye, 2005).

Developing Group Identity

In group interactions, people may identify with subgroups or on the basis of larger social groups. People may identify with others on the interpersonal relational dimension (SIP, Walther, 1992) or on the basis of social identity with a group. Because in new media there is frequently visual anonymity, the SIDE theory (social identity model of deindividuation effects) predicts that people behave in a depersonalized, deindividuated manner and this leads them to identify with a salient group identity, whether in an ad hoc group or larger social groupings. Having a disliked in-group participant reduced group member's identification with the in-group (Wang, Walther & Hancock, 2009). They suggest that interpersonal behaviors may influence and direct in-group identification.

An intriguing study by Ruelle and Peverelli (2016) explored the development of collective group identity at a Chinese NGO through using WeChat. Online interactions included both instrumental-digital comments as well as phatic-analogous discussion, thus building a group identity as well as group solidarity. They suggest that it is important to explore the social construction of cognitive and social elements: "instrumental or digital communication continuously constructs and re-constructs the cognitive element of a social-cognitive group while phatic or analogous communication is constructive of the social elements" (Ruelle & Peverelli, 2016, p. 17). Finally, they note that WeChat blurs the "boundaries between physical and digital spaces, instrumental-digital and phatic-analogous communication, and even between weak and strong ties" (Ruelle & Peverelli, 2016, p. 17).

Chinese cultural identity was influenced by mainstream media (books and television) as well media content (educational and political) although foreign information was also present (Wu, Shi & Yan, 2013). Liu (2011) found that Chinese urban youth used the internet as a cultural tool for developing the self, study, sociability and learning. Professional, group, organizational and cultural identity are also developed on new media (Sangwan, 2005). Chen and Collier (2012) found that two nonprofit organizations negotiated identity positioning, cross-status relationships and hierarchies, and minority status in their collaborative mediated communication.

As we have seen thus far, cultural influences on social media are present and influence how users interact online. In some cases, social media serve to mitigate the pressure of face-to-face interactions. Identity is managed by agency, self-presentation and an idealized self-image. Identities vary as a function of relational orientation, group identity, cultural and ethnic heritage, and concerns about trust and privacy. And differences in how identity is expressed vary across Eastern and Western countries. Thus, culture plays a significant role in how, where and in what forms identity is developed and expressed. And culture influences both personal, professional and group identities.

More awareness and appreciation of such differences will promote more effective interactions through an enhanced understanding of the different contexts in which people live and how their identities develop. Identity is the foundation from which we interact with one another, and new media provides new sources of information as well as new venues for expression of identity. It is important for effective cross-cultural and intercultural communication to understand others' perspectives. In a world of increasing differentiation and conflict, enhanced understanding of different perspectives is necessary for effective interaction and can provide a clearer basis for cooperation.

We next turn to another strong influence on social media use, the type of communication platform utilized. At the outset, however, we should note that internet penetration and governmental policies limit access to various social media platforms. Modernization and globalization of countries influence a particular country's access to various forms of media with wealthier countries having more access as well as more varied access. For example, as is well known, Facebook is banned in China. Several countries have developed their own social media platforms, like Mixi in Japan and Cyworld in South Korea. Each of these platforms presents their own internal structures and guidelines for use. The development of new media platforms is rapidly increasing worldwide, and at present one can discern some patterns of media usage although there is widespread change within and across countries.

Cultural Variation in New Media Platforms

Platform Affordances

New media users have cultural preferences in selecting what media platforms they use (Kline & Liu, 2005). Specific platforms have been developed for particular countries, such as Mixi in Japan or SinaWeibo in China. For example, Hispanic students were more likely to use MySpace while Asian students were more likely to use Xanga and Friendster (Boyd & Ellison, 2008). Miller and Madianou (2012, p. 148) argue that users rely on a variety of media platforms in which "media are mediated by the relationship as well as the other way around." They suggest that individuals will be judged by why and how they use a particular media: thus, affordances of a media may significantly influence its use. At present, new platforms and preferences are proliferating because of the rapid changes in mediated communication. And Sundar and Limperos (2013) argue that the affordances of new media may create new needs and gratifications among users. The qualities (affordances) of the platforms themselves limit how one's identity may be presented. For example, Facebook has a standard template for presenting information on profiles.

Design Preferences

The platform features offered by various networks and social network sites (SNSs) directly influence the construction of cultural and personal identity by the features (affordances) offered. Brivio, Ibarra and Galimberti (2010) found that the template, layout and username were significant factors influencing new media users. Home pages were found to be "building blocks" for later blogs. Users also prefer Web sites designed by members of their own cultures (Gevorgyan & Manucharova, 2009) and can locate individualistic/collectivist elements in web design (Kim, Coyle & Gould, 2009).

Language may be considered a design feature because different languages are "read" differently (e.g., from left to right, right to left, top to bottom). Such features shape the platforms' format and overall design. In addition, social identity is linked to one's language which serves as a social marker for a group's distinctiveness (Noel, Yashima & Zhang, 2013), even though there may be multiple ethnolinguistic identities being referenced in an encounter. Odejobi and Adegbola (2010) also discuss the difficulties of new media in supporting African languages and their concomitant platform difficulties (both in computation and engineering) . They suggest that language technologies should be developed around culture and ethnicity.

Blogging

Blogging has long been recognized for its social networking capacity and for providing alternative sources of information (Baym, 2010; Chen, 2010). Blogs alter media content by enabling individual voices on the internet and also help form new electronic communities that exist across time and space (Barnes, 2008). Blogs create, manage and negotiate identities by making and checking arguments, posting on going conversations about events, and presenting strategically edited content about the author. Papacharissi (2004) found that blogs displayed personal expressiveness and social utility more than home pages did. Blogs were also found to contain substantial self-revelation and items that revealed personal identification (Huffacker & Calvert, 2005).

In a cross-cultural comparison, Chen (2010) found that Taiwanese bloggers revealed far less personal information on their blogs and presented a self-image anchored in a relational self. Gender also influences blogging, with male teenagers using active, direct language and more emoticons (Huffaker & Calvert, 2005).

In sum, new media—particularly social media---provide an important source for developing and expressing personal and cultural identity. New media open up new opportunities for developing, managing and negotiating identity. Identity may express one's uniqueness as well as reflect one's cultural roots and may manifest itself across personal, group and/or work environments. Although platform design and affordances may limit the options for expressing identity, great creativity and adaptability can be seen on new media. The context and cultural norms surrounding new media also influence the expression of identity.

Some cultural factors influencing the presentation of identity include platform selection, design features, self-as-a-source of information, the variety of cultural strategies that can be utilized, anonymity vs. nonymity, individualism vs. collectivism, the context in which the information is presented, trust and self-disclosure. Users of large public internet platforms, like Facebook or SinaWeibo, allow individuals to present a careful self-edited portrayal of themselves. Perhaps the most openness in expressing identity is found on blogs, where bloggers control the available content. New media users are thus able to express multiple facets of their identities over diverse venues provided by new media.

CONCLUSION

With worldwide globalization, cultures are experiencing continual change, particularly from the increased flow of information, the emergence of transnational cultures, and both divergence and hybridization across cultures. The landscape of communication has been profoundly altered with the increasing importance of mediated communication in our daily lives. New media continue to provide new information that challenges how we view culture and our own identities. Both cultures and identities have been changed through new media's capacity to encourage reflexivity, enhance distanciation and enable disembedding. Culture, communication and identity are complex constructs in and of themselves, and in constant flux, with new developments continuously emerging.

This chapter argues that structuration theory (ST) provides an excellent overarching perspective which contextualizes the complexity and speed of social change across cultures and individuals. In particular, ST focuses on cultural, social, economic and political changes in modernity which have been driven by changes in communication and transportation. Transportation enables relatively easy and rapid connections throughout the world and mediated communication facilitates instantaneous rapid interactions throughout the world. These new interconnections involve us in a worldwide community with exposure to multiple lifestyles and different ideas; identities have been challenged by this new influx of information. With its emphasis on interaction as building cultures and cultural institutions, ST focuses attention on the centrality of interpersonal and mediated communication in identity. The processes of distanciation and disembedding explain how we can form identities across time and space.

With structurational interaction, integrating Goffman's interaction order with Giddens' structuration, attention is also directed to the daily interactions of individuals and groups and how they create and maintain social structures that undergird cultural institutions. This integration connects micro- and macro-levels of analysis and promotes a deeper appreciation of the multiple layers of culture, from individuals to groups to institutions and to the broad overview of culture. For example, we can observe how micro-level interactions, such as the beginning of social protest movements, can build up into widespread forces of change, such as in the Arab spring or protests in the U.S. against the Vietnam War.

'Who am I?' changes over one's lifespan, but simultaneously reflects facets of a self that is consistent over multiple contexts. In this process of constructing the self, identity is critically important because it affects every thought and action one takes. Through new media significant new venues for the expression and development of identity are presented. As new media evolve and change, new venues for identity management and negotiation will continue to appear.

The information and arguments set out in this chapter suggest that culture, communication and identity are intertwined processes and that they have been transformed by new media. Culture and communication are inextricably linked because we learn our cultures via communication, and cultures are reinforced, modified or profoundly changed by communication. In turn, cultures shape communicative processes and styles. This fundamental interconnection between communication and culture is ongoing. Giddens' structuration theory is particularly useful because it enhances our understanding of the critical role of communication in establishing, maintaining and changing cultures and identities.

Initially, communication and culture are learned through face-to-face interaction in family contexts. Identity also develops in this manner. Through new media, communicative processes have been altered such that new knowledge, lifestyles and ideas are now available that go well beyond the limits of familial or immediate cultural contexts. Mediated communication enables one to visit other cultures virtually such that we can be both 'here and there, and now and then'. Transportation has also facilitated intertwined economies. Thus, mediated communication and transportation, as Giddens suggests, have profoundly altered our world.

Because both communication and culture are being transformed, identity is also being transformed. Individuals have access to information about other lifestyles, cultures, music and so forth which present a wide array of new choices. Identities are also expressed, negotiated and managed online. Through social media individuals can engage one another directly, and adapt, change or reject ideas from others. One can have both offline and online identities, and the lines between them have become blurred. Through mediated communication, one can separate from one's real life circumstances and experience other identities, develop new identities and new self-concepts.

Online development of identity, however, functions as a result of platform design features and restrictions. Another fundamental limitation is due to the digital divide in which less economically developed economies have less access to mediated communication and individuals may lack the necessary media literacy skills to use media platforms effectively (Hargiatti & Hsieh, 2013). Cultures will also vary in terms of what is considered appropriate in online interaction.

This chapter has argued that culture, communication and identity influence one another and that all of them are in continuous transformation. The development of new media has also experienced tremendous growth and change. These interconnections are so closely interwoven that a change in one aspect alters the other areas as well. And thus 'Who am I?' is also in continuous flux.

FUTURE RESEARCH DIRECTIONS

Serious concerns have developed during the transformation of culture, communication and identity. Future research is needed to explore such areas as privacy and security. How can information be protected and shared only with selected others? Trust is another major research interest—how is trust established online and how do we verify the identities of others? Trust is an integral part of how identity is developed and maintained. We trust our families and cultures in the earliest stages of development and, subsequently, trust is a major factor in how we assess and use new media. Are sources of information trusted (think of 'alternative facts'), and do we trust the individuals we meet in cyberspace? And most importantly, more scholarship is needed to analyze the profound shifts in how we communicate with one another, and on the interconnections between mediated and face-to-face communication (Turkle, 2011).

Researchers could analyze the links between culture and identity in more detail by examining how specific aspects of culture, such as individualism/collectivism or values like openness and conservatism, influence identity development and maintenance. Although there is some research detailing these more fine-grained influences, such investigations could represent a new promising line of research.

In a similar fashion, comparisons across social media platforms, such as Facebook versus blogging, could explore how identity develops and is maintained across these two platforms.

Another area of research interest is that of authenticity: what is the relationship between offline and online identity? Are such identities separate or fused, and what are the implications of this for both culture and communication?

Research also needs to explore the digital divide. This division, of course, is a major underlying concern for media use as well as economic development and must be addressed by political and economic interests. Individuals without digital access experience major disadvantages in competing for jobs and enriching their own lives (Hargiatti, 2008; Hargiatti & Hsieh, 2013; Haslett, forthcoming).

There is also a pressing need for integration of research on identity, culture and new media. The theory of structurational interaction (Haslett, 2012) synthesizes Giddens' structuration theory and Goffman's interaction order, and offers the theoretical breadth and depth needed for integrating these research areas. This synthesis extends structuration theory to tocus on agency, culture and communication, both face-to-face and mediated communication. Structurational interaction thus provides a framework for both macro-level and micro-level analyses of media, communication and culture. While media scholars have used both Giddens and Goffman's work, their potential integration on multiple levels has been overlooked. Such integration is needed to enrich our understanding of the interconnections among culture, new media and identity.

Future research also needs to focus on careful development of constructs such as identity and culture, and to clearly articulate the underlying assumptions in these constructs and how they are operationalized. In addition, more attention needs to be given to finding research measures that translate across different cultures and to addressing response biases that may limit the accuracy of responses. Bhawuk (2008) also emphasizes the need for multiparadigmatic research approaches in which various facets of intercultural connections can be assessed.

The importance of intracultural differences must also be acknowledged because indigenous research reveals the complex nuances of value differences within nation-states (Bhawuk, 2008). And with the shift of economic power and media development to the East (especially China and India) alternative theorizing might look at the "other" globalization (Thussu, 2011, p. 234; see also Rakow, 2013).

REFERENCES

Bargiela-Chiappini, F. (2006). (Whose) English(es) for Asian business discourse? *Journal of Asian Pacific Communication*, *16*(1), 1–23. doi:10.1075/japc.16.1.02bar

Barnes, S. (2008). Understanding social media from the media ecological perspective. In E. Konjin, S. Utz, M. Tanis, & S. Barnes (Eds.), *Mediated interpersonal communication* (pp. 14–33). New York: Routledge.

Bauman, Z. (2000). *Liquid modernity*. Cambridge, UK: Polity Press.

Baym, N. (2010). *Personal connections in the digital age*. Cambridge, UK: Polity.

Baym, N., & boyd, . (2012). Socially mediated publicness: An introduction. *Journal of Broadcasting & Electronic Media*, *56*(3), 320–329. doi:10.1080/08838151.2012.705200

Belay, G. (1996). The (re)construction and negotiation of cultural identities in the age of globalization. In H. Mokros (Ed.), *Interaction and identity*. New Brunswick, NJ: Transaction.

Bhawuk, D. (2008). Globalization and indigenous cultures: Homogenization or differentiation? *International Journal of Intercultural Relations*, *32*(4), 305–312. doi:10.1016/j.ijintrel.2008.06.002

Bouvier, G. (2012). How Facebook users select identity categories for self-presentation. *Journal of Multicultural Discourses*, *7*(1), 37–57. doi:10.1080/17447143.2011.652781

boyd, d., & Ellison, N. (2008). Social network sites: Definition, history and scholarship. *Journal of Computer-Mediated Communication, 13*(1), 210-230.

Brewer, M., & Gardner, W. (1996). Who is this 'we'? Levels of collective identity and self-representations. *Journal of Personality and Social Psychology*, *71*(1), 83–93. doi:10.1037/0022-3514.71.1.83

Brivio, E., Ibarra, F., & Galimberti, C. (2010). An integrated approach to interactions in cyberplaces: The presentation of self in blogs. In R. Taiwo (Ed.), *Handbook of research on discourse behavior and digital communication* (Vol. 2, pp. 810–829). New York: Information Science Reference. doi:10.4018/978-1-61520-773-2.ch052

Bruggemann, M., & Wessler, H. (2014). Transnational communication as deliberation, ritual, and strategy. *Communication Theory*, *24*(4), 394–414. doi:10.1111/comt.12046

Castells, M. (1996). *The rise of the networked society: The information age: Economy, society and culture*. Oxford, UK: Blackwell.

Chapman, C., & Lahav, M. (2008). International ethnographic observations of social networking sites. *Proceedings of CHI 2008* (pp. 3123-3128). New York, NY: Association for Computing Machinery. doi:10.1145/1358628.1358818

Chen, G.-M., & Dai, X. (2014). New media and asymmetry in cultural identity negotiations. In P. Cheong, J. Martin, & L. Macfayden (Eds.), *New media and intercultural communication* (pp. 123–138). New York, NY: Peter Lang.

Chen, G.-M., & Zhang, K. (2010). New media and cultural identity in the global society. In R. Taiwo (Ed.), *Handbook of research on discourse behavior and digital communication* (Vol. 2, pp. 801–815). New York, NY: Information Science Reference. doi:10.4018/978-1-61520-773-2.ch051

Chen, L. (2011). Cultural identity as a production in process. *Journal of Asian Pacific Communication*, *21*(2), 213–237. doi:10.1075/japc.21.2.04che

Chen, Y.-N. (2010). Examining the presentation of self in popular blogs: A cultural perspective. *Chinese Journal of Communication*, *3*(1), 28–41. doi:10.1080/17544750903528773

Chen, Y.-W., & Collier, M. J. (2012). Intercultural identity positioning: Interview discourses from two identity-based nonprofit organizations. *Journal of International and Intercultural Communication*, *5*(1), 43–63. doi:10.1080/17513057.2011.631215

Church, A., Katigbak, M., Del Prado, A., Ortiz, F., Mastor, K., Harumi, Y., ... Cabrera, H. F. (2006). Implicit theories and self-perceptions of traitedness across cultures. *Journal of Cross-Cultural Psychology*, *37*(6), 694–716. doi:10.1177/0022022106292078

Collier, M. (2000). Reconstructing cultural diversity in global relationships: Negotiating in the borderlands. In G. M. Chen & W. Starosta (Eds.), *Communication and global society* (pp. 215–236). New York, NY: Peter Lang.

Collier, M. (2009). Contextual negotiation of cultural identifications and relationships: Interview discourse about Palestinian, Israeli, and Palestinian/Israeli young women in a U.S. peace-building program. *Journal of International and Intercultural Communication*, *2*(4), 344–368. doi:10.1080/17513050903177292

Coretti, L., & Pica, D. (2015). The rise and fall of collective identity in networked movement: Communication protocols, Facebook, and the anti-Berlusconi protest. *Information Communication and Society*, *18*(8), 951–967. doi:10.1080/1369118X.2015.1043317

Croucher, S. (2011). Social networking and cultural adaptation: A theoretical model. *Journal of International and Intercultural Communication*, *4*(4), 259–264. doi:10.1080/17513057.2011.598046

Croucher, S., & Cronn-Mills, D. (2011). *Religious misperceptions: The case of Muslims and Christians in France and Britain*. New York, NY: Hampton Press.

DeFleur, M., & Dennis, E. (2010). *Understanding media in the digital age: connections for communication, society and culture*. New York, NY: Allyn and Bacon.

Del Prado, A., Church, A., Katigbak, M., Miramonies, L., Whitty, M., Curtis, G., & … . (2007). Culture, method and the content of self-concepts: Testing trait, Individual self-primacy, and cultural psychology perspectives. *Journal of Research in Personality*, *47*(6), 1119–1160. doi:10.1016/j.jrp.2007.02.002 PMID:19050737

Dervin, F. (2012). Cultural identity, representation and othering. In J. Jackson (Ed.), The Routledge handbook of language and intercultural communication (pp. 181-194). New York, NY: Routledge.

English, R., & Chen, S. (2007). Culture and self-concept stability: Consistency across and within contexts among Asian Americans and European Americans. *Journal of Personality and Social Psychology*, *93*(3), 478–490. doi:10.1037/0022-3514.93.3.478 PMID:17723061

Ess, C., Kawabata, A., & Kurosaki, H. (2007). Cross-cultural perspective on religion and computer-mediated communication. *Journal of Computer-Mediated Communication*, *12*(3), 939–955. doi:10.1111/j.1083-6101.2007.00357.x

Georgalou, M. (2010). "Pathfinding" discourses of self in social network sites. In R. Taiwo (Ed.), *Handbook of research on discourse behavior and digital communication* (Vol. 1, pp. 39–61). New York, NY: Information Science Reference. doi:10.4018/978-1-61520-773-2.ch003

Gergen, K. (1991). *The saturated self: Dilemmas of identity in contemporary life*. New York, NY: Basic Books.

Gevorgyan, G., & Manucharova, N. (2009). Does culturally adapted online communication work? A study of American and Chinese Internet users' attitudes and preferences toward culturally customized web design elements. *Journal of Computer-Mediated Communication*, *14*(2), 393–413. doi:10.1111/j.1083-6101.2009.01446.x

Giddens, A. (1984). *The constitution of society*. Berkeley, CA: University of California Press.

Giddens, A. (1987). *Social theory and modern sociology*. Cambridge, MA: Polity Press.

Giddens, A. (1990). *The consequences of modernity*. Cambridge, MA: Polity Press.

Giddens, A. (1991). *Modernity and self-identity: Self and society in the late modern age*. Cambridge, UK: Polity Press.

Giddens, A. (2000). Goffman as a systematic social theorist. In G. Fine & G. Smith (Eds.), *Erving Goffman* (Vol. 4, pp. 151–175). Thousand Oaks, CA: Sage.

Giddens, A. (2003). *The runaway world*. New York, NY: Routledge.

Goffman, E. (1974). *Frame analysis*. New York, NY: Basic Books.

Goffman, E. (1983). The interaction order. *American Sociological Review*, *48*(1), 1–17. doi:10.2307/2095141

Grasmuck, S., Martin, J., & Shanyand, Z. (2009). Ethno-racial identity displays on Facebook. *Journal of Computer-Mediated Communication*, *15*(1), 158–188. doi:10.1111/j.1083-6101.2009.01498.x

Gudykunst, W., & Kim, Y. Y. (2003). *Communicating with strangers*. New York, NY: McGraw-Hill.

Guo, C. & Yu, J. (2009). Socializing online in various cultural contexts: A cross nation study of social network service development. *AMCIS 2009 Proceedings*, paper 514.

Hall, E. (1976). *Beyond culture*. New York: Doubleday.

Hall, S. (1989). Cultural identity and diaspora. In J. Rutherford (Ed.), *Community, culture, difference* (pp. 222–237). London: Lawrence & Wishart.

Harb, C., & Smith, P. (2008). Self-construals across cultures: Beyond independence and interdependence. *Journal of Cross-Cultural Psychology*, *39*(2), 178–197. doi:10.1177/0022022107313861

Hargiatti, E. (2008). Whose space? Differences among users and non-users of social network sites. *Journal of Computer-Mediated Communication*, *13*(1), 276–297. doi:10.1111/j.1083-6101.2007.00396.x

Hargiatti, E., & Hsieh, Y. (2013). Digital inequality. In W. H. Dutton (Ed.), *Oxford handbook for internet research* (pp. 129–150). Oxford, UK: Oxford University Press.

Haslett, B. (1987). *Communication: Strategic action in context*. Hillsdale, NJ: Lawrence Erlbaum Associates.

Haslett, B. (2012). *Communicating and organizing in context: The theory of structurational interaction*. New York, NY: Taylor & Francis.

Haslett, B. (2014a). Social media, communication and culture. In C. Litang & M. Prosser (Eds.), *Social media in Asia*. Lake Oswego, OR: Dignity Press.

Haslett, B. (2014b). A structurational interaction approach to investigating culture, identity, and mediated communication. In P. Cheong, J. Martin, & L. Macfayden (Eds.), *New media and intercultural communication: Identity, community and politics* (pp. 39–60). New York, NY: Peter Lang.

Haslett, B. (forthcoming). Multilayered interactions: Culture, communication and the new media. In A. Atay & M. D'Silva (Eds.), *Mediated intercultural communication in a digital age*. New York, NY: Peter Lang.

Haslett, B. (forthcoming). Who am I? Culture, identity and new media. In N. Bilge & M. Marino (Eds.), *Reconceptualizing media and culture.*

Hecht, M., Collier, M. J., & Ribeau, S. (1993). *African American communication: Ethnic identity and cultural interpretation*. Newbury, CA: Sage.

Hecht, M., Warren, J., Jung, E., & Krieger, J. (2005). A communication theory of identity: development, theoretical perspective, and future directions. In W. Gudykunst (Ed.), *Theorizing about Intercultural Communication* (pp. 257–278). Thousand Oaks, CA: Sage.

Hofstede, G. (2001). *Culture's consequences: Comparing values, behaviors, institutions and organizations across nations (2nd ed.)*. Thousand Oaks, CA: Sage.

Hofstede, G., & Hofstede, G. F. (2005). *Cultures and organizations: Software of the mind.* New York, NY: McGraw Hill.

Hogg, M. A., Abrams, D., Otten, S., & Hinkle, S. (2004). The Social Identity Perspective: Intergroup Relations, Self-Conception, and Small Groups. *Sage, 35*(3), 246-276.

Huffaker, D., & Calvert, S. (2005). Gender, identity, and language use in teenage blogs. *Journal of Computer-Mediated Communication, 10*(2), 1.

Hwang, K. (2005). A Chinese perspective on face. In K. Yang, K. Hwang, & Z. Yang (Eds.), *Indigenous psychological research in Chinese societies* (pp. 365–405). Taipei, Taiwan: Yuan-Liou Publishing Company.

Imahori, T., & Cupach, W. (2005). Identity management theory: Facework in intercultural relationships. In W. Gudykunst (Ed.), *Theorizing about intercultural communication* (pp. 195–210). Thousand Oaks, CA: Sage.

Internet World Statistics. (2017). Retrieved from http://www.internetworldstats.com/links10.html

Iwabuchi, K. (2010). Taking "Japanization" seriously: Cultural globalization reconsidered. In D. Thussu (Ed.), *International Communication: A reader* (pp. 410–433). New York, NY: Routledge.

Jetten, J., Postmes, T., & McAuliffe, B. (2002). 'We're all individuals': Group norms individualism and collectivism, levels of identification and identity threat. *European Journal of Social Psychology*, *32*(2), 189–208. doi:10.1002/ejsp.65

Kagitcibasi, C. (2005). Autonomy and relatedness in cultural context: Implications for self and family. *Journal of Cross-Cultural Psychology*, *36*(4), 403–422. doi:10.1177/0022022105275959

Kaplan, A. & Haenlein, M. (2010). Users of the world, unite! The challenges and opportunities of social media. *Business Horizons, 53*(1), 61.

Kim, H., Coyle, J., & Gould, S. (2009). Collectivist and individualistic influences on web-site design in South Korea and the US: A cross-cultural content analysis. *Journal of Computer-Mediated Communication*, *14*(3), 581–601. doi:10.1111/j.1083-6101.2009.01454.x

Kim, K., & Yun, H. (2008). Crying for me, crying for us: Relational dialectics in a Korean social network site. *Journal of Computer-Mediated Communication*, *13*(1), 298–318. doi:10.1111/j.1083-6101.2007.00397.x

Kim, Y. Y. (2007). Ideology, identity, and intercultural communication: An analysis of differing academic conceptions of cultural identity. *Journal of Intercultural Communication Research*, *36*(3), 237–253. doi:10.1080/17475750701737181

Kim, Y. Y. (2008). Intercultural personhood: Globalization and a way of being. *International Journal of Intercultural Relations*, *32*(4), 359–368. doi:10.1016/j.ijintrel.2008.04.005

Kim, Y. Y., & Bhawuk, D. (2008). Globalization and diversity: Contributions from intercultural research. *International Journal of Intercultural Relations*, *32*(4), 301–304. doi:10.1016/j.ijintrel.2008.06.001

Kline, S., & Liu, F. (2005). The influence of comparative media use on acculturation, acculturative stress, and family relationships of Chinese International students. *International Journal of Intercultural Relations*, *29*(4), 367–390. doi:10.1016/j.ijintrel.2005.07.001

Kraidy, M., & Murphy, P. (2008). Shifting Geertz. *Communication Theory*, *18*(3), 335–355. doi:10.1111/j.1468-2885.2008.00325.x

Kramsch, C., & Uryu, M. (2012). Intercultural contact, hybridity, and third space. In J. Jackson (Ed.), *The Routledge handbook of language and intercultural communication* (pp. 211–226). New York, NY: Palgrave.

Kyto, M., & McGookin, D. (2017). Investigating user-generated presentations of self in face-to-face interaction between strangers. *International Journal of Human-Computer Studies, 104*, 1–15. doi:10.1016/j.ijhcs.2017.02.007

Lagerkvist, A. (2013). *Media and memory in new Shanghai*. New York, NY: Palgrave. doi:10.1057/9781137014658

Lee, H., Kim, J., & Min, E. (2009). Hybridization of reality: Re-imaging the communicative environment in South Korea. *Asian Journal of Communication, 19*(2), 133–136. doi:10.1080/01292980902836459

Lee, W., & Choi, S. (2005). The role of horizontal and vertical individualism and collectivism in online consumers' response toward persuasive communication on the web. *Journal of Computer-Mediated Communication, 11*(1), 15. doi:10.1111/j.1083-6101.2006.tb00315.x

Liang, H., Shen, F., & Fu, K. (2017). Privacy protection and self-disclosure across societies: A study of global Twitter users. *New Media & Society, 19*(9), 1476–1497. doi:10.1177/1461444816642210

Liu, F. (2011). Wired for fun. *Young: Nordic Journal of Youth Studies, 19*(1), 69–89. doi:10.1177/110330881001900105

Liu, H. (2007). Social network profiles as taste performances. *Journal of Computer-Mediated Communication, 13*(1), 13. doi:10.1111/j.1083-6101.2007.00395.x

Lucas, D. (2014). Social media and protest—the Indian spring. In C. Litang & M. Prosser (Eds.), *Social media in Asia*. Lake Oswego, OR: Dignity Press.

Machin, D., & VanLeeuwen, T. (2008). Branding the self. In C. Caldas-Coulthard & R. Iedema (Eds.), Identity trouble (pp. 43-56). Basingstoke, UK: Palgrave Macmillan. doi:10.1057/9780230593329_3

Manovich, L. (2001). *The language of new media*. Cambridge, MA: MIT Press.

Marcus, A., & Krishnamurthi, N. (2009). Cross-cultural analysis of social network services in Japan, Korea, and the USA. *DID '09 Proceedings of the 3rd. International Conference on Internationalization, design and global development.*

Markus, H., & Kitayama, S. (1991). Culture and the self: Implications for cognition, emotion, and motivation. *Psychological Review*, *98*(2), 223–253. doi:10.1037/0033-295X.98.2.224

Marwick, A., & boyd, . (2010). I tweet honestly, I tweet passionately: Twitter users, context collapse and the imagined audience. *New Media & Society*, *13*(1), 114–133. doi:10.1177/1461444810365313

McEwan, B., & Sobre-Denton, M. (2011). Virtual cosmopolitanism: Constructing third cultures and transmitting social and cultural capital through social media. *Journal of International and Intercultural Communication*, *4*(4), 252–258. doi:10.1080/17513057.2011.598044

Miller, D., & Madianou, M. (2012). *Migration and new media: Transnational families and polymedia*. London: Routledge.

Morley, D. (2006). Globalisation and cultural imperialism reconsidered: old questions in new guises. In J. Curran & D. Morley (Eds.), *Media and cultural theory* (pp. 30–43). New York, NY: Routledge.

Mussell, J. (2012). Social media. *Journal of Victorian Culture*, 1.

Neuman, W. R. (1991). *The future of the mass audience*. Cambridge, UK: Cambridge University Press.

Ng, K. (2014). Asian American new media communication as cultural engagement: E-mail, vlog/blogs, mobile applications, social networks, and YouTube. In P. Cheong, J. Martin, & L. Macfadyen (Eds.), *New media and intercultural communication* (pp. 255–274). New York, NY: Peter Lang.

Noels, K., Yashima, T., & Zhang, R. (2012). Language, identity and intercultural pragmatics. In J. Jackson (Ed.), *The Routledge handbook of language and intercultural communication* (pp. 52–66). New York, NY: Routledge.

Obar, J., & Wildman, S. (2015). Social media definition and the governance challenge: An introduction to the special issue. *Telecommunications Policy*, *39*(9), 745–750. doi:10.1016/j.telpol.2015.07.014

Odejobi, R., & Adegbola, T. (2010). Computational and engineering issues in human computer interaction systems for supporting communication in African languages. In R. Taiwo (Ed.), *The handbook of research on discourse behavior digital communication: Language structures and social interaction* (Vol. 2, pp. 876–881). New York, NY: Information Science Reference. doi:10.4018/978-1-61520-773-2.ch056

Ogilvy. (2010). *Infographic: China's social media evolution*. Retrieved from http://www.thomascrampton.com/china/china-social-evolution

Oyserman, D., Coon, H., & Kemmelmeier, M. (2002). Rethinking individualism and collectivism: Evaluation of theoretical assumptions and meta-analyses. *Psychological Bulletin, 128*(1), 3–72. doi:10.1037/0033-2909.128.1.3 PMID:11843547

Oyserman, D., & Lee, S. (2008). "Does culture influence what and how we think?" Effects of priming individualism and collectivism. *Psychological Bulletin, 134*(2), 311–342. doi:10.1037/0033-2909.134.2.311 PMID:18298274

Papacharissi, Z. (2004, May). *The blogger revolution? Audience as media producers*. Paper presented, International Communication Association, New Orleans, LA.

Qui, J. (2010). Mobile communication research in Asia: Changing technological and intellectual geopolitics. *Asian Journal of Communication, 20*(2), 213–229. doi:10.1080/01292981003693393

Rakow, L. (2013). Worldviews and mediatization: In search of a metatheory. *Journal of Multicultural Discourses, 8*(3), 190–194. doi:10.1080/17447143.2013.849712

Rantanen, R. (2005). Giddens and the 'G-word': An interview with Anthony Giddens. *Global Media and Communication, 1*(1), 63–77. doi:10.1177/1742766505050173

Rettie, R. (2009). Mobile phone communication: Extending Goffman to mediated interaction. *Sociology, 43*(3), 421–438. doi:10.1177/0038038509103197

Roccas, S., & Brewer, M. B. (2002). Social identity complexity. *Personality and Social Psychology Review, 6*(2), 88–106. doi:10.1207/S15327957PSPR0602_01

Ruelle, O., & Peverelli, P. (2016). The discursive construction of identity through interaction on social media in a Chinese NGO. *Chinese Journal of Communication, 8*, 1–26.

Rybas, N. (2014). Producing the self at the digital interface. In P. Cheong, J. Martin, & L. Macfayden (Eds.), *New media and intercultural communication: Identity, community and politics* (pp. 93–108). New York, NY: Peter Lang.

Sangwan, S. (2005). Virtual community success: A uses and gratifications perspective. *Proceedings of the 38yh Hawaii International Conference on System Sciences,* 1-10. doi:10.1109/HICSS.2005.673

Schwartz, S., & Bardi, A. (2001). Value hierarchies across cultures: Taking a similarities perspective. *Journal of Cross-Cultural Psychology, 32*(3), 268–290. doi:10.1177/0022022101032003002

Shao, G. (2009). Understanding the appeal of user-generated media: A uses and gratification perspective. *Internet Research, 19*(1), 7–25. doi:10.1108/10662240910927795

Shuter, R. (2012). Intercultural new media studies: The next frontier in intercultural communication. *Journal of Intercultural Communication Research, 41*(3), 219–237. doi:10.1080/17475759.2012.728761

Simon, B. (2004). *Identity in modern society: A social psychological perspective.* Oxford, UK: Blackwell. doi:10.1002/9780470773437

Singh, C. (2010). New media and cultural identity. *China Media Research, 6*(1), 86–90.

Smith, P. (2011). Cross-cultural perspectives on identity. In V. Vignoles, S. Schwartz, & K. Luyckx (Eds.), *Handbook of identity theory and research* (pp. 249–265). London: Springer. doi:10.1007/978-1-4419-7988-9_11

Sobre-Denton, M. (2016). Virtual intercultural bridgework: Social media, virtual cosmospolitanism, and activist community-building. *New Media & Society, 18*(8), 1715–1731. doi:10.1177/1461444814567988

Spencer-Oatey, H. (2007). Theories of identity and the analysis of face. *Journal of Pragmatics, 39*(4), 639–656. doi:10.1016/j.pragma.2006.12.004

St. Amant, K. (2014). Culture, context, and cyberspace: Rethinking identity and credibility in international virtual teams. In P. Cheong, J. Martin, & L. Macfadyen (Eds.), *New media and intercultural communication: Identity, community and politics* (pp. 75–92). New York, NY: Peter Lang.

Sundar, S. S. (2008). Self as source: Agency and customization in interactive media. In E. Konjin, S. Utz, M. Tanis, & S. Barnes (Eds.), *Mediated interpersonal communication* (pp. 58–74). New York, NY: Routledge.

Sundar, S. S., & Limperos, A. (2013). Uses and grats 2.0: New gratifications for new media. *Journal of Broadcasting & Electronic Media, 57*(4), 504–525. doi:10.1080/08838151.2013.845827

Takemura, K., Yuki, M., & Ohtsubo, Y. (2010). Attending inside or outside: A Japan-US comparison of spontaneous memory of group information. *Asian Journal of Social Psychology, 13*(4), 303–307. doi:10.1111/j.1467-839X.2010.01327.x

Thussu, D. (2011). Media identities in a "post-American" world. In R. Chopra & R. Gajjala (Eds.), *Global media, cultures and identity* (pp. 235–249). New York, NY: Routledge.

Ting-Toomey, S. (2005). Identity negotiation theory. In W. Gudykunst (Ed.), *Theorizing about intercultural communication* (pp. 211–233). Thousand Oaks, CA: Sage.

Ting-Toomey, S., Yee-Jung, K., Shapiro, R., Wright, T., & Oetzel, J. (2000). Ethnic/cultural identity salience and conflict styles in four US ethnic groups. *International Journal of Intercultural Relations, 24*(1), 47–81. doi:10.1016/S0147-1767(99)00023-1

Tokunga, R. (2009). High-speed internet access to the other: The influence of cultural orientation on self-disclosures in offline and online relationships. *Journal of Intercultural Communication Research, 38*(3), 133–147. doi:10.1080/17475759.2009.505058

Tomlinson, J. (1997). A phenomenology of globalization? Giddens on global modernity. In C. Bryant & D. Jary (Eds.), Anthony Giddens: Critical assessments (vol. 4, pp. 116-136). New York: Routledge.

Triandis, H. C. (1995). *Individualism-collectivism.* Boulder, CO: Westview.

Tufekci, Z. (2008). Grooming, gossip, Facebook, and Myspace: What can we learn about those sites from those who don't assimilate? *Information Communication and Society, 11*(4), 544–564. doi:10.1080/13691180801999050

Turkle, S. (2011). *Alone together: Why we expect more from technology and less from each other.* New York, NY: Basic Books.

Utz, S. (2010). Show me your friends and I will tell you the type of person you area; How one's profile, number of friends, and type of friendships influence impression formation. *Journal of Computer-Mediated Communication, 15*(2), 314–335. doi:10.1111/j.1083-6101.2010.01522.x

Vignoles, V., Schwartz, S., & Luyckx, K. (2011). Introduction: Toward an integrative view of identity. In V. Vignoles, S. Schwartz & K. Luyckx (Eds.), Handbook of identity theory and research (pp. 1-19). New York: Springer.

Waisbord, S. (2013). A metatheory of mediatization and globalization? *Journal of Multicultural Discourses, 8*(3), 182–189. doi:10.1080/17447143.2013.822504

Walther, J. (1992). Interpersonal effects in computer-mediated interaction: A relational perspective. *Human Communication Research, 19*(1), 52–90. doi:10.1177/009365092019001003

Wan, C., Chin, C.-y., & Tam, K. (2007). Perceived cultural importance and actual self-importance of values in cultural identification. *Journal of Personality and Social Psychology*, *92*(2), 337–354. doi:10.1037/0022-3514.92.2.337 PMID:17279853

Wang, Z., Walther, J., & Hancock, J. (2009). Social identification and interpersonal communication in computer-mediated communication: What you do versus who you are in virtual groups. *Human Communication Research*, *35*(1), 59–85. doi:10.1111/j.1468-2958.2008.01338.x

Wu, S., Shi, Y., & Yan, Y. (2013). Media exposure and Chinese cultural identity. *Studies in Communication Sciences*, *13*(2), 129–132. doi:10.1016/j.scoms.2013.11.007

Yamagishi, T., & Yamagishi, M. (1998). Trust and commitment in the United States and Japan. *Motivation and Emotion*, *18*(2), 129–166. doi:10.1007/BF02249397

Yin, J. (2017). Rethinking cultural identity in the context of globalization: Comparative insights from the Kemetic and Confucian traditions. In X. Dai & G.-M. Chen (Eds.), *Conflict management and intercultural communication: The art of intercultural harmony* (pp. 155–174). New York, NY: Routledge.

Yuan, E. (2013). Recent literature on new media and intercultural communication. *Journal of Multicultural Discourse*, *8*(3), 260–265. doi:10.1080/17447143.2013.829480

Yum, Y., & Hara, K. (2006). Computer-mediated relationship development. A cross-cultural comparison. *Journal of Computer-Mediated Communication*, *11*(1), 133–152. doi:10.1111/j.1083-6101.2006.tb00307.x

Zhang, S., & Prosser, M. (2012). Globalization, Asian modernity, values and Chinese civil society. *Chinese Media Research*, *8*, 18–25.

Zhao, S., Grasmuck, S., & Martin, J. (2008). Identity construction on Facebook: Digital empowerment in anchored relationships. *Computers in Human Behavior*, *24*(5), 1816–1836. doi:10.1016/j.chb.2008.02.012

Chapter 5
Dynamic Social Impact Theory:
Heterophily and Homophily in Socio-Culturally Mediated Communication (SCMC)

Binod Sundararajan
Dalhousie University, Canada

Elizabeth Tetzlaff
Dalhousie University, Canada

ABSTRACT

Following the sociocultural traditions of communication, the authors explore the commonalities between Latané's dynamic social impact theory (DSIT), and the concepts of homophily and heterophily, and find that the markers of DSIT appear quite strikingly similar to the concepts similarity espoused by homophily (i.e., clustering, correlation, and consolidation), while the continuing diversity in DSIT is very similar to heterophily, which exists in groups and cultures. The authors test these concepts by analyzing two different blog conversations and find support to the above propositions. In the process, the authors suggest that social media should be retitled sociocultural media as this media aids in the creation and maintenance of cultures that coexist with those of differing viewpoints.

INTRODUCTION

Individual and collective identities are in a constant state of flux, particularly in the modern socio-culturally mediated communication environment that spans a range of communication channels, each with its own idiosyncratic qualities and challenges. From the whimsical Snapchat, to the voyeuristic Reddit and Instagram,

DOI: 10.4018/978-1-5225-3784-7.ch005

from the staid Facebook updates to the tremulous tweets of Twitter, from the un-nuanced, asynchronous pronouncements of traditional email to the unavoidable 'Good mornings", or incessant forwards of family Whatsapp groups, and many more, far too numerous to mention, each has established a presence in our socio-cultural landscape as a mediator, moderator, soother and instigator of our waking selves.

Latané (1996) presents a theory (Dynamic Social Impact Theory – DSIT) of, "how individuals located in social space influence each other to create higher patterns of structure", and demonstrates how "culture could emerge from individual experience and everyday interaction". He outlined four phenomena, (i) clustering, or regional differences in cultural elements; (ii) correlation, or emergent associations between elements; (iii) consolidation, or a reduction in variance; and (iv) continuing diversity that can serve as indicators of DSIT. Harton and Bullock (2007), reviewing DSIT, suggest that cultures can be created and changed from the bottom-up through everyday communication with neighbors, friends, and coworkers.

Using the socio-cultural tradition, one can view the individual, their relationships with others, the channel, the message, and the collective (culture, sub-culture, smaller cliques or the broader organization) that allows individuals and groups to weave a tapestry of cross-cultural identities, ranging from simple alter egoistic identities to undetectable and undecipherable no-nyms adopted by internet trolls and their ilk (Phillips, 2012).

Using the lens of dynamic social impact theory (Latané, 1996), the authors of this chapter wishes to demonstrate the existence of heterophily and homophily among individuals and groups, as they navigate their individual and collective identities in the socio-cultural landscapes provided by modern media. Heterophilous groups tend to become homophilous over time, yet maintain the primary diversity that brought the group together (Sundararajan, Finch, & O'Reilly, 2016). However, like the DSIT has posited, there is constant tension between the consolidation (reduction in variance or tendency towards homophily) of individual and group identities in socio-cultural media, and continuing diversity (heterophily) as individuals strive to maintain their individuality in the face of pressure to conform from their group or collective.

Sundararajan and Macdonald (2016, pp 202) state: "we are at the threshold of the next generation of web and mobile tools, applications and services, possibly Web 3.0". The phrase "social media" came to stand for the entire collection of online and mobile applications that allowed everyday people to create and share content with pretty much everyone else, engage with one another, create shared commons, and eventually, cultural enclaves. Many of these cultural enclaves came to exist as the online space resulting from real world offline activities, but many others were primarily created online and may have migrated to offline meetups, action organizations, and other small and large entities. As witnesses to the constantly evolving cultural landscape, precipitated partly because of the proliferation of social media communication, it behooves us to retitle this as sociocultural media. Communication in this socioculturally mediated landscape assumes an even larger role in our daily lives, regardless of who we are, what we do, and what our station in life is.

TODAY'S SOCIOCULTURALLY MEDIATED COMMUNICATION LANDSCAPE

Hainla (2017), details a host of statistics about current internet and social media usage across the globe, and the numbers are no less than staggering. While many of the statistics are around brand recognition, the following subset is more general. For context, as of October 2017, total worldwide population is 7.6 billion

Social Media Statistics (Hainla, 2017)

1. 2.56 billion global mobile social media users, equaling 34% penetration; globally with 1 million new active mobile social users added every day
2. Visual content is more than 40 times more likely to get shared on social media than other types of content. 6. In 2015 Facebook influenced 52 per cent of consumers' online and offline purchases, up from 36 per cent in 2014.
3. There are now more than 50 million small businesses using Facebook Pages to connect with their customers 4 million of those businesses pay for social media advertising on Facebook.
4. There were over 4.4 million videos uploaded directly to Facebook in February 2016, generating over 199 billion views.
5. There is a total of 1.3 billion accounts on Twitter, but only 328 million are active.
6. 90% of Instagram users are younger than 35
7. Posts tagged with another user (56%) or location (79%) have significantly higher engagement rates
8. There are 1.5 billion logged-in YouTube monthly active users visiting the website at least once a month.
9. In 2015 YouTube posted the figure of 40 billion all-time views for branded content.
10. More than half of YouTube views come from mobile devices and the average mobile viewing session lasts more than 40 minutes.

Organizations, governments (from the municipal to the national), community groups, self-interest, self-help and support groups all had a presence in at least one, if not more, such social networking sites (Sundararajan & Macdonald, 2016, pp 203). As we can see from the statistics above, a large percentage of these users access the online world using their mobile devices (smartphones, tablets etc.). Citizen journalism had taken the world by storm with real time updates of events, and of course "alternative news", "alternative realities", and "alternative facts".

Elsewhere in China, Baidu offers several services including an online encyclopedia, search features and a searchable keyword-based discussion forum, and provides over 740 million indexed web pages, over 80 million images and over 10 million media files, and these numbers are from 2014 (Alexa.com). In the fiscal year ending March 31, 2016, Chinese e-commerce corporation Alibaba recorded consolidated revenues of 101.14 billion yuan. This translates to approximately 15.69 billion U.S. dollars (Statista, 2017). We see from these statistics that users wish to maintain an online presence, connect with friends, families, and even organizations, want access to information and would like to use this information for personal consumption (news, entertainment and shopping). The increasing use of mobile apps is an indication of the need for users to have access to information, news, entertainment and shopping as they are moving about. Fei and Kuo (2013) discuss the presence of communication or information grey zones among China's internet users. They feel that the popular trend of "fast and easy consumption" among China's internet users is possibly one of the reasons for the decline of local communities in China, and put forward the idea of community media to help stem this decline.

Throughout the evolution of the internet or the world wide web, two things have been common to all users, whether individual or organizational – 1] Identity and 2] Content. Every time an individual created an online profile on any site produced a blog or wiki, they were creating and establishing their identity. This identity is their key to gaining acceptance, credibility and relevance in this online sociocultural communication landscape. While individuals, especially millennials/ young adults, have an assumed/presumed ability of navigating their online profiles and managing their sociocultural identities, too often they are unable to manage both their social identities and professional identities well enough. A clearer awareness that a LinkedIn profile requires a different approach, as compared to the individual's Facebook, Twitter or Instagram profile, is still lacking in many individuals. This has led to much grief for people who have said something inappropriate on a social networking site and has come back to haunt them via their professional networks and jobs (Sundararajan & Macdonald, 2016, pp 205).

Next, the authors briefly review what social presence, identity, image, brand and reputation are, followed by a discussion of Dynamic Social Impact Theory (DSIT), its relation to homophily and heterophily, and how these are relevant to our central discussion of socioculturally mediated communication (SCMC).

SOCIAL PRESENCE, IDENTITY, BRAND, IMAGE AND REPUTATION

Before we discuss identity, image, brand and reputation, particularly in the context of social media or sociocultural media, we need to look at the concept of "presence", and more specifically "online or social presence". The Oxford English Dictionary (2017e) defines "presence" as "the state or fact of existing, occurring or being present". The original definition of social presence is "the degree of salience (the quality or state of being there) between two communicators using a communication medium". Other definitions include, "the sense of being with another" (Biocca, Harms & Burgoon, 2003); "the degree to which a person is perceived as a real person" (Gunawardena, 1995); "a student's sense of being in and belonging in a course and the ability to interact with other students and the instructor" (Picciano, 2002). Lowenthal (2009) has presented the idea that social presence is the sum of an individual's affective responses (emotions, humor and self-disclosure), cohesive responses (vocatives, use of inclusive pronouns and social task oriented communication or salutations), and interactive responses (continuing a thread, quoting to other messages, asking questions, expressing agreement or appreciation).

While social presence has all these definitions, it has predominantly been used in the context of social learning and social interactions, particularly in technologically mediated and online environments and specifically with reference to individuals present in these environments. The organizational version of this would then be "online corporate presence". Corporations can very well use emotions, humor, and self-disclosure to connect with its key users or stakeholders to establish their identity and create an image or brand. A corporation can also use inclusive pronouns and salutations to directly address its key stakeholders and likewise use interactive responses to engage with its users. When a corporation does all this online, it begins to establish an online corporate presence, to the extent that it becomes a significant presence in its stakeholders' personal or professional networks. Just as individuals need to maintain their singular identities and image, create brand awareness (of being smart, informative, funny, silly etc.) and enhance their reputations, so too do corporations strive to enhance their corporate identities, image, brand awareness and reputations. Table 1 lists the definitions of identity, image, brand and reputation for individuals and corporations. Regardless of whether it is the individual or an organization, the image, credibility and reputation of the identity or brand depends wholly on how consistently individuals or organizations can demonstrate quality of

Table 1. Identity, image, brand and reputation

	Individual	Organization/Corporate
Identity	The fact of being who or what a person or thing is. This is typically conveyed by what a person does or how they behave and in the case of a thing, what it does and how it performs. It can be self-identity or whether one identifies with someone or something other than themselves. (Oxford English Dictionary, 2017a)	The profile and values of an organization conveyed through symbolism, communication and behaviour.
Image	A representation of the external form or a person or a thing. It is also a representation or an idea and can be self-image or a projected one. (Oxford English Dictionary, 2017b)	An individual's perception of an organization, product or service at a certain point in time.
Brand	A particular identity or image regarded as an asset. For an individual seeking a particular job or career, developing a unique brand can work to their advantage and let them stand out from the crowd. (Oxford English Dictionary, 2017c)	The set of physical attributes of a product or service, together with the beliefs and expectations surrounding it – a unique combination which the name or logo of the product or service should evoke in the mind of the audience
Reputation	The beliefs or opinions that are generally held about someone or something. An individual's actions can lead to either increasing their reputation and credibility or notoriety. A reputation of having integrity is good, while being known to be chronically late can be bad. (Oxford English Dictionary, 2017b)	An individual's collective representation of past images of an organization (induced through either communication or past experiences) established over time. The general evaluation of an organization (compared to its rivals), leading to likeability and preference.

Data Source: (Oxford English Dictionary, 2017a, 2017b, 2017c, 2017d; Cornelissen, 2014)

work or product/service, and how ethical they are when producing the work, product or service, not just at any one point in time, but over time.

When we view these with the sociocultural lens of communication, we can name this as sociocultural identity, image, brand or reputation. Each entity (individual or organization) is striving to create a culture around their social and corporate behaviors, communication, norms, symbols, and actions, and obtain a set of followers who can subscribe to these points of view. These followers, will exhibit similar sociocultural behaviors, and over time congeal into groups that believe in similar things, act similarly, communicate in a similar manner, and have shared understandings of the world through language, symbols and actions. These groups in the online/offline sociocultural commons begin to exist as new sociocultural entities. The longevity of these entities would then depend on the strength of these sociocultural bonds, and how well these individuals/groups, often acting in concert, can resist the macro-cultural forces. This phenomenon is aptly described by Latané's (1996) Dynamic Social Impact Theory (DSIT).

DYNAMIC SOCIAL IMPACT THEORY (DSIT)

Latané (1981) developed social impact theory (SIT), and described it as a phenomenon in which people affect one another in social situations, and how these situations are governed by the presence and actions of others. The effect on people in social situations due to the presence and actions of others can manifest itself visibly, and internally by changing behaviors, thoughts, attitudes and even physiological states, and these can be the result of social influence. Latané (1981) developed this theory to contain three laws, social forces, physio social law, and multiplication/division of impact. Over time, this social influence was determined by the strength, immediacy, and number of actors present in a cultural or sub-cultural sphere to describe how majority and minority group members influence one another.

Latané (1996) developed Dynamic Social Impact Theory – DSIT, as an extension of Social Impact Theory, to describe "how individuals located in social space influence each other to create higher patterns of structure". He demonstrates how "culture could emerge from individual experience and everyday interaction", by outlining the four phenomena, (i) clustering, or regional differences in cultural elements; (ii) correlation, or emergent associations between elements; (iii) consolidation, or a reduction in variance; and (iv) continuing diversity. Harton and Bullock (2007), reviewing DSIT, suggest that cultures can be created and changed from the bottom-up through everyday communication with neighbors, friends, and coworkers.

"DSIT proposes that culture is created from the bottom-up through everyday communication between people. 'Communication' refers to any of the countless ways people get across their beliefs, attitudes, preferences, and behaviors to others. This communication can be verbal (a conversation) or behavioral" (Harton & Bullock, 2007; pp 2), or it can be sharing a particular photograph on Instagram, giving an update on Facebook, urging friends to follow someone on Twitter, forwarding jokes on family WhatsApp groups, watching particular videos on YouTube, creating, writing and/or subscribing to certain blogs and wikis, and actively participating in them or posting recipes on Pinterest, or doing a myriad activities on social media that contributes to ongoing conversations or create new ones.

What has transformed these seemingly simple acts of communication between friends and family within short geographical distances of one another, is the advent of social media that allows random people, geographically co-located or dispersed, yet brought together by common interest, to engage in such communication episodes, and create cultural aspects around each of these interests. In that sense, it is now sociocultural media, rather than just social media. Harton and Bullock (2007) stated that the geographical proximity effect leads to regional differences in cultural elements. But in the case of modern sociocultural media, as opposed to just social media, people will, "influence each other on these different elements" (Harton &

Bullock, 2007, pp 2), regardless of geographical/spatial proximity or distance, and collectively give rise to cultures or sub-cultures.

Latané (1981), who created the earlier theory of social influence - Social Impact Theory (SIT), describes social impact as the amount of social influence individuals have on one another and is a multiplicative function of strength (such as expertise, physical attractiveness, or personality), immediacy, and number. Latané (1995) argued that social space is constrained by physical space. However, with respect to modern sociocultural media, there is no longer any constraint on this social space, and influence can increase even if social space increases. Thousands of blogger moms, many of whom have probably never met one another, and probably never will, have organized themselves into a group called "momsrising.org" to influence government and corporations at the local, state and even federal levels, particularly in the context of healthcare and healthcare products (Momsrising.org). Harton and Bullock (2007) state that each additional person adds a little less unique influence, and that one "can be more influenced by two people arguing a position than one person, but the 301st person probably will not have much influence beyond the 300th". But in the case of modern sociocultural media, particularly in the case of collective action, each additional person adds to the overall influence the collective will have on whatever social cause the collective wishes to espouse, and bring about a cultural change. Writing about this in 2007, Harton and Bullock do indicate that the Internet, "may introduce more outside influences on some issues, but it is unlikely to threaten the effects of daily, local communication for most people." However, we can see today that this was a vast underestimation of the local and global influences of modern sociocultural media on communication and culture. The Arab Spring, collectives organized around social and environmental causes using Twitter, Facebook and other such online platforms, disaster relief communication (Potts, 2013), corporations responding to consumer requests to change product lines or services, citizen journalists reporting on events and many such instances are a result of individuals and groups, with opinions and causes, mobilizing as a cultural or sub-cultural collective to organize themselves in this sociocultural media to effect outcomes that are aimed to benefit large portions of society.

The Four Indicators of DSIT:Clustering, Correlation, Consolidation and Continuing Diversity

As discussed earlier, Latané's DSIT has four elements that can be called indicators or predictors – clustering, correlation, consolidation and continuing diversity.

Clustering, considered to be one of the strongest predictors of DSIT, highlights the presence of regional differences in attitudes and behaviors. As people influence those closest to them, they will come to be more like them than those further away, resulting in spatial distributions of cultural elements, (Bullock, Okdie, & Harton, 2007). Clustering thus can arise in a variety of situations and contexts, and in the sociocultural media outlets of today, people tend to cluster around ideas, trends, products, services, and corporate brands, social, cultural, political, economic, regional, and global issues.

Correlation occurs when there are emergent associations between cultural elements because of communication episodes. These elements or attributes tend to be correlated with one another over time. Clusters tend to make people form into social or sociocultural groups, and member attitudes in these groups begin to look alike. Since any belief system depends on people arriving at a shared understanding of the meanings and intents of the elements of that belief system, clustering will tend to have groups that have members whose ideas correlate quite strongly with one another. So as time progresses, individuals with similar views will tend to join these groups, and group will tend to become homogeneous, and exhibit homophily. We will address this shortly, when we discuss homophily and heterophily.

Consolidation and continuing diversity – in groups and clusters there is a tendency for viewpoints to converge, and slowly, but surely, minority opinions begin to mimic those of the majority opinions and there is a consolidation, and the size of the majority increases over time.

But contra-intuitively, despite this consolidation of the majority opinion over time, pockets of diversity continue to exist. The dominant cultural worldview will never be completely able to subsume or consume the various diverse sub-cultures within its fold, and these sub-cultures, with their own world views on the issue at hand, continue to exist. There is often tension at the borders of these sub-cultural orbs and the larger cultural sphere of influence, and a movement of ideas and conversions continue at these cultural border crossings. But the overall systems continue to exist as an independent sociocultural and contextual entity, at least for the lifetime of the context or issue. Such a diversity of opinion is an indication of heterophily.

Consolidation occurs regularly in small discrete groups if there is an initial majority (Binder & Bourgeois, 2006; Conway, 2004). In spatially distributed groups, it often depends on how much minority opinion holders are exposed to majority positions. Overtime, it is also possible that minority opinions can become the dominant world views within this sociocultural context, often seen in groundswell support for socio-economic causes, or even the mom bloggers getting together to rally against Johnson & Johnson about a banned chemical being present in their baby shampoo sold in various markets (Hartman, 2011).

Harton and Bullock (2007), state that attributes that are more important to people, less genetically transmitted, easier to observe, and 'true' are more likely to be among those that define cultures. They identify *involvement, heritability, observability and demonstrability* as four such elements that are likely to become part of a culture. In the case of *involvement,* they suggest that attitudes or attributes that are at least somewhat involving should be more likely to cluster, correlate, and consolidate (Harton & Bourgeois, 2004). They indicate that the speed and level of involvement varies according to the seriousness or gravity of the issue at hand, i.e. quicker for lighter issues (ice cream flavors, and fashion trends), and more involved for deeper societal issues like religion, corporate social responsibility etc. (Latané & Nowak, 1997) suggest that if attitudes are at least somewhat 'nonlinear', stable regional differences will emerge.

Heritability, as a genetic component, is often seen innate in cultural norms, practices, attitudes and behaviors, even though some of this might have been learned early in the group or culture formation period. Because highly heritable attitudes are less open to influence (Tesser, 1993), they may also be less likely to self-organize and become defining elements of cultures (Harton & Bullock, 2007). *Observability,* is the ability for onlookers to discern overt behaviors as a part of cultural mores and practices, and hence determine the extent of social influence in a culture and/ or sub-culture. And, finally, d*emonstrability* is the degree to which we show that an opinion or answer is 'correct' also affects self-organization (Harton et al., 2006; Heath & Heath, 2007; Rogers, 2003). Harton and Bullock (2007) state that although 'truth' may make an element more likely to spread, different interpretations of that 'truth' ensure continuing diversity, and in the modern socioculturally mediated communication ethos, this includes "fake news", where the existence of a divergent opinion, no matter its lack of veracity, demonstrates the manifestations of not just continued diversity but DSIT in general.

HOMOPHILY AND HETEROPHILY

The role of homophily and heterophily in team composition has been central to a highly debated discussion in management literature. Homophily is the concept that individuals who are like one another tend to develop close interpersonal relationships as it facilitates information flow between actors (Rogers, 1995). In contrast, heterophilous relationships and networks are difficult to form, as they possess natural barriers such as language, education and social status (Rogers, 1996). Therefore, it is important to understand both heterophily and homophily communication. Another aspect of homophily, particularly in such collaborative efforts, is the ability to trust the collaborators with key pieces of information. The assumption here is that when people work together on various projects and communicate with one another in these contexts, they invest in the relationships, and build trust and social capital. Trust and social capital then become embedded resources in these relationship networks, and form the basis of the longevity of these, possibly homophilous networks. According to Mollering (2001: 404), trust is "a state of favorable expectation regarding other people's actions and intentions." It has been viewed as the basis for individual risk-taking Coleman (1988), social capital (Coleman, 1988; Burt, 1992; Lin, 2000; Cook, 2001; Putnam, 1995), and cooperation (Gambetta, 1988). Sundararajan, Finch and O'Reilly (2016), studying the collaborative cosmopolitanism in author team networks, in the context of choosing the knowledge dissemination outlet (KDO – peer-reviewed journal), found that smaller author teams tend to display higher tendencies for homophily, and author teams that tended to start out as heterophilous, over time began to exhibit homophily.

This discussion of homophily and heterophily is extremely relevant to the ideas presented so far about DSIT. The DSIT components of clustering, correlation and consolidation are nearly identical to the characteristics of homophily, in that people with similar likes, behaviors, and attitudes tend to gravitate towards one another, and behave in a homophilous manner. And just as clustering, correlation and consolidation is determined by the reciprocity of communication between the actors, so too it is in homophilous relationships. However, regardless of the extent of homophily extant in a network or culture, there continues to be diversity, or heterophily, whether at the borders/edges of cultural sub-spheres or rampant throughout the cultural sphere of influence, existing as pockets of fierce resistance and non-capitulation to the dominant culture. While reciprocity is evident in heterophilous relationships, it is however, not truly bidirectional, allowing for the continuation of the diversity. We can see this even more in today's sociocultural communication landscape.

SOCIOCULTURALLY MEDIATED COMMUNICATION LANDSCAPE AND THE SOCIOCULTURAL TRADITIONS

The authors have dubbed the modern social media landscape as the sociocultural communication landscape for very specific reasons, some of which have been mentioned above. The fact that everything that is discussed in various online outlets, whether they are corporate blogs or private posts, special interest groups, or wandering online minstrels, all of them constantly exercise and exhibit their sociocultural preferences by not only how they create and share content, but more so how they portray themselves, create and maintain their identities, and grow their individual and collective spheres of influence. We would then be remiss if we do not recollect which aspects of the sociocultural theory are applicable here.

Theories in the sociocultural tradition have explored the relationships between external and internal processes, and focus on the creation and usage of mediating tools that play a role in how humans think, act, behave, and create spheres of influence that may or may not morph into sociocultural phenomena. In the sociocultural view, human development is viewed as a socially mediated process that varies from culture to culture, and the authors espouses that this socially mediated process is rife with socioculturally mediated communication, which, in and of itself, is both a mediator and moderator, mover and shaker, instigator, and pacifier for the various contexts in which it is used.

Thus, the sociocultural tradition, has concerned itself with relations between micro communication practices and macro communication structures, where specific interactions are indicative of communication practices and sociocultural roles and rituals determine communication processes and structures. Six theories form part of the sociocultural tradition, *Ethnomethodology, Symbolic Interactionism, Social Constructionism, Ethnography of Communication, Structuration Theory,* and *Actor Network Theory* (Tora-Joy, 2013).

Ethnomethodology (EM) (Garfinkel, 1967) seeks to understand the methods and procedures people use to conduct rational and orderly ways of conducting everyday life. Research in this space is done through observations, interviews, and the analysis of notes taken during these processes. Conversation analysis is a key research tool to help understand the nuances in any human, sociocultural undertaking.

Symbolic Interactionism (SI), coined by George Herbert Mead, revolves around the aspect that meaning arises directly from social interaction, and identity is a key aspect. Research is done through online ethnography or participant observation, like signing up as a member in a disease support group network, to observe interactions among online group members.

Social Constructionism, also known as *social constructivism,* assumes that reality is a social construction, and that communication is *the* fundamental activity by which humans *constitute* their social world as a "real" phenomenon. According to Vygotsky (1978), social interaction is the source of learning and development, which is not found solely in the mind of an individual. Humans can be studied or understood only as a part of society, culture or history and not in isolation. In this approach, an individual identity is not just a product of the individual in isolation; rather, it is the sum of learned behaviors and experiences that the individual acquires by being part of or being immersed in one or more sociocultural environments. Also, these experiences are resultant of the social and reflexive nature of human beings, and keeping in mind the individual, social and contextual issues is critical when studying sociocultural human behavior and resultant identities.

Ethnography of Communication (EOC), regards social actors as simultaneously using multiple channels (i.e., verbal and nonverbal) and codes (rules for creating and interpreting signs) to create meaningful interaction (such as that required for determining group membership).

Structuration Theory – ST, (Giddens, 1984), studies how social actors draw upon structures of meaning, power, and norms and defines practices, systems and structure.

And finally, *Actor Network theory (ANT),* developed by Michael Callon, Bruno Latour, and John Law at various times, have espoused the role of non-human artifacts in human social interaction.

Reviewing the various sociocultural theories, albeit briefly, allows us to situate the communication in today's sociocultural media landscape as one that exhibits the various elements of dynamic social impact theory, and that these elements are not different from homophilous and heterophilous tendencies exhibited by various groups and cultures. The key aspect of this is how can individuals, groups and organizations maintain their individual, group and corporate identities in such a constantly changing sociocultural communication landscape? Figure 1 illustrates the underpinning of homophily and heterophily amongst the various components of DSIT.

DEMONSTRATION 1

Figure 1 places all the elements of DSIT, homophily and heterophily together, and one can go a step further and parse these elements into a simple table that can be used as thematic codes for content analysis of online conversations. Taken as such, Clustering, Correlation, Consolidation and Continuing Diversity are the main components of DSIT. What then could be the components of homophily and

Figure 1. DSIT components: Homophily and heterophily

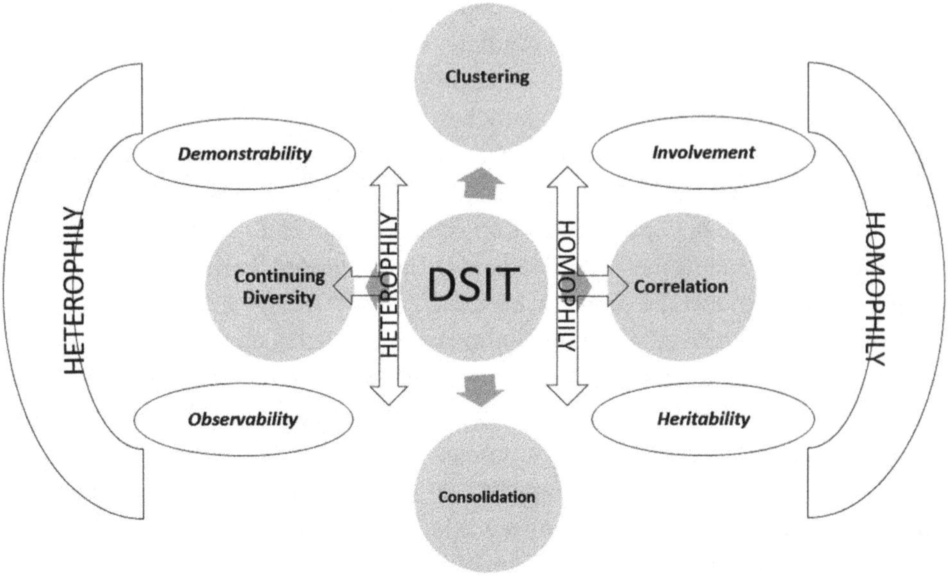

heterophily? With respect to homophily, one can expect to see convergence of ideas, similarity in thoughts, actions, and behaviors, and agreement for many suggestions within the group. In the case of heterophily, one can expect to see divergence of views, dissimilarity in thoughts, actions and behaviors, and consensus instead of disagreement or outright disagreement for suggestions within the group. Table 2 shows the markers of DSIT, homophily and heterophily as discussed above.

To test the efficacy of these markers as possible thematic codes for content analysis of online, socio-culturally mediated conversations, and demonstrate the presence of DSIT, homophily and heterophily in these conversations, the authors conducted a rudimentary exploratory analysis of an online blog that dispensed advice on homemade remedies for arthritis.

Claire Goodall, has a blog post called "14 Home Remedies for Arthritis and Joint Pain" on the website "everydayroots.com/arthritis-remedies", and provides information on various natural approaches to help people cope with arthritis and joint pain. Claire Goodall's page has over 450 or so comments. However, the "14 Home Remedies…" post has 68 comments, with the first comment posted on October 15, 2013, and the most recent comment posted on April 28, 2016. These comments are mostly from commenters having discovered this blog site and having tried the suggested remedies with varying levels of success. The nature of this disease and the lack of an established cure in mainstream medicine, has prompted many chronic sufferers of arthritic pain to seek alternatives. Having arrived at this site, and finding rather simple ways to help them manage the pain by following the suggestions, many of the commenters are either ebullient about the success they have had, or are happy to suggest other alternatives. Some of it is validation, while other commenters report more effective alternatives. Moreover, both regular visitors and new comers to the site post comments. Claire Goodall regularly responds with more suggestions, and accepts new variants as well. While this is not indicative of a sub-culture in and of itself, this context of alternative approaches to a chronic condition, has certainly drawn a variety of visits, comments, regulars, converts, and those with divergent opinions, making this collection of online conversations rather emblematic of a socioculturally mediated communication scenario, and thus a suitable collection of online artifacts to test the DSIT, homophily and heterophily markers. This small sample was used to test the thematic codes.

The authors collected these posts/comments in a word document and input them into QDAMiner®, and performed the coding of the blog post comments. Figure 2 shows the column chart of the coding by variables (as a percentage of all the codes).

It is immediately evident from Figure 2 that the DSIT markers, Clustering, Correlation, and Consolidation are present as expected in higher frequencies, and Continuing Diversity, while also present, is substantially lower in frequency of occurrence. If Clustering, Correlation and Consolidation are present, items that were

Table 2. Markers of DSIT, homophily and heterophily

Phenomenon	Marker/Thematic Code for Content Analysis
Dynamic Social Impact Theory (DSIT)	Clustering
	Correlation
	Consolidation
	Continuing Diversity
Homophily	Similarity
	Convergence
	Agreement
Heterophily	Dissimilarity
	Divergence
	Consensus/Disagreement

Figure 2. Frequency of occurrence of thematic codes: Arthritis remedies blog

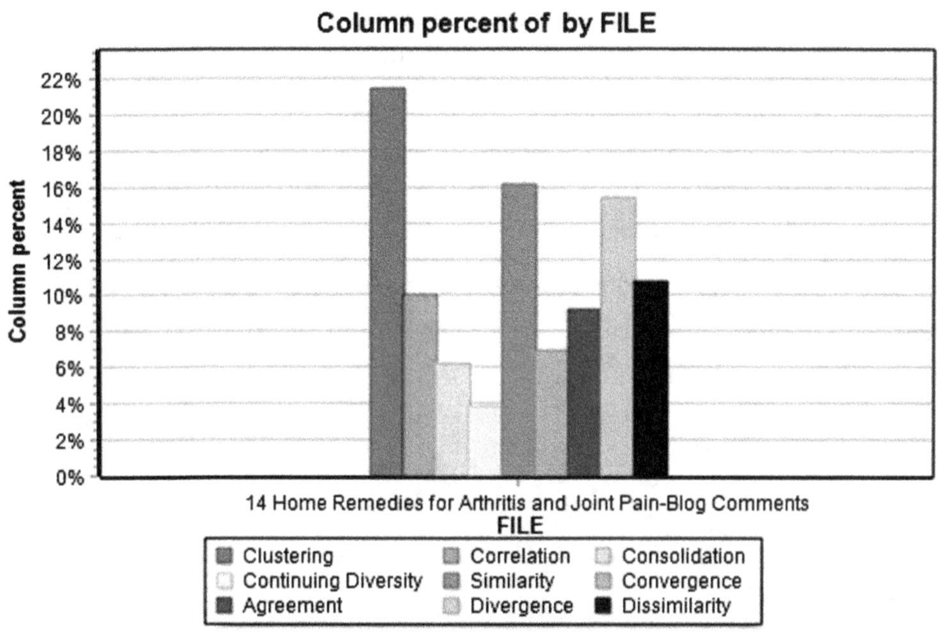

"similar", indicated "convergence", and "agreement" were coded as such, affirming the presence of homophily. Where commenters offered differing or "divergent" opinions, and displayed "dissimilarity" to the suggested remedies, heterophily markers were detected.

For example, one snippet from all the comments centered on dogs with arthritis. Figure 3 is a screenshot of the conversation set and the coding.

The coded conversation snippet in figure 5 shows similarity and convergence, but when we look at figure 6, we see dissimilarity and divergence, when one commenter confirms (correlation and consolidation) that they tried the "gin and raisins" remedy, but did not find success (disagreement or dissimilarity) and they go on to suggest another approach – "olive oil rub" (divergence). Throughout the various comments, we see the presence of these markers.

Figure 6 shows a word cloud, with the largest size of the code indicating the highest frequency of occurrence of the code. We see that "Clustering" and "Similarity" have a comparable size, "Correlation" and "Agreement" have a comparable word size, and "Consolidation", and "Convergence" have a comparable word size. These DSIT and Homophily markers can thus possibly be used interchangeably, and we can purport to say that when DSIT is evident in a socioculturally mediated communication episode, you will also detect homophily. However, DSIT is not complete without the presence of "Continuing Diversity". While this is present, so are the heterophily markers, "Divergence", "Dissimilarity", and to a very minor extent, "Consensus". So, heterophily is also present in these conversations, confirming that "Continuing Diversity" is indeed like "heterophily", particularly in socio-culturally mediated communication.

Figure 3. Coding snippet from 14 remedies blog post: Showing divergence

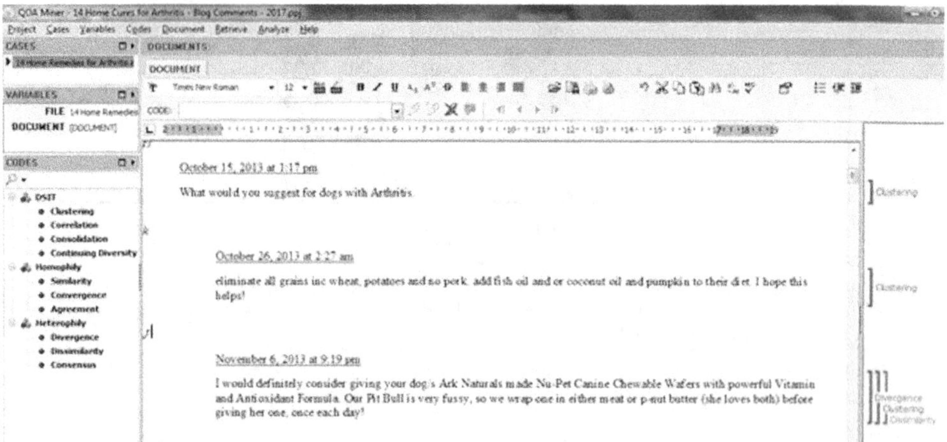

Figure 4. Coding snippet showing clustering and similarity

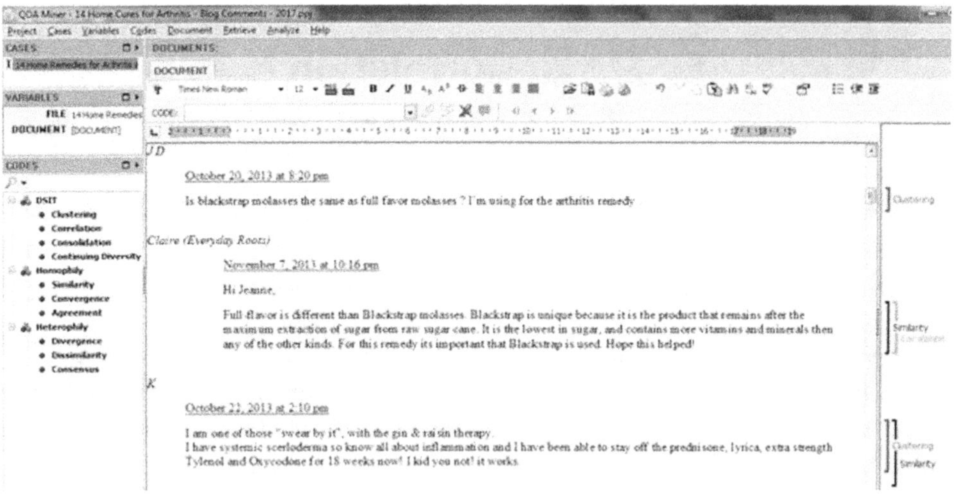

Figure 5. Coding snippet showing similarity, convergence, dissimilarity and divergence

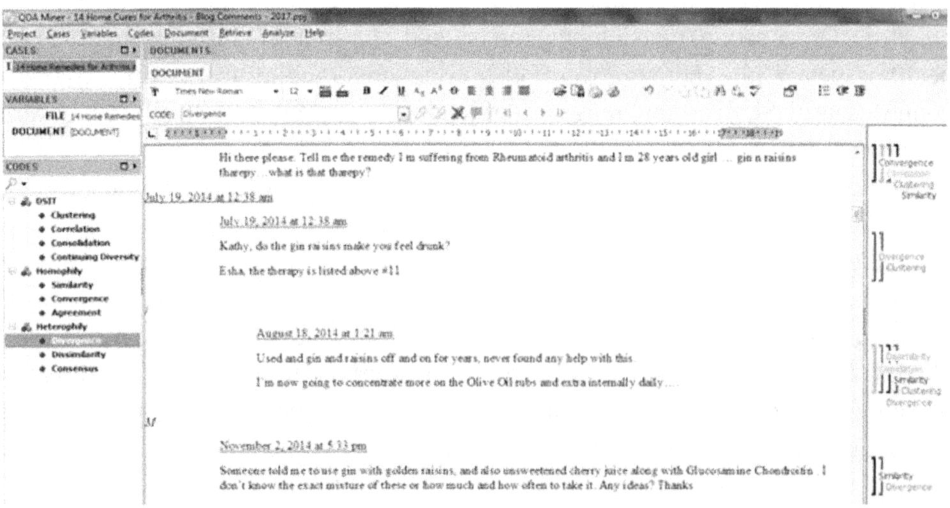

DEMONSTRATION 2

We have investigated the presence of DSIT, Homophily and Heterophily markers in one random blog post. To test these thematic markers, it behooves us to test them again in another random set online of conversations. The authors looked for other

Figure 6. Word cloud of thematic codes:14 home remedies for Arthritics-joint pain

recent events and selected a news story about the recent killings in Las Vegas (The Canadian Press, 2017). This story, while grim, is another in a long of line of similar stories where readers tend to post comments based on their perceptions, beliefs, cultural orientations and other proclivities. At the time of the retrieval of the blog comments there were 288 comments and the analysis was performed on this set of 288 comments. Subsequently, the number of comments has risen to 449.

The comments, as expected, are quite polarizing, with comments either reinforcing or validating prior held beliefs. Three major clusters of conversations emerged, 1] gun laws need to be changed or addressed, 2] conspiracy theory that this is more the work of a larger group, than a lone gunman, and 3] a smaller cluster around mental health issues. While there are/were other comments ranging from events in other countries vs. the US, around religion and random comments from trolls, none were numerous enough to form significant clusters.

The dominant cluster was around comments related to gun laws in the US, like "when will the US change its gun laws", or "was Sandy Hook, Columbine etc. not enough?" The opposing viewpoints (continuing diversity and divergence/dissimilarity) centered around "something's not right, this has to be the work of more than one person", or "maybe the gunman was already dead, and someone else did the firing", "Manchurian Candidate or similar mind control". The third set of opinions revolved around "possible mental health issues, possibly triggered by gambling", or "his father was a bank robber and diagnosed with psychosis, so the son probably had a similar condition".

Figure 7 presents the overall frequency distribution of all the thematic codes in a pie chart. 29% of the codes were around Clustering (4.1%), Correlation (13.4%) and Consolidation (11.5%). Comparably, the indicators of Homophily, Similarity (9.1%), Convergence (11%) and Agreement (12.5%) totaled to 32.5%. Continuing Diversity, the DSIT marker indicating the presence of differing opinions appears about 12.9% of the time. Comparably, the Heterophily markers, Dissimilarity (4.6%),

Figure 7. Yahoo news:Vegas shooter –DSIT, homophily and heterophily markers

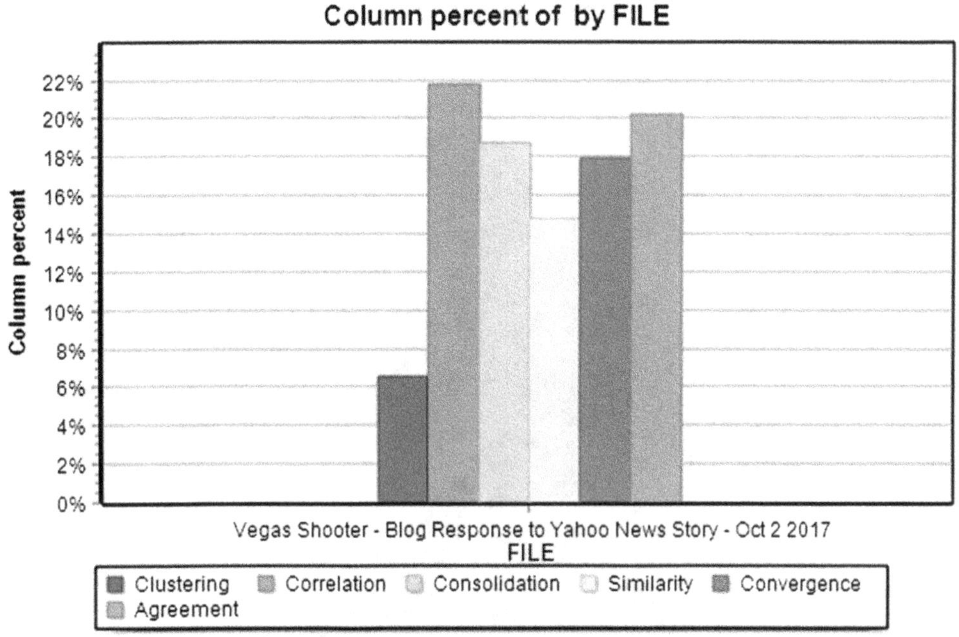

Divergence (8.2%) and Consensus (12.7%) appears 25.5% of the time. Consensus appears to be prevalent because of commenters agreeing with the divergent opinions and grouping around this contrary opinion. The word cloud depicted in Figure 8 will show these markers in relation to each other.

One final comparison will involve looking at the presence of the Continuing Diversity marker whenever the Heterophily markers are present. Figure 8 shows the occurrence of the Continuing Diversity marker, alongside the Heterophily markers, Dissimilarity, Divergence and Consensus.

Seen in comparison to the code distribution of the DSIT markers Clustering, Correlation and Consolidation, the Homophily markers of Similarity, Convergence and Agreement (Figure 10), the spread of these markers indicate that where DSIT is present in these online conversations, homophily and heterophily are also present.

In Figure 10, the Similarity marker appears about 14% of the time in comparison to the Clustering marker (~ 6%). The Convergence marker (~ 18%) is comparable to the Correlation marker (~ 22%) and the Agreement marker (~ 20%) is comparable to the Consolidation marker (~ 18%). This is possible due to coding differences and future studies can ensure better inter-coder reliability.

Figure 8. Yahoo news: Vegas shooter – DSIT, homophily and heterophily markers

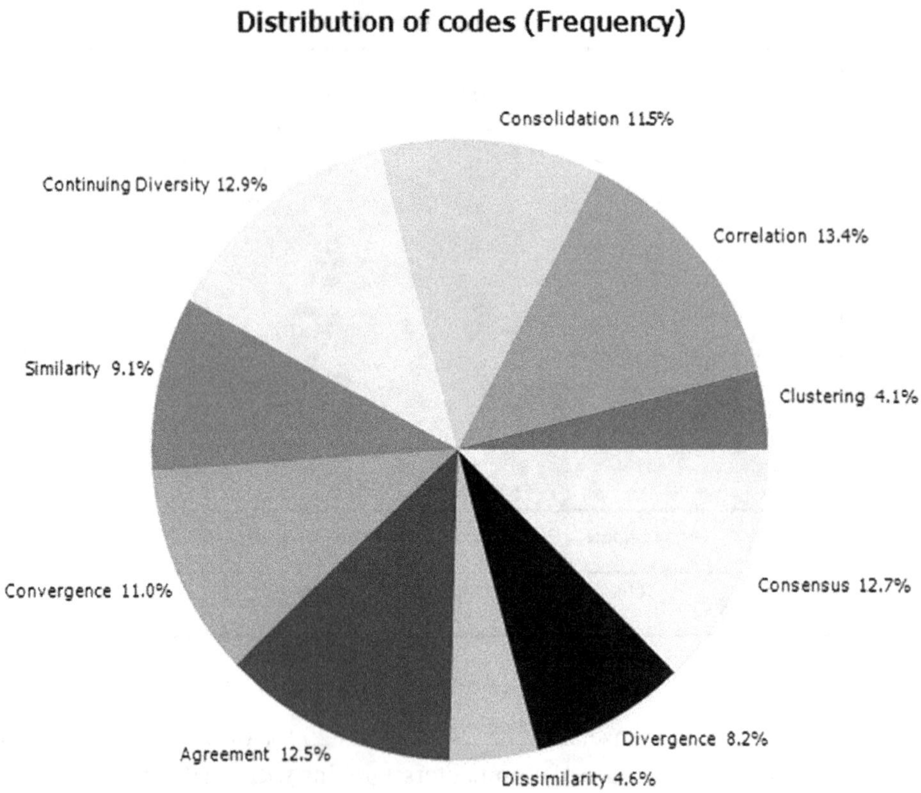

Figure 9. Continuing diversity vs. heterophily markers: Yahoo news Vegas shooter story

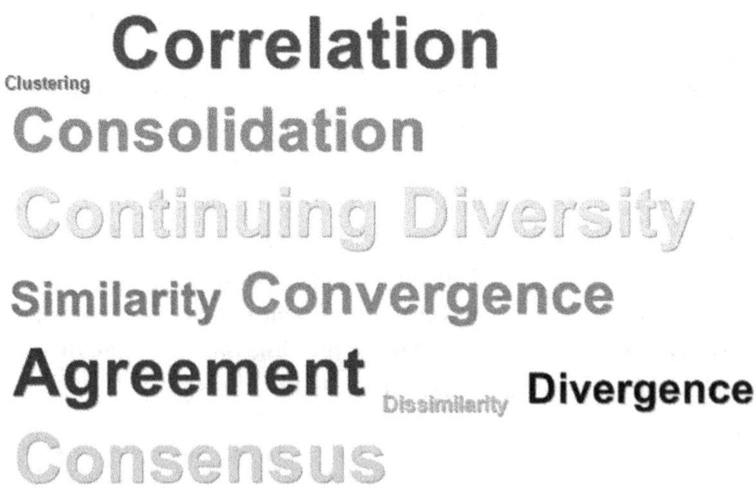

Figure 10. DSIT: Clustering, correlation and consolidation vs. homophily-Similarity, convergence and agreement

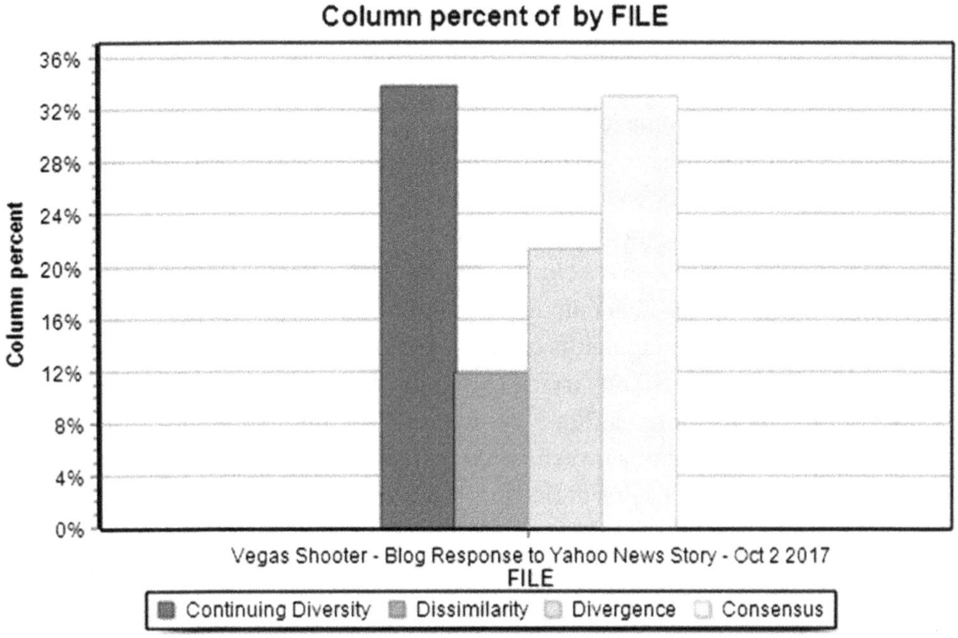

CONCLUSION

Reflecting on the preliminary analysis of two blog posts and the comments related to these posts, the authors venture to say that DSIT, homophily and heterophily are two approaches to studying the same phenomenon, that of similarity and diversity coexisting in a tenuous tussle, in modern socioculturally mediated communication environments. The authors feel that these rudimentary analyses do have merit and warrants further investigation.

Harton and Bullock (2007) state that, "culture can emerge merely through every day social influence from people who live close to us", and advocate that DSIT can "provide insights into how cultures form and change and which elements are most likely to proliferate and delineate cultures". This chapter explored, the theoretical linkages between DSIT, and the concepts of homophily and heterophily. Further, by viewing these two theoretical concepts from the sociocultural tradition, the authors note that social media should be renamed as sociocultural media. In this context, it is the "*sociocultural*" presence of individuals, and possibly even groups and organizations that will determine the longevity of any groups or cultures that these entities wish to perpetuate. This approach will allow them to create new sociocultural communities, not unlike those suggested by Fei and Kuo (2013), where local causes can surface amidst the cacophony of internet broadcasts and blog pronouncements, and communication grey zones can be minimized.

The authors would then define "*sociocultural presence*" for the individual, as the ability of the individual to create a unique sociocultural identity for themselves, by a sustained use of language, symbols, metaphors and other cultural elements, to espouse a personal, organizational, social, or societal cause, and perpetuate this sociocultural persona, using every means of socioculturally mediated communication available to them. There is much to unpack in this definition, as it not only attempts to encompass a lot, but also gives clues as to how DSIT, homophily and heterophily all play a role in how well this unique sociocultural identity will garner followers. Over time, how well this uniqueness can be spread by like-minded others/followers, while each of them are constantly trying to remain unique themselves, can determine the fate of both their efforts and the sociocultural medium itself. This waits to be seen, and the next stage of this investigation will attempt to delve into these matters, and allow the unpacking of this definition, with more evidence.

FUTURE RESEARCH DIRECTIONS

While there are obvious limitations to this study, researcher bias would have played a part in the coding, and the next stage would involve even larger datasets, multiple coders, probably Claire Goodall's 457 comments page, and the 449 and counting posts on the Vegas shooter story on Yahoo news, and other such online repositories of sociocultural conversation episodes. The thematic codes presented here, and the sub-markers of DSIT (Involvement, Heritability, Observability and Demonstrability, as cited in Harton & Bullock, 2007), can be deployed in the investigation to further ascertain that these phenomena are indeed present and social media is sociocultural media. One can then begin to look at effective strategies for individuals, groups, and even organizations to maintain their respective identities, image, brand and reputation on the sociocultural media landscape. These are but a few of the various communication events on sociocultural media that merit further investigation for the presence of DSIT, homophily and heterophily.

ACKNOWLEDGMENT

This research received no specific grant from any funding agency in the public, commercial, or not-for-profit sectors.

REFERENCES

Alexa.com. (n.d.). Retrieved from http://www.alexa.com/topsites/global

Biocca, F., Harms, C., & Burgoon, J. (2003). Towards a more robust theory and measure of social presence: Review and suggested criteria. *Presence: Teleoperators and Virtual Environments*, *12*(5), 456 – 480. doi: 10.1162/105474603322761270

Bullock, M., Okdie, B. M., & Harton, H. C. (2007). *Self-organization of attitudes as a function of issue relevance*. Poster presented at the meeting of the Society for Personality and Social Psychology, Memphis, TN.

Burt, R. S. (1992). *Structural Holes*. Cambridge, MA: Harvard University Press.

Chapman, M. (2014). Target Corp reveals full scale of payment card theft: 70 million customers' data stolen. *Associated Press, Financial Post*. Retrieved from http://business.financialpost.com/2014/01/10/target-corp-credit-card-breach/

Clifford, S. (2009). Video Prank at Domino's Taints Brand. *The New York Times*. Retrieved from http://www.nytimes.com/2009/04/16/business/media/16dominos.html?_r=0

Coleman, J. S. (1988). Social Capital in the Creation of Human Capital. *American Journal of Sociology*, *94*, S95–S120. doi:10.1086/228943

Cook, K. (2001). *Trust in Society*. New York: Russell Sage Foundation.

Cornelissen, J. (2014). *Corporate Communication: A Guide to Theory & Practice* (4th ed.). London: Sage Publications.

Fei, J., & Kuo, H. (2013). Community Media in China: Communication, Digitalization, and Relocation. *Journal of International Communication*, *19*(1), 2013.

Gambetta, D. (1988). *Trust: Making and Breaking Co-Operative Relations*. Oxford, UK: Basil Blackwell.

Garfinkel, H. (1967). *Studies in Ethnomethodology*. Englewood Cliffs, NJ: Prentice-Hall.

Giddens, A. (1984). *The constitution of society: Outline of the theory of structuration*. Cambridge, UK: Polity Press.

Gunawardena, C. N. (1995). Social presence theory and implications for interaction collaborative learning in computer conferences. *International Journal of Educational Telecommunications*, *1*(2/3), 147–166.

Hainla, L. (2017). *21 Social Media Marketing Statistics You Need to Know in 2017*. Retrieved from https://www.dreamgrow.com/21-social-media-marketing-statistics/

Harjani, A., & Min, W. (2014). *Alibaba to smash Single's Day sales record*. Retrieved from https://ca.finance.yahoo.com/news/alibaba-smash-singles-day-sales-record-223605524.html

Hartman, M. (2011). *Johnson & Johnson Gently Poisons Babies With Its Shampoo*. Retrieved from http://jezebel.com/5855115/johnson--johnson-gently-poisoning-babies-with-its-shampoo

Harton, H. C., & Bullock, M. (2007). Dynamic Social Impact: A Theory of the Origins and Evolution of Culture. *Social and Personality Psychology Compass*, *1*(1), 521–540. doi:10.1111/j.1751-9004.2007.00022.x

Heath, C., & Heath, D. (2007). *Made to Stick: Why Some Ideas Survive and Others Die*. Random House.

Karstens-Smith, G., & Rushowy, K. (2013). *'Blackface' controversy at Mayfield Secondary School in Caledon not the first*. Retrieved from http://www.thestar.com/news/gta/2013/11/12/blackface_controversy_at_mayfield_secondary_school_in_caledon_not_the_first.html

Latané, B. (1981). The psychology of social impact. *The American Psychologist*, *36*, 343–356. doi:10.1037/0003-066X.36.4.343

Latané, B. (1996). Dynamic social impact: The creation of culture by communication. *Journal of Communication*, *46*(4), 13–25. doi:10.1111/j.1460-2466.1996.tb01501.x

Latané, B., & Nowak, A. (1997). Self-organizing social systems: Necessary and sufficient conditions for the emergence of consolidation and clustering. In G. Barnett & F. Boster (Eds.), *Progress in Communication Sciences: Persuasion* (pp. 43–74). Norwood, NJ: Ablex.

Lin, N. (2000). *Social Capital*. Cambridge, UK: Cambridge University Press.

Loranger, H. (2014). *Break Grammar Rules on Websites for Clarity*. Retrieved from http://www.nngroup.com/articles/break-grammar-rules/

Lowenthal, P. (2009). *Social Presence: What Is It and Why Does It Matter?* Retrieved from http://www.slideshare.net/plowenthal/social-presence-what-is-it-and-why-does-it-matter

Mollering, G. (2001). The Nature of Trust: From Georg Simmel to a Theory of Expectation, Interpretation and Suspension. *Sociology*, *35*(2), 403–420. doi:10.1177/S0038038501000190

Oxford English Dictionary. (2017a). *Identity*. Retrieved from https://en.oxforddictionaries.com/definition/identity

Oxford English Dictionary. (2017b). *Image*. Retrieved from https://en.oxforddictionaries.com/definition/image

Oxford English Dictionary. (2017c). *Brand*. Retrieved from https://en.oxforddictionaries.com/definition/brand

Oxford English Dictionary. (2017d). *Reputation*. Retrieved from https://en.oxforddictionaries.com/definition/reputation

Oxford English Dictionary. (2017e). *Presence*. Retrieved from https://en.oxforddictionaries.com/definition/presence

Phillips, W. (2012). What an Academic Who Wrote Her Dissertation on Trolls Thinks of Violentacrez. *The Atlantic*. Retrieved from https://www.theatlantic.com/technology/archive/2012/10/what-an-academic-who-wrote-her-dissertation-on-trolls-thinks-of-violentacrez/263631/

Picciano, A. G. (2002). Beyond student perceptions: Issues of interaction, presence, and performance in an online course. *Journal of Asynchronous Learning Networks*, *6*(1).

Potts, L. (2013). *Social media in disaster response: How experience architects can build for participation*. Routledge.

Putnam, R. (1995). Bowling Alone: America's Declining Social Capital. *Journal of Democracy*, *6*(1), 65–78. doi:10.1353/jod.1995.0002

Rogers, E. M. (2003). *Diffusion of Innovations* (5th ed.). New York: Free Press.

Shontell, A. (2013). *Actually, Snapchat Doesn't Delete Your Private Pictures And Someone Found A Way To Resurface Them*. Retrieved from http://www.businessinsider.com/snapchat-doesnt-delete-your-private-pictures-2013-5

Statista. (2017). Annual Revenue of Alibaba Group from 2010-2016. *The Statista Portal*. Retrieved from https://www.statista.com/statistics/225614/net-revenue-of-alibaba/

Sundararajan, B., Finch, D., & O'Reilly, N. (2016). *Homophily in Authors Team Networks: A Network Analysis of Authors and Authors Teams in Leading Management Journals*. Presented at the *2016 Administrative Sciences Association of Canada (ASAC) Conference*, Edmonton, Canada.

Sundararajan, B., & Macdonald, L. (2016). *Lean, Ethical Business Communication*. Toronto, Canada: Oxford University Press.

Sundararajan, B., & Sundararajan, M. (2012). Like us on Facebook and follow us on Twitter: Corporate identity management across social media platforms. In C. Cunningham (Ed.), *Social Networking and Impression Management* (pp. 129–146). Lexington Books.

Tesser, A. (1993). The importance of heritability in psychological research: The case of attitudes. *Psychological Review*, *100*(1), 129–142. doi:10.1037/0033-295X.100.1.129 PMID:8426878

The Canadian Press. (2017). Brother: Las Vegas gunman was wealthy real-estate investor. *Yahoo News*. Retrieved from https://ca.news.yahoo.com/gunman-killed-50-las-vegas-151003919.html

Tora-Joy, P. (2013). Socio-Cultural Tradition. *Communication Theory Blog*. Retrieved from https://torajoypatrick.wordpress.com/2013/10/07/socio-cultural-tradition/comment-page-1/

Vygotsky, L. (1978). *Mind in Society: The Development of Higher Psychological Processes*. Cambridge, MA: Harvard University Press.

ADDITIONAL READING

Craig, R. T., & Muller, H. L. (2007). Theorizing Communications: Reading Across Traditions. *Sage (Atlanta, Ga.)*, (April): 5.

Lin, T.-B., Chen, V., & Chai, C. S. (2015). *New Media and Learning in the 21st Century: A Socio-Cultural Perspective*. Springer. doi:10.1007/978-981-287-326-2

KEY TERMS AND DEFINITIONS

Agreement: A situation when everyone in the group is of the same opinion.

Clustering: Grouping together of ideas, people, or groups based on common features, likes, characteristics, and behavior.

Consensus: A situation where the majority vote is accepted as the group decision.

Consolidation: A firming of ideas or likes or commonalities.

Continuing Diversity: The phenomena of maintaining a different or minority view or idea, despite pressure to conform to a majority opinion or viewpoint.

Convergence: The tendency of ideas and characteristics to start being similar.

Correlation: A strong similarity in behavior between people's ideas, likes, dislikes, aspirations.

Dissimilarity: The tendency of ideas and characteristics to be different from the expected views.

Divergence: The tendency of ideas and characteristics to start being dissimilar.

Similarity: The tendency of ideas and characteristics to be the same as the expected views.

Chapter 6
Use of New Media in Intercultural Communication Classes:
"I Have to Text My Classmate in China!"

Sachiyo Morinaga Shearman
East Carolina University, USA

Mariko Eguchi
University of Shimane, Japan

ABSTRACT

Since the term intercultural communication was first used by Edward T. Hall in 1959, more than half a century has passed, and the context of intercultural communication has gone through dramatic changes. With the advent of the internet and the digital media technologies, instructors can offer students computer-mediated intercultural communication using a variety of new media such as video-conferencing and instant messaging. Drawing from contact theory, learning cycle theory, and new media theory, the authors examine the use of computer-mediated intercultural communication, report various ways that new media are used in classrooms based on an online survey, discuss its benefit and limitations, and review a best practice example, a case of "Global Understanding Course" coordinated by East Carolina University and Global Partners in Education. The authors believe that integrating the use of new media in intercultural communication education helps prepare students for the global society.

DOI: 10.4018/978-1-5225-3784-7.ch006

INTRODUCTION

Since the term "intercultural communication" was first used by Edward T. Hall in 1959 (Rogers, Hart, & Miike, 2002), more than half a century has passed, and the context of intercultural communication has gone through dramatic changes. Development of transportation systems and decreased airfares have made international tourism much more affordable for many people. In 2012, one billion tourists traveled the world (UNWTO, 2012), impacting local cultures on remote corners of the world. Nearly 13% of the U.S. population was foreign-born in 2014 when it was only 5.4% in 1960 (Brown & Stepler, 2016). Due to economic globalism, the world is becoming more and more interconnected with the increased flow of goods and services. Advancements in information technology (IT) make it common to communicate with colleagues and business partners working around the globe via email, text messaging, video conferencing, and social media.

BACKGROUND

Intercultural communication competence, the ability to communicate effectively with people who have different cultures, is now embraced not only in the field of international business and international diplomacy, but it is also needed in personal and professional lives in the domestic context. The negative impact of increased intercultural exchanges harbors new concerns in various settings. In Palau, local residents are not happy with a sudden influx of international tourists who affect the local environment (South China Morning Post, 2015). Images of beach volleyball athletes wearing different types of bathing suits raised the eyebrows of many spectators at the Rio Olympic Games in Brazil (BBC News, 2016). Hate crimes frequently occur when intolerant perpetrators attack victims who belong to different cultural groups (BBC News, 2017). Increased contacts between individuals with diverging cultures could be a great resource for human prosperity, but this wonderful opportunity also harbors the unexpected negative consequences due to misunderstanding, power struggles, and heightened protectionism and ethnocentrism. Cultures that have had little contact with each other are now coming into contact, creating a clash of cultures. It raises the question of how educators can help today's young people to become more interculturally competent.

Increasing intercultural contacts via new media have the potential to improve education in intercultural communication for a larger number of students. In addition to intercultural courses, intercultural training, and study abroad programs, educators now can provide computer-mediated intercultural contacts using a variety of new media, such as video conferencing and instant messages. Since Internet-based communication tools are instantaneous and inexpensive, students can virtually "study abroad" to multiple countries online so that they can experience not just one foreign culture, but a variety of cultures. The use of new media in intercultural communication education can create opportunities for intercultural contacts, helping students become more competent in cross-cultural situations.

MAIN FOCUS OF THE CHAPTER

The purpose of this chapter is to examine various uses of new media in intercultural communication courses in order to foster students' intercultural communication competence. We will review three conventional approaches to intercultural communication education: the lecture, intercultural training, and study abroad programs. Then, we will examine the definition of new media and their characteristics, and possible theoretical frameworks which help us understand the use of new media in intercultural communication education by specifically analyzing computer-mediated intercultural contacts, and reviewing the process through experiential learning theory. We will share the results of the survey on the use of new media in intercultural communication classes. Various ways of incorporating new media in intercultural communication as well as some of the best practice examples are reviewed. We believe that integrating the use of new media in intercultural communication education help prepare our students for the global society and that investing in new platforms that enable international collaboration among educational institutions is beneficial for higher education institution and is necessary for the successful integration of the new media format into the curriculum.

Reconceptualizing of New Media in Instructional Contexts

New Media Defined

It is not easy to define the term "new media," since the adjective "new" or what is perceived as "new or relatively new" evolves as time passes and contexts change. In this digital age where we constantly have new innovations, it is more so the case that the concept of "newness" changes rapidly. As Anyanwu (2003) commented, the distinction of new media is historically relative. During the time when people used fire and drums for communication, the paper was a new medium. At the beginning of 20th century, the newspaper, the typewriter, the telephone, and the telegraph used to be the brand new technologies (Hatchen & Scotten, 2016). Marshal McLuhan examined television as a new medium, which was new in his time (Logan, 2010).

Today, the most dominant understanding of new media refers to digital communication technologies (Peters & Lubken, 2011). In this context, the traditional media, or the "old" media include newspapers, magazines, radio, and television, while examples of "new" media are the Internet, World Wide Web, search engines, blogs, email, texting, social networking, smartphones, and various application programs. The scholars who examine the trend of new media research in the field of communication also define new media as the Internet and related digital technologies (e.g., cell phones, PDAs [Personal Digital Assistants]) and applications (e.g., video-conferencing, file-sharing programs), (Tomasello, Lee, & Bear, 2010). In this chapter, we define "new media" loosely as the digital communication technologies that allow people to send and receive information instantly via the Internet. With this definition, we now examine the potential of new media use in the intercultural communication instruction.

Educational Value of New Media Use

The difference between the old media and the new media is revolutionary in multiple ways. The first characteristics of new media are their empowering nature. The power that only selected and educated individuals have had as 'creators of the text' in old media is now shifted to the traditionally powerless group of the audience. Anyone who has access to the Internet can now voice his or her opinions publicly to many other people. In 2009, the citizens of Iran mobilized themselves using the social media such as Twitter and the series of protests was called "Twitter Revolution". As social media helped mobilize them, the Iranian people received direct support from people in the rest of the world who were connected to the protests via social media (Pew Research Center, 2009). Not long after, the other citizens in the Middle East and North Africa mobilized themselves for political reform using the Internet and social media, and the media and the world reacted in support of them, calling these democratic uprisings as "Arab Spring". The movement began in Tunisia and spread to Egypt, Yemen, Bahrain, Libya, and Syria. In early 2011, the long-standing leader of Tunisia, Zine el-Abidine Ben Ali and the authoritarian president of Egypt, Hosni Mubarak, were forced to resign (Amnesty International, 2016).

Also, new media offer the heightened interactivity of the creator and audience. Cover (2004) claims that the author-text-audience sequence is now re-conceptualized with a continuity of interactivity between author and audience and that the democratization of user participation is seen in the creation and transformation of the text in online communities such as in gaming. While people are passive receivers of information in the context of the traditional media, people can be active contributors in the context of the new media by using convenient and easily accessible tools, such as YouTube, and Twitter, and by using various free blog sites, such as Blogger, Weebly, and WordPress. For instance, Kirk and Schill (2011) claimed that communication via new media created an electronic gathering place for the US citizens, a "digital agora," as they participated and setting agenda in 2008 presidential debate. In another continent, Somolu (2007) reported that African women are starting to have a presence on the Internet by, for example, blogging for information-sharing, setting their own agendas, and raising the possibility for social change, despite the many significant obstacles that they face.

Additionally, the heightened interactivity is not limited to one-to-one communication, since new media provide an easy platform for many-to-many communication where participatory expertise is exercised, as we see in Wikipedia (Pfister, 2011). The Wiki platform allows multiple contributors to join in and create shared knowledge and meaning. Instead of "intercultural dialogue" that we often imagine as in a typical face-to-face conversation between two individuals, new media's information and communication technology provide us the platform where one can communicate to a mass audience at an instant.

Another characteristic of the new media is their cost-efficient nature. Unlike print media, we are freed from the format and limitation of space. Communicating using new media is instant and relatively inexpensive. Thanks to the Internet, we are more interconnected than ever before. Kovarik (2011, p. 315) states that "for the first time in human history, digital networks allowed the billions of people to communicate across national boundaries, instantly, at no cost, in any media format—from text to video." Unfortunately, we need to acknowledge the digital divide issue. The division of "haves" and "have-nots" when it comes to the access to the Internet due to individual and national economic status and national infrastructure is an important issue that we face. This is seen in the Internet penetration rates. For Demark, for example, it is 96.3% of the population, but in Myanmar, it is only 2.5%, according to data reported on July 1st of 2016 (Internet Live Stats, 2016). If we are to establish computer-mediated intercultural contacts with the partners around the world, we need to acknowledge this very issue.

Theoretical Frameworks for Computer-Mediated Intercultural Communication

Using new media and information and communication technologies, the instructors of intercultural communication can provide opportunities for their students to have computer-mediated encounters with a variety of international partners. This type of computer-mediated intercultural encounter costs less than an actual study abroad program, so students who cannot afford it can still learn to communicate effectively with those who are culturally different from them. The computer-mediated intercultural interaction can be an additional approach for the educators who teach intercultural communication competence.

Contact Theory and Computer-Mediated Intercultural Communication Contact

In his book titled *The Nature of the Prejudice*, Allport (1954) theorized that we could reduce prejudice toward out-group members and possibly improve inter-group relations if we can increase the inter-group contact under certain conditions. His intuitive and important thesis was that when members of different cultural groups come into contact with one another, and as they increase their contacts, they may develop more positive attitudes toward each other while reducing negative perception of each other. Naturally, the contact in and of itself is not enough, and the contact should meet certain conditions. Specifically, the premise of the contact theory holds true, if we engage in contact with other out-group members under the right conditions, such as engaging in cooperative interaction, aiming for common goals, under the equal status, and with institutional support. These "right conditions" certainly are not easy to achieve under the real social contexts, however, so many experimental and quasi-experimental studies have been conducted to examine this hypothesis.

The contact theory has been applied various contexts including in educational contexts. A meta-analytic review of more than 500 studies by Pettigrew and Tropp (2008) found that increased contact reduces prejudice with mediated variables such as increased knowledge about outgroups, reduced anxiety about intergroup contact, and increased empathy and perspective taking.

An integrative theory of intergroup contact improves Allport's contact theory by incorporating a related theoretical understanding of the dimensions of contact, group salience following inter-group contact, the importance of psychological mediators, and generalized outcomes for intergroup relations (Brown & Hewstone, 2005).

Harwood (2010) added explanations for the variations of contacts using two-dimensional space of 1) the degree of self-involvement in contact and 2) media richness of self-outgroup experience. He specifically reviewed multiple channels such as interpersonal (or face-to-face contact), mass-mediated, computer-mediated, and imagined contact, to provide more integrated ways to understand different types of contacts and mediated factors. Harwood's application of contact space can provide an in-depth understanding of how one's involvement in communication (or a contact) and the level of media richness that one may enjoy depends on the impact of different channels on the contact experience itself.

Amichai-Hamburger and McKenna (2006) point out three major issues of contact hypothesis (i.e., lack of practicality in creating a contact situation, participants' sense of anxiety in contact situations, and the lack of generalizability, since the artificially created contact may be limited). They then reconsider the contact hypothesis via the Internet. Specifically, Amichai-Hamburger and McKenna (2006) claim that computer-mediated intercultural contact is better-suited to provide contact situations that meet Allport's conditions. In most face-to-face contacts, people are keenly attuned to the status difference or power difference even just by looking at the attire or physical appearance of individuals. Contrary, the Internet could level the playing field in a sense, since various cues associated with the power or status differences are excluded in the mediated communication. Although the environment created for divergent groups to get together at the same time and place can be artificial, and in turn create anxiety among participants, the computer-mediated communication environment is accessible from participants' homes, where they feel secure, comfortable and less anxious. Cooperation via computer-mediated contacts is possible, and some studies have indicated that members of electronic work groups or virtual teams tend to share more information than face-to-face teams (Dennis, 1996; Dennis & Kinney, 1998).

Learner-Centered Pedagogy of Experiential Learning

Among philosophies of learning, experiential learning provides a framework to understand the online intercultural interaction. A central premise of experiential learning is that experience plays the central role in the learning process. In the experiential learning literature, learning is defined learning as "the process whereby knowledge is created through the transformation of experience." (Kolb, 1984, p. 38). Kolb, after reviewing traditions of experiential learning, identified four stages of learning, which he called the Learning Cycle theory (1984): "concrete experience," "reflective observation," "abstract conceptualization," and "active experimentation". Individuals' encounters a concrete experience, which contradicts their previous understanding about such an experience, they reflect on the experience and form a new theory to explain the experience, whereby they create new knowledge. Then they actively use the newly gained knowledge in another situation. This cycle continues as the individuals learn and adapt to new knowledge and skills.

Intercultural Contacts, Applying Kolb's (1984) Experiential Learning Model

In the context of online intercultural communication, the combination of intercultural communication experiences via online and theoretical understanding in the classroom can complete the cycle. Via new media, students will have "concrete experience" when they are connected with people in other cultures. They can exchange ideas or work on a project together via new media. Then the students will have "reflective

Figure 1. Process of learning intercultural communication competence through computer-mediated interaction

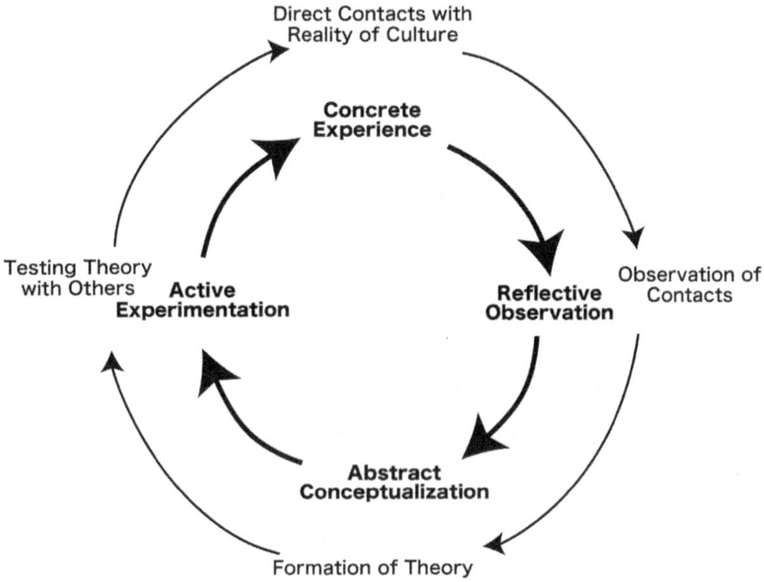

observation" when they share their views about their concrete experience either via new media or in the classroom. Next, the students will have "abstract conceptualization" when they form hypotheses about the experience with help of previous intercultural communication theories via teachers' lecture or textbooks. Finally, the students will have "active experimentation" when they apply their newly gained hypotheses in other intercultural contacts with the culturally different via new media.

For example, an American student may experience ambiguous responses from Japanese students, which can be interpreted as both "yes" and "no." In the second phase, the students reflect such an observation; they share what was confusing with classmates and the teacher. In the third phase, the teacher debriefs the class by giving a lecture on differences in communication styles based on theories of intercultural communication. In the fourth phase, the students experiment with the newly gained knowledge and skills in another interactive situation via new media. In this context, students are not passive learners, but they are actively engaging, and they gain more knowledge, and change motivational, affective attitudes toward students in other countries, as they learn how to function effectively in communicating with those who are culturally different.

The benefits of using new media in the intercultural communication instruction lie in new media's ability to overcome barriers to intercultural communication by making intercultural contacts possible. Samovar, Porter, and McDaniel (2007) listed various issues in intercultural communication including biased human perception against out-groups, such as stereotyping and prejudice, and the human tendency to seek similarity. As the proverb goes "birds of a feather flock together," people tend to seek out others who are similar. When we do not feel familiar, we tend to withdraw from communication rather than engaging in an open-minded interaction with the unfamiliar. New media provide an opportunity for students to meet with someone whom they usually do not choose to meet; namely the unfamiliar. In addition, the new media do it in the comfort of the classroom, reducing the anxiety of meeting the unfamiliar others face to face (Amichai-Hamburger & McKenna, 2006). Computer-mediated intercultural communication may have the potential to overcome barriers to intercultural communication by making optimal intercultural contacts possible.

Conventional Approaches in Intercultural Communication Pedagogy

Before answering in detail the question of how new media can enhance intercultural communication education, let us review some of the conventional approaches to intercultural communication instruction. As the field of intercultural communication is interdisciplinary, and scholars like anthropologists, linguists, psychologists, educational philosophers and communication researchers are involved in the field. In the following sections, approaches to intercultural communication are reviewed, and their characteristics and limitations are discussed.

Lecture-Based Approaches to Intercultural Communication Instruction

The field of intercultural communication emerged in response to the needs of American diplomats to effectively communicate with foreign nationals after the World War II (Leeds-Hurwitz, 1990). While most of the ambassadors and staff of Russian embassies were able to communicate in local languages, a lot of their American counterparts were ignorant of the culture and language of the country of assignment (Rogers, Hart & Miike, 2002). Faced with this serious lack of cultural knowledge, in 1946, the Foreign Service Institute (FSI) was established to provide the staff of the Foreign Service with knowledge of the host culture to which foreign service officers were about to be sent.

In the 1980s, Beebe and Biggers (1986) surveyed introductory intercultural courses at U.S. colleges and found that the lecture was the most common teaching method. In the lecture format, the instructors of intercultural communication courses introduce knowledge, perspectives, behaviors, customs, and languages of other cultures so that students can further understand their own cultures, and ultimately become effective communicators in intercultural contexts. In the lecture, instructors use a variety of traditional media such as printed materials ranging from textbooks, journal articles, literature, travelogues, newspapers, and magazines. Audio-visual materials such as

TV programs, movies, and videos of intercultural conflicts are excellent mediums to examine culturally-bound nonverbal cues such as paralanguage, facial expressions, and gestures. In addition, individuals who represent target cultures are often invited to the classroom to interact with students. Although Beebe and Biggers' study is dated, the content of intercultural communication courses and use of the lecture are still prevalent among intercultural communication courses.

According to Gudykunst and Hammer (1983), "this 'university model' (the didactic approach) of cross-cultural training design assumes that a cognitive understanding of a culture's people, customs, and institutions is of major importance if one is to live effectively in a foreign culture" (p. 122). Lecture-based instruction is an indispensable format, yet with it, students often are expected to take a role of passive learner. In addition, although we teach that communication is a process and is dynamic in nature and that culture is not static, in the context of lecture-based approach to teaching intercultural communication, communication and culture seem rather static. The cognitive approach of intercultural communication education tends to focus more on theoretical aspects of culture and communication, rather than on the development of intercultural communication skills.

The Intercultural Training

When the Foreign Service Institute was established in 1946, Edward Hall lectured on abstract concepts in anthropology to the trainees, but they demanded concrete knowledge and skills that they could quickly apply to their overseas assignments (Leeds-Hurwitz, 1990). Hall utilized culture shock stories that the trainees experienced in foreign countries. In this context, the trainees were active participants and not passive learners.

In addition to stories of participants, the training format utilized simulation games, exercises and the participants themselves. These tools are used to help students "experience" a culture shock by entering into an unfamiliar setting from a familiar setting. For example, a simulation game called Barnga lets participants experience the moment when previously learned rules do not work in a new culture, and also experience the added stress of not being able to communicate verbally when they are asked to communicate using only nonverbal cues (Thiagarajan & Steinwachs, 1990). BaFa BaFa is another simulation game where participants can experience being en-cultured in one culture while negotiating with an individual from other culture (Shirts, 1977). There are variations of simulation games like BaFa BaFa. Although some activities may work better for some instructors than others, there are varieties of options for experiential learning activities compiled in various books such as Kohls and Knight's (1994) *Developing Intercultural Awareness: A cross-cultural training handbook* and Seelye's (1996) *Experiential Activities for Intercultural Learning*.

There is also a website with various experiential learning activities that professor Thiagarajan shares on his website, (The Thiagi Group, 2014).

Intercultural simulation activities offer a valuable means of providing participants with an opportunity to experience interactions with different cultures. Students can be actively participating in these activities while they gain first-hand experience of what it is like to be "out of the element" and feeling a sense of loss due to cultural differences. Students and instructors do not have to leave the classroom, as they simulate these experiences and brief students on what it means to have such experiences, and what they can do about them.

Naturally, however, these experiential learning activities can lack authenticity and realism. The participants who agreed to join in an activity experience the fictional culture shock of an imaginary setting that is artificially constructed. The intercultural training is conducted in a classroom in a country where participants live where they share certain cultural values, although there may be individuals of diverse backgrounds. Therefore, participants do not have to negotiate shared meanings with those who are culturally different. The intercultural training, conducted in the class of students with relatively homogeneous backgrounds, does not offer the students an opportunity to try out what they have learned in an authentic situation.

Study Abroad

Studying abroad is one way to help students become interculturally competent by immersing students in real cultural experiences. Study abroad programs are gaining popularity, and more and more American colleges have begun to integrate study abroad into the curriculum (Haynes, 2011). The study abroad movement in the United States dates back to the 1950s, decreasing airfares made traveling overseas more accessible. In addition to its benefits, such as personal growth, cross-cultural awareness, broader perspectives, and development of future careers, studying abroad offers students a lot of authentic situations where they can try out what they have learned in the classroom. Study abroad is considered to be "the best means of developing intercultural communication skills" (Sterns, 2009, p. 65).

However, there are several disadvantages of this approach: limited number of participating students, a limited number of destinations, and a natural tendency among students for self-segregation. Although spending a year or semester in a foreign university is a wonderful learning experience, not everyone can afford it. Naffziger, Bott, and Mueller (2008) examined barriers to of study abroad decision and found that the financial cost of studying abroad is the most significant. Current students face increasing college tuition and fees, and more and more students want to graduate college as quickly as possible to start paying back their education loans. It is no wonder why only a small percentage of students can study abroad.

The limited number of countries that students can go to is also an issue. Students tend to participate in study abroad programs in popular locations, such as Italy, Spain, the United Kingdom, and France. In 2016, over 54.5% of the American students who studied abroad chose European countries, while only 2.2% of them traveled to Middle East (Institute of International Education, 2016). It is understandable for American students to be attracted to European destinations because these places are traditionally popular tourist destinations, having great cultural attractions and fewer language barriers and cultural distance, and having concerns for safety during the trip. Today's young people need to gain multiple perspectives not just European perspectives through exposure to diverse cultures including the cultures of less popular travel destinations.

Another issue with studying abroad is its effect on the students' intercultural communication ability. Study abroad experiences do not always result in fostering intercultural flexibility. According to Finchilescu (2010), there is a high degree of self-segregation among international students and they tend to avoid interaction with other cultural groups even though they are on the same campus. Gareis (2012) reported that 38% of the international students in the study answered that they did not have meaningful personal connections with people in their host country. Some students, unfortunately, develop negative emotions for their host countries. Dan (2003) found that Chinese students who studied at Japanese universities developed anti-Japanese sentiments during their stay.

There are many factors to such disappointing results from study abroad experiences. For example, international students may not have language proficiency, and are busy with school work, while local students may not be interested in international students. People tend to do something familiar in unfamiliar environments to make them feel secure. So interaction with other cultural groups does not occur naturally. Even though cross-cultural interaction does occur, the interaction may not produce a good result for better intercultural relations. Researchers generally agree with Allport's Contact Theory, which predicts that intercultural contact is effective to reduce stereotypes (Pettigrew & Tropp, 2006). It can be hard, however, for study abroad coordinators to ensure the "right conditions" for intercultural contacts to happen during the study abroad program.

Use of New Media in Intercultural Communication Education

Online Survey

In order for us to learn more about how often and in what way the instructors of intercultural communication offers actual and computer-mediated intercultural contacts in contrast to face-to-face contacts and in-class simulation games, we conducted an online survey of instructors of intercultural communication, cross-cultural communication, and any other courses with different title but which deal with culture and communication. We invited participation through the list-serve member emailing lists among members of the National Communication Association and the Center for Intercultural Dialogue (https://centerforinterculturaldialogue.org/) and the Center for Intercultural New Media Research (http://www.interculturalnewmedia.com/). The email solicitation and announcements explained the goal of the survey and provided the link to the Web-based survey. When the link was clicked, participants saw the first page of the survey as the informed consent statement, which included basic information about the study, the anonymous and confidential nature of the survey, and how participation was voluntary. The survey questionnaire included basic demographic information about the instructor, instructional goals for using new media in intercultural communication, including specific examples, and perceived benefits and challenges of using new media technologies in intercultural communication instruction.

Participants

Forty-eight instructors participated in the survey. Thirty-percent of them were male. The age of the participants ranged from 27 to 79, with the average age being 47 years old (SD = 11.8). Their position titles ranged from adjunct/part-time instructor (8%), full time instructor (6%), assistant professor (20%), associate professor (29%), full professor (23%), and other (15%), which included director, PhD candidate, TA, and no response. Seventy percent of the participants were from the communication discipline, though a few were from psychology, anthropology, linguistics, business, education, international studies, and cultural studies. All 48 participants stated that they teach courses that touch on culture and communication, and the sample course titles were intercultural communication, international communication, cross-cultural communication, communication and culture, intercultural business communication, global communication, international studies, inter-ethnic communication, and study abroad. The number of students in the courses ranged from 8 to 240, averaged 40 students.

Survey Results

Out of the 48 instructors who participated in the study, 29.2% said they “always” create a face-to-face intercultural encounter for their students. Another 18.8% of the instructors said that they do that “most of the time,” and 14.6% said they do that “sometimes.” In total, 62.6% of them reported that they have created a face-to-face intercultural encounter for students using various methods. For example, instructors have assignments that require their students to interact with the international students on campus, participate in multiple on-campus intercultural events, and to match-up with international students as conversation partners for the duration of the semester. Some instructors choose to invite various types of guest speakers who are from either different cultures (e.g., international students on campus), or have a significant intercultural experience (e.g., those who have worked in non-profit organizations to assist refugees). A few instructors stated that they invite multiple guest speakers who represent different cultures to class and then tasks students with different types of questions. A few instructors mentioned offering service learning activities in intercultural contexts.

When asked if the instructors use in-class experiential learning activities, 63.3% of instructor stated that they do. Among them, 12.5% use it “always,” 10.3% use it “most of the time,” and 26.7% use it “sometimes.” Instructors who participated in the study listed a varieties of activities that can be categorized under the experiential learning or simulation games, including role play, case studies, and simulation game such as Barnga (Thiagarajan & Steinwachs, 1990), watching and analyzing foreign movies (specifically made for foreign audience and not American movie dealing with international topics), situational or scenario based questions and discussion, application journals kept by students, and cultural simulations of several days in length.

Out of the 48 instructors, only 31.3% of them stated that they have provided computer-mediated intercultural contacts. Among them, 12.5% said they provide such contacts “always,” while 4.2% said “most of the time,” and 14.6% said “sometimes.” The instructors reported using video-recorded lecture exchanges, video-conferencing, in-class activities and discussions to connect with students in other countries, email, instant messaging between their students and those in other countries. One of the instructors mentioned that inviting several international experts (i.e., individuals representing different countries) to class for interview and discussion sessions, where students ask similar types of questions for further understanding of a specific culture and for a comparative understanding of various cultures. Some instructors reported using gamification programs such as diversophy (https://diversophy.com/) and the Soliya connect program (https://www.soliya.net/). These online programs and many others like them can provide more opportunities for instructors to incorporate computer-mediated intercultural encounters in their courses to enrich students’ learning experiences.

Compared to their use of face-to-face intercultural contact (62.6%) and experiential learning activities (63.3%) in class, only one-third of the instructors (31.3%) in the survey reported using new media tools. We asked for the reasons why some instructors have not yet incorporated computer-mediated encounters in class, and we also asked about the perceived benefits of providing such opportunities for students regardless of the instructors' previous experience with offering computer-mediated intercultural communication.

Many of the instructors said they believe that offering computer-mediated intercultural encounters may be valuable, but they have not yet actually provided those opportunities in class, or they are currently exploring the options. Many instructors listed possible benefits of incorporating computer-mediated intercultural contacts. The benefits include its ability to offer intercultural encounters without leaving their classroom, instant-feedback from the other party, the immediacy with those with whom that they are communicating with, and realism for the millennial students.

The instructors gave us reasons for why they have not yet been able to incorporate computer-mediated intercultural encounters in their classes. The reasons include not having appropriate facilities for it, not having viable international contacts, or simply not having a chance to do so. Some instructors stated that they have tried it but met with difficulties (i.e., issues with technology, and issues in scheduling with others in different time zones). Some instructors said and it was way too time-consuming, and the contact in itself can be hit or miss in terms of quality of communication. Instructors who have used emailing and text-messaging stated that those methods can be hugely dependent on the willingness of students and their intercultural partners to contribute and continue. Many instructors mentioned that the language barrier is one of the key challenges, as oftentimes English is a global language used in academia but it entails the power structure between those who speak English well and those who do not. In addition, the instructors mentioned that simply providing one encounter is not good enough for students to experience and understand those who are from other cultures. Although with some technical difficulties, some participants indicated that they are in the process of planning the intercultural contacts and others are compiling the databases of questions and answers about intercultural communication issues to provide online.

Computer-Mediated Intercultural Communication Examples

There are varieties of ways that we can offer computer-mediated intercultural encounters, synchronous and asynchronous as well as text-based or audio-visual based technology. Chun (2008) categorized the computer-mediated discourse in the instructional environment into four main types using three elements: synchronicity, media-richness (test, audio/visual), and first or second generation web technology. Let us review the four types collapsing first or second generation web technology: asynchronous text-based (i.e., email, bulletin board, wikis, and blogs), asynchronous audio/visual-based (i.e., audio board, social websites sharing photos and videos like YouTube), synchronous text-based (i.e., instant messaging, chatbots), and synchronous audio/visual-based (i.e., desktop video-conferencing, web-based

Figure 2. Typologies of computer-mediated communication (Chun, 2008)

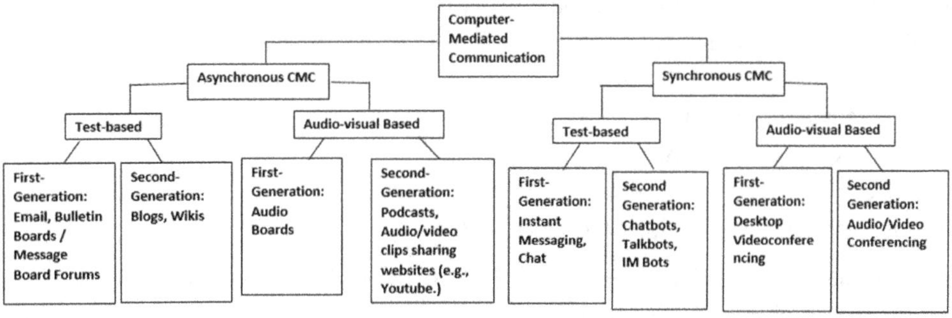

video-conferencing). Varieties of instructors have used these different new media technologies in their instruction, such as blog writing, bulletin board, wikis, YouTube, and video-conferencing, for possible computer-mediated collaborative learning. Chun (2008) offers a summary of previous studies using these varieties of new media in various educational contexts.

Asynchronous Text-Based Technology

Asynchronous text-based technology includes email, bulletin boards forums, blogs, and wikis. The email has been applied in educational contexts especially in language education, and various studies have reported both positive and negative aspects (e.g., Itakura, 2004; Kramshe & Thorne, 2002; O'Dowd, 2003). For instance, Itakura (2004) facilitated Japanese university students with Hong Kong University learners of Japanese to engage in a collaborative intercultural email projects, and reported that students became more aware of the problems of cultural stereotypes, while some students confirmed their negative attitude, or stereotypes, or even formed new stereotypes after the computer-mediated intercultural interaction. Kramsh and Thorne (2002) offered email exchanges between high school French students and American students who were learning French on a variety of topics during the semester and reported that different styles of discourse were a challenge, and the email as a medium may have accentuated cultural differences. O'Dowd (2003) examined long-term email exchanges between Spanish language learners and English learners and reported that successful learners who have engaged in positive and open communication gained intercultural communication competence, while some students' intercultural contacts simply confirmed their negative attitudes and stereotypes.

Asynchronous text-based technology has its benefits in that instructors and students in different time zones can utilize this technology without worrying about matching their respective course schedule. In the contexts of email, students who may have higher intercultural communication anxiety or low English language proficiency (if English was the language of communication) can take time to interpret the message received, and also carefully compose text in response. Email allows for a longer and deeper conversation than synchronous media such as texting or instant messaging, where timeliness of the response is expected.

Asynchronous Audio/Visual Technology

Asynchronous audio/visual technology includes recorded video lectures or recorded videos on streaming and social websites such as on YouTube. Blackboard, a popular distance education tool in the US, provides varieties of ways for instructors to incorporate the recorded lecture to be posted on the medium. The first author of this chapter has used the recorded lectures along with video-conferencing. Two professors in Hiroshima, Japan, shared the recorded lectures regarding the current status of atomic bombs in the world, and the analysis of media coverage regarding atomic bombs. Students observed these recorded lectures in the United States during the class time and later join in a scheduled video-conferencing session via Skype where American students had the opportunity to ask questions, share their responses, and hold discussion sessions with this professor who resided in Hiroshima. This is an example using asynchronous audio/visual technology (video-recorded lecture), followed by synchronous audio/visual technology (video-conferencing session). The second author of this chapter used Voice Thread in her classroom to connect students in the US with the students in Russia. The two sets of respective students created audio files with images of their choice, audio-recorded their introduction, and then share the files with the students in their partner country.

Now that many individuals record audio and video casually and with a use of smartphones, we may be able to incorporate the use of audio-visual asynchronous technology more in the classroom context. The benefits of this asynchronous audio/visual tool are its flexibility, so an instructor in different time zones with different course schedules does not have to worry about matching their class times. Another benefit is the ease of sharing. Now various tools to record the lectures, such as Camtasia, QuickTime, or MediaSite, are available and can easily be shared between instructors in different countries or time zones via file sharing tools, such as Dropbox. The limitations of this technology are that it is possible that some instructors may be reluctant to video-record their lectures and shared it with other instructors, and some students may not engage as much if a recorded lecture is provided without a follow-up interaction session like the example above.

Synchronous Text-Based Technology

Synchronous text-based technology includes texting, chatting, and, instant messaging. Kramsch, A'Ness, and Lam (2000) examined the use of Internet chat which offers synchronous two-way communication through text messages. Thorne (2003) examined language learners using instant messaging. Since visual and audio signals are absent in Internet chat, some students may feel less intercultural communication anxiety, thus enabling less confident speakers to experience text-based intercultural communication. Internet chat is also a good tool for teachers to use to communicate in the background of students' communication because it is unobtrusive in nature. The literature on teaching intercultural communication via Internet chat also support the effectiveness of using Internet chat on the motivational dimension of intercultural communication competence. Contrary to face-to-face communication, where outgoing and confident students tend to dominate the discussion, reticent or less proficient students participate in intercultural communication rather than withdrawing from it (Freiermuth & Huang, 2012).

The obvious benefits of this type of technology include its speed and interactive nature. Students can instantly hear from the other person with whom they are communicating, and students can instantly share clarification or ask probing questions. The instant and dynamic nature of the communication is closer to actual face-to-face communication, although students can still stay in their respective classrooms. Possible limitations include technology issues and students' ability to respond quickly and appropriately. The instructors can assist their students in texting (giving advice and interpretations), if or when students face possible intercultural miscommunication. As with any synchronous communication, instructors need to match course schedule and/or time differences.

Synchronous Audio/Visual Technology

Synchronous audio/visual technology includes desktop based or web-based video-conferencing. Video-conferencing is a technology that allows people to experience the atmosphere of similar to face-to-face meetings, and it is now widely used in corporations, medical institutions, and educational institutions for meetings, medical services, and lectures (Ferran & Watts, 2008). In a study of transforming negative perceptions of others, Eguchi (2016) used videoconferencing discussion sessions between Japanese students and Chinese students and reported that the method effectively transformed negative perceptions toward out-group members into positive ones. Eguchi (2016) discussed that one of the characteristics of online intercultural exchanges as being the ability to structure online meetings carefully, unlike the case of casual contacts.

This medium usually consists of multiple digital tools that support real-time audio and visual communication such as cameras, microphones, speakers, computer, software, screens, projectors, and the Internet connection. When these components work well, students could feel as if they were sharing the same space with those who live in a different part of the world, so authenticity and realism are benefits to this technology. Also, the instructor can program content, speaking turns, and language depending on the goal of the interaction and the structure of the video-conference. The authors of this article have engaged in computer-mediated in-class activity game (e.g., introduction game), and it not only gives a structure to a class but also give a realistic experience of having collaborative classrooms among students in different countries. Possible limitations include scheduling issues, availability of technology and facilities. At the minimum, for synchronous audio/video conferencing, instructors need a good Internet connection, a PC, projector or a TV, and a good camera to capture students and speakers. Students who have high intercultural communication anxiety may not perform as well in this context, especially when they first communicate. Instructors can consider using different media in steps, so students can start with an asynchronous text-based or audio/visual technology, and then move on to use synchronous text-based or audio/visual technology.

These examples of intercultural communication exchanges via new media suggest promising venues for fostering intercultural communication competence in addition to other approaches to intercultural communication education. Clearly, the use of new media solves the costs of time and money of physical travel to another country to meet people from other cultures. In addition, computer-mediated intercultural communication exchanges provide students with unique intercultural experiences that they cannot have from physical study abroad programs, lectures, or intercultural training in their home countries. Each medium has different characteristics: synchronous media enables instant feedback, audio-visual media appeal to vision and hearing, and text media allows careful composition. Students do not hesitate to speak during real-time video-conferencing, but they become suddenly self-conscious when they are asked to record their videos and upload them to a video sharing platform. Students with intercultural communication anxiety may not be willing to speak in video-conferencing, but they express their ideas fully in text-based chat or email exchanges.

Every medium has unique properties and it is the educator's decision on how to use the variety of media to maximize the effect of an intercultural encounter for each learning objective. As we have mentioned in some of the examples above, many educators have been combining multiple types of tools to offer computer-mediated intercultural communication experiences for students. In the next section, we explain a successful example where the combination of synchronous, asynchronous, text-based, and audio-visual based technologies was incorporated to offer students intercultural encounters.

Global Understanding of Global Partners in Education as Best Practice

Global Understanding Course Overview

Let us describe Global Understanding (GU), created by East Carolina University as a successful example of offering computer-mediated intercultural communication in courses using new media technologies (Chia, Poe & Biwu, 2011). GU was first piloted between China and United States in 2003, and it grew in following year to include four countries of China, Gambia, Switzerland, and United States. The partner institutions have increased since then, and GU is currently offered in 50 plus partner institutions in 30 or more countries worldwide. The office of Global Academic Initiative at East Carolina University created the Global Partners in Education (GPE), where participating institutions can engage in creating collaborative classrooms through international lecture exchanges and online discussions among students in the various countries, using Internet-based videoconferencing and instant messaging technology (Chia, Poe, & Singh, 2008; Chia, Poe, & Yang, 2011).

GU uses a variety of new media technologies: synchronous, asynchronous, text-based, and audio-visual based media, including video-conferencing (e.g., Skype, IMO, and Zoom), individual chats (e.g., as Internet Relay Chat), and emails (typically a university provided platform), and texting of their choice outside of the classrooms. Instructors typically pair students in the different countries, and the students connect individually in and outside of the class, as well as engaging in the video conferencing discussion during class.

The duration of a class lasts about 70 minutes depending on the time that each institution is available. In order to allow all students to interact with their partners, the class is divided into two groups. Each day, half of the class starts the video-conferencing session by sitting in front of the camera, while the other half uses computers to exchange text messages. After 30 minutes, the groups switch technologies. In this way, everyone is able to "meet" their partners and exchange ideas, via both video and text chat. Students are required to exchange ideas outside of the classroom. They generally use email to share ideas, but they use a variety of communication technologies such as Facebook, Instagram, LINE, WhatsApp, WeChat, and SnapChat. The main goal of the course is to give students basic knowledge of other cultures, help them become more open-minded, and have them experience the act of working collaboratively with students from other cultures (Chia, Poe & Yang, 2011).

In GU, students generally meet partners in one country for 5 to 6 times during three weeks. Their discussion progress from familiar topics such as "college life" and "family and traditions" to deeper topics such as "meaning of life" and "stereotypes and prejudice." The last meeting is saved for the presentation of the collaborative project. The students must negotiate with each other on what to do with their collaborative project outside of the classroom and they must present their joint works at the end of their exchanges. GU enables students to form relationships with a variety of cultures, leading students to gain not just the perspective of one foreign country, but multiple perspectives from around the world. At ECU, this is an introductory undergraduate course, but GU might be treated as an upper-level course in other countries because GU is conducted in English. GU offers key discussion topics and discussion questions, and ideas for collaborative projects so that students at partner institutions are prepared to discuss and work on shared topics.

Scheduling With Countries in Different Time Zones

The creators of the GU course invented a novel method aimed at reconciling the differences in time and the partner institutions' academic calendars. Due to the fact that universities begin at different times of the year, the degree of bilateral collaboration between different countries can be difficult to achieve. For example, the spring semester in Japan lasts between April and July, while it extends from January to May in the United States. These differences limit bilateral collaboration between Japan and the United States because there is only one month in which there is an overlapping schedule.

ECU's GPE created a system in which each partner could be linked with three other partners throughout the semester in order to remedy the calendar differences. For example, during the first 4 to 5 video-conferencing links, Japan is paired with the United States. After the links with the U.S., Japan is paired with China for 4 to 5 links, which would be followed by the third 4 to 5 links with Russia. In the meantime, the partner institutions are matched to connect other partners throughout the semester. Even though different countries have different academic calendars, ECU's GPE made organizing multiple connections throughout the academic year feasible. In GU course, students in the United States would meet students from multiple countries (e.g., Russia, China, and Japan) during one semester, and they would have assigned topics to communicate on assignments to complete video-conferencing and instant messaging chat. In the meantime, the partner institutions are matched to connect other partners throughout the semester.

GU embodies the power of new media to reach the diversity of cultures. Students taking GU can establish "contact" with the people in other countries that are not so popular study abroad destinations such as Algeria, Cambodia, Lebanon, Gambia, Kyrgyzstan, Macedonia, and Nigeria. With new media, any student can virtually study abroad using new media, even to the countries not commonly chosen as study abroad destinations. Chia, Elmer, and Wuensch (2009) stated that the online intercultural communication class is "not only feasible for American students but also welcomed by higher education institutions from other countries." The online international communication course enables a variety of cultures to interact, leading students to gain not just the perspective of a host country, but multiple perspectives from around the world.

GU does not simply provide computer-mediated intercultural contact. It also provides the stages of learning cycle theory. In the process of discussion, students experience misunderstanding, stress, confusion, and culture shocks. Students have more power to control the learning process; they can create their own questions, ask questions when they want to, get immediate feedback, and test their knowledge and skills with their intercultural partners in a realistic context. They can exchange ideas, negotiate meaning, share photos, create videos, and form relationships, just by clicking a button on the computer screen. The online intercultural interaction via new media offers an educational space that is learner-centric, authentic, and motivating, transforming passive recipients of information into an active agent of culture.

Both of the authors of this chapter have taught GU and experimented with offering different methods of computer-mediated intercultural contacts and communication. As it was revealed from our survey, it is difficult to establish and maintain intercultural communication exchanges via new media due to factors such as technical difficulties, and time zone differences, academic calendar differences, and course scheduling differences, and language barriers and varying commitments by partners in offering computer-mediated intercultural communication. While it may be easy to conduct one-time intercultural exchange via new media, maintaining such an endeavor requires something more than enthusiasm and the effort of teachers. The maintenance of communication and relationships with partner institutions and related institutional, technical, and administrative support such as ECU's GPE is indispensable. The success of GU offers valuable suggestions regarding how to design and maintain online intercultural communication exchanges via new media.

CONCLUSION

In this chapter, we have reviewed the approaches of intercultural communication courses, discussed characteristics of new media, and examined the use of computer-mediated intercultural encounters in intercultural communication courses using two theoretical frameworks: Allport's Contact Theory and Kolb's Experiential Learning Theory. We have reported the results of a survey study among the instructors of intercultural communication courses and reviewed various ways that the instructors of intercultural communication can provide actual intercultural encounters in class along with other experiential learning courses. It seems that majority of professors and instructors who we have surveyed use some form of experiential learning, ranging from in-class role-playing, case studies, and simulation games, and to the assignments that involve intercultural contacts. Only about one-third of instructors who we surveyed actually have incorporated computer-mediated intercultural encounter into their classes and some ideas include online guest lectures, in-class video-conferencing interview sessions, and using programs such as Soliya Net.

We have listed different types of computer-mediated intercultural contacts using a variety of new media: asynchronous or synchronous platforms, text-based or audio/video based, or first generation or second generation web technology. We discussed benefits and limitations for each type of new media technologies, as we shared examples of our own experiences and others. As a best practice of combining multiple online intercultural contacts among partner institutions, we reviewed the model of the Global Understanding courses offered by East Carolina University and Global Partners in Education.

Our intention is not to say that new media technology is better than the conventional approaches to the intercultural pedagogy. All of the approaches to intercultural communication teaching – lectures, intercultural training, and study abroad programs are indispensable. We propose that the use of new media in intercultural communication provides us with an additional valuable approach for us to facilitate students' learning at the multi-dimensional level. When computer-mediated intercultural contacts are provided, students are actively engaged as they interact with students in other countries. Students take initiative in questions that they ask, in the way they communicate and collaborate as they complete the collaborative assignments. Students not only gain more knowledge, and change attitudes toward students in other countries, they can also learn to function effectively in communicating those who are culturally different. In sum, the computer-mediated intercultural encounter can provide students with multi-dimensional (i.e., cognitive, affective, and skill-based) learning opportunities.

FUTURE RESEARCH DIRECTIONS

As Shuter (2012) calls the intercultural new media studies as "new frontier" since the intersection of new media and intercultural communication needs to be further examined. Our understanding of traditional intercultural communication process may change, as the available technology changes. The ICT (Information and Communications Technology) continues to evolve and many successful innovations are to follow. Many of the new media technology categorizations blur as various technologies are now combined in one platform. This pace of innovation in media technologies is creating a new paradigm for our way of life, as it necessitates us to engage in life-long learning and adaptation.

With this fast-paced innovation of new technologies, we also face difficulties in theoretical understanding of the process as well as practical applications in changing the environment. For the instructors to offer constant computer-mediated intercultural contacts with varieties of countries around the world, the administrative and institutional support becomes indispensable. As we reviewed in the survey, there are such innovative ideas and efforts in use by instructors of intercultural communication. We may benefit from having venues for the instructors and higher education institutions to share examples of best practices and use of new media in classroom instruction of intercultural communication.

As we move on to more inter-connected and globalized society, it is critical that we educate ourselves and young leaders to be culturally competent and flexible communicators. To this end, the intercultural exchange is critical, so that mutual understanding and respect between countries can be possible. Further intercultural contacts offered to students either in face-to-face contexts, in simulation game activities, or computer-mediated contexts, can help deepen the understanding of who we are and as we relate to others. Our hope is that this chapter provides some insights for those who are teaching intercultural communication courses or other courses that deal with culture and communication, and help them make students more prepared for the globalized society.

ACKNOWLEDGMENT

Authors would like to acknowledge Dr. Robert Shuter, director of the Center for Intercultural New Media Research, and Dr. Wendy Leeds-Hurwitz, director of the Center for Intercultural Dialogue, for their assistance in distributing the survey. Authors would also like to thank Dr. Jami Leibowitz, the Interim Director of ECU Academic Initiative, and the Director of Global Understanding, for her encouragement and initial contribution to this piece, as well as Dr. Linda Kean, the director of the School of Communication at the East Carolina University, for her support and for providing the SOC research award in completing this project.

REFERENCES

Allport, G. W. (1954). *The nature of prejudice*. Cambridge, MA: Addison-Wesley.

Amichai-Hamburger, Y., & McKenna, K. Y. A. (2006). The contact hypothesis reconsidered: Interacting via the Internet. *Journal of Computer-Mediated Communication*, *11*(3), 825–843. doi:10.1111/j.1083-6101.2006.00037.x

Amnesty International. (2016). *The 'Arab Spring': Five years on*. Retrieved from https://www.amnesty.org/en/latest/campaigns/2016/01/arab-spring-five-years-on/

Anyanwu, C. (2003). Myth and realities of new media technology: Virtual classroom education premise. *Television & New Media*, *40*(4), 289–409. doi:10.1177/1527476403256210

BBC News. (2016). *Volleyball in a hijab: Does this picture show a culture clash?* Retrieved from http://www.bbc.com/news/magazine-37009324

BBC News. (2017). *Quebec City mosque shooting: Six killed, eight wounded.* Retrieved from http://www.bbc.com/news/world-us-canada-38793071

Beebe, S. A., & Biggers, T. (1986). The status of the introductory intercultural communication course. *Communication Education*, *35*(1), 56–60. doi:10.1080/03634528609388319

Brown, A., & Stepler, R. (2016). Statistical portrait of the foreign-born population in the United States. *Pew Research Center*. Retrieved from http://www.pewhispanic.org/2016/04/19/statistical-portrait-of-the-foreign-born-population-in-the-united-states-key-charts/

Brown, R., & Hewstone, M. (2005). An integrative theory of intergroup contact. In M. P. Zanna (Ed.), Advances in experimental social psychology (Vol. 37, pp. 255–342). San Diego, CA: Elsevier.

Chen, G. M. (2012). The impact of new media on intercultural communication in global context. *China Media Research*, *8*(2), 1–10.

Chia, R. C., Poe, E., & Singh, P. (2008). An interactive virtual global cultural course: Building a real-time cost-effective global collaborative learning environment. *International Journal of Emerging Technologies in Learning*, *3*(1), 32–35. Retrieved from http://online-journals.org/i-jet/article/view/187/239

Chia, R. C., Poe, E., & Wuensche, K. L. (2009). Attitude change after taking a virtual global understanding course. *World Academy of Science, Engineering and Technology*, *31*, 722–726.

Chia, R. C., Poe, E., & Yang, B. (2011). History of Global Partners in Education. *Global Partners in Education Journal, 1*(1), 3–7.

Chun, D. M. (2008). Computer Mediated Discourse in Instructed Environment. In S.S. Magnan (Ed.), Mediating Discourse Online (pp. 15-45). John Benjamins Publishing. doi:10.1075/aals.3.04chu

Cover, R. (2004). New Media Theory: Electronic games, Democracy and Reconfiguring the Author-Audience Relationship. *Social Semiotics, 14*(2), 173–188. doi:10.1080/1035033042000238268

Dan, Y. (2003). *Gendai chugokujinno nihon ryugaku* [Modern Chinese study abroad in Japan]. Tokyo: Akashi Shoten.

Dennis, A. R. (1996). Information exchange and use in group decision making: You can lead a group to information but you can't make it think. *Management Information Systems Quarterly, 20*(4), 433–455. doi:10.2307/249563

Dennis, A. R., & Kinney, S. T. (1998). Testing media richness theory in the new media: The effects of cues, feedback, and task equivocality. *Information Systems Research, 9*(3), 256–274. doi:10.1287/isre.9.3.256

Eguchi, M. (2016). Using video-conferencing to change Japanese high school students' perceptions of China. *Journal of Policy Studies, 32*, 1–15.

Ferran, C., & Watts, S. (2008). Videoconferencing in the field: A heuristic processing model. *Management Science, 54*(9), 1565–1578. doi:10.1287/mnsc.1080.0879

Finchilescu, G. (2010). Intergroup anxiety in interracial interaction: The role of prejudice and meta-stereotypes. *The Journal of Social Issues, 6*(2), 334–351. doi:10.1111/j.1540-4560.2010.01648.x

Freiermuth, M. R., & Huang, H. (2012). Bringing Japan and Taiwan closer electronically: A look at an intercultural online synchronic chat task and its effect on motivation. *Language Teaching Research, 16*(1), 61–88. doi:10.1177/1362168811423341

Gareis, E. (2012). Intercultural friendship: Effects of home and host region. *Journal of International and Intercultural Communication, 5*(4), 309–328. doi:10.1080/17513057.2012.691525

Global Partners in Education (GPE). (2014). *The purpose of GPE.* Retrieved from http://thegpe.org/about-gpe/purpose/

Gudykunst, W. B., & Hammer, M. R. (1983). Basic Training Design: Approaches to intercultural training. In D. Landis & R. S. Bhagat (Eds.), *Handbook of intercultural training* (pp. 118–147). Elmsford: Pergamon Press. doi:10.1016/B978-0-08-027533-8.50011-7

Harwood, J. (2010). The Contact Space: A novel framework for intergroup contact. *Journal of Language and Social Psychology*, *29*(2), 147–177. doi:10.1177/0261927X09359520

Hatchen, W. A., & Scotten. (2016). *The world news prism: digital, social and interactive.* Malden, MA: Wiley Blackwell.

Haynes, C. (2011). Overcoming the study abroad hype. *Journal of the National Collegiate Honors Council*, *12*(1), 17–24. Retrieved from http://digitalcommons.unl.edu/nchcjournal/305

Institute of International Education. (2016). *Open Doors Data - Fast Fact 2016.* Retrieved from http://www.iie.org/Research-and-Publications/Open-Doors/Data/Fast-Facts#.WHPHULnMJs8

Internet Live Stats. (2016). *Internet Users by Country (2016).* Retrieved from http://www.internetlivestats.com/internet-users-by-country/

Itakura, H. (2004). Changing cultural stereotypes through e-mail assisted foreign language learning. *System*, *32*(1), 37–51. doi:10.1016/j.system.2003.04.003

Kirk, R., & Schill, D. (2011). A digital agora: Citizen participation in the 2009 presidential debates. *The American Behavioral Scientist*, *55*(3), 325–347. doi:10.1177/0002764210392167

Kohls, L. R., & Knight, J. M. (1994). *Developing intercultural awareness: A cross-cultural training handbook* (2nd ed.). Yarmouth, ME: Intercultural Press.

Kolb, D. A. (1984). *Experiential Learning: experience as the source of learning and development.* Englewood Cliffs, NJ: Prentice-Hall.

Kovarik, B. (2011). *Revolutions in Communication: Media history from Gutenberg to the digital age.* New York: Continuum.

Kramsch, C., A'Ness, A., & Lam, E. (2000). Authenticity and authorship in the computer-mediated acquisition of L2 Literacy. *Language Learning & Technology*, *4*(2), 78–104.

Kramsch, C., & Thorne, S. L. (2002). Foreign language learning as global communicative practice. In D. Block & D. Cameron (Eds.), *Globalization and language teaching* (pp. 83–100). London: Routledge.

Leeds-Hurwitz, W. (1990). Notes in the history of intercultural communication: The Foreign Service Institute and the mandate for intercultural training. *The Quarterly Journal of Speech*, *76*(3), 262–281. doi:10.1080/00335639009383919

Logan, R. (2010). *Understanding New Media*. New York: Peter Lang.

Naffziger, D. W., Bott, J. P., & Mueller, C. B. (2008). Factors influencing study abroad decisions among college of business students. *International Business: Research Teaching and Practice*, *2*(1), 39–52.

O'Dowd, R. (2003). Understanding the "other side": Intercultural learning in a Spanish-English email exchange. *Language Learning & Technology*, *7*(2), 118–144.

Peters, B., & Lubken, D. (2011). New Media in Crises: Discursive instability and emergency communication. In D. W. Park, N. W. Jankowski, & S. Jones (Eds.), *The long history of new media: technology, historiography, and contextualizing newness* (pp. 193–209). New York: Peter Lang.

Pettigrew, T. F., & Tropp, L. R. (2006). A meta-analytic test of intergroup contact theory. *Journal of Personality and Social Psychology*, *90*(5), 751–783. doi:10.1037/0022-3514.90.5.751 PMID:16737372

Pettigrew, T. F., & Tropp, L. R. (2008). How does intergroup contact reduce prejudice? Meta-analytic tests of three mediators. *European Journal of Social Psychology*, *28*(6), 922–934. doi:10.1002/ejsp.504

Pew Research Center. (2009). *Iran and the "Twitter Revolution": PEJ New Media Index*. Retrieved from http://www.journalism.org/2009/06/25/iran-and-twitter-revolution/#

Pfister, D. S. (2011). Networked Expertise in the Era of Many-to-Many Communication: On Wikipedia and Invention. *Social Epistemology*, *25*(3), 217–231.

Pfister, D. S., & Soliz, J. (2011). (Re)conceptualizing Intercultural Communication in a Networked Society. *Journal of International and Intercultural Communication*, *4*(4), 246–251. doi:10.1080/17513057.2011.598043

Rogers, E. M., Hart, W. B., & Miike, Y. (2002). Edward T. Hall and the history of intercultural communication: The United States and Japan. *Keio Communication Review, 24*, 3–26. Retrieved from http://www.mediacom.keio.ac.jp/publication/pdf2002/review24/2.pdf

Samovar, L. A., Porter, R. E., & McDaniel, E. R. (2007). *Communication between cultures*. Belmont, CA: Thomson Wadworth.

Seelye, H. N. (1997). *Experiential activities for intercultural learning*. Boston, MA: Intercultural Press.

Shirts, R. G. (1977). *BaFa BaFa: A cross cultural simulation*. Delmar, CA: Smile II.

Shuter, R. (2012). Intercultural New Media Studies: The next frontier in intercultural communication. *Journal of Intercultural Communication Research, 41*(3), 219–237. doi:10.1080/17475759.2012.728761

Somolu, O. (2007). Telling our own stories: African women blogging for social change. *Gender and Development, 15*(3), 477–489. doi:10.1080/13552070701630640

South China Morning Post. (2015). *Chinese tourist invasion transforms remote Palau and not everyone is happy*. Retrieved from http://www.scmp.com/news/china/foreignrelations/article/1738288/chinese-descend-remote-palau-wanderlust-deepens

Sterns, P. N. (2009). *Educating global citizens in colleges and universities: challenges and opportunities*. New York, NY: Routledge.

The Thiagi Group. (2014). *Training Games*. Retrieved from http://www.thiagi.com/games.html

Thiagarajan, S., & Steinwachs, B. (1990). *Barnga: A simulation game on cultural clashes. Yarmouth*. Intercultural Press.

Thorne, S. L. (2003). Artifacts and cultures of use in intercultural communication. *Language Learning & Technology*, *7*(2), 38–67. Retrieved from http://llt.msu.edu/vol7num2/thorne/

Tomasello, T. K., Lee, Y., & Bear, A. P. (2010). "New media" research publication trends and outlets in communication, 1990-2006. *New Media & Society*, *12*(4), 531–548. doi:10.1177/1461444809342762

UNWTO. (2012). *International tourism hits one billion*. Retrieved from http://media.unwto.org/en/press-release/2012-12-12/international-tourism-hits-one-billion

KEY TERMS AND DEFINITIONS

Asynchronous Computer-Mediated Communication: Refers to the communication where interactants engage in a conversation at a different time allowing for delayed access using some type of mediated technology such as emails, bulletin board, audio board, blogs, wikis, and YouTube.

Contact Theory: Examines the process of prejudice reduction due to increased contact with the out-group members, given certain conditions such as cooperative interaction, aiming for common goals, under the equal status, and with institutional support.

Intercultural Communication: Refers to the process of interaction where individuals with diverging ethnic and cultural background are communicating with each other.

Intercultural Communication Competence: Refers to one's ability to adapt, be flexible in a given context, and communicate effectively and appropriately with someone whose background may be different from one's own. Intercultural communication has three key components: affective components (emotional reaction), cognitive component (information and knowledge), and psych-motor components (behavior and skills).

Intercultural Communication Pedagogy: Refers to an examination and a study of teaching methods used to make individuals learn more about culture, communication, and intercultural communication processes.

Learner-Centered Pedagogy: Refers to an educational method where the emphasis is placed on the initiative and the engagements of learners, rather than that of teachers/instructors.

Learning Cycle Theory: Refers to the steps that a learner takes in learning new knowledge or adapting new skills, which include concrete experience, reflective observation, abstract conceptualization, and active experimentation.

New Media: Is defined, in this chapter, as the digital communication technologies that allow people to send and receive information instantly via the internet and some type of digital technologies (such as personal computers, personal digital assistants, and cell phones) and applications, though the definition of "newness" changes over time as with technological advancement.

Synchronous Computer-Mediated Communication: Refers to the communication where interactants engage in a conversation at the same time using some type of mediated technology such as instant messaging, video-conferencing, and chatbots.

Section 3

New Media, Culture and Conflict

This section presents chapters exploring the connection between culture and conflict using new media, specifically focusing on conflict formation, conflict management, and conflict resolution in the new media platform.

Chapter 7
The Benefits and Challenges of New Media for Intercultural Conflict

Amy Janan Johnson
University of Oklahoma, USA

Sun Kyong Lee
University of Oklahoma, USA

Ioana A. Cionea
University of Oklahoma, USA

Zachary B. Massey
University of Oklahoma, USA

ABSTRACT

This chapter examines current research on intercultural interactions over new media with a particular emphasis on those studies involving conflict. Two main points are emphasized: 1) new media have several characteristics that differentiate them from traditional forms of media and shape intercultural conflict, providing benefits but also creating challenges not encountered before; and 2) traditional theoretical explanations of the relationship between media and conflict are inadequate for explaining the role that individual and group characteristics play in intercultural conflict in the digital age. Certain theories are discussed in relation to the second point. Overall, the chapter proposes questions that could advance research in this emerging area.

DOI: 10.4018/978-1-5225-3784-7.ch007

INTRODUCTION

The advent of new media has shortened the space between people of differing ethnic and cultural backgrounds, providing them with new and diverse ways of interacting with one another. For instance, users can now connect through visual image sharing sites (e.g., YouTube, Vimeo, Flickr), social network sites (e.g., Facebook, Twitter, Instagram), discussion forums (e.g., Reddit, 4chan, Gaia online), and online dating services (e.g., eHarmony, Match.com, Tinder). Furthermore, new media have been the catalytic force in the emergence of several intergroup conflicts or the success of social movements across the world (Zeitzoff, 2017), such as the Moldovan "Twitter revolution" of 2009, the Arab Spring movements of 2011 (Kharroub & Bas, 2015; Van Niekerk & Maharaj, 2013), and more recently, the use of YouTube by rebels in the Syrian civil war (Meis, 2017). Given the interactivity facilitated by new media platforms, contact via new media may be just as visceral, if not more so, than actual physical contact. Against this background, this chapter advances two main arguments: 1) new media's characteristics create a complex context, with new opportunities and challenges, that shapes intercultural conflict in novel ways; and 2) the relationship between new media and conflict needs updated theoretical explanations as traditional theories cannot explain how individual and group characteristics combine to drive intercultural conflict in the digital age.

BACKGROUND

Before delving into further discussion, however, it is useful to define some key terms. First, *intercultural communication* refers to communicative exchanges between members of different cultural groups. *Culture* is defined as an abstract, socially derived system of shared beliefs, values, and behaviors that a group of people who speak the same language and usually inhabit the same territory have devised (Kluckhohn & Kelly, 1945; Triandis, 1995). The authors use the term *culture* broadly, to include national cultures, ethnic groups, and any other cultural groups. *Intercultural contexts* are those situations that involve culturally different individuals or groups that come into contact, physically or digitally. Intercultural contexts also capture situations in which culture is a key consideration that shapes the interaction between individuals or groups. With respect to conflict, Hocker and Wilmot (1978) define *conflict* as, "an expressed struggle between at least two interdependent parties who perceive incompatible goals, scarce resources, and interference from others in achieving their goals" (p. 9). Finally, Shuter (2012) speaks of information communication technologies when discussing *new media* and provides the following examples: social media, text messaging, Skype, blogs, virtual worlds, and multiplayer online games. Thus, the examination of intercultural conflict and new media involves discussions about the incompatibilities or struggles of culturally distinct groups or individuals that are undertaken through or facilitated by these new forms of communication technology.

Chen (2012) argues that there are five different characteristics of new media. *Digitality* refers to the conversion of media from analog to digital forms. *Convergency* means that various forms of information and media are reunited, blending their functions, and yielding new, powerful information technologies, such as the Internet and mobile phones. *Interactivity* captures the new ways in which users and information platforms interact, the freedom of producing, exchanging, and controlling information, and the convenience of such exchanges. *Hypertextuality* refers to the global network of information that can move instantaneously and freely among users. Finally, *virtuality* refers to the cyberspace new media have generated, giving users the opportunity to experience virtual realities (Chen, 2012). Besides these five characteristics, *anonymity* (i.e., the sender of the message is unknown) and *asynchronicity* (i.e., a time gap between message sent and message received) can be considered features of some new media, such as anonymous discussion forums; however, due to the wide adoption and usage of social media that require users to have authentic profiles and allow both synchronous and asynchronous interactions, anonymity and asynchronicity cannot represent all new media. Also, social media tend to have various affordances that separate them from other forms of new media (Treem & Leonardi, 2012).

Shuter (2012) suggests that the "next frontier in intercultural communication" is intercultural new media studies (p. 219). To this end, this chapter examines how various features (i.e., convergency, interactivity, hypertextuality, anonymity, asynchronicity) and affordances (e.g., visibility, editability, spreadability, persistence, searchability, association) of new media affect how individuals of different cultures engage in conflict. By comparing and combining aspects of both previous intercultural research and computer-mediated communication research, this chapter provides a blueprint for fruitful directions for future research.

Examining new media from an intercultural perspective is essential for scholars who want to understand how conflict is performed across cultural groups in this increasingly globalized and digitized world. Shuter (2012) claims, "new media play a major role in the ebb and flow of intercultural encounters" (p. 122). As individuals use new media to build relationships across cultural lines, intercultural conflict within these relationships is inevitable. In addition, differences in how members of various cultures engage with new media also influence how these channels affect broader aspects of cultural systems (such as relationships between different countries) worldwide. This chapter presents both benefits and challenges in engaging in intercultural conflict using new media. As such, new media are not conceptualized as a panacea for intercultural conflict.

In addition, traditional theories of intercultural communication need to be reconceptualized based on the advent and use of new media (Shuter, 2012). For example, Shuter discusses how computer-mediated communication in general, and virtual gaming worlds in particular, improve acculturation and increase intercultural competence. More and more communication is being mediated, and new media are increasingly becoming the site of intercultural and interpersonal conflict. Therefore, this chapter addresses both the opportunities and the challenges that new media create for reducing prejudice toward culturally different groups, as well as the potential of certain theories to help in this endeavor.

The next section provides a brief overview of the existing research concerning new media and intercultural conflict, first focusing on the benefits and then challenges of new media.

MAIN FOCUS OF THE CHAPTER

Current Research on the Benefits of New Media for Intercultural Conflict

The blooming literature on new media mainly examines how its affordances change the emergence, management, and consequences of conflict. New media, particularly social media, offer multiple affordances not available to interactants in offline contexts, such as persistence, visibility, association, and editability (Treem & Leonardi, 2012), besides anonymity and asynchronicity, which are associated with certain online discussion forums. These affordances change how models of conflict should map and explain behaviors. As Tufekci (2017) explains, older media (e.g., TV, newspapers, radio) would not have been able to offer individuals the flexibility in organizing, publicizing, and breaking censorship that new media do. Due to these new communication technologies, social movements and activism have taken new trajectories, previously impossible.

Considering the affordances of social media provides an illustration of how new media are affecting intercultural conflict. The *persistence* of social media refers to the permanent nature of Internet-based records as people can view messages on social media over a long period of time (Treem & Leonardi, 2012). One can access another's past history easily when they make connections on social media. The *visibility* of social media indicates a person's knowledge, expertise, preferences, and even personality may become visible through his or her activities on social media, such as sharing behaviors. *Association* is about the network connectivity allowed by social media and how people can create new contacts and maintain/strengthen their existing ties. *Editability* pertains to how social media users can delete contents on their own social media accounts, potentially based on self-surveillance or impression management concerns (Treem & Leonardi, 2012). boyd (2014) adds *searchability* and *spreadability* as unique affordances of social media; *searchability* speaks to how one's digital records are easily searchable by other people/entities, whereas *spreadability* refers to how certain contents on social media become viral and spread through the network quickly.

Due to these affordances, increased contact through new media may have many benefits for individuals, groups, and organizations. Gilboa (2009) argues that new media may have created new possibilities for conflict resolution because they offer a more neutral and balanced reporting of events, as compared to traditional forms of media. Furthermore, the visibility and association of social media enables various perspectives and opinions to become more easily accessible through social media and the network connections afforded by them. Similarly, Zeitzoff (2018) contends that social media can be used as a strategic tool in conflict and can improve the likelihood of conflict resolution. He offers the example of the Libyan rebellion of 2011 when the rebels' Twitter campaign increased American support. The network associations (direct or indirect) between Libyans and Americans as well as the spreadability of viral social media contents (boyd, 2014) likely contributed to this phenomenon.

The existing discussion in the literature concerning conflict and new media has been carried out at two levels. The first is a macro level in which new media forms, such as Twitter, Facebook, or YouTube, are linked to global, inter-state, or national conflicts between groups. For example, Van Niekerk and Maharaj (2013) examined the role of social media in civil disturbances. The second is a micro level in which new media are connected to interpersonal conflict in relationships. For example, Shah, Chauhan, Gupta, and Sen (2016) reported increased intergenerational conflict in India among adolescents and their parents as the latter disagreed with the former's use of Facebook.

The benefits of new media, in general, are closely related to the features of *convergency*, *interactivity*, and *hypertextuality* (Chen, 2012), which allow new media to be used as a strategic tool in the management of conflict. Zeitzoff (2018) has argued that new information technologies have changed the role that international audiences play in conflict. New media's *interactivity* and *hypertextuality* and social media's affordance of *association* give conflict participants access to wider, global audiences. Thus, other international actors besides the initial protagonists may become involved, which can increase support for a particular side. Similarly, Gray and Gordo (2014) argue that new media constitute an essential component of modern social movements that incorporate them into their social justice actions.

Zeitzoff, Kelly, and Lotan (2015) propose that new media can reveal information about foreign policy, which relates to the *hypertextuality* function of new media, and the *spreadability* of social media, allowing information to move instantaneously around the world. In their case study of the Israeli-Iranian conflict of 2012-2013 over Iran's nuclear program, Twitter discussions served as a useful source of information about foreign policy issues; new media offered a new arena for political discussion regarding this conflict.

The *interactivity* feature of new media has been perhaps one of its most beneficial characteristics. New media can facilitate higher level of social interactivity among individuals, allowing them to share ideas and experiences much faster, across time and space, in a global network. Examples of new media-facilitated interactivity include user-generated content in the form of tweets, amateur video recordings, and pictures that are uploaded instantaneously to the web. The ability to interact in these new ways has shaped various conflicts, and has even led to changes in regimes in the past two decades. According to Van Niekerk and Maharaj (2013), some of the earliest uses of social media to mobilize physical protests were in the 1994 Zapatista uprising and the Chiapas conflict in Mexico. Since then, the use of Twitter, YouTube, or Facebook to fuel protests has increased (Bennett & Segerberg, 2011).

According to Van Niekerk and Maharaj (2013), new media are used in social disturbances to transform online discourse into physical protest. In the Arab Spring, for instance, online conversations preceded physical protests. Howard et al. (2011) claim that online conversations on blogs and Twitter spiked right before mass protests on the ground. Similarly, Alaimo (2015) explains that the owner of the Egyptian Facebook page "We Are All Khaled Said" used this platform to raise awareness among individuals, and then mobilized them to take the movement to the streets. Thus, the *interactive* platforms of new media allow for faster and more efficient organization of collective social movement and the viral diffusion of information, prior to, concurrently, or after physical demonstrations in national and international conflicts.

Connected to the beneficial feature of interactivity is the tremendous increase in citizen journalism and amateur reporting permitted and facilitated by new media. Kavanaugh, Sheetz, Sandoval-Almazan, Tedesco, and Fox (2016) found that, when political information was uncertain (as may be the case when citizens challenge their governments, or when conflict occurs within or between nations), social networks and online sources were perceived to be more reliable than traditional forms of mass media. The information found on these platforms is often uploaded by users who are on the scene, broadcasting "live" from amid the masses, as in the Arab Spring (Howard et al., 2011; Kharroub & Bas, 2015). Information posted by citizens on the ground can be publicly transmitted worldwide much faster than in the past (Howard et al., 2011).

Another benefit of new media is that it enables information to travel *freely* across borders, which relates to *hypertextuality* (Chen, 2012), *association* (Treem & Leonardi, 2012), and *spreadability* (boyd, 2014). Even when governments try to block Internet access, the blackouts are usually short and unsustainable given the vast network connectivity options. For example, during the Egyptian revolution, the Muslim Brotherhood relied on servers hosted outside Egypt to blog information about the conflict (Howard et al., 2011).

Features of new media (e.g., interactivity and hypertextuality) and social media affordances (e.g., spreadability, association, visibility) have provided many benefits to those who seek certain goals from intercultural conflict. However, the same features that might be seen as a benefit to one group (being able to broadcast the crackdown of a new regime) might not be perceived as beneficial by others (such as the regime in question). There are certain challenges of new media that may exacerbate and/or complicate intercultural conflict, which will be discussed in the next section.

Current Research on Challenges of New Media for Intercultural Conflict

Despite the aforementioned benefits, new media also pose several challenges related to intercultural conflict. For example, Gladwell (2010) questions whether the type of "revolution" that new media facilitates is truly a form of activism that can accomplish the same results as lunch counter sit-ins or the Freedom Schools. Gladwell argues that these new forms of so-called activism center around weak ties between members enmeshed in networks, not hierarchical forms of organization, like traditional activism. He argues that new forms of media manage to spread awareness and increase virtual participation in low-risk circumstances, but do not translate into the actual action needed to sustain a social movement. Terms such as *slacktivism* or *clicktivism* illustrate the shallow involvement of online activists in a cause (Morozov, 2009). Thus, one of the challenges of new media is the need to transform digital forms of awareness and support into concrete tools for intercultural conflict management. Moreover, Alaimo (2015) argues that social media (by likely extension other forms of new media, too) cannot function as or foster governance in the aftermath of a revolution.

Second, the *accessibility* of platforms can be used to promote extremist agendas, to encourage radical movements, and to exacerbate intercultural conflict. As Zeitzoff (2018) explains, the Islamic State of Iraq and the Levant (ISIL) are competent and heavy users of new forms of media, such as Twitter (Klausen, 2015) and YouTube for seeking support, recruiting and mobilizing members, and publicly displaying their acts of violence. Social media can be an effective force for terrorist organizations to establish their credibility and legitimacy (Blaker, 2015; Farwell, 2014; Stern & Berger, 2015), which exacerbates global intercultural conflict. *Convergency* and *hypertextuality* of new media in general, and *association* and *visibility* of social media in particular, can operate to promote negative agendas, whereas the *anonymity* of new media can provide a haven for extremists.

Similarly, it is not only citizens who can coordinate and organize online. Governments and regimes have also tried blocking access, shutting down the Internet, or targeting individuals or groups based on their online activity (Gohdes, 2015; Howard et al., 2011; Meis, 2017). Although some of these tactics may be short-lived, Gohdes (2015) argues that they are part of a governmental or military strategy to manage conflict for their gains. As Tufekci (2017) explains, "many governments have come a long way in understanding and learning how to control the new public sphere and its digital ecology" (p. 225).

In addition, new media may also have unintended negative consequences. Moghaddam (2005), for instance, has noted that exposure to Western media has contributed to feelings of resentment, deprivation, and anger in non-Western youths who find the secular ideals of consumer culture both unattainable and culturally offensive. Warren (2015) argues that the horizontal connections that new media afford among individuals actually increase the likelihood of collective violence, especially in areas where no other forms of mass media can be accessed. As new media platforms grow in both sophistication and accessibility, the virtual space between individuals will continue to shrink, such that increased interactivity may not always have positive consequences.

Another way that new media may increase interethnic conflict is through "contamination" (Weidmann, 2015). The presence of ethnic conflict in a country's partners (not necessarily geographic, neighboring countries) can increase the likelihood that ethnic conflict will erupt in said country, too, because new media permit the unobstructed diffusion of information (i.e., hypertextuality). For example, Snow Bailard (2015) has found that the availability of mobile communication increased the potential for interethnic violent conflicts. It eliminated various barriers that would have otherwise stood in the way of collective organization for action. Furthermore, Snow Bailard argues, for ethnic groups that are excluded from power and those in less developed countries, the presence of mobile phone technologies provides a unique opportunity to mobilize and, hence, increases the probability of interethnic conflict.

In summary, new media have both benefits and challenges in respect to intercultural conflict. The authors have highlighted a few of them. The most important conclusion that can be drawn from this discussion is that new media's affordances and constraints have expanded our understanding of what intercultural conflict is and how it can be carried out, beyond in-person, physical forms. In what follows, the authors discuss theoretical perspectives from both intercultural and computer-mediated communication research that can offer a deeper understanding of intercultural conflict involving new media.

Theories Related to New Media and Intercultural Conflict

Contact Hypothesis: Re-Categorizing Social Differences

Originally proposed by Allport (1954), the *contact hypothesis* argues that positive social contact between people from different groups can lead to decreased prejudice, if certain conditions are present: (a) support from institutional authorities, (b) shared goals between interactants, (c) intergroup cooperation, and (d) equal status between groups. Re-categorization tends to occur because positive contact presents a challenge to rigid outgroup categorizations. Through de-categorization, individuals come to see each other in terms of individual characteristics instead of group-based generalizations (Brewer & Miller, 1984). Positive intergroup contact, then, shifts communicative behavior from intergroup orientations to interpersonal ones (see Tajfel & Turner, 1986). The interactants are forced to reevaluate the groups attached to the stereotypes. Thus, positive contact decreases prejudice toward the outgroup as a whole (Bettencourt, Brewer, Croak, & Miller, 1992).

Findings from over 60 years of contact research highlight key areas where intercultural contact and new media intersect. For instance, while most research focuses on the ability of positive interpersonal contact to generalize to intergroup reevaluations, a smaller body of research indicates that negative (i.e., unfriendly, unpleasant) interactions increase intergroup category salience (Paolini, Harwood, & Rubin, 2010) and have disproportionate influence on future intergroup encounters (Paolini et al., 2014). Such findings indicate that intergroup contact under less than ideal conditions (which may include over new media) may increase hostilities.

Indeed, some features of new media may contribute to negative contact rather than positive contact. For instance, *anonymity* allows users to freely change their gender, ethnicity, age, and so on. However, the Hewstone-Brown model of intergroup contact (see Hewstone & Brown, 1986) has shown that for positive interpersonal contact to generalize to intergroup evaluations, the ingroup identity of each interactant must be salient to allow erosion of group categorizations. Anonymity, though, potentially allows people to interact without anxiety (Amichai-Hamburger, Hasler, & Shani-Sherman, 2015), which has been found to mediate contact effects (Pettigrew & Tropp, 2006). Therefore, the function of anonymity in intergroup contact in new media contexts remains an empirical question awaiting future research.

The affordances of new media may encourage positive contact between groups. For example, *interactivity* allows members of social networks that may be separated by physical distance to interact instantaneously. Kim (2015) found that contact with dissimilar others through the exchange of different political opinions via discussion networks counteracted selective exposure to similar ideas, and subsequent intergroup polarization. If anonymity potentially strips away one factor necessary for positive contact, interactivity may provide another possibility for possibility to reduce polarized attitudes, which could have a positive effect on conflict.

Similarly, the affordance of *visibility* includes category information that may help or hinder intergroup contact. The visibility of social media provides the relevant ingroup identification cues necessary for the generalization of positive contact effects. However, the visibility of one's social media may include information that conflicts with the ethnic, religious, or cultural orientation of another user. The affordance of *association* may allow users to create new contacts and larger social networks. At the same time, a preoccupation with association may encourage rigid ingroup boundaries as users seek like-minded and culturally similar others. Indeed, as Awan (2017) has noted, the "cyber jihadists" of ISIS have been hugely successful at disseminating propaganda and attracting recruits via social media to adopt a rigid worldview. Finally, *editability* allows one to edit expressions that may cause strife or misunderstanding. The same function may allow users to "edit" their networks, banishing people who do not share consensus on social, political, or cultural issues. In short, technology provides an avenue for people to initiate contact across physical, ideological, and cultural distances. Whether such contact inflames or ameliorates intercultural conflict depends on the user.

In a relevant study of intergroup contact via new media channels, Walther, Hoter, Ganayem, and Shonfeld (2015) examined intergroup contact between Israeli Jews and Arabs working together in virtual teams. Contact was initiated over the course of an academic year via six member workgroups—two from each educational/religious center (e.g., Arab, secular Jewish, and religious Jewish). Overall, participants' negative attitudes toward their most disliked group diminished over time, as literature on intergroup contact would suggest. Importantly, the work teams were designed to meet the boundary conditions necessary to facilitate positive contact. Finally, the contact was facilitated through new media channels, providing evidence that intergroup contact, under certain conditions, can generate positive results in new media contexts.

The Internet was imagined by its initial designers as a place where people can meet and communicate with various others, regardless of their background and orientation (Rheingold, 1994). However, contextual factors such as one's gender, race/ethnicity, and religion still matter as people do not necessarily hide their background (except for anonymous or fake interactions), and use new media to find similar others who share similar interests and background. Thus, new media users do not necessarily seek out contact with different others, so the reduction of prejudice through the use of new media is not necessarily guaranteed. Next, theories related to computer-mediated communication will be considered for their applicability to intercultural conflict.

SIDE and SIP/Hyperpersonal Model of Computer-Mediated Communication

Bou-Franch and Blitvich (2014) argue that the study of conflict in digital environments requires new theoretical models to be developed. However, before researchers consider completely new models, one potential avenue of fruitful integration pertains to the applicability of current computer-mediated communication theories to intercultural conflict over new media. Two theoretical approaches from this area are potentially relevant: the social identity model of deindividuation effects (SIDE; Lea & Spears, 1992), which focuses on how visual anonymity influences online group interaction, and social information processing theory/the hyperpersonal communication model (Walther, 1992; 1996), which focus more on interpersonal processes in computer-mediated communication. Hoter, Shonfeld, and Ganayem (2009) have suggested that the hyperpersonal communication model is particularly promising due to implications for interethnic/intercultural conflict resolution.

SIDE

When researchers think of groups and computer-mediated communication (CMC), the SIDE model (Lea & Spears, 1992; Reicher, Spears, & Postmes, 1995) often comes to mind due to its focus on group-level factors. This model specifies two ways in which CMC changes social relationships: users' social identification and self-categorization (Tajfel & Turner, 1986). The first necessary component for deindividuation effects is the visual *anonymity* of text-based CMC in which communicators lose awareness of their own and others' individuality. The second component of the theory refers to how CMC users identify themselves with a salient social category or group when they are deindividuated. If they experience a *social identification*, users relating to other CMC users form a unified perception of others online based on whether they belong to the same group or not (i.e., salient ingroup). SIDE originally predicted this unified perception causes systemic attraction toward ingroup members (Lea, Spears, & de Groot, 2001). However, the research on social identification in visually anonymous settings has not produced consistent findings, especially on members' identification with general social categories (e.g., nationality, gender; Postmes, Spears, & Lea, 2002; Tanis & Postmes, 2003). This led to revisions of the theory and SIDE theorists now argue that it is the inability to tell who is online (i.e., depersonalization), not necessarily deindividuation, that causes unified perceptions and attractions toward ingroup members.

SIDE can be promising for intercultural conflict associated with intergroup animosities as prejudices between groups may decrease based on anonymous online group-based interactions (Amichai-Hamburger & McKenna, 2006; Walther,

2009). Nevertheless, most SIDE studies did not conduct their experiments with participants from different offline social groups; even when they employed such a setting (e.g., Rogers & Lea, 2004; English vs. Dutch), the research outcome did not support increased social identification. In addition, Wang, Walther, and Hancock (2009) and Walther et al. (2015) showed stronger support for interpersonal rather than intergroup dynamics. Therefore, whether anonymous online interaction will usually lead to attraction toward ingroup members (who may be from different cultural groups) is not certain.

In order to test further SIDE-like effects in the context of interethnic/intercultural communication, research should examine whether being informed about the cultural outgroup membership of interaction partners *before* or *after* anonymous online interactions (during which members from different cultures are put into one task group) influences people's post-hoc attitudes toward the other cultural group/members. If participants learn their group members' cultural background *before* the interaction, their preexisting opinions may influence their interactions. If they learn multicultural membership of their virtual groups *after* the interaction, they may be pleasantly surprised and form more favorable attitudes toward cultural outgroups (to justify or make sense of their positive interactions within the group). Distinguishing the valence of the interaction, similar to the case of the contact hypothesis (Allport, 1954), may help clarify when group-level identification predicts group members' beliefs.

Manipulating visual aspects in CMC, such as the uniform appearance of avatars, can also induce group identification and perceived deindividuation (Kim & Park, 2011), providing opportunities to decrease intercultural conflict. However, individuals also desire to maintain their balance between assimilation with others and uniqueness as individuals (Brewer, 1991; Kim, 2010); thus, being too similar with other group members can trigger unwillingness to follow group norms (Kim & Park, 2011). Simultaneously, excessive amounts of idiosyncrasy within a group make members seek a common frame of reference, such as a larger collective (e.g., gender, nationality, human race). Therefore, the effects of visual cues in CMC groups are contingent upon the composition of the group, one factor being the uniformity (or idiosyncrasy) of members' appearances.

Thus, the importance of the SIDE theory to intercultural conflict seems to lie in its potential effect on group members' communication patterns, depending on the composition of groups and visual settings (e.g., anonymous, visible with uniform or idiosyncratic appearance).

Walther (2009) argues that the greatest contribution of SIDE lies in the intersection between social identification and interpersonal communication. Walther et al. (2015) challenged the assumptions of SIDE by showing that group identification was not significantly associated with virtual group members' attitude change toward their cultural "outgroup" (e.g., Israeli Jews toward Arabs, and vice versa). The study found identification with one's virtual group did not predict outgroup attitudes. However, relational communication, social attraction, and task attraction were all significantly correlated with attitudes towards outgroups. Walther et al. concluded that liking of individual virtual group members, not liking of one's group as a whole, decreased prejudicial attitudes toward cultural outgroups after successful task performance over a year. Therefore, they suggested that individual factors were more important than group factors when decreasing intergroup prejudice. The next section will examine CMC theories that focus more on interpersonal factors to explore how various features and affordances of new media affect intercultural conflict given Walther et al.'s (2015) findings.

SIP/Hyperpersonal Communication

Social information processing (SIP) theory (Walther, 1992) claims that face-to-face and computer-mediated groups can reach similar levels of closeness, if the computer-mediated group is provided sufficient time to build relationships among members. As such, SIP theory illustrates that it is possible to build close, personal relationships online. The hyperpersonal model of CMC (Walther, 1996) explains how CMC may foster impression and relationship development online that *exceeds* the intimacy and desirability of offline interactions. The hyperpersonal model includes the influences of (1) receiver effects; (2) sender effects; (3) channel effects; and (4) feedback effects.

Receiver effects relate to the message receivers' exaggerated perceptions of similarities between themselves and their online communication partners, which lead to the formation of idealized images of their partners. This distorted perception is based on the lack of visual and/or social cues of most CMC settings in which receivers fill in missing information to form certain impressions of their interaction partners. If members from different ethnic/cultural groups meet in *visually anonymous* online settings to discuss common interests, such as hobbies that are not directly related to ethno-political conflicts among them, their perception of similarity may contribute to the formation of idealized images of each other. Even in the age of social media when users are required to have an authentic profile with photos and real names, people sometimes lie about themselves by creating fake profiles. Also, even if we have "visual" information on social media, most communication on social media is still text-based; thus, as long as interactants are separated by a certain physical distance, and mostly communicate through mediated means, it is possible to form idealized images of the other.

Sender effects indicate how CMC users construct certain images of themselves in preferential ways so that they will be perceived as desirable interaction partners.

Selective disclosure about oneself and asking personal questions during CMC breed more intimacy than in face-to-face communication. The *editability* of social media is related to this optimal self-presentation as users can edit their profile information and posts to strategically manage online impressions.

Channel effects relate to the ability to make optimal self-presentations based on the mechanical features (e.g., asynchronicity, lack of social cues) and affordances (e.g., editability, visibility, and association) of CMC. Users can take time to contemplate and construct favorable online messages without interfering with conversational flow (unlike the case of in-person interactions) thanks to *asynchronicity*. They can also *edit* posts as they discover their interaction partners may not perceive certain contents favorably.

Last, *feedback effects* are based on behavioral confirmation (Snyder, Tanke, & Berscheid, 1977): how one interactant's impression of the other leads the former to behave in a certain way, and how that behavior influences, in return, the responses of the latter. A CMC user's idealized impression of a partner may lead the user to reciprocate based on such a positive impression, delivering messages that may positively influence the partner's responses. Feedback processes, facilitated by the high *interactivity* of CMC users, can intensify hyperpersonal effects of receiver idealization, sender's selective presentation, and channel usage.

Hoter et al.'s (2009) study with virtual groups formed across colleges attended by religious Jews, secular Jews, or Islamic Arabs showed support for the hyperpersonal model. Group members interacted over the term and formed relatively strong bonds despite their distinctive religious orientations. Participants acknowledged the benefit of initial online interactions that allowed them to "feel less threatened and be more open and frank with one another" (Hoter et al., 2009, p. 9). The component of later in-person interactions also contributed to their positive relationship formation.

Walther (2009) suggests connections between CMC and a particular type of intercultural conflict by relating the hyperpersonal effect to the contact hypothesis' requirements for reducing intergroup prejudice. First, the *focus of discussion* over CMC may affect whether a reduction in prejudice occurs. When CMC members are not reminded of their intergroup differences, and collaborate on external tasks, they are more likely to develop interpersonal relationships with one another compared to the case when intergroup (or intercultural) differences or conflict become salient to them (Walther, 1995). For example, research by Ellis and Maoz (2007) on CMC between Israeli Jews and Palestinians was conducted in a setting where participants were aware of each other's background and were asked to discuss conflict resolution between the two ethnopolitical groups. Participants were less engaged in the issue and only exchanged short sequences of counter arguments and disagreements that did not contribute to articulation of their points, suggesting that focusing the discussion in this manner was not effective.

Second, the *process of failure and blame* may occur differently when communicating over CMC (Walther, 2009). When virtual group members collaborate and problems occur, they often blame their remotely located partners (Walther & Bazarova, 2008); however, if they are constantly reminded to look for some external reason that may be influencing their partners' performances, their dispositional attributions decline (Walther, 2009). This may suggest that a third-party mediation may often be needed to make online interactions between partners from different cultures smooth and productive.

Third, the *time* spent interacting over CMC makes a difference (Walther, 2009). As stated previously, SIP theory (Walther, 1992) predicts that it is possible to develop equally close interpersonal relationships over time via text-based CMC. Ad hoc, short-term online groups are known to have negative communication (Walther, 2009) that can develop into cyberbullying and trolling. People are more likely to engage in such antisocial behaviors online when they do not expect to meet the target in the near future (i.e., anonymity). Therefore, when facilitating intercultural collaboration online, a sufficient amount of time needs to be assigned to the interacting group, and interactants need to respond to each other promptly.

Fourth, the *interaction patterns* between the communicators using computer-mediated means affect whether a reduction in outgroup prejudice occurs (Walther, 2009). Research has found group members' communication patterns influence their trust, liking, and work output (Chen, Chiu, & Wang, 2012; Walther, 2009; Weisband & Atwater, 1999). Contrary to SIDE theory's original predictions about irrelevance or minimal effect of interpersonal dynamics, group members' frequent message exchanges, showing interest in other members' responses, and taking initiative and providing feedback all mattered to their liking and performance (Walther, 2009). For example, Chen et al. (2012) found agreements in online discussion increased the likelihood of positive social cue usage, whereas disagreements increased the likelihood of negative social cue usage. Also, in terms of the content of the online discussions, justifications reduced positive social cues usage, whereas new ideas reduced negative social cues usage. Walther and Bunz's (2005) study also demonstrated that virtual group members' interaction patterns could be managed by providing participants rules to facilitate positive outcomes such as higher trust, better self-evaluation of work quality, and higher external evaluation of the work quality. Based on these research findings, setting up rules of interactions (e.g., positive social cues, respectful disagreement, encouraging new ideas and limiting justification) has the potential to enhance intercultural conflict resolution over CMC.

Finally, the degree to which individuals use multimedia (i.e., *convergency* of new media) affects intergroup prejudice (Walther, 2009). For short-term groups, seeing participants' photos increased their attraction to one another; however, distributed groups without photos developed higher levels of affection and attraction over time, whereas seeing photos at later time points decreased their liking (Walther, Slovacek, & Tidwell, 2001). Based on these research findings, visually anonymous online settings such as chat room, Reddit, or blogs may be more suitable than social network sites or video chats (e.g., Skype, Facetime) for developing interethnic/intercultural relationships with less room for prejudice and stereotyping.

This section has suggested ways in which traditional intercultural and computer-mediated communication theories may be relevant to understanding intercultural conflict over new media. The next section will suggest additional future directions for research in this area and practical applications of the material discussed in this chapter.

SOLUTIONS AND RECOMMENDATIONS

White, Harvey, and Hisham (2015) provide some specific suggestions for using new media to reduce intercultural conflict between cultures that have traditionally had challenging relationships, such as Israeli Jews and Arabs. They suggest that communicating over CMC is particularly conducive for potentially positive interaction between groups with high intergroup tension or those separated geographically. However, White et al. (2015) caution that the nature of CMC can lead to negative interactions between groups due to anonymity and problems with coordination, such as different expected response patterns. They suggest that researchers who wish to use CMC to improve intergroup relations consider how the aspects of each particular medium allow one to implement Allport's (1954) necessary conditions for contact that can lead to decreased prejudice. For example, equal status can be implemented by having equal numbers of ingroup and outgroup members who are similar to each other on demographic variables communicate. Different types of computer-mediated contacts encourage various degrees of attention to intergroup differences; individuals may feel less anxiety engaging initially over text-based methods. In addition, researchers can allow individuals from different cultures to pursue a common goal and provide enough time to potentially develop online friendships (similar to suggestions based on SIP; Walther, 1992). All of the above suggestions by White et al. (2015) could be implemented using new media, providing blueprints for researchers who wish to design projects using new media to decrease intergroup conflict.

However, when considering everyday (not structured) intercultural interaction between individuals, such careful design is not possible. Considering the absence of the above conditions in some new media may help researchers understand why intercultural conflict is occurring in certain instances. For example, as stated earlier, social media often provide access to one's networks. As such, the extended contact hypothesis (Wright, Aron, McLauglin-Volpe, & Ropp, 1997) may be more relevant in such situations. This hypothesis states that having a friend who has a friend in one's outgroup reduces outgroup prejudices. Researchers could examine whether overlapping social media networks (based on the affordance of association) lead to less conflict and prejudice between groups from different cultures.

FUTURE RESEARCH DIRECTIONS

In the same way that intercultural theories may need to be updated to explain more adequately how individuals engage in conflict across cultures using new media, this chapter has discussed that CMC theories also need to be examined to determine whether their boundary conditions include new media use to reduce intercultural conflict. This chapter has discussed three CMC theories and existing research on these theories that applies to new media. Next, the authors will suggest future research directions specifically related to intercultural conflict that would help expand the reach and question the applicability of these traditional theories. For example, SIDE (Lea & Spears, 1992) focuses on group-level variables and visual anonymity. However, further theorizing and empirical tests related to this theory (e.g., Walther, 2009; Walther et al., 2015) provide evidence that the interpersonal relationships formed between individuals from different cultures and the interaction patterns between them may have greater implications for intercultural conflict over new media.

Whether traditional CMC theories apply especially to social media must be examined. Both SIDE theory and the hyperpersonal model of CMC were proposed before the age of social media. Although not always, social media usually have a component in which users upload photos of themselves or other representatives of themselves (e.g., pet, landscape, etc.). Much social media communication is a combination of texts and visuals (photos or videos) that users post with updates about their daily lives, or to share news. Hyperpersonal communication effects may still be observed on social media as users can strategically present themselves by selecting their best visual images or describing their lives as socially desirable (i.e., editability). However, on social media, individuals are judged by the company they keep. If a social media profile owner's friends' photos are not perceived as attractive, that can affect the profile owner's image negatively (Walther, Van Der Heide, Kim, Westerman, & Tong, 2008). Also, friends' comments about the profile owner have more weight on others' perceptions of the owner than the owner's comments about himself or herself (Walther, Van Der Heide, Hamel, & Shulman, 2009). Reminding each other of one's ethnic and cultural background with visual information on social media is likely to make social categories more salient; thus, it is possible that ingroup-outgroup dynamics and intergroup conflicts worsen online.

On the other hand, boyd and Ellison (2008) argue group identification may be *less* relevant, overall, in the age of social media when users are connected person-to-person by online social networks. Despite the available visual information that cues one's social and cultural background, social media users may pay more attention to individual and personal characteristics of their contacts due to connections between mutual friends (i.e., association). If so, hyperpersonal communication on social media between members from different ethnic/cultural groups may contribute to reducing intergroup prejudice. One caveat exists, though: connections through social media are mainly based on people's offline social networks, which are heavily influenced by their social and group identifications (e.g., race, ethnicity, gender, nationality) and homophily (i.e., a dominant networking principle that social ties are more likely to be formed between similar people than between different people; McPherson, Smith-Lovin, & Cook, 2001). Therefore, the basic question of how much contact individuals have with people from other cultures through social network sites also needs to be examined.

Idealization of one's partner through CMC (as predicted by the hyperpersonal model) may have particular relevance to understanding conflict between individuals of different cultures. Positive online interactions, including selective self-presentations and positive responses to such presentations, reinforce hyperpersonal CMC processes based on behavioral confirmation (i.e., feedback). Message senders experience identity shifts in line with reinforced positive self-images. How and whether those who may be prejudiced against some ethnic/cultural groups experience hyperpersonal CMC needs to be further examined (Walther et al., 2015).

Another possible impact of new media on hyperpersonal effects includes the increasing number of individuals playing computer games over distance. Computer games specifically developed for peace education seem promising as research has shown increased knowledge acquisition and attitude changes about proximate and distant intercultural conflicts (Kampf & Cuhadar, 2015). By enabling perspective- and role-taking of the other side based on various game scenarios, Israeli-Jewish, Palestinian, and Guatemalan students learned more about intergroup conflict issues, reappraised their ingroups, and understood the outgroups better. Similarly, being immersed in a virtual environment, such as Second Life, and learning about new cultures by interacting with avatars was found to be effective in nurturing intercultural sensitivity (Coffey, Kamhawi, Fishwick, & Henderson, 2013). Further research about the influences of online games is needed.

Finally, White et al. (2015) suggest that researchers examine how moving from text-based, to audio-based, to web-cam computer-mediated channels affects interaction between outgroups. Because various forms of new media incorporate each of these types of relating, they provide a powerful tool for examining such questions as whether synchronous versus asynchronous contact affects intercultural conflict, or whether richer media that allow more nonverbal cues, such as Skype, affect intercultural conflict differently than leaner media (e.g., email, discussion forums). Some CMC research has suggested that how individuals engage in conflict with interpersonal partners may differ based on whether the conflict is initiated face-to-face or is mediated (e.g., Lee, Bassick, & Wilson Mumpower, 2016). Such findings should be incorporated into future research concerning how intercultural partners engage in conflict using multiple types of new media.

CONCLUSION

The use of new media is expanding rapidly, and to understand fully how intercultural conflict occurs today, a focus on these types of media must occur. New media have certain features and affordances that can affect interaction between individuals of different cultures. This review has focused on areas where research has been conducted regarding new media and intercultural conflict, such as planned interventions using new media to seek to reduce this type of conflict, and research that has examined how individuals naturally use new media to engage in conflict. Many further research questions remain for scholars interested in understanding more fully and in more depth how new media influence the process of intercultural conflict.

REFERENCES

Alaimo, K. (2015). How the Facebook Arabic page “We Are All Khaled Said” helped promote the Egyptian revolution. *Social Media & Society*, *1*(2), 1–10. doi:10.1177/2056305115604854

Allport, G. W. (1954). *The nature of prejudice*. Cambridge, MA: Perseus Books.

Amichai-Hamburger, Y., Hasler, B. S., & Shani-Sherman, T. (2015). Structured and unstructured intergroup contact in the digital age. *Computers in Human Behavior*, *52*, 515–522. doi:10.1016/j.chb.2015.02.022

Amichai-Hamburger, Y., & McKenna, K. Y. A. (2006). The contact hypothesis reconsidered: Interacting via the Internet. *Journal of Computer-Mediated Communication*, *11*(3), 825–843. doi:10.1111/j.1083-6101.2006.00037.x

Awan, I. (2017). Cyber-extremism: ISIS and the power of social media. *Society*, *54*(2), 138–149. doi:10.1007/s12115-017-0114-0

Bennett, W. L., & Segerberg, A. (2011). Digital media and the personalization of collective action: Social technology and the organization of protests against the global economic crisis. *Information Communication and Society*, *14*(6), 770–799. doi:10.1080/1369118X.2011.579141

Bettencourt, B. A., Brewer, M. B., Croak, M. R., & Miller, N. (1992). Cooperation and the reduction of intergroup bias: The role of reward structure and social orientation. *Journal of Experimental Social Psychology*, *28*(4), 301–309. doi:10.1016/0022-1031(92)90048-O

Blaker, L. (2015). The Islamic State's use of online social media. *Military Cyber Affairs*, *1*(1). doi:10.5038/2378-0789.1.1.1004

Bou-Franch, P., & Blitvich, P. G.-C. (2014). Conflict management in massive polylogues: A case study from YouTube. *Journal of Pragmatics*, *73*, 19–36. doi:10.1016/j.pragma.2014.05.001

boyd, d., & Ellison, N. B. (2008). Social network sites: Definition, history, and scholarship. *Journal of Computer-Mediated Communication, 13*, 210-130. doi:10.1111/j.1083-6101.2007.00393.x

boyd, d. (2014). *It's complicated: The social lives of networked teens*. New Haven, CT: Yale University Press.

Brewer, M. B. (1991). The social self: On being the same and different at the same time. *Personality and Social Psychology Bulletin*, *17*(5), 475–482. doi:10.1177/0146167291175001

Brewer, M. B., & Miller, N. (1984). Beyond the contact hypothesis: Theoretical perspectives on desegregation. In N. Miller & M. B. Brewer (Eds.), *Groups in contact: The psychology of desegregation* (pp. 281–302). Orlando, FL: Academic Press. doi:10.1016/B978-0-12-497780-8.50019-X

Chen, G. M. (2012). The impact of new media on intercultural communication in global context. *China Media Research, 8,* 1-10. Retrieved from http://www.chinamediaresearch.net/index.php/submission/10-china-media-research/back-issues/54-vol-8-no-2

Chen, G. M., Chiu, M. M., & Wang, Z. (2012). Predicting social cues during online discussions: Effects of evaluations and knowledge content. *Computers in Human Behavior*, *28*(4), 1497–1509. doi:10.1016/j.chb.2012.03.017

Coffey, A. J., Kamhawi, R., Fishwick, P., & Henderson, J. (2013). New media environments' comparative effects upon intercultural sensitivity: A five-dimensional analysis. *International Journal of Intercultural Relations*, *37*(5), 605–627. doi:10.1016/j.ijintrel.2013.06.006

Ellis, D. G., & Maoz, I. (2007). Online argument between Israeli Jews and Palestinians. *Human Communication Research*, *33*(3), 291–309. doi:10.1111/j.1468-2958.2007.00300.x

Farwell, J. P. (2014). The media strategy of ISIS. *Survival > Global Politics and Strategy*, *56*. doi:10.1080/00396338.2014.985436

Gilboa, E. (2009). Media and conflict resolution: A framework for analysis. *Marquette Law Review*, *93*, 87–110. Retrieved from http://scholarship.law.marquette.edu/cgi/viewcontent.cgi?article=4927&context=mulr

Gladwell, M. (2010, October 4). Small change. *The New Yorker*, 42-49.

Gohdes, A. R. (2015). Pulling the plug: Network disruptions and violence in civil conflict. *Journal of Peace Research*, *52*(3), 352–367. doi:10.1177/0022343314551398

Gray, C. H., & Gordo, A. J. (2014). Social media in conflict: Comparing military and social-movement technocultures. *Cultural Politics*, *10*(3), 251–261. doi:10.1215/17432197-2795645

Hewstone, M., & Brown, R. J. (1986). Contact is not enough: An intergroup perspective on the contact hypothesis. In M. Hewstone & R. J. Brown (Eds.), *Contact and conflict in intergroup encounters* (pp. 1–44). Oxford, UK: Basil Blackwell.

Hocker, J. L., & Wilmot, W. W. (1978). *Interpersonal conflict*. Dubuque, IA: W. C. Brown.

Hoter, E., Shonfeld, M., & Ganayem, A. (2009). ICT in the service of multiculturalism. *International Review of Research in Open and Distance Learning*, *10*(2). Retrieved from http://www.irrodl.org/index.php/irrodl/article/view/601/1207

Howard, P. N., Duffy, A., Freelon, D., Hussain, M., Mari, W., & Mazaid, M. (2011). *Opening closed regimes: What was the role of social media during the Arab Spring?* Retrieved from http://pitpi.org/index.php/2011/09/11/opening-closed-regimes-what-was-the-role-of-social-media-during-the-arab-spring/

Kampf, R., & Cuhadar, E. (2015). Do computer games enhance learning about conflicts? A cross-national inquiry into proximate and distant scenarios in global conflicts. *Computers in Human Behavior*, *52*, 541–549. doi:10.1016/j.chb.2014.08.008

Kavanaugh, A. L., Sheetz, S. D., Sandoval-Almazan, R., Tedesco, J. C., & Fox, E. A. (2016). Media use during conflicts: Information seeking and political efficacy during the 2012 Mexican elections. *Government Information Quarterly*, *33*(3), 595–602. doi:10.1016/j.giq.2016.01.004

Kharroub, T., & Bas, O. (2015). Social media and protests: An examination of Twitter images of the 2011 Egyptian revolution. *New Media & Society*, *18*(9), 1973–1992. doi:10.1177/1461444815571914

Kim, J. (2010). Balancing uniqueness and assimilation in computer-mediated groups. *Computers in Human Behavior*, *26*(4), 778–784. doi:10.1016/j.chb.2010.02.001

Kim, J., & Park, H. (2011). The effect of uniform virtual appearance on conformity intention: Social identity model of deindividuation effects and optimal distinctiveness theory. *Computers in Human Behavior*, *27*(3), 1223–1230. doi:10.1016/j.chb.2011.01.002

Kim, Y. (2015). Does disagreement mitigate polarization? How selective exposure and disagreement affect political polarization. *Journalism & Mass Communication Quarterly*, *92*(4), 915–937. doi:10.1177/1077699015596328

Klausen, J. (2015). Tweeting the Jihad: Social media networks of western foreign fighters in Syria and Iraq. *Studies in Conflict and Terrorism*, *38*(1), 1–22. doi:10.1080/1057610X.2014.974948

Kluckhohn, C., & Kelly, W. H. (1945). The concept of culture. In R. Linton (Ed.), *The science of man in the world crisis* (pp. 78–106). New York, NY: Columbia University Press.

Lea, M., & Spears, R. (1992). Paralanguage and social perception in computer-mediated communication. *Journal of Organizational Computing*, *2*(3-4), 321–341. doi:10.1080/10919399209540190

Lea, M., Spears, R., & de Groot, D. (2001). Knowing me, knowing you: Anonymity effects on group polarization in CMC within groups. *Personality and Social Psychology Bulletin*, *27*, 526–537. doi:10.1177/0146167201275002

Lee, S., Bassick, M. A., & Wilson Mumpower, S. (2016). Fighting electronically: Long-distance romantic couples' conflict management over mobile communication. *Electronic Journal of Communication, 26*(3-4). Retrieved from http://www.cios.org/www/ejc/v26n34toc.htm

McPherson, M., Smith-Lovin, L., & Cook, J. M. (2001). Birds of a feather: Homophily in social networks. *Annual Review of Sociology*, *27*(1), 415–444. doi:10.1146/annurev.soc.27.1.415

Meis, M. (2017). When is a conflict a crisis? On the aesthetics of the Syrian civil war in a social media context. *Media, War & Conflict*, *10*(1), 69–86. doi:10.1177/1750635216653903

Moghaddam, F. M. (2005). The staircase to terrorism: A psychological exploration. *The American Psychologist*, *60*(2), 161–169. doi:10.1037/0003-066X.60.2.161 PMID:15740448

Morozov, E. (2009, May 19). Foreign policy: Brave new world of slacktiv-ism. *NPR*. Retrieved from http://www.npr.org/templates/story/ story.php?storyId=104302141

Paolini, S., Harwood, J., & Rubin, M. (2010). Negative intergroup contact makes group memberships salient: Explaining why intergroup conflict endures. *Personality and Social Psychology Bulletin*, *36*(12), 1723–1738. doi:10.1177/0146167210388667 PMID:21051766

Paolini, S., Harwood, J., Rubin, M., Husnu, S., Joyce, N., & Hewstone, M. (2014). Positive and extensive intergroup contact in the past buffers against the disproportionate impact of negative contact in the present. *European Journal of Social Psychology*, *44*(6), 548–562. doi:10.1002/ejsp.2029

Pettigrew, T. F., & Tropp, L. R. (2006). A meta-analytic test of intergroup contact theory. *Journal of Personality and Social Psychology*, *90*(5), 751–783. doi:10.1037/0022-3514.90.5.751 PMID:16737372

Postmes, T., Spears, R., & Lea, M. (2002). Inter-group differentiation in computer-mediated communication: Effects of depersonalization. *Group Dynamics*, *6*(1), 3–16. doi:10.1037/1089-2699.6.1.3

Reicher, S., Spears, R., & Postmes, T. (1995). A social identity model of deindividuation phenomena. *European Review of Social Psychology*, *6*(1), 161–198. doi:10.1080/14792779443000049

Rheingold, H. (1994). *The virtual community*. Retrieved from http://www.rheingold.com/vc/book/3.html

Rogers, P., & Lea, M. (2004). Cohesion in online groups. In K. Morgan, C. A. Brebbia, J. Sanchez, & A. Voiskounsky (Eds.), *Human perspectives in the Internet society: Culture, psychology and gender* (pp. 115–124). Southampton, UK: WIT Press.

Shah, R., Chauhan, N., Gupta, A. K., & Sen, M. S. (2016). Adolescent-parent conflict in the age of social media: Case reports from India. *Asian Journal of Psychiatry*, *23*, 24–26. doi:10.1016/j.ajp.2016.07.002 PMID:27969073

Shuter, R. (2012). Intercultural new media studies: The next frontier in intercultural communication. *Journal of Intercultural Communication Research*, *41*(3), 219–237. doi:10.1080/17475759.2012.728761

Snow Bailard, C. (2015). Ethnic conflict goes mobile: Mobile technology's effect on the opportunities and motivations for violent collective action. *Journal of Peace Research*, *52*(3), 323–337. doi:10.1177/0022343314556334

Snyder, M., Tanke, E. D., & Berscheid, E. (1977). Social perception and interpersonal behavior: On the self-fulfilling nature of social stereotypes. *Journal of Experimental Social Psychology*, *35*, 656–666. doi:10.1037/0022-3514.35.9.656

Stern, J., & Berger, J. M. (2015). *ISIS: The state of terror*. New York, NY: Harper Collins.

Tajfel, H., & Turner, J. (1986). The social identity theory of intergroup behavior. In S. Worchel & W. Austin (Eds.), *Psychology of intergroup relations* (2nd ed.; pp. 7–24). Chicago, IL: Nelson-Hall.

Tanis, M., & Postmes, T. (2003). Social cues and impression formation in CMC. *Journal of Communication*, *53*(4), 676–693. doi:10.1111/j.1460-2466.2003.tb02917.x

Treem, J. W., & Leonardi, P. M. (2012). Social media use in organizations: Exploring the affordances of visibility, editability, persistence, and association. *Communication Yearbook*, *36*, 143–189. doi:10.2139/ssrn.2129853

Triandis, C. H. (1995). *Individualism and collectivism*. Boulder, CO: Westview Press.

Tufekci, Z. (2017). *Twitter and tear gas: The power and fragility of networked protest*. New Haven, CT: Yale University Press.

Van Niekerk, B., & Maharaj, M. (2013). Social media and information conflict. *International Journal of Communication, 7,* 1162-1184. doi:1932–8036/20130005

Walther, J. B. (1992). Interpersonal effects in computer-mediated interaction: A relational perspective. *Communication Research*, *19*(1), 52–90. doi:10.1177/009365092019001003

Walther, J. B. (1995). Relational aspects of computer-mediated communication: Experimental observations over time. *Organization Science*, *6*(2), 186–203. doi:10.1287/orsc.6.2.186

Walther, J. B. (1996). Computer-mediated communication: Impersonal, interpersonal, and hyperpersonal interaction. *Communication Research*, *23*(1), 3–43. doi:10.1177/009365096023001001

Walther, J. B. (2009). Computer-mediated communication and virtual groups: Applications to interethnic conflict. *Journal of Applied Communication Research*, *37*(3), 225–238. doi:10.1080/00909880903025937

Walther, J. B., & Bazarova, N. (2008). Validation and application of electronic propinquity theory to computer-mediated communication in groups. *Communication Research*, *35*(5), 622–645. doi:10.1177/0093650208321783

Walther, J. B., & Bunz, U. (2005). The rules of virtual groups: Trust, liking, and performance in computer-mediated communication. *Journal of Communication*, *55*(4), 828–846. doi:10.1111/j.1460-2466.2005.tb03025.x

Walther, J. B., Hoter, E., Ganayem, A., & Shonfeld, M. (2015). Computer-mediated communication and the reduction of prejudice: A controlled longitudinal field experiment among Jews and Arabs in Israel. *Computers in Human Behavior*, *52*, 550–558. doi:10.1016/j.chb.2014.08.004

Walther, J. B., Slovacek, C., & Tidwell, L. C. (2001). Is a picture worth a thousand words? Photographic images in long term and short term virtual teams. *Communication Research*, *28*(1), 105–134. doi:10.1177/009365001028001004

Walther, J. B., Van Der Heide, B., Hamel, L., & Shulman, H. (2009). Self-generated versus other-generated statements and impressions in computer-mediated communication: A test of warranting theory using Facebook. *Communication Research*, *36*(2), 229–253. doi:10.1177/0093650208330251

Walther, J. B., Van Der Heide, B., Kim, S., Westerman, D., & Tong, S. T. (2008). The role of friends' appearance and behavior on evaluations of individuals on Facebook: Are we known by the company we keep? *Human Communication Research*, *34*(1), 28–49. doi:10.1111/j.1468-2958.2007.00312.x

Wang, Z., Walther, J. B., & Hancock, J. T. (2009). Social identification and interpersonal communication in computer-mediated communication: What you do versus who you are in virtual groups. *Human Communication Research*, *35*(1), 59–85. doi:10.1111/j.1468-2958.2008.01338.x

Warren, T. C. (2015). Explosive connections? Mass media, social media, and the geography of collective violence in African states. *Journal of Peace Research, 52*(3), 297–311. doi:10.1177/0022343314558102

Weidmann, N. B. (2015). Communication networks and the transnational spread of ethnic conflict. *Journal of Peace Research, 52*(3), 285–296. doi:10.1177/0022343314554670

Weisband, S., & Atwater, L. (1999). Evaluating self and others in electronic and face-to-face groups. *The Journal of Applied Psychology, 84*(4), 632–639. doi:10.1037/0021-9010.84.4.632

White, F. A., Harvey, L. J., & Hisham, A.-R. M. (2015). Improving intergroup relations in the Internet age: A critical review. *Review of General Psychology, 19*(2), 129–139. doi:10.1037/gpr0000036

Wright, S. C., Aron, A., McLaughlin-Volpe, T., & Ropp, S. A. (1997). The extended contact effect: Knowledge of cross-group friendships and prejudice. *Journal of Personality and Social Psychology, 73*(1), 73–90. doi:10.1037/0022-3514.73.1.73

Zeitzoff, T. (2017). How social media is changing conflict. *Journal of Conflict Resolution, 61*(9), 1970–1991. doi:10.1177/0022002717721392

Zeitzoff, T. (2018). Does social media influence conflict? Evidence from the 1012 Gaza conflict. *The Journal of Conflict Resolution, 62*(1), 29–63. doi:10.1177/0022002716650925

Zeitzoff, T., Kelly, J., & Lotan, G. (2015). Using social media to measure foreign policy dynamics: An empirical analysis of the Iranian-Israeli confrontation (2012-13). *Journal of Peace Research, 52*(3), 368–383. doi:10.1177/0022343314558700

ADDITIONAL READING

Orbe, M. P., & Everett, M. A. (2006). Interracial and interethnic conflict and communication in the United States. In J. G. Oetzel & S. Ting-Toomey (Eds.), *The SAGE handbook of conflict communication* (pp. 575–594). Thousand Oaks, CA: Sage. doi:10.4135/9781412976176.n21

KEY TERMS AND DEFINITIONS

Affordances: The characteristics of an object that allow one to use the object for specific purposes.

Contact Hypothesis: The prediction that, given that certain requirements are met, contact between individuals of different cultures should result in less prejudice.

Hyperpersonal Model: Predicts that in certain cases, relationships developed over computer-mediated channels can actually be emotionally closer than those that develop face-to-face.

Intercultural Communication: Communicative exchanges between members of different cultural groups.

Slacktivism: Shallow involvement that online activists are perceived to have in a cause.

Social Identity Model of Deindividuation Effects (SIDE): A theory that focuses on group-level characteristics and how the perception of these characteristics affects individuals' perceptions of their in-group.

Social Information Processing Model (SIP): Predicts that face-to-face and computer-mediated groups can reach similar levels of performance and relationship development as long as the computer-mediated group is given sufficient time to interact.

Chapter 8
Facebook and the Interaction of Culture and Conflict

Godfrey A. Steele
The University of the West Indies, Trinidad and Tobago

ABSTRACT

The intersection of culture and conflict is relatively understudied in communication, focusing on mass-self communication and power relations and new media scholarship. Conflict and the cultural dimensions in media coverage are well documented, but with less attention to new media cultural settings, often limited to use as one-way broadcasting media or as audiencing participants in social media marketing. Potentially more interactive communication exists within a closed community, especially because Facebook has defining cultural, psychological, and psychosocial characteristics. Conflict message interactions facilitate studying the intersection of culture and conflict within a new media setting. This chapter focuses on conflict within the cultural context of Facebook closed communities, theorizes about this relationship, and tests its application.

INTRODUCTION

This chapter reviews the literature on conflict and culture, focusing on their intersection. It integrates concepts from culture and conflict to analyse their mutual influence and develops a theoretical framework for studying culture and conflict. Adopting a methodological approach to investigating and understanding the intersection between culture and conflict in interactions, this chapter presents an empirical test of this methodological framework, reports the results of studying culture and conflict, discusses the thematic results and discusses their significance

DOI: 10.4018/978-1-5225-3784-7.ch008

and implications for theorizing and testing a model of studying culture and conflict. It concludes with a commentary on the intersection of culture and conflict within online closed communities in Facebook.

BACKGROUND

Why Study Culture and Conflict on Facebook?

Overview

The intersection of culture and conflict is a relatively understudied area of new media communication research. Embedded within such research are paradigms of mass-self communication and power relations (Castells, 2013) and new media scholarship (Boyd & Ellison, 2008). Conflict in media coverage is well documented (Arno, 2009), but there has been less attention to conflict within a new media cultural setting or to intractable conflict (Bar-Tal, Abutbul-Selinger, & Raviv, 2014), or to imagining such communities in newer media settings (Conboy, 2006). Even when such communities exist in social media networks such as Facebook, they are often limited to being used as one-way broadcasting media, among politicians for example, without real interaction (Ross, Fountaine & Comrie, 2015) or as audience participants in social media marketing (Fisher, 2015). There is potentially more interactive communication, with resulting opportunities for the intersection of culture and conflict within a closed community, especially as research on Facebook has defining cultural (Köhl & Götzenbrucker, 2014), psychological (Anderson, Fagan, Woodnutt, & Chamorro-Premuzic, 2012) and psychosocial characteristics such as oversharing (Agger, 2015). The conflict messages in interactions among members of a community offer an opportunity to study the intersection of culture and conflict within a new media setting. This chapter focuses on conflict within the cultural context of Facebook closed communities, theorizes about this relationship and tests its application.

A SYSTEMATIC REVIEW OF THE CULTURE AND CONFLICT LITERATURE IN NEWER MEDIA SETTINGS

A systematic review of the literature derived from a search of "Facebook AND culture" published between 1978 and 2017 produced extensive results for peer-reviewed journal articles (n=19,811). Refinement of this scoping search yielded fewer, but substantially high results for peer-reviewed articles for the period 2004-

2017(n=19076). Prior to the research for this chapter, extensive studies had been conducted on the definition, history, development and features of social networking sites for the period 1997-2006 (Boyd & Ellison, 2008) and a narrative review of scholarship on social support based on SNS platforms for the period 2004-2017 (Meng et al., 2017).

For the purpose of this chapter's focus on culture and conflict on Facebook and the implications for reconceptualizing new media, it was decided to narrow the search to "Facebook AND culture AND conflict". This refinement yielded 5,810 peer-reviewed articles from several databases such as ProQuest, Social Sciences Citation Index (Web of Science), Science Citation Index, Medline, Emerald, Informa, Taylor and Francis, Springer and JSTOR among the top 20. Further refinement led to 4,747 peer-reviewed articles. An additional refinement to include only 2004-2017 led to 4728 results. Another refinement for the period 2004-2017, focusing on studies yielded 956 results, of which there were experimental/theoretical (n=336), social networks (n=255), communication (n=70) items and social media (n=65).

A decision was made to restrict the search to "Facebook AND culture AND conflict" with filters focusing on experimental/theoretical and social network studies for the period 2007-2017. This strategy yielded substantially fewer results (n=97). Fifty-nine (59) were directly relevant. These articles were analysed thematically and resulted in seven major emphases. These seven themes included social business/marketing potential and threats, online communities (brand love and social identity on Facebook, members' contribution of knowledge to online communities, country of origin (COO) and image, brand loyalty, social media love and the look of the Other, social media's potential for supporting virtue friendship, collaborative learning, and intergroup intractable conflict), approaches to studying social media platforms, organization members' use of social networks, comparing young users, online privacy, and social information behaviour. These seven themes are presented as findings in the fifth section based on the systematic literature review in this section.

EXPLORING AND DEFINING CONFLICT, CONFLICT MESSAGES AND INTERACTIONS IN NEWER MEDIA AND SOCIAL NETWORKING SITES

Conflict in Newer Media and Social Networking Sites

Few studies have addressed conflict within closed social media groups. Conflict in media coverage is well documented, but there has been less attention to conflict within a new media cultural setting. For example, conflict in traditional media coverage such as daily news reporting is often presented as a conflictual anthropological phenomenon (Arno, 2009). When intergroup conflict occurs over an extended period such as a generation and is unresolvable it may be described as intractable (Bar-Tal, Abutbul-Selinger, & Raviv, 2014), but there has been less attention to this phenomenon in newer media. In an alternative media setting it may be presented as contestation (Couldry & Curran, 2003), but there has been less attention to conflict in newer media environments. Similarly, while the imagining of a community of daily newspaper audiences captures the culture of such a community (Conboy, 2006), there has been less attention to imagining such communities in newer media settings. In a study of collaborative learning in the social media environment, Borstnar (2012) explored motivation, trust, and conflict among 24 students working in groups. It was theorized that an unstructured social media environment facilitates problem solving. For example, Borstnar (2012, p. 102) argued "based on the assumption that collaborative learning can be efficiently supported in a rule-free and social media unstructured environment, and that it has a positive impact on the self-organizing of the group and thus contributes to problem solving and learning."

Studying Conflict in Facebook

Borstnar's (2012) study of collaborative learning in the social media environment noted that although the effective use of ICT to support group collaboration was well-researched, there was less understanding of what happens in a less structured, rule-free and perhaps more chaotic social media environment. Borstnar (2012) investigated whether group knowledge in the group-learning process in a social media environment could be elicited. This was done by assigning 24 students to three groups and giving them tasks, conducting naturalistic observation, and measuring attitudes towards collaborative work using a questionnaire. The study's results suggested that motivation and trust were positively associated with self-management. However, increases in conflicts were associated with a decrease in formal structure and facilitation.

The rapid increase in social network sites, and their increasing popularity have brought new concerns about conflict. Will new media provide new platforms for the staging and working out of conflicts? Will new media be transformed by enduring human issues such as conflict or will they have a transformative impact on how conflict is managed? Intergroup intractable conflict occurs when groups have mutually incompatible goals which they each regard as essential to their survival (Bar-Tal, Abutbul-Selinger, & Raviv, 2014). Bar-Tal, Abutbul-Selinger, and Raviv (2014) reviewed intergenerational intractable conflicts across nationalities, states and over the course of history. They concluded that this type of conflict is often violent, and because of their long-lasting nature, the collective impact upon groups is the creation of a culture of conflict in which the conflicts are perceived to be zero-sum in nature. The question, then, for new media, is whether they can exert a new influence over the presence of intractable conflict or merely provide new arenas and tools for the perpetuation of conflict.

EXPLORING AND DEFINING CULTURE IN NEWER MEDIA AND SOCIAL NETWORKING SITES

Facebook Communities and Group Culture

Newer media not only offer opportunities to exert cultural influences and be influenced by cultural forces, but they constitute and evolve into cultures of their own. Affordances refer to the interface between the potential for action created by newer media and their tendency to predict the intensity of usage of aspects of the newer media (Kuo, Tseng, Tseng, & Lin, 2013). It is quite feasible to consider the extent to which the availability of the means to use social networks sites such as Facebook can influence the ways in which they are used and the degree to which such facilities, as afforded by these sites, actually predict user behavior.

This issue may be explored by considering what has been happening in the culture of the Facebook community of users. One way which SNS are involved is in the creation of social business and opportunities for marketing and innovation. Accordingly, there has been a call for business organizations as networks of communities interacting with clients to ensure that there is alignment between their leaders and their culture to facilitate this role for SNS.

Studying Culture in Facebook

Kuo et al.'s (2013) study investigated three social information affordances for expressive information control, privacy information control, and image information control in Facebook. The results demonstrated gender differences among users. Commenting on this outcome, the researchers noted

The results showed that the three affordances can significantly explain how Facebook's interface designs facilitate users' self-presentation activities. In addition, the findings reveal that males are more engaged in expressing information than females, while females are more involved in privacy control than males. A practical application of our study is to compare and contrast the level of affordances offered by various social network sites (SNS) like Facebook and Twitter, as well as differences in online self-presentations across cultures. Our approach can therefore be useful to investigate how SNS design features can be tailored to specific gender and culture needs (p. 635).

Thus, Kuo et al.'s (2013) study exemplifies a method for investigating the cultural dimension on Facebook.

A THEORETICAL FRAMEWORK FOR STUDYING CULTURE AND CONFLICT WITHIN AN ONLINE CLOSED COMMUNITY

Social Presence

Social presence (SP) has emerged as an area of interest related to culture and conflict in studying online closed communities such as Facebook (Rourke, Anderson, Garrison, & Archer, 2000). It consists of affective, interactive and cohesive components. The affective component is indicated by emotional expression, the use of humor, and disclosure behaviors. The interactive component is indicated by behaviors such as continuing or making links to previous conversation such as a reply to a thread, quoting from others' messages, referring explicitly to others' messages, asking questions, complimenting or expressing appreciation, and expressing agreement. The cohesive component consists of vocatives or direct ways of addressing participants by name, addressing a group using inclusive pronouns, using phatic communication and salutations that fulfil a social function, and using greetings and closures.

Conflict Messages

Conflict messages are embodied in posts among users. They may occur as elements within a post. These conflict messages may have integrative and disintegrative effects (Horton & Hunt, 1984). Participation in conflict messages could involve the creation and response to messages. Conflict messages are indicated by statements of mutually incompatible goals and are characterised by cognitive, behavioral and affective behaviors (Barki & Hartwick, 2004). These messages may be reflective of integrative and disintegrative outcomes (Horton & Hunt, 1984) and a range of conflict styles (Euwema, van der Vliet, & Bakker, 2003; Rahim, 1983). The degree and extent of participation are worth exploring. The production of conflict messages can be evident in the frequency and type of conflict style handling expressed in posts and responses to posts.

In searching the literature, the results of the search strategies, keywords such as culture and conflict were combined with Facebook and focused on experimental/theoretical studies and social network studies were reviewed for thematic patterns.

SOLUTIONS AND RECOMMENDATIONS:

Purpose, Objectives, Research Questions, and Method

This methodological approach utilises a systematic literature review to explore concepts and characteristics of culture and conflict in Facebook use among members of closed communities. The main objective is to identify patterns of concerns and research findings in relation to these variables. This approach seeks to answer the emergent research question focusing on the major themes in the literature review which offer perspectives on reconceptualization of new media such as Facebook. Details of the method adopted were provided in the first section.

Findings

1. **Social Business/Marketing Potential and Threats Emerged as a Major Theme**: The first aspect of this theme focuses on the role of the culture within organizations that seek to benefit from the use of social media to capitalize on opportunities for capturing value in marketing and innovation, as well as operations and leadership. Thus for online communities, it is recommended that the leadership and the culture of the communities should be aligned (Kiron, Palmer, Phillips, & Kruschwitz, 2012). A potentially negative dimension to the reliance on social media is posed by threats to a brand. These threats are referred to as "collaborative brand threats" which are planned, deliberate attacks on brands by large numbers of social media users (Rauschnabel, Kammerlander, & Ivens, 2016). In this regard, research is being developed to anticipate what can signal or anticipate these attacks (triggers), how these attacks can develop momentum (amplifiers) and how brand and reputation managers can respond effectively (reaction strategies) (Rauschnabel, Kammerlander, & Ivens, 2016). These two aspects of social business have implications for how online communities think of, and use social media. The first aspect, the social business/marketing potential, helps us to think of the positive uses to which online creators and users of content might put social media, and the role of organizational culture in facilitating marketing and innovation, especially. The second aspect alerts us to the potential danger and the strategic ways in which brand management can be challenged to be more resilient and adaptive in dealing with new arenas of conflict during interactions with users within their communities. This theme reflects a focus on culture as a critical variable in studying Facebook.
2. **Online Communities:** There were several aspects of this theme, not surprisingly, owing to the presence of online communities as a keyword among 26% or

roughly 1 in 4 of the 956 studies found. First, the formation and development of online communities has attracted attention among researchers. In one study (Goggins, Laffey, & Gallagher, 2011) researchers investigated the formation of patterns of interaction and the development of online group practices using six case studies. This study suggests another key role for culture as a key variable.

Second, another study (Ch'Ng, 2015) explored the formation, maintenance and disintegration of a fringe Twitter community to understand whether offline community structure applies to online communities – laboratory case using Big Data to track user-generated content to assess the significance of "particular user nodes" with centrality measures and to track "ego centralities" with time –series analysis. This method was used to determine whether online communities of this type are sustained by specific ego characteristics of users that support opposing ideologies and the creation of resilience among "desperate online users" who find ways to overcome social media limitations. This focus emphasizes both cultural and conflict variables.

Third, the role of brand love and social identity on Facebook was addressed in another study (Vernuccio, Pagani, Barbarrosa, & Pastore, 2015). This study identified the value of leveraging customers' social identity with experiences that engage them in a social-interactive manner to strengthen their emotional bond with a brand among online communities such as Facebook. Such engagement was further explored and confirmed in an experiential study (Wondwesen, 2016). This third aspect reflects a focus on culture. Fourth, this research highlights members' contribution of knowledge to online communities (Chou, 2010). This emphasis suggests the value of taking into account individual differences, extrinsic and intrinsic motivation, and how they relate to the knowledge members might wish to contribute in building online communities. Culture is once more accentuated in this aspect of online communities. Fifth, the focus is on the role of country of origin (COO) and how that relates to image and brand loyalty when globally recognized sports teams, for example, are associated positively with brands from that country (White & Absher, 2013). Culture is again reflected in this fifth aspect. Sixth, this example relates to how our perception of how the Other judges us (based on Sartre's social communication framework) is often influential in online communities (Lopato, 2016). Culture and identity are reflected in this aspect of research on online communities. Seventh, another aspect of online community research addresses social media's potential for supporting virtue friendship based on Aristotle's work (Elder, 2014). This aspect reflects the perspective of culture and its link to philosophy. Thus, these five aspects of research on online communities (examples 3-7) reflect a focus on culture as a key variable.

The eighth aspect of this research focuses on collaborative learning (Borstnar, 2012). This focus embraces both culture and conflict as key variables. The ninth aspect of online community research explores the role of intergroup intractable conflicts and the implications for social media (Bar-Tal, Abutbul-Selinger, & Raviv, 2014), with a focus on conflict as a variable. Altogether, these nine aspects of online community research, five focusing on culture and four on both culture and conflict, suggest that this is a fertile and generative area of research. Such interest implies that a potentially useful avenue for exploring and developing reconceptualizations of new media may exist in this line of research.

3. Approaches to studying uses of social media platforms include the data on user statistics, and their motivations for using specific aspects of online platforms that focus, for example, on understudied areas such as Twitter hashtags and Facebook favorites and more "destructive" activities as unfollowing (Weller, 2016). Both culture and conflict are reflected in this theme.
4. Organizational members' use of social networks has generated debate over its value (Moqbel, Nevo & Kock, 2013). This debate can be explored by investigating the role of organizational members' use of SNS and its effect on job satisfaction, perceived organizational commitment and job performance. Similar research has been conducted in relation to supervisor-subordinate communication (Steele & Plenty, 2015) but not with a focus on the context of SNS. Moqbel, Nevo and Kock (2013) contend that SNS rather than promoting presenteeism, or being at the workplace but working below peak capacity, can foster work-life balance, and demonstrate organizational commitment. Another aspect of members' contribution of knowledge to SNS lies in concerns about employee ignorance. One study found employees' ignorance could have a negative impact on their intention to share knowledge. This results in poor decision-making and communication in organizations, and can "limit the organizational ability to repel external threats, implement innovation and manage future risks" (Israilidis, Siachou, Cooke, & Lock, 2015, p. 1109). This research focus suggests the key role of culture as a variable in studying an online community such as Facebook.
5. Another interesting research theme lies, firstly, in comparing young users of social media. In one such comparison in France social platform use and cyber bullying was investigated and the researchers' findings recommended educating young users about a positive and safe use of the Internet seriously, and providing appropriate guidance, especially for primary school children (Blaya & Fartoukh, 2016). Secondly, the adolescent perspective is taken into account in proposing a "a conceptual model of social media consumption" to help them "identify positive and negative outcomes and the behavioral strategies of media selection and differentiation used to cope with them" (Hübner Barcelos & Vargas Rossi, 2014, p. 275). This theme reflects culture and conflict.

6. Online privacy (a component of the culture variable) is another critical research theme relating to SNS. There are two dimensions worth noting. There is a distinction between types of online privacy. In the context of online social networks (OSN), privacy between users is different from privacy between a user and a third party. Researchers explain the difference between interpersonal and third-party disclosure. In the first instance, based on symbolic interactionist accounts of privacy, "users are performing dramaturgically for an intended audience" (Heyman, De Wolf, & Pierson, 2014, p. 18). In the second instance, "third-party privacy is based on the data that represent the user in data mining and knowledge discovery processes, which ultimately manipulate users into audience commodities" (Heyman, De Wolf, & Pierson, 2014, p. 18). When these distinctions were applied to the privacy settings of Facebook, LinkedIn and Twitter the findings indicated "that users are granted more options in controlling their interpersonal information flow towards other users than third parties or service providers" (Heyman, De Wolf, & Pierson, 2014, p. 18). Related to online privacy is the issue of self-disclosure. Research on self-disclosure, (another component of the culture variable) focuses on personality factors which influence SNS users' motivation to disclose information about themselves as well as share information (Chen, Pan, & Guo, 2016).
7. **Social Information Behavior (SIB):** Various aspects of social information behavior have been researched. Six of them are described and are linked to issues of tension; fake identities, treats and attacks; the extent of national cultural influence; photo sharing; restrictions on occupational use of social media; and benefits and dangers. They reflect the culture and conflict perspectives.
    a. Serendipity and disruption (conflict): The rise in popularity of social media has led to its promotion as a platform for serendipity, but ironically this feature has been accompanied by disruption (Skågeby, 2012). According to Skågeby (2012), there are five prevalent tensions relating to social disruption: market logic and social logic; public and private; work and non-work; individual and collective; and IRL (In Real Life) or AFK (Away From Keyboard). These tensions reflect the conflict variable.
    b. Fake identities, threats, attacks (conflict): Modern challenges to security are posed by the use of fake identities, threats and attacks on SNS such as Facebook (Hoehle, Zhang, & Venkatesh, 2015; Krombholz, Merkl, & Weippl, 2012). This theme reflects the conflict variable.
    c. National culture has little effect on the relationship between usability constructs and continued intention to use mobile social media applications (Hoehle, Zhang, & Venkatesh, 2015). The culture variable is reflected in this theme.

d. Facebook photo sharing especially among adolescent users emerged as a popular activity on Facebook since its launch in 2005, and requires research (Malik, Dhir, & Nieminen, 2015). The culture variable is reflected in this theme.
e. As an example of occupational use, certified public accountants tend to never use Facebook, LinkedIn, Twitter, and chat rooms. They prefer traditional communication channels such as written documents and telephone call and electronic mail is used frequently with a few significant differences among gender, age, education level achieved, and number of employees in the firm (Rollins & Lewis, 2012). Culture is reflected in this theme.
f. The benefits and dangers of enjoyment of social networking sites were predicted (Turel & Serenko, 2012), but this has become an increasingly important area of research interest on new media. Culture is reflected in this theme.

Overall, these six aspects of social information behavior (SIB) reflect the underlying influence of conflict (examples 1-2) and culture (examples 3-6) on social media and SNS, and suggest six subthemes of SIB for reconceptualising new media.

FUTURE RESEARCH DIRECTIONS

Seven broad thematic areas have emerged from an analysis based on a systematic literature review of research on culture, conflict and Facebook focusing on selected studies. In some themes there are extensive subsections or subtopics associated with them, for example, online communities, and social information behaviour. These clusters suggest that these two areas have attracted much interest and perhaps reflect the most developed aspects of research. Perhaps they signal the potential significance of these themes and subtopics as areas for emphasis which may have implications for the reconceptualization of new media. Next, the implications for online communities and SIB, as two major themes, are discussed in some detail and reference is made to the other five.

In the case of online communities their formation, maintenance and dissolution can influence how new media develop and the trajectories of knowledge that are being developed. Reflection on this observation suggests that both culture and conflict exert considerable influence and are influenced by a focus on online communities on Facebook. In the case of closed communities, there are prospects for using current understandings and new knowledge to study and gain a better grasp of how such online communities are being shaped as cultural phenomena and may function as sites of mediatized conflict. These insights have relevance for users, co-creators of content, and managers and researchers studying new media. However, issues of access, privacy and ethical and practical issues related to insider research can create new, but not insurmountable challenges.

The focus on social information behaviour alerts researchers assessing and studying new media to the complexity and range of issues that have emerged. Again culture and conflict offer contextual groundings for this line of research. For example, issues relating to the potentially serendipitous and disruptive nature of new media, the related benefits and dangers of enjoying social media, and other issues such as privacy, disclosure, fake identities and threats indicate that these variables are likely to play a significant role in how new media are engaged, and are shaped, even as they shape cultural connections and conflict interactions on a platform such as Facebook, the largest SNS.

The influence of social media in changing the way persons connect or reconnect with others, entertain themselves, pursue leisure activities, shop and find jobs is recognized (Yusuf, Al-Banawi, & Rahman Al-Imam, 2014), but several challenges exist which can have implications for the reconceptualization of new media. A review and research agenda for understanding Generation Y and their use of social media (Bolton et al., 2013) acknowledged that prior research on Generation Y's social media use raised more questions than it answered. Bolton et al.'s (2013) critique of such research argued that its primary focus was on the USA and perhaps one or other country, "ignoring other regions with large and fast-growing Generation Y populations where social-media use and its determinants may differ significantly"; tended to "study students whose behaviors may change over their life cycle stages"; relied on "self-reports by different age groups to infer Generation Y's social media use"; and did "not examine the drivers and outcomes of social-media use". These reviewers noted that their paper provided a conceptual framework for considering the antecedents and consequences of Generation Y's social media usage. This chapter argues that one problematic consequence or impact relates to the use of social media in negative ways.

One particularly problematic and negative impact is that social media may be used to perpetuate and promote online threats such as cyber bullying, bullying and victimization. These practices pose risks to children and young people and more generally to persons in workplace settings. These risks include cyber bullying, privacy breaches, reputational damage and assault on personal dignity on SNS, in addition to hazards associated with geo-tagging, facial recognition techniques and the spreading of viruses using social media (Haynes & Robinson, 2015). In critiquing commonly used definitions of risk such as "a situation involving exposure to danger" or "the possibility that something unpleasant or unwelcome will happen", Haynes and Robinson observed that these examples are "not very specific and need to be pinned down (Pearsall & Hanks, 1999, p. 1602)." Haynes and Robinson (2015, p. 97) offered this definition: "risk is defined as an uncertain event which has an adverse impact on an activity or outcome. Applied here, risk is an event of unknown probability of occurrence involving personal data on an SNS that has a negative impact on that person". Haynes and Robinson recommended that for regulatory purposes concerned with the management and mitigation of risk, an analysis of the occurrence of risk events and their consequences can provide a basis for evaluating different regulatory approaches. This approach offers a way to reconceptualize treating with cyber bullying and bullying on SNS and via social media.

One consequence of the negative use of new media is workplace bullying. An examination of whether job satisfaction and work-related depression played a role in mediating the relationship between workplace bullying and job satisfaction, and work-related depression, play a role in mediating the relationship between workplace bullying 'and three forms of employee performance or behaviors: task performance, individual-targeted citizenship behavior (OCB-I), and interpersonal counterproductive work behavior (CWB-P)" in a small developing Caribbean country found that "job satisfaction alone partially mediated the relationship between workplace bullying and task performance, whereas work-related depression alone partially mediated the relationship between workplace bullying and OCB-I. Both job satisfaction and work-related depression partially mediated the relationship between workplace bullying and CWB-P." (Devonish, 2013).

Another consequence is the impact on children and youth. Using self-report survey data from over 3000 middle and high school students in a Midwest US city, Baker and Pelfrey (2016) explored the effect of experiencing the strains of traditional bullying victimization and cyber bullying victimization on adolescents' self-reported soft drug use, hard drug use, and weapon carrying behavior among both frequent and infrequent users of social networking sites. The results indicated that cyber bullying victimization and the anticipated strain of feeling unsafe at or on the way to or from school were significantly and positively associated with the three ways of delinquent coping among both sets of social network users (Baker & Pelfrey, 2016). This finding suggests there are similar negative consequences of traditional bullying and cyber bullying via social media and confirms an earlier finding (Lampert & Donoso, 2012). Given this finding of similar negative consequences, it would be useful to explore the impact of strategies used to counteract traditional bullying when applied in new media environments. It raises the possibility of reconceptualizing new media as parallel or complementary vehicles for social support for victims.

Social support affords victims of bullying a recourse to help from family and friends in (77% of online cases, or about four out of five children), but the most common responses were solving the problem on one's own (31%) or hoping the problem would go away (24%) (Livingstone, Haddon, Görzig, & Ólafsson, 2011,

p. 71). Interestingly "children who experience more psychological difficulties are more likely to be victims or perpetrators of cyberbullying" (Lampert & Donoso, 2012, p. 146). Despite the acknowledged value of social support in helping bullying victims to cope, there is some inconsistency in what kind of social support is actually helpful and a lack of understanding of why there is inconsistency (Matsunaga, 2011). Possible theoretical ways of understanding such inconsistency include learning about the extent of victims' positive appraisal, and to a lesser extent, esteem support or network support, and the gap between desired and received support. To date these issues have been studied in the context of post bullying adjustment in a retrospective (recall-based) study of four face-to-face bullying situations (collectively, physical, indirect, material harm, and online) among college students under 20 (Matsunaga, 2011), but not specifically in a separate social media or SNS context using actual *in situ* online bullying experiences. Conceivably, just as cyber bullying and bullying can occur via social media and SNS, bullied victims can also seek support from their online networks to cope with this phenomenon, but the extent to which they do so and the outcomes of such efforts are largely unknown. Some important questions for the reconceptualization of new media include developing an understanding of whether social support provided through social media has the same or different impact and variation in outcomes on bullied victims and bullies.

A third consequence of the use of social media in negative ways is found in social groups in various cultural contexts. Using multilevel analysis of data from four racial/ethnic groups, Williams and Peguero (2013) found that bullying is more frequent among blacks who are higher achievers, but is just as harmful on later achievers among all groups studied. In a study of rural African American youth, where the incidence rates for bullying, victimization and aggressive victimization paralleled other population groups, bullies are often rated as aggressive, hyperactive and manipulative, and are likely to be members of both aggressive and non-aggressive groups and popular and unpopular groups (Estell, Farmer, & Cairns, 2007). Bullies tend to use humiliation, intimidation, and terrorization to target persons and may do so repeatedly and systematically with the intention of inflicting an emotional burden on the victim, and are successful, innovative, informed and trained persons (Altinöz, et al., 2010).

An analysis of European gymnasium students' perceptions of online threats such as cyber bullying, bullying abuse, sexual harassment, revealing of personal information and the sharing of harmful content, indicated that social networks are widely used for social and leisure purposes (Žibėnienė & Brasienė, 2013). In that study, while most young persons thought that they were aware of these threats and knew how to protect themselves, they revealed information that could put them at risk such as their surnames (94.5%), uploaded photos in which their faces are visible (87.2%), identified their school (84.1%) and their real age (72.2%). More boys than girls tended to set their profiles as public and were more likely to receive abusive messages but other studies suggested girls were more likely to be targeted and to report being targeted (Lampert & Donoso, 2012; Livingstone, Haddon & Görzig, 2012). Only 1 in every 5 students would opt not to seek help if their rights were violated. A study of pre-school teachers' perceptions of online risks for EU children found similar results with 85% of the sample being concerned about the revelation of sensitive information, encountering inappropriate sexual content (13%), and cyber bullying (3%) as noted previously (Dönmez, Odabaşi, Yurdakul, Kuzu, & Girgin, 2017; Kabakçı, Odabaşı, & Çoklar, 2008; Odabaşı, Kabakçi, & Çoklar, 2007). Even when there are existing legal and regulatory frameworks the risk persists. It has been recommended that a useful approach stresses the "importance of multi-stakeholder involvement, proportionality of measures, procedural guarantees (such as transparency) and the careful combination of regulatory strategies targeted at illegal as well as harmful conduct and content risks for a balanced protection of minors in social networks" (Lievens, 2011, p. 43).

Another study, this time of Taiwanese 7th graders found that boys compared to girls were more likely to be both bullies and victims (Wei & Lee, 2014). Employing social network analysis Wegge, Vandebosch and Eggermont (2014) found that cyber bullying is a reflection of traditional bullying among adolescents in Europe, may occur mutually, and is more likely to occur in same-gender and same-class contexts. Using secondary qualitative data, Ephraim (2013) found that children and youth aged 13-30 in Africa are the largest users of social networks. This study, having found that SNS are used in cyber bullying and violence against girls and women, proposes a culture –centered approach that stresses ethical use of these media and respect for the dignity and rights of other users. Based on an in depth survey of 25,000 children in Europe, it was found that, contrary to popular expectations, children were developing the skills to cope with and counteract bullying and sexual exploitation but certain challenges remained and some were still vulnerable (Livingstone, Haddon & Görzig, 2012).

Based on a review of the literature that showed bullying is a group process that is dependent on context (Sentse, Kiuru, Veenstra, & Salmivalli, 2014), researchers used statistical procedures and found that levels of bullying were inversely related to likability among Finnish adolescents in evaluating an anti-bullying program "in grades 7-9 (N = 9,183, M age at wave 1 = 13.96 years; 49.2% boys; M classroom size = 19.47) from 37 intervention and 30 control schools". Higher levels of bullying were related to lower levels of likability. This effect also held in cases of lower levels of bullying and greater likability after controlling for perceived popularity and gender. Finally, higher levels of bullying predicted higher levels of likability among peers also after controlling for popularity and gender. Social network positions based on peer nominations such as being an isolate or a clique member, for example, often relates to bullying experiences (physical, verbal or relational) (Lin, Wu, Lee, Lin, & Chiang, 2014). These findings suggest that indicators such as likability, perceived popularity, and social position indices are related to social networks and bullying. Thus, if social media are employed in cyber bullying or bullying, it would be interesting to explore whether these influences are impacting social media use or whether social media use are impacting the role of these influencers. Theoretically one might posit the view that social media, when used as tools for cyber bullying and bullying, may be investigated further in the case of Facebook using likability and dislikability metrics. In this vein an interesting issue is whether the indices are related to conflict situations that exist in cyber bullying and bullying, and whether these indices could be used to anticipate, predict and better understand and manage online conflict behaviors.

An investigation into whether adolescents learn to become morally disengaged or practice self-justifying behavior as a result of socialization found that gender, bullying and perceived popularity did not moderate the influence of friends on moral disengagement over time except in early adolescence (Sijtsema, Rambaran, Caravita, & Gini, 2014). The implication of this finding is that by the time persons use social media in conflict situations cyber bullying, gender and perceived popularity may not have influential roles. Adopting a social network perspective to study cyber bullying in classroom-based friendships of young people, investigators found that more cyber bullying occurs in high closeness concentration in offline and online friendship networks but there was less cyber bullying in high global clustering settings (Heirman et al., 2015).

Changing the public behavior of a randomly selected group of social referents, who exert influence over their peers in everyday social interaction, changes their peers' perceptions of collective norms and their harassment behavior (Paluck, Shepherd, & Smith, 2012). A follow-up study based on network analyses of peer-to-peer influence found that social referent students or students who attract more student attention can be incorporated into anti-bullying programs to spread perceptions of conflict as less socially normative among their peers (Paluck, Shepherd, & Aronow, 2016). This finding confirms an earlier suggestion by other researchers (Mouttapa, Valente, Gallaher, Rohrbach, & Unger, 2004) that when bullying and aggression prevention efforts target highly aggressive students, this may have a positive influence on their friends, in conjunction with assertiveness training in handling aggressive situations.

The other five themes, though not as evenly represented as the foregoing ones discussed, offer possibilities for identifying new areas for research exploration and growth. If the research on comparisons of users, online privacy, approaches to studying uses of social media platforms, organizational members' use of SNS, social business/marketing potential applications across the range of uses and preferences for SNS such as Facebook, appears to be less prevalent, this may signal that these five themes may not be active areas of interest or are understudied areas, or may be exciting new areas to be explored. Asking questions about the current status and future implications of these issues and why they have come to be so, pose several avenues for interrogation of new media. They offer opportunities for exploring taken for granted assumptions about these five themes and critiquing both popular wisdom and scientific inquiry on new media.

Growing interest in incivility in the US and elsewhere (Anderson, Brossard, Scheufele, Xenos, & Ladwig, 2014) is increasingly being associated with new media online discourse and rhetoric. Referring to a world characterised as increasingly volatile, uncertain, complex, and ambiguous (VUCA), International Communication Association President Peng Hwa Ang (2017) appropriated a post-Cold War term to express the view that populist sentiments are reversing the trends began almost 30 years ago in removing barriers and promoting freedom and movement. He noted the work of communication scholars, communicated powerfully, is one way of addressing the VUCA challenge by shining a light and clarifying what is not known in a VUCA world. This can be achieved, not by making issues more difficult to understand or by being unquestioning, for the people and the world they inhabit.

New media have a role to play in defining and shaping the world in which humans communicate. The challenge is to ask the right questions, critiquing assumptions, in searching for new meanings and new interpretations in reconceptualizing new media. The seven themes identified and linked to culture and conflict on Facebook, discussed earlier, offer possible avenues for further research and making sense of how new media are being reconceptualized and how they impact human communication. They also offer further exciting opportunities to understand, embrace and learn more about humanity and what makes communication, despite the presence and affordances of new media, a fundamentally human phenomenon.

CONCLUSION

This chapter explored cultural connections and conflict interactions using research conducted on Facebook. A systematic literature review spanning several databases identified, analysed and discussed seven major themes that present perspectives on the reconceptualization of new media. The emergent findings and discussion offer possibilities for better understanding, challenging and further investigating issues pertaining to culture and conflict on one SNS platform such as Facebook.

REFERENCES

Agger, B. (2015). *Oversharing: Presentations of self in the internet age*. London: Routledge.

Altinöz, M., Parildar, C., Çakiroglu, D., Barlas, M., Çaliskan, G., & Özdil, G. (2010). Bullying encountered during workplace training: Comparison of bullying level perceived by trainees whose workplace managers are women and men (Sample of Hacettepe University). *Selcuk Üniversitesi Sosyal Bilimler Enstitüsü Dergisi, 24*, 63-74. Retrieved from dergisosyalbil.selcuk.edu.tr/susbed/article/download/212/196

Anderson, A. A., Brossard, D., Scheufele, D. A., Xenos, M. A., & Ladwig, P. (2014). The "nasty effect:" Online incivility and risk perceptions of emerging technologies. *Journal of Computer-Mediated Communication, 19*(3), 373–387. doi:10.1111/jcc4.12009

Anderson, B., Fagan, P., Woodnutt, T., & Chamorro-Premuzic, T. (2012). Facebook psychology: Popular questions answered by research. *Psychology of Popular Media Culture, 1*(1), 23–37. doi:10.1037/a0026452

Ang, H. P. (2017). *Communicating with Power in a VUCA World*. Retrieved from http://www.icahdq.org/blogpost/1523657/272158/Communicating-With-Power-in-a-VUCA-World

Arno, A. (2009). *Alarming reports: Communicating conflict in the daily news*. Oxford, UK: Berghahn Books.

Baker, T., & Pelfrey, W. Jr. (2016). Bullying victimization, social network usage, and delinquent coping in a sample of urban youth: Examining the predictions of general strain theory. *Violence and Victims, 31*(6), 1021–1043. doi:10.1891/0886-6708.VV-D-14-00154 PMID:28661374

Bar-Tal, D., Abutbul-Selinger, G., & Raviv, A. (2014). The culture of conflict and its routinization. In P. Nesbitt-Larking, C. Kinnvall, T. Capelos, & H. Dekker (Eds.), *The Palgrave handbook of global political psychology* (pp. 369–387). London: Palgrave Macmillan.

Barki, H., & Hartwick, J. (2004). Conceptualizing the construct of interpersonal conflict. *International Journal of Conflict Management, 15*(3), 216–224. doi:10.1108/eb022913

Blaya, C., & Fartoukh, M. (2016). Digital uses, victimization and online aggression: A comparative study between primary school and lower secondary school students in France. *European Journal on Criminal Policy and Research, 22*(2), 285–300. doi:10.1007/s10610-015-9293-7

Bolton, R., Parasuraman, A., Hoefnagels, A., Migchels, N., Kabadayi, S., Gruber, T., ... Solnet, D. (2013). Understanding Generation Y and their use of social media: A review and research agenda. *Journal of Service Management, 24*(3), 245–267. doi:10.1108/09564231311326987

Borstnar, M. (2012). Towards understanding collaborative learning in the social media environment. *Organizacija, 45*(3), 100–106. doi:10.2478/v10051-012-0010-8

Boyd, D., & Ellison, N. B. (2008). Social network sites: Definition, history, and scholarship. *Journal of Computer-Mediated Communication, 13*(1), 210–230. doi:10.1111/j.1083-6101.2007.00393.x

Castells, M. (2013). *Communication power* (2nd ed.). Oxford, UK: Oxford University Press.

Ch'Ng, E. (2015). The bottom-up formation and maintenance of a Twitter community: Analysis of the #FreeJahar Twitter community. *Industrial Management & Data Systems, 115*(4), 612–624. doi:10.1108/IMDS-11-2014-0332

Chen, X., Pan, Y., & Guo, B. (2016). The influence of personality traits and social networks on the self-disclosure behavior of social network site users. *Internet Research, 26*(3), 566–586. doi:10.1108/IntR-05-2014-0145

Chou, S.-W. (2010). Why do members contribute knowledge to online communities? *Online Information Review, 34*(6), 829–854. doi:10.1108/14684521011099360

Conboy, M. (2006). *Tabloid Britain: Constructing a community through language*. London: Routledge.

N. Couldry, & J. Curran (Eds.). (2003). *Contesting media power: Alternative media in a networked world*. Oxford, UK: Rowman and Littlefield.

Devonish, D. (2013). Workplace bullying, employee performance and behaviors. *Employee Relations, 35*(6), 630-647.doi: 10.1108/ER-01-2013-0004

Dönmez, O., Odabaşi, H., Yurdakul, I., Kuzu, A., & Girgin, U. (2017). Development of a scale to address perceptions of pre-service teachers regarding online risks for children. *Kuram Ve Uygulamada Egitim Bilimleri, 17*(3), 923-943. doi: 10.12738/estp.2017.3.0022

Elder, A. (2014). Excellent online friendships: An Aristotelian defense of social media. *Ethics and Information Technology, 16*(4), 287–297. doi:10.1007/s10676-014-9354-5

Ephraim, P. (2013). African youths and the dangers of social networking: A culture-centered approach to using social media. *Ethics and Information Technology*, *15*(4), 275–284. doi:10.1007/s10676-013-9333-2

Estell, D., Farmer, T., & Cairns, B. (2007). Bullies and victims in rural African American youth: Behavioral characteristics and social network placement. *Aggressive Behavior*, *33*(2), 145–159. doi:10.1002/ab.20176 PMID:17441015

Euwema, M. C., van de Vliert, E., & Bakker, A. B. (2003). Substantive and relational effectiveness of organizational conflict behavior. *International Journal of Conflict Management*, *14*(2), 119–139. doi:10.1108/eb022894

Fisher, E. (2015). 'You media': Audiencing as marketing in social media. *Media Culture & Society*, *37*(1), 50–67. doi:10.1177/0163443714549088

Goggins, S., Laffey, J., & Gallagher, M. (2011). Completely online group formation and development: Small groups as socio-technical systems. *Information Technology & People*, *24*(2), 104–133. doi:10.1108/09593841111137322

Haynes, D., & Robinson, L. (2015). Defining user risk in social networking services. *Aslib Journal of Information Management*, *67*(1), 94–115. doi:10.1108/AJIM-07-2014-0087

Heirman, W., Angelopoulos, S., Wegge, D., Vandebosch, H., Eggermont, S., & Walrave, M. (2015). Cyberbullying-entrenched or cyberbully-free classrooms? A class network and class composition approach. *Journal of Computer-Mediated Communication*, *20*(3), 260–277. doi:10.1111/jcc4.12111

Heyman, R., De Wolf, R., & Pierson, J. (2014). Evaluating social media privacy settings for personal and advertising purposes. *Info*, *16*(4), 18–32. doi:10.1108/info-01-2014-0004

Hoehle, H., Zhang, X., & Venkatesh, V. (2015). An espoused cultural perspective to understand continued intention to use mobile applications: A four-country study of mobile social media application usability. *European Journal of Information Systems*, *24*(3), 337–359. doi:10.1057/ejis.2014.43

Horton, P. B., & Hunt, C. L. (1984). *Sociology* (6th ed.). New York: McGraw Hill.

Hübner Barcelos, R., & Alberto Vargas Rossi, C. (2014). Paradoxes and strategies of social media consumption among adolescents. *Young Consumers*, *15*(4), 275–295. doi:10.1108/YC-10-2013-00408

Israilidis, J., Siachou, E., Cooke, L., & Lock, R. (2015). Individual variables with an impact on knowledge sharing: The critical role of employees' ignorance. *Journal of Knowledge Management*, *19*(6), 1109–1123. doi:10.1108/JKM-04-2015-0153

Kabakçı, I., Odabaşı, H. F., & Çoklar, A. N. (2008). Parents' views about Internet use of their children. *International Journal of Education and Information Technologies*, *4*(2), 248–255. http://www.naun.org/main/NAUN/educationinformation/eit-75.pdf

Kiron, D., Palmer, D., Phillips, A., & Kruschwitz, N. (2012). Social business: What are companies really doing? *MIT Sloan Management Review*, *53*(4), 1–32. Retrieved from http://sloanreview.mit.edu/article/what-managers-really-think-about-social-business/

Köhl, M. M., & Götzenbrucker, G. (2014). Networked technologies as emotional resources? Exploring emerging emotional cultures on social network sites such as Facebook and Hi5: A trans-cultural study. *Media Culture & Society*, *36*(4), 508–525. doi:10.1177/0163443714523813

Krombholz, K., Merkl, D., & Weippl, E. (2012). Fake identities in social media: A case study on the sustainability of the Facebook business model. *Journal of Service Science Research*, *4*(2), 175–212. doi:10.1007/s12927-012-0008-z

Kuo, F.-Y., Tseng, C. Y., Tseng, F.-C., & Lin, C. S. (2013). A study of social information control affordances and gender difference in Facebook self- presentation. *Cyberpsychology, Behavior, and Social Networking*, *16*(9), 635–644. doi:10.1089/cyber.2012.0345 PMID:23849000

Lampert, C., & Donoso, V. (2012). Bullying. In S. Livingstone, L. Haddon, & A. Görzig (Eds.), *Children, risk and safety on the internet* (pp. 141–150). Bristol, UK: Policy Press at the University of Bristol. doi:10.1332/policypress/9781847428837.003.0011

Lievens, E. (2011). Risk-reducing regulatory strategies for protecting minors in social networks. *Info*, *13*(6), 43–54. doi:10.1108/14636691111174252

Lin, Y., Wu, W., Lee, C., Lin, D., & Chiang, Y. (2014). Effects of social network indicators and positions in class on bullied experiences among junior high school students in Taiwan. *Taiwan Gong Wei Sheng Za Zhi, 33*(4), 397- 409. https://search.proquest.com/docview/1561743546

S. Livingstone, L. Haddon, & A. Görzig (Eds.). (2012). *Children, risk and safety on the internet*. Bristol, UK: Policy Press at the University of Bristol. doi:10.1332/policypress/9781847428837.001.0001

Livingstone, S., Haddon, L., Görzig, A., & Ólafsson, K. (2011). *Risks and safety on the internet. The perspective of European children. Full findings*. London: London School of Economics and Political Science.

Lopato, M. (2016). Social media, love, and Sartre's look of the Other: Why online communication is not fulfilling. *Philosophy & Technology*, *29*(3), 195–210. doi:10.1007/s13347-015-0207-x

Malik, A., Dhir, A., & Nieminen, M. (2015). Uncovering Facebook photo tagging culture and practices among digital natives. *Global Media Journal, 13*(24), 1-21. Retrieved from http://www.globalmediajournal.com/open-access/uncovering-facebook- photo-tagging-culture-and-practices-among-digital-natives.pdf

Matsunaga, M. (2011). Underlying circuits of social support for bullied victims: An appraisal-based perspective on supportive communication and postbullying adjustment. *Human Communication Research*, *37*(2), 174–206. doi:10.1111/j.1468-2958.2010.01398.x

Meng, J., Martinez, L., Holmstrom, A., Chung, M., & Cox, J. (2017). Research on social networking sites and social support from 2004 to 2015: A narrative review and directions for future research. *Cyberpsychology, Behavior, and Social Networking*, *20*(1), 44–51. doi:10.1089/cyber.2016.0325 PMID:28002686

Moqbel, M., Nevo, S., & Kock, N. (2013). Organizational members' use of social networking sites and job performance. *Information Technology & People*, *26*(3), 240–264. doi:10.1108/ITP-10-2012-0110

Mouttapa, M., Valente, T., Gallaher, P., Rohrbach, L. A., & Unger, J. B. (2004). Social network predictors of bullying and victimization. *Adolescence*, *39*(154), 315–335. PMID:15563041

Odabaşı, H. F. I., Kabakçı, I., & Çoklar, A. N. (2007). *İnternet, aile ve çocuk* [The internet, family and children]. Ankara, Turkey: Nobel Yayıncılık.

Paluck, E., Shepherd, H., & Aronow, P. (2016). Changing climates of conflict: A social network experiment in 56 schools. *Proceedings of the National Academy of Sciences of the United States of America*, *113*(3), 566–571. doi:10.1073/pnas.1514483113 PMID:26729884

Paluck, E., Shepherd, H., & Smith, E. R. (2012). The salience of social referents: A field experiment on collective norms and harassment behavior in a school social network. *Journal of Personality and Social Psychology*, *103*(6), 899–915. doi:10.1037/a0030015 PMID:22984831

Rahim, A. (1983). A measure of styles of handling interpersonal conflict. *Academy of Management Journal, 26*(2), 368–376. doi:10.2307/255985 PMID:10263067

Rauschnabel, P., Kammerlander, N., & Ivens, B. (2016). Collaborative brand attacks in social media: Exploring the antecedents, characteristics, and consequences of a new form of brand crises. *Journal of Marketing Theory and Practice, 24*(4), 381–410. doi:10.1080/10696679.2016.1205452

Rollins, M., & Lewis, S. (2012). Communication practices of certified public accountants. *Journal of Organizational Culture, Communications and Conflict, 16*(1), 107-112. Retrieved from https://search.proquest.com/docview/1037693138

Ross, K., Fountaine, S., & Comrie, M. (2015). Facing up to Facebook: Politicians, publics and the social media(ted) turn in New Zealand. *Media Culture & Society, 37*(2), 251–269. doi:10.1177/0163443714557983

Rourke, L., Anderson, T., Garrison, D. R., & Archer, W. (2000). Assessing social presence in asynchronous text-based computer conferencing. *International Journal of E-Learning and Distance Education, 14*(2), 50–71. Retrieved from http://www.ijede.ca/index.php/jde/article/view/153/341

Sentse, M., Kiuru, N., Veenstra, R., & Salmivalli, C. (2014). A social network approach to the interplay between adolescents' bullying and likeability over time. *Journal of Youth and Adolescence, 43*(9), 1409–1420. doi:10.1007/s10964-014-0129-4 PMID:24752280

Sijtsema, J. J., Rambaran, J. A., Caravita, S. C. S., & Gini, G. (2014). Friendship selection and influence in bullying and defending: Effects of moral disengagement. *Developmental Psychology, 50*(8), 2093–2104. doi:10.1037/a0037145 PMID:24911569

Skågeby, J. (2012). The irony of serendipity: Disruptions in social information behavior. *Library Hi Tech, 30*(2), 321–334. doi:10.1108/07378831211239988

Steele, G. A., & Plenty, D. (2015). Supervisor-subordinate communication competence and job and communication satisfaction. *International Journal of Business Communication, 52*(3), 294–318. doi:10.1177/2329488414525450

Turel, O., & Serenko, A. (2012). The benefits and dangers of enjoyment with social networking websites. *European Journal of Information Systems, 21*(5), 512–528. doi:10.1057/ejis.2012.1

Vernuccio, M., Pagani, M., Barbarossa, C., & Pastore, A. (2015). Antecedents of brand love in online network-based communities. A social identity perspective. *Journal of Product and Brand Management*, *24*(7), 706–719. doi:10.1108/JPBM-12-2014-0772

Wegge, D., Vandebosch, H., & Eggermont, S. (2014). Who bullies whom online: A social network analysis of cyberbullying in a school context. *Communications-European Journal of Communication Research, 39*(4), 415-433. doi: 10.1515/commun-2014-0019

Wei, H., & Lee, W. (2014). Individual and social network predictors of physical bullying: A longitudinal study of Taiwanese early adolescents. *Violence and Victims*, *29*(4), 701–716. doi:10.1891/0886-6708.VV-D-12-00173 PMID:25199395

Weller, K. (2016). Trying to understand social media users and usage. *Online Information Review*, *40*(2), 256–264. doi:10.1108/OIR-09-2015-0299

White, D., & Absher, K. (2013). Red Devils, Royals, and the River Thames. *Sport, Business and Management*, *3*(4), 312–326. doi:10.1108/SBM-05-2013-0011

Williams, L., & Peguero, A. (2013). The impact of school bullying on racial/ethnic achievement. *Race and Social Problems*, *5*(4), 296–308. doi:10.1007/s12552-013-9105-y

Wondwesen, T. (2016). An experiential model of consumer engagement in social media. *Journal of Product and Brand Management*, *25*(5), 424–434. doi:10.1108/JPBM-05-2015-0879

Yusuf, N., Al-Banawi, N., & Rahman Al-Imam, H. (2014). The social media as echo chamber: The digital impact. *Journal of Business & Economics Research (Online)*, *12*(1). Retrieved from https://search.proquest.com/docview/1477975226

Žibėnienė, G., & Brasienė, D. (2013). Using the Internet, online social networks and potentially incurred risk: Student opinions. *Social Technologies, 3*(1), 53-67. Retrieved from https://search.proquest.com/docview/1426562879

KEY TERMS AND DEFINITIONS

Closed Community: A private group of persons who use social platforms and web-based infrastructure and service and networking or connections to create personal profiles that have restricted access.

Conflict: A situation in which at least two parties have perceived mutually incompatible goals and interests and which can be managed using strategies ranging from integrative or win-win to competitive or win-lose approaches.

Conflict Interactions: Behaviors of parties whose goals and interests are perceived to be mutually incompatible. These interactions may include cognitive (thought), behavioral (action), and affective (feeling) dimensions.

Culture: The characteristic visible and invisible ties that bind its members and which are reflected in the shared assumptions, beliefs, interests, practices, and patterns of behavior.

Facebook: A social networking site that facilitates interactivity and connectivity, immediate and instantaneous content creation and sharing, and supports user updated private and public profiles.

Intercultural Connections: Social relationships facilitated by social media platforms that allow users to match their interests and preferences based on the online profiles they create.

Social Networking Sites (SNS): A term that refers to both networks or web-based infrastructure and services, and networking or connections among users of SNS.

Social Presence: Consists of affective (feeling, emotion, humour, disclosure), interactive (connecting or linking or replying), and cohesive (forms of address, salutations, greetings, and closures fulfilling a social function) components of behavior.

Chapter 9
The Influence of Groupthink on Culture and Conflict in Twitter

Godfrey A. Steele
The University of the West Indies, Trinidad and Tobago

Niekitta Zephyrine
The University of the West Indies, Trinidad and Tobago

ABSTRACT

Groupthink puts pressure on individuals to conform to social norms, but anonymity has been found to reduce or lessen such influence. Apart from anonymity, the significance of the topic and self-censorship may or may not contribute to the influence of groupthink. Groupthink has been studied in the context of social media using various approaches, but to date it remains unclear how much and to what extent it influences the conflict among users within this cultural context. This chapter describes approaches to studying the influence of groupthink on the users of an open social media platform (e.g., Twitter) and proposes a methodology for conducting a study. Using data from a selected hashtag, it reports on the application of theory to research, considers the role and influence of groupthink, and discusses the implications of the findings for reconceptualizing approaches to the study of new media.

INTRODUCTION

In six main sections, this chapter systematically reviews contemporary research on groupthink, exploring its influence on culture and conflict to formulate a theoretical framework for studying the influence of groupthink on culture and conflict. It reports

DOI: 10.4018/978-1-5225-3784-7.ch009

on an empirical test of that model within an online open community and discusses the findings and implications for understanding and reconceptualizing new media, before concluding.

BACKGROUND

A Review of the Groupthink Literature in Newer Media Settings

Overview

This chapter presents the outcomes of conducting a keyword search of groupthink, social networking sites (SNS), culture, conflict and related terms in selected databases in communication, focusing on Twitter. The rationale for focusing on Twitter is based on the growing prevalence and use of Twitter as a social diary and as a popular site for intercultural connection and conflict interaction. Twitter is a medium for intercultural connections and expressions and conflict interactions that may be integrative and disruptive. In the absence of a comprehensive review of social media since the review of scholarship on SNS (Boyd & Ellison, 2008) and later research on social networking sites spanning 2004-2015 (Meng, Martinez, Holmstrom, Chung, & Cox, 2017), there is need for an overarching theoretical framework and a method for studying SNS as an evolving aspect of new media reconceptualization in human communication. Current concepts are presented in this first section. This presentation begins with defining groupthink, its precursors or predisposing conditions, and proceeds by defining culture, intercultural connections, conflict, conflict interactions, social networking sites and Twitter.

Concepts

Groupthink, based on Janis' (1972) social psychological theory, is characterized by a:

mode of thinking in which individual members of small cohesive groups tend to accept a viewpoint or conclusion that represents a perceived group consensus, whether or not the group members believe it to be valid, correct, or optimal. Groupthink reduces the efficiency of collective problem solving within such groups (Schmidt, 2013).

Groupthink is associated with the desire to fit in, modifying our individual opinions so that they move in the direction of a consensus, avoiding speaking out based on one's beliefs to keeping quiet to avoid causing problems (Katopol, 2015). When there is dissent on social media such as Twitter, how do persons respond? It has been suggested that two main themes emerge in organizational settings (Garner, 2017). First, prior dissent events chain together and a dissent event can be understood in the context of other events, thereby influencing the expression of future dissent. Second, the channel of expression seems to be guided by unwritten rules about what is appropriate and when channels such as emails or social media are used. In the case of Twitter, it is unclear whether these themes are applicable.

Culture is the shared assumptions, beliefs, practices and patterns of behavior among groups of persons. Within any culture there may be subgroups. Intercultural communication occurs among subgroups within a cultural context, and between groups within and between cultures. Interactions between ideas and issues across various contexts of communication such as computer-mediated and political communication and other forms of communication are essentially manifestations and expressions of intercultural communication broadly defined. Intercultural connections are facilitated by social media platforms which allow users to match their interests and preferences based on the online profiles they create. These connections are possible because persons are willing to publicly display their connections via the views they express and respond to online via tweets and retweets on Twitter.

Conflict is a situation in which at least two parties have perceived mutually incompatible goals and interests and which can be managed using strategies ranging from integrative or win-win to competitive or win-lose approaches. Conflict interactions are characterized by the behaviors of parties whose goals and interests are mutually incompatible. These conflict interactions may include cognitive, behavioral and affective dimensions (Barki & Hartwick, 2004). Various approaches to conflict management range from integrative or win-win to competitive or win-lose approaches incorporating avoiding, dominating, compromising, obliging and integrating conflict styles (Rahim, 1983). Conflict may lead to positive or integrative outcomes or negative of disintegrative outcomes. Sometimes a combination of approaches or episodes utilising different approaches may be used in what is described as conglomerative conflict behavior (Euwema, van der Vliet, & Bakker, 2003).

Social pollution refers to the presence of abusive posts (Liao, Squicciarini, Griffin, & Rajtmajer, 2016). Persons respond to abusive posts in various ways. Some may reply, ignore or retweet the abusive post. It is not always clear how persons may respond to abusive posts, other than by calling them or their authors out or by flagging or reporting them. One possible response is dissent. Dissent is useful in organizational contexts, particularly as a mechanism to improve decision-making and as a counter to groupthink behavior. The expression of dissent may differ on social media when compared to face-to-face situations (Garner, 2017). The expression of dissent may be pursued or avoided. The avoidance of dissent can create conditions for conformity, the creation of apparent consent by non-dissent, and can encourage groupthink. Dissent can also lead to healthy, respectful debate, perhaps even fostering intercultural connections between persons who agree to disagree. It can also lead to conflict interactions, which embody integrative and disintegrative dimensions.

Social networking sites (SNS) is a term used to refer to both networks or web-based infrastructure and services, and networking or the connections among users of SNS (Boyd & Ellison, 2008). According to Meng et al. (2017, p. 45), "SNS refers to all web-based services that allow for creating personal profiles, making and publicly displaying personal connections within a bounded system.". Younger persons tend to be more receptive to SNS than older adults. A survey of SNS use and attitudes among Italian academics found SNS such as Facebook and Twitter were more restricted and limited (Manca & Ranieri, 2016). Cultural resistance, pedagogical issues or institutional constraints were the main factors underlying the obstacles facing academics. The attitudes were influenced by academic discipline, reflected ambivalence and obstacles were more prevalent than benefits among this generation.

Twitter is a microblog limited to 140 characters. It is a platform on which networks of users (or tweepers) share and update information, and engage in social networking and real-time communication using tweets. Users of Twitter vary in their preferences by age (Korhan & Ersoy, 2016), and differ from Facebook users (Petrocchi, Asnaani, Martinez, Nadkarni, & Hofmann, 2015). Persons engaged in active Twitter use tend to experience greater Twitter-related conflict which in turn has been associated with relationship infidelity, breakup and divorce in romantic relationships (Clayton, 2014). It is not known whether the same relationships that exist among active Twitter use, conflict and dissolution of the relationship also hold in non-romantic situations among tweepers who may have created online identities, may be anonymous and are users of a network.

Approaches to Studying Groupthink in the Context of Newer Media, e.g. Twitter

Methodology: Conducting a Systematic Literature Review and Content Analysis

A search was undertaken to identify and content analyze directly relevant articles spanning 20 databases including Directory of Open Access Journals (DOAJ), Elsevier, Informa, Medline/PubMed, ProQuest, Science Citation Index, Social Science Citation Index, and Taylor and Francis in the social, medical sciences and humanities. An initial search of the term "social network* sites" (which would yield network or networking hits) yielded: "Social network sites" n=156,252; peer-reviewed journals n= 149,905 articles; 2004-2017 n = 127,855; and "Social network sites AND Twitter" n=14,489.

Next, refined searches were undertaken for 2004-2017 articles with the following keywords and yielded: "SNS and Twitter" n= 14, 470. A pilot review of the first 50 articles showed a relevance rate of 80% (selected articles n=40/50). The peer-reviewed articles were identified (n= 9561) and the most relevant peer reviewed articles were selected from the first fifty articles (n= 40/50): "SNS AND Twitter AND groupthink" (n=233) with the following selected for analysis from peer reviewed journal articles (n=65); selected articles (n=20/65): "Groupthink" (n=13, 276); peer-reviewed journal articles (n = 5,120); groupthink AND Twitter (n=82); groupthink AND Twitter AND conflict (selected articles n=46).

Then, the search results were used to identify and summarize the prevalence of main theories used, their functions, references to them and their associated methodologies (including research design and measurement) and roles and interplay among groupthink, culture and conflict on social networking sites, particularly Twitter. This approach has been used by other researchers (Gurman, Rubin, & Roess, 2012; Meng et al., 2017).

Integrating Concepts: A Literature Review

The study of the use of SNS including Twitter and other networks has been proposed, theorized or tested in various contexts. For example, a proposal for the active participation of citizens in solving simulated Homeland Security problems in the US (Ford, 2011), the relationship between online campaigning and political involvement (Kruikemeier, Van Noort, Vliegenthart, & de Vreese, 2016), and perceptions of the effect of social cues and interactivity on journalistic credibility on Twitter (Jahng & Littau, 2016) were reported. SNS have been used in providing social support (Meng et al., 2017; Myrick, Holton, Himelboim & Love, 2016), and highlighting accomplishments in areas such as thoracic surgery (Antonoff, 2015) and developing a measure of reported patient success (Tour et al., 2014) in health communication. Twitter is widely used in medicine and health care (Baumann, 2009), and is often used in medical education, conferences and health care delivery (Grajales, Sheps, Ho, Novak-Lauscher, & Eysenbach, 2014). A review of the use of SNS, and particularly a microblog such as Twitter, in medicine and health care has identified unanswered issues of governance, ethics, professionalism, privacy, confidentiality, and information quality (Grajales et al., 2014). These issues have the potential to vary across cultural contexts and generate conflict. In turn these issues can impact the reconceptualization of newer media.

SNS are sources of studying online virus propagation control in probabilistic communities (Liu, Hsu, & Ke, 2014). The potential for comparing Twitter with Facebook in exploring social information affordances and gender difference was also proposed (Kuo, Tseng, Tseng, & Lin, 2013). SNS networks were also identified as potential sites for image and multimedia mining (Mishra & Silakari, 2012) and as a source for studying the social relationships underlying social media sites (Hansen, 2011). SNS are sources of investigation of anonymity, privacy and online identity and their impact on behavior and psychological well-being among younger users (Binns, 2014; Dogan, 2016), and trust among heterogeneous communities (Wu, Chen, Yu, Han, & Wu, 2015).

Thus, the role, value and potential of SNS as both sources and sites of connection and interaction, and opportunities for research have been demonstrated. The nature and dynamics of these connections and interactions have been indirectly referenced in these examples, but a direct focus on these phenomena has not received as much attention. This chapter explores the nature and dynamics of connections and interactions in an online public community, Twitter. This exploration uses the study of intercultural connections and conflict interactions in Twitter to review, summarize and formulate theoretical and methodological approaches and to propose how these developments contribute to the reconceptualization of newer media. A content analytic approach based on a systematic literature review is used to ground this discussion regarding culture in the next section.

EXPLORING AND DEFINING GROUPTHINK'S INFLUENCE ON CULTURE IN NEWER MEDIA AND SOCIAL NETWORKING SITES

Groupthink and Culture in Newer Media and Social Networking Sites

To recap, groupthink is a tendency for one's views to be influenced by a perceived norm and to move toward a perceived consensus among group members, despite doubts about validity, correctness or the best option when decisions are being made. It is associated with fulfilling a desire to fit in, keeping silent to avoid problems, and avoiding expressing dissent. With respect to intercultural connections on SNS such as Twitter, groupthink is expected to exert some influence, but its precise and predictable impact is difficult to hypothesize in this cultural context owing to the range and complexity of variables. The cultural context among Twitter microblog users is marked by attributes that connect and bind members as a result of age, interests, online identity and profile, issues of anonymity, significance of the topic and self-censorship and an interest in sharing and updating information within a community of persons who choose, create and participate in social networking connections on this platform.

Studying Groupthink and Culture in Twitter

How then does one approach the study of groupthink and culture using the Twitter platform as an SNS network and networking context? A review of one research effort to do so may be helpful. In studying cross-ideology exposure on Twitter, Himelboim, McCreery and Smith (2013) conducted network and content analyses. These researchers mapped the Twitter networks of ten controversial political topics, discovered clusters of highly self-connected users and coded messages and links in them for political orientation. Reporting on their findings the researchers observed,

We found that Twitter users are unlikely to be exposed to cross-ideological content from the clusters of users they followed, as these were usually politically homogeneous. Links pointed at grassroots web pages (e.g.: blogs) more frequently than traditional media websites. Liberal messages, however, were more likely to link to traditional media. Last, we found that more specific topics of controversy had both conservative and liberal clusters, while in broader topics, dominant clusters reflected conservative sentiment. (McCreery & Smith, 2013, p. 154)

It seems, then, that owing to the politically homogenous nature of the clusters, there was less likelihood of users in one cluster being influenced by the ideological views of other clusters. This suggests that groupthink on Twitter may function differently from other SNS. Patterns of links to webpages according to political ideology (Liberal or conservative) were discernible. This finding suggests ideologically political underpinnings are fairly stable and predictable among Twitter users regarding controversial political topics. The nature of the topic can be linked to ideological clusters with narrower topics attracting a wider range of ideological interests (liberal and conservative) and broader topics attracting conservative interests.

The researchers concluded (McCreery & Smith, 2013, p. 171)

Political talk on Twitter does not occur in a strictly political environment, and individuals create social ties based on a wide range of interests, not only based on political opinions. Political content, nonetheless, was overall confined to like-minded clusters of users. On Twitter, individuals may interact with others who do not share their political ideology. But, at least for the issues analyzed for this study, this potential does not lead to meaningful cross-ideological interaction.

It seems that like-minded clusters of users, owing to their highly connected social ties that extend beyond political boundaries, appear to be predisposed to groupthink behaviors and to resistance to cross-ideological influences. As the researchers acknowledge, the real-time nature of Twitter creates limitations because of the short nature of the posts (140 characters) although users often use links to websites to supplement this brevity, the eventual disappearance of posts and the uncertainty as to whether all posts are read when only the most recent are featured. These limitations affect the ability to conduct longitudinal studies that would garner data on enduring ideologies and the maintenance or change of groupthink behavior, and thus caution is recommended in interpreting the results of studies based on real-time data. The next section focuses the discussion on the relevance to conflict.

EXPLORING AND DEFINING GROUPTHINK'S INFLUENCE ON CONFLICT IN NEWER MEDIA AND SOCIAL NETWORKING SITES

Groupthink, Twitter Communities and Group Conflict

The like-minded hypothesis is supported by a view which regards online debates as echo chambers (Sunstein, 2001, 2007). According to this view, in an online debate, persons selectively avoid arguments that oppose theirs, opting to seek out like-minded persons, particularly as algorithms purposely provide content that is linked to their previous preferences (Bücher, 2012) owing to strong differences marked by reciprocated and non-reciprocated ties based on political homophily (Colleoni, Rozza, & Arvidsson, 2014). Thus, Karlsen, Steen-Johnsen, Wollebæk, and Enjolras (2017, p. 2) observe "According to several key observers, such features do not foster a democratized and enlightened debate, but rather group mentality, polarization, and extremism.". However contrary to the echo chambers position, which has been challenged (Brundidge, 2010), another view argues that when presented with opposing arguments, online debaters may not critique and change their initial opinion, but develop a stronger belief in the previously held opinion, known as "trench warfare dynamics" (Karlsen et al., 2017, p. 2). Trench warfare dynamics can have the effect of reinforcing entrenched positions and maintaining polarities, leading to the creation of intractable conflict.

Another possible groupthink influence on conflict is the extent to which social bonds are created. These social bonds can offer two main ways of managing conflict if it arises. First, exploring what SNS participants do to construct sociable bonds with each other using the technological affordances available, specifically those connected to second screens, can be worthwhile (Kroon, 2017). In a multi-platform broadcasting environment there are opportunities for broadcast audiences to interact with broadcasters using social media as second screens "as a thoroughly sociable activity" (Kroon, 2017, p. 670) and to experience a sense of presence while the main event is on a primary screen such as television. Second, Twitter, users can have multiple communication circuits for interacting with each other to develop informal social bonds outside of their main professional or occupational activities. These social bonds can create conditions for groupthink or like-minded behavior.

Studying Groupthink and Conflict in Twitter

Kroon's (2017) case study of a series of Swedish football commentary webcasts examined how producers and users engage in communication with each other during the FIFA World Cup in 2014. It explored how users and producers adopt strategies of inclusion oriented to creating a joint sense of "being here together" in an online community based on the official hashtag expressenvm. The study found that "second screen setups of this kind have the potential of displacing the big TV screen and its live sports event, at least for a specific user crowd." (Kroon, 2017, p. 1).

In studying groupthink and conflict on Twitter, findings from two other previous studies can be helpful. Waheed, Anjum, Rehman, and Khawaja (2017, p. 1) found that "activities performed on SNS are either associated with user behavior or reflect personality characteristics. The researchers noted one implication of these findings is that practitioners can use this information to evaluate their SNS platforms and develop more user-centered applications, and help organizations to understand better the needs of their employees." In another study Kenski, Coe and Rains (in press) investigated incivility in public discourse. Noting that most incivility research had focused narrowly on incivility in elite discourse, the researchers focused on how the lay public perceives incivility. The results from two surveys to track differences in perceptions of specific types of uncivil speech and identify predictors of those perceptions, demonstrated that "different types of incivility elicit different responses. Name-calling and vulgarity were rated as more uncivil than were other speech acts" and that "several demographic, personality, and news consumption variables were analyzed as predictors of incivility perceptions." (Kenski, Coe, & Rains, in press, p. 1).

Thus, both user behavior and user personality characteristics may be useful variables worth exploring in groupthink and conflict research on newer media. With respect to user behavior, name calling and vulgarity are perceived as more uncivil than other behaviors. It may be worthwhile to explore how these variables interact, and to account for their influence on conflict among Twitter users. Theoretically, the concepts of echo chambers or non-dissenting behavior and trench warfare dynamics which potentially lead to entrenched positions (O'Hara & Stevens, 2015) or polarized political positions (Ems, 2014; Gruzd & Roy, 2014; Lee, Choi, Kim, & Kim, 2014) and intractable conflict may be explored as aspects of groupthink that have special application to reconceptualizing the study of social media. Additionally, the creation of social bonds may have a moderating influence on the role of groupthink and its influence on conflict on an SNS platform such as Twitter. Next, one possible theoretical framework is presented as an example.

TOWARDS A THEORETICAL FRAMEWORK FOR STUDYING THE INFLUENCE OF GROUPTHINK ON CULTURE AND CONFLICT WITHIN AN ONLINE COMMUNITY

Anonymity

Anonymity was once a preferred way of preserving identity online but there has been a growing tendency among teenagers to upload personal information, resulting in concerns about abandonment of privacy and obsessive self-grooming of online identities (Binns, 2014). Using SNS poses security threats, particularly if users' passwords are weak or if these sites have no complexity checks (Eston, 2010). Additionally, an examination of the ethical dimensions of tracking SNS users' movements reveals threats to privacy (Sar & Al-Saggaf, 2014) and privacy concerns in balancing their private and public spheres (Balleys & Coll, 2016).

Binns (2014) studied whether different SNS affect behavior and happiness differently by examining Facebook, Twitter and Q&A site usage by 342 teenage girls. This study found that site architecture influences behavior which, in turn, creates new media environments. These environments can be characterized as "choice architecture" or "persuasive design". Young persons are more concerned about privacy and protection issues involving authority figures such as parents rather than those they do not know such as marketers, advertisers and those in distant relations (Jeong & Coyle, 2014), or with using social media for instrumental reasons such making quick connections and building relationships among high school seniors (Agosto & Abbas, 2010). Thus, there appears to be less concern with anonymity, particularly among younger female Twitter users and/or teens.

Social media allows users to create content. In doing so, social media users create opportunities for social surveillance by examining the content produced by others and by examining one's content through the eyes of others (Marwick, 2012). Social surveillance is distinguished from traditional surveillance. In the former case users have a different kind of control, hierarchical power and reciprocity from those who are under traditional surveillance. Marwick (2012) argues that social surveillance, unlike traditional surveillance, through the affordances of social media facilitates a collapse of social contexts and social cues, complicating boundary work, and relying more on informal everyday revelation, disclosure and concealment of personal information. This behavior is described as routine among highly connected communities. This suggests that although Twitter is an SNS which conforms to the definition advanced by Boyd and Ellison (2008, p. 211) as

web-based services that allow individuals to (1) construct a public or semi-public profile within a bounded system, (2) articulate a list of other users with whom they share a connection, and (3) view and traverse their list of connections and those made by others within the system. The nature and nomenclature of these connections may vary from site to site, it may have some unique characteristics as an SNS it has some unique features.

Message features such as the use of the hashtag, and local network properties, message content and message style influence greater retransmission of messages in an imminent crisis situation (Sutton et al., 2015), but it is not clear whether these features are applicable in a different setting such as those involving cultural connections or conflict interactions among members of a public online community such as #BlackLivesMatter on Twitter. The online identity and anonymity of users can also possibly influence the retransmission rates of tweets.

Thus, anonymity, which originated as a key variable in theorizing about the influence of groupthink on Twitter users and their behavior, has evolved in various ways with different meanings and applications for users and marketers. Issues of privacy, confidentiality and security have emerged. Social surveillance, as distinct from traditional surveillance, has afforded opportunities for self-monitoring and creating an online identity viewed through one's eyes and the eyes of others. These developments suggest an ongoing reconceptualization of newer media as not a mere tool but as a facilitator and shaper of connections and interactions among users creating content that has become a commodity and a merchandising apparatus for those who promote and benefit from the political economy of newer media.

Significance of the Topic

Social media has grown to become a primary means by which persons contribute to the public discussions on social issues and the current social, political and environmental climate. According to Tsikerdekis (2012), "The opportunity for a young generation to actively contribute and share content has affected individuals, their families and society as a whole that can now share information free from restrictions of the physical world (Palfrey & Gasser, 2010)." (as cited in Tsikerdekis, 2012, p. 1). This exemplifies social media's large impact on communication in general. Thus, as a growing field, it is important that social media along with the means of communicating online is observed as human communication evolves and changes. This contributes to how new media are reconceptualized.

As the term social media has grown to encompass a prevalent and newer media, the study of racism, race and racial divisions is also significant. One can also observe that racism and racial discussions, as universal phenomena, can be applied to the Caribbean experience, specifically to the context of Trinidad and Tobago and elsewhere, such as the BlackLivesMatter movement in the US discussed later.

Current research focuses on social media and social behaviors and how social media has contributed to the significant change in how persons communicate internationally and the medium's impact in the formation of groups, which may lead to the emergence of groupthink behaviors amongst an online community (Hui & Buchegger, 2009; Kosur, 2014; Tsikerdekis, 2013). However, it has been observed that there is limited research linking the #BlackLivesMatter and groupthink behaviors on the social media website Twitter. Thus, this research's significance lies in seeking to link racism, racial discussion and groupthink in relation to intercultural connection and conflict interaction which occur online on Twitter.

Self-Censorship

Irving Janis (1972, 1982), in conceptualising groupthink theory, identified several symptoms, one of which is self-censorship, which occurs when group members do not voice their opposing views for fear of disrupting group cohesion (Littlejohn & Foss, 2008, p. 242; Salazar, 2009, p. 461). Kosur (2014) identified behaviors which are associated with self-censorship where it is stated that persons may not post their views on an issue if they are uncertain that the rest of the community may agree with it. Exposure to social media may allow for the users to be aware of varying opinions on social issues. However, persons may hesitate to voice these opposing opinions for fear of causing offense to other users and friends online (Kosur, 2014). This can also be a mechanism to avoid conflict within these online spaces and may emerge during conflict discussions and sensitive topics.

According to Vincent (2014) self-censorship is a common behavior on social media websites such as Twitter and Facebook, which is referred to as the 'spiral of silence'. Using Twitter as an example Vincent commented that

Although the hubbub of comment threads and Twitter timelines might seem to contain a wide variety of opinion, the researchers suggest that internet users tend to clump together with like-minded individuals (a tendency that internet experts have previously suggested is reinforced by online search algorithms that cater to our views). (Vincent, 2014, para. 6)

which according to Janis' (1972) definition of the term is a common practice of persons who are victims of groupthink.

Self-censorship has emerged as a critical variable in theorizing about how new media are influenced by groupthink, and are being reconceptualized. Self-censorship can have a limiting impact on individual expression, particularly if anonymity is difficult to create and maintain or is in doubt. In turn, in highly connected communities, this impact can potentially moderate the nature and quality of intercultural connections. Apart from the potential impact on intercultural connections, self-censorship can facilitate the way conflict is managed and privilege certain styles of conflict handling (e.g. avoiding, compromising) on a platform such as Twitter. This impact may be relevant to all SNS, but may have a unique manifestation on Twitter where brevity, and sharing and updating of information, and a focus on recent updates, could lead to reduced or limited collective memory, and can also potentially impact conflict interactions.

The Social Identity Model of Deindividuation Effects

The social identity model of deindividuation effects (SIDE) was developed by Martin Lea and Russell Spears. As an extension of deindividuation theory, SIDE, like groupthink theory, attempts to observe and understand individual behavior within large groups as well as the impact on anonymity on individual behavior (Levine & Hogg, 2010, p. 794).

Martin Lea and Russell Spears thus theorised that persons who perceive themselves to be anonymous due to their part in a large group are less likely to adhere to social norms. One such example of this in current, global news is the Venezuelan anti-government protests which escalated on April 19th, 2017 (López & Watts, 2017). According to Romo and Brocchetto (2017), protestors participated in actions such as attacking authorities and utilizing homemade arson such as molotov cocktails (petrol bombs). The demonstrations caused the deaths of approximately nine persons and also resulted in several injuries. As thousands of persons participated in these protests, according to SIDE, it would be easy for persons to view themselves as anonymous and this would explain violent behaviors against the authorities. Thus, this example indicates the relevance of the model in explaining human behavior or more so misbehavior in large groups.

Although on social media websites, users are free to use their names and images, there is also the option to use pseudonyms and images which are non-identifiable with the users thus allowing the users to perceive themselves to be anonymous. According to the SIDE model persons on these websites would be less likely to adhere to the norm and or dominant view as they perceive themselves to be anonymous.

SOLUTIONS AND RECOMMENDATIONS

Methodological Approach: A Case Study

This section provides a methodological case study for studying SNS, Twitter, as an example of exploring opportunities for reconceptualization of new media. It reports selected data from a larger study of #BlackLivesMatter on Twitter conducted by the second author and supervised by the first author.

Purpose, Objectives, Research Questions and Method

In this regard, the research aimed to investigate the extent to which groupthink behaviors exist on the #BlackLivesMatter on the social media website, Twitter during a selected time period. The time-period was March 1st, 2016 and March 2nd, 2016. The selection of this time-period was based on a story/conflict which emerged between Trump supporters and #BlackLivesMatter protesters at a Trump rally in Louisville.

The video, which went viral, showcased a young, possibly teenaged female being assaulted at a Trump rally. The video which was selected for this study was a news report clip. The report showed various angles of the alleged assault as well as a brief summary of the events which occurred at the rally. Thus, it was an ideal reference point for this study.

Witnesses noted that the victim was verbally and physically abused due to her protest at the event (Howard, 2016). Following the conversation threads on Twitter, paired with a review of research on groupthink, social media and anonymity, research questions were conceptualized. These questions consisted of 1. To what extent are groupthink behaviors exhibited on the social media website Twitter on the #BlackLivesMatter (Hashtag Black Lives Matter)? and 2. To what extent does anonymity impact groupthink behaviors on #BlackLivesMatter on the social media website, Twitter?

With these questions in mind, the following objectives were determined: (1) To observe and record Twitter discussions which were posted on the identified dates (March 1st, 2016 to March 2nd, 2016). (2) To use the groupthink coding categories instrument which was developed to explore the extent to which groupthink behaviors emerged; and (3) To observe and record usernames, profile images, etc. to determine the impact of anonymity on groupthink behaviors.

The data were collated using the top tweet search option which, according to Twitter (2017, para. 2), *are the most relevant Tweets for your search. We determine relevance based on the popularity of a Tweet (e.g., when a lot of people are interacting with or sharing via Retweets and replies), the keywords it contains, and many other factors.*

Top Tweets are most relevant to the user's past interest (Twitter, 2017, para. 4). Thus, to avoid Twitter's algorithm creating a top tweet list based on the user's interest, the researcher logged out of the website before the search was conducted, to avoid tailored results.

The advanced search option on Twitter also facilitated collection of the data as it allowed for the specification of which tweets would appear, according to date (March 1st, 2016 – March 2nd, 2016) and hashtag (#BlackLivesMatter). The top twenty tweets which appeared between March 1st, 2016 and March 2nd, 2016 and which used #BlackLivesMatter (hashtag Black Lives Matter) along with corresponding tweets were captured.

Although it would have been ideal to observe and collect over twenty top tweets over an extended period of time, to collect and analyze raw data and their corresponding responses would be difficult for one person to complete. Internet Live Stats (2017), a social media monitoring platform, estimates that approximately six-thousand (6,000) tweets are sent out each second which are estimated at three-hundred and fifty thousand (350,000) tweets per minute. Therefore, to allow for the sample to be manageable for the researcher, the top twenty tweets and their corresponding responses were chosen. This was based on eligibility criteria developed by the researcher which were as follows:

1. Tweets which were posted on and between March 1st, and March 2nd, 2016.
2. Tweets which appeared in the "Top Tweets" margin.
3. Tweets which had #BlackLivesMatter.

Sixty-eight (68) tweets were collected via screen capture and text. During the analytical process, the tweets were separated into labelled conversation threads (e.g.: CH1), resulting in twenty conversation threads in February 2017. Using the groupthink coding categories, an instrument based on Janis' eight symptoms of groupthink and an additional category for neutral tweets/data, the sixty-eight tweets were then categorised using qualitative content analysis. The nine categories included

1. **C1:** Illusion of Invulnerability occurs when an individual is willing to take extreme risks for the benefit of the group (Littlejohn & Foss, 2008, p. 242; Salazar, 2009, p. 461). On social media, an example of this symptom is the expression of radical views and allegations without considering legal and/or other implications.

2. **C2:** Collective Efforts to Rationalise occurs when group members and or persons who agree with the dominant view, attempt to discredit opposing, rational viewpoints (Littlejohn & Foss, 2008, p. 242; Salazar, 2009, p. 461). On social media websites, users may resort to name calling or discrediting opposing views, diminishing other users' character/personality.
3. **C3:** Illusion of Morality, according to Littlejohn and Foss (2008, p. 242; Salazar, 2009, p. 461), occurs when group members express a strong belief that the group's view is the only ethical view and is the only moral compass for group members.
4. **C4:** Excessive Stereotyping occurs when group members construct negative stereotypes of group rivals and persons who oppose the group's dominant view. Group members may also view group rivals and/or persons who oppose the dominant view as unworthy of discussion and debate (Littlejohn & Foss, 2008, p. 242; Salazar, 2009, p. 461).
5. **C5:** Pressure to Conform occurs when group members pressure persons and/or groups to agree with the dominant view using tactics such as associating persons who disagree with the dominant view as disloyal (Littlejohn & Foss, 2008, p. 242; Salazar, 2009, p. 461).
6. **C6:** Self-Censorship occurs when persons withhold their opposing view for fear of persecution from fellow group members. This symptom also encompasses persons who withhold their opinions with the goal of maintaining group cohesion (Littlejohn & Foss, 2008, p. 242; Salazar, 2009, p. 461).
7. **C7:** Illusion of Unanimity is a false perception that members have achieved a consensus as persons do not express views outside or opposing the dominant view, indicating silence is consent (Littlejohn & Foss, 2008, p. 242; Salazar, 2009, p. 461).
8. **C8:** Self-appointed 'Mindguards', according to Littlejohn and Foss (2008, p. 242) and Salazar (2009, p. 462) consist of group members who view themselves as the protectors or informants of the group. These group members tend to dispense limited and sometimes biased information to the group, leading to stereotyping and morality issues as group members are not exposed to the complexities of the issue and/or argument.
9. **C9:** Neutral-This category was developed to encompass tweets and responses outside any of the above-mentioned categories, as well as tweets which do not express an opinion on an issue such as news reports, links and media files without commentary.

Findings

Groupthink behaviors emerged based on the findings of this data. First, the most common groupthink category was excessive stereotyping which, according to Janis, occurs when persons construct negative stereotypes of group rivals or persons who may disagree with the "group's" view. One such example is referring to persons who did not agree with the #BlackLivesMatter Movement's actions regarding the Trump rally, as racist or Trump supporters (Littlejohn & Foss, 2008 p. 242; Salazar, 2009, p. 461).

Second, although various symptoms of groupthink emerged in the data, several of Janis' symptoms of groupthink did not emerge in the sample such as self-censorship, illusion of unanimity and pressure to conform. This, however, can be attributed to the method chosen (content analysis) and the small sample size.

Specifically, after coding the raw data, six categories emerged. There were twenty-six (26) cases of excessive stereotyping; eighteen (18) instances of neutral tweets; seven (7) instances of illusion of invulnerability; twenty-four (24) instances of self-appointed mindguards; five (5) instances of illusion of morality and three (3) instances of collective efforts to rationalise. Notably, some tweets fell into two or more categories. One such example from the sample is, "Racist Matthew Heimbach admits to pushing black woman at Trump rally, blames #BlackLivesMatter #MatthewHeimbach" was categorised as, C1: Illusion of invulnerability as allegations without certain evidence were made which could have legal implications; and C8: Self-appointed 'mindguards' as biased information which suited the group's narrative and viewpoint was presented. To ensure the accuracy of the findings, coding was done on two separate occasions; (1) January 12th, 2017; and (2) April 10th, 2017 by the second author and reviewed for consistency by the first author.

Third, several conflict words also emerged in the data such as "racist" which occurred six (6) times in the same tweet, "punch/shove/push" which occurred nine (9) times, and protest which occurred nine (9) times. Observations of which key words were used in relation to each other were also noted. The key-word "white" was followed by the word "supremacist" in two instances. One such example is TweetSample 1 which stated "Oh look Black girl assaulted by white supremacist at Trump rally". Other key-words used in conjunction with each other include the key-words "racist" used with the key-word "Trump" which occurred twice and "white" occurred in relation to the word "Trump" three (3) times.

Finally, identifiability was another factor which was observed and recorded in the raw data. Initially, it was assumed that only two users were unidentifiable based on their username and images. However, upon careful inspection of the data via both the text document version and the word document version created, it was observed that nineteen (19) users (30%) utilized usernames which were unidentifiable. This increase is attributed to the revelation that a display picture does not equate identifiability alone. Other factors which would contribute to the identifiability of a user include username, name associated with the account, as well as media files associated with the account (pictures, videos, etc.). After analyzing the data, forty-four (44) users, (70%) of users were identifiable to some extent, based on the factors outlined above.

FUTURE RESEARCH DIRECTIONS

As mentioned previously, one symptom which did not emerge was self-censorship. However, despite the lack of evidence of this symptom occurring in this study, it does not dismiss the fact that this behavior occurs on social media. According to Vincent (2014) self-censorship is a common behavior on social media websites such as Twitter and Facebook which is referred to as the 'spiral of silence'. Spiral of silence theory (Noelle-Neumann 1974, 1984) has been critically assessed (Salmon & Kline, 1985). Panayırcı (2016), citing Mcdevitt et al. (2003), argues "scholars have promoted spiral of silence theory as a bridge between macro and individual level processes, as it describes how a person's motivation for opinion expression is a function of his/her surveillance of mass media and other cues about the opinion climate." (p. 55). The theory, therefore, identifies the pressure persons feel to remain silent based on the dominant view. This offers a potential account of individual and group characteristics. Gearhart and Zhang (2015, p. 208) explained that this behavior is motivated by fear of isolation and disapproval from online associates and friends, stating, "Those who share the perceived dominant opinion are likely to speak out, while the minority is silenced, beginning a spiraling process that establishes the prevailing opinion."

Thus, the similarities between the spiral of silence and groupthink symptoms emerge. The spiral of silence also aligns with the groupthink symptom of self-censorship, where persons withhold their opposing views to ensure that group cohesion is maintained (Littlejohn & Foss, 2008, p. 242). However, recent evidence suggests groupthink may not be as influential over the wisdom of the crowd when opinion leaders hold sway (Becker, Brackbill, & Centola, 2017).

Thus, as this is a small sample, it would be interesting to see if future research on social media, with emphasis on Twitter, would reveal this symptom as appearing within the context of tweets collected or if this symptom can only be determined through direct interaction with the authors of social media posts.

Based on the sample of sixty-eight tweets, there was only one instance of a person who had an unidentifiable profile, who did not openly agree with the view that the female was assaulted at the rally. Notably, there was an instance of one user who neither had a username which was identifiable as a name nor a profile photo which was a person and this user agreed with the dominant view that the female was assaulted and identified the actions of the #BlackLivesMatter movement with the actions of the protestors. This finding, based on limited examples, therefore contrasts with the SIDE model which states that persons are less likely to adhere to social norms if they perceive themselves to be anonymous (Levine & Hogg, 2010, p. 794).

Regarding anonymity, there were users who disagreed that the female was assaulted but did not do so behind a profile where they could perceive themselves to be anonymous. This finding contrasts with Tsikerdekis' (2012) findings that users were less likely to adhere to groupthink behaviors if they perceived themselves to be anonymous. Based on the sample, persons do not withhold their controversial opinions on #BlackLivesMatter on Twitter, even if they are identifiable by other users.

One reasoning behind this behavior could be attributed to the user's online persona and the expectations of their online persona. This is supported by Cho and Kim (2012, p. 3043) who averred,

Highly linkable public pseudonyms indicate that the link between a pseudonym (or nickname) and a real identity is publicly known or easy to discover. Unlinkable pseudonyms mean that system operators or third parties cannot detect a certain pseudonym's real identity.

This may explain one part of the sample where despite persons' unidentifiability, the user still practised groupthink and adhered to the dominant view that the female was assaulted as the person may have established an online persona. Cho, Kim and Acquisti's (2012, p. 3043), observation "the notion that identity shapes behavior has been affirmed in diverse fields, such as psychology, economics, organizational behavior, marketing, and information systems" reinforces the view that despite the user's anonymity, the expectation to maintain a certain persona is present.

It was assumed at the beginning of the research project that persons who used pseudonymous and unidentifiable profiles may be less likely to adhere to groupthink according to Tsikerdekis (2013) and the SIDE model which state that persons counter the norm of the group and or society if they perceive themselves to be anonymous. It was assumed this was so, as persons' public persona would not be at risk if they perceived themselves to have some level of anonymity when expressing views or conducting actions which were against the established group and societal norm. However, based on Cho et al. (2012), it can be inferred that a profile still has an attached identity. Secondly, it can also be inferred based on the results and analysis of the sample, that anonymity is not a firm deterrent of groupthink behaviors within an online space as these users may have adhered to the view that the female was assaulted, in order to protect their online persona and behave in accordance with their established reputation.

CONCLUSION

This chapter systematically reviewed the literature on groupthink and new media, specifically Twitter, focusing on the role of culture and conflict in this context. In doing so, concepts were integrated from both fields. A theoretical framework was advanced for studying groupthink and new media and investigating the influence of groupthink on new media. An empirical test of the theoretical approach was presented in a field study of Twitter posts on the #BlackLivesMatter. Social media impacts an individual's behavior and expression of views. Based on the limited sample, however, anonymity does not seem to impact groupthink behaviors online. However, one can determine that groupthink symptoms are viewed and practised within the online space when discussing sensitive social issues. The evidence indicates that groupthink continues to be a powerful influence on new media since it was described by Janis (1972) more than 45 years ago. Since groupthink ideas were first presented, new media have emerged, evolved and become an important part of contemporary human communication. This research is a modest first step towards a better understanding of groupthink within social media and online spaces and further develops an understanding of individual and group behaviors online. As we seek to understand, explain and interpret new media, a consideration of groupthink's influence on the culture and conflict in Twitter offers opportunities for discussing the reconceptualization of new media.

REFERENCES

Agosto, D. E., & Abbas, J. (2010). High school seniors' social network and other ICT use preferences and concerns. *Proceedings of the American Society for Information Science and Technology*, *47*(1), 1–10. doi:10.1002/meet.14504701025

Antonoff, M. (2015). Thoracic Surgery Social Media Network: Bringing thoracic surgery scholarship to Twitter. *The Annals of Thoracic Surgery*, *100*(2), 383–384. doi:10.1016/j.athoracsur.2015.06.049 PMID:26142909

Balleys, C., & Coll, S. (2016). Being publicly intimate: Teenagers managing online privacy. *Media Culture & Society*, *39*(6), 885–901. doi:10.1177/0163443716679033

Barki, H., & Hartwick, J. (2004). Conceptualizing the construct of interpersonal conflict. *International Journal of Conflict Management*, *15*(3), 216–244. doi:10.1108/eb022913

Baumann, P. (2009). *140 healthcare uses for Twitter*. Retrieved from http://philbaumann.com/140-health-care-uses-for-twitter/

Becker, J., Brackbill, D., & Centola, D. (2017). Network dynamics of social influence in the wisdom of crowds. *Proceedings of the National Academy of Sciences of the United States of America, 114*(26), E5070–E5076. Retrieved from www.pnas.org/cgi/doi/10.1073/pnas.1615978114 PMID:28607070

Binns, A. (2014). Twitter City and Facebook Village: Teenage girls' personas and experiences influenced by choice architecture in social networking sites. *Journal of Media Practice*, *15*(2), 71–91. doi:10.1080/14682753.2014.960763

Boyd, D. M., & Ellison, N. B. (2008). Social network sites: Definition, history, and scholarship. *Journal of Computer-Mediated Communication*, *13*, 208–230. doi:10.1111/j.1083-6101.2007.00393.x

Brundidge, J. (2010). Encountering 'difference' in the contemporary public sphere: The contribution of the Internet to the heterogeneity of political discussion networks. *Journal of Communication*, *60*(4), 680–700. doi:10.1111/j.1460-2466.2010.01509.x

Bücher, T. (2012). Want to be on the top? Algorithmic power and the threat of invisibility on Facebook. *New Media & Society*, *14*(7), 1164–1180. doi:10.1177/1461444812440159

Cho, D., Kim, S., & Acquisti, A. (2012). Empirical analysis of online anonymity and user behaviors: the impact of real name policy. *45th Hawaii International Conference on System Sciences*, 3041-3050. doi:10.1109/hicss.2012.241

Clayton, R. (2014). The third wheel: The impact of Twitter use on relationship infidelity and divorce. *Cyberpsychology, Behavior, and Social Networking*, *17*(7), 425–430. doi:10.1089/cyber.2013.0570 PMID:24690067

Colleoni, E., Rozza, A., & Arvidsson, A. (2014). Echo chamber or public sphere? Predicting political orientation and measuring political homophily in Twitter using big data. *Journal of Communication*, *64*(2), 317–332. doi:10.1111/jcom.12084

Dogan, U. (2016). Effects of social network use on happiness, psychological well- being, and life satisfaction of high school students: Case of Facebook and Twitter. *Egitim Ve Bilim-Education and Science*, *41*(183), 217–231. doi:10.15390/EB.2016.4616

Ems, L. (2014). Twitter's place in the tussle: How old power struggles play out on a new stage. *Media Culture & Society*, *36*(5), 720–731. doi:10.1177/0163443714529070

Eston, T. (2010, October 30). The social network threat. *Information Week*, *64*(1284), 66. Retrieved from http://www.darkreading.com/vulnerabilities-and-threats/social-networks-threat-to-security/d/d-id/1093707

Euwema, M. C., van de Vliert, E., & Bakker, A. B. (2003). Substantive and relational effectiveness of organizational conflict behavior. *International Journal of Conflict Management*, *14*(2), 119–139. doi:10.1108/eb022894

Ford, C. M. (2011). Twitter, Facebook, and ten red balloons: Social network problem solving and Homeland Security. *Homeland Security Affairs, 7*(1), Article 3. Retrieved from https://www.hsaj.org/articles/54

Garner, J. T. (2017). An examination of organizational dissent events and communication channels: Perspectives of a dissenter, supervisors, and coworkers. *Communication Reports*, *30*(1), 26–38. doi:10.1080/08934215.2015.1128454

Gearhart, S., & Zhang, W. (2015). 'Was it something I said?' 'No, it was something you posted!' A study of the spiral of silence theory in social media contexts. *Cyberpsychology, Behavior, and Social Networking*, *18*(4), 208–213. doi:10.1089/cyber.2014.0443 PMID:25879378

Grajales, F. III, Sheps, S., Ho, K., Novak-Lauscher, H., & Eysenbach, G. (2014). Social media: A review and tutorial of applications in medicine and health care. *Journal of Medical Internet Research*, *16*(2), e13. doi:10.2196/jmir.2912 PMID:24518354

Gruzd, A., & Roy, J. (2014). Investigating political polarization on Twitter: A Canadian perspective. *Policy and Internet*, *6*(1), 28–45. doi:10.1002/1944-2866.POI354

Gurman, T. A., Rubin, S. E., & Roess, A. A. (2012). Effectiveness of mHealth behavior change communication interventions in developing countries: A systematic review of the literature. *Journal of Health Communication*, *17*(1), 82–104. doi:10.1080/10810730.2011.649160 PMID:22548603

Hansen, D. L. (2011). Exploring social media relationships. *On the Horizon*, *19*(1), 43–51. doi:10.1108/10748121111107726

Himelboim, I., McCreery, S., & Smith, M. (2013). Birds of a feather tweet together: Integrating network and content analyses to examine cross-ideology exposure on Twitter. *Journal of Computer-Mediated Communication*, *18*(2), 40–60. doi:10.1111/jcc4.12001

Howard, H. (2016, March 2). Donald Trump's supporters assaulted a Black girl at a campaign rally. *Teen Vogue*. Retrieved March 12, 2016, from http://www.teenvogue.com/story/black-girl-assaulted-donald-trump-rally

Hui, P., & Buchegger, S. (2009). Groupthink and peer pressure: Social influence in online social network groups. In *Proceedings 2009 International Conference on Advances in Social Network Analysis and Mining* (pp. 53 – 59). IEEE. doi:10.1109/ASONAM.2009.17

Internet Live Stats. (2017). *Twitter Usage Statistics*. Retrieved August 24, 2017, from http://www.internetlivestats.com/twitter-statistics/

Jahng, M., & Littau, J. (2016). Interacting is believing: Interactivity, social cue, and perceptions of journalistic credibility on Twitter. *Journalism & Mass Communication Quarterly*, *93*(1), 38–58. doi:10.1177/1077699015606680

Janis, I. L. (1972). *Victims of groupthink*. New York: Houghton Mifflin.

Janis, I. L. (1982). *Groupthink: Psychological studies of policy decisions and fiascoes* (2nd ed.). New York: Houghton Mifflin.

Jeong, T., & Coyle, E. (2014). What are you worrying about on Facebook and Twitter? An empirical investigation of young social network site users' privacy perceptions and behaviors. *Journal of Interactive Advertising*, *14*(2), 51–59. doi:10.1080/15252019.2014.930678

Karlsen, R., Steen-Johnsen, K., Wollebæk, D., & Enjolras, B. (2017). Echo chamber and trench warfare dynamics in online debates. *European Journal of Communication*, *32*(3), 257–273. doi:10.1177/0267323117695734 PMID:28690351

Katopol, P. (2015). Groupthink: Group dynamics and the decision-making process. *Library Leadership & Management (Online), 30*(1), 1-6. Retrieved from https://journals.tdl.org/llm/index.php/llm/article/view/7172/6350

Kenski, K., Coe, K., & Rains, S. A. (in press). Perceptions of uncivil discourse online: An examination of types and predictors. *Communication Research*. doi:10.1177/0093650217699933

Korhan, O., & Ersoy, M. (2016). Usability and functionality factors of the social network site application users from the perspective of uses and gratification theory. *Quality & Quantity*, *50*(4), 1799–1816. doi:10.1007/s11135-015-0236-7

Kosur, J. (2014, August 29). *Facebook and Twitter have created political groupthink, study claims*. Retrieved February 02, 2016, from http://www.business2community.com/social-buzz/facebook-twitter-created- political-silence-study-claims-0993862#gPzLYHIUh3UhPXSt.97

Kroon, Å. (2017). More than a hashtag: Producers' and users' co-creation of a loving "we" in a second screen TV sports production. *Television & New Media*, *18*(7), 670–688. doi:10.1177/1527476417699708

Kruikemeier, S., Van Noort, G., Vliegenthart, R., & de Vreese, H., C. (. (2016). The relationship between online campaigning and political involvement. *Online Information Review*, *40*(5), 673–694. doi:10.1108/OIR-11-2015-0346

Kuo, F. Y., Tseng, C. Y., Tseng, F. C., & Lin, C. S. (2013). A study of social information control affordances and gender difference in Facebook self-presentation. *Cyberpsychology, Behavior, and Social Networking*, *16*(9), 635–644. doi:10.1089/cyber.2012.0345 PMID:23849000

Lee, J. K., Choi, J., Kim, C., & Kim, Y. (2014). Social media, network heterogeneity, and opinion polarization. *Journal of Communication*, *64*(4), 702–722. doi:10.1111/jcom.12077

Levine, J., & Hogg, M. (2010). *Encyclopedia of group processes & intergroup relations*. New Delhi: SAGE Publications. doi:10.4135/9781412972017

Liao, C., Squicciarini, A., Griffin, C., & Rajtmajer, S. (2016). A hybrid epidemic model for deindividuation and antinormative behavior in online social networks. *Social Network Analysis and Mining*, *6*(1), 1–11. doi:10.1007/s13278-016-0321-5

Littlejohn, S. W., & Foss, K. A. (2008). *Theories of human communication*. Belmont, CA: Thomson Wadsworth Cengage Learning.

Liu, B., Hsu, Y., & Ke, W. (2014). Virus infection control in online social networks based on probabilistic communities. *International Journal of Communication Systems*, *27*(12), 4481–4491. doi:10.1002/dac.2630

López, V., & Watts, J. (2017, April 19). *Deaths and injuries reported amid 'mother of all marches' in Venezuela*. Retrieved April 20, 2017, from https://www.theguardian.com/world/2017/apr/19/venezuela-protest-mother-of-all-marches-maduro-violence

Manca, S., & Ranieri, M. (2016). Facebook and the others. Potentials and obstacles of social media for teaching in higher education. *Computers & Education*, *95*, 216–230. doi:10.1016/j.compedu.2016.01.012

Marwick, A. (2012). The public domain: Social surveillance in everyday life. *Surveillance & Society*, *9*(4), 378–393. Retrieved from https://ojs.library.queensu.ca/index.php/surveillance-and-society/article/view/pub_dom

Meng, J., Martinez, L., Holmstrom, A., Chung, M., & Cox, J. (2017). Research on social networking sites and social support from 2004 to 2015: A narrative review and directions for future research. *Cyberpsychology, Behavior, and Social Networking*, *20*(1), 44–51. doi:10.1089/cyber.2016.0325 PMID:28002686

Mishra, N., & Silakari, S. (2012). Image mining in the context of content based image retrieval: A perspective. *International Journal of Computer Science Issues*, *9*(4), 69–76. Retrieved from http://ijcsi.org/papers/IJCSI-9-4-3-69-76.pdf

Myrick, J., Holton, A., Himelboim, I., & Love, B. (2016). #Stupidcancer: Exploring a typology of social support and the role of emotional expression in a social media community. *Health Communication*, *31*(5), 596–605. doi:10.1080/10410236.2014.981664 PMID:26453480

Noelle-Neumann, E. (1974). The spiral of silence: A theory of public opinion. *Journal of Communication*, *24*(2), 43–51. doi:10.1111/j.1460-2466.1974.tb00367.x

Noelle-Neumann, E. (1984). *The spiral of silence: Public opinion – Our social skin*. Chicago, IL: University of Chicago Press.

O'Hara, K., & Stevens, D. (2015). Echo chambers and online radicalism: Assessing the Internet's complicity in violent extremism. *Policy and Internet*, *7*(4), 401–422. doi:10.1002/poi3.88

Panayırcı, U. (2016). Are communication theories affected by new communication technologies? A look at spiral of silence theory. *Online Academic Journal of Information Technology*, *7*(22), 51–66. doi:10.5824/1309-1581.2016.1.004.x

Petrocchi, N., Asnaani, A., Martinez, A., Nadkarni, A., & Hofmann, S. (2015). Differences between people who use only Facebook and those who use Facebook plus Twitter. *International Journal of Human-Computer Interaction*, *31*(2), 157–165. doi:10.1080/10447318.2014.986640 PMID:26997849

Rahim, A. (1983). A measure of styles of handling interpersonal conflict. *Academy of Management Journal*, *26*(2), 368–376. doi:10.2307/255985 PMID:10263067

Romo, R., & Brocchetto, M. (2017, April 20). *Venezuela protests: What you need to know*. Retrieved April 20, 2017, from http://edition.cnn.com/2017/04/18/americas/venezuela-protest-explainer/

Salazar, A. J. (2009). Groupthink. In S. W. Littlejohn & K. A. Foss (Eds.), *Encyclopedia of Communication Theory* (Vol. 2, pp. 461–462). Thousand Oaks, CA: SAGE Publications. doi:10.4135/9781412959384.n169

Salmon, C. T., & Kline, F. G. (1985). The spiral of silence ten years later: An examination and evaluation. In K. R. Sanders, L. L. Kaid, & D. Nimmo (Eds.), *Political Communication Yearbook 1984* (pp. 3–30). Carbondale, IL: Southern Illinois University Press.

Sar, R., & Al-Saggaf, K. (2014). Contextual integrity's decision heuristic and the tracking by social network sites. *Ethics and Information Technology*, *16*(1), 15–26. doi:10.1007/s10676-013-9329-y

Schmidt, A. (2013). Groupthink. In *Britannica Online Academic Edition.* Encyclopædia Britannica, Inc. Retrieved from https://www.britannica.com/contributor/Anna-Schmidt/9345859

Sunstein, C. (2001). *Republic.com.* Princeton, NJ: Princeton University Press.

Sunstein, C. (2007). *Republic.com 2.0.* Princeton, NJ: Princeton University Press.

Sutton, J., Gibson, C., Phillips, N., Spiro, E., League, C., Johnson, B., ... Butts, C. (2015). A cross-hazard analysis of terse message retransmission on Twitter. *Proceedings of the National Academy of Sciences of the United States of America*, *112*(48), 14793–14798. doi:10.1073/pnas.1508916112 PMID:26627233

Tour, S., Thomas, K., Walker, D., Leighton, P., Yong, A., & Batchelor, J. (2014). Survey and online discussion groups to develop a patient-rated outcome measure on acceptability of treatment response in vitiligo. *BMC Dermatology*, *14*(1), 10. doi:10.1186/1471-5945-14-10 PMID:24929563

Tsikerdekis, M. (2012). *Social interaction design for social media: The case of groupthink and aggression* (Unpublished doctoral dissertation). Masaryk University.

Tsikerdekis, M. (2013). The effects of perceived anonymity and anonymity states on conformity and groupthink in online communities: A Wikipedia study. *Journal of the American Society for Information Science and Technology*, *64*(5), 1001–1015. doi:10.1002/asi.22795

Twitter. (2017). *FAQs about top search results*. Retrieved August 24, 2017, from https://support.twitter.com/articles/131209

Vincent, J. (2014, August 27). *The 'spiral of silence': How social media encourages self-censorship online.* Retrieved February 27, 2017, from http://www.independent.co.uk/life-style/gadgets-and-tech/the-spiral-of-silence how-social-media-encourages-self-censorship-online-9693044.html

Waheed, H., Anjum, M., Rehman, M., & Khawaja, A. (2017). Investigation of user behavior on social networking sites. *PLoS One, 12*(2), e0169693. doi:10.1371/journal.pone.0169693 PMID:28151963

Wu, J., Chen, L., Yu, Q., Han, P. P., & Wu, Zh. (2015). Trust-aware media recommendation in heterogeneous social networks. *World Wide Web-Internet and Web Information Systems, 18*(1), 139–157. doi:10.1007/s11280-013- 0243-3

KEY TERMS AND DEFINITIONS

Conflict: A situation in which at least two parties have perceived mutually incompatible goals and interests and which can be managed using strategies ranging from integrative or win-win to competitive or win-lose approaches.

Conflict Interactions: Behaviors of parties whose goals and interests are perceived to be mutually incompatible. These interactions may include cognitive (thought), behavioral (action), and affective (feeling) dimensions.

Culture: The characteristic visible and invisible ties that bind its members and which are reflected in the shared assumptions, beliefs, interests, practices, and patterns of behavior.

Groupthink: A behavior associated with a way of thinking in which members of groups uncritically accept a dominant view or position perceived to be the consensus of such groups in order to maintain group cohesion.

Intercultural Connections: Social relationships facilitated by social media platforms which allow users to match their interests and preferences based on the online profiles they create.

Online Open Community: A public and accessible group of persons who use social platforms and web-based infrastructure and service and networking or connections to create personal profiles which are available to the public with unrestricted access.

Social Networking Sites (SNS): A term that refers to both networks or web-based infrastructure and services, and networking or connections among users of SNS.

Twitter: A microblog limited to 140 characters. A social networking site that functions as a social diary. It is a popular site for intercultural connection and conflict interaction. Twitter users or tweepers explore, form, and maintain connections within groups of persons with similar cultural interests, and between and across cultures. These connections may also include conflict interactions such as dissent and responses to it.

Section 4

New Media, Culture and Politics and Policies

This section presents chapters exploring the connection between culture and politics using new media, specifically focusing on political identities, political conflict, and communication of politics in the new media platform.

Chapter 10
American People vs. Politicians:
Group Vitality Achieved Through the Construction and Realignment of Political Cultural Identity in Online Comments About "Obamacare"

Anastacia Dawn Kurylo
St. Joseph's College, USA

ABSTRACT

To study political identity construction, a thematic analysis is used to explore online reviews of the book Beating Obamacare. Themes that emerged construct four political identities relevant to the construction Obamacare, the American public, President Obama and politicians, and those in opposition to Obamacare. The construction of these identities contributes to group vitality. This process is facilitated by the juxtaposition of the construction of the American public with those who oppose Obamacare versus politicians. Notably, this construction is accomplished with the near absence of reference to political party affiliation creating a realignment of political identity in a way that provides stronger group vitality than would be achieved across traditional partisan lines. This chapter has implications for understanding how identity is constructed online to demonstrate group vitality in ways that facilitate intracultural and intercultural communication.

DOI: 10.4018/978-1-5225-3784-7.ch010

INTRODUCTION

The Affordable Care Act (ACA) was signed into law on March 23, 2010. This controversial legislation has been received with mixed reviews and has been a lightning rod for political ideological debate and grandstanding from those espousing various political perspectives (e.g., Goldzwig, 2013; Johnston, Hillygus, & Bartels, 2014). In this way, the Affordable Care Act is more than a law; it provides a talking point that can help establish political alignment as evidenced by its politically loaded nickname 'Obamacare' that references, or rather attributes blame to, Barack Obama, the 44th President of the United States (Hopper, 2015). As a construct used for political alignment, the way in which the Affordable Care Act is discussed can inform about current American political identities. This chapter exposes how communication about ACA constructs political identities. This construction process has high stakes because it facilitates the group vitality (Giles, 1978) of political groups within the American political system as they vie for power and compete to exist within the current American political climate.

BACKGROUND

The Social Construction of Political Identity

From a social construction approach (e.g., Gergen, 1991), identity is not viewed as a personal static aspect of self that is independent from others. Instead, identity is viewed as a product of collaborative communication processes (Mokros, 2003; Tracy, 2002; Galanes & Leeds-Hurwitz, 2009). Much work has explored the ways in which identity- particularly related to cultural group memberships including but not limited to race, ethnicity, gender, or sexual orientation- is a product of communication (e.g., Lee, 1996; Reyes, 2007; Shi & Babrow, 2007). Together the members of a cultural group work to create a shared cultural identity through communication. In other words, how cultural group members verbally and nonverbally communicate about their cultural group and about characteristics of their cultural group identity, amongst each other and with members of other groups, collaboratively constructs that group identity. This construction of identity occurs regardless of intent to express a particular identity. Furthermore, construction does not inherently and only involve the identity of one's self. Rather, through communication, a person can not only attempt to construct their own identity but the identity of co-present and non-co-present others as well. Furthermore, communication by a single person does not in itself construct identity. Rather, it is the collaborative work of multiple people working together, more often than not outside of their awareness of doing so, to construct identity. This construction process occurs regardless of whether interaction takes place face-to-face or in mediated environments such as online social networking sites (Kurylo & Shuter, 2015).

Perhaps particularly because social media interconnects people from disparate locations, identity construction independent from an objective reality, as argued by Gergen (1991) among others, is epitomized in social media. Identity is constructed through online communication in the absence of the physical and tangible ways in which identity has historically been constructed before, as Gergen (1991) argues, the technologies of social saturation. In other words, with the ubiquity of online environments in which to be social, the assertion of identity for one's self and others becomes ever more reliant on words and, increasingly, images and ever distanced from the presumption of an objective reality underlying this assertion. In this way, within a site of social meaning, communicators construct identity for various cultural group members regardless of how others might view that group in any statistically and scientifically verifiable way. Indeed, in as much as identity construction of groups can often invoke stereotypes, this is not a new claim about identity. LaPierre (1936) found in his study testing the assertion that stereotypes have a kernel of truth that stereotypes of cultural groups can exist not only in the absence of evidence for a stereotype but also in the presence of evidence that directly contradicts the stereotype. Thus, the construction of identity through communication is a mechanism through which to assert the reality of that identity.

Cultural identity has traditionally been associated with ethnic and geographic groups. Still today, intercultural purists espouse this view. However, increasingly race, gender, and sexual orientation are amongst cultural groups studied by intercultural scholars. The groups permitted to be studied as intercultural communication are indeed ever increasing. For example, Harris (2013) identifies rape survivors as a co-cultural. Similarly, Kurylo (2013; 2017) argues for an inclusive definition of what groups can be identified as cultural in nature (i.e., having a distinct way of life). Towards this end, a clarification is necessitated about the cultural group studied in the current chapter. Although the political identities discussed are constructed in American culture and are asserted as part of American culture, American culture is not the cultural group under study. Rather, the chapter identifies political cultural groups as communicating intraculturally amongst themselves and interculturally to other cultural groups. In this way, the political parties are in and of themselves, regardless of existing within an American context, cultural groups whose communication with each other constitute inter-cultural communication.

A person's political identity is complex. Depending on the issues being discussed a person may vary across a spectrum of political ideology rather than holding firm allegiance to just one. Research shows that on many economic and social issues there is moderation and centrism (Fiorina, 2010); yet, the political topics that arguably are most visible and garner the most attention in the media, speeches, and interpersonal communication communicate a divide amongst the left (i.e., democrats and liberals) and right (i.e., Tea Party members, libertarians, conservatives, and republicans). This seemingly bipartisan divide has been exacerbated by the relatively recent arrival of the Tea Party into American politics, the boundary breaking election and re-election of the first bi-racial president (more commonly constructed as the first black president), a poor economy, a 'war on terror' as well as on Afghanistan and Iraq, and the passing of controversial healthcare legislature. Despite the complexity of any one person's avowed political identity, the construction of political identity is often reductionist.

The Affordable Care Act provides a point of intersection amongst many current politically charged topics on which there is much misunderstanding (Pasek, Sood, & Krosnick, 2015) and about which people may be divided along bipartisan lines including but not limited to issues related to the economy, class, and race. The law is such a driving force in politics that opposition to the healthcare law is one of the reasons for a 16-day government shut down in the United States from October 1 to October 16, 2013. This occurred despite the legality of the law which was vetted through all three branches of the federal government (i.e., executive, legislative, and judicial), all members of which hold offices as representatives of the citizenship of the United States at large. In 2016, President Trump made repealing the Affordable Care Act a basic part of his stump speech while running for office and as president repeatedly makes Obamacare a subject of his political activity. As such a strong force in today's political climate, Obamacare provides an ideal topic through which to study the identity construction of political groups. It should be noted, however, that the current chapter does not claim as the focus of its study the topic of Affordable Care Act or healthcare more broadly. Rather, the present chapter takes as its focus political identities that are constructed during discussion about the Affordable Care Act wherein the legislation serves as an opportunity for speakers to claim meaning for various political identities. Specifically, the Affordable Care Act serves as the mechanism through which communicators are able to demonstrate group vitality for their cultural identity.

Group Vitality

Group vitality refers to the strength of a cultural group identity (Giles, 1978; Harwood, Giles & Bourhis, 1994). Group vitality is achieved through intragroup and intergroup communication. The concept of group vitality was originally conceptualized as ethnolinguistic vitality theory (Giles, 1978; Ehala, 2010). In this form, this theory proposed that an ethnic or geographically delimited cultural group gained and preserved a sense of its identity through distinctive and collective linguistic patterns

(Giles, 1978). Group vitality is integral for cultural groups because the more vitality a group has "the more likely it will survive and thrive as a collective entity in the intergroup context" (Harwood, Giles & Bourhis, 1994, p. 168). Thus, group vitality informs about a group's ability to maintain itself in existence over time. The ability to survive amongst so many other cultural groups is akin to extinction faced by different species. Although the comparison is seemingly extreme, the precedent exists for the extinction of entire cultural groups over time because of decreased group vitality. This has occurred with ancient cultures such as the Mayan, Aztec, Arawak, and Rapa Nui cultures. The threat of extinction of a cultural group exists within systems wherein groups vie for economic, political, and social resources.

The concept of group vitality has been broadened since its original iteration related to ethnic and geographic groups (e.g., Pornsakulvanich, 2007; Yaeger-Dror, 1988). The theory has now been stretched to allow it to have applicability to cultural groups whose identities are not tied to ethnicity or geographic location. For example, studies have been conducted applying the concept of group vitality even to religious groups (e.g., Croucher, Austin, Fang, & Holody, 2011) and age based groups (e.g., Ota, Giles, & Gallois, 2002). Group vitality, then, can be applied through non-ethnic non-geographic groups including political groups. Understanding how members of political groups foster their group's survival through how they communicate is insightful to understanding the current political climate in the United States, one which has perplexed many in the media, politics, and the citizenry itself.

Three basic tenants of group vitality have remained consistent regardless of the type of group to which the concept is applied: demography, institutional support, and social status. *Demography* refers to the sheer numbers of members of the group. Thus, vitality is dependent upon maintaining and increasing the number of people in the group. *Institutional support* refers "to the extent that the community has gained formal and informal representation in the various institutions of a community, region, state or nation" (Harwood, Giles & Bourhis, 1994, p. 168) in such a way as to provide group members with power and influence over current and future decisions that affect the group. *Social status* refers to a "community's social prestige, its socio-historical status and the prestige of its language and culture" (Harwood, Giles & Bourhis, 1994, p. 170). The extent to which a group holds prestige and social status in the community contributes to its group vitality accordingly.

With regard to political identity, as with all cultural identity, communicators working collaboratively are able to demonstrate to their group vitality to fellow group members as well as to those outside their group. Group vitality provides for a cultural group, even a political culture, a way to claim a right to existence amongst other cultural groups. This is particularly important to understand, and group vitality provides a useful tool through which to do so, for those groups that are not geographically or nationally identified and, thus, without the presumed physical tangible reality to rely on to claim a right to existence. Moreover, the ability to invoke group vitality is particularly important for cultural groups who congregate online rather than in physical locations. In the latter, the pure mass of physically co-present people would help demonstrate group vitality; however, in the absence of physical co-presence in social media, group vitality must be demonstrated through communication. Thus, understanding how group vitality is demonstrated for political identity in a social media context extends previous understanding of the ways in which ethnic and national cultural groups demonstrate group vitality to themselves and others (Giles & Giles, 2013, 2016) to those groups who are not defined ethnically or nationally demonstrating group vitality in online contexts.

CONSTRUCTION AND REALIGNMENT OF POLITICAL CULTURAL IDENTITY

To explore the construction of political identity and the role this construction plays in the group vitality of political groups, the current study explores how political cultural identity is constructed through communication about the Affordable Care Act, as a vital lightning rod piece of legislation to which various political groups have proffered an ideological viewpoint. Moreover, because the theoretical construct of group vitality provides a lens through which to interpret group identity construction and to understand its necessity for the survival of political groups, the study seeks to answer the following research questions about the construction of political identity and group vitality. The method used to answer these research questions is discussed in the following section.

- **Research Question One:** *How is political identity constructed through communication related to ACA?*
- **Research Question Two:** *How does the construction of political identity through communication about ACA play a role in the group vitality of the constructed political group(s)?*

Method

An exploration of communication messages centered on the topic of ACA to explore the construction of political identity requires a sample of messages centered on Obamacare. Ideally these messages would be communicated by members of a non-political, non-media, and non-entertainment based population that represent the general public so that the data would better represent a cross section of the population rather than those privileged with access to voice their opinions on

Obamacare. Towards this end, new media provides a platform through which people can express viewpoints as well as provide a location for which unobtrusive data can be collected unobtrusively. The research presented here explores identity construction enacted through online book reviews posted on Amazon.com. Vàsquez (2014) demonstrates the value of utilizing customer reviews for research. Amazon.com reviews were selected because of its interactive book review functionality available to anyone with access to the internet and because Amazon.com "has built itself into the world's largest online marketplace thanks in part to the recommendations and reviews of its users" (Dumova, 2016; see also Ante, 2009). Online reviews involve the characteristics of new media in that they are digital, interactive, hypertextual, virtual, networked, and simulated (Lister, Dovey, Giddings, Grant, & Kelly, 2009).

Book Reviews

The research presented here explores identity construction enacted through online book reviews of a particular book on Obamacare, which serves as the unit of analysis. Dumova discusses the appropriateness of activity driven sampling for research. According to Dumova, "event driven [sampling occurs when] the choice of units is dictated by certain activities or events in which people are engaged rather than affiliations or the existence of enumerated subgroups in the population" (Dumova, 2016; Scott, 2013). Reviews were selected for three reasons. First, reviews are accessible online and delineated with dates thereby providing a finite unobtrusively collected data set that is easily retrieved and converted to text based computer software programs. Second, reviews provide an outlet for opinions that are necessarily rich with data. The anonymity of the review process through the voluntary use of pseudonyms allows even opinions that might remain unspoken in a conversation due to social and conversational norms to be given the opportunity to be shared with others. Third, reviews are fundamentally offered to provide advice, to sway potential buyers to one outcome or another. Moreover, Merchant (2016) notes, "consumer reviews [show] how subscribers provide advice, warning, and public endorsement" embedded into the review.

The Book

To determine which book to use as the basis of the study, Amazon.com's search tool was used to search for the word 'Obamacare.' This yielded 825 hits. Of these, only those that included Obamacare in the title, whose main content was about Obamacare rather than President Obama more broadly as indicated by the words 'handbook' and 'guide' for example, and that were published after 2010 when the law was passed were further considered. Of these there appeared a natural split in the popularity of the books. Most books had up to 125 reviews. Only three books had over 300 reviews. No books fell in between these two ranges. This natural split suggested the three were the most popular books in the Amazon marketplace on the topic of Obamacare. As a check on this process, two other searches were conducted with the more neutral words 'healthcare' and 'Affordable Care Act' rather than 'Obamacare,' which is potentially a loaded term indicative of the political right. The results for all three searches with the same restrictions on the results yielded the identical three books. Thus, only these three books were further considered. Although some might argue for the benefit of incorporating all three books into the current study, the reader is reminded that the goal of the study is not to analyze the Affordable Care Act though this would be an admirable aim for another study, but rather to study how political identity is constructed through discussion about the Affordable Care Act. For the latter, any of these books may suffice as a location of this identity construction process and only one was ultimately selected.

Of the three books, two were written by authors known to be right of center and one known to be left of center. Yet, all three books were promoted with the politically neutral utilitarian sounding terms of either 'guide' or 'handbook' in the title presumably in an attempt to appeal to a broader audience than the author's own political affiliation would suggest. All three books sell for between $10 and $15.00 on Amazon.com. Two books -- *The Healing of America: A Global Quest for Better, Cheaper, and Fairer Health Care* by T.R. Reid and *ObamaCare Survival Guide: The Affordable Care Act and What It Means for You and Your Healthcare* by Nick J. Tate were published in August 31, 2010 and October 1, 2012 respectively. The most recent book, *Beating Obamacare: Your Handbook for the New Healthcare Law,* was published January 14, 2013. This latter book was chosen for two reasons. First, because of its recency at the time the research was conducted it would potentially contain the most recent comments and provide the most up-to-date information for readers and reviewers to reference. Second, Dr. Betsy McCaughey, the author, a conservative policy advocate, and former Lt. Governor of New York State, was touted as one of the only people to have read the healthcare law in its entirety and, so, the book might arguably contain the most accurate information related to the law and perhaps appear to prospective readers as providing the most credible and thorough discussion and, thus, appear to be the most politically neutral of all three books.

Data

As of November 4, 2013, *Beating Obamacare: Your Handbook for the New Healthcare Law* had received a copious amount of review comments (327) on the Amazon.com website. One identical review was posted twice. The second instance was removed from the dataset resulting in N = 326 reviews used in the study. Amazon reviews provide considerable information about their reviewers. However, self-reported gender, race, age, and ethnicity were indeterminable based on the limits of the information requested in Amazon's review interface. The database created for the current study included the text of these reviews, the date posted, and the title given by the reviewer for the review, the reviewer user name, the number of reviews the reviewer has written for Amazon.com in total, the state self-identified by the reviewer when indicated, and the number of stars the book received by the reviewer out of five total. State was inconsistently provided by reviewers and so were not sufficient to explore related patterns in the data and, so, was not further considered. Similarly, reviewer username, which varied from "Stephan" to "Quadrocycle" to, simply, "F." were not substantive and, so, were not further considered.

The number of reviews that each reviewer had written was also not particularly informative. The minimum number of reviews and the mode was one and the maximum number 302. Only five reviewers had written more than 100 reviews which skewed the average considerably ($x = 15.5$). Of the 326 reviewers, 48 (15%) had never reviewed on Amazon before but were willing to do so for this book alone. All 326 reviews published starting with the first posted on February 11, 2013 through November 4, 2013 were analyzed. About half of these (48%) were rated 5 star (n=157); the remaining were more evenly divided with the following ratings: 4 star (n = 49), 3 star (n = 52), 2 star (n = 33), and 1 star (n = 35).

It should be noted that reviews do not represent people who read the book in its entirety and provided unsolicited feedback about it, although some reviewers may. The nature of the review process on Amazon.com is such that buyers can be prompted via email to provide a review of their product. This prompting can occur in two ways. Amazon's Vine program which launched in 2007 invites a select group of unpaid panelists to review products for their site with the invitation based on how Amazon customers have rated the usefulness of reviewer's reviews in the past. This is not likely to be what occurred for the majority of reviewers of *Beating Obamacare* who mentioned receiving prompts to review the book since Vine reviewers would not likely be annoyed by prompts to review by Amazon and would be cognizant of not mentioning the prompts to review by Amazon. In lieu of Vine, Amazon customers may receive prompts by vendors themselves. These prompts would be sent through a vendor's Amazon portal and may have the appearance of being from Amazon. These prompts can be emailed as frequently and with whatever content a vendor prefers to include in order to motivate a reviewer to respond except that incentives for reviews and too frequent or unprofessional prompts would warrant censure from Amazon. Vendor sent prompts could be ignored and reviewing a purchase would remain as an option on the person's account for them to undertake (or not) at a later time. However, people who have not read the book fully either out of ethical obligation, mistaken understanding that a review is required, or a motivation to post may be more likely to review the book at the time when they receive this prompt from a vendor. These prompts by a vendor are most likely to happen within a few weeks of a purchase.

Indeed, although the comments included as part of the data set used in this study cover nearly a year, more than half were written within the first four months after the book's publication date suggesting that there was a motivation to post comments to provide feedback to other potential Amazon customers who might want to purchase the book. For some reviewers, the urgency to share their opinion was paramount regardless of whether they had read the book such that some reviews indicated versions of the following statements: "skimmed the book," "only on p. 29," "I haven't read it," "my son is reading it," "I did not read it yet," or otherwise indicated that they have not begun to read the book at all. Regardless of whether they had read the book, some reviewers used the opportunity for the reviews to comment on ACA. For example:

*After you read this book, send the copy to one of your *$@# representatives or Senator who voted for this abomination with a note inside the cover asking them to read this and to reverse this law. If you have a business, convert your employees to independent contractors and pay them the employer's share of benefits and social security. Nothing wakes up people like seeing what employers really pay them but they don't see or get because it goes to government, as well as the paper work have to do for them. This will also permit your employees to remain full time instead of having their hours or jobs cut, so this isn't hurting them but can be welcome. A kind former employer will provide some training to transition and make people aware of what they have to do now that they are in business for themselves. I gave this a neutral rating only because I haven't read it.*

Other reviewers both read the book and used their review as a platform for commentary on ACA. Unfortunately, while the excerpted reviewer indicated their status of having read/not read the book, many do not. Therefore, the reviews related to ACA are treated as sites of construction about political identity, regardless of whether a reviewer did or did not read the book in its entirety.

Thematic Analysis

A thematic analysis was conducted in order to explore the content of the reviews. Thematic analysis is used in communication research (e.g., Dougherty, 2001; Orbe & Warren, 2000; Wright, 2000) as a "process for encoding qualitative information" (Boyatzis, 1998, p. vi; see also Strauss & Corbin, 1998). Thematic analysis requires the constant comparison of one theme to another in order to delimit where each begins and ends. This process incorporates what Glaser and Strauss (1967) termed the constant comparative method which allows some themes to be subsumed under more inclusive ones as the process is undertaken. It is through this deeper analysis that overt and subtle meanings in the form of themes can inductively emerge. The themes produced from this process prove insightful about the construction of political identity.

To begin this process, each title and review was read repeatedly and notes were taken on the initial impressions of the researcher. Reflexivity is important to this process as a way for researcher bias to come to the fore so that a deeper analysis can be attained. Through the initial process of reading and rereading the data one particular assumption became obvious. With regard to political identity, the researcher initially assumed that the data would include overt mention of political identity (e.g., republican or democrat) guided the process. However, the data had a surprising dearth of reference to political parties. The word ‘democrat’ was only used four times in all 326 reviews with one of these being a reviewer self-identifying as a democrat. The word ‘liberal’ was only used twice with one of these being a reviewer self-identifying as a liberal. The word ‘left’ was not used at all to refer to political side. The words ‘right,’ ‘conservative,’ and ‘republican’ were each used only three times. Thus, an overwhelming majority of reviewers did not align themselves in an overt partisan way despite the researcher’s initial assumption that this would be the case. As such, political party affiliations were not themes which emerged as meaningful in the data.

As reviews were studied, it became clear that despite the absence of political party affiliation being overtly invoked, reviewers were constructing political identities as they provided feedback on the book itself. In this way, reviews were a conduit through which reviewers could express their thoughts and emotions about topics related to the book. Reviews that were rated two to four stars tended to stay focused discussing the merits and pitfalls of the book itself whereas reviews at the extremes rated one or five tended to provide more commentary unrelated to the book itself. In particular, five-star reviews in tended towards commentary beyond the book and, not surprisingly, incorporated a more dramatic communication style including the use of caps, ellipses, rhetorical questions, statistics, quotes, dates, and exclamation points for emphasis. The emphatic nature of these reviews suggest further motivation on the part of these reviewers to make certain their opinion was heard.

All 326 reviews, regardless of how many stars the review was accompanied by, were further analyzed. In order to reduce this data, the researcher focused on commentary in each review that was unrelated to a most basic review of the book itself as opinion about the quality of the book was not the focus of the study and did not substantively contribute to the construction of political identity. In this way parts of a review that related to simply whether the book being liked or disliked was not further considered although the other aspects of that review were. Each review and title were carefully and repeatedly read until themes reflective of the data began to emerge. The delineation of these emergent themes required constant comparison between each theme to determine how each word, phrase, or sentence of the commentary seemed to fit amidst these emerging themes. These themes were compared, re-articulated, and reduced to have clearly defined and identifiable definitions and distinctions. Ultimately, these themes were delimited through this constant comparison method and used to code the database to assure saturation was reached. Despite how short the reviews were, multiple themes were able to be applied even in a single review.

Once themes identified through a constant comparative method, reviews themselves, rather than titles for the reviews were coded. The titles were not used because these were more generic, often reiterated the book title, or were dramatic presumably to attract readers. Each review was coded present or absent for the four political identities that emerged. The presence of these four identities served as a filter for whether the review would be coded further. Reviews that discussed one of the four identities were further coded manually with the relevant themes related to that identity. This resulted in the creation of a subset of reviews that were further analyzes with those that stayed focused on the quality of the book itself and/or the author not considered further as this was not the focus of the study. Finally, to cross-check the coding to ensure consistency, an automated search using the software program functionality was conducted for the root word (i.e., code) for all terms relevant to each theme. Reviews in which the code appeared that were not originally coded as the relevant theme, were interrogated to determine the extent to which context warranted coding and, when appropriate, the coding was changed.

Findings

The Construction of Four Political Identities

The first research question explored in the current study looked to determine how political identity is constructed through communication related to Obamacare. Through the thematic analysis conducted, themes relevant to the following four political identities emerged: Obamacare, Obama and politicians, the opposition to Obamacare, and the American people. Each theme associated with these four political identities is defined and discussed in the following section.

The Construction of Obamacare (N = 244; 75%)

Obamacare was not surprisingly the dominant topic for commentary in the reviews. To explore this concept, reviews were coded for whether they explicitly mention Obamacare. Four themes emerged related to how Obamacare was discussed. Although Obamacare is a law rather than an individual, reviewers personified Obamacare in a way reminiscent of Frankenstein's monster. As such, Obamacare was constructed as having an identity and as a being with volition. When "Obamacare," "American Health Care Act," or other reference to it was coded in the data, it was constructed as inevitable (n = 87; 36%), threatening (n = 80; 33%), complex (n = 34; 14%), and fraudulent (n = 15; 6%).

- *Inevitable*

These reviews suggest that Obamacare has agency to act upon them and that this was unavoidable. Reviewers referred to Obamacare as an "inevitable" catastrophe that "will happen" and is "going to cause damage." Reviewers used words like "submission," "foisted," and "forced" to express this point. For some reviewers there is a sense of fait accompli expressed in complaints such as stating the "noose [is] around the neck," the "downward spiral" has begun, and people should "buckle up" to prepare for the inevitability of Obamacare. Reviews that mention "deep trouble," "rapids," "train wreck," and "quagmire" invoke the image of a situation in which one is trapped by Obamacare against their will or better judgment with no way out. At the extreme, one reviewer opined,

In Nancy Pelosi's words. "It is a Christmas present to the American people." I never had a Christmas gift shoved down my throat against my will before but Santa got re-elected again and intends to redistribute all the wealth to all his voters so I guess tyranny is here to stay."

Reviewers lamented that Obamacare had "power over your entire lives" and that "there is really nothing you can do."

- *Threatening*

Obamacare is constructed as something threatening that imminently has the potential to cause harm and, therefore, should be feared. Particularly in the reviews with a four or five star rating and sprinkled throughout some of the middle star ratings, Obamacare is personified as a "monstrosity" or "abomination" that threatens people's lives and for which people must "prepar[e]." For example, one reviewer stated "no one can survive Obamacare." The threat that emerged from the reviews that reflect this theme is that Obamacare will make "Americans suffer" and "lower the life expectancy of the average American" in no small part to its "death panels." Obamacare is constructed in these reviews as all powerful and capable of large scale destruction to America. Reviewers reference images of "Armageddon," "catastrophe," "horror," "nightmare[s]," "devastation," "destruction," and "ruin." These words invoke images of annihilation. Reviewers whose comments fall within this theme are unambiguous about their concerns. Obamacare, for them, is the "worst thing that can happen," an "unmitigated disaster" that will have "horrible repercussions." In part, according to reviewers, Obamacare is "scary," and causes "concern," "worry," and "fear" because, as one reviewer stated, "Obamacare is coming."

- *Complex*

Reviews in this theme reference a need to understand the full breadth and the enormity of ACA. Reviews that incorporated the idea of "complex[ity]" involved talking about how "complicat[ed]" the law is and incorporated words like "mess" and "mindboggling." Reviewers appreciate the author's ability to decipher this "mindbogglingly complex" law with its legal "jargon." This view is often supported by the mention that the author was the only one to have read the entire law including those who voted on it. Reviewers, especially those who provided a one or a five star rating, emphasized the issue of how "confus[ed]" and "overwhelm[ed]" they are by this "onerous" law. For these reviewers, Obamacare was like a Frankenstein monster comprised of things that do not belong together, do not make sense to them and are not easily understood.

- *Fraudulent*

A recurring theme, particularly in the highest star reviews, was that the law was "fraud[ulent]" or "illegal." In these reviews, it was "unconstitutional," and a "scheme" or "robbery" of the American people. Reviewers said this while even acknowledging that the Supreme Court upheld the law's legality. The idea of fraud arises, even if not explicitly called such, when reviewers commented that politicians are lying about two aspects of the law and its benefits. First, reviewers refer to the law as inevitably more expensive for average Americans than current health plans with one reviewer calling it the "(un)affordable care act." Second, reviewers refer to the law as an overreach of the government because of its perceived potential to violate privacy of Americans and force them into actions they may not want to take (i.e., being fined if they do not secure healthcare). Reviewers referred to these as "infringements on liberties and freedoms." The phrase "ugly fraud" captures some of the depth of reviewers' contempt about this perceived overreach. Here, though perhaps more subtly, the Frankenstein monster image may still be envisioned. Consider that for something to be fraudulent there is a presumption that a legitimate version could have or should have existed. A quote not from the data but from Mary Wollstonecraft Shelley, author of *The Modern Prometheus* (a.k.a. *Frankenstein*), encapsulates the idea of fraud that emerged in the data. The Frankenstein monster laments, "I ought to be thy Adam, but I am rather the fallen angel."

Overall, the four subcategories personify Obamacare and construct the law as something that is destined to wreak havoc upon the United States populace. Obamacare is constructed as complex, compiled of too many pieces so as to be incomprehensible. Obamacare is constructed as illegitimate, a fraud trying to look like a legal law but not fooling anyone. The inevitability of Obamacare wreaking havoc on the American public is a construction which presents Obamacare as threatening to the American public. In this way, the way the themes related to Obamacare build upon one another to construct a cohesive story about Obamacare, as if it is a Frankenstein monster poised to attack the American people. In creating this personified identity for Obamacare, reviewers warn the American public that Obamacare "is coming" and they should be "scared."

The Construction of the American People (N = 95; 29%)

Reviewers constructed themselves collectively as Americans through the following terminology that appeared in reviews: "America[ns]," "people," (e.g., "ordinary people," "lay people") "citizen[s]," "everyone," "public," and "million[s]." The generalized pronouns "us," "we," and "our" were also coded as part of a construction of the American people when they occurred without immediate referents to give the pronoun specificity, were generalized to an ambiguous "we" or "us," or were specific to something all-encompassing that could apply to everyone such as "our lives" or "our ongoing fight" rather than something more specific such as "our healthcare" or "our government" which would not inherently by definition apply to everyone in the country. Based on these codes for the identity of the American people, the following themes emerged: in this situation together (n = 78; 82%), unaware/uninformed/ignorant (n = 76; 80%), and victims (n = 67; 71%).

- *In this situation together*

The American people are constructed through reviews as in this situation together and, therefore, bound together by the need to read the book, understand the law, be aware of what is coming and how we are affected, and, at the extreme, be in opposition to the ACA. This is evidenced most obviously in one review that stated,

"This is (y)our life, (y)our health care she's talking about." Another emphasizes "WE THE PEOPLE." This theme highlights collective benefit or loss rather than drawing exceptions for selected groups such as the young or the elderly, those who read or didn't read, and so forth. Instead this theme collapses all distinctions and constructs the American populace to be homogeneous and sharing the same outcomes with regards to Obamacare.

- *Unaware/uninformed/ignorant*

The American people are constructed as unaware/uninformed/ignorant of what the politicians and President Obama are doing to them with Obamacare. In the most neutral way, the American public is considered to be uninformed and needing to be made aware of what is going on. One reviewer articulates this in the following way, "That's the problem we had with the election; too many uninformed voters." Less forgiving reviewers note that the American public is in need of a "total wake up call." In another review, Americans are spoken to directly: "Wake up America, you will find out that you have been duped!" The American people are constructed as "blissfully ignorant of what is coming at them and their families." Yet, another reviewer calls the American public "puppets" suggesting their inability to act on their own to make educated decisions. In this way, the American people are constructed as naïve of what is presumably to come with Obamacare.

- *Victims*

The American public is constructed through reviews as victims who are suffering and will suffer in the face of ACA. From this positioning, some reviewers argue that the suffering of the "American people" will "weep." Regularly the title of the book "beating" is discounted and instead suggested replacements suggest the victim status of the American people such as "Beaten by Obamacare." The American people, according to reviewers, must try to "survive" their "sad," "depressing," and "desperate" situation in which they are being "screw[ed]" by an institutional system that has "fail[ed]" them and "punish[ed] by the government." Reviewers invoke "God" appealing for help pleading "heaven help us" and "God help us." Praying is provided as an option for how to respond to the "suffer[ing]" that reviewers suggest that the ACA will cause. By constructing the American people as victims, reviewers imply that they are helpless to change what is going to occur.

Reviewers invoked two large groups involved in the ACA. Reviewers contrast the American people from the politicians who make the laws. The former, discussed in this section, involves the American people. The American people are constructed as naïve victims who must work to survive the ACA together if they are to stand a chance against it. The latter, discussed in the following section, includes President Obama and politicians. This contrast constructs the American-ness of the American people while simultaneously denying American identity to politicians by constructing them as incompetent, undemocratic, and are hurting the American people.

The Construction of President Obama and Politicians (N = 42; 13%)

Reviews were coded to determine whether they mentioned some iteration of "politicians," "legislator[s]," "congress," the "senate," "government," "our representatives," "this administration," "Washington" (e.g., "Washington crowd"), "president," or "Obama." Context was taken into consideration such that "government regulation" was not coded as present but "federal government" was coded as present. If these terms were present, the reviews were coded for the following themes which emerged through the constant comparison method: not having read the bill ($n = 13$; 31%), undemocratic ($n = 20$; 48%), and working to hurt America ($n = 26$; 62%).

- *Not having read the bill*

Although President Obama is constructed in some reviews as the person who authored the health care law, politicians in general and occasionally President Obama specifically, are accused repeatedly of not having read the bill. This is likely salient to reviewers because the book's author has been extensively promoted as the only person to have read the entire bill. For example, one reviewer notes that Obamacare "passed the Congress along party lines without a single member of Congress actually having read the bill." Insinuated by this idea that politicians have not read the bill is that they are not performing an essential part of their job function and that they are indifferent to this. Moreover, the reason for this seeming incompetence may be self-serving. Reviewers repeatedly comment about this at times insinuating about why the bills are not read. For example, one reviewer provides an explanation saying, "politicians rarely read the bills they vote on, as long as a hat is tipped to their special projects." Thus, even the most conservative interpretation of these accusations constructs President Obama and his fellow politicians as bad at their jobs.

- *Undemocratic*

Reviewers couple politicians in general with President Obama as undemocratic. Politicians and President Obama are labeled as "socialist[s]," "Marxist[s]" and referred to as part of a "regime." Politicians were also labeled "communist[s]" and anarchist[s]." President Obama is called "tyran[ical]" and accused of orchestrating a "medical takeover" and "taking our freedom away!" Another reviewer comments that there is a "power grab and manipulation pouring out of DC." One review states politicians are "avoid[ing] the wishes of the voters and push[ing] laws/policies based on lobbyists wishes" Another states that politicians seek "exemptions for political pals (Democrats)." One reviewer states that President Obama is "redistribut[ing] all the wealth to all his voters." President Obama and politicians were constructed as acting in dictatorial ways against the will of the American populace in ways that serve others instead.

- *Working to hurt America*

Both President Obama and politicians more broadly are constructed as working to hurt America either through their incompetence or through intentional manipulation. One reviewer states politicians are "politically dysfunctional" turning "everything in this country upside down." Reviewers argue that politicians are "harmful . . . to all our citizens" and that President Obama has "truly declared war on senior citizens" and is "a person that wants to destroy America." Another reviewer notes, "Not surprising that it took almost 3000 pages for Obama to tell the public how we are being screwed." In this way, both accusations of incompetence and being undemocratic are not sufficient as characteristics for this identity because they may be presumed to be innocuous, having little tangible effect. Instead, reviewers who make comments in this theme imply that regardless of the cause (i.e., incompetence or being undemocratic), the outcome of these is consequential resulting in the construction of President Obama and politicians as working actively, potentially even intentionally, to hurt the American people.

Overall, President Obama and politicians are constructed as working in tandem to harm the American people with a combination of indifference (i.e., not reading the law), incompetence (i.e., being dysfunctional), and corruption (i.e., benefiting). Despite being two of three essential parts of American government, President Obama and politicians are constructed as undemocratic and, hence, an illegitimate government that does not represent or work on behalf of the American people.

The Construction of the Opposition to Obamacare (N = 96; 29%)

Another prominent political identity constructed in the data was the construction of the opposition to Obamacare. Whereas the American public is constructed as in need of help and the politicians as the cause of the impending danger, the opposition to Obamacare is the protagonist who is in the position to fight on behalf of the American people. Three themes emerged to construct the identity of the opposition to Obamacare: finding a cure for Obamacare ($n = 49$; 51%), the power of knowledge ($n = 48$; 51%), and legislative action ($n = 11$; 11%). Each of the themes that construct the identity of the opposition to Obamacare is discussed below.

- *Finding a Cure for Obamacare*

The opposition to Obamacare is beating or "seeking a 'cure' to the problem of Obamacare." Words like "prepare," "solution[s]," "navigate," "survive," "beat," "protect," "cure" identified this theme. They are trying to "beat" the Obamacare system. This theme often appeared in the data as a complaint waged against the author of the book and appears throughout the reviews, though mostly at the one star rating. While the consensus, even at the one star rating, is that the book is "informative," reviewers protest that the book offers no "suggestions," "solution[s]," "advice," "tips," "help," or "guidance" for "what to do" to "maneuver" or "get around the new law." Unfortunately, they are left "disappointed" by the book because the title is "misleading" and a "misrepresentation" because it is "not what it's advertised to be." The frustration in these reviews is palpable as they point out that even the author -- an "educated," "smart," "intelligent," "qualified," "expert," with a "PhD" and "great credentials" who "did her research" and is one of the only people to read the entire law -- cannot offer a "cure" for how to "beat" Obamacare. As such, the opposition to Obamacare is constructed as stymied in their search for a cure.

- *The Power of Knowledge*

Although some reviewers invoke God for assistance in this search for a cure, other reviewers invoke the power of knowledge to create an informed populace as a way to affect change. Some reviewers offer specific suggestions for what recourse the American public has to "beat" Obamacare. As one reviewer states, "knowledge is power." Discerning "accurate" information and "facts" is offered as a specific suggestion. Many of the reviews which mention this theme indicate that information will help them prepare for and survive Obamacare.

- *Legislative Action*

Various legislative options were recommended by reviewers including "repealing," "reversing the law," "defund[ing]" the law as well as "call[ing] senators," creating "replacement legislation," and being more careful about "who you vote for." One more fatalistic reviewer giving in to the perceived inevitability of Obamacare encourages the enlistment of "high school students" who should read *Beating Obamacare* so that they can find ways to change the law in the future. Although this theme appeared in the data, it was infrequent with most reviewers, who discussed the future of Obamacare, acquiescing that there was nothing anyone could do to beat Obamacare.

The construction of the opposition to Obamacare occurs in the absence of overt reference to political party. Rather than invoking the common bipartisan political sides of left and right, democrat and republican, liberal and conservative, it is noteworthy that reviewers chose not to align themselves overtly with either of these polarized political sides. Instead, the construction of the opposition to Obamacare is accomplished through the creation of a new polarized dichotomy: the American people versus politicians. On one side are the constructions of Obamacare personified as well as the President and politicians who are vilified for their support of the law. On the other side, sits the American people and the opposition to Obamacare. The opposition to Obamacare is constructed as representing and fighting for the American people against a monolith, Obamacare, which is attacking them.

A Demonstration of Group Vitality for a Political Culture

The second research question sought to understand how the construction of political identity through communication about ACA plays a role in group vitality. Four elements bolster group vitality, all of which are manifested in this study: demographics, institutional support, social status, and linguistic markers. Through these elements, groups are able to demonstrate their vitality, necessary for a group's survival amongst so many other competing groups. This competition is particularly poignant in a political context in which there appears to be only two main competing identities both of which are historically well defined, culturally embedded, and taken-for-granted. In the American political system, the notion of a bi-partisan political system is integral and ingrained. Nonetheless, the construction process as occurred in the data demonstrates a considerably different political divide than would be expected. Rather than left and right wing political polarization, reviewers construct four alternate political identities. Through these, reviewers perform a political alignment that establishes a substantially stronger group vitality than either left or right could potentially construct otherwise. The constructions of the political identities of Obamacare, the American people, President Obama and politicians, and the opposition to Obamacare invoke each of four elements to demonstrate the strong group vitality of the opposition to Obamacare.

Demographics

The value of demography to group vitality is that it suggests that the amount of members of the group is significant thereby contributing to the strength and longevity of the group. Reviewers aligned themselves with the American people rather than with the political right. The former reflects a much larger group of people than alignment with the political right alone might have afforded. Moreover, the American people are juxtaposed against politicians, a much smaller group of people than the entirety of the political left. The more members of the group, then the stronger that the group might be perceived to be to itself in terms of its subjective vitality. By shifting from the political alignment of left and right, reviewers are able to align themselves with a much bigger group without the necessity of statistical evidence to support these demographic claims. The production allows the critiques of the ACA to appear to have considerable group vitality in juxtaposition to a vilified group that comprises a much smaller number of people.

Institutional Support

A second component of group vitality is the extent the group is perceived as having institutional support. Politicians could be considered to be formal representations of institutional support because of their ability to control the American people with laws. However, reviewers undermine and discredit the power of politicians as part of a governmental institution. Reviewers imply that despite their official roles in government President Obama and politicians are essentially anti-American. First, this is accomplished by attacking politicians as acting counter to the principles of democracy. Second, this is accomplished by accusing politicians of hurting the American people. Thus, although the opposition to Obamacare constructs itself in opposition to the government, a powerful institution, they are able to minimize the value of this institution constructing it as impotent as an institutional system and, as such, not a risk to their group vitality.

In place of the government, reviewers align themselves with two much more important institutions to construct the appearance of institutional support. First, reviewers align themselves with totality of the American people as informal representations of institutional support. One reviewer goes so far as to beseech the reader to "please comment about the book to increase awareness by others of this most important treasure in our ongoing fight against this devastating and most illegal legislation." Reviewers demonstrate the ability of the opposition to Obamacare to exert power an influence through the systematic power of the American people as an institution, albeit an informal one, capable of accomplishing large scale social action. Second, reviewers align themselves with social media as an institution capable of being a mechanism for group vitality. Through social media, reviewers demonstrate that, indeed, they can exert pressure on the American people. The very act of writing the reviews on the Amazon website embodies the pressure that the opposition to Obamacare is able to exert on the American public. This direct outreach to the American public reifies their ability to have informal institutional support and demonstrates the strength of their group vitality.

Social Status

Social status is relevant to the reviews in that it affords reviewers an opportunity for another sleight of hand to be performed. Consider that the identity of the American people constructed in the reviews requires their status as victims and, therefore, powerless (i.e., without social status). Although the politicians can be presumed to have social status, reviewers have collectively constructed politicians in a high-status position, albeit a discredited one, in opposition to the American people. Between these groups, there is little place for status to emerge. Nonetheless, reviewers' constructions align the American people with God in seeking guidance and help to persevere in the face of ACA. God can be attributed to have a considerably higher social status than politicians (i.e., even the American dollar states "In God we trust"). By invoking God and aligning with God as someone who can and, in theory, would, offer them help, reviewers are able to exert affiliation with a higher social status than politicians. Although politicians may have social status in American culture, the group vitality of the American people benefits considerably from an alignment with God.

Linguistic Markers

Findings of this thematic analysis expose the 'ways of speaking' characteristic of the reviewers' comments that construct the opposition to Obamacare in particular and the American people more broadly. Specifically, there are three communication markers that facilitate the appearance of group vitality. First, the vilification of President Obama and Obamacare are important communication markers of what it means to be a group member. Second, the avoidance of invoking political partisanship is an equally important communication marker of this group identity because it enables the appearance of distance between a group member and the government. Third, invoking an alignment with the American public is a necessary way of speaking to construct a large community of members for the group. These three linguistic markers suggest that group vitality can be constructed as much through what is not communicated (i.e., political party affiliation) as by what is communicated. Combined, the three linguistic markers which emerged in this study work together to help reviewers construct a strong group vitality.

Whereas the political cultural groups most known in American culture would represent a left/right divide, reviewers align in a way different than is typically identifiable in the traditional notions of bipartisan politics in American culture: the opposition to Obamacare versus politicians. In doing so, reviewers demonstrate a strong group vitality for the opposition to Obamacare. Group vitality serves two main purposes as discussed by Giles and Giles (2016). Intraculturally, the demonstration of group vitality suggests to members their ability to survive as a cultural group. This provides the opportunity for members to predict their sustainability over time and determine the best course of action for the group collectively such as, for example, fighting against rival groups or joining them in order to align with a group with greater potential for longevity. Interculturally, the demonstration of group vitality serves as an indication of the competitive stance of that cultural group vis-à-vis others. Messages demonstrating group vitality help another cultural group to know, for example, whether a fight will be easily won or be drawn out of centuries. The political alignment evidenced in the data demonstrates a strong group vitality that can both bolster the sense of attachment amongst ingroup members (i.e., those who oppose Obamacare) as well as serve as a threat to outgroup members (i.e., politicians).

DISCUSSION

This study identified four identities that are constructed through the online reviews of the book *Beating Obamacare*. The thematic analysis conducted in the current study produced a description of the way in which Obamacare, the American people, President Obama and politicians, and the opposition to Obamacare are constructed. At a meta level, the study provides further evidence that new media is a bountiful site of identity construction even, in this case, predominantly utilizing words as a tool for this construction process. That identity can be constructed in online environments is particularly important for cultural groups who are not geographically located as ethnic or national cultures often are. Cultures more closely tied to physically tangible co-presence and space might more easily give the impression of a reality underlying the cultural group whereas a cultural group unrelated to physical geographic location, like political cultures, must find alternate ways to demonstrate group vitality.

The study also shows that identity can be constructed online not only in the absence of evidence but also in the presence of contradicting rationale evidence (i.e., there are some benefits to the law at least in the view of some people in America). While research has shown most Americans to be centrist, the construction of identities in the reviews analyzed here performs a magical sleight of hand which allows a bipartisan system to disappear and centrism not to exist while instead constructed a political stance against ACA as a non-partisan position espoused by all of the American people.

The four identities which emerged from this study work together in order to tell a story about the current American political climate. In this story, Obamacare is constructed as a complex and inevitable fraud perpetrated by ineffectual politicians that poses a threat to the victimized American people who can only be protected by those who work in opposition to Obamacare, if at all. The story involves a protagonist (i.e., the American people), an antagonist (i.e., politicians), a plot (i.e., Obamacare attacking a defenseless populace), and a hero (i.e., the opposition to Obamacare) and is told without invoking traditional partisan political identities. This story allows reviewers to demonstrate a strong group vitality for the opposition to Obamacare, although unaffiliated with a traditional bipartisan divide, by aligning with all of the American people against a handful of inept or ill-intentioned politicians. Intraculturally this political alignment bolsters ingroup bonds. Interculturally this political alignment poses a more imposing threat to outgroup members.

FUTURE RESEARCH DIRECTIONS

The results of the study suggest that the identities constructed were essentially able to be reduced to a dichotomy of those in favor of the ACA and those opposed. While this dichotomy rather than a more complex identity construction process emerged from the data, it should be noted that other identities were constructed in the data. For example, it could be argued that a dispassionate reviewer identity was constructed by those who did not comment on the ACA and instead chose to focus on the book and the author. However, that identity was not analyzed in this study as it was not inherently a political identity. Reviewers that were motivated to provide commentary beyond this contributed to the construction of the political identities presented here. As a result of the limitations noted here, the topic would benefit from additional work in extension areas in which other methods are incorporated to further explore whether the same dichotomy in how political identities are constructed emerges in the media, in everyday talk, or from focus groups or interviews.

CONCLUSION

The current study sought to understand political identities and explore the role that this construction process plays in group vitality. The thematic analysis incorporated into this study produced suggestive findings about the ways in which constructions of Obamacare and President Obama and politicians are juxtaposed against constructions of the American people aligned with opposition to Obamacare to contribute to the appearance of a strong group vitality. The theoretical construct of group vitality provides a lens through which to interpret the online construction of political identity. The political alignment evidenced in the data is fascinating and poignant for American culture, which is founded on a bi-partisan premise that equates to a zero-sum game in terms of elections and governmental control. In the current political climate, the alignment of political cultural identities and the demonstrated group vitality that emerged from the study may provide a microcosm of a political shift in alignment being constructed on the larger scale within American culture.

ACKNOWLEDGMENT

This research received no specific grant from any funding agency in the public, commercial, or not-for-profit sectors. The author would like to acknowledge research assistants Samantha Laine and Leon Shek, both from St. Joseph's College, for their assistance on this project.

REFERENCES

Ante, S. E. (2009, October 19). *Amazon: Turning Consumer Opinions into Gold*. Retrieved from http://www.bloomberg.com/bw/magazine/content/09_43/b4152047039565.htm

Boyatzis, R. E. (1998). *Transforming qualitative information: Thematic analysis & code development*. Thousand Oaks, CA: Sage.

Croucher, S. M., Austin, M., Fang, L., & Holody, K. J. (2011). Interpersonal attraction and religious identification: A comparative analysis of Muslims and Hindus in India. *Asian Journal of Communication, 2011*(6), 564–574. doi:10.1080/01292986.2011.609600

Dougherty, D. S. (2001). Women's discursive construction of a sexual harassment paradox. *Qualitative Research Reports*, *2*, 6–13.

Dumova, T. (2016). Social network research methods: Approaches and key issues. In A. Kurylo & T. Dumova (Eds.), *Redefining communication in the era of social networking: Cultural, social, and political perspectives*. Madison, NJ: Fairleigh Dickinson University Press.

Ehala, M. (2010). Ethnolinguistic vitality and intergroup processes. *Multiligua*, *29*(2), 203–221. doi:10.1515/mult.2010.009

Fiorina, M. P., Abrams, S. J., & Pope, J. C. (2010). *Culture War? The Myth of a Polarized America*. London: Longman.

Galanes, G. J., & Leeds-Hurwitz, W. (2009). *Socially constructing communication*. Cresskill, NJ: Hampton Press.

Gergen, K. (1991). *The saturated self*. New York: Basic Books.

Giles, H. (1978). Linguistic differentiation in ethnic groups. In H. Tajfel (Ed.), *Differentiation between social groups: Studies in the social psychology of intergroup relations* (pp. 361–394). London: Academic Press.

Giles, H., & Giles, J. (2016). Ingroups and outgroups. In A. Kurylo (Ed.), *Inter/cultural communication representation and construction of culture* (pp. 141–162). Thousand Oaks, CA: SAGE.

Giles, H., & Giles, J. (2016). *Communication theories of group membership and the research process. In Negotiating group identity in the research process: Are you in or are you out?* New York: Lexington Books.

Glaser, B. G., & Strauss, A. L. (1967). *The discovery of grounded theory: Strategies for qualitative research*. New York: Aldine Atherton.

Goldzwig, S. R. (2013). The U.S. Catholic Bishops, "Religious Freedom," and the 2012 Presidential election campaign: A reflection. *Rhetoric & Public Affairs*, *16*(2), 369–384. doi:10.14321/rhetpublaffa.16.2.0369

Harris, T. M. (2013). Co-cultural group membership. In A. Kurylo (Ed.), *Inter/cultural communication representation and construction of culture* (pp. 185–210). Thousand Oaks, CA: SAGE.

Harwood, J., Giles, H., & Bourhis, R. Y. (1994). The genesis of vitality theory: Historical patterns and discoursal dimensions. *International Journal of the Sociology of Language*, *108*(1), 167–206. doi:10.1515/ijsl.1994.108.167

Hopper, J. (2015). Obamacare, the news media, and the politics of 21st- century presidential communication. *International Journal of Communication*, *9*, 1275–1299.

Johnston, C. D., Hillygus, D. S., & Bartels, B. L. (2014). Ideology, the Affordable Care Act ruling, and Supreme Court legitimacy. *Public Opinion Quarterly*, *78*(4), 963–973. doi:10.1093/poq/nfu036

A. Kurylo (Ed.). (2013). *Inter/cultural communication: Representation and construction of culture*. Thousand Oaks, CA: SAGE.

Kurylo, A. (2017). Stereotyping the field: The case for disentangling interpersonal and inter/cultural communication. *Atlantic Journal of Communication*, *25*(4), 232–243. doi:10.1080/15456870.2017.1350681

Kurylo, A., & Shuter, R. (2015). Special issue: Intercultural new media research. *International Journal of Interactive Communication Systems and Technologies, 5*. Retrieved from http://www.igi-global.com/journal/international-journal-interactive-communicationsystems/41029

LaPiere, R. T. (1936). Type-rationalizations of group antipathy. *Social Forces, 15*(2), 232–237. doi:10.2307/2570963

Lee, S. J. (1996). *Unraveling the "model minority" stereotype: Listening to Asian American youth*. New York: Teachers College Press.

Lister, M., Dovy, J., Giddings, S., Grant, I., & Kelly, K. (2009). *New media: A critical introduction*. London: Routledge.

Macrae, C. N., Milne, A. B., & Bodenhausen, G. V. (1994). Stereotypes as energy-saving devices: A peek inside the cognitive toolbox. *Journal of Personality and Social Psychology, 66*(1), 37–47. doi:10.1037/0022-3514.66.1.37

McCaughey, B. (2013). *Beating Obamacare: Your handbook for the new healthcare law*. Washington, DC: Regnery Publishing.

Merchant, G. (2016). Together and apart: Social and technical networks. In A. Kurylo & T. Dumova (Eds.), *Redefining communication in the era of social networking: Cultural, social, and political perspectives*. Madison, NJ: Fairleigh Dickinson University Press.

Mokros, H. B. (2003). *Identity matters: Communication based explorations and explanations*. Cresskill, NJ: Hampton Press.

Orbe, M. P., & Warren, K. T. (2000). Different standpoints, different realities: Race, gender, and perceptions of intercultural conflict. *Qualitative Research Reports, 1*, 51–57.

Ota, H., Giles, H., & Gallois, C. (2002). Perceptions of Younger, Middle-aged, and Older Adults in Australia and Japan: Stereotypes and age group vitality. *Journal of Intercultural Studies (Melbourne, Vic.), 23*(3), 253–266. doi:10.1080/07256860216390

Pasek, J., Sood, G., & Krosnick, J. A. (2015). Misinformed about the Affordable Care Act? Leveraging certainty to assess the prevalence of misperceptions. *Journal of Communication, 65*(4), 660–673. doi:10.1111/jcom.12165

Pornsakulvanich, V. (2007). Television portrayals of ethnic minorities in the United States: The analysis of individual differences, media use, and group identity and vitality. *ABAC Journal, 27*, 22–28.

Reyes, A. (2007). *Language, identity, and stereotype among Southeast Asian American youth: The other Asian*. Mahwah, NJ: Erlbaum.

Scott, J. (2013). *Social network analysis* (3rd ed.). London: Sage.

Shi, X., & Babrow, S. A. (2007). Challenges of adolescent and young adult Chinese American identity construction: An application of problematic integration theory. *Western Journal of Communication, 71*(4), 316–335. doi:10.1080/10570310701672935

Strauss, A., & Corbin, J. (1998). *Basics of qualitative research: Techniques and procedures for developing grounded theory*. London: Sage.

Tracy, K. (2002). *Everyday talk: Building and reflecting identities*. New York: Guilford Press.

Wright, K. (2000). The communication of social support within an on-line community for older adults: A qualitative analysis of the senior net community. *Qualitative Research Reports, 1*, 33–43.

Yaeger-Dror, M. (1988). The influence of changing group vitality on convergence toward a dominant linguistic form: An Israeli example. *Language & Communication, 8*(3-4), 285–305. doi:10.1016/0271-5309(88)90023-7

KEY TERMS AND DEFINITIONS

Group Vitality: Group vitality refers to the strength of a cultural group identity, which is achieved through intragroup and intergroup communication. Group vitality informs about a group's ability to maintain itself in existence over time. Three basic tenants of group vitality have remained consistent regardless of the type of group to which the concept is applied: demography, institutional support, and social status.

Obamacare: The politically loaded nickname for the Affordable Care Act (ACA) signed into law on March 23, 2010. It references, or rather attributes blame to, Barack Obama, the 44th President of the United States.

Social Construction of Identity: From this perspective identity is viewed as a product of collaborative communication processes and not as a personal static aspect of self that is independent from others. Together the members of a cultural group verbally and nonverbally communicate to create a shared cultural identity.

Stereotypes: An association between a group and the characteristics attributed to members of that group which can be thought as part of a cognitive process or communicated. Researchers have found no evidence that stereotypes can be applied to every member of a group. Therefore, stereotypes cannot be claimed to be accurate representations of members of the stereotyped group.

Thematic Analysis: A methodology used in qualitative communication research to code data. It requires the constant comparison of one theme to another in order to delimit where each begins and ends. This process incorporates the constant comparative method which allows some themes to be subsumed under more inclusive ones as the process is undertaken to produce an exhaustive list of emergent themes that encompass the ideas represented in the data.

Chapter 11
Becoming Citizens in the Age of Online Social Networks:
Youths' Civic Engagement in China and Japan

Ping Yang
Millersville University, USA

Mito Ogawa
Millersville University, USA

ABSTRACT

New media studies have attracted increasing scholarly attention as communication technologies become integrated into our everyday lives. New media provide unique contexts to share, record, and extend civic life and motivate civic commitment in the digital era. This chapter addresses the intersection of new media, culture, and political communication by exploring youths' civic engagement in China and Japan through individual voluntarism, civic participation, and political activism. It interrogates the civic use of social network sites in the digital age so as to increase our understanding of intercultural online interactions. Through the case studies of China and Japan, this research adds to the knowledge of intercultural communication in the networked society, with its potential to promote more democratic forms of engagement between citizens and states in the contexts of new media.

INTRODUCTION

New media have become important online communication venues for people across the world. A growing number of individuals, especially young people, interact, connect, explore, participate, and negotiate by using this new mode of online

DOI: 10.4018/978-1-5225-3784-7.ch011

communication. New media and culture now have a permanent place on research agendas and in intellectual inquiry.

New media provide unique contexts to share, record, extend civic life and motivate civic commitment in the digital era. They are interrelated with civic engagement to analyze the interactive process concerning the transmission of information among citizens, new media, and cultures (Gastil, 2008; Moraru & Rusu, 2017; Dahlgren, 2005). Advance in communication technologies influences the ways people engage in political participation and volunteer engagement. New media have afforded novel opportunities for people to connect with each other on political issues and allow them to benefit positively from community development through participation, activism, information processing, and livelihood skills development (Thurlow, Lengel, & Tomic, 2004; Campbell, 2004; Campbell, Levinson & Frederick, 2012). As Bala (2014) indicates, this digital civic engagement leads to a wide range of phenomena, from using social networks to access information to the use of digital platforms to exchange views, from the use of mobile application to access government services to organizing protests on social networks.

This research project emphasizes volunteer engagement, citizen participation, information processing, and political activism with the use of social media in intercultural communication contexts. It investigates the civic use of social network sites among youths in China and Japan so as to increase our understanding of what East Asian youths do online, by emphasizing the understudied area of their civic use of new media. Previous research has examined how social networks have been used to engage in cultural conversations, political activism, and political activities, for example, by African Americans in the U.S., youths in *Arab Spring* in Egypt and Tunisia, and people and politicians in Turkey (Brock, 2012; Carty, 2014; Sancar, 2013). Civic participation and political activism of young people have been explored in places such as Mexico, South Africa, Europe, Chile, and Spain (Malila & Oelofsen, 2016; Sloam, 2014; Rocha, Gutiérrez, & Cortés, 2017; Sola-Morales & Hernández-Santaolalla, 2017). With the rapid development of digital technologies, it is important to investigate how social networks extend the context of civic life and how participation in civic engagement looks like in the rest of the world such as countries in East Asia. In the rapidly developing digital era, young people are experiencing increasing gaps between the technological haves and have-nots, and changing social connections. Scholars have pointed out that Asian youths are experiencing digital connectivity and dis-connectivity as a result of rapid economic and technological developments (Yang, 2009; Lin, Cheong, Kim & Jung, 2010; Hommerich, 2014). Therefore, as Chinese and Japanese youths are embracing communication technologies at unprecedented rate, civic engagement in the age of online social networks remains an important area of scholarly inquiry. A qualitative analysis through interviews provides a rich and in-depth understanding of the youths' civic experiences in the contexts of new media. It adds to the knowledge of intercultural communication in the networked society by empowering political participation and relationship building in the digital age and has the potential to promote more democratic forms of engagement between citizens and states in China and Japan.

BACKGROUND

This section reviews existing literature in online social networks and civic engagement relevant to the current study. Three sets of research are presented: 1) civic engagement and new media, 2) net citizens of the digital generation, and 3) use of online social networks in China and Japan. These strands of previous literature provide theoretical foundation and important context for the current research.

Civic Engagement and New Media

Civic engagement is a multifaceted concept related to individual and collective behaviors in issues of public concerns (Cheng, Liang, & Leung, 2015; Campbell, 2004; Levinson, 2010; Theiss-Morse & Hibbing, 2005). Civic engagement includes forming beliefs, achieving the desired result (taking actions), as well as processing of the information as a progression (Theiss-Morse & Hibbing, 2005). It includes ways in which people participate in public life, learning, and getting involved in various social and community activities (Bala, 2014; Campbell, 2004; Levinson, 2010; Theiss-Morse & Hibbing, 2005). Civic engagement refers to all the ways in which individuals participate in public life, such as how they learn, how they get involved in various problems and contexts beyond anyone's privacy or intimacy (Bala, 2014).

Civic engagement is of particular significance for youth development and smooth transition to adulthood because of its emphasis on individual voluntarism, organizational involvement, and electoral participation (Cheng et al., 2015). Activities in civic engagement range from acquiring information to formulating views on civic issues, from expressing beliefs about civic life to taking measures with social institutions such as corporations, political parties, government, and communities (Campbell et al., 2012). The increasing use of the Internet and social network sites has created a new context for investigation of civic engagement in the digital age.

The fast development of communication technologies has allowed individuals to interact in different ways. With the use of new media, people can explore, hide, evaluate, connect, negotiate, and coordinate to a greater extent than before (Bala, 2014). Researchers have found that online communication can help increase mutual tolerance, open dialogues, participatory mind-set, and political awareness (Cheng et al., 2015; Thurlow et al., 2004; Bala, 2014). More and more people can communicate online, receive and process vast amount of information, simultaneously or asynchronously interact and engage each other in civic activities. The use of new media frees people to communication in domestic and international settings without having to travel and enables the reception of unprecedented amount of information from various sources (MacKinnon, 2008; Hu, 2012; Thurlow et al., 2004)

Previous research has examined the relationships between the use of new media and civic participation (Swanson, 2000; Lupia & Philpot, 2005; Hu, 2012; Yang, 2009; Stanley & Weare, 2004; Nie & Erbring, 2000). Some of them have addressed that new media have the capacity to facilitate civic deliberation and communication, thus allowing citizens to engage in political debate and decision-making process (Lupia & Philpot, 2005; Norris, 2000; Stanley & Weare, 2004; Swanson, 2000). However, some other scholars have found either no relationship between Internet usage and civic participation (Kohut, 2000; Wyatt, Katz, & Kim, 2000) or negative association between the two (Nie & Erbring, 2000). Recent studies have focused on the increasing use of the Internet and how it leads to a greater involvement degree of civic activities (Cheng et al., 2015; Bala, 2014; Shao, Lu & Wu, 2012; Roldan & Gracia, 2015). The use of new media has opened up a new forum for public discussion and citizen participation, and enabled people to speak for underrepresented group, challenge authority, and express their views more easily (Thurlow et al., 2004). It encourages online activism and allows citizens to express dissent as well as to challenge dominant discourse (MacKinnon, 2008; Hu, 2012; Yang, 2009). Research on civic engagement and new media has been extended to examine the impact of social network sites on social interaction, community cooperation, political activities, and democratic participation of citizens, especially the younger generations who grow up with the communication technologies.

Net Citizens of the Digital Generation

According to the Pew Internet and American Life Project (2017), among Internet users 18 and older in the United States, young adults (aged 18 – 29) are continuously leading all age groups in using the Internet. Around seven out of ten Americans use social media to connect with one another, share information, and entertain themselves. Almost 90% of young adults are social network users, greatly overpassing all other age groups in using the social media. Digital technologies have tremendously changed the ways that youths and adolescents communicate (Lauricella, Cingel, Blackwell, Wartella, & Conway, 2014). Lin and her colleagues (2010) call the young generation who grows up with the Internet and computers the "wired" generation. In fact, because the digital generation is so highly connected in the 21st century and mobile devices are replacing or reinforcing traditional Internet use through computers, scholars also argue that the digital generation is transforming from a "wired" generation to a "wireless" one (Lin, Zhang, Jung, & Kim, 2013).

Previous research has explored the association of new media use and online activities of young people (Jones & Fox, 2009; Livingston & Bober, 2005; Taylor, 2012; Middaugh & Kahne, 2013; Spurgeon, Ferrier, Gunders, & Graham, 2012). Research findings have shown that young people mostly use the Internet for entertainment and communication purposes (Jones & Fox, 2009). When it comes to political engagement, over half of the surveyed participants visited civic or political website, although they have little interest in political participation for fear of not being listened to by politicians (Livingston & Bober, 2005). Like other Americans, young people express more interest in politics and voting than they did in the past, however, the digital generation's attitudes and opinions on civic and political participation may change with the political, economic, and social trends (Taylor, 2012). Some studies argue that new media provide popular venues for young people to receive citizenship education, service learning, and develop sense of agency and efficacy as civic actors, but at the same time, new media also contribute to public anxiety because they may disrupt the capacity of transmission media to tie nations (Middaugh & Kahne, 2013; Spurgeon et al., 2012).

New media studies have explored the civic participation and political activism of young people in many parts of the world (Malila & Oelofsen, 2016; Sloam, 2014; Carty, 2014; Rocha, Gutiérrez & Cortés, 2017; Sola-Morales & Hernández-Santaolalla, 2017). Malila and Oelofsen (2016) have examined how young citizens in South Africa negotiate their political and civic engagement in the new and liberated online world unknown to them and their parents. There is a paradoxical relationship between political participation and use of new media during their effort to deepen a culture of meaningful citizenship within the context of media use and consumption (Malila & Oelofsen, 2016). Youth activism has also become a major focus in European political communication. According to Sloam (2014), new media play a significant role in the development of the protest movements across Europe such as demonstration of the "outraged young" against political corruption, the *Occupy* movement against the excesses of global capitalism, and the emergence of new political parties. During the *Arab Spring* movement in Tunisia and Egypt, Carty (2014) notes that new media platform has played a significant role in the planning and mobilizing efforts. New media has influenced the political environment and motivated young citizens to participate in protest activities. Rocha, Gutiérrez, and Cortés (2017) have focused their study on civic and political activities of young students in Mexico. Their research explores the habits, attitudes, perspectives, and experiences of university students in using social networks to mobilize the *'oSoyiyz* student movement. Sola-Morales and Hernández-Santaolalla (2017) have conducted a comparative analysis of the youths' political participation between Chile and Spain. They draw the conclusion that young people in both countries are seeking greater participation as net citizens, though Chileans and Spaniards are exploring the new forms of participation online, their political engagement is still not high compared to public figures.

Research on civic engagement in the contexts of new media is of great importance in exploring what civic engagement is like for cultures around the world. Internet users in Asia reached 1.85 billion by the end of March 2017, with a penetration rate of 44.7% (Internet World Stats, 2017). An exploration of the youth civic participation in China and Japan is significant in providing a cross-cultural perspective in understanding the changing political landscape in both countries.

Use of Online Social Networks in China and Japan

New media are ubiquitous, changing people's communication practices and their relationships with one another (Shuter, 2012; Hepp, Hjarvard, & Lundby, 2015). The increasing use of new media throughout the globe, including social networking sites, smart phones, Skype, text messaging, computer-mediated communication, multi-player online games are revolutionizing the ways communicators interact with one another in the digital age. The Internet World Stats (2017) states that China has witnessed an increase of Internet users from 22.5 million in 2000 to 731 million by March 2017, making up 39% of total users in Asia. Internet users in Japan have grown from 47.1 million in the year 2000 to 118 million by March 2017, with a penetration rate of 94% (Internet World Stats, 2017). China and Japan are ideal places to examine the ways that new media are associated with youth's civic practices because of their exponential growth of young Internet users and non-Western perspectives in new media studies.

Researchers have pointed out the specific social characteristics of new technologies that lead to a greater involvement in civic life (Klopfer, Squire, & Jenkins, 2002; Wellman, Quan-Haase, Witt, & Hampton, 2001). The development and increasing use of online social networks, which are available on interactive, portable, and individual technologies, makes it possible for civic activities, such as for individuals to learn together, exchange views, and cooperate and act in unprecedented ways (Gordon & Baldwin-Philippi, 2013). It is important to view East Asian culture and communication as a changing and dynamic phenomenon influenced by its past histories, present conditions, and new media uses. The online social networks provide huge opportunities for connections and interactions in its cultural settings.

The use of social network sites increases social connectivity, but also mediates our understanding of space, geography, and community. Some researchers have examined the change in East Asia brought about by digital technologies (Hommerich, 2014;

Cheng et al., 2015). Hommerich (2014) has explored the role of social connectedness in motivating citizens of Japan to take an active interest in society and to engage in community activities. She notes that Japanese society has been diagnosed with a weakening of social bonds in the digital era, as well as with an increase in social inequality and precarity. This feeling of disconnectedness has exerted a negative effect on civic engagement in Japanese society (Hommerich, 2014). Cheng, Liang, and Leung (2015) have investigated the relationships between social network service and civic attitudes and engagement in China. The researchers conducted a survey of 760 college students in China and found that civic attitudes and social network service use on mobile devices are positively related to civic engagement (Cheng et al., 2015).

Existing literature has relied on quantitative analysis by comparing Internet usage among cities and regions in Asia (Lin et al., 2010; Lin et al., 2013; Chen, Chan, & Lee, 2016; Kim & Chen, 2015). This study fills the gap by examining the civic cultures of two countries that have been understudied in this area. The qualitative approach helps demonstrate the complexity of the contexts and complication of the issue in both places. In the recent decades, China and Japan have witnessed exponential growth of young populations using social network sites. At the same time, they have also been experiencing large discrepancies in society, by gender, economic development, regional differences, and digital divide (Hommerich, 2014; Cheng et al., 2015). Through the studies of Chinese and Japanese youth's use of online social networks, this paper analyzes experiences, practices, opportunities, and initiatives among young people who participate in civic activities. Research findings demonstrate the role of social network sites in civic participation and provide an in-depth understanding of the changing civic cultures in both countries in the digital era.

RESEARCH METHOD

This research explores stability and change as reflected in new media practices on social network sites such as *WeChat* and *Weibo* in China, and *Line* and *Mixi* in Japan. These social network sites have become everyday tools of transmission of message for young people. They provide opportunities for human interactions occurring with a changing cultural landscape and civic engagement. Interpretive approach has been employed to generate detailed understandings of the civic engagement of youths with online social networks. The data for this project were collected through respondent interviews. Respondent interviews focus on experiences, expressions, and explanations (Lindlof & Taylor, 2002). Respondent interview is a good fit for this study because this research method meets the objective of the project: to help explore and interpret the behaviors of Chinese and Japanese youths when they act. Respondents have personal experiences in terms of civic engagement and social network sites. In addition, it helps the researchers to explore how the Chinese and Japanese students' civic attitudes and actions are related to the outer social, political, and economic contexts.

A total of fourteen interviewees participated in the current research project. Interview participants were recruited through friends, acquaintances and students, through snowball sampling. Snowball sampling as a form of volunteer sampling helps recruit participants who are interested in the project and willing to be interviewed (Treadwell, 2017). After introducing the project, the researchers informed the participants of their role in the study and asked for their consent for participation. A letter of consent was provided before the start of the interview. Interview participants included 8 Japanese young adults (5 female, 3 male) and 6 Chinese youths (3 female, 3 male) whose age ranges from eighteen to twenty-five. Respondents are university undergraduate and graduate students, varied in majors and the number of years studying at Japanese universities in Osaka and Kyoto, Chinese universities in Beijing, Henan, and Chinese exchange students studying in a public university at the Northeast of the United States. Fourteen interviews have generated rich, nuanced data. Data collection was conducted in the fall of 2016, at places such as a university library, cafeteria, and office. Each interview lasted for approximately 60 minutes and was conducted in English. An interview guide structured the interview process, consisting of four sections of questions. The first section focused on the backgrounds of the participants. The second was related to their experiences of social network sites. Questions in the third section were centered on the description of the community engagement and volunteer work. The fourth section included questions on the participants' civic attitudes and political activities. Interview transcripts have been processed for data analysis to generate research findings.

Transcription of the data was conducted immediately after the interview completed, with a total of 105 single-spaced pages of text. Since the goal of this research is to explore how young people in China and Japan experience civic engagement in online social networks, grounded theory is used for data analysis. Grounded theory looks at ideas and themes that emerge from texts and assign each idea to a category (Treadwell, 2017). It applies constant comparative method as the data analysis proceeds. Grounded theory provides the opportunity to do coding and collecting data at the same time because new experiences in the field continuously alter the scope of analysis (Lindlof & Taylor, 2002). The researchers collected data and read it many times to come up with different levels of themes and categories. During the analysis and writing processes, pseudonyms have been used to ensure anonymity of the research participants. The following section presents research findings and analysis. Research results have revealed the complicated roles that new media play in civic engagement and how young people may be empowered by digital technologies to make contributions to their communities, societies, and to change their lives.

USE OF ONLINE SOCIAL NETWORKS FOR INDIVIDUAL VOLUNTARISM

Research findings have revealed both similarities and differences between young people's use of online social networks for civic activities in China and Japan. The most frequently used SNS (social network sites) are *WeChat*, *Weibo*, *QQ*, and *What'sApp* in China and *Line*, *Twitter*, *Facebook*, *Instagram*, *Snapchat*, and *What'sApp* in Japan. One of the categories generated from research findings is individual voluntarism. It shows that with the use of SNS, individuals receive more information about volunteering, become agents of their own actions, and have more control over what they do. The following section discusses research results based on two themes emerging from the data regarding individual voluntarism: volunteer opportunities and voluntary actions.

Volunteer Opportunities

Online social networks provide a vast variety of volunteer opportunities for young people. Volunteer information is constantly posted by individuals, groups, organizations, and governments. Chinese and Japanese students have agreed that there are rich opportunities of engaging in civic life and community activities. In both countries, the government, civil society, institutions of higher education, and individuals have been taking a lot of effort in promoting youth civic participation.

In China, for example, there are individuals who post and repost information about volunteer opportunities on social network sites. Haitao shares his experience receiving such information from school, "once my school had a basketball game. They needed a volunteer to discipline the crowd. I got this information from my classmates through *WeChat*. So I volunteered." Mei shares her experience receiving information on SNS through friends, "Your friends tell you what their friends post [on SNS]. We exchange [volunteer] information and post it again." This particular volunteer information that Mei refers to is an opportunity to work overseas to teach English in Africa and South Asia,

There are posts about helping undergraduate students to do volunteer jobs in Africa and South Asia. It is inviting college students to do volunteer jobs. Some people like to post it. It's about volunteer teaching – teaching English in Africa and South Asia.

Not only do individuals post information on SNS to recruit volunteer participants, so do organizations. Some groups and organizations post information on social network sites in order to reach more people. For example, Xiaolei from China shares that "Sometimes there are volunteer groups sending you information on protecting wildlife animals in other countries or taking care of the old people. Maybe they get our contacts from our school website, so they send it." In addition, local communities and even the government also send young people the volunteer information. According to Haitao, "The G20 meeting was held in China in 2016. They needed volunteers. The government sent us the information. It was from the local government – they wanted college students to volunteer." Sometimes volunteer information also comes from students' organizations. Students' organizations, associations, and clubs at the university also send them lots of information, as noted by Xiaolei,

It is sometimes university students who build this group, and they always post information about donating money, helping the old, and volunteer activities like these. It is student organizations that send me WeChat information about these volunteer opportunities. My home university is Beijing Institute of Graphic Communication. It is not just my school, but in Beijing, all universities have these groups. Who wants to be volunteers can get information this way.

In Japan, young people receive vast amount of volunteer information generally from friends. People recruit participants by sending individual messages online to those people they know. These messages read like "My friend [need] people who want help for recitals" or "I found a volunteer work from [social network] site – on *Line*, and I recommended one of my friends to join a volunteer work on SNS," according to one of the Japanese interviewees, Yurika. At the same time, there is also information posted by organizations. Rita shares her experience receiving voluntary information from online social networks,

[Volunteer information] is created by an organization or a company which establishes a volunteer group. It is like a page. Advertisements about volunteer work are clicked "like" by people and they are spread. On Facebook, people post pictures and comments. There are pictures and comments about volunteer work and there is a usually link under them.

This information sent via social network sites serves as a significant initiator of people's civic behaviors and participatory actions. It is related to the second theme of individual voluntarism: volunteer actions.

Volunteer Actions

In regard to volunteer actions among young people in China, most interviewees have shown their willingness to lend a hand. Reasons for taking actions in volunteer work include feeling of happiness, being able to help, building of confidence, and benefits for the community. For example, Xiaolei has volunteered to visit the elderly home to help with housework and donated money to the poor areas to build elementary schools, after learning these information from *QQ* and *WeChat*. Xiaolei states that the reason she volunteers is because "I think it makes me happy, and when you help other people, it can also improve your confidence." The feeling of being helpful is also shared by Weicheng, who says that he has donated money to the earthquake stricken areas because he and his friends all thought they needed to be helped. He reveals "anywhere in the world if it gets earthquake, I should help….I don't know other ways [to help], we just gave clothes and money." In a similar vein, Haitao says that he has volunteered for the school basketball tournament in October 2015 through *WeChat*, because "it is helpful. I can help other people and I feel it is very good for me and for the school." When sometimes an individual student sees volunteer information on SNS but does not take immediate action, it is a common practice among Chinese youths to respond to their friends by "like" it or repost it, as indicated by Mei,

I respond to my friend's call by 'like' it. Lots of people click 'like". We can see a list of so many of your friends under the post ['like']. It depends on how big the group - maybe 20% or 30% [like it]. I also reposted some articles [about volunteer information]. It's about going to South Asia to do volunteer jobs, for example, I posted articles like this, or, teaching some students in South Asia, Cambodia. Lots of people click 'like" to show 'I like it," and to show their feelings."

Along the same lines, many Japanese students express their excitement and interest in volunteer work when they see comments about volunteer opportunities on SNS. As Takeshi notes, "I often have heard that many people who came from different areas joined volunteer work after big earthquake happened. I feel this is because of the power of SNS. Actually there are some of my friends who joined. I think SNS is a start for young people to join volunteer work easily." Some interviewees, on the other hand, have concerns over taking immediate volunteer actions. Reasons related to hesitation to participate include uncertainty, cost, time, lack of credibility, and little interest. For instance, one of the reasons seems to be uncertainty over the information on SNS. Yurika says,

I have met people who put these comments [on SNS] about volunteer work, but I do not know them much. I feel like I am not sure whether it is okay to join these volunteer work or not. I do not join volunteer work from information on SNS because I do not know them so much.

Cost and time are other factors that prevent people from taking immediate actions. Research participants have expressed their interest in the work but could not afford it, "there are many volunteer work which I have to go to foreign countries and it is too expensive to do it. I am interested in it and I want to do it, but I cannot afford it. I do not have enough money and time." Takeshi shows his interest in volunteer work but also explains the reason for his hesitation,

I am not sure whether information on SNS is true or not. There is no credibility. Sometimes it is not safe because the information is on SNS.... I check situation of place before I join. No matter how I am interested in, I think we should check safety before making a decision. It is possible that people are in danger while doing volunteer work, but of course, information on SNS is really useful. It depends on people whether they join or not.

According to research participants in both China and Japan, without SNS, they have to search for information about volunteer work themselves, either offline or online. Now with SNS such as *WeChat*, *QQ*, *Line*, and *Twitter*, it is easier to send information and spread the words to lots of people within a short period of time. Exposure to vast amount of volunteer opportunities is likely to have a positive association with the civic actions taken to answer those volunteer calls, though there are uncertainty and hesitation in participation among young interviewees. More detailed discussion of civic participation is presented in the next section.

IMPACT OF ONLINE SOCIAL NETWORKS ON CIVIC PARTICIPATION

This section explores the influence of social network sites on interviewees' attitudes and actions to address issues of public concern. In terms of the impact of SNS on civic participation, there are two themes revealed from the data in this category: helpful information and growing interest.

Helpful Information

Interview participants from both China and Japan have expressed appreciation of the large amount of information that SNS offers for volunteer activities. As Haitao from China indicates, SNS makes it easier for people to practice civic activism because people can get volunteer information almost all the time, when they eat, play, or lie in beds – "more and more people can get volunteer information from social networks easily." Mei echoes by saying, "there is a lot of helpful information on SNS, for example, a lot of political news about American presidential candidates Clinton and Trump." Xiaolei also shares her opinions regarding political information,

[SNS] make more people know political things. If students just receive information from their university, it is different from receiving information on SNS because on SNS, you receive messages from all universities and resources. Those information is very real, instant, and letting more people know things quickly.

In addition to political information, messages about community events are also emphasized by Chinese interviewees. Xiaolei continues to share experience of hers and her friends in helping elderly people and engaging in other civic activities by making use of the information online,

There are some volunteer groups sending you information protecting wildlife animals in other countries or to take care of the old people. They always post information like that in WeChat and QQ. In my high school, I had been to old people's house to visit them, help them do housework, and make things for them.... I have some friends who go to other countries to be teacher or to protect animals. Some go to villages in China or other countries, such as in Africa or Vietnam, to teach basic knowledge such as Maths or English for kids. As for protecting animals, some volunteers go to the beach. They protect turtles, turtle's eggs, and the small turtles, because after turtles are born, they need to go to the sea. They protect the eggs so they won't be eaten by birds.

This information not only helps young people learn about these opportunities, but also lets them do research and get information they need in order to make decisions. Everyone can send volunteer information on SNS at any time, as Weicheng notes, "if someone needs help, you can just send a *Weibo*. If you need help, you can write it on *Weibo* and you can get help from lots of people immediately." It helps people receive volunteer information and organizations who need volunteers. These organizations, as Jianfei states, by using SNS, can contact a lot of potential young volunteers, including strangers.

Yuta is a boy from Japan. He emphasizes that SNS allows information to be spread fast and efficiently. SNS assists his friends and him to receive and share information and sometimes political opinions and viewpoints,

Information can spread easily, so we know what we want to know about volunteer work. I get information from retweeting or sharing. Usually people share it with their opinions and it is interesting to read comments people share. I think politicians have been posting political comments [on SNS] for many years. In this one-year and a half, I think I follow more people who post political comments. That is why I see more political comments online.

Addition to information about politics, civic engagements, and public opinions, another impact of online social networks is the increase of interest of individuals in engaging in civic activities.

Growing Interest

Participants have indicated that SNS makes it easier for civic engagement because of the interest it inspires in people. After reading other people's SNS posts on participation and volunteer work, an individual is more likely to wish to do the same. There arises a growing interest in civic engagement because of the posts on SNS. Haitao from China has shared his experience learning about G20 Summit being held in Hangzhou, China in 2016. From organizations and local governments, he got to know this volunteer opportunity on *WeChat*, so that he and his ten friends have volunteered. SNS seems to inspire high motivation for young people to join in civic activities. For example, Weicheng has told the researchers that in the year 2008, there was a big earthquake in Sichuan Province, China. As soon as he got the information from *QQ* and *WeChat*, he donated clothes and money. Mei describes a similar experience of hers – when she sees any volunteer jobs on *WeChat*, for example, about teaching work, environmental protection activities such as cleaning the river, or earthquake assistance work, she is eager to do it. If she sees other people's comments such as "like" or posts about going, those would greatly motivate her to respond and take actions immediately. The huge impact and immediacy of information on SNS is also revealed by Rita from Japan who emphasizes her positive attitudes and strong motivation after seeing information about volunteer work and someone who has just participated,

We have higher motivation for volunteer work when we see comments about volunteer work, such as 'I did volunteer work', on SNS. When I want to do volunteer work, but I cannot take actions, comments about volunteer work on SNS encourages me to have high motivation to take actions. Like, 'I wanna do it too!

Regarding growing interests, Yuta states that information posted on SNS is a very good start to attract people's attention and develop their interest,

We can get information [on SNS]. We can know what volunteer groups do. I think information on SNS is a start to be interested in volunteer work. Volunteer work is close to us because of SNS. People could know only from advertisements in the train before, but now, everyone get information about volunteer work from SNS.

The power of SNS, the high motivation it inspires, as well as the growing interest that information on SNS starts in people is shown in other Japanese students' experiences. Takeshi often hears of volunteers who help victims during the earthquake. He believes that SNS provides a good opportunity for young people to start interest in community engagement and to grow interest in volunteer activities.

The previous sections have discussed the use of online social networks for individual voluntarism and civic participation. One other important component of civic engagement involves political participation (Cheng et al., 2015; Campbell et al., 2012). Analysis of the Chinese and Japanese youths' experience of political engagement and expressions are presented in the following section.

POLITICAL ACTIVISM IN ONLINE SOCIAL NETWORKS

Political activism relates to political information, political awareness, electoral participation, democratic movement, activities of political parties, and political reforms (Thurlow et al., 2004; Bala, 2014; Cheng et al., 2015; Campbell et al., 2012). Analysis of the interview data of Chinese and Japanese youths has demonstrated the following themes regarding political activism in the contexts of social networks: a platform for political information, (dis)engaging in political expressions, and lack of political participation.

A Platform for Political Information

Interviewees have noted that SNS are serving as an effective platform for political information, sometimes information not accessible from official sources. Online social networks are places to speak up and sharing information and opinions on politics. For example, one student from China indicates that SNS provides multiple perspectives of information about politics. Bai provides an example about Tianjin

Explosion that took place in Tianjin Harbor on August 12, 2015. According to New York Times (Hernandez, 2016), the blast killed 165 people at Tianjing, China's busiest seaports, as a man-made disaster resulting from a mismanagement of a chemical warehouse and lax oversight by regulators. Soon after the tragedy occurred, according to Bai, there were a lot of posts about what happened and a vast number of political comments on SNS,

I know there is some information in China the public want to know. I think some articles posted on WeChat are about things I don't know. I don't know how these articles get around. I think if these are things the government wouldn't want to show to everybody, but on WeChat people share articles like this, not the same as government posted-articles. People can still read as they want and choose what they read [on WeChat], sometimes to understand what's going on.

Students from Japan generally think SNS make it easier to post political comments. As Yurika notes, young people in Japan are more used to posting political comments online than in face-to-face conversations, "we can write what we want to say on SNS easily without hesitation." This is actually a good thing for young people to learn more information about politics and politicians, as well for the general public to learn political attitudes and opinions of youths, as Yurika adds,

There are some TV programs which collect comments about politics from SNS, and consider them public opinion, and broadcast it. Then, many people watch those TV programs and they know comments about politics from SNS. I think it is better than before if more people know young people's opinions about politics in this way.

Social network sites have changed the political landscape not only by providing a platform for more political information, but also the opportunity for young generations to openly express their political viewpoints, no matter they make use of it or not.

(Dis)Engaging in Political Expressions

Interview participants in both countries have expressed their lack of interest in political issues. They contribute their low engagement in political activities to the fact that online communication easily leads to misunderstandings and miscommunication, especially about complex issues over politics. However, when chances arise, these same group of young people are willing to express their political opinions on elections of other countries such as the United States. In terms of little interest in political issues, Niko from Japan attributes his lack of expressions of political opinions on SNS to language barriers. He seldom expresses his political beliefs and attitudes online in order to avoid misunderstandings from his friends. He acknowledges that political topics are sensitive to a lot of people,

On SNS even short sentences, that means when I use words such as 'I do not like that politician', I think there can be a gap of degrees of how much we do not like that politician among us. Some people do not like [the politician] so much, but I do not like a little bit. On SNS, because words can be misleading, this can be the cause to problems. And, politics is a sensitive topic. I do not want my opinions to be misunderstood by other people because of the gap. I do not want to have problems because of the gap. That is why I do not do it.

Even though young people in Japan and China are reluctant to engage in political expressions online, they both like to post political opinions on American politicians and policies. One interviewee from Japan, Yuta, points out that he often reads other people's comments about politics on Facebook, not about Japanese elections, but about elections in the U.S.,

I do not remember exactly, but they often put comments about how American people criticize their politics. After people read American people's comments about their politics, they write their opinions about American people's comments.

Jianfei has attested similar practice on SNS in China. Rather than discussing political issues in China, young Chinese are engaged in candid conversations over presidential debate and elections in the United States. During the U.S. presidential election, for example, Jianfei says "some of my Chinese friends posted which people they liked online. It is to show their personal opinions." It seems a common practice to read other people's comments about politics on SNS and their personal views toward political issues in the United States. However, most interviewees still hesitate to speak up about politics themselves, although they consider SNS a place with more comfort and freedom to speak up and express political opinions, attitudes, and comments.

Lack of Political Participation

Throughout the interviews, students have repeatedly expressed their lack of interest in political activities. Participants from China and Japan have offered different reasons to explain why they are not engaged in political participation. Students in China emphasize personal reasons as well as pressure from the government. Interviewees in Japan are reluctant to participate mainly because of personal reasons, such as their indifference to politics or need to care for other people's feelings. For instance,

Rita from Japan feels that it is possible that some people may get hurt because of her political opinions.

Yurika adds,

I am not interested in politics, so I have nothing to write about politics. If someone asks me to write about politics on SNS, I cannot write anything because I do not know about it so much.

Lack of power is another reason revealed by Japanese participants to explain why they are uninterested in politics. It is too hard to make a change no matter what they say or do about politics online. As Ichika states, "to be honest, I go to the election to vote, but I feel like I do not care who wins the election." Ichika believes that politics in Japan will not change even if she speaks up or actively takes part in political activities,

Elderly people have big power to decide politics in Japan. There are many elderly politicians and there are many old ideas. They also do not like to accept new ideas. It is my opinion, but I think even though they say they will change, they do not change. Many politicians are lax about money. So I feel like politics in Japan does not change even though I speak up. I feel like it does not matter which party becomes a ruling party. I realize that it is no use trying to speak up.

In addition to lack of personal interest, Chinese interviewees have added that the political system in China and parental forces have prevented them from engaging in more political activities. They are afraid of getting into trouble by participating in political activities with the use of SNS. Mei describes her experience,

I want to post [political comments]. My father always stops me. I did [post on SNS], but I don't think they are about my political views. I just posted my ideas about some social issues, maybe related to political things but not really political. My father is in the army. He stops me. He never says 'you can't do it.' He often says 'you probably should not do it.'

These examples and experiences shared by research participants have revealed similarities and differences between Chinese and Japanese young people's behaviors regarding political activism on social networks in their cultural contexts. They give related yet different reasons for political expressions, activism, or lack of engagement in political activities online.

CONCLUSION

The current research has explored experiences of young people in China and Japan with civic engagement influenced by their use of online social networks. It has analyzed the civic culture in both countries based on (1) individual voluntarism, including volunteer opportunities and volunteer actions, (2) impact of SNS on civic participation, including helpful information and growing interest, and (3) political activism, including a platform for political information, (dis)engaging in political expressions, and lack of political participation. Rich descriptive data from participants' experiences have been provided to support each theme and category, helping examine and interpret the behaviors of the youths, analyze their acts at the macro-level social and political contexts, and assist the research findings to reach a wider audience. In the fast developing and rapidly changing world with digital technologies, this current research on new media, culture, and civic engagement allows readers to better understand Chinese and Japanese youth behaviors on SNS and how technologies play significant roles in influencing their civic activities. This paper fills in the void in the literature by investigating the impact of online social networks on youth civic culture in two countries that are understudied in the field. A qualitative approach to explore these two culturally related yet socially and politically different countries helps generate new perspectives and knowledge in reconceptualizing culture and new media. It allows us to explore what opportunities new media technologies may embrace in our society and how they can inspire us to push boundaries, explore possibilities, and think imaginatively about what our future can be and should be.

REFERENCES

Bala, M. (2014). Civic engagement in the age of online social networks. *Contemporary Readings in Law and Social Justice*, *6*(1), 767–774.

Brock, A. (2012). From the blackhand side: Twitter as a cultural conversation. *Journal of Broadcasting & Electronic Media*, *56*(4), 529–549. doi:10.1080/08838151.2012.732147

Campbell, D. E. (2004, April). *What you do depends on where you are: Community heterogeneity and participation.* Paper presented at the Annual Meeting of the Midwest Political Science Association, Chicago, IL.

D. E. Campbell, M. H. Levinson, & M. Frederick (Eds.). (2012). *Making civics count: Citizenship education for a new generation.* Cambridge, MA: Harvard Education Press.

Carty, V. (2014). Arab spring in Tunisia and Egypt: The impact of new media on Contemporary social movements and challenges for social movement theory. *International Journal of Contemporary Sociology*, *51*(1), 51–80.

Chen, H., Chan, M., & Lee, F. L. (2016). Social media use and democratic engagement: A comparative study of Hong Kong, Taiwan, and China. *Chinese Journal of Communication*, *9*(4), 348–366. doi:10.1080/17544750.2016.1210182

Cheng, Y., Liang, J., & Leung, L. (2015). Social network service use on mobile devices: An examination of gratification, civic attitudes and civic engagement in China. *New Media & Society*, *17*(7), 1096–1116. doi:10.1177/1461444814521362

Dahlgren, P. (2005). The internet, public spheres, and political communication: Dispersion and deliberation. *Political Communication*, *22*(2), 147–162. doi:10.1080/10584600590933160

Gastil, J. (2008). *Political communication and deliberation.* Thousand Oaks, CA: Sage Publications. doi:10.4135/9781483329208

Gordon, E., & Baldwin-Philippi, J. (2013). Making a habit out of engagement: How the culture of open data is reframing civic life. In B. Goldstein & L. Dyson (Eds.), *Beyond transparency: Open data and the future of civic innovation* (pp. 139–148). San Francisco, CA: Code for America Press.

Hepp, A., Hjarvard, S., & Lundby, K. (2015). Mediatization: Theorizing the interplay between media, culture and society. *Media Culture & Society*, *37*(2), 314–324. doi:10.1177/0163443715573835

Hernandez, J. C. (2016, February 5). Tianjin explosions were result of mismanagement, China finds. *New York Times.* Retrieved from https://www.nytimes.com/2016/02/06/world/asia/tianjin-explosions-were-result-of-mismanagement-china-finds.html

Hommerich, C. (2014). Feeling disconnected: Exploring the relationship between different form of social capital and civic engagement in Japan. *Voluntas*, *26*(1), 45–68. doi:10.1007/s11266-014-9525-3

Hu, Y. (2012). The Internet and social mobilization in China. In F. F. Lee, L. Leung, J. L. Qiu, & D. C. Chu (Eds.), *Frontiers in new media research* (pp. 93–112). New York, NY: Routledge.

Internet World Stats. (2017). *Asia stats*. Retrieved from http://www.internetworldstats.com/stats.htm

Jones, S., & Fox, S. (2009). *Generations online in 2009*. Retrieved from http://www.pewinternet.org/Reports/2009/Generations-Online-in-2009.aspx

Kim, Y., & Chen, H. (2015). Discussion network heterogeneity matters: Examining a moderated mediation model of social media use and civic engagement. *International Journal of Communication*, *9*, 2344–2365.

Klopfer, E., Squire, K., & Jenkins, H. (2002). *Environmental detectives PDAs as a window into a virtual simulated world.* Paper presented at International Workshop on Wireless and Mobile Technologies in Education. doi:10.1109/WMTE.2002.1039227

Kohut, A. (2000). Internet users are on the rise, but public affairs interest isn't. *Columbia Journalism Review*, *38*(5), 68–69.

Lauricella, A. R., Cingel, D. P., Blackwell, C., Wartella, E., & Conway, A. (2014). The mobile generation: Youth and adolescent ownership and use of new media. *Communication Research Reports*, *31*(4), 357–364. doi:10.1080/08824096.2014.963221

Levinson, M. (2010). The civic empowerment gap: Defining the problem and locating solutions. In L. R. Sherrod, J. Torney-Purta, & C. A. Flanagan (Eds.), *Handbook of research on civic engagement in youth* (pp. 393–423). Hoboken, NJ: John Wiley & Sons. doi:10.1002/9780470767603.ch13

Lin, W., Cheong, P. H., Kim, Y., & Jung, J. (2010). Becoming citizens: Youths civic uses of new media in five digital cities in East Asia. *Journal of Adolescent Research*, *25*(6), 839–857. doi:10.1177/0743558410371125

Lin, W., Zhang, X., Jung, J., & Kim, Y. (2013). From the wired to wireless generation? Investigating teens' Internet use through the mobile phone. *Telecommunications Policy*, *37*(8), 651–661. doi:10.1016/j.telpol.2012.09.008

Lindlof, T., & Taylor, B. (2002). *Qualitative communication research methods*. Thousand Oaks, CA: Sage.

Livingstone, S., & Bober, M. (2005). *UK children go online: Final report of key project findings*. London: London School of Economics and Political Science.

Lupia, A., & Philpot, T. S. (2005). Views from inside the net: How websites affect young adults' political interest. *The Journal of Politics*, *67*(4), 1122–1142. doi:10.1111/j.1468-2508.2005.00353.x

MacKinnon, R. (2008). Blogs and China correspondence: Lessons about global Information flows. *Chinese Journal of Communication*, *1*(2), 242–157. doi:10.1080/17544750802288081

Malila, V., & Oelofsen, M. (2016). Young citizens in South Africa: A paradox of engagement with politics and the media. *Journal of African Media Studies*, *8*(2), 187–203. doi:10.1386/jams.8.2.187_1

Middaugh, E., & Kahne, J. (2013). New media as a tool for civic learning. *Comunicar*, *20*(40), 99–107. doi:10.3916/C40-2013-02-10

Moraru, V., & Rusu, L. (2017). New media – The reforming factor of political communication. *International Journal of Communication Research*, *7*(1), 50–57.

Nie, N. E., & Erbring, L. (2000). *Internet and society: A preliminary report*. Los Altos, CA: Stanford Institute for the Quantitative Study of Society.

Norris, P. (2000). *A virtuous circle: Political communications in postindustrial societies*. Cambridge, UK: Cambridge University Press. doi:10.1017/CBO9780511609343

Pew Internet and American Life Project. (2017). *Internet and Technology: Fact Sheets*. Retrieved from http://www.pewinternet.org

Rocha, M. E. M., Gutiérrez, E. O., & Cortés, G. U. (2017). Youth and political participation: #Yosoy132 and the struggle for freedom of expression in Mexico. *Communicatio Socialis*, *30*(1), 87–105.

Roldan, Z., & Gracia, M. D. (2015). Locating civic engagement through social media during calamities: The Philippine experience. *International Journal of Interdisciplinary Studies in Communication*, *10*(2), 1–7. doi:10.18848/2324-7320/CGP/v10i02/53611

Sancer, G. A. (2013). Political public relations 2.0 and the use of Twitter of political leaders in Turkey. *Online Journal of Communication and Media Technologies*, *3*(1), 181–194.

Shao, G., Lu, J., & Wu, J. (2012). New media and civic engagement in China: The case of the Xiamen PX event. *China Media Research*, *8*(2), 76–82.

Shutter, R. (2012). Research and pedagogy in intercultural new media studies. *China Media Research*, *8*(4), 1–5.

Sloam, J. (2014). "The outraged young": Young Europeans, civic engagement and the new media in a time of crisis. *Information Communication and Society*, *17*(2), 127–231. doi:10.1080/1369118X.2013.868019

Sola-Morales, S., & Hernández-Santaolalla, V. (2017). Voter turnout and new forms of political participation of young people: A comparative analysis between Chile and Spain. *Revista Latina de Comunicación Social*, *72*, 629–648.

Spurgeon, C., Ferrier, L., Gunders, L., & Graham, P. (2012). Young citizens, values and new/s media. *Journal of Media & Cultural Studies*, *26*(6), 911–922. doi:10.1080/10304312.2012.734598

Stanley, J. W., & Weare, C. (2004). The effects of Internet use on political participation: Evidence from an agency online discussion forum. *Administration & Society*, *36*(5), 503–527. doi:10.1177/0095399704268503

Swanson, D. L. (2000). The homologous evolution of political communication and civic engagement: Good news, bad news, and no news. *Political Communication*, *17*(4), 409–414. doi:10.1080/10584600050179031

Taylor, P. (2012). *Young people and political engagement*. Retrieved from http://www.pewresearch.org/2012/07/16/ask-the-expert-young-people-and-political-engagement/

Theiss-Morse, E., & Hibbing, J. R. (2005). Citizenship and civic engagement. *Annual Review of Political Science*, *8*(1), 227–249. doi:10.1146/annurev.polisci.8.082103.104829

Thurlow, C., Lengel, L., & Tomic, A. (2004). *Computer-mediated communication: Social interaction and the Internet*. Thousand Oaks, CA: Sage Publications.

Treadwell, D. (2017). *Introducing communication research: Paths of inquiry*. Los Angeles, CA: Sage Publications.

Wellman, B., Quan-Haase, A., Witt, J., & Hampton, K. N. (2001). Does the Internet increase, decrease, or supplement social capital? Social networks, participation, and community commitment. *The American Behavioral Scientist*, *45*(3), 436–455. doi:10.1177/00027640121957286

Wyatt, R. O., Katz, E., & Kim, J. (2000). Bridging the spheres: Political and personal conversation in public and private spaces. *Journal of Communication*, *50*(1), 71–92. doi:10.1111/j.1460-2466.2000.tb02834.x

Yang, G. (2009). *The power of the Internet in China: Citizen activism online*. New York, NY: Columbia University Press.

Chapter 12
A Critical Discourse Analysis of "Minority Women for Trump" Campaigns on Social Media

Wei Sun
Howard University, USA

ABSTRACT

Political communication in the digital age has brought new insights and challenges to American citizens across parties, genders, and ethnicity. The 2016 Presidential election has drawn global attention just as previous US presidential campaigns. Moreover, with two opposing and controversial candidates for the presidency, voters are divided across a wide range of issues. This chapter is interested in various minority women for Trump campaigns on social media sites, in the time frame when Trump's lewd comments about women were made headlines before the third Presidential Debate until Election Day. Selective and sampled posts from Facebook, Twitter, and Instagram are analyzed. How did minority women position themselves in Trump's campaign on social media discourse? How did minority women make decisions to support Trump's campaign? How did minority women relate to Trump's lewd comments about women? These research questions are answered to offer readers insights of minority women's political engagement.

INTRODUCTION

On October 8, 2016, four weeks before Election Day, Republican presidential candidate Donald Trump's lewd comments about women made headlines. Despite protests from feminists and other activist groups and additional controversies, Trump

DOI: 10.4018/978-1-5225-3784-7.ch012

won the election to become the 45th president of the United States. The majority of Trump's voter base consisted of White males and he won with the lowest number of minority votes in decades (Kahn, 2016). However, despite insulting women in several recorded instances, Trump won a significant percentage of women's votes, especially those of minority women. News sources indicate that 54% of women voted for Hillary Clinton and 41% of women voted for Donald Trump. Among Trump's college educated women supporters, 6% were African American, 28% Hispanic, 19% non-White, and 45% White. The percentage of non-college graduated women voters of Trump were 3% African American, 25% Hispanic women, 16% non-White, and 62% White (CNN, 2016; BBC, 2016; New York Times, 2016).

BACKGROUND

From 1980 to 2012, American women voters have typically shown support for Democratic candidates. Women are 8% more likely than men to vote for a Democratic candidate (Chaturvedi, 2016). Women's votes greatly influenced U.S. politics in the past two decades. In recent presidential elections, among Asian Pacific Islanders, Blacks, Hispanics, and Whites, the number of female voters have exceeded that of male voters (American Women and Politics, 2015). In 2012, 2.1 million Asian women as compared to 1.8 million Asian men, 10.4 million Black women as compared to 7.4 million Black men, 6 million Hispanic women as compared to 5.2 million Hispanic men, and 51.8 million White women as compared to 46.3 White men voted. Women outnumbered men as registered voters and have higher turnout rates. Omero and McGuinness (2012) believe that women's votes have changed the outcome of American elections.

Hillary Clinton was the first female presidential candidate in American history. Polls before the election consistently predicted that Clinton would win, but results were otherwise. Clinton won the popular vote by 3 million, but Trump won the electoral votes. The 2016 election raised many questions. This study examines minority women's standpoint on a campaign which did not seem to represent minority women's best interests. The implication behind the voters' decision-making is worthy of critical scrutiny. Women's participatory roles in democratic society are becoming more and more important in modern American politics. Minority women's voting behaviors, the ideologies they follow, and their political discourses in a hegemonic political system deserves attention.

MAIN FOCUS OF THE CHAPTER

New Media and Political Engagement

Though scholars still debate the effectiveness of social media as a public sphere where citizens become more engaged in civic life and political communication (Dahlgren, 2005; Fuchs, 2017; Habermas, 1991; Jenkins, 2014), the popularity of social media and its effect on users' political engagement have been widely recognized (Bennett, 2012; Bherer, et al, 2016; Blumlet & Kavanagh, 1999; Lee, et al, 2015). A meta-analysis of 36 studies has examined the relationship between social media use and political and civic participation. The result concluded that there is a correlation of more than 80% between the above two variables (Boulianne, 2015). In the 2008 and 2012 presidential elections, Barack Obama's campaigns made effective use of social media. Compared to John McCain's and Mitt Romney's internet campaigns, Obama's campaigns stayed current and active on social media. This contributed significantly to his overall win (Chang, 2010; Dalton-Hoffman, 2012).

Sanders (2016) has questioned the overall effectiveness of social media usage during the 2016 election. Take Twitter for example: with a 140-character limit, candidates' and teams' tweets and re-tweets become more and more combative with each iteration on the social media platform. On October 9, 2016, the day after Trump's lewd comments came to public view, Trump was mentioned 4,002,730 times on Twitter, whereas Clinton was mentioned 2,138,470 times. On October 19, the day of the third presidential debate, Trump was mentioned 2,920,810 times and Clinton was mentioned 1,949,260 times. The scandal increased Trump's popularity on social media. Sanders (2016) asserts that citizens' actions on social media might have driven attention away from the issues at stake during the election because users became combative and personal over the points being discussed and the candidates. Supporters often take personal offence when their candidate's stance is challenged. This trend permeates both traditional and new media. MacCabe (2016) claims that social media has overtaken traditional news outlets to lead the 2016 election. Facebook, Twitter and Instagram are major battlefields for candidates' campaigns to the White House.

According to a Pew Research study, two-thirds of young Americans between the ages of 18-29 agreed that social media helped them learn new things about politics and 44% of adults affirmed they learned something new about the election from social media in the previous week (Lang, 2016). Social media creates a user generated democracy: "equipped with social media, the citizen no longer has to be a passive consumer of political party propaganda, government spin or mass media news, but is instead actually enabled to challenge discourses, share alternative perspectives and publish their own opinions" (Loader & Mercea, 2011, p.762). In regards to participatory democracy, Palletta (2015) believes that social media's loosely coordinated networks empower individuals with information and direct interaction with activists.

Minority Women and Political Communication

Women leaders around the world are still a minority. According to the World Economic Forum, only 46 out of 146 countries have had a female chief executive head of government in the past fifty years. The United States has never had a female president (Geiger & Kent, 2017; Ryle, 2018). As of 2017, American women are still underrepresented in leadership positions. For example, only 19% of congressional politicians, 4 out of 50 state governors, and 5% of the Fortune 500 company CEOs are women. Women are still at higher risk for sexual abuse and poverty than their male counterparts (Live Your Dream, 2017). As America becomes more diverse, the minority demographic grows ever more quickly. Today, more than one-third of Americans are non-White. Racial minority groups are underrepresented in the local, state, and federal government in the U.S (Lien, 2016). Minority women are slowly entering public offices with their distinct experiences and backgrounds and work on improving social inequalities in gender representation (Brown & Gershon, 2016). In 2015, minority women made up 33 members of congress, 9 members of the statewide elective executive office, and 390 members in state legislatures. Race and gender are usually double disadvantages for minority women who run for office. Minority women tend to win low legislature office elections. After they win the election, however, within the traditionally male dominated power structure, they still face the challenge of equal access to power and influence (Geiger & Kent 2017; Political Parity, 2017).

Political critics suggest that Hillary Clinton failed to effectively draw minority and young people to turn out and vote. Many African American, Latino, and young voters did not show up to cast ballots. Black voter turnout dipped for the first time in twenty years in the 2016 election (Luhby, 2016). The political activities and images of minority women and other disadvantaged groups rarely receive fair coverage in the news. They are either ignored or their images are distorted (Graber & Dunaway, 2015; Graber & Smith, 2005). The gendered coverage of female candidates influences the outcomes of the elections. Despite the fact that more women than ever are engaging in politics, the media still favors women taking traditional gender roles in society. The negative gendered coverage of women candidates often make their running for higher political positions more difficult (Ryan, 2013; Wasburn & Wasburn 2011; Ward, 2017). In past U.S. elections, Hillary Clinton, Elizabeth Dole, and Sarah Palin have all been subjected to gender bias in media coverage. Women candidates receive different gendered coverage than their male peers. Femininity is a disadvantage in campaigns. They are either considered weak in comparison with their male counterparts (Ryan, 2013; Meeks, 2012). Through an analysis of 162 narratives collected from 49 U.S. local government officials, Portillo (2010) found out that minority women in authority positions have lower social status with the public. And within their own organizations, they have to establish their authority through formal and explicit rules. Race, sex, and age intersect with their political identity. Acknowledging that women candidates encountered stereotypes when running for offices, researchers suggest that to win women voters, women candidates should stress issues to comply. However, this might further isolate them from male voters (Hermson, Lay and Stokes, 2003). Harell (2017) examines the gender gap in political participation between men and women among various ethno-racial groups in Canada. She found that there was little difference between men and women at federal level voting regardless their racial backgrounds. Minority members tend to vote at lower levels than those of European descents among first and second generation immigrants.

Women, Hegemony Discourse and Intersectionality

Throughout American history, the political elite have always been White males (Ryan, 2013; Ryle, 2018). Barack Obama's presidency as the first African American male challenged the White male elitism. The most dominant discourse suggests that the election of a Black leader has eased the racial inequality in America. 83% of White Americans believe that racial equality has been achieved or soon will be achieved (BoBo, 2012; Brown, 2011; Mendible, 2012). According to Roberts and Ely (2016), Donald Trump's campaign appealed to White women in two ways. His proposal for tighter immigration laws and anti-Muslim rhetoric created an "Us vs.Them" dichotomy which regards "diversity as an impediment to American greatness." This further isolated the poor and non-college educated White Americans in rural states who did not have many opportunities to embrace cultural diversity. As for college graduated White women, Trump presented himself as a successful businessman, a typical masculine image that most women associate with strong leadership. 25% of voters did not believe Trump was qualified to be president but voted for him anyway (Roberts & Ely, 2016).

The hegemonic definition of masculinity is "a man in power, a man with power, and a man of power" (Kimmel, 1994). Political power in the United States is institutional and where women often struggle to seek representation among the political male elite. Substantive representation is the representation of group interests, whereas numerical representation is the number of members of a particular group who hold offices (Ryle, 2018). "Democracy should also encourage political parties to include more female candidates and to give more weight to women's issues. This argument takes the basic position that democracy creates more space for women's political involvement and for the articulation of concerns related to gender inequality than that which exists in authoritarian regimes" (Ryle, 2018, p.25). Women leaders often face intimidation and verbal abuse throughout their campaigns. Their efficiency in leadership positions has frequently been questioned and challenged (Wasburn & Wasburn 2011; Ward, 2017; Yoon, 2005).

Stoddard (2007) has reviewed the discourse evolution from ideology to hegemony. Ideology represents the dominant class's ideas and interests, whereas hegemonic power makes people accept the social class and social values in the term of "common sense" that guides everyday life. Institutions such as churches, schools, and mass media disseminate ideologies to their affiliated members. A sense of political identity does not always come from one's class position. People "construct a collective political identity through discourses that create relations of 'equivalence' between subject positions. There is no preordained reason why the working class should adopt a left politics" (p.207). Americans have become more polarized in terms of equality, economic status, and political views. Traditionally the poor and middle class identify with the Democratic Party while the wealthy identify with the Republican Party. This trend has changed in recent elections. While wealthy urban liberals vote for Democrats, the poorer and the rural voters side with the Republicans (Gelman, et al, 2009).

Radical feminists regard gender as a fundamental factor by which power and resources are distributed among people. Inequality is built into all aspects of societal value systems. "Gender affects our social and personal lives as well as our political and economic institutions. Men directly benefit from the subordination of women, and men's superior position in many societies is premised on ensuring women's inferiority" (Ryle, 2018, p. 23). Verloo (2013) and Lombardo, Meier & Verloo (2009) argue that in the process of setting up policies to achieve equality for marginalized groups, it is hard to eliminate the impact of dominant discourse. They suggest four political approaches that will interfere with inequalities and intersectionality: imposing marginalizing effects, highlighting possibilities for intersectional politics within the existing political instruments, calling for structural change, and including marginalized members in the discussion.

Since 1970s, scholars have discussed the intersectionality aspect in race, gender, politics, social economic status, and power relations in various communication areas (Byerly 2017; Collins & Bilge, 2017). Scholars agree that gender issues should be examined with an intersectional aspect, which means in order to fully understand the marginalized, stereotyped, and disempowered group members' experiences, scholars need to apply multiple categories of their identity. No single factor could explain the complex issues of minority women's political engagement in a post-racial

America. Their experiences need to be studies in context (Byerly, 2017; Collins & Bilge, 2017). Brown (2014) asserts that in an ideal society, "equal participation among groups would allow citizens to voice their concerns and political preferences on par with each other. However, the structures and institutions of democracy are not neutral, and those with greater resources and privileged identities (i.e., White male) participate at higher rates" (p. 315). Through a quantitative study using an intersectional analysis of identity, Brown (2014) examines the way in which gender intersects with race and ethnicity to influence the political participation of women of color. Brown analyzed responses of Black, non-White Latino, and Asian women. She concludes that resource rich Asian women's political engagement is most closely aligned to that of White women's participation. Of all three groups, Black women's political engagement is impacted the most by her racial identity. English-speaking households are more likely to influence political participation for Asian and Latino women, and while education is a significant factor in political participation for Black and Latino women, it is not a statistically significant factor for Asian women.

Many factors have intertwined in 2016 election. In this study, the researcher is especially interested in examining the following research questions:

RQ1: How did minority women position themselves in Trumps' campaign on social media discourse?
RQ2: How did minority women make decisions to support Trump's campaign?
RQ3: How did minority women relate their gender to Trump's lewd comments about women?

THEORETICAL FRAMEWORK AND RESEARCH METHOD

The theoretical framework for this study is minority discourse and feminist theory. Minority discourse asserts that minority groups share a common marginalized identity in a White dominant culture and that they should collectively examine the nature and content of their marginalized experience to come up with strategies to empower themselves (JanMohamed & Lloyd, 1987). Feminist theory studies gender inequality. In the time of social change, feminist theory understands gender as a communicative process (Rakou & Wakwitz, 2004).

The research method used in this study is critical discourse analysis. Critical discourse analysis aims to analyze the interrelationship among language, power, and ideology to describe the practice and convention behind texts and are committed to social change and intervention (Marchin & Myer, 2012).

RESEARCH APPROACH AND ANALYSIS/DISCUSSION

Selective and sampled postings and tweets/re-tweets from Facebook, Twitter, and Instagram between October 8 and November 8, 2016, the time range between Trump's lewd comments about women made headlines, to Election Day were analyzed. A few messages which were one or two days beyond this time range were included as they were closely related to the issue.

Keyword searches for "minority women for Trump" on the above mentioned social media platforms resulted in few hashtag findings. But searches for "Women for Trump" resulted in dozens of community and organizational pages under the name "Women for Trump" or "Women against Trump." From the images and video links available on social media sites, the majority of these pages seemed to be created and managed by White women. The largest online minority for Trump community, "National Minority Association for Trump" (pseudonym name) has more than 3,600 likes and followers. One specific women for Trump organization has more than 120,000 likes and followers. The researcher sought out minority women's comments and messages which clearly indicated their ethnicity. The names of the posters have been replaced with letters and numerals for privacy protection purposes in data displaying and analysis. The information cited in the following section are all publicly available on selected social media sites. The origins of the social media site were not included in the selected quoted posts. The posts quoted for this study are originals with no additional editing.

After carefully reading over 200 posts on social media platform, the researcher quoted 27 of the posts as a sample group used to analyze the self-identified minority women's discourses to support Trump's campaign. Discussions follow the arrangement of the research questions.

RQ1: How Did Minority Women Position Themselves in Trump's Campaign on Social Media Discourse?

Minority women for Trump distinguish themselves from those who support Hillary Clinton through "Otherness". They embrace Trump's "Make America Great Again" campaign as part of their American Dream.

1. Trump's Minority Women Supporters Distinguish Themselves From "Others"

Most minority women for Trump discourses echo those of mainstream White American for Trump campaign ideologies. They accept Trump as a leader who can make America great again. This rhetoric implies that America faced many problems under Obama's leadership in the past eight years. Trump's minority women supporters, like other conservatives, agree with the harsh policies Trump planned to implement as national policy, even though their own ethnic groups would be targeted. There are Muslim Americans who supported Trump's proposals to ban Muslims and there are Hispanic immigrants who support Trump's plan to build a wall at the Mexico-U.S. border. One "Moderate Muslim for Trump" social media page claims that it is "a page for Moderate Muslims who support Donald Trump's clear stance against extremist Wahhabi and Deobandi Muslims." On this particular page, there is a post of an image of Trump overlaid with one of his quotes from Fox News' *O'Reilly Factor*: "You've got fabulous Muslims, I know many Muslims. They're fabulous people. They're smart. They are industrious, they are great." Trump has labeled the above group as "model minorities". Muslim Trump supporters may believe that Trump has created an "us" from "them" distinction and may think that as long as they continue to work hard, be nice and be quiet, they would avoid being troubled and feared. Asian Americans have been labeled as a "model minority" since the 1980s. "Model minority" is double edged sword which silences the designated minority group and is also used as a way to confront the "non-model minority". The label is used to encourage the minority member to mind his or her own business and not mess with the mainstream (Sun & Starosta, 2006). The label of "model minority" resembles the implication of "Other" in the rhetoric of "us versus them". Critchfield (2010) has defined the "Other" as:

[the Other] is directly related to personal identity and how a person defines himself or herself. Typically the Other is perceived negatively and is deemed different from and less admired or respected than the self. However, the Other can also be a positive disassociation. When a person deems another Other, he or she has decided that their identities are different. The person rendered Other may or may not be aware of the person's contempt because the process of Othering may be a direct communication, such as a racial slur, or an unspoken disdain for, or avoidance of the Other. (p.169)

The groups who distinguish themselves from the "Others" called themselves the "silent Trump supporters."

Post 1: *A lot is being said now about the "silent secret Trump supporters." This is my confession and explanation: I, a 51 year old, a Muslim, an immigrant woman "of color"-am one of those silent voters for Donald Trump. And I'm not a "bigot," "racist," "chauvinist" or "White supremacist," as Trump voters are being called, nor part of some "Whitelash."* –November 10

Some posters asserted that the traditional media did not reflect "the silent majority's" true thoughts about the campaign. They believed that Hillary Clinton's campaign overshadowed Donald Trump's. Sharing a picture of several Black women holding a sign of "Women for Trump," one poster excitedly proclaimed:

Post 2: *It's true, women support Trump and his policies. #MAGA#WomenForTrump. "Everywhere I go, I see hundreds of 'Women for Trump' signs, and then I see these polls!"* --October. 12

Another poster shared a news article entitled "Blacks vote for Trump surged-Doubled in Ten Days." The article included a picture of several minority women holding posters read "the silent majority STAND WITH TRUMP". The article indicated that between October 9 and October 13, Trump's Blacks vote rate increased from 9% to 24%":

Post 3: *This is what the media is not showing. The media is just as corrupt as Hillary Clinton because they are aiding and abiding her!!* -October 22

After results finalized on Election Day, a woman expressed her happiness towards Trump's win:

Post 4: *This morning I put my elephant sweatshirt on and went to vote! Deep down inside I had this glimmer of hope, I tried to ignore because I had already accepted defeat. But all day election anxiety took control. I can't believe we did it, but I couldn't be happier. Finally. It's my third election and the first time my choice won.* –November 8

2. Trump's Minority Women Supporters Embraced His "Make America Great Again" Slogan as Part of Their American Dream

Trump's campaign slogan, "Make America Great Again", not only appealed to White Americans, but also for non-White women. Some immigrants even emphasized that as "legal immigrants", they fully supported Trump's policies to ban Muslims and illegal immigration, believing that the new policies make it fairer for the hard working legal immigrants.

The following poster shared a blog link entitled "Trump and Pence voted best CEO-President and VP by American business women leaders. Bottom line: jobs and security":

Post 5: *American Business WOMEN Leaders Vote Trump and Pence CEO-President and VP-COO Team! Bottom Line: WE Care about Jobs and Security! READ FULL ARTICLE HERE*-October 8

Two other posters shared their concerns:

Post 6: *The U.S. has voted for a Black liberal president the last two times, people don't change their leanings that's drastically. If people were really listening to what was going on and not the headlines, it was obvious Clinton was going to lose this election to him. That being said, only a minority wants his actual policies, I guarantee you he knows that and will immediately become more moderate.*-October 25

Post 7: *I know I'm of the minority in my state of California...but...this girl is a Latina deplorable voting Trump because...*
I'm a God fearing woman who loves my country
Let's build the wall and keep our citizens safe from illegals and terrorists
Let's stop the corrupt politicians in office... -November 4

One poster left a harsh message to her fellow immigrants:

Post 8: *If you don't think this country is great. LEAVE*- October 29

As for minority women who are usually under the influence of masculine culture values, Trump's campaign projected that he is a "manly" leader, or a strong leader who could make America great again, proud again. A race unspecified woman posted Trump's slogan "Make America great again, make America strong again" under almost every "minority women for Trump" post on the "National Minority Association for Trump" page to reinforce the ideology. Some posters seem to believe that since there existed so many likeminded "model minorities" who support Trump so passionately, it is impossible for him to be racist or sexist.

Post 9*: (Chinese American for Trump) Think! If Trump is racist, anti this and anti that, why so many minority groups (Asian, Legal immigrants, Blacks, Latinos and women) are so passionately supporting him?*-October 29

RQ2: How Do Minority Women Make Decisions to Support Trump's Campaign?

Based on their discourse, some minority women seem to have made the decision to support Trump's campaign based on their beliefs that as a White male, Trump could provide security (Make America Great Again); that other minority voters supported him; and due to the fact that there were other minority celebrities and leaders who chose to support Trump.

The persuasion theory of Elaboration Likelihood Model (ELM) explains that people are persuaded in two routes. The central route persuasion depends on people being persuaded by core values. If a persuader shares the same core values with the audience, the persuasion will be effective. Peripheral process persuasion relies on the speaker's communication skills and credibility appeal to audiences (Petty & Cacciopo, 1986). Donald Trump's campaign persuaded from conservatives' central value: Make America Great Again. His emphasis on "USA First" and "American First" gained him lots of supporters. Past successful American presidential campaign finalists all had short and concise slogans, like President Obama's 2008 "Hope" and "Yes we can", and "Forward" in 2012. Trump's promises to strengthen America's homeland security, to build a wall at U.S and Mexico border, to block Muslim terrorist/refugees, to provide more jobs, to reduce tax and medical care, etc., are core values many conservative Americans care about and many minority members accept as "American values." Those who did not support Trump should leave the country (*Post 8*).

Identity formation is constructed through the process of one's own experiences. Immigrants share a common identity. Their hyphenated American identity is ascribed to their acculturation. This identity functions to provide an understanding about themselves, a sense of personal control, consistency and harmony between values and beliefs, and ability to recognize future choices (Adams & Marshall, 1996; Schwartz, et al, 2006). Though non-White immigrants may receive limited help from their own ethnic community during acculturation, they are not fully accepted by the mainstream dominant culture. Their hard-earned American citizenship makes them angry for those who "took the free train" immigration path, which many believed was condoned by President Obama's temporary protections for undocumented illegal immigrants from being deported. And Hillary Clinton seemed to wish to continue Obama's policies. In one exit poll interview, one minority woman indicated that she always voted for Democrats in the past several elections. But this time she and her other immigrant friends switched to vote for Trump. She did not believe that the exit poll results were accurate: even though certain minority group members voted for Trump, the poll did not include their opinions, and they remain as an invisible minority (Yin, 2016).

When searching for "Asian American Women for Trump" on one social media site, one news item came out show that Trump supporters harassed one Asian American woman in November 2016. When she fought them off, police came to handcuff her, the victim. Another incident noted Trump supporters throwing eggs at an Asian girl as she walked her dog in the street. She was yelled at to "go back to Asia!"

This irony speaks a lot about the Trump's promised America: a country that is racially divided and where intolerance presents everywhere. When dealing with issues of illegal immigration, Trump's harsh language used to condemn illegal immigrants, Muslims, terrorists, and refugees, made minority women feel safer. The masculine leadership and a greater America promise worked to their central value. Clinton's slogans such as "Making America work for you" or "Moving ahead, together" did not sounds masculine enough to this group of women. These following posts show the example of such beliefs:

Post 10: *If Trump as president, it will be good not only for America but for the whole world! I hope that he will be the best president who will celebrate and remember the humanity as such. Jesus is our savior, But That I believe God is working through Donald Trump Our country to rescue. God bless you.* –October 7

Post 11: *She is Black, she is Latina, she is Asian, but mostly she is White — and she is middle-class. In many ways, she resembles an intersectional feminist, even if she does not use the term herself. Her theological posture is one of acceptance, of belonging — not of shame and condemnation. And amongst this current generation of Christian women, she is legion.*–November 6

Post 12*: Pastor Darrell Scott shared a powerful message regarding his belief in Christ and how he feels. Mr. Trump is fit to be the next President. Over 12,000 in the stadium REJOICED!*–November 7

In a newspaper article titled "Don't be duped again: an open letter to Black clergy", Bishop Harry Jackson offers seven reasons why African Americans should vote for Trump. This article generated over 2,400 likes. Many minority women supporters shared or left comments on the article to ally with the bishop.

Trump's minority women supporters held representatives from almost every ethnic group. Religious groups also show their loyalty to Trump. On the official site of "Minority for Trump Association", each ethnic group has at least one post to support Trump. There were posts from Native Americans for Trump, Japanese Americans for Trump, Korean Americans for Trump, Muslim women for Trump, etc. Minority women who were harassed by their own ethnic group members by being a Trump supporter often portrayed themselves as heroes. One poster shared a story of a Filipina beauty queen who risked her beauty queen title when she publicly announced that she supported Trump received negative feedback on the Internet:

Post 13: *Here is the message from a Filipina beauty queen. She is a hero*–October 26

In another post, an Indian American woman shared news of support for Donald Trump in capitalized letters:

Post 14: *Shared the news "OVER 5,000 HINDU AMERICANS Turn Out to See DONALD TRUMP in New Jersey (VIDEO)". This event was COMPLETELY IGNORED By the DNC Mainstream Media—OVER 5,000 INDIAN AMERICANS TURNED OUT TO SEE DONALD TRUMP IN NEW JERSEY ON SATURDAY!!* –October 17

Little could be found for why African American women and Native American women support Trump. There are a few social media pages named "Black women for Trump", but the pages were blank when this analysis was conducted. On one social media site, there was only one posting during the sampled time period, which shared a video share from the "Women for Trump" group. There were no posts from the Native American Women for Trump groups. There were few hashtags found on this subject on Black Twitter at the time this research was conducted. Since the majority of African American women voted for Clinton, the few Black minority voters for Trump might have been shunned or the messages may have been deleted by the authors after or during the election. The most prominent Black women supporters for Trump groups, including the Diamond & Silk duo and Omarosa Manigault, have generated lots of praise as well as criticism whenever their Trump-supporter discourse were made public.

Due to Trump's unpopularity among liberals, celebrity endorsements for Trump were fewer than that of Clinton. Women supporters seem to approve when news spread that Trump was connected with the female leaders of civil right movement:

Post 15: *[National Minority Association for] Trump welcomes Alveda King "Spiritual Advisor" Dr. Martin Luther King Jr. niece*–October 26

Post 16: *1986 Donald Trump awarded the Ellis Island Medal of Honor with Rosa Parks & Muhammad Ali*–October 23

To counter the Obama influence on Black voters, some posted direct attacks:

Post 17: *[shared a Washington Post article entitled "Black people, if you really like the Obamas, you'll vote for Hillary"] The most divisive & insulting headline I've seen this entire election, by @washingtonpost. This is genuine racism in its most current form.* –November 4

RQ3: How Do Minority Women Relate Their Gender to Trump's Lewd Comments About Women?

Trump has been criticized as racist and sexist and has been labeled the most controversial presidential candidate in American history. Trump's minority women supporters either separate themselves from Trump, or show forgiveness. Some even turned against Hillary Clinton.

There was a short period of silence from Trump's campaign after his lewd comments about women made headlines. Even Trump's political partners could not excuse what he had said. On October 8, Trump supporter posts were hard to find among the targeted research social media groups. The Democratic Party immediately began to attack Trump's character. President Obama, First Lady Michelle Obama, and Hillary Clinton all pointed out that the lewd comments were not acceptable. Several days after, posters started to either directly or indirectly brush away the topic. Some religious minority women supporters forgave Trump's insults against women because they believed his becoming president was necessary for a godly cause. Some male minority pastors' messages were shared and retweeted by minority women to confirm their beliefs that Trump was the calling of God to fix America's problems (*Post 12*).

Post 18: *The New Evangelical Woman Vs. Trump. In recent weeks, several prominent female Christian authors, bloggers, and musicians have denounced Trump — one part of a larger renovation and rejuvenation of old-fashioned ideas of evangelical Christianity. But that doesn't mean these women, or their followers, are voting for Hillary.* –November 7

There were some minority women directly pointed out that "it is not a dealbreaker" (*Post 19*), or "I like Trump because he is politically incorrect" (*Post 20*). One minority woman got angry. Her messages used all capital letters and stated that by constantly quoting Trump's lewd comments to certain women, Hillary Clinton insulted millions of women (*Post 21*).

Post 19: *[In October, a message about Muslims support Trump despite his anti-Muslim were shared on the social media.] "Meet the Muslims support Trump" 'The Kelly File' why sexual assault controversies are not a dealbreaker.*–October 14

Post 20: *[Sharing of Fox news "I like Trump because he's politically incorrect"]*– October 14

The news item showed an interview with an Asian American woman, a self-declared proud Trump Deplorable. She was upset about Trump's lewd comments, but still supported him anyway. And there were some women saying by confronting Trump of his lewd comment, it brought back the wounds, and it was an insult to millions of women:

Post 21: *HILLARY CLINTON ULTIMATELY "INSULTED" MILLIONS OF WOMEN BY CONSTANTLY REMINDING THEM ABOUT DONALD TRUMP'S "INSULTS/COMMENTS" CONCERNING ONLY "SOME" WOMEN!*–October 20

Some US Muslim women planned to vote for Trump, despite his reputation of anti-Muslim position:

Post 22: *For some of America's 3.3 million Muslims, New York developer remains their choice for president in November's election*–October 16

The quickest way to discredit a political candidate is to publicize negative campaign against him or her. Minority women Trump supporters attacked Hillary Clinton from all grounds, from her character, to her competence, and to her political issues. The following posts display their anger and include name-calling against Hillary Clinton:

Post 23: *SHE'S NOT THE WOMAN WE WANT REPRESENTING US.*–October 11

Post 24: *It's hard to watch these videos when Wolf Blitzer continues to not listen and continue to talk negative about Trump. If Hillary wins, we the people, will continue to be divided because we know how evil Hillary will be to Americans.*–October 24

Post 25: *Taco bowls for Hillary, are you foolish enough to fall for her lies, she cares about nothing but money and power and will do nothing for Latinos*–November 8

Post 26: *I don't trust Hillary for a second. The Clinton machine will stoop as low as they can. She controls the media. The democrats will hire people to say and do anything. They have the money to bribe whoever they want. Think of the big picture. [shared the link of story a boy was murdered by illegal immigrant]*–November 1

Post 27: *Crooked thinks that just because she gives a free concert using Beyonce & Jay Z that black people will vote for her. Hell Naw! #NeverHillary*–November 6

A poll of 1,000 adults in UK indicated that 50% of women blamed the rape victim instead of rapist in reported rape crimes (Camber, 2010). One study on perceptions of rape victims indicated that men and women, but especially women, tend to blame victims for inappropriate behaviors which lead to the self- inflicted crimes (Abrams et al, 2003). Trump's lewd comments did not destroy his campaign. Instead, supporters came to him anyway, especially from religious communities. Endorsements from Christian leaders have generated lots of votes for Trump. *Post 10* is representative statement from the Christian world: "Jesus is our savior, But That I believe God is working through Donald Trump Our country to rescue." Post 15: "Her (Christian minority women in general) theological posture is one of acceptance, of belonging — not of shame and condemnation. And amongst this current generation of Christian women, she is legion." One post speaks of God's plan, another of forgiving. Those two doctrines work together in church communities to back up Trump's conservative policies on the LGBT community and abortion. The Democratic Party's 2016 federal government public school guidelines of "providing transgender students access to sex-segregated activities and facilities consistent with their gender identity" agitated some parents and churches. Church and State have always not always been separate in American presidential elections. A mid-2016 survey found out that 62% of Americans agreed that it is important for U.S. president to have strong religious beliefs, 47% of people believe that their churches or worship institutions should express social and political views, 49% think that churches should not discuss political issues. 33% of Republicans and 26% of Democrats think that churches should endorse a candidate (Smith, 2017).

Besides their strong perceptions about sexual harassment victims and their church community's reasoning, women supporters also seem to employ change of topic as a technique when showing their support for Trump. Take for example the silent majority supporters' expressions in Post 1. They may not have a voice and may feel embarrassed about backing a candidate with a tarnished image, but they support him anyway.

Trump's minority women supporters blamed Hillary Clinton for almost everything, from ISIS intrusions, to an illegal immigrant who killed an American school boy. Post 23 claimed that Clinton is not a woman who represents women. Hillary Clinton was insulted with various name callings. To these minority women, Clinton is not competent as a woman leader. If she is tough, she becomes evil. This paradox showed up in early campaign. 49% of women did not support Clinton (Mohdin, 2016). A Bernie Sanders supporter believed that the Clinton campaign did not address issues of low-income women, immigrant women, and women of color (Chapin, 2016). Post 24 denounced Clinton's credibility as a leader, and her character was attacked.

After Trump's lewd comments leaked on October 8, there were no posts from the NMA official account for two days. Trump's campaign also remained awkwardly silent on the day of the leak. Some "women for Trump" communities formed after October 9 and took shots at Hillary Clinton about her private email investigations, WikiLeaks, and her role as the Secretary of State in Benghazi attack. On social media sites, various "White Women for Trump" campaigns took the lead and the minority women for Trump groups and individuals mainly echoed their White allies' campaign discourses.

IMPLICATION, LIMITATION AND FUTURE RESEARCH

The controversial 2016 election leaves future historians a lot to explore. The nation became divided in age, gender and ethnicity. What are the implications of minority women for Trump campaigns to the future of American politics?

van dijk (1993) indicates that institutional elites contribute to the formation of a persuasive dominant discourse. In regard to minority relations, such discourse is persuasive, "speakers or writers may justify or legitimate specific cognitions or actions of themselves or other in-group members, or derogate those of out-group members'' (p. 30). American political discourse is elite discourse. In its 241 years' history, besides President Obama's two terms in the White House, America has always had a White male president. The 2016 election was between a White man and a White woman. Eventually the majority of White men and nearly half of White women elected Trump to the office. In minority women for Trump campaigns, it is hard for minority women to relate to a White male candidate. Their discourse mostly echoes those of White women or White men for Trump campaigns discourses. Their voices were weak and unheard, did not matter, and were unappreciated. Their assumed participation in democracy is an illusion. Minority women's concerns will not be reflected in this president's agenda. Politicians, advocates, and activists should acknowledge the phenomenon, and in the future political campaigns, to address specifically to this diverse group.

This study has its limits. First, lack of minority women's representation on traditional media and social media have created difficulties to "sample" fairly from the new media sites. The available data in this study are confined to several major popular American social media sites. There are minority groups using their native languages to create communities and post their opinions. Due to the limited language variety of the research, campaign pages using languages other than English were unavailable for scrutiny. There are many more ethnic language campaigns on other social media platforms. Future studies might include non-English native speakers as co-authors to examine campaign discourses in other ethnic languages. Second, the study examined one fraction of the campaign discourses, minority women for Trump campaign. What was the minority women's discourse in Clinton's campaign? The findings of such a study might not simply counter-prove the results. How did minority women identify themselves with a woman leader who has been a veteran for women and minority rights? That deserves a full study. Third, due to the anonymous nature on social media, it is hard to identify posters' real age or ethnic identity unless it is specified. Fourth, the silent majority who sided with Trump, but may not say it in public, remain a mystery. Who are these silent majority not reflected in polls? In-depth interviews and focus group studies may be conducted for deep understanding.

CONCLUSION

This study answers the research questions such as: How did minority women position themselves in Trumps' campaign on social media discourse? How did minority women make decisions to support Trump's campaign? How did minority women relate their gender to Trump's lewd comments about women? Minority women for Trump distinguish themselves from those who support Hillary Clinton through "Otherness". The study finds that minority women for Trump campaigns embrace Trump's "Make America Great Again" campaign as part of their American Dream. They have made the decision to support Trump's campaign based on their beliefs that as a White male, Trump could provide security (Make America Great Again); that other minority voters supported him; and due to the fact that there were other minority celebrities and leaders who chose to support Trump. Trump's minority women supporters chose to separate themselves from Trump's sexist languages, show forgiveness, and turn against Hillary Clinton in responding to Trump's lewd comments about women. The sampled minority women's voting behaviors, the ideologies they follow, and their political discourses in a hegemonic political system are under scrutiny.

REFERENCES

Abrams, D., Viki, G. T., Masser, B., & Bohner, G. (2003). Perceptions of Stranger and Acquaintance Rape: The Role of Benevolent and Hostile Sexism in Victim Blame and Rape Proclivity. *Journal of Personality and Social Psychology*, *84*(1), 111–125. doi:10.1037/0022-3514.84.1.111 PMID:12518974

Adams, G. R., & Marshall, S. K. (1996). A developmental social psychology of identity: Understanding the person-in-context. *Journal of Adolescence*, *19*(5), 429–442. doi:10.1006/jado.1996.0041 PMID:9245296

American Women Politics. (2015). Retrieved from http://www.cawp.rutgers.edu/

BBC. (2016, November 9). *Reality Check: Who voted for Donald Trump?* Retrieved from http://www.bbc.com/news/election-us-2016-37922587

Bennett, W. L. (2012). The Personalization of Politics: Political Identity, Social Media, and Changing Patterns of Participation. *The ANNALS of American Academy, 644*(1), 20–38. doi:10.1177/0002716212451428

Bherer, L., Dufour, P., & Montambeault, F. (2016). The participatory democracy turn: An introduction. *Journal of Civil Society, 1*(3), 225–230. doi:10.1080/17448689.2016.1216383

Blumler, J. G., & Kavanagh, D. (1999). The Third Age of Political Communication: Influences and Features. *Political Communication, 16*(3), 209–230. doi:10.1080/105846099198596

Bobo, L. (2011). Somewhere between Jim Crow and Post-Racialism: Reflections on the Racial Divide in America Today. *Daedalus, 140*(2), 11–31. doi:10.1162/DAED_a_00091 PMID:21465840

Boulianne, S. (2015). Social media use and participation. A meta-analysis of current research. *Information Communication and Society, 18*(5), 524–538. doi:10.1080/1369118X.2015.1008542

Brown, C. B. (2011). Barack Obama as the Great Man: Communicative constructions of racial transcendence in White-male elite discourses. *Communication Monographs, 78*(4), 535–556. doi:10.1080/03637751.2011.618140

Brown, N. E. (2014). Political participation of women of color: An intersectional analysis. *Journal of Women, Politics & Policy, 35*(4), 315–348. doi:10.1080/1554477X.2014.955406

Brown, N. E., & Gershon, S. N. (2016). *Distinct identities: minority women in U.S. politics*. Routledge.

Byerly, C. M. (2017). Feminist Intersectionality Research in Communications: Origins, Contributions and Tensions. *Ex Aequo, 35*, 23–31.

Camber, R. (2010, February 15). Rape? It's the fault of the victims, say 50% of women. *Daily Mail.*

Center for American Women and Politics. (n.d.). Retrieved from http://www.cawp.rutgers.edu/sites/default/files/resources/genderdiff.pdf

Chang, V. (2010, May). Obama and the power of social media and technology. *European Business Review*, 16–21.

Chapin, A. (2016, May 23). "I am not with her": Why women are wary of Hillary Clinton? *The Guardian.*

Chaturvedi, R. (2016). *A closer look at the gender gap in presidential voting.* Pew Research Center.

CNN. (2016, November 23). *Presidential Results.* Retrieved from http://www.cnn.com/election/results/president

Collins, P. H., & Bilge, S. (2017). *Intersectionality.* Malden, MA: Polity Press.

Critchfield, A. J. (2010). The Other. In R. L. Jackson II & M. A. Hogg (Eds.), *Encyclopedia of Identity.* Thousand Oaks, CA: Sage Publications.

Dahlgren, P. (2005). Internet, public spheres and political communication: Dispersion and deliberation. *Political Communication, 22*(2), 147–162. doi:10.1080/10584600590933160

Dahlgren, P. (2009). *Media and Political Engagement: Citizens, Communication, and Democracy.* Cambridge, UK: Cambridge Press.

Dalton-Hoffman, M. (2012). *The Effect of Social Media in the 2012 Presidential Election. In The First-Year Papers (2010 - present).* Hartford, CT: Trinity College Digital Repository.

Ferrari, F. (2012). 'Through a woman's eyes' narratives of the nation: Gender as and beyond a category of analysis. *Journal of Multicultural Discourses, 7*(3), 243–262. doi:10.1080/17447143.2012.720258

Fuchs, C. (2017). *Social media: a critical introduction.* Thousand Oaks, CA: Sage Publications.

Geiger, A., & Kent, L. (2017). *Number of women leaders around the world has grown, but they're still a small group.* Pew Research.

Gelman, A., Park, D., Shor, B., & Cortina, J. (2009). *Red state, blue state, rich State, poor state.* Princeton, NJ: Princeton University Press. doi:10.1515/9781400832118

Gerodimos, R., & Ward, J. Rethinking online youth civic engagement. In B. Loader (Ed.), Young citizens in digital age: Political engagement, young people and new media (pp. 114-126). Routledge.

Graber, D. A., & Dunaway, J. (2015). *New media and American politics.* Thousand Oaks, CA: Sage.

Graber, D. A., & Smith, J. M. (2005). Political communication faces the 21st century. *Journal of Communication*, *55*(3), 479–507. doi:10.1111/j.1460-2466.2005.tb02682.x

Habermas, J. (1991). *The structural transformation of public sphere*. Cambridge, MA: MIT Press.

Harell, A. (2017). Intersectionality and gendered political behaviour in a multicultural Canada. *Canadian Journal of Political Science*, *50*(2), 495–514. doi:10.1017/S000842391700021X

Hermon, P. S., Lay, J. C., & Stoke, A. K. (2003). Women running "as women": Candidate gender campaign issues, and voter-targeting strategies. *The Journal of Politics*, *65*(1), 244–255. doi:10.1111/1468-2508.t01-1-00013

JanMohamed, A.R., & Lloyd, D. (1990). The nature and context of minority discourse. Oxford University Press.

Jenkins, H. (2014). Rethinking 'Rethinking Convergence/Culture'. *Journal of Cultural Studies*, *28*(2), 267–297. doi:10.1080/09502386.2013.801579

Kahn, C. (2016, November 28). Trump won with lowest minority vote in decades, fueling divisions. *Hoffton Post.*

Kimmel, M. S. (1994). Masculinity as homophobia. In P. S. Rothenberg (Ed.), Race, Class, and Gender in the United States: An Integrated Study (pp. 431-440). Academic Press.

Kofman, E., Vacchelli, E., & Saharso, S. (2015). Gendered Perspectives on Integration Discourses and Measures. *International Migration (Geneva, Switzerland)*, *53*(4), 77–89. doi:10.1111/imig.12102

Lang, M. (2016, April 5). 2016 Presidential Election Circus: Is Social Media the Cause? *San Francisco Chronicle.*

Lee, C. W., McQuarrie, M., & Walker, E. T. (Eds.). (2015). Democratizing inequalities: Dilemmas of the new public participation. New York: New York University Press. doi:10.18574/nyu/9781479847273.001.0001

Lien, P. T. (2015). Reassessing Descriptive Representation by Women and Men of Color: New Evidence at the Subnational Level. *Urban Affairs Review*, *51*(2), 239–262. doi:10.1177/1078087414529124

Live Your Dream. (2017). Retrieved from http://www.liveyourdream.org/

Loader, B. D., & Mercea, D. (2011). Networking democracy? Social media innovations in participatory politics. *Information Communication and Society*, *14*(6), 757–769. doi:10.1080/1369118X.2011.592648

Lombardo, E., Meier, P., & Verloo, M. (2009). *The Discursive Politics of Gender Equality: Stretching, Bending and Policy*. Routledge.

Luhb, T. (2016, November 9). How Hillary Clinton lost? *CNN News*.

Marchin, D., & Myer, A. (2012). *How to do critical discourse analysis*. Thousand Oaks, CA: Sage Publication.

McCabe, D. (2015, August 17). Welcome to social media election. *The Hill*.

Meeks, L. (2012). Is she "man enough"? Women candidates, executive political offices, and news coverage. *Journal of Communication*, *62*(1), 175–193. doi:10.1111/j.1460-2466.2011.01621.x

Mohdin, A. (2016, Nov. 9). American women voted overwhelmingly for Clinton, except the White ones. *Quartz*.

Omero, M., & McGuinness, T. (2012). *How women changed the outcome of the election*. Center for American Progress.

Petty, R. E., & Cacciopo, J. (1986). The elaboration likelihood model of persuasion. *Advances in Experimental Social Psychology*, *19*, 123–205. doi:10.1016/S0065-2601(08)60214-2

Political Parity. (2017). *Women of color in American politics*. Retrieved from https://www.politicalparity.org/wp-content/uploads/2015/08/Parity-Research-Women-Of-Color.pdf

Polletta, F. (2015). Public deliberation and political contention. In C. W. Lee, M. McQuarrie, & E. T. Walker (Eds.), *Democratizing inequalities: Dilemmas of the new public participation* (pp. 222–246). New York: New York University Press. doi:10.18574/nyu/9781479847273.003.0012

Portillo, S. (2010). How race, sex, and age frame the use of authority by local government officials. *Law & Social Inquiry*, *35*(3), 603–623. doi:10.1111/j.1747-4469.2010.01197.x

Rakou, L. F., & Wakwitz, L. A. (2004). *Feminist Communication Theory*. Thousand Oaks, CA: Sage Publication.

Roberts, L. M., & Ely, R. J. (2016, November 23). Why Did So Many White Women Vote for Donald Trump? *Fortune*.

Ryan, K. (2013). The media's war on women: Gendered coverage on women candidates. *Xavier Journal of Politics*, *4*(1), 13–25.

Ryle, R. (2018). *Questioning gender* (4th ed.). Thousand Oaks, CA: Sage Publication.

Sanders, S. (2016, Nov. 8). Did Social Media Ruin Election 2016? *National Public Radio*.

Schwartz, S. J., Montgomery, M. J., & Briones, E. (2006). The Role of Identity in Acculturation among Immigrant People: Theoretical Propositions, Empirical Questions, and Applied Recommendations. *Human Development*, *49*(1), 1–30. doi:10.1159/000090300

Smith, G. A. (2017). *Most Americans oppose churches choosing sides in elections.* Pew Research.

Stoddard, M. C. J. (2007). Ideology, Hegemony, Discourse: A Critical Review of Theories of Knowledge and Power. *Social Thought & Research*, *28*, 191–225.

Sun, W., & Starosta, W. J. (2006). Perceptions of Minority Invisibility Among Asian American Professionals. *The Howard Journal of Communications*, *17*(2), 119–142. doi:10.1080/10646170600656870

van dijk, T. (1993). *Elite Discourse and the Reproduction of Racism*. Thousand Oaks, CA: Sage Publication.

Verloo, M. (2013). Intersectional and Cross-Movement Politics and Policies: Reflections on Current Practices and Debates. *Intersectionality: Theorizing Power, Empowering Theory*, *38*(4), 893–915.

Ward, O. (2017). Intersectionality and press coverage of political campaigns. *The International Journal of Press/Politics*, *22*(1), 43–66. doi:10.1177/1940161216673195

Wasburn, P. C., & Wasburn, M. H. (2011). Media coverage of women in politics: The curious case of Sarah Palin. *Media Culture & Society*, *33*(7), 1127–1041. doi:10.1177/0163443711415744

Yin, S. (2016, November 9). Exit polls were wrong about how many Asian Americans supported Trump. *Fusion*.

Yoon, M. Y. (2005). Sub-Saharan Africa. In Y. Galligan & M. Tremblay (Eds.), *Sharing power: Women, parliament, democracy* (pp. 79–90). Burlington, VT: Ashgate.

KEY TERMS AND DEFINITIONS

Critical Discourse Analysis: A type of research method analyzing the interrelationship among language, power, and ideology in texts.

Donald Trump: The Republican Party's presidential candidate of 2016 Election.

Feminism: A theory studies the gender inequality.

Hillary Clinton: The Democratic Party's presidential candidate of 2016 Election.

Intersectionality: A social identity theory that applies multiple categories of identities to fully understand the experiences of marginalized, stereotyped, and disempowered group members.

Minority Women: Women from non-White ethnic groups.

Presidential Campaigns: In modern democracies, various political parties use strategies to influence and promote their candidates to become the head of the government.

Social Media: Social networking which allows internet users to exchange ideas freely.

Women in Politics: Women who have participated political communication either through running offices as candidates or through voting.

Chapter 13
Social Media and Infectious Disease Perceptions in a Multicultural Society

Maria Elena Villar
Florida International University, USA

Elizabeth Marsh
Florida International University, USA

ABSTRACT

Mass media is recognized in health communication as a gatekeeper, alerting the public to what is important with a focus on accuracy and relevancy. This is done through media framing, by which mass media sets the tone through which the public will view the message. Social media has emerged as a force in health communication with the same potential for media framing as mass media; however, with social media there is no formal gatekeeper. Looking at two major disease outbreaks, Ebola and Zika, this chapter examines the influence and effect of social media on health communication. The Zika outbreak in Miami was examined with social listening methods to determine both the effect of mass media on social media and of social media on the effectiveness of traditional health communication outlets to spread their message. The authors conclude that social media is both an asset and a liability during disease outbreaks, and its effect depends on audiences' cultural attitudes and trust toward authorities and the media.

DOI: 10.4018/978-1-5225-3784-7.ch013

INTRODUCTION

There will always be new and recurring disease outbreaks. Although most are relatively predictable in their transmission and evolution, information about outbreaks or epidemics seems to take on a life of its own, with its unfolding drama narrated to the public by the media, and publicly interpreted by audiences through social media. This chapter examines the role of media, and particularly social media, in shaping the public's understanding and interpretation of infectious diseases and how this relationship between media and public perception may be influenced by cultural attitudes toward risk and trust in sources of information. The interaction of media with infectious disease perceptions occurs on two levels. First, how the media frames a health issue influences the public's attitude, which in turn influences the public's behavior on social media and ultimately public opinion. Second, health authorities count on the media to disseminate information about health policies, which influences what people think and how they behave. However, these messages are often adapted or distorted as they make their way through social media.

The media serve as the main source of information in crisis situations, alerting the public to risks to the community and explaining implementation of health policies. In communicating this information, health authorities and policymakers use a variety of media channels -both traditional and social media - to help the public interpret a situation involving infectious disease through media framing, including the choice of language, quoted sources, emphasized perspectives (e.g. behavioral prevention versus medical treatment), groups associated with the disease, and general tone (e.g. alarmist, optimistic, etc.).

To discuss the relationship between public reaction and media coverage on infectious disease, it is first necessary to provide a working definition of mass media, social media, and further describe the two main theoretical constructs at work: the agenda setting function of the media and media framing of health issues. Mass media refers to all outlets relaying information to a large population simultaneously. In our times, this includes print media, such as newspapers and magazines; broadcast media, including television and radio; films; and an ever-growing range of new media outlets applications available on the Internet and through mobile devices. Generally speaking, social media refers to websites and applications that enable users to create and share content. Ellison (2007) defined social network sites as web-based services that allow individuals to construct a public or semi-public profile within a bounded system, and articulate a list of other users with whom they share a connection.

Regardless of the channel, the purpose of media is to disseminate information, particularly news, entertainment and advertising, to a mass audience. While the leading media conglomerates are commercial enterprises, in a democracy, media outlets are also expected to uphold minimal standards of social responsibility such as telling the truth and respecting the audience. Because social media consists largely of audience-generated content, the standards of social responsibility range widely. The relationship between media and the government varies by country and political climate. In democracies with open media systems, traditional media are expected to serve as a watchdog of the government on behalf of the citizens; in some systems, media is used as a propaganda tool by the government to control information; in the libertarian model, the media is controlled by private elites with may or may not support the government. These multiple roles create challenges not only for the media industry, but also for the public, which has to interpret the information presented through the media and use it to make personal choices and participate in the economic and political process. As will be discussed later in this chapter, how the public interpret media messages depends on the cultural attitudes toward authorities, including vertical trust in media. Social media entered into the equation in the early 2000s, and was widely regarded as a democratization of mass media, giving audiences the

Media disseminates information through a variety of vehicles, such as news articles, television and radio programs, web pages, and many others. Then the public further disseminates and replicates the information through social media. The content of the message is only part of the knowledge acquisition process. How the content is presented is equally important (McCombs & Shaw, 1993). In traditional media, the lines between news and entertainment often blur, with news attempting to capture audiences with dramatic coverage, and entertainment trying to engage media consumers with relatable facts and realistic depictions. In social media, news issues are often compounded with humor, through memes and edited images. The conveyors of information are often ridiculed or otherwise discredited through comments and engagement with the content.

Essentially, media - both mass and social media - facilitate communication between message senders and the audience. Modern life now includes near-constant exposure to media, with print and television being traditionally the most important outlets and web pages and social media consistently and rapidly gaining influence. This initially applied to the developed world, but is fast becoming a global phenomenon as less-developed regions find that it is cheaper to access information online through mobile phones than through traditional broadcast and print media. In today's technologically-connected world, more knowledge is gained through media than through personal experience. Social media adds a layer of complexity to disseminating information about disease outbreaks and helping audiences interpret risks associated with it.

BACKGROUND

Gatekeeping, the Media Agenda, and Social Media

Media gatekeeping is the process through which content creators decide what stories will be covered and reported, what information is released to consumers (Westerman et al., 2014), and therefore, whose voice will be amplified. It is carried out through the selective inclusion of facts, qualitative interpretation and editorializing, and the amount of space and time devoted to an issue (DeFleur & Everett, 2002). Presumably, gatekeepers (including journalists, editors, media owners and even advertisers) are concerned with veracity and credibility of the information disseminated through their media outlets, because they are concerned with their reputation required for their continued existence.

Gatekeeping decisions are intentional, but many factors can impact their effect. For example, external events occurring in a given time span may result in the emphasizing or deemphasizing of a story or event. Additionally, a reporter's conscious or subconscious biases and interests further shape how a message is presented. In traditional media, both editorial perspectives and commercial goals guide these decisions. However, in social media the process of information gatekeeping is turned on its head. Content consumers, instead of content producers, become their own gatekeepers. Veracity and credibility are no longer the concern of the media organization but are something the content consumer must determine for his or herself.

While there are different approaches to studying the social effects of mass communication, the idea that media interprets the world for the audience is a common thread. As early as the 1920s, journalist Walter Lippmann cited the agenda-setting function of the media, and the eventual link to policy and political action. He believed that the media creates pictures in people's heads, and that the public - which is typically removed from the actual events - react, not to 'reality,' but to the pictures in their heads (Lippmann, 1922, p. 37).

The pictures inside the heads of these human beings, the pictures of themselves, of others, of their needs and purposes, and relationship, are their public opinions. Those pictures which are acted upon by groups of people, or by individuals acting in the name of groups, are Public Opinion, with capital letters.

Agenda-setting theory was first proposed by McCombs and Shaw in 1972, and operationalizes a classic quote from Bernard Cohen (1963, p. 13), stating: "The press may not be successful much of the time in telling people what to think, but it is stunningly successful in telling its readers what to think about." This assertion is consistently supported by the correlation between frequency of media coverage on a topic and the perceived importance of that topic among the members of the audience. The concept of agenda setting has been expanded to include second level agenda setting (McCombs & Shaw, 1993), which suggests that the way media content frames an issue will ultimately influence *how* people think about that particular issue. Yet another expansion of the theory is the concept of inter-media agenda setting, where media outlets cover stories from other outlets, and even social media as news items in themselves. Twitter users from traditional media outlets may have more agenda setting power than the outlets themselves (Harder, Sevenans, & Van Aelst, 2017). Even Instagram, a non-textual social media platform, was found to have an agenda setting role in the 2016 U.S. presidential elections (Towner & Muñoz, 2017).

General consensus among media scholars is that media portrayal affects individuals' views of issues and the world, but that individuals have control the extent of the influence through their ability to select the media they consume and by corroborating information across media channels, comparing media content with personal experience, and by exercising their own judgment about the credibility of media sources. Personal experience, interpersonal contacts, and overarching social processes in the "real world," such as economic, scientific, or social events, interact with the media agenda to create the public's perception of reality, or the public agenda. The extent to which the public participates in the political process helps shape the policy agenda. McQuail and Windahl (1993) proposed a conceptual model of the interrelationships between the real world, the media agenda, the public agenda and the policy agenda (Figure 1).

Figure 1. McQuail and Windah'sl (1993) conceptual model of agenda setting

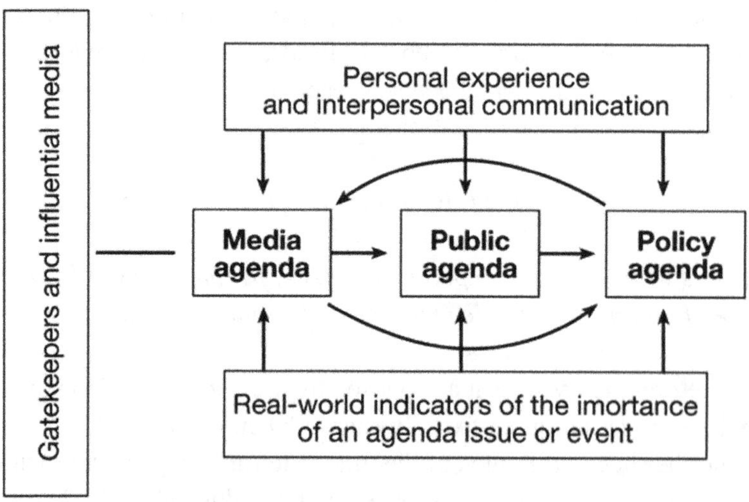

This model shows the bi-directional links between the gatekeepers in media organizations, the media content or media agenda, world events, the public agenda and the policy agenda. Policies and policy debates are covered by the media, which places policy issues on the public agenda. Because infectious disease outbreaks are typically newsworthy events that trigger policy action and public concern, this model provides a conceptual framework to discuss the links between infectious disease in the media and public health policies.

Albalawi and Sixsmith (2015) proposed an updated model of agenda setting incorporating social media (see Figure 2). They argue that, unlike classic agenda setting, agenda setting in the social media age involves rich interactions among many different actors. "Agenda setting via social media is a new sphere of social interaction that represents any member who desires to participate in the process" (Albalawi & Sixsmith, 2015). Given this interactive, multi-actor setting, they view social media as an "independent agenda-formulating body within the agenda-setting process" (Albalawi & Sixsmith, 2015), setting the agenda for the public, and even for policy, at an equal level as the traditional media.

Figure 2. Albalawi and Sixsmith (2015) agenda setting model in the social media era

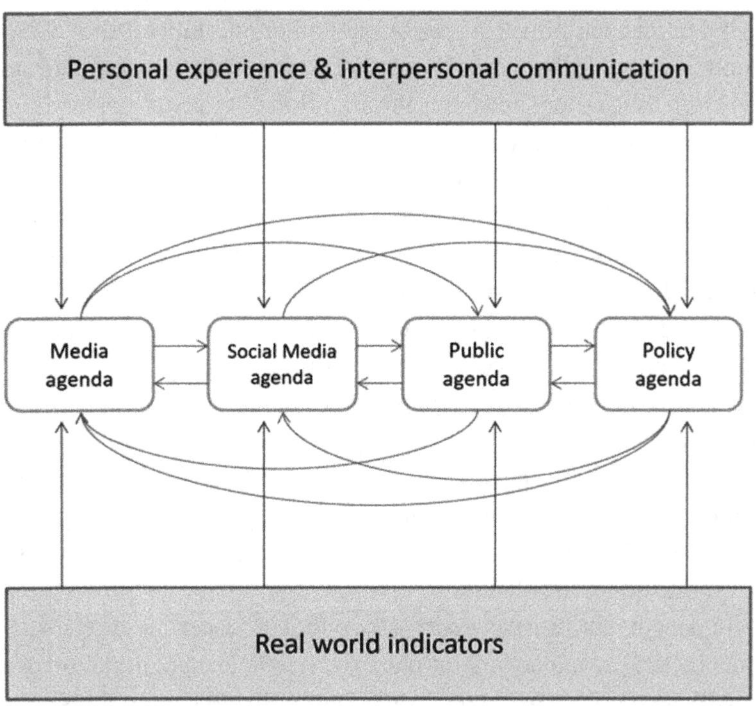

Health Crises, Media and the Public Agenda

Since the time of the bubonic plague, epidemics and plagues have decimated populations. Not surprisingly, the fear of contagion, often with no identified solution or mechanism of prevention fueled the public agenda on these health issues. As mass media evolved, it has become a key tool to educate the public on disease prevention and to alert them regarding disease outbreaks for their protection. The oral tradition of sharing information among family and acquaintances was replaced by mass media channels as the main source of information, including health information (Bomlitz & Brezis, 2008). Individuals rely on mass media to learn about their world, and make choices about their behaviors based on what was presented to them. Should they avoid certain areas to avoid infection? Are there measures they can take, such as hand washing or water boiling, to prevent contagion? What groups are most affected? How severe are the potential consequences?

What is presented in the media influences what media users know with respect to health and disease beyond their personal experience. Only a small portion of all diseases are experienced firsthand, and those are generally locally based. About 65% of the world's first news about infectious disease now comes from informal sources (as opposed to health authorities), including press reports and the Internet (Heymann & Rodier, 2001). How epidemics are presented in the media plays an important role in the importance they ascribe to the issues presented, and the perceived personal risk or susceptibility. A media phenomenon, dubbed the "CNN effect," occurs when coverage of an issue by powerful news media organizations such as CNN provokes public outcry and gains the attention of government leaders (Natsios, 1996; Robinson, 1999). Commercial news outlets' tendency to show emotionally-charged images of suffering and devastation in an effort to boost ratings also has the power to arouse the public to demand action from policy makers. Conversely, when coverage ceases, the pressure on policymakers drops. An example of this is the 2010 earthquake in Haiti. As the news media covered the destruction, the public agenda became focused on the issue and brought about policy action, such as monetary commitment, deployment of troops, and temporary protective status for Haitian immigrants. Once the novelty wore off and the news media no longer deemed the issue newsworthy, the call for policies in support of Haiti abated from the public agenda. The same phenomenon has been repeatedly exhibited in coverage of recent infectious disease outbreaks around the globe, such as the SARS epidemic in Asia, the Avian flu, Ebola, MRSA, and Zika. When the media moves on to the next story, public concern subsides.

Entertainment media also play a part in the public's concern over germs, evidenced, for example, by the prevalence of antibacterial hand cleaners in public places. This coincided with an increase in content related to viral and bacterial diseases in news coverage, advertisements, and entertainment media (Tomes, 2000). Television programming featuring forensic scientists tracking the source of infectious agents, advertisements calling attention to invisible germs, documentary series showcasing obscure infections, and news coverage of outbreaks such as salmonella, influenza and methicillin resistant Staphylococcus Aureus (MRSA), are all examples of recent media attention to viruses and bacteria. Media scholars enjoy lively debates about the directionality of these associations: Does public interest in bacterial and viral infections guide the nature of media content, or is it the other way around?

Media Framing: Setting the Tone for Risk Perceptions

As discussed above, media coverage is critical to management of outbreaks and epidemics to draw attention to unmet needs, educate the public about prevention behaviors and rapidly communicate policies and recommendations. However, the way this information is communicated frames the issue and sets the tone among mass audiences for the discussion of issues. Once the tone it set, however, it is difficult to change. The frame is communicated through a variety of contextual cues, which constitute a sort of interpretive commentary to the informational content. For example, television and news frequently use music, sound bites and catch phrases to refer to a news story (e.g. "Gulf Oil Disaster" and "H1N1: Fighting the Flu"). Print media uses magnified images of bacteria or emotional depictions of victims. Colors, fonts and theme songs are carefully selected to match the intended tone of the story. All of these tactics helps create an identity for the story and illustrate the drama of an unfolding crisis, which is then run rampant on social media, often without important contextual information.

Metaphors are often coined that exaggerate and change the actual meaning of the situation. The metaphors selected communicate meaning about the intensity of a threat (Sontag, 1988; Wallis & Nerlich, 2005; Larson, Nerlich, & Wallis, 2005). The wording used by mass media conveys meaning, and can provoke misguided perceptions, which are then promulgated and often exaggerated on social media. When discussing the mutation of viruses, for example, the media created the term "superbug," generating the image of an invincible opponent in the mind of the public (Washer & Joffe, 2006; Nerlich & Richard, 2009). Describing a disease as a "retrovirus," versus "pandemic," or a "killer" communicates different connotations, and which can have significant effects on other areas of society, such as travel, the economy, health policies, and law enforcement (Verghese, 2004). Bovine Spongiform Encephalopathy (BSE) and the derivative Creutzfeld-Jacob Disease (CJD) was referred to as "Mad Cow Disease," which, cast the British meat industry in a negative light (Washer, 2005). SARS was portrayed in the UK as a Chinese disease, and the appearance of "third world" diseases, such as tuberculosis, malaria, and leprosy, in the U.S. was often attributed to illegal immigration. Attributing the disease to "others" cast blame in order to calm fears (Washer, 2004). These strategies are successful in gaining attention, but do not necessarily provide education or accurate information, and most importantly, have the potential to harm groups through stigma and discrimination. Another example is the pork industry's call to refer to so-called "swine flu" as H1N1 to remove the stigma from their product (Johnson, 2009).

MEDIA AND DISEASE RISK COMMUNICATION

Disease Outbreaks and Social Panic

During a public health emergency, people expect traditional news media to know how serious the situation is and how to avoid infection (Fischhoff *et al.*, 2006). Risk communication deals with providing knowledge that people need to understand risk, influencing risk related behavior and facilitating cooperation among stakeholders (Rohrmann, 1992). When there is an infectious disease outbreak, authorities use the media to communicate with the public, help them interpret the situation, and appease them with assurances that something is being done. Used effectively, risk communication is one of the most important responsibilities of government to respond to the public's needs (Leiss, 2004). Positive crisis communication includes scientific information translated into layman's terms, addressing uncertainties and handling the interface of science and public policy (Leiss, 2004). This process closes the circle between the policy agenda and the media agenda illustrated by McQuail and Windahl (1993) in Figure 1. While the media coverage of a disease may influence the policy agenda, in this case, it is the policy agenda that determines the media content. Authorities can now also use social media to promulgate their health messages. For better or for worse, once messages are out there on social media, so can everyone else, along with their comments and personal interpretations.

When properly used, crisis communication can not only avoid the spread of a disease, but also to prevent panic. The important aspects of preventing panic include gaining the public's trust, understanding each public, planning and preparation, and getting each message out as early as possible (WHO, 2005). Unfortunately, at times the media achieve the opposite effect. According to Young, Norman & Humphreys (2008), the public's perception of disease risk is impacted by high levels of media reporting. Bomlitz and Brezis (2008) examined the relationship between the intensity of media coverage and the actual risk of an event to public health. In some cases, the amount of media coverage was inversely correlated with actual numbers of deaths for the specific public health risks. For example, SARS, bioterrorism, and West Nile Fever killed only a handful of people in 2003. However, together, they generated over 100,000 media reports (Bomlitz & Brezis, 2008), arguably generating disproportionate concern among audiences. Villar and Zamith (2011) compared the frequency of health issues covered by major national online media outlets, worldwide mortality and the public's perception of risk. Frequency of media coverage was found to be correlated with both worldwide mortality and with perceived risks for specific diseases and injuries. Results also showed that for all causes of death, the public's perception of risk to self was significantly lower than the perceived risk to society.

Diseases frequently portrayed in media, even when actually infrequent, gain higher status in the public's mind and are perceived to be more dangerous than they actually are. This "top-of-mind" effect created by mass media is multiplied on social media, exacerbating the perception that the disease is more widespread that it actually may be. Obscure or emerging infectious diseases have mass media appeal, which results in greater salience of these issues in the media. These topics then spread on social media exponentially, contributing to the perception that these outbreaks are as widespread as the information about them. Far less time, money and media space are spent on the most common and deadly health threats, such as smoking and obesity.

It is a challenge for the media to strike a reasonable balance between accurately communicating risk and reporting "sexy" stories that may be deemed more newsworthy. As mentioned above, what is newsworthy is determined in traditional media by gatekeepers who in turn are influenced by corporate mandates, proximity, and other events in the news. In the AIDS epidemic, new media fueled social panic and instigating moral outrage by adequately communicating the risk of doctor to patient transmission, rather than basing their reporting on calculable risk (Brown, Chapman & Lupton, 1996). Another example of risk overstatement is the global outbreak of Severe Acute Respiratory Syndrome (SARS) in the early 2000s. Extensive media coverage, combined with the disease's ease of transmission through air travel, led to international travel restrictions and ultimately had a negative financial impact on several continents. While SARS did infect about 10,000 people, it only killed about 1,000 (Smith, 2006), pointing again to the fact that the real impact of SARS arguably was less harmful than the global economic losses created by fear.

Outbreaks, Social Media, and Crisis/Risk Communication

The role of social media such as Facebook, Twitter, Instagram and other such applications on global infectious disease communication merits special attention. Social media enables open access to a virtually infinite number of contacts through the Internet and mobile devices, which can be a tremendous help to disseminate information. Indeed, the proliferation of increasingly-capable mobile devices allows for instant mass communication from almost any source. This immediacy can be beneficial in disseminating information in an emergency and helping educational materials reach a vast audience in a very short amount of time. Social media has already been used by health officials to communicate symptom identification information, food recalls and vaccination sites. Indeed, through Twitter alone, the U.S. Centers for Disease Control and Prevention has accumulated almost one million followers and was often cited during news coverage of the H1N1 flu pandemic in 2009 (CDC, 2017). Social media and the Internet allow for instant sharing of visual information and images, which aids educational messages, particularly among low-literacy audiences. This communication revolution rivals the advent of the printing press and television, and has great opportunities to advance health communication strategies.

Nevertheless, the open nature of social media can also serve as a source of misinformation because it is often difficult to verify the validity and credibility of the source. Although scholarly research lags behind these ever-evolving technologies, emerging research shows that social media users are less concerned with the credibility of the original source, and rely more on the trust they have in the person who sent them the information. Internet users may not have the background or the interest in assessing the quality of the information provided. Consequently, these events may generate misinformation and cause unnecessary panic. Rumors and "grapevine" information have always had potentially negative implications, and the speed of messaging through social media can exacerbate this risk.

Organizations and individuals communicating information about outbreaks need to be aware that messages intended to educate can cause social panic, create stigma and point blame. Audiences should be active media consumers, verify information across several sources, evaluate the credibility and validity of the messages and images they see. The more sources one accesses, the more accurate the picture becomes. In addition to the large media conglomerates, there are now a wide range of independent news outlets and generators of quality health information, both through traditional media and social media. However, not everyone avails themselves of these other sources. Just as information dissemination prior to the advent of mass media was centered around friends and family, social media allows an individual to surround themselves with friends and family and like-minded individuals and still feel as if they are connected to the wider world. This contradiction between the potential for global reach and the reality of choosing a small trusted inner circle means social media will certainly have both a positive and negative effect on health communication on a global level.

Culture, Social Media and Risk Amplification

Kasperson et al. (1988) established a framework of risk amplification that whereby psychological, social, cultural and political factors interact to create ripple effects beyond the actual risk or hazard. The perceived seriousness of an issue is related to the media coverage that it gets, and the associated signals communicated about the event or issue. Specifically, amplification occurs in the transfer of information about the risk, and in the publics' response mechanisms. The risk situation is interpreted by individuals and groups, including the scientist who communicates the risk assessment, the news media, cultural groups, interpersonal networks, and others. The amplified risk leads to behavioral responses, and policy actions.

Public perception of risk is multidimensional incorporating considerations of controllability, catastrophic potential, equity and threat to future generations (Slovic, 2016). Sunstein (2006) uses the term "misfearing" to refer to the tendency to fear instinctively rather than factually. Humans often fear hazards that sound tragic or sensational, beyond any measure of realistic risk. "Tornadoes. Terrorist attacks. Homicides. The big, the dramatic, and the memorable occupy far more of our worry budget than the things that kill with far greater frequency: strokes, diabetes, heart disease" (Rosenbuam, 2014, p.595). Rosenbaum (2014) identifies a force that interacts with these fear factors: our commitment to our cultural groups. If a hazard impacts our cultural group (gender, ethnic group, geographic area), we have a greater likelihood of "misfearing." Since most people connect on social media with people who are similar to them, the perceived impact on a cultural group may be amplified.

Worldviews are orienting dispositions serving to guide people's responses in complex situations (Dake, 1992), and are important in determining people's risk attitudes and perceptions. For example, Peters and Slovic (1996) found that people with a more egalitarian world view had a higher perceived risk for a wide range of hazards than people who prefer a hierarchical social order. Because people's risk perceptions and actions are greatly influenced by worldviews, technical communication often has little effect on the public's attitudes toward hazards such as nuclear power plants or nuclear waste (Slovic, 2016). Therefore, health authorities communicating on social media must have an understanding of their audiences' worldviews when framing messages about risk during disease outbreaks.

A person's individual life experiences may influence their perception of risk. For example, men are less concerned about hazards than women, and white men are less concerned about risks than non-white men. Kim, Schroeder, and Pennington-Gray (2016) found that age and gender, as well as uncertainty avoidance significantly influenced travel risk perceptions. Risk perceptions may also be related to an individual's power to influence decisions about specific hazards, and trust in those managing the risk. Besides cultural and individual predispositions toward risk, crisis and risk communication efforts are often unsuccessful due to lack of trust. Discussions of risk often pit expert against expert, contradicting each other's risk assessment, further destroying the public's trust. (Slovic, 2016). The public often rejects scientists' risk assessment due to lack of trust. Trust in risk management has been found to correlate with gender, race, and worldview (Slovic, 2016).

Trust in media may actually be an important determinant of health, beyond simple access to media content. Mass media campaigns are central to disseminating health health-related information. However, the effectiveness of these campaigns greatly depends on the public's trust in the information received. This was supported by a recent study that found that trust in mass media is associated with better health among Asian people (Tokuda et al., 2017). Therefore, lack of trust in media can actually result in dismissing important health information and consequently, poor health outcomes. Unfortunately, trust in media, including social media is quite low. In the United States, trust in national news has declined significantly, and the extent of the decline differs by political affiliation. Republicans report more trust in friends, family and acquaintances than national news. Trust in social media at large is very low (3%) among Republicans, but trust in local news is higher than all other news sources at 24%. Democrats trust national and local news sources almost equally, and have a relatively higher (6%) trust of social media as a news source (Greenwood, 2017).

A 2014 study found that the amount of funding provided by public health agencies to support information about the H1N1 outbreak was positively related to media attention to the H1N1 disease, as well as the salience of the severity of the disease in the messaging. However, there was no relationship between salience of the severity as covered in the media and public risk perceptions. In other words, media coverage increased awareness of the issue, but did not influence perceptions of severity despite the salience of the severity attributes in the media coverage. This raises questions about the ability of traditional media to adequately convey information about disease severity (Rim, Ha, & Kiousis, 2014). This may support the importance of social media to help transfer the agenda from the media to the public for important health issues. It may also speak to the lack of trust in media, that results in selective attention and perception of what is presented.

Examples of Social Media and Risk Information During Outbreaks

The immediacy and ubiquity of social media opens unprecedented opportunities to promote infectious disease prevention and mitigation policies, but also creates its own set of challenges. In an environment where the audience receives information from a multitude of individual sources, rather than a few large sources, there are no clear gatekeepers and there may not be an overarching media agenda as the public agenda blurs with the media agenda. The Pew Research Center reported in 2016 that 62% of US adults gets news from social media and 18% do so often. However, the level of trust in that information is particularly low. Only about two-in-ten Americans (22%) trust the information they get from local news organizations a lot, whether online or offline, and 18% say the same of national organizations, slightly higher than the 14% who say this of the information they get from their friends and family. While the portion saying they have a lot of trust in each group is low, large majorities have at least some trust (Greenwood, 2017).

Social media, is trusted by a slim minority – only 4% of web-using adults have a lot of trust in the information they find on social media. And that rises to only 7% among those who get news on these sites. When those who get news online from each source type were asked specifically about each's accuracy, news organizations again sit at the top; 15% of those who get news from news organizations online find them very accurate, compared with 7% who say the same about people they are close with and just 2% for people with whom they are not particularly close (Greenwood, 2017).

The flat, nonhierarchical nature of social media does allow health authorities to communicate directly with the public. This removed the media from its role as gatekeeper and so mitigates the effects an exaggerated media narrative might have. However, social media may also complicate a health authority's ability to manage the message about a crisis by adding the unfiltered diverse opinions of an audience without any expertise in a forum easily viewed by the public. Further on social media, like traditional media, excitement and novelty can generate more interest than drier yet more accurate information. Sharma et al. (2017) found that while the clear majority (81%) of Facebook posts about Zika were accurate, the inaccurate ones were shared at a much higher rate suggesting that legitimate health information risks being drowned out on social channels by misinformation or conspiracy theories.

During the Ebola outbreak in Africa the World Health Organization found itself fighting a second "virtual epidemic" of misinformation carried on social media (Allgaier & Svalastog, 2015). Following the first diagnosis of Ebola in the United States on September 30, 2014 mentions of Ebola on Twitter jumped from 100 to over 6000. Even though Ebola was at the time confined to one patient in Dallas, TX, the Department of Health in Iowa had to refute rumors that Ebola was spreading through that state.

In 2014, The Lancet examined Twitter use in relation to the Ebola outbreak and found that 21,037,331 tweets were about the nine cases of Ebola in the USA and only 13, 480 concerned Ebola in the West African countries that were suffering a massive health crisis. This can be attributed to the lopsided number of social media users in the United States as compared to West Africa. This also meant that misinformation was spread through social media at a much higher rate in the U.S. leading to an undesirable wave of panic where none was warranted (Lancet, 2014.)

Examining the 2016 Zika outbreak in Miami, Florida further illuminates the nuanced role of social media in the United States. On August 1st, 2016 fifteen cases of Zika were diagnosed in Miami. Zika had been a significant topic in social media conversation earlier in the year when the first cases were found in Brazil, but interest had faded after the Olympics. But once Zika had been diagnosed in the United States, specifically in Miami, FL, both traditional media coverage and social media exploded in a parallel yet asymmetrical fashion. The first spike in news coverage, shortly after the outbreak in Miami began, represented a 1000% increase in articles from 43 to 424. On that same day Zika mentions on Twitter and Facebook reached 20,000, which was a 1300% increase from the day prior which saw only 1455. Other smaller spikes in media coverage were each closely followed by comparable increases in social media conversations, primarily on Twitter. Just looking at the social media exposure, a viral effect is apparent showing a significantly increased reach when a subject is of sufficient interest, and further there is some indication that this increased reach in social media can be linked to an increase in interest by traditional media sources. That increased reach is an important tool for health authorities, however as with Ebola there were some problematic aspects in social media communication which either ignored or exaggerated health concerns and claims. For instance, a prominent theme in Zika coverage from the traditional media at that time was disease prevention and control, a theme which was utterly absent from social media. Social media did reinforce messages from reliable healthcare communicators and that formed the majority of the social media conversations on Zika. But it also propagated alarmist false information by retweeting headlines such as: "Gestapo Sprays Gas Chamber Aerosols Over Miami Using ZIKA Hoax as Excuse" which was a misleading representation of the genuine concern about the pesticide being used to combat Zika (Chemtrail, 2016). This misleading information about the aerial spraying was corrected in traditional media, but the corrections were not reflected by the social source that had spread the misinformation, meaning the misinformation and the correction may have reached two different audiences.

The CDC (@cdcgov) made a sustained effort to communicate via social media offering tips on preventing Zika and describing symptoms well before the outbreak in Miami. They began correcting misinformation with responses to individuals once false information began to appear in the United States, which corresponded with that outbreak. The Florida Department of Health (@healthyFla) followed the same pattern, making direct responses to offer correct information once Zika was diagnosed in Miami. The actual top posters driving most of the conversation, or at least occupying most of the bandwidth, were not healthcare communicators. The top

Twitter poster using the word "Zika" from July 28th 2016 to February 28th 2017 was an exterminator, who retweeted accurate information from reliable news and health communication sources but with attention grabbing headlines stressing the threat of Zika such as: Check it OUT! | #*Zika* virus can 'SHRINK a man's #testicles - leaving them #infertile' #NYC #FL #*Miami* #AZ #TX #NC (Downey, 2017)

The drop-in hotel bookings in Miami suggests that the CDC warnings, media coverage and the resultant amplification on social media was effective in convincing tourists not to come to Miami (Herrera, 2016). This may not have been the intended result as much of the information presented concerned prevention not avoidance.

One difference between the impact of social media on awareness and discussion of Zika as opposed to Ebola was that South America, where Zika became a significant health issue in 2016, has a well-entrenched social media presence at least in the upper classes. While the United States still generated 18% of the world wide social media Zika conversation, Brazil had the second largest number of social media mentions of Zika at 4%, followed by India, Argentina and Mexico, all countries with significant social media penetration. Clearly the digital divide remains a pervasive concern when using social media as a health communication tool, but one that can be anticipated.

FUTURE RESEARCH DIRECTIONS

To fully understand the agenda setting relationship between social media and traditional media, we require comparative content analyses of infectious disease topics on traditional and social media. More information is needed on the adoption of new media among different groups, and whether this form of health communication increases or decreases the tendency to create myths, stigmatize groups and find scapegoats. Other areas of research include exploring the possibility of an increased knowledge gap between those with access to information and communication technologies and those without, as well as the need for enhanced cross-cultural competence in interpreting health related messages originating from all parts of the world, accessible at the tap of a finger on a smartphone.

With social media serving as the voice of the audience, it can be a valuable source of outbreak information from the field, as well as a tool for dissemination for authorities. There is increasing interest in crowdsourcing for public health reporting and surveillance (Brabham et al., 2014; Kraemer et al., 2017), sharing knowledge during emergency events, and even to create collective databases on the earth's microbes form around the world (Raes, 2017). Bernardo et al. (2013) examined the research on internet search engines searches and social media posts as a complement to disease surveillance. The potential of social media as a credible source of crowdsourced data needs to be further explored.

Finally, more research is needed to explore the influence of culture on risk perceptions, and the susceptibility or resilience of different cultural groups to disease information spread on social media. This essay serves as a first look on the role of culture in outbreak communication through social media. However more systematic research must be conducted to inform health and risk communicators on the most appropriate, ethical and effective ways to accurately communicate with publics about how to manage infectious disease risk and prevent contagion without contributing to social panic. The threshold between rational scientific interpretation of calculable risk and unwarranted fear due to erroneous interpretations of risk may very well be, at least in part, determined by cultural attitudes. Uncertainty avoidance, trust and respect for authorities and the media, access to social capital, social media dependence, among other factors, may be determinants in the effect of social media content relating to disease outbreaks. We need research that distinguishes audience characteristics and social media uses, so that health communicators can best use these tools for their intended effect.

CONCLUSION

Social media appears to be both an asset and a liability during disease outbreaks, and its effect depends on audiences cultural attitudes and trust toward authorities and the media. When reacting to an infectious disease outbreak in the media, it is critical to consider the impact and spread of information through social media. Social media best practices including transparency and increased engagement initially appear vitally important to health communicators. They are also important to help audiences adequately interpret risk, filtered through the different voice present on social media. Public health and crisis communication officials can use the lessons learned from previous outbreaks and the impact of media coverage to help the media "strike the right balance between timely and frequent risk communication and placing risk in the proper context" (Wilder-Smith, 2006, p. 59).

Research shows that people tend to fear more about issues that impact people from their same cultural group. People who cannot relate to the technical information being disseminated by authorities are more likely to disregard them. People with a more egalitarian worldview tend to have a higher perception of risk that people with a hierarchical world view. Lack of trust in the media may also lead to dismissing official health information, and lead audiences to rely more on information on social media that has been filtered by people with whom they share a culture and worldview.

It makes sense that the tactics - including tactics meant to build trust - that work for corporate social community managers would also work for health communicators. Making sure that reliable health information is readily available on social media makes it more likely it will be seen and passed on. Since authority on social media rests at the individual level and peers are sometimes more trusted than expert sources, it is important to work at that individual level when communicating. Working to establish trusted relationships with less media savvy communities could also be important, but ultimately it must be remembered that the best, if imperfect, way to counter misinformation on social media is to put out accurate information on both traditional and social media.

Regardless of the type of media, it is imperative that media gatekeepers gain a greater understanding of health issues, analyze their framework in which it will be presented, and understand the possible social implications of how they address infectious diseases. Similarly, national and global health organizations need to garner a deeper appreciation the changing media environment and its potential as a tool to disseminate information on public health risk, policies and prevention behaviors. Policymakers also need to be cognizant that media is global and will affect more than just one specific region or sector of society.

REFERENCES

Albalawi, Y., & Sixsmith, J. (2015). Agenda Setting for Health Promotion: Exploring an Adapted Model for the Social Media Era. *JMIR Public Health and Surveillance*, *1*(2), e21. doi:10.2196/publichealth.5014 PMID:27227139

Allgaier, J., & Svalastog, A. L. (2015). The communication aspects of the Ebola virus disease outbreak in Western Africa–do we need to counter one, two, or many epidemics? *Croatian Medical Journal*, *56*(5), 496–499. doi:10.3325/cmj.2015.56.496 PMID:26526888

Bernardo, T. M., Rajic, A., Young, I., Robiadek, K., Pham, M. T., & Funk, J. A. (2013). Scoping review on search queries and social media for disease surveillance: A chronology of innovation. *Journal of Medical Internet Research*, *15*(7), e147. doi:10.2196/jmir.2740 PMID:23896182

Bomlitz, L. J., & Brezis, M. (2008). Misrepresentation of health risks by mass media. *Journal of Public Health*, *30*(2), 202–204. doi:10.1093/pubmed/fdn009 PMID:18281322

Brabham, D. C., Ribisl, K. M., Kirchner, T. R., & Bernhardt, J. M. (2014). Crowdsourcing applications for public health. *American Journal of Preventive Medicine*, *46*(2), 179–187. doi:10.1016/j.amepre.2013.10.016 PMID:24439353

Brown, J., Chapman, S., & Lupton, D. (1996). Infinitesimal risk as public health crisis: News media coverage of a doctor-patient HIV contact tracing investigation. *Social Science & Medicine*, *43*(12), 1685–1695. doi:10.1016/0277-9536(95)00402-5 PMID:8961412

CDC (@CDCgov). (2017, November 12). [Twitter post]. Retrieved from https://twitter.com/CDCgov

Chemtrail. (2016). *Gestapo Sprays Gas Chamber Aerosols Over Miami Using ZIKA Hoax as Excuse*. Retrieved from: chemtrailsplanet.net/2016/08/06/gestapo-sprays-gas-chamber-aerosols-over-miami-using-zika-hoax-as-excuse/.

Cohen, B. (1963). *The Press and Foreign Policy*. Princeton, NJ: Princeton University Press.

Dake, K. (1992). Myths of nature: Culture and the social construction of risk. *The Journal of Social Issues*, *48*(4), 21–37. doi:10.1111/j.1540-4560.1992.tb01943.x

DeFleur, M. L., & Everett, E. D. (2002). *Understanding Mass Communication*. Houghton Mifflin Company.

Downey, A. (2017). Zika Virus Can 'SHRINK a Man's Testicles - Leaving Them Infertile'. *The Sun*. Retrieved from www.thesun.co.uk/living/2940013/zika-virus-can-shrink-a-mans-testicles-leaving-them-infertile/

Ellison, N. B. (2007). Social network sites: Definition, history, and scholarship. *Journal of Computer-Mediated Communication*, *13*(1), 210–230. doi:10.1111/j.1083-6101.2007.00393.x

Fischhoff, B., Bruine de Bruin, W., & Guvenc, U. (2006). Analyzing disaster risks and plans: An avian flu example. *Journal of Risk and Uncertainty*, *33*(1-2), 133–151. doi:10.1007/s11166-006-0175-8

Florida Dept. Health (@HealthyFla). (2017, November 2). [Twitter post]. Retrieved from https://twitter.com/HealthyFla

Greenwood, S. (2017). Trust in the News Media. *Pew Research Center's Journalism Project*. Retrieved from www.journalism.org/2017/05/10/americans-attitudes-about-the-news-media-deeply-divided-along-partisan-lines/pj_2017-05-10_media-attitudes_a-05/

Harder, R. A., Sevenans, J., & Van Aelst, P. (2017). Intermedia Agenda Setting in the Social Media Age: How Traditional Players Dominate the News Agenda in Election Times. *The International Journal of Press/Politics*.

Herrera, C. (2016). Miami Beach Tourism Takes a Hit from Zika: Demand Drops, Cancellations Rise. *Miami Herald*. Retrieved from www.miamiherald.com/news/health-care/article103553277.html

Heymann, D. L., & Rodier, G. R. (2001). Hot spots in a wired world: WHO surveillance of emerging and re-emerging infectious diseases. *The Lancet Infectious Diseases*, *1*(5), 345–353. doi:10.1016/S1473-3099(01)00148-7 PMID:11871807

Johnson, R. (2009). Potential Farm Sector Effects of 2009 H1N1 "Swine Flu": Questions and Answers. *Congressional Research Service*. Retrieved from http://assets.opencrs.com/rpts/R40575_20100112.pdf

Kasperson, R. E., Renn, O., Slovic, P., Brown, H. S., Emel, J., Goble, R., ... Ratick, S. (1988). The social amplification of risk: A conceptual framework. *Risk Analysis*, *8*(2), 177–187. doi:10.1111/j.1539-6924.1988.tb01168.x

Kim, H., Schroeder, A., & Pennington-Gray, L. (2016). Does Culture Influence Risk Perceptions? *Tourism Review International*, *20*(1), 11–28. doi:10.3727/154427216X14581596798942

Kraemer, J. D., Strasser, A. A., Lindblom, E. N., Niaura, R. S., & Mays, D. (2017). Crowdsourced data collection for public health: A comparison with nationally representative, population tobacco use data. *Preventive Medicine*, *102*, 93–99. doi:10.1016/j.ypmed.2017.07.006 PMID:28694063

Larson, B. M. H., Nerlich, B., & Wallis, P. (2005). Metaphors and Biorisks: The War on Infectious Diseases and Invasive Species. *Science Communication*, *26*(3), 243–268. doi:10.1177/1075547004273019

Leiss, W. (2004). Effective risk communication practice. *Toxicology Letters*, *149*(1-3), 399–404. doi:10.1016/j.toxlet.2003.12.050 PMID:15093287

Lippmann, W. (1922). *Public Opinion*. New York: Macmillan.

McCombs, M. E., & Shaw, D. L. (1972). The Agenda-Setting Function of Mass Media. *Public Opinion Quarterly*, *36*(2), 176–187. doi:10.1086/267990

McCombs, M. E., & Shaw, D. L. (1993). The Evolution of Agenda-Setting Research: Twenty-Five Years in the Marketplace of Ideas. *Journal of Communication*, *43*(2), 58–67. doi:10.1111/j.1460-2466.1993.tb01262.x

McQuail, D., & Windahl, S. (1993). *Communication Models* (2nd ed.). New York: Routledge.

Natsios, A. (1996). *Illusions of Influence: The CNN Effect in Complex Emergencies. In From Massacres to Genocide: The Media, Public Policy, and Humanitarian Crises* (pp. 149–168). Brookings Institution.

Nerlich, B., & Richard, J. (2009). "The post-antibiotic apocalypse" and the "war on superbugs": Catastrophe discourse in microbiology, its rhetorical form and political function. *Public Understanding of Science (Bristol, England)*, *18*(5), 574–590. doi:10.1177/0963662507087974 PMID:20027773

Peters, E., & Slovic, P. (1996). The role of affect and worldviews as orienting dispositions in the perception and acceptance of nuclear power. *Journal of Applied Social Psychology*, *26*(16), 1427–1453. doi:10.1111/j.1559-1816.1996.tb00079.x

Raes, J. (2017). Microbiology: Crowdsourcing Earth's microbes. *Nature*. Retrieved on Nov 12, 2017 from https://www.nature.com/articles/nature24756

Rim, H., Ha, J. H., & Kiousis, S. (2014). The evidence of compelling arguments in agenda building: Relationships among public information subsidies, media coverage, and risk perceptions during a pandemic outbreak. *Journal of Communication Management*, *18*(1), 101–116. doi:10.1108/JCOM-05-2012-0044

Robinson, P. (1999). The CNN effect: Can the news media drive foreign policy? *Review of International Studies*, *25*(2), 301–330. doi:10.1017/S0260210599003010

Rohrmann, B. (1992). The evaluation of risk communication effectiveness. *Acta Psychologica*, *81*(2), 169–192. doi:10.1016/0001-6918(92)90004-W

Rosenbaum, L. (2014). "Misfearing"—culture, identity, and our perceptions of health risks. *The New England Journal of Medicine*, *370*(7), 595–597. doi:10.1056/NEJMp1314638 PMID:24521105

Sharma, M., Yadav, K., Yadav, N., & Ferdinand, K. C. (2017). Zika virus pandemic—analysis of Facebook as a social media health information platform. *American Journal of Infection Control*, *45*(3), 301–302. doi:10.1016/j.ajic.2016.08.022 PMID:27776823

Slovic, P. (2016). *The perception of risk*. New York: Routledge.

Smith, R. D. (2006). Responding to global infectious disease outbreaks: Lessons from SARS on the role of risk perception, communication and management. *Social Science & Medicine*, *63*(12), 3113–3123. doi:10.1016/j.socscimed.2006.08.004 PMID:16978751

Sontag, S. (1988). *Illness as Metaphor & AIDS and Its Metaphors*. New York: Farrar, Strauss, and Giroux.

Sunstein, C. R. (2005). Misfearing: A reply. *Harvard Law Review, 119*, 1110.

The Lancet. (2014). The medium and the message of Ebola [editorial]. *Lancet, 384*(9955). Retrieved from http://www.thelancet.com/journals/lancet/article/PIIS0140-6736(14)62016-X/fulltext

Tokuda, Y., Fujii, S., Jimba, M., & Inoguchi, T. (2017). The Relationship Between Trust in Mass Media and the Healthcare System and Individual Health: Evidence from the Asia Barometer Survey. In T. Inoguchi & Y. Tokuda (Eds.), *Trust with Asian Characteristics: Interpersonal and Institutional* (pp. 191–207). Springer Singapore. doi:10.1007/978-981-10-2305-7_12

Tomes, N. (2000). The making of a germ panic, then and now. *American Journal of Public Health, 90*(2), 191–198. doi:10.2105/AJPH.90.2.191 PMID:10667179

Towner, T. L., & Muñoz, C. L. (2017). The Role of Instagram in Issue Agenda Setting during the 2016 Presidential Primary Campaign. In The Internet and the 2016 Presidential Campaign (pp. 263-284). Academic Press.

Verghese, A. (2004). What Is in a Word? *Clinical Infectious Diseases, 38*(7), 932–933. doi:10.1086/382365 PMID:15034822

Villar, M. E., & Zamith, R. (2011). Comparing frequency of online news coverage, worldwide mortality and perceived risk of leading diseases and injuries: Challenging paradigms in the new media landscape. *Journal of Health & Mass Communication, 3*(1-4), 193.

Wallis, P., & Nerlich, B. (2005). Disease metaphors in new epidemics: The UK media framing of the 2003 SARS epidemic. *Social Science & Medicine, 60*(11), 2629–2639. doi:10.1016/j.socscimed.2004.11.031 PMID:15814187

Washer, P. (2004). Representations of SARS in the British newspapers. *Social Science & Medicine, 59*(12), 2561–2571. doi:10.1016/j.socscimed.2004.03.038 PMID:15474209

Washer, P. (2005). Representations of mad cow disease. *Social Science & Medicine, 62*(2), 457–466. doi:10.1016/j.socscimed.2005.06.001 PMID:16046039

Washer, P., & Joffe, H. (2006). The "hospital superbug": Social representations of MRSA. *Social Science & Medicine, 63*(8), 2141–2152. doi:10.1016/j.socscimed.2006.05.018 PMID:16782254

Westerman, D., Spence, P. R., & Van Der Heide, B. (2014). Social media as information source: Recency of updates and credibility of information. *Journal of Computer-Mediated Communication, 19*(2), 171–183. doi:10.1111/jcc4.12041

Wilder-Smith, A. (2006). The severe acute respiratory syndrome: Impact on travel and tourism. *Travel Medicine and Infectious Disease*, *4*(2), 53–60. doi:10.1016/j.tmaid.2005.04.004 PMID:16887725

World Health Organization. (2005). *Outbreak Communications Guidelines.* Communicable Disease Cluster, WHO document number WHO/CDS/2005.28. Retrieved from http://www.who.int/infectious-disease-news/IDdocs/whocds200528/whocds200528en.pdf

Xu, Z., Zhang, H., Hu, C., Mei, L., Xuan, J., Choo, K. K. R., ... Zhu, Y. (2016). Building knowledge base of urban emergency events based on crowdsourcing of social media. *Concurrency and Computation*, *28*(15), 4038–4052. doi:10.1002/cpe.3780

Young, M. E., Norman, G. R., & Humphreys, K. R. (2008). Medicine in the Popular Press: The Influence of the Media on Perceptions of Disease. *PLoS One*, *3*(10), e3552. doi:10.1371/journal.pone.0003552 PMID:18958167

KEY TERMS AND DEFINITIONS

Agenda Setting: The theory that what the public thinks about is set by the media, developed by McCombs and Shaw in 1968.

Epidemic: Refers to a widespread occurrence of an infectious disease in a community at a particular time.

Infectious Disease: A disease caused by pathogenic microorganisms, such as bacteria, viruses, parasites, or fungi, that can be spread, directly or indirectly, from one person to another.

Mass Media: All outlets relaying information to a large population simultaneously.

Outbreak (Disease): The occurrence of cases of disease in excess of what would normally be expected in a defined community, geographical area, or season.

Risk Perceptions: The subjective judgements that people make about the characteristics and severity of a risk.

Social Media: Websites and digital applications that enable users to create and share content.

Zika: A disease is caused by a virus transmitted primarily by Aedes mosquitoes.

Compilation of References

Abrams, D., Viki, G. T., Masser, B., & Bohner, G. (2003). Perceptions of Stranger and Acquaintance Rape: The Role of Benevolent and Hostile Sexism in Victim Blame and Rape Proclivity. *Journal of Personality and Social Psychology*, *84*(1), 111–125. doi:10.1037/0022-3514.84.1.111 PMID:12518974

Adams, G. R., & Marshall, S. K. (1996). A developmental social psychology of identity: Understanding the person-in-context. *Journal of Adolescence*, *19*(5), 429–442. doi:10.1006/jado.1996.0041 PMID:9245296

Agger, B. (2015). *Oversharing: Presentations of self in the internet age*. London: Routledge.

Agosto, D. E., & Abbas, J. (2010). High school seniors' social network and other ICT use preferences and concerns. *Proceedings of the American Society for Information Science and Technology*, *47*(1), 1–10. doi:10.1002/meet.14504701025

Aitchison, J., & Lewis, D. (Eds.). (2006). New Media Language. London: Routledge.

Alaimo, K. (2015). How the Facebook Arabic page "We Are All Khaled Said" helped promote the Egyptian revolution. *Social Media & Society*, *1*(2), 1–10. doi:10.1177/2056305115604854

Alanen, L. (2001). Explorations in Generational Analysis. In L. Alanen & B. Mayall (Eds.), *Conceptualizing Child-Adult Relations* (pp. 11–22). London: Routledge.

Albalawi, Y., & Sixsmith, J. (2015). Agenda Setting for Health Promotion: Exploring an Adapted Model for the Social Media Era. *JMIR Public Health and Surveillance*, *1*(2), e21. doi:10.2196/publichealth.5014 PMID:27227139

Alexa.com. (n.d.). Retrieved from http://www.alexa.com/topsites/global

Allgaier, J., & Svalastog, A. L. (2015). The communication aspects of the Ebola virus disease outbreak in Western Africa–do we need to counter one, two, or many epidemics? *Croatian Medical Journal*, *56*(5), 496–499. doi:10.3325/cmj.2015.56.496 PMID:26526888

Allport, G. W. (1954). *The nature of prejudice*. Cambridge, MA: Addison-Wesley.

Alonso, A., & Oiarzabal, P. J. (2010). *Diasporas in the new media age: Identity, politics, and community*. Reno, NV: University of Nevada Press.

Altinöz, M., Parildar, C., Çakiroglu, D., Barlas, M., Çaliskan, G., & Özdil, G. (2010). Bullying encountered during workplace training: Comparison of bullying level perceived by trainees whose workplace managers are women and men (Sample of Hacettepe University). *Selcuk Üniversitesi Sosyal Bilimler Enstitüsü Dergisi, 24*, 63-74. Retrieved from dergisosyalbil.selcuk.edu.tr/susbed/article/download/212/196

American Women Politics. (2015). Retrieved from http://www.cawp.rutgers.edu/

Amichai-Hamburger, Y., Hasler, B. S., & Shani-Sherman, T. (2015). Structured and unstructured intergroup contact in the digital age. *Computers in Human Behavior, 52*, 515–522. doi:10.1016/j.chb.2015.02.022

Amichai-Hamburger, Y., & McKenna, K. Y. A. (2006). The contact hypothesis reconsidered: Interacting via the Internet. *Journal of Computer-Mediated Communication, 11*(3), 825–843. doi:10.1111/j.1083-6101.2006.00037.x

Amnesty International. (2016). *The 'Arab Spring': Five years on.* Retrieved from https://www.amnesty.org/en/latest/campaigns/2016/01/arab-spring-five-years-on/

Anderson, A. A., Brossard, D., Scheufele, D. A., Xenos, M. A., & Ladwig, P. (2014). The "nasty effect:" Online incivility and risk perceptions of emerging technologies. *Journal of Computer-Mediated Communication, 19*(3), 373–387. doi:10.1111/jcc4.12009

Anderson, B. (1991). *Imagined Communities.* New York, NY: Verso.

Anderson, B. (2006). *Imagined communities: Reflections on the origin and spread of nationalism.* London: Verso Books.

Anderson, B., Fagan, P., Woodnutt, T., & Chamorro-Premuzic, T. (2012). Facebook psychology: Popular questions answered by research. *Psychology of Popular Media Culture, 1*(1), 23–37. doi:10.1037/a0026452

Ang, H. P. (2017). *Communicating with Power in a VUCA World.* Retrieved from http://www.icahdq.org/blogpost/1523657/272158/Communicating-With-Power-in-a-VUCA-World

Ang, I. (1990). The nature of the audience. In J. D. H. Downing, A. Mohammadi, & A. Sreberny (Eds.), *Questioning the media: A critical introduction* (pp. 155–165). Thousand Oaks, CA: Sage Publications.

Ante, S. E. (2009, October 19). *Amazon: Turning Consumer Opinions into Gold.* Retrieved from http://www.bloomberg.com/bw/magazine/content/09_43/b4152047039565.htm

Antonoff, M. (2015). Thoracic Surgery Social Media Network: Bringing thoracic surgery scholarship to Twitter. *The Annals of Thoracic Surgery, 100*(2), 383–384. doi:10.1016/j.athoracsur.2015.06.049 PMID:26142909

Antunovic, D., Parsons, P., & Cooke, T. R. (2016). 'Checking' and googling: Stages of news consumption among young adults. *Journalism*, 1–17.

Anyanwu, C. (2003). Myth and realities of new media technology: Virtual classroom education premise. *Television & New Media, 40*(4), 289–409. doi:10.1177/1527476403256210

Aoki, A., & Takeda, O. (2008). *Asian American Politics* (Vol. 1). Cambridge, UK: Polity Press.

Appadurai, A. (1996). *Modernity at large: Cultural dimensions of globalization.* Minneapolis, MN: University of Minnesota Press.

Applegate, J. L., & Sypher, H. E. (1988). A constructivist theory of communication and culture. In Y. Y. Kim & W. B. Gudykunst (Eds.), *Theories in intercultural communication* (pp. 41–65). Newbury Park, CA: Sage.

Arno, A. (2009). *Alarming reports: Communicating conflict in the daily news.* Oxford, UK: Berghahn Books.

Awan, I. (2017). Cyber-extremism: ISIS and the power of social media. *Society, 54*(2), 138–149. doi:10.1007/s12115-017-0114-0

Aydıngün, A. (2007). Resettlement and belonging among cultural and ethnic kin: The Meskhetian Turks in Turkey. In T. Trier & A. Khanzihn (Eds.), *Meskhetian Turks at a crossroads: Integration, reparation or resettlement?* (pp. 340–377). Berlin, Germany: Lit Verlag.

Baker, T., & Pelfrey, W. Jr. (2016). Bullying victimization, social network usage, and delinquent coping in a sample of urban youth: Examining the predictions of general strain theory. *Violence and Victims, 31*(6), 1021–1043. doi:10.1891/0886-6708.VV-D-14-00154 PMID:28661374

Bala, M. (2014). Civic engagement in the age of online social networks. *Contemporary Readings in Law and Social Justice, 6*(1), 767–774.

Ball, J. (2012, April 22). Me and my data: How much do the Internet giants really know? *The Guardian.* Retrieved from: http://www.theguardian.com/technology/2012/apr/22/me-and-my-data-Internet-giants

Balleys, C., & Coll, S. (2016). Being publicly intimate: Teenagers managing online privacy. *Media Culture & Society, 39*(6), 885–901. doi:10.1177/0163443716679033

Bargiela-Chiappini, F. (2006). (Whose) English(es) for Asian business discourse? *Journal of Asian Pacific Communication, 16*(1), 1–23. doi:10.1075/japc.16.1.02bar

Barki, H., & Hartwick, J. (2004). Conceptualizing the construct of interpersonal conflict. *International Journal of Conflict Management, 15*(3), 216–224. doi:10.1108/eb022913

Barnes, S. (2008). Understanding social media from the media ecological perspective. In E. Konjin, S. Utz, M. Tanis, & S. Barnes (Eds.), *Mediated interpersonal communication* (pp. 14–33). New York: Routledge.

Baron, N. S., & Segerstad, Y. A. F. (2010). Cross-cultural patterns in mobile-phone use: Public space and reachability in Sweden, the USA and Japan. *New Media & Society, 12*(1), 13–34. doi:10.1177/1461444809355111

Bar-Tal, D., Abutbul-Selinger, G., & Raviv, A. (2014). The culture of conflict and its routinization. In P. Nesbitt-Larking, C. Kinnvall, T. Capelos, & H. Dekker (Eds.), *The Palgrave handbook of global political psychology* (pp. 369–387). London: Palgrave Macmillan.

Barthel, M., Shearer, E., Gottfried, J., & Mitchell, A. (2015, July 14). *The Evolving Role of News on Twitter and Facebook.* Retrieved from http://www.journalism.org/2015/07/14/the-evolving-role-of-news-on-twitter-and-facebook/

Basaran Ince, G. (2014). Digital Culture, New Media and The Transformation of Collective Memory. *Iletisim, 21*, 9–29.

Basaran Ince, G. (2014). Digital Culture, New Media, and The Transformation of Collective Memory. *Iletisim, 21*, 9–29.

Bates, B. R., Romina, S., Ahmed, R., & Hopson, D. (2006). The effect of source credibility on consumers' perceptions of the quality of health information on the Internet. *Medical Informatics and the Internet in Medicine, 31*(1), 45–52. doi:10.1080/14639230600552601 PMID:16754366

Baumann, P. (2009). *140 healthcare uses for Twitter.* Retrieved from http://philbaumann.com/140-health-care-uses-for-twitter/

Bauman, Z. (2000). *Liquid modernity.* Cambridge, UK: Polity Press.

Baym, N. (2010). *Personal connections in the digital age.* Cambridge, UK: Polity.

Baym, N., & boyd, . (2012). Socially mediated publicness: An introduction. *Journal of Broadcasting & Electronic Media, 56*(3), 320–329. doi:10.1080/08838151.2012.705200

BBC News. (2016). *Volleyball in a hijab: Does this picture show a culture clash?* Retrieved from http://www.bbc.com/news/magazine-37009324

BBC News. (2017). *Quebec City mosque shooting: Six killed, eight wounded.* Retrieved from http://www.bbc.com/news/world-us-canada-38793071

BBC. (2016, November 9). *Reality Check: Who voted for Donald Trump?* Retrieved from http://www.bbc.com/news/election-us-2016-37922587

Becker, J., Brackbill, D., & Centola, D. (2017). Network dynamics of social influence in the wisdom of crowds. *Proceedings of the National Academy of Sciences of the United States of America, 114*(26), E5070–E5076. Retrieved from www.pnas.org/cgi/doi/10.1073/pnas.1615978114 PMID:28607070

Beebe, S. A., & Biggers, T. (1986). The status of the introductory intercultural communication course. *Communication Education, 35*(1), 56–60. doi:10.1080/03634528609388319

Belanger, S., & Pinard, M. (1991). Ethnic movements and the competition model: Some missing links. *American Sociological Review, 56*(4), 446–457. doi:10.2307/2096267

Belay, G. (1996). The (re)construction and negotiation of cultural identities in the age of globalization. In H. Mokros (Ed.), *Interaction and identity.* New Brunswick, NJ: Transaction.

Benítez, J. L. (2012). Salvadoran transnational families: ICT and communication practices in the network society. *Journal of Ethnic and Migration Studies*, *38*(9), 1439–1449. doi:10.1080/1369183X.2012.698214

Benkler, Y. (2006). *The wealth of networks: How social production transforms markets and freedom*. New Haven, CT: Yale University Press.

Bennett, I. (2017, Nov 12). Artist's 'sexual' robin redbreast Christmas cards banned by Facebook. *The Guardian*. Retrieved from: https://www.theguardian.com/technology/2017/nov/12/artists-sexual-robin-redbreast-christmas-cards-banned-by-facebook

Bennett, W. L. (2012). The Personalization of Politics: Political Identity, Social Media, and Changing Patterns of Participation. *The ANNALS of American Academy*, *644*(1), 20–38. doi:10.1177/0002716212451428

Bennett, W. L., & Segerberg, A. (2011). Digital media and the personalization of collective action: Social technology and the organization of protests against the global economic crisis. *Information Communication and Society*, *14*(6), 770–799. doi:10.1080/1369118X.2011.579141

Bernal, V. (2006). Diaspora, cyberspace and political imagination: The Eritrean diaspora online. *Global Networks*, *6*(2), 161–179. doi:10.1111/j.1471-0374.2006.00139.x

Bernardo, T. M., Rajic, A., Young, I., Robiadek, K., Pham, M. T., & Funk, J. A. (2013). Scoping review on search queries and social media for disease surveillance: A chronology of innovation. *Journal of Medical Internet Research*, *15*(7), e147. doi:10.2196/jmir.2740 PMID:23896182

Berry, J. W. (1980). Acculturation as varieties of adaptation. In A. M. Padilla (Ed.), *Acculturation: Theory, models, and some new findings* (pp. 9–25). Boulder, CO: Westview Press.

Bettencourt, B. A., Brewer, M. B., Croak, M. R., & Miller, N. (1992). Cooperation and the reduction of intergroup bias: The role of reward structure and social orientation. *Journal of Experimental Social Psychology*, *28*(4), 301–309. doi:10.1016/0022-1031(92)90048-O

Bhawuk, D. (2008). Globalization and indigenous cultures: Homogenization or differentiation? *International Journal of Intercultural Relations*, *32*(4), 305–312. doi:10.1016/j.ijintrel.2008.06.002

Bherer, L., Dufour, P., & Montambeault, F. (2016). The participatory democracy turn: An introduction. *Journal of Civil Society*, *1*(3), 225–230. doi:10.1080/17448689.2016.1216383

Bilge, N. (2017). Secondary Cultures and Their Impact as Intermediaries on Refugee Adaptation to Host Cultures: Connections of Community. *Journal of Intercultural Communication Research*, *46*(2), 130–146. doi:10.1080/17475759.2016.1275029

Binns, A. (2014). Twitter City and Facebook Village: Teenage girls' personas and experiences influenced by choice architecture in social networking sites. *Journal of Media Practice*, *15*(2), 71–91. doi:10.1080/14682753.2014.960763

Biocca, F., Harms, C., & Burgoon, J. (2003). Towards a more robust theory and measure of social presence: Review and suggested criteria. *Presence: Teleoperators and Virtual Environments, 12*(5), 456 – 480. doi: 10.1162/105474603322761270

Blaker, L. (2015). The Islamic State's use of online social media. *Military Cyber Affairs, 1*(1). doi:10.5038/2378-0789.1.1.1004

Blaya, C., & Fartoukh, M. (2016). Digital uses, victimization and online aggression: A comparative study between primary school and lower secondary school students in France. *European Journal on Criminal Policy and Research, 22*(2), 285–300. doi:10.1007/s10610-015-9293-7

Blumler, J. G., & Kavanagh, D. (1999). The Third Age of Political Communication: Influences and Features. *Political Communication, 16*(3), 209–230. doi:10.1080/105846099198596

Bobo, L. (2011). Somewhere between Jim Crow and Post-Racialism: Reflections on the Racial Divide in America Today. *Daedalus, 140*(2), 11–31. doi:10.1162/DAED_a_00091 PMID:21465840

Bolton, R., Parasuraman, A., Hoefnagels, A., Migchels, N., Kabadayi, S., Gruber, T., ... Solnet, D. (2013). Understanding Generation Y and their use of social media: A review and research agenda. *Journal of Service Management, 24*(3), 245–267. doi:10.1108/09564231311326987

Bomlitz, L. J., & Brezis, M. (2008). Misrepresentation of health risks by mass media. *Journal of Public Health, 30*(2), 202–204. doi:10.1093/pubmed/fdn009 PMID:18281322

Bonfadelli, H., Bucher, P., & Piga, A. (2007). Use of old and new media by ethnic minority youth in Europe with a special emphasis on Switzerland. *Communications, 32*(2), 141–170. doi:10.1515/COMMUN.2007.010

Booth, P. (2015). Fans' list-making: Memory, influence, and argument in the "event" of fandom. *MATRIZes, 9*(2), 85–107. doi:10.11606/issn.1982-8160.v9i2p85-107

Borstnar, M. (2012). Towards understanding collaborative learning in the social media environment. *Organizacija, 45*(3), 100–106. doi:10.2478/v10051-012-0010-8

Bou-Franch, P., & Blitvich, P. G.-C. (2014). Conflict management in massive polylogues: A case study from YouTube. *Journal of Pragmatics, 73*, 19–36. doi:10.1016/j.pragma.2014.05.001

Boulianne, S. (2015). Social media use and participation. A meta-analysis of current research. *Information Communication and Society, 18*(5), 524–538. doi:10.1080/1369118X.2015.1008542

Bouvier, G. (2012). How Facebook users select identity categories for self-presentation. *Journal of Multicultural Discourses, 7*(1), 37–57. doi:10.1080/17447143.2011.652781

Boyatzis, R. E. (1998). *Transforming qualitative information: Thematic analysis & code development*. Thousand Oaks, CA: Sage.

boyd, d. (2014). *It's complicated: The social lives of networked teens*. New Haven, CT: Yale University Press.

boyd, d., & Ellison, N. (2008). Social network sites: Definition, history and scholarship. *Journal of Computer-Mediated Communication, 13*(1), 210-230.

boyd, d., & Ellison, N. B. (2008). Social network sites: Definition, history, and scholarship. *Journal of Computer-Mediated Communication, 13*, 210-130. doi:10.1111/j.1083-6101.2007.00393.x

Brabham, D. C., Ribisl, K. M., Kirchner, T. R., & Bernhardt, J. M. (2014). Crowdsourcing applications for public health. *American Journal of Preventive Medicine, 46*(2), 179–187. doi:10.1016/j.amepre.2013.10.016 PMID:24439353

Brewer, M. B. (1991). The social self: On being the same and different at the same time. *Personality and Social Psychology Bulletin, 17*(5), 475–482. doi:10.1177/0146167291175001

Brewer, M. B., & Miller, N. (1984). Beyond the contact hypothesis: Theoretical perspectives on desegregation. In N. Miller & M. B. Brewer (Eds.), *Groups in contact: The psychology of desegregation* (pp. 281–302). Orlando, FL: Academic Press. doi:10.1016/B978-0-12-497780-8.50019-X

Brewer, M., & Gardner, W. (1996). Who is this 'we'? Levels of collective identity and self-representations. *Journal of Personality and Social Psychology, 71*(1), 83–93. doi:10.1037/0022-3514.71.1.83

Brinkerhoff, J. M. (2009). *Digital diasporas: Identity and transnational engagement*. Cambridge, UK: Cambridge University Press. doi:10.1017/CBO9780511805158

Brivio, E., Ibarra, F., & Galimberti, C. (2010). An integrated approach to interactions in cyberplaces: The presentation of self in blogs. In R. Taiwo (Ed.), *Handbook of research on discourse behavior and digital communication* (Vol. 2, pp. 810–829). New York: Information Science Reference. doi:10.4018/978-1-61520-773-2.ch052

Brock, A. (2012). From the blackhand side: Twitter as a cultural conversation. *Journal of Broadcasting & Electronic Media, 56*(4), 529–549. doi:10.1080/08838151.2012.732147

Brown, A., & Stepler, R. (2016). Statistical portrait of the foreign-born population in the United States. *Pew Research Center*. Retrieved from http://www.pewhispanic.org/2016/04/19/statistical-portrait-of-the-foreign-born-population-in-the-united-states-key-charts/

Brown, C. B. (2011). Barack Obama as the Great Man: Communicative constructions of racial transcendence in White-male elite discourses. *Communication Monographs, 78*(4), 535–556. doi:10.1080/03637751.2011.618140

Brown, J., Chapman, S., & Lupton, D. (1996). Infinitesimal risk as public health crisis: News media coverage of a doctor-patient HIV contact tracing investigation. *Social Science & Medicine, 43*(12), 1685–1695. doi:10.1016/0277-9536(95)00402-5 PMID:8961412

Brown, N. E. (2014). Political participation of women of color: An intersectional analysis. *Journal of Women, Politics & Policy, 35*(4), 315–348. doi:10.1080/1554477X.2014.955406

Brown, N. E., & Gershon, S. N. (2016). *Distinct identities: minority women in U.S. politics.* Routledge.

Brown, R., & Hewstone, M. (2005). An integrative theory of intergroup contact. In M. P. Zanna (Ed.), Advances in experimental social psychology (Vol. 37, pp. 255–342). San Diego, CA: Elsevier.

Bruggemann, M., & Wessler, H. (2014). Transnational communication as deliberation, ritual, and strategy. *Communication Theory, 24*(4), 394–414. doi:10.1111/comt.12046

Brundidge, J. (2010). Encountering 'difference' in the contemporary public sphere: The contribution of the Internet to the heterogeneity of political discussion networks. *Journal of Communication, 60*(4), 680–700. doi:10.1111/j.1460-2466.2010.01509.x

Bruns, A. (2005). *Gatewatching. Collaborative Online News Production.* New York: Peter Lang Publishing.

Bücher, T. (2012). Want to be on the top? Algorithmic power and the threat of invisibility on Facebook. *New Media & Society, 14*(7), 1164–1180. doi:10.1177/1461444812440159

Bullock, M., Okdie, B. M., & Harton, H. C. (2007). *Self-organization of attitudes as a function of issue relevance.* Poster presented at the meeting of the Society for Personality and Social Psychology, Memphis, TN.

Bungey, S. (2014, September 30). Some Facts About the Listicle. *The Morning News.* Retrieved from http://www.themorningnews.org/article/some-facts-about-the-listicle

Burt, R. S. (1992). *Structural Holes.* Cambridge, MA: Harvard University Press.

Byerly, C. M. (2017). Feminist Intersectionality Research in Communications: Origins, Contributions and Tensions. *Ex Aequo, 35,* 23–31.

Camber, R. (2010, February 15). Rape? It's the fault of the victims, say 50% of women. *Daily Mail.*

Campbell, D. E. (2004, April). *What you do depends on where you are: Community heterogeneity and participation.* Paper presented at the Annual Meeting of the Midwest Political Science Association, Chicago, IL.

D. E. Campbell, M. H. Levinson, & M. Frederick (Eds.). (2012). *Making civics count: Citizenship education for a new generation.* Cambridge, MA: Harvard Education Press.

Campbell, S. W. (2007). A cross-cultural comparison of perceptions and uses of mobile telephony. *New Media & Society, 9*(2), 343–363. doi:10.1177/1461444807075016

Candau, J. (1998). *Mémoire et Identité.* Paris: Presses Universtaires de France.

Carty, V. (2014). Arab spring in Tunisia and Egypt: The impact of new media on Contemporary social movements and challenges for social movement theory. *International Journal of Contemporary Sociology, 51*(1), 51–80.

Cassidy, W. P. (2007). Online news credibility: An examination of the perceptions of newspaper journalists. *Journal of Computer-Mediated Communication, 12*(2), 478–498. doi:10.1111/j.1083-6101.2007.00334.x

Castells, M. (2004). Informationalism, Networks and the Network Society: A Theoretical Blueprint. In The Network Society, A Cross-cultural Perspective. Edward Elgar Publishing. doi:10.4337/9781845421663.00010

Castells, M. (1996). *The network society* (Vol. 469). Oxford, UK: Blackwell.

Castells, M. (1996). *The rise of the networked society: The information age: Economy, society and culture*. Oxford, UK: Blackwell.

Castells, M. (2010). *The Rise of the Network Society*. Wiley Blackwell Publishing.

Castells, M. (2013). *Communication power* (2nd ed.). Oxford, UK: Oxford University Press.

CDC (@CDCgov). (2017, November 12). [Twitter post]. Retrieved from https://twitter.com/CDCgov

Center for American Women and Politics. (n.d.). Retrieved from http://www.cawp.rutgers.edu/sites/default/files/resources/genderdiff.pdf

Ch'Ng, E. (2015). The bottom-up formation and maintenance of a Twitter community: Analysis of the #FreeJahar Twitter community. *Industrial Management & Data Systems, 115*(4), 612–624. doi:10.1108/IMDS-11-2014-0332

Chadwick, A. (2013). *The Hybrid Media System: Politics and power*. Oxford, UK: Oxford University Press. doi:10.1093/acprof:oso/9780199759477.001.0001

Chalaby, J. K. (2005). From internationalization to transnationalization. *Global Media and Communication, 1*(1), 28–33. doi:10.1177/1742766505001000107

Chambers, C. W. (2006). Writing Patient Education Content for the Web. *AMWA Journal: American Medical Writers Association Journal, 21*(3), 108–109.

Chang, T., & Lim, J. (2002). Cross-cultural communication and social presence in asynchronous learning processes. *e-Service Journal, 1*(3), 83–105.

Chang, V. (2010, May). Obama and the power of social media and technology. *European Business Review*, 16–21.

Chapin, A. (2016, May 23). "I am not with her": Why women are wary of Hillary Clinton? *The Guardian*.

Chapman, M. (2014). Target Corp reveals full scale of payment card theft: 70 million customers' data stolen. *Associated Press, Financial Post*. Retrieved from http://business.financialpost.com/2014/01/10/target-corp-credit-card-breach/

Chapman, C., & Lahav, M. (2008). International ethnographic observations of social networking sites. *Proceedings of CHI 2008* (pp. 3123-3128). New York, NY: Association for Computing Machinery. doi:10.1145/1358628.1358818

Chaturvedi, R. (2016). *A closer look at the gender gap in presidential voting*. Pew Research Center.

Chemtrail. (2016). *Gestapo Sprays Gas Chamber Aerosols Over Miami Using ZIKA Hoax as Excuse*. Retrieved from: chemtrailsplanet.net/2016/08/06/gestapo-sprays-gas-chamber-aerosols-over-miami-using-zika-hoax-as-excuse/.

Chen, G. M. (2012). The impact of new media on intercultural communication in global context. *China Media Research, 8,* 1-10. Retrieved from http://www.chinamediaresearch.net/index.php/submission/10-china-media-research/back-issues/54-vol-8-no-2

Chen, G. M. (2012). The impact of new media on intercultural communication in global context. *China Media Research*, *8*(2), 1–10.

Chen, G. M., Chiu, M. M., & Wang, Z. (2012). Predicting social cues during online discussions: Effects of evaluations and knowledge content. *Computers in Human Behavior*, *28*(4), 1497–1509. doi:10.1016/j.chb.2012.03.017

Chen, G. M., & Dai, X.-d. (2014). New media and asymmetry in cultural identity negotiation. In P. H. Cheong, J. N. Martin, & L. Macfadyen (Eds.), *New media and intercultural communication: Identity, community and politics* (pp. 123–138). New York, NY: Peter Lang.

Chen, G.-M., & Dai, X. (2014). New media and asymmetry in cultural identity negotiations. In P. Cheong, J. Martin, & L. Macfayden (Eds.), *New media and intercultural communication* (pp. 123–138). New York, NY: Peter Lang.

Chen, G.-M., & Zhang, K. (2010). New media and cultural identity in the global society. In R. Taiwo (Ed.), *Handbook of research on discourse behavior and digital communication* (Vol. 2, pp. 801–815). New York, NY: Information Science Reference. doi:10.4018/978-1-61520-773-2.ch051

Cheng, Y., Liang, J., & Leung, L. (2015). Social network service use on mobile devices: An examination of gratification, civic attitudes and civic engagement in China. *New Media & Society*, *17*(7), 1096–1116. doi:10.1177/1461444814521362

Chen, H. T., Ping, S., & Chen, G. (2015). Far from reach but near at hand: The role of social media for cross-national mobilization. *Computers in Human Behavior*, *53*, 443–451. doi:10.1016/j.chb.2015.05.052

Chen, H., Chan, M., & Lee, F. L. (2016). Social media use and democratic engagement: A comparative study of Hong Kong, Taiwan, and China. *Chinese Journal of Communication*, *9*(4), 348–366. doi:10.1080/17544750.2016.1210182

Chen, L. (2011). Cultural identity as a production in process. *Journal of Asian Pacific Communication*, *21*(2), 213–237. doi:10.1075/japc.21.2.04che

Chen, X., Pan, Y., & Guo, B. (2016). The influence of personality traits and social networks on the self-disclosure behavior of social network site users. *Internet Research*, *26*(3), 566–586. doi:10.1108/IntR-05-2014-0145

Chen, Y.-N. (2010). Examining the presentation of self in popular blogs: A cultural perspective. *Chinese Journal of Communication*, *3*(1), 28–41. doi:10.1080/17544750903528773

Chen, Y.-W., & Collier, M. J. (2012). Intercultural identity positioning: Interview discourses from two identity-based nonprofit organizations. *Journal of International and Intercultural Communication*, *5*(1), 43–63. doi:10.1080/17513057.2011.631215

Cheong, P. H. Martin. J. N., & Macfadyen, L. (Eds.). (2012). New media and intercultural communication: Identity, community and politics. New York, NY: Peter Lang.

Chia, R. C., Poe, E., & Singh, P. (2008). An interactive virtual global cultural course: Building a real-time cost-effective global collaborative learning environment. *International Journal of Emerging Technologies in Learning*, *3*(1), 32–35. Retrieved from http://online-journals.org/i-jet/article/view/187/239

Chia, R. C., Poe, E., & Wuensche, K. L. (2009). Attitude change after taking a virtual global understanding course. *World Academy of Science, Engineering and Technology*, *31*, 722–726.

Chia, R. C., Poe, E., & Yang, B. (2011). History of Global Partners in Education. *Global Partners in Education Journal*, *1*(1), 3–7.

Cho, D., Kim, S., & Acquisti, A. (2012). Empirical analysis of online anonymity and user behaviors: the impact of real name policy. *45th Hawaii International Conference on System Sciences*, 3041-3050. doi:10.1109/hicss.2012.241

Choi, J. H., Watt, J. H., & Lynch, M. (2006). Perceptions of News Credibility about the War in Iraq: Why War Opponents Perceived the Internet as the Most Credible Medium. *Journal of Computer-Mediated Communication*, *12*(1), 209–229. doi:10.1111/j.1083-6101.2006.00322.x

Cho, J. (2015). Roles of Smartphone App Use in Improving Social Capital and Reducing Social Isolation. *Cyberpsychology, Behavior, and Social Networking*, *18*(6), 350–355. doi:10.1089/cyber.2014.0657 PMID:26075923

Cho, J., Shah, D. V., Nah, S., & Brossard, D. (2009). “Split Screens” and “Spin Rooms”: Debate Modality, Post-Debate Coverage, and the New Videomalaise. *Journal of Broadcasting & Electronic Media*, *53*(2), 242–261. doi:10.1080/08838150902907827

Chou, S.-W. (2010). Why do members contribute knowledge to online communities? *Online Information Review*, *34*(6), 829–854. doi:10.1108/14684521011099360

Chun, D. M. (2008). Computer Mediated Discourse in Instructed Environment. In S.S. Magnan (Ed.), Mediating Discourse Online (pp. 15-45). John Benjamins Publishing. doi:10.1075/aals.3.04chu

Chung, C. J., Kim, H., & Kim, J. H. (2010). An anatomy of the credibility of online newspapers. *Online Information Review*, *34*(5), 669–685. doi:10.1108/14684521011084564

Chung, C. J., Nam, Y., & Stefanone, M. A. (2012). Exploring Online News Credibility: The Relative Influence of Traditional and Technological Factors. *Journal of Computer-Mediated Communication*, *17*(2), 171–186. doi:10.1111/j.1083-6101.2011.01565.x

Church, A., Katigbak, M., Del Prado, A., Ortiz, F., Mastor, K., Harumi, Y., ... Cabrera, H. F. (2006). Implicit theories and self-perceptions of traitedness across cultures. *Journal of Cross-Cultural Psychology*, *37*(6), 694–716. doi:10.1177/0022022106292078

Clayton, R. (2014). The third wheel: The impact of Twitter use on relationship infidelity and divorce. *Cyberpsychology, Behavior, and Social Networking*, *17*(7), 425–430. doi:10.1089/cyber.2013.0570 PMID:24690067

Clifford, S. (2009). Video Prank at Domino's Taints Brand. *The New York Times*. Retrieved from http://www.nytimes.com/2009/04/16/business/media/16dominos.html?_r=0

Clothier, I. M. (2005). Created identities: Hybrid cultures and the internet. *Convergence (London)*, *11*(4), 44–59. doi:10.1177//1354856505061053

CNN. (2016, November 23). *Presidential Results*. Retrieved from http://www.cnn.com/election/results/president

Coffey, A. J., Kamhawi, R., Fishwick, P., & Henderson, J. (2013). New media environments' comparative effects upon intercultural sensitivity: A five-dimensional analysis. *International Journal of Intercultural Relations*, *37*(5), 605–627. doi:10.1016/j.ijintrel.2013.06.006

Cohen, B. (1963). *The Press and Foreign Policy*. Princeton, NJ: Princeton University Press.

Coleman, J. S. (1988). Social Capital in the Creation of Human Capital. *American Journal of Sociology*, *94*, S95–S120. doi:10.1086/228943

Colleoni, E., Rozza, A., & Arvidsson, A. (2014). Echo chamber or public sphere? Predicting political orientation and measuring political homophily in Twitter using big data. *Journal of Communication*, *64*(2), 317–332. doi:10.1111/jcom.12084

Collier, M. (2000). Reconstructing cultural diversity in global relationships: Negotiating in the borderlands. In G. M. Chen & W. Starosta (Eds.), *Communication and global society* (pp. 215–236). New York, NY: Peter Lang.

Collier, M. (2009). Contextual negotiation of cultural identifications and relationships: Interview discourse about Palestinian, Israeli, and Palestinian/Israeli young women in a U.S. peace-building program. *Journal of International and Intercultural Communication*, *2*(4), 344–368. doi:10.1080/17513050903177292

Collier, M. J., & Thomas, M. (1988). Cultural identity: An interpretive perspective. In Y. Y. Kim & W. B. Gudykunst (Eds.), *Theories in intercultural communication* (pp. 99–122). Newbury Park, CA: Sage.

Collins, P. H., & Bilge, S. (2017). *Intersectionality*. Malden, MA: Polity Press.

Conboy, M. (2006). *Tabloid Britain: Constructing a community through language*. London: Routledge.

Conradson, D., & McKay, D. (2007). Translocal subjectivities: Mobility, connection, emotion. *Mobilities*, *2*(2), 167–174. doi:10.1080/17450100701381524

Cook, K. (2001). *Trust in Society*. New York: Russell Sage Foundation.

Coretti, L., & Pica, D. (2015). The rise and fall of collective identity in networked movement: Communication protocols, Facebook, and the anti-Berlusconi protest. *Information Communication and Society*, *18*(8), 951–967. doi:10.1080/1369118X.2015.1043317

Cornelissen, J. (2014). *Corporate Communication: A Guide to Theory & Practice* (4th ed.). London: Sage Publications.

Couldry, N. (2003). *Media rituals: a critical approach*. London: Routledge.

N. Couldry, & J. Curran (Eds.). (2003). *Contesting media power: Alternative media in a networked world*. Oxford, UK: Rowman and Littlefield.

Cover, R. (2004). New Media Theory: Electronic games, Democracy and Reconfiguring the Author-Audience Relationship. *Social Semiotics*, *14*(2), 173–188. doi:10.1080/1035033042000238268

Creswell, J. W., & Clark, V. L. P. (2011). *Designing and conducting mixed methods research*. Thousand Oaks, CA: Sage Publications.

Critchfield, A. J. (2010). The Other. In R. L. Jackson II & M. A. Hogg (Eds.), *Encyclopedia of Identity*. Thousand Oaks, CA: Sage Publications.

Croucher, S. M. (2011). Social networking and cultural adaptation: A theoretical model. *Journal of International and Intercultural Communication*, *4*(4), 259–264. doi:10.1080/17513057.2011.598046

Croucher, S. M., Austin, M., Fang, L., & Holody, K. J. (2011). Interpersonal attraction and religious identification: A comparative analysis of Muslims and Hindus in India. *Asian Journal of Communication*, *2011*(6), 564–574. doi:10.1080/01292986.2011.609600

Croucher, S. M., & Rahmani, D. (2015). A longitudinal test of the effects of Facebook on cultural adaptation. *Journal of International and Intercultural Communication*, *8*(4), 330–345. doi:10.1080/17513057.2015.1087093

Croucher, S., & Cronn-Mills, D. (2011). *Religious misperceptions: The case of Muslims and Christians in France and Britain*. New York, NY: Hampton Press.

Cuéllar, I., Arnold, B., & Maldonado, R. (1995). Acculturation Rating Scale for Mexican Americans-II: A revision of the original ARSMA Scale. *Hispanic Journal of Behavioral Sciences*, *17*(3), 275–304. doi:10.1177/07399863950173001

Cunningham, S. (2001). Popular media as public "sphericules" for diasporic communities. *International Journal of Cultural Studies*, *4*(2), 131–147. doi:10.1177/136787790100400201 d'Haenens, L., Van Summeren, C., Kokhuis, M., & Beentjes, J. W. (2002). Ownership and use of old and new media among ethnic minority youth in the Netherlands: The role of the ethno-cultural position. *Communications*, *27*(3), 365–393. doi:10.1515/comm.27.3.365

Dahlgren, P. (2005). The internet, public spheres, and political communication: Dispersion and deliberation. *Political Communication*, *22*(2), 147–162. doi:10.1080/10584600590933160

Dahlgren, P. (2009). *Media and Political Engagement: Citizens, Communication, and Democracy*. Cambridge, UK: Cambridge Press.

Dake, K. (1992). Myths of nature: Culture and the social construction of risk. *The Journal of Social Issues*, *48*(4), 21–37. doi:10.1111/j.1540-4560.1992.tb01943.x

Dalisay, F. (2012). Media use and acculturation of new immigrants in the United States. *Communication Research Reports*, *29*(2), 148–160. doi:10.1080/08824096.2012.667774

Dalrymple, J. (2015a, April 2). Here's How California Will Enforce Its First-Ever Statewide Water Restrictions. *BuzzFeed News*. Retrieved from https://www.buzzfeed.com/jimdalrympleii/heres-how-california-will-enforce-its-first-ever-statewide-w?utm_term=.byn8eaoEOY#.mnJ3yMYR7b

Dalrymple, J. (2015b, April 16). How Severe Is California's Drought Really? *BuzzFeed News*. Retrieved from https://www.buzzfeed.com/jimdalrympleii/how-severe-is-californias-drought-really?utm_term=.knddvqPbAm#.olZOGBxXj2

Dalrymple, J. (2015c, May 7). Extreme Drought Prompts Starbucks To End California Water Bottling. *BuzzFeed News*. Retrieved from https://www.buzzfeed.com/jimdalrympleii/starbucks-ends-water-bottling-operations-in-california-citin?utm_term=.aud1dq5pnE#.ea072Vz3KY

Dalrymple, J. (2015d, August 3). Thousands of Water Wasters In California Hit With Fines. *BuzzFeed News*. Retrieved from https://www.buzzfeed.com/jimdalrympleii/california-cities-are-handing-out-thousands-of-fines-for-ove?utm_term=.jr9XKY6jRm#.lcpDq5l72a

Dalton-Hoffman, M. (2012). *The Effect of Social Media in the 2012 Presidential Election. In The First-Year Papers (2010 - present)*. Hartford, CT: Trinity College Digital Repository.

Dan, Y. (2003). *Gendai chugokujinno nihon ryugaku* [Modern Chinese study abroad in Japan]. Tokyo: Akashi Shoten.

DATUB. (2017). Retrieved from https://fr-fr.facebook.com/groups/datubburhanozkosar/about/

Davis, D. C. (2007). My Space Isn't Your Space: Expanding the Fair Credit Reporting Act to Ensure Accountability and Fairness in Employer Searches of Online Social Networking Services. *The Kansas Journal of Law & Public Policy*, *16*, 237–256.

de Block, L., & Buckingham, D. (2007). *Global children, global media: Migration, media and childhood*. New York: Palgrave Macmillan. doi:10.1057/9780230591646

De la Llama, V., Barreto, C., Trueba, I., Voges, C., & Park, D. (2012). At Face(book) value: Uses of Facebook in hiring processes and the role of identity in social networks. *International Journal of Work Innovation*, *1*(1), 114–136. doi:10.1504/IJWI.2012.047984

De Vos, G. A. (2006). Introduction: Ethnic pluralism: Conflict and accomodation. In L. Romanucci-Ross, G. A. De Vos, & T. Tsuda (Eds.), *Ethnic identity* (pp. 1–36). Oxford, UK: AltaMira.

De Vos, G. A., & Romanucci-Ross, L. (2006). Conclusion: Ethnic identity: A psychocultural perspective. In L. Romanucci-Ross, G. A. De Vos, & T. Tsuda (Eds.), *Ethnic identity* (pp. 375–401). Oxford, UK: AltaMira.

DeFleur, M. L., & Everett, E. D. (2002). *Understanding Mass Communication*. Houghton Mifflin Company.

DeFleur, M., & Dennis, E. (2010). *Understanding media in the digital age: connections for communication, society and culture*. New York, NY: Allyn and Bacon.

Del Prado, A., Church, A., Katigbak, M., Miramonies, L., Whitty, M., Curtis, G., & … . (2007). Culture, method and the content of self-concepts: Testing trait, Individual self-primacy, and cultural psychology perspectives. *Journal of Research in Personality*, *47*(6), 1119–1160. doi:10.1016/j.jrp.2007.02.002 PMID:19050737

Denning, S. (2014, August 29). Five Reasons Why Millennials Love Listicles. *Forbes*. Retrieved from http://www.forbes.com/sites/stevedenning/2014/08/29/five-reasons-why-millennials-love-listicles/#ea901f851aad

Dennis, A. R. (1996). Information exchange and use in group decision making: You can lead a group to information but you can't make it think. *Management Information Systems Quarterly*, *20*(4), 433–455. doi:10.2307/249563

Dennis, A. R., & Kinney, S. T. (1998). Testing media richness theory in the new media: The effects of cues, feedback, and task equivocality. *Information Systems Research*, *9*(3), 256–274. doi:10.1287/isre.9.3.256

Dervin, F. (2012). Cultural identity, representation and othering. In J. Jackson (Ed.), The Routledge handbook of language and intercultural communication (pp. 181-194). New York, NY: Routledge.

Desjardins, F. (2017). Chart: Here's how 5 tech giants make their billions. *Virtual Capitalist.* Retrieved from: http://www.visualcapitalist.com/chart-5-tech-giants-make- billions/

Devonish, D. (2013). Workplace bullying, employee performance and behaviors. *Employee Relations, 35*(6), 630-647.doi: 10.1108/ER-01-2013-0004

Dijk, J. V. (2007). *Mediated Memories in the Digital Age*. Stanford University Press.

Dijk, J. V. (2012). *The Network Society*. London: Sage Publications.

Dogan, U. (2016). Effects of social network use on happiness, psychological well- being, and life satisfaction of high school students: Case of Facebook and Twitter. *Egitim Ve Bilim-Education and Science*, *41*(183), 217–231. doi:10.15390/EB.2016.4616

Dönmez, O., Odabaşi, H., Yurdakul, I., Kuzu, A., & Girgin, U. (2017). Development of a scale to address perceptions of pre-service teachers regarding online risks for children. *Kuram Ve Uygulamada Egitim Bilimleri, 17*(3), 923-943. doi: 10.12738/estp.2017.3.0022

Dougherty, D. S. (2001). Women's discursive construction of a sexual harassment paradox. *Qualitative Research Reports*, *2*, 6–13.

Downey, A. (2017). Zika Virus Can 'SHRINK a Man's Testicles - Leaving Them Infertile'. *The Sun*. Retrieved from www.thesun.co.uk/living/2940013/zika-virus-can-shrink-a-mans-testicles-leaving-them-infertile/

Dredge, S. (2014, March 7). Eric Schmidt to dictators: 'You don't turn off the Internet: you infiltrate it'. *The Guardian*. Retrieved from http://www.theguardian.com/technology/2014/mar/07/google-eric-schmidt-jared-cohen

Dumova, T. (2016). Social network research methods: Approaches and key issues. In A. Kurylo & T. Dumova (Eds.), *Redefining communication in the era of social networking: Cultural, social, and political perspectives*. Madison, NJ: Fairleigh Dickinson University Press.

Dyer-Witheford, N. (1999). Cyber-Marx: Cycles and circuits of struggle in high-technology capitalism. Chicago: University of Illinois Press.

Edmunds, J., & Turner, B. S. (2002). *Generations, Culture, and Society*. Philadelphia: Open University Press.

Edwards, B., & Foley, M. W. (1998). Civil society and social capital beyond Putnam. *The American Behavioral Scientist*, *42*(1), 124–139. doi:10.1177/0002764298042001010

Eguchi, M. (2016). Using video-conferencing to change Japanese high school students' perceptions of China. *Journal of Policy Studies*, *32*, 1–15.

Ehala, M. (2010). Ethnolinguistic vitality and intergroup processes. *Multiligua*, *29*(2), 203–221. doi:10.1515/mult.2010.009

Elder, A. (2014). Excellent online friendships: An Aristotelian defense of social media. *Ethics and Information Technology*, *16*(4), 287–297. doi:10.1007/s10676-014-9354-5

Elgesem, D., Steskal, L., & Diakopoulos, N. (2015). Structure and content of the discourse on climate change in the blogosphere: The big picture. *Environmental Communication*, *9*(2), 169–188. doi:10.1080/17524032.2014.983536

Elias, N. (2013). Immigrant children and media. *The Routledge international handbook on children and media*, 336–343.

Ellis, D. G., & Maoz, I. (2007). Online argument between Israeli Jews and Palestinians. *Human Communication Research*, *33*(3), 291–309. doi:10.1111/j.1468-2958.2007.00300.x

Ems, L. (2014). Twitter's place in the tussle: How old power struggles play out on a new stage. *Media Culture & Society*, *36*(5), 720–731. doi:10.1177/0163443714529070

English, R., & Chen, S. (2007). Culture and self-concept stability: Consistency across and within contexts among Asian Americans and European Americans. *Journal of Personality and Social Psychology*, *93*(3), 478–490. doi:10.1037/0022-3514.93.3.478 PMID:17723061

Ephraim, P. (2013). African youths and the dangers of social networking: A culture- centered approach to using social media. *Ethics and Information Technology*, *15*(4), 275–284. doi:10.1007/s10676-013-9333-2

Espiritu, Y. L. (1993). *Asian American panethnicity: Bridging institutions and identities.* Philadelphia: Temple University Press.

Espiritu, Y. L. (1994). The intersection of race, ethnicity, and class: The multiple identities of second generation Filipinos. *Identities (Yverdon)*, *1*(2–3), 249–273. doi:10.1080/1070289X.1994.9962507

Ess, C., Kawabata, A., & Kurosaki, H. (2007). Cross-cultural perspective on religion and computer-mediated communication. *Journal of Computer-Mediated Communication*, *12*(3), 939–955. doi:10.1111/j.1083-6101.2007.00357.x

Estell, D., Farmer, T., & Cairns, B. (2007). Bullies and victims in rural African American youth: Behavioral characteristics and social network placement. *Aggressive Behavior*, *33*(2), 145–159. doi:10.1002/ab.20176 PMID:17441015

Eston, T. (2010, October 30). The social network threat. *Information Week*, *64*(1284), 66. Retrieved from http://www.darkreading.com/vulnerabilities-and-threats/social-networks-threat-to-security/d/d-id/1093707

Euwema, M. C., van de Vliert, E., & Bakker, A. B. (2003). Substantive and relational effectiveness of organizational conflict behavior. *International Journal of Conflict Management*, *14*(2), 119–139. doi:10.1108/eb022894

Farwell, J. P. (2014). The media strategy of ISIS. *Survival > Global Politics and Strategy, 56.* doi:10.1080/00396338.2014.985436

Fei, J., & Kuo, H. (2013). Community Media in China: Communication, Digitalization, and Relocation. *Journal of International Communication*, *19*(1), 2013.

Ferran, C., & Watts, S. (2008). Videoconferencing in the field: A heuristic processing model. *Management Science*, *54*(9), 1565–1578. doi:10.1287/mnsc.1080.0879

Ferrari, F. (2012). 'Through a woman's eyes' narratives of the nation: Gender as and beyond a category of analysis. *Journal of Multicultural Discourses*, *7*(3), 243–262. doi:10.1080/17447143.2012.720258

Finchilescu, G. (2010). Intergroup anxiety in interracial interaction: The role of prejudice and meta-stereotypes. *The Journal of Social Issues*, *6*(2), 334–351. doi:10.1111/j.1540-4560.2010.01648.x

Fiorina, M. P., Abrams, S. J., & Pope, J. C. (2010). *Culture War? The Myth of a Polarized America*. London: Longman.

Fischer, A. R., & Moradi, B. (2001). Racial and ethnic identity: Recent development and needed directions. In J. G. Ponterotto, J. M. Casas, L. Suzuki, & C. M. Alexander (Eds.), *Handbook of multicultural counseling* (2nd ed.; pp. 341–370). Thousand Oaks, CA: Sage Publications.

Fischhoff, B., Bruine de Bruin, W., & Guvenc, U. (2006). Analyzing disaster risks and plans: An avian flu example. *Journal of Risk and Uncertainty*, *33*(1-2), 133–151. doi:10.1007/s11166-006-0175-8

Fisher, A. (2009). Bullets with butterfly wings: Tweets, protest networks, and the Iranian election. In Y. R. Kamalipour (Ed.), *Media, power, and politics in the digital age* (pp. 105–118). Rowman & Littlefield.

Fisher, E. (2015). 'You media': Audiencing as marketing in social media. *Media Culture & Society*, *37*(1), 50–67. doi:10.1177/0163443714549088

Florida Dept. Health (@HealthyFla). (2017, November 2). [Twitter post]. Retrieved from https://twitter.com/HealthyFla

Fong, M. (2004). Identity and speech community. In M. Fong & R. Chuang (Eds.), *Communicating ethnic and cultural identity* (pp. 3–19). Lanham, MD: Rowman & Littlefield.

Fong, M., & Chuang, R. (2004). *Communicating ethnic and cultural identity*. Lanham, MD: Rowman & Littlefield.

Forbush, E., & Foucault-Welles, B. (2016). Social media use and adaptation among Chinese students beginning to study in the United States. *International Journal of Intercultural Relations*, *50*, 1–12. doi:10.1016/j.ijintrel.2015.10.007

Ford, C. M. (2011). Twitter, Facebook, and ten red balloons: Social network problem solving and Homeland Security. *Homeland Security Affairs*, *7*(1), Article 3. Retrieved from https://www.hsaj.org/articles/54

Foti, S., & Ring, G. (2000). Portfolios: Beyond Assessment. *Teaching and Learning: The Journal of Natural Inquiry*, *14*(2), 18–22.

Freiermuth, M. R., & Huang, H. (2012). Bringing Japan and Taiwan closer electronically: A look at an intercultural online synchronic chat task and its effect on motivation. *Language Teaching Research*, *16*(1), 61–88. doi:10.1177/1362168811423341

Fuchs, C. (2017). *Social media: a critical introduction*. Thousand Oaks, CA: Sage Publications.

Galanes, G. J., & Leeds-Hurwitz, W. (2009). *Socially constructing communication*. Cresskill, NJ: Hampton Press.

Gambetta, D. (1988). *Trust: Making and Breaking Co-Operative Relations*. Oxford, UK: Basil Blackwell.

Ganesh, S., & Holmes, P. (2011). Positioning intercultural dialogue – theories, pragmatics, and an agenda. *Journal of International and Intercultural Communication*, *4*(2), 81–86. doi:10.1080/17513057.2011.557482

Garcia, A. (2015, Sept. 27). Mark Zuckerberg: Internet access can eradicate extreme poverty. *CNN.com*. Retrieved from: http://money.cnn.com/2015/09/26/news/mark-zuckerberg-united-nations-poverty-internet/index.html

Gareis, E. (2012). Intercultural friendship: Effects of home and host region. *Journal of International and Intercultural Communication*, *5*(4), 309–328. doi:10.1080/17513057.2012.691525

Garfinkel, H. (1967). *Studies in Ethnomethodology*. Englewood Cliffs, NJ: Prentice-Hall.

Garner, J. T. (2017). An examination of organizational dissent events and communication channels: Perspectives of a dissenter, supervisors, and coworkers. *Communication Reports*, *30*(1), 26–38. doi:10.1080/08934215.2015.1128454

Gastil, J. (2008). *Political communication and deliberation*. Thousand Oaks, CA: Sage Publications. doi:10.4135/9781483329208

Gearhart, S., & Zhang, W. (2015). 'Was it something I said?' 'No, it was something you posted!' A study of the spiral of silence theory in social media contexts. *Cyberpsychology, Behavior, and Social Networking*, *18*(4), 208–213. doi:10.1089/cyber.2014.0443 PMID:25879378

Geiger, A., & Kent, L. (2017). *Number of women leaders around the world has grown, but they're still a small group*. Pew Research.

Gelman, A., Park, D., Shor, B., & Cortina, J. (2009). *Red state, blue state, rich State, poor state*. Princeton, NJ: Princeton University Press. doi:10.1515/9781400832118

Georgalou, M. (2010). "Pathfinding" discourses of self in social network sites. In R. Taiwo (Ed.), *Handbook of research on discourse behavior and digital communication* (Vol. 1, pp. 39–61). New York, NY: Information Science Reference. doi:10.4018/978-1-61520-773-2.ch003

Georgiou, M. (2001). Crossing the boundaries of the ethnic home: Media consumption and ethnic identity construction in the public space: The case of the Cypriot Community Centre in North London. *Gazette*, *63*(4), 311–329. doi:10.1177/0016549201063004003

Georgiou, M. (2006). *Diaspora, identity and the media: Diasporic transnationalism and mediated spatialities*. New York: Hampton Press.

Gergen, K. (1991). *The saturated self*. New York: Basic Books.

Gergen, K. (1991). *The saturated self: Dilemmas of identity in contemporary life*. New York, NY: Basic Books.

Gerodimos, R., & Ward, J. Rethinking online youth civic engagement. In B. Loader (Ed.), Young citizens in digital age: Political engagement, young people and new media (pp. 114-126). Routledge.

Gevorgyan, G., & Manucharova, N. (2009). Does culturally adapted online communication work? A study of American and Chinese Internet users' attitudes and preferences toward culturally customized web design elements. *Journal of Computer-Mediated Communication, 14*(2), 393–413. doi:10.1111/j.1083-6101.2009.01446.x

Giddens, A. (1984). *The constitution of society*. Berkeley, CA: University of California Press.

Giddens, A. (1984). *The constitution of society: Outline of the theory of structuration*. Cambridge, UK: Polity Press.

Giddens, A. (1987). *Social theory and modern sociology*. Cambridge, MA: Polity Press.

Giddens, A. (1990). *The consequences of modernity*. Cambridge, MA: Polity Press.

Giddens, A. (1991). *Modernity and self-identity: Self and society in the late modern age*. Redwood City, CA: Stanford University Press.

Giddens, A. (2000). Goffman as a systematic social theorist. In G. Fine & G. Smith (Eds.), *Erving Goffman* (Vol. 4, pp. 151–175). Thousand Oaks, CA: Sage.

Giddens, A. (2003). *The runaway world*. New York, NY: Routledge.

Gilboa, E. (2009). Media and conflict resolution: A framework for analysis. *Marquette Law Review, 93*, 87–110. Retrieved from http://scholarship.law.marquette.edu/cgi/viewcontent.cgi?article=4927&context=mulr

Giles, H. (1978). Linguistic differentiation in ethnic groups. In H. Tajfel (Ed.), *Differentiation between social groups: Studies in the social psychology of intergroup relations* (pp. 361–394). London: Academic Press.

Giles, H., & Giles, J. (2016). *Communication theories of group membership and the research process. In Negotiating group identity in the research process: Are you in or are you out?* New York: Lexington Books.

Giles, H., & Giles, J. (2016). Ingroups and outgroups. In A. Kurylo (Ed.), *Inter/cultural communication representation and construction of culture* (pp. 141–162). Thousand Oaks, CA: SAGE.

Gillespie, M. (2000). Transnational communications and diaspora communities. *Ethnic minorities and the media*, 164–178.

Gilliland, M. K. (2006). Ethnic nationality in the former Yugoslavia: Ethnogenesis, ethnic cleansing, and present-day identities among Croats, Serbs, and Bosniacs. In L. Romanucci-Ross, G. A. De Vos, & T. Tsuda (Eds.), *Ethnic identity* (pp. 88–118). Oxford, UK: AltaMira.

Gladwell, M. (2010, October 4). Small change. *The New Yorker,* 42-49.

Glaser, B. G., & Strauss, A. L. (1967). *The discovery of grounded theory: Strategies for qualitative research*. New York: Aldine Atherton.

Global Partners in Education (GPE). (2014). *The purpose of GPE*. Retrieved from http://thegpe.org/about-gpe/purpose/

Goffman, E. (1974). *Frame analysis*. New York, NY: Basic Books.

Goffman, E. (1978). *The presentation of self in everyday life* (p. 56). Harmondsworth, UK: Penguin Books.

Goffman, E. (1983). The interaction order. *American Sociological Review*, *48*(1), 1–17. doi:10.2307/2095141

Goggins, S., Laffey, J., & Gallagher, M. (2011). Completely online group formation and development: Small groups as socio-technical systems. *Information Technology & People*, *24*(2), 104–133. doi:10.1108/09593841111137322

Gohdes, A. R. (2015). Pulling the plug: Network disruptions and violence in civil conflict. *Journal of Peace Research*, *52*(3), 352–367. doi:10.1177/0022343314551398

Goldzwig, S. R. (2013). The U.S. Catholic Bishops, "Religious Freedom," and the 2012 Presidential election campaign: A reflection. *Rhetoric & Public Affairs*, *16*(2), 369–384. doi:10.14321/rhetpublaffa.16.2.0369

Goodstein, A. (2007). *Totally Wired*. New York: St. Martin's Press.

Gordon, E., & Baldwin-Philippi, J. (2013). Making a habit out of engagement: How the culture of open data is reframing civic life. In B. Goldstein & L. Dyson (Eds.), *Beyond transparency: Open data and the future of civic innovation* (pp. 139–148). San Francisco, CA: Code for America Press.

Gottfried, J., & Shearer, E. (2016, May 26). News Use Across Social Media Platforms 2016. *Pew Research Center*. Retrieved from http://www.journalism.org/2016/05/26/news-use-across-social-media-platforms-2016/?utm_content=bufferae870&utm_medium=social&utm_source=twitter.com&utm_campaign=buffer

Graber, D. A., & Dunaway, J. (2015). *New media and American politics*. Thousand Oaks, CA: Sage.

Graber, D. A., & Smith, J. M. (2005). Political communication faces the 21st century. *Journal of Communication*, *55*(3), 479–507. doi:10.1111/j.1460-2466.2005.tb02682.x

Grajales, F. III, Sheps, S., Ho, K., Novak-Lauscher, H., & Eysenbach, G. (2014). Social media: A review and tutorial of applications in medicine and health care. *Journal of Medical Internet Research*, *16*(2), e13. doi:10.2196/jmir.2912 PMID:24518354

Grasmuck, S., Martin, J., & Shanyand, Z. (2009). Ethno-racial identity displays on Facebook. *Journal of Computer-Mediated Communication*, *15*(1), 158–188. doi:10.1111/j.1083-6101.2009.01498.x

Graves, T. D. (1967). Acculturation, access, and alcohol in a tri-ethnic community. *American Anthropologist*, *69*(3–4), 306–321. doi:10.1525/aa.1967.69.3-4.02a00030

Gray, C. H., & Gordo, A. J. (2014). Social media in conflict: Comparing military and social-movement technocultures. *Cultural Politics*, *10*(3), 251–261. doi:10.1215/17432197-2795645

Greenwood, S. (2017). Trust in the News Media. *Pew Research Center's Journalism Project*. Retrieved from www.journalism.org/2017/05/10/americans-attitudes-about-the-news-media-deeply-divided-along-partisan-lines/pj_2017-05-10_media-attitudes_a-05/

Gruzd, A., & Roy, J. (2014). Investigating political polarization on Twitter: A Canadian perspective. *Policy and Internet*, *6*(1), 28–45. doi:10.1002/1944-2866.POI354

Gudykunst, W. B., & Hammer, M. R. (1983). Basic Training Design: Approaches to intercultural training. In D. Landis & R. S. Bhagat (Eds.), *Handbook of intercultural training* (pp. 118–147). Elmsford: Pergamon Press. doi:10.1016/B978-0-08-027533-8.50011-7

Gudykunst, W., & Kim, Y. Y. (2003). *Communicating with strangers*. New York, NY: McGraw-Hill.

Gumpert, G., & Cathcart, R. (1985). Media Grammars, Generations, and Media Gaps. *Critical Studies in Mass Communication*, *2*(1), 23–35. doi:10.1080/15295038509360059

Gunawardena, C. N. (1995). Social presence theory and implications for interaction collaborative learning in computer conferences. *International Journal of Educational Telecommunications*, *1*(2/3), 147–166.

Gunduz, U., & Erdem, B. K. (2017). The concept of virtual nationalism in the digital age: Social media perspectives of Turkey. *Communication Today*, *8*, 18–28.

Gunn, S.E. & Thumim, N. (2012). Socializing and self-representation online: Exploring Facebook. *Observatorio Journal*, *6*(1), 87-105. doi: 1646-5954/ERC123483/2012 087

Gunter, B. (2006). Who do online news consumers trust? *Library and Information Update*, *5*(9), 40–41.

Gunter, B., Campbell, V., Touri, M., & Gibson, R. (2009). Blogs, news and credibility. *Aslib Proceedings*, *61*(2), 185–204. doi:10.1108/00012530910946929

Guo, C. & Yu, J. (2009). Socializing online in various cultural contexts: A cross nation study of social network service development. *AMCIS 2009 Proceedings*, paper 514.

Gurman, T. A., Rubin, S. E., & Roess, A. A. (2012). Effectiveness of mHealth behavior change communication interventions in developing countries: A systematic review of the literature. *Journal of Health Communication*, *17*(1), 82–104. doi:10.1080/10810730.2011.649160 PMID:22548603

Habermas, J. (1991). *The structural transformation of public sphere*. Cambridge, MA: MIT Press.

Hainla, L. (2017). *21 Social Media Marketing Statistics You Need to Know in 2017*. Retrieved from https://www.dreamgrow.com/21-social-media-marketing-statistics/

Ha, L., Xu, Y., Yang, C., Wang, F., Yang, L., Abuljadail, M., ... Gabay, I. (2016). Decline in news content engagement or news medium engagement? A longitudinal analysis of news engagement since the rise of social and mobile media 2009–2012. *Journalism*, 1–22.

Hall, E. (1973). *The silent language*. Garden City, NY: Doubleday.

Hall, E. (1990). *Understanding cultural differences: Germans, French, and Americans*. Yarmouth, ME: Intercultural Press.

Hall, E. T. (1989). *Beyond culture*. New York: Anchor Books.

Hall, S. (1989). Cultural identity and diaspora. In J. Rutherford (Ed.), *Community, culture, difference* (pp. 222–237). London: Lawrence & Wishart.

Hall, S. (1990). Cultural identity and diaspora. In J. Rutherford (Ed.), *Identity: Community, Culture, Difference* (pp. 222–237). London: Lawrence & Wishart.

Hansen, D. L. (2011). Exploring social media relationships. *On the Horizon*, *19*(1), 43–51. doi:10.1108/10748121111107726

Harb, C., & Smith, P. (2008). Self-construals across cultures: Beyond independence and interdependence. *Journal of Cross-Cultural Psychology*, *39*(2), 178–197. doi:10.1177/0022022107313861

Harder, R. A., Sevenans, J., & Van Aelst, P. (2017). Intermedia Agenda Setting in the Social Media Age: How Traditional Players Dominate the News Agenda in Election Times. *The International Journal of Press/Politics*.

Harell, A. (2017). Intersectionality and gendered political behaviour in a multicultural Canada. *Canadian Journal of Political Science*, *50*(2), 495–514. doi:10.1017/S000842391700021X

Hargiatti, E. (2008). Whose space? Differences among users and non-users of social network sites. *Journal of Computer-Mediated Communication*, *13*(1), 276–297. doi:10.1111/j.1083-6101.2007.00396.x

Hargiatti, E., & Hsieh, Y. (2013). Digital inequality. In W. H. Dutton (Ed.), *Oxford handbook for internet research* (pp. 129–150). Oxford, UK: Oxford University Press.

Harjani, A., & Min, W. (2014). *Alibaba to smash Single's Day sales record*. Retrieved from https://ca.finance.yahoo.com/news/alibaba-smash-singles-day-sales-record-223605524.html

Harris, T. M. (2013). Co-cultural group membership. In A. Kurylo (Ed.), *Inter/cultural communication representation and construction of culture* (pp. 185–210). Thousand Oaks, CA: SAGE.

Hartman, M. (2011). *Johnson & Johnson Gently Poisons Babies With Its Shampoo*. Retrieved from http://jezebel.com/5855115/johnson--johnson-gently-poisoning-babies-with-its-shampoo

Harton, H. C., & Bullock, M. (2007). Dynamic Social Impact: A Theory of the Origins and Evolution of Culture. *Social and Personality Psychology Compass*, *1*(1), 521–540. doi:10.1111/j.1751-9004.2007.00022.x

Harwood, J. (2010). The Contact Space: A novel framework for intergroup contact. *Journal of Language and Social Psychology*, *29*(2), 147–177. doi:10.1177/0261927X09359520

Harwood, J., Giles, H., & Bourhis, R. Y. (1994). The genesis of vitality theory: Historical patterns and discoursal dimensions. *International Journal of the Sociology of Language*, *108*(1), 167–206. doi:10.1515/ijsl.1994.108.167

Haslett, B. (1987). *Communication: Strategic action in context*. Hillsdale, NJ: Lawrence Erlbaum Associates.

Haslett, B. (2012). *Communicating and organizing in context: The theory of structurational interaction*. New York, NY: Taylor & Francis.

Haslett, B. (2014a). Social media, communication and culture. In C. Litang & M. Prosser (Eds.), *Social media in Asia*. Lake Oswego, OR: Dignity Press.

Haslett, B. (2014b). A structurational interaction approach to investigating culture, identity, and mediated communication. In P. Cheong, J. Martin, & L. Macfayden (Eds.), *New media and intercultural communication: Identity, community and politics* (pp. 39–60). New York, NY: Peter Lang.

Haslett, B. (forthcoming). Multilayered interactions: Culture, communication and the new media. In A. Atay & M. D'Silva (Eds.), *Mediated intercultural communication in a digital age*. New York, NY: Peter Lang.

Haslett, B. (forthcoming). Who am I? Culture, identity and new media. In N. Bilge & M. Marino (Eds.), *Reconceptualizing media and culture*.

Hasnat, M. O. (2014). Credibility of Social Online Media: In the Eyes of Finnish Professional Journalists. *Communicacao e Sociedade*, *25*(0), 220–235. doi:10.17231/comsoc.25(2014).1870

Hatchen, W. A., & Scotten. (2016). *The world news prism: digital, social and interactive*. Malden, MA: Wiley Blackwell.

Haynes, C. (2011). Overcoming the study abroad hype. *Journal of the National Collegiate Honors Council*, *12*(1), 17–24. Retrieved from http://digitalcommons.unl.edu/nchcjournal/305

Haynes, D., & Robinson, L. (2015). Defining user risk in social networking services. *Aslib Journal of Information Management*, *67*(1), 94–115. doi:10.1108/AJIM-07-2014-0087

Heath, C., & Heath, D. (2007). *Made to Stick: Why Some Ideas Survive and Others Die*. Random House.

Hecht, M. L., Collier, M. J., & Ribeau, S. A. (2003). *African American Communication: Exploring Identity and Culture*. Mahwah, NJ: Lawrence Erlbaum Associates.

Hecht, M., Collier, M. J., & Ribeau, S. (1993). *African American communication: Ethnic identity and cultural interpretation*. Newbury, CA: Sage.

Hecht, M., Warren, J., Jung, E., & Krieger, J. (2005). A communication theory of identity: development, theoretical perspective, and future directions. In W. Gudykunst (Ed.), *Theorizing about Intercultural Communication* (pp. 257–278). Thousand Oaks, CA: Sage.

Heirman, W., Angelopoulos, S., Wegge, D., Vandebosch, H., Eggermont, S., & Walrave, M. (2015). Cyberbullying-entrenched or cyberbully-free classrooms? A class network and class composition approach. *Journal of Computer-Mediated Communication*, *20*(3), 260–277. doi:10.1111/jcc4.12111

Hendrickson, B., & Rosen, D. (2017). Insights into new media use by international students: Implications for cross-cultural adaptation theory. *Social Networking*, *6*(02), 81–106. doi:10.4236/sn.2017.62006

Hepp, A. (2009). Localities of diasporic communicative spaces: Material aspects of translocal mediated networking. *Communication Review*, *12*(4), 327–348. doi:10.1080/10714420903344451

Hepp, A., Hjarvard, S., & Lundby, K. (2015). Mediatization: Theorizing the interplay between media, culture and society. *Media Culture & Society*, *37*(2), 314–324. doi:10.1177/0163443715573835

Hermon, P. S., Lay, J. C., & Stoke, A. K. (2003). Women running “as women”: Candidate gender campaign issues, and voter-targeting strategies. *The Journal of Politics*, *65*(1), 244–255. doi:10.1111/1468-2508.t01-1-00013

Hernandez, J. C. (2016, February 5). Tianjin explosions were result of mismanagement, China finds. *New York Times*. Retrieved from https://www.nytimes.com/2016/02/06/world/asia/tianjin-explosions-were-result-of-mismanagement-china-finds.html

Herrera, C. (2016). Miami Beach Tourism Takes a Hit from Zika: Demand Drops, Cancellations Rise. *Miami Herald*. Retrieved from www.miamiherald.com/news/health-care/article103553277.html

Herskovits, M. J. (1948). *Man and his works: The science of cultural anthropology*. New York: Knopf.

Hewstone, M., & Brown, R. J. (1986). Contact is not enough: An intergroup perspective on the contact hypothesis. In M. Hewstone & R. J. Brown (Eds.), *Contact and conflict in intergroup encounters* (pp. 1–44). Oxford, UK: Basil Blackwell.

Heymann, D. L., & Rodier, G. R. (2001). Hot spots in a wired world: WHO surveillance of emerging and re-emerging infectious diseases. *The Lancet Infectious Diseases*, *1*(5), 345–353. doi:10.1016/S1473-3099(01)00148-7 PMID:11871807

Heyman, R., De Wolf, R., & Pierson, J. (2014). Evaluating social media privacy settings for personal and advertising purposes. *Info*, *16*(4), 18–32. doi:10.1108/info-01-2014-0004

Hiller, H. H., & Franz, T. M. (2004). New ties, old ties and lost ties: The use of the internet in diaspora. *New Media & Society*, *6*(6), 731–752. doi:10.1177/146144804044327

Himelboim, I., McCreery, S., & Smith, M. (2013). Birds of a feather tweet together: Integrating network and content analyses to examine cross-ideology exposure on Twitter. *Journal of Computer-Mediated Communication*, *18*(2), 40–60. doi:10.1111/jcc4.12001

Hocker, J. L., & Wilmot, W. W. (1978). *Interpersonal conflict*. Dubuque, IA: W. C. Brown.

Hoeffel, E. M., Rastogi, S., Kim, M. O., & Hasan, S. (2012). *The Asian Population: 2010*. US Department of Commerce, Economics and Statistics Administration, US Census Bureau. Retrieved from: http://www.census.gov/prod/cen2010/briefs/c2010br-11.pdf

Hoehle, H., Zhang, X., & Venkatesh, V. (2015). An espoused cultural perspective to understand continued intention to use mobile applications: A four-country study of mobile social media application usability. *European Journal of Information Systems*, *24*(3), 337–359. doi:10.1057/ejis.2014.43

Hofstede, G. (2001). *Culture's consequences: Comparing values, behaviors, institutions and organizations across nations (2nd ed.)*. Thousand Oaks, CA: Sage.

Hofstede, G. (2003). *Culture's consequences: Comparing values, behaviors, institutions and organizations across nations*. Thousand Oaks, CA: Sage Publications.

Hofstede, G., & Hofstede, G. F. (2005). *Cultures and organizations: Software of the mind*. New York, NY: McGraw Hill.

Hogg, M. A., Abrams, D., Otten, S., & Hinkle, S. (2004). The Social Identity Perspective: Intergroup Relations, Self-Conception, and Small Groups. *Sage, 35*(3), 246-276.

Holic, N. (2014, January 23). An Open Letter to List Articles. *Huffington Post*. Retrieved from http://www.huffingtonpost.com/the-university-of-central-florida-forum/an-open-letter-to-list-articles_b_4268725.html

Hommerich, C. (2014). Feeling disconnected: Exploring the relationship between different form of social capital and civic engagement in Japan. *Voluntas*, *26*(1), 45–68. doi:10.1007/s11266-014-9525-3

Hopper, J. (2015). Obamacare, the news media, and the politics of 21st- century presidential communication. *International Journal of Communication*, *9*, 1275–1299.

Horton, P. B., & Hunt, C. L. (1984). *Sociology* (6th ed.). New York: McGraw Hill.

Hoter, E., Shonfeld, M., & Ganayem, A. (2009). ICT in the service of multiculturalism. *International Review of Research in Open and Distance Learning*, *10*(2). Retrieved from http://www.irrodl.org/index.php/irrodl/article/view/601/1207

Howard, H. (2016, March 2). Donald Trump's supporters assaulted a Black girl at a campaign rally. *Teen Vogue*. Retrieved March 12, 2016, from http://www.teenvogue.com/story/black-girl-assaulted-donald-trump-rally

Howard, P. N., Duffy, A., Freelon, D., Hussain, M., Mari, W., & Mazaid, M. (2011). *Opening closed regimes: What was the role of social media during the Arab Spring?* Retrieved from http://pitpi.org/index.php/2011/09/11/opening-closed-regimes-what-was-the-role-of-social-media-during-the-arab-spring/

Hübner Barcelos, R., & Alberto Vargas Rossi, C. (2014). Paradoxes and strategies of social media consumption among adolescents. *Young Consumers*, *15*(4), 275–295. doi:10.1108/YC-10-2013-00408

Huffaker, D., & Calvert, S. (2005). Gender, identity, and language use in teenage blogs. *Journal of Computer-Mediated Communication*, *10*(2), 1.

Hui, P., & Buchegger, S. (2009). Groupthink and peer pressure: Social influence in online social network groups. In *Proceedings 2009 International Conference on Advances in Social Network Analysis and Mining* (pp. 53 – 59). IEEE. doi:10.1109/ASONAM.2009.17

Hu, Y. (2012). The Internet and social mobilization in China. In F. F. Lee, L. Leung, J. L. Qiu, & D. C. Chu (Eds.), *Frontiers in new media research* (pp. 93–112). New York, NY: Routledge.

Hwang, K. (2005). A Chinese perspective on face. In K. Yang, K. Hwang, & Z. Yang (Eds.), *Indigenous psychological research in Chinese societies* (pp. 365–405). Taipei, Taiwan: Yuan-Liou Publishing Company.

Hwang, W. C., & Ting, J. Y. (2008). Disaggregating the effects of acculturation and acculturative stress on the mental health of Asian Americans. *Cultural Diversity & Ethnic Minority Psychology*, *14*(2), 147–154. doi:10.1037/1099-9809.14.2.147 PMID:18426287

Imahori, T., & Cupach, W. (2005). Identity management theory: Facework in intercultural relationships. In W. Gudykunst (Ed.), *Theorizing about intercultural communication* (pp. 195–210). Thousand Oaks, CA: Sage.

Information Observatory. (2016). Billionaires who owe their wealth to information. *Information Observatory*. Retrieved from: http://informationobservatory.info/2016/05/01/billionaires-who-owe-their-wealth-to-information/

Ingraham, C., & Reeves, J. (2016). New media, new panics. *Critical Studies in Media Communication*, *33*(5), 455–467. doi:10.1080/15295036.2016.1227863

Institute of International Education. (2016). *Open Doors Data - Fast Fact 2016*. Retrieved from http://www.iie.org/Research-and-Publications/Open-Doors/Data/Fast-Facts#.WHPHULnMJs8

Internet Live Stats. (2016). *Internet Users by Country (2016)*. Retrieved from http://www.internetlivestats.com/internet-users-by-country/

Internet Live Stats. (2017). *Twitter Usage Statistics*. Retrieved August 24, 2017, from http://www.internetlivestats.com/twitter-statistics/

Internet World Statistics. (2017). Retrieved from http://www.internetworldstats.com/links10.html

Internet World Stats. (2017). *Asia stats*. Retrieved from http://www.internetworldstats.com/stats.htm

Israilidis, J., Siachou, E., Cooke, L., & Lock, R. (2015). Individual variables with an impact on knowledge sharing: The critical role of employees' ignorance. *Journal of Knowledge Management*, *19*(6), 1109–1123. doi:10.1108/JKM-04-2015-0153

Itakura, H. (2004). Changing cultural stereotypes through e-mail assisted foreign language learning. *System*, *32*(1), 37–51. doi:10.1016/j.system.2003.04.003

Ito, M. (2008). *Living and Learning with New Media*. Cambridge, MA: MIT Press.

Iwabuchi, K. (2010). Taking "Japanization" seriously: Cultural globalization reconsidered. In D. Thussu (Ed.), *International Communication: A reader* (pp. 410–433). New York, NY: Routledge.

Jahng, M., & Littau, J. (2016). Interacting is believing: Interactivity, social cue, and perceptions of journalistic credibility on Twitter. *Journalism & Mass Communication Quarterly*, *93*(1), 38–58. doi:10.1177/1077699015606680

Jaldemark, J. (2008). Participation and genres of communication in online settings of higher education. *Education and Information Technologies*, *13*(2), 129–146. doi:10.1007/s10639-008-9057-9

Janis, I. L. (1972). *Victims of groupthink*. New York: Houghton Mifflin.

Janis, I. L. (1982). *Groupthink: Psychological studies of policy decisions and fiascoes* (2nd ed.). New York: Houghton Mifflin.

JanMohamed, A.R., & Lloyd, D. (1990). The nature and context of minority discourse. Oxford University Press.

Jenkins, H. (2006). *Convergence Culture: Where Old and new media Collide*. New York: New York University Press.

Jenkins, H. (2014). Rethinking 'Rethinking Convergence/Culture'. *Journal of Cultural Studies*, *28*(2), 267–297. doi:10.1080/09502386.2013.801579

Jeong, T., & Coyle, E. (2014). What are you worrying about on Facebook and Twitter? An empirical investigation of young social network site users' privacy perceptions and behaviors. *Journal of Interactive Advertising*, *14*(2), 51–59. doi:10.1080/15252019.2014.930678

Jetten, J., Postmes, T., & McAuliffe, B. (2002). 'We're all individuals': Group norms individualism and collectivism, levels of identification and identity threat. *European Journal of Social Psychology*, *32*(2), 189–208. doi:10.1002/ejsp.65

Johnson, R. (2009). Potential Farm Sector Effects of 2009 H1N1 "Swine Flu": Questions and Answers. *Congressional Research Service*. Retrieved from http://assets.opencrs.com/rpts/R40575_20100112.pdf

Johnson, T. J., & Kaye, B. K. (2015). Reasons to believe: Influence of credibility on motivations for using social networks. *Computers in Human Behavior*, *50*, 544–555. doi:10.1016/j.chb.2015.04.002

Johnson, T., & Kaye, B. (2010). Choosing is believing? How web gratifications and reliance affect Internet credibility among politically interested users. *Atlantic Journal of Communication*, *18*(1), 1–21. doi:10.1080/15456870903340431

Johnston, C. D., Hillygus, D. S., & Bartels, B. L. (2014). Ideology, the Affordable Care Act ruling, and Supreme Court legitimacy. *Public Opinion Quarterly*, *78*(4), 963–973. doi:10.1093/poq/nfu036

Jones, S., & Fox, S. (2009). *Generations online in 2009*. Retrieved from http://www.pewinternet.org/Reports/2009/Generations-Online-in-2009.aspx

Jones, S. (1998). *Cybersociety 2.0 revisiting computer-mediated communication and community*. Sage.

Ju, H., & Lee, S. (2015). The Korean Wave and Asian Americans: The ethnic meanings of transnational Korean pop culture in the USA. *Journal of Media & Cultural Studies*, *29*(3), 323–338. doi:10.1080/10304312.2014.986059

Kabakçı, I., Odabaşı, H. F., & Çoklar, A. N. (2008). Parents' views about Internet use of their children. *International Journal of Education and Information Technologies*, *4*(2), 248–255. http://www.naun.org/main/NAUN/educationinformation/eit-75.pdf

Kagitcibasi, C. (2005). Autonomy and relatedness in cultural context: Implications for self and family. *Journal of Cross-Cultural Psychology*, *36*(4), 403–422. doi:10.1177/0022022105275959

Kahn, C. (2016, November 28). Trump won with lowest minority vote in decades, fueling divisions. *Hoffton Post*.

Kalsbeek, W. D. (2003). Sampling minority groups in health surveys. *Statistics in Medicine*, *22*(9), 1527–1549. doi:10.1002/sim.1510 PMID:12704614

Kampf, R., & Cuhadar, E. (2015). Do computer games enhance learning about conflicts? A cross-national inquiry into proximate and distant scenarios in global conflicts. *Computers in Human Behavior*, *52*, 541–549. doi:10.1016/j.chb.2014.08.008

Kaplan, A. & Haenlein, M. (2010). Users of the world, unite! The challenges and opportunities of social media. *Business Horizons, 53*(1), 61.

Karim, K. H. (2003). *The media of diaspora* (Vol. 7). New York: Routledge.

Karlsen, R., Steen-Johnsen, K., Wollebæk, D., & Enjolras, B. (2017). Echo chamber and trench warfare dynamics in online debates. *European Journal of Communication*, *32*(3), 257–273. doi:10.1177/0267323117695734 PMID:28690351

Karstens-Smith, G., & Rushowy, K. (2013). *'Blackface' controversy at Mayfield Secondary School in Caledon not the first*. Retrieved from http://www.thestar.com/news/gta/2013/11/12/blackface_controversy_at_mayfield_secondary_school_in_caledon_not_the_first.html

Kasperson, R. E., Renn, O., Slovic, P., Brown, H. S., Emel, J., Goble, R., ... Ratick, S. (1988). The social amplification of risk: A conceptual framework. *Risk Analysis*, *8*(2), 177–187. doi:10.1111/j.1539-6924.1988.tb01168.x

Katopol, P. (2015). Groupthink: Group dynamics and the decision-making process. *Library Leadership & Management (Online), 30*(1), 1-6. Retrieved from https://journals.tdl.org/llm/index.php/llm/article/view/7172/6350

Katz, E., Haas, H., & Gurevitch, M. (1973). On the use of the mass media for important things. *American Sociological Review, 38*(2), 164–181. doi:10.2307/2094393

Katz, V. S. (2010). How children of immigrants use media to connect their families to the community: The case of Latinos in South Los Angeles. *Journal of Children and Media, 4*(3), 298–315. doi:10.1080/17482798.2010.486136

Kavanaugh, A. L., Sheetz, S. D., Sandoval-Almazan, R., Tedesco, J. C., & Fox, E. A. (2016). Media use during conflicts: Information seeking and political efficacy during the 2012 Mexican elections. *Government Information Quarterly, 33*(3), 595–602. doi:10.1016/j.giq.2016.01.004

Kenski, K., Coe, K., & Rains, S. A. (in press). Perceptions of uncivil discourse online: An examination of types and predictors. *Communication Research*. doi:10.1177/0093650217699933

Kharroub, T., & Bas, O. (2015). Social media and protests: An examination of Twitter images of the 2011 Egyptian revolution. *New Media & Society, 18*(9), 1973–1992. doi:10.1177/1461444815571914

Kibria, N. (2003). *Becoming Asian American: Second-generation Chinese and Korean American identities*. Baltimore, MD: Johns Hopkins University Press.

Kim, B. S. K. (2007). Acculturation and enculturation. In F. T. L. Leong, A. G. Inman, A. Ebreo, L. H. Yang, L. M. Kinoshita, & M. Fu (Eds.), *Handbook of Asian American psychology* (2nd ed., pp. 141–158). Thousand Oaks, CA: Sage Publications.

Kim, B. S. K., & Abreu, J. M. (2001). Acculturation measurement: Theory, current instruments, and future directions. In J. G. Ponterotto, J. M. Casas, L. Suzuki, & C. M. Alexander (Eds.), *Handbook of multicultural counseling* (2nd ed.; pp. 394–424). Thousand Oaks, CA: Sage Publications.

Kim, H., Coyle, J., & Gould, S. (2009). Collectivist and individualistic influences on web-site design in South Korea and the US: A cross-cultural content analysis. *Journal of Computer-Mediated Communication, 14*(3), 581–601. doi:10.1111/j.1083-6101.2009.01454.x

Kim, H., Schroeder, A., & Pennington-Gray, L. (2016). Does Culture Influence Risk Perceptions? *Tourism Review International, 20*(1), 11–28. doi:10.3727/154427216X14581596798942

Kim, J. (2010). Balancing uniqueness and assimilation in computer-mediated groups. *Computers in Human Behavior, 26*(4), 778–784. doi:10.1016/j.chb.2010.02.001

Kim, J., & Park, H. (2011). The effect of uniform virtual appearance on conformity intention: Social identity model of deindividuation effects and optimal distinctiveness theory. *Computers in Human Behavior, 27*(3), 1223–1230. doi:10.1016/j.chb.2011.01.002

Kim, K., & Yun, H. (2008). Crying for me, crying for us: Relational dialectics in a Korean social network site. *Journal of Computer-Mediated Communication*, *13*(1), 298–318. doi:10.1111/j.1083-6101.2007.00397.x

Kimmel, M. S. (1994). Masculinity as homophobia. In P. S. Rothenberg (Ed.), Race, Class, and Gender in the United States: An Integrated Study (pp. 431-440). Academic Press.

Kim, Y. (2015). Does disagreement mitigate polarization? How selective exposure and disagreement affect political polarization. *Journalism & Mass Communication Quarterly*, *92*(4), 915–937. doi:10.1177/1077699015596328

Kim, Y. Y. (1988). *Communication and cross-cultural adaptation: An integrative theory*. Philadelphia: Multilingual Matters.

Kim, Y. Y. (2001). *Becoming intercultural: An integrative theory of communication and cross-cultural adaptation*. Thousand Oaks, CA: Sage Publications.

Kim, Y. Y. (2007). Ideology, identity, and intercultural communication: An analysis of differing academic conceptions of cultural identity. *Journal of Intercultural Communication Research*, *36*(3), 237–253. doi:10.1080/17475750701737181

Kim, Y. Y. (2008). Intercultural personhood: Globalization and a way of being. *International Journal of Intercultural Relations*, *32*(4), 359–368. doi:10.1016/j.ijintrel.2008.04.005

Kim, Y. Y. (2015). Finding a "home" beyond culture: The emergence of intercultural personhood in the globalizing world. *International Journal of Intercultural Relations*, *46*, 3–12. doi:10.1016/j.ijintrel.2015.03.018

Kim, Y. Y., & Bhawuk, D. (2008). Globalization and diversity: Contributions from intercultural research. *International Journal of Intercultural Relations*, *32*(4), 301–304. doi:10.1016/j.ijintrel.2008.06.001

Kim, Y., & Chen, H. (2015). Discussion network heterogeneity matters: Examining a moderated mediation model of social media use and civic engagement. *International Journal of Communication*, *9*, 2344–2365.

Kirk, R., & Schill, D. (2011). A digital agora: Citizen participation in the 2009 presidential debates. *The American Behavioral Scientist*, *55*(3), 325–347. doi:10.1177/0002764210392167

Kiron, D., Palmer, D., Phillips, A., & Kruschwitz, N. (2012). Social business: What are companies really doing? *MIT Sloan Management Review*, *53*(4), 1–32. Retrieved from http://sloanreview.mit.edu/article/what-managers-really-think-about-social- business/

Kissau, K. (2012). Structuring migrants' political activities on the internet: A two-dimensional approach. *Journal of Ethnic and Migration Studies*, *38*(9), 1381–1403. doi:10.1080/1369183X.2012.698207

Klausen, J. (2015). Tweeting the Jihad: Social media networks of western foreign fighters in Syria and Iraq. *Studies in Conflict and Terrorism*, *38*(1), 1–22. doi:10.1080/1057610X.2014.974948

Kline, S., & Liu, F. (2005). The influence of comparative media use on acculturation, acculturative stress, and family relationships of Chinese International students. *International Journal of Intercultural Relations*, *29*(4), 367–390. doi:10.1016/j.ijintrel.2005.07.001

Klopfer, E., Squire, K., & Jenkins, H. (2002). *Environmental detectives PDAs as a window into a virtual simulated world.* Paper presented at International Workshop on Wireless and Mobile Technologies in Education. doi:10.1109/WMTE.2002.1039227

Kluckhohn, C., & Kelly, W. H. (1945). The concept of culture. In R. Linton (Ed.), *The science of man in the world crisis* (pp. 78–106). New York, NY: Columbia University Press.

Knutson, T., Komolsevin, R., Chatiketu, P., & Smith, V. (2003). A cross-cultural comparison of Thai and US American rhetorical sensitivity: Implications for intercultural communication effectiveness. *International Journal of Intercultural Relations*, *27*(1), 63–78. doi:10.1016/S0147-1767(02)00060-3

Koc, M. (2006). Cultural identity crisis in the age of globalization and technology. *The Turkish Online Journal of Educational Technology*, *5*, 37–43.

Kofman, E., Vacchelli, E., & Saharso, S. (2015). Gendered Perspectives on Integration Discourses and Measures. *International Migration (Geneva, Switzerland)*, *53*(4), 77–89. doi:10.1111/imig.12102

Köhl, M. M., & Götzenbrucker, G. (2014). Networked technologies as emotional resources? Exploring emerging emotional cultures on social network sites such as Facebook and Hi5: A trans-cultural study. *Media Culture & Society*, *36*(4), 508–525. doi:10.1177/0163443714523813

Kohls, L. R., & Knight, J. M. (1994). *Developing intercultural awareness: A cross-cultural training handbook* (2nd ed.). Yarmouth, ME: Intercultural Press.

Kohut, A. (2000). Internet users are on the rise, but public affairs interest isn't. *Columbia Journalism Review*, *38*(5), 68–69.

Kok, S., & Rogers, R. (2017). Rethinking migration in the digital age: Transglocalization and the Somali diaspora. *Global Networks*, *17*(1), 23–46. doi:10.1111/glob.12127

Kolb, D. A. (1984). *Experiential Learning: experience as the source of learning and development.* Englewood Cliffs, NJ: Prentice-Hall.

Kolko, B., & Reid, E. (1998). Dissolution and fragmentation: Problems in on-line communities. In S. Jones (Ed.), *Cybersociety 2.0 revisiting computer-mediated communication and community* (pp. 129–158). Sage. doi:10.4135/9781452243689.n8

Korhan, O., & Ersoy, M. (2016). Usability and functionality factors of the social network site application users from the perspective of uses and gratification theory. *Quality & Quantity*, *50*(4), 1799–1816. doi:10.1007/s11135-015-0236-7

Kosur, J. (2014, August 29). *Facebook and Twitter have created political groupthink, study claims*. Retrieved February 02, 2016, from http://www.business2community.com/social-buzz/facebook-twitter-created- political-silence-study-claims-0993862#gPzLYHIUh3UhPXSt.97

Koteyko, N., Jaspal, R., & Nerlich, B. (2013). Climate change and 'climategate' in online reader comments: A mixed methods study. *The Geographical Journal*, *179*(1), 74–86. doi:10.1111/j.1475-4959.2012.00479.x

Kovarik, B. (2011). *Revolutions in Communication: Media history from Gutenberg to the digital age*. New York: Continuum.

Kraemer, J. D., Strasser, A. A., Lindblom, E. N., Niaura, R. S., & Mays, D. (2017). Crowdsourced data collection for public health: A comparison with nationally representative, population tobacco use data. *Preventive Medicine*, *102*, 93–99. doi:10.1016/j.ypmed.2017.07.006 PMID:28694063

Kraidy, M., & Murphy, P. (2008). Shifting Geertz. *Communication Theory*, *18*(3), 335–355. doi:10.1111/j.1468-2885.2008.00325.x

Kramsch, C., A'Ness, A., & Lam, E. (2000). Authenticity and authorship in the computer-mediated acquisition of L2 Literacy. *Language Learning & Technology*, *4*(2), 78–104.

Kramsch, C., & Thorne, S. L. (2002). Foreign language learning as global communicative practice. In D. Block & D. Cameron (Eds.), *Globalization and language teaching* (pp. 83–100). London: Routledge.

Kramsch, C., & Uryu, M. (2012). Intercultural contact, hybridity, and third space. In J. Jackson (Ed.), *The Routledge handbook of language and intercultural communication* (pp. 211–226). New York, NY: Palgrave.

Kreijns, K., Kirschner, P., & Jochems, W. (2003). Identifying the pitfalls for social interaction in computer-supported collaborative learning environments: A review of the research. *Computers in Human Behavior*, *19*(3), 335–353. doi:10.1016/S0747-5632(02)00057-2

Krombholz, K., Merkl, D., & Weippl, E. (2012). Fake identities in social media: A case study on the sustainability of the Facebook business model. *Journal of Service Science Research*, *4*(2), 175–212. doi:10.1007/s12927-012-0008-z

Kroon, Å. (2017). More than a hashtag: Producers' and users' co-creation of a loving "we" in a second screen TV sports production. *Television & New Media*, *18*(7), 670–688. doi:10.1177/1527476417699708

Kruikemeier, S., Van Noort, G., Vliegenthart, R., & de Vreese, H., C. (. (2016). The relationship between online campaigning and political involvement. *Online Information Review*, *40*(5), 673–694. doi:10.1108/OIR-11-2015-0346

Ksiazek, T. B., Malthouse, E. C., & Webster, J. G. (2010). News-seekers and Avoiders: Exploring Patterns of Total News Consumption Across Media and the Relationship to Civic Participation. *Journal of Broadcasting & Electronic Media*, *54*(4), 551–568. doi:10.1080/08838151.2010.519808

Kuo, F.-Y., Tseng, C. Y., Tseng, F.-C., & Lin, C. S. (2013). A study of social information control affordances and gender difference in Facebook self- presentation. *Cyberpsychology, Behavior, and Social Networking, 16*(9), 635–644. doi:10.1089/cyber.2012.0345 PMID:23849000

Kurylo, A. (2017). Stereotyping the field: The case for disentangling interpersonal and inter/cultural communication. *Atlantic Journal of Communication, 25*(4), 232–243. doi:10.1080/15456870.2017.1350681

A. Kurylo (Ed.). (2013). *Inter/cultural communication: Representation and construction of culture*. Thousand Oaks, CA: SAGE.

Kurylo, A., & Shuter, R. (2015). Special issue: Intercultural new media research. *International Journal of Interactive Communication Systems and Technologies, 5*. Retrieved from http://www.igi-global.com/journal/international-journal-interactive-communicationsystems/41029

Kyto, M., & McGookin, D. (2017). Investigating user-generated presentations of self in face-to-face interaction between strangers. *International Journal of Human-Computer Studies, 104*, 1–15. doi:10.1016/j.ijhcs.2017.02.007

Lagerkvist, A. (2013). *Media and memory in new Shanghai*. New York, NY: Palgrave. doi:10.1057/9781137014658

Lampert, C., & Donoso, V. (2012). Bullying. In S. Livingstone, L. Haddon, & A. Görzig (Eds.), *Children, risk and safety on the internet* (pp. 141–150). Bristol, UK: Policy Press at the University of Bristol. doi:10.1332/policypress/9781847428837.003.0011

Landolt, P., & Portes, A. (1996). The downside of social capital. *The American Prospect, 26*, 18–21.

Lang, M. (2016, April 5). 2016 Presidential Election Circus: Is Social Media the Cause? *San Francisco Chronicle.*

LaPiere, R. T. (1936). Type-rationalizations of group antipathy. *Social Forces, 15*(2), 232–237. doi:10.2307/2570963

Larson, B. M. H., Nerlich, B., & Wallis, P. (2005). Metaphors and Biorisks: The War on Infectious Diseases and Invasive Species. *Science Communication, 26*(3), 243–268. doi:10.1177/1075547004273019

Latané, B. (1981). The psychology of social impact. *The American Psychologist, 36*, 343–356. doi:10.1037/0003-066X.36.4.343

Latané, B. (1996). Dynamic social impact: The creation of culture by communication. *Journal of Communication, 46*(4), 13–25. doi:10.1111/j.1460-2466.1996.tb01501.x

Latané, B., & Nowak, A. (1997). Self-organizing social systems: Necessary and sufficient conditions for the emergence of consolidation and clustering. In G. Barnett & F. Boster (Eds.), *Progress in Communication Sciences: Persuasion* (pp. 43–74). Norwood, NJ: Ablex.

Lauricella, A. R., Cingel, D. P., Blackwell, C., Wartella, E., & Conway, A. (2014). The mobile generation: Youth and adolescent ownership and use of new media. *Communication Research Reports*, *31*(4), 357–364. doi:10.1080/08824096.2014.963221

Lazzari, M. (2012, July). The role of social networking services to shape the double virtual citizenship of young immigrants in Italy. In *IADIS International Conference ICT, Society and Human Beings* (pp. 11–18). IADIS.

Lea, M., & Spears, R. (1992). Paralanguage and social perception in computer-mediated communication. *Journal of Organizational Computing*, *2*(3-4), 321–341. doi:10.1080/10919399209540190

Lea, M., Spears, R., & de Groot, D. (2001). Knowing me, knowing you: Anonymity effects on group polarization in CMC within groups. *Personality and Social Psychology Bulletin*, *27*, 526–537. doi:10.1177/0146167201275002

Lee, C. W., McQuarrie, M., & Walker, E. T. (Eds.). (2015). Democratizing inequalities: Dilemmas of the new public participation. New York: New York University Press. doi:10.18574/nyu/9781479847273.001.0001

Lee, S., Bassick, M. A., & Wilson Mumpower, S. (2016). Fighting electronically: Long-distance romantic couples' conflict management over mobile communication. *Electronic Journal of Communication, 26*(3-4). Retrieved from http://www.cios.org/www/ejc/v26n34toc.htm

Leeds-Hurwitz, W. (1990). Notes in the history of intercultural communication: The Foreign Service Institute and the mandate for intercultural training. *The Quarterly Journal of Speech*, *76*(3), 262–281. doi:10.1080/00335639009383919

Lee, H., Kim, J., & Min, E. (2009). Hybridization of reality: Re-imaging the communicative environment in South Korea. *Asian Journal of Communication*, *19*(2), 133–136. doi:10.1080/01292980902836459

Lee, J. K., Choi, J., Kim, C., & Kim, Y. (2014). Social media, network heterogeneity, and opinion polarization. *Journal of Communication*, *64*(4), 702–722. doi:10.1111/jcom.12077

Lee, R. M. (2003). Do ethnic identity and other-group orientation protect against discrimination for Asian Americans? *Journal of Counseling Psychology*, *50*(2), 133–141. doi:10.1037/0022-0167.50.2.133

Lee, R. M., Yoon, E., & Liu-Tom, H. T. (2006). Structure and measurement of acculturation/enculturation for Asian Americans using the ARSMA-II. *Measurement & Evaluation in Counseling & Development*, *39*(1), 42–55. doi:10.1080/07481756.2006.11909789

Lee, S. J. (1996). *Unraveling the "model minority" stereotype: Listening to Asian American youth*. New York: Teachers College Press.

Lee, W. N., & Tse, D. K. (1994). Changing media consumption in a new home: Acculturation patterns among Hong Kong immigrants to Canada. *Journal of Advertising*, *23*(1), 57–70. doi:10.1080/00913367.1994.10673431

Lee, W., & Choi, S. (2005). The role of horizontal and vertical individualism and collectivism in online consumers' response toward persuasive communication on the web. *Journal of Computer-Mediated Communication*, *11*(1), 15. doi:10.1111/j.1083-6101.2006.tb00315.x

Leiss, W. (2004). Effective risk communication practice. *Toxicology Letters*, *149*(1-3), 399–404. doi:10.1016/j.toxlet.2003.12.050 PMID:15093287

Levin, S. (2017, June 13). Pay to sway: Report reveals how easy it is to manipulate elections with fake news. *The Guardian.* Retrieved from: https://www.theguardian.com/media/2017/jun/13/fake-news-manipulate-elections-paid-propaganda

Levine, J., & Hogg, M. (2010). *Encyclopedia of group processes & intergroup relations*. New Delhi: SAGE Publications. doi:10.4135/9781412972017

Levinson, M. (2010). The civic empowerment gap: Defining the problem and locating solutions. In L. R. Sherrod, J. Torney-Purta, & C. A. Flanagan (Eds.), *Handbook of research on civic engagement in youth* (pp. 393–423). Hoboken, NJ: John Wiley & Sons. doi:10.1002/9780470767603.ch13

Liang, H., Shen, F., & Fu, K. (2017). Privacy protection and self-disclosure across societies: A study of global Twitter users. *New Media & Society*, *19*(9), 1476–1497. doi:10.1177/1461444816642210

Liao, C., Squicciarini, A., Griffin, C., & Rajtmajer, S. (2016). A hybrid epidemic model for deindividuation and antinormative behavior in online social networks. *Social Network Analysis and Mining*, *6*(1), 1–11. doi:10.1007/s13278-016-0321-5

Lien, P. T. (2015). Reassessing Descriptive Representation by Women and Men of Color: New Evidence at the Subnational Level. *Urban Affairs Review*, *51*(2), 239–262. doi:10.1177/1078087414529124

Lien, P. T., Conway, M. M., & Wong, J. (2004). *The politics of Asian Americans: Diversity and community*. New York: Routledge.

Lievens, E. (2011). Risk-reducing regulatory strategies for protecting minors in social networks. *Info*, *13*(6), 43–54. doi:10.1108/14636691111174252

Lin, Y., Wu, W., Lee, C., Lin, D., & Chiang, Y. (2014). Effects of social network indicators and positions in class on bullied experiences among junior high school students in Taiwan. *Taiwan Gong Wei Sheng Za Zhi, 33*(4), 397- 409. https://search.proquest.com/docview/1561743546

Lindlof, T., & Taylor, B. (2002). *Qualitative communication research methods*. Thousand Oaks, CA: Sage.

Lin, J., Peng, W., Kim, M., Kim, S., & LaRose, R. (2012). Social networking and adjustments among international students. *New Media & Society*, *14*(3), 421–440. doi:10.1177/1461444811418627

Lin, N. (2000). *Social Capital*. Cambridge, UK: Cambridge University Press.

Lin, W., Cheong, P. H., Kim, Y., & Jung, J. (2010). Becoming citizens: Youths civic uses of new media in five digital cities in East Asia. *Journal of Adolescent Research*, *25*(6), 839–857. doi:10.1177/0743558410371125

Lin, W., Zhang, X., Jung, J., & Kim, Y. (2013). From the wired to wireless generation? Investigating teens' Internet use through the mobile phone. *Telecommunications Policy*, *37*(8), 651–661. doi:10.1016/j.telpol.2012.09.008

Lippmann, W. (1922). *Public Opinion*. New York: Macmillan.

M. Lister, J. Dovey, S. Giddings, I. Grant, & K. Kelly (Eds.). (2009). *New Media: A Critical Introduction* (2nd ed.). London: Routledge.

Lister, M., Dovy, J., Giddings, S., Grant, I., & Kelly, K. (2009). *New media: A critical introduction*. London: Routledge.

Littlejohn, S. W., & Foss, K. A. (2008). *Theories of human communication*. Belmont, CA: Thomson Wadsworth Cengage Learning.

Liu, B., Hsu, Y., & Ke, W. (2014). Virus infection control in online social networks based on probabilistic communities. *International Journal of Communication Systems*, *27*(12), 4481–4491. doi:10.1002/dac.2630

Liu, F. (2011). Wired for fun. *Young: Nordic Journal of Youth Studies*, *19*(1), 69–89. doi:10.1177/110330881001900105

Liu, H. (2007). Social network profiles as taste performances. *Journal of Computer-Mediated Communication*, *13*(1), 13. doi:10.1111/j.1083-6101.2007.00395.x

Live Your Dream. (2017). Retrieved from http://www.liveyourdream.org/

Livingstone, S., & Bober, M. (2005). *UK children go online: Final report of key project findings*. London: London School of Economics and Political Science.

S. Livingstone, L. Haddon, & A. Görzig (Eds.). (2012). *Children, risk and safety on the internet*. Bristol, UK: Policy Press at the University of Bristol. doi:10.1332/policypress/9781847428837.001.0001

Livingstone, S., Haddon, L., Görzig, A., & Ólafsson, K. (2011). *Risks and safety on the internet. The perspective of European children. Full findings*. London: London School of Economics and Political Science.

Loader, B. D., & Mercea, D. (2011). Networking democracy? Social media innovations in participatory politics. *Information Communication and Society*, *14*(6), 757–769. doi:10.1080/1369118X.2011.592648

Loehwing, M., & Motter, J. (2012). Utilizing co-cultures & counterpublics in Intercultural new media research. *China Media Research*, *8*, 29–38.

Logan, R. (2010). *Understanding New Media*. New York: Peter Lang.

Logan, R. K. (2010). *Understanding New Media, Extending Marshall McLuhan*. Peter Lang Publishing.

Lombardo, E., Meier, P., & Verloo, M. (2009). *The Discursive Politics of Gender Equality: Stretching, Bending and Policy*. Routledge.

Lopato, M. (2016). Social media, love, and Sartre's look of the Other: Why online communication is not fulfilling. *Philosophy & Technology*, *29*(3), 195–210. doi:10.1007/s13347-015-0207-x

López, V., & Watts, J. (2017, April 19). *Deaths and injuries reported amid 'mother of all marches' in Venezuela.* Retrieved April 20, 2017, from https://www.theguardian.com/world/2017/apr/19/venezuela-protest-mother-of-all-marches-maduro-violence

Loranger, H. (2014). *Break Grammar Rules on Websites for Clarity*. Retrieved from http://www.nngroup.com/articles/break-grammar-rules/

Lowenthal, P. (2009). *Social Presence: What Is It and Why Does It Matter?* Retrieved from http://www.slideshare.net/plowenthal/social-presence-what-is-it-and-why-does-it-matter

Lucas, D. (2014). Social media and protest—the Indian spring. In C. Litang & M. Prosser (Eds.), *Social media in Asia*. Lake Oswego, OR: Dignity Press.

Luhb, T. (2016, November 9). How Hillary Clinton lost? *CNN News*.

Lupia, A., & Philpot, T. S. (2005). Views from inside the net: How websites affect young adults' political interest. *The Journal of Politics*, *67*(4), 1122–1142. doi:10.1111/j.1468-2508.2005.00353.x

Machin, D., & VanLeeuwen, T. (2008). Branding the self. In C. Caldas-Coulthard & R. Iedema (Eds.), Identity trouble (pp. 43-56). Basingstoke, UK: Palgrave Macmillan. doi:10.1057/9780230593329_3

MacKinnon, R. (2008). Blogs and China correspondence: Lessons about global Information flows. *Chinese Journal of Communication*, *1*(2), 242–157. doi:10.1080/17544750802288081

MacKinnon, R. (2013). *Consent of the networked: The worldwide struggle for Internet freedom*. Basic Books.

Macrae, C. N., Milne, A. B., & Bodenhausen, G. V. (1994). Stereotypes as energy-saving devices: A peek inside the cognitive toolbox. *Journal of Personality and Social Psychology*, *66*(1), 37–47. doi:10.1037/0022-3514.66.1.37

Malik, A., Dhir, A., & Nieminen, M. (2015). Uncovering Facebook photo tagging culture and practices among digital natives. *Global Media Journal, 13*(24), 1-21. Retrieved from http://www.globalmediajournal.com/open-access/uncovering-facebook- photo-tagging-culture-and-practices-among-digital-natives.pdf

Malila, V., & Oelofsen, M. (2016). Young citizens in South Africa: A paradox of engagement with politics and the media. *Journal of African Media Studies*, *8*(2), 187–203. doi:10.1386/jams.8.2.187_1

Manca, S., & Ranieri, M. (2016). Facebook and the others. Potentials and obstacles of social media for teaching in higher education. *Computers & Education, 95*, 216–230. doi:10.1016/j.compedu.2016.01.012

Mannheim, K. (1952). The Problem of Generations. In P. Kecskemeti (Ed.), *Essays on the Sociology of Knowledge* (pp. 276–320). London: Routledge.

Manovich, L. (2001). *The language of new media*. Cambridge, MA: MIT Press.

Manovich, L. (2001). *The Language of New Media*. London: The MIT Press.

Marchin, D., & Myer, A. (2012). *How to do critical discourse analysis*. Thousand Oaks, CA: Sage Publication.

Marcus, A., & Krishnamurthi, N. (2009). Cross-cultural analysis of social network services in Japan, Korea, and the USA. *DID '09 Proceedings of the 3rd. International Conference on Internationalization, design and global development.*

Markus, H., & Kitayama, S. (1991). Culture and the self: Implications for cognition, emotion, and motivation. *Psychological Review, 98*(2), 223–253. doi:10.1037/0033-295X.98.2.224

Marlowe, J. M., Bartley, A., & Collins, F. (2017). Digital belongings: The intersections of social cohesion, connectivity and digital media. *Ethnicities, 17*(1), 85–102. doi:10.1177/1468796816654174

Martin, J., & Nakayama, T. (1999). Thinking dialectically about culture and communication. *Communication Theory, 9*(1), 1–25. doi:10.1111/j.1468-2885.1999.tb00160.x

Marwick, A. (2012). The public domain: Social surveillance in everyday life. *Surveillance & Society, 9*(4), 378–393. Retrieved from https://ojs.library.queensu.ca/index.php/surveillance-and-society/article/view/pub_dom

Marwick, A., & boyd, . (2010). I tweet honestly, I tweet passionately: Twitter users, context collapse and the imagined audience. *New Media & Society, 13*(1), 114–133. doi:10.1177/1461444810365313

Ma, S. M. (2000). *The deathly embrace: Orientalism and Asian American identity*. Minneapolis, MN: University of Minnesota Press.

Mason, R. L., Gunst, R. F., & Hess, J. L. (1989). *Statistical design and analysis of experiments: With applications to engineering and science*. New York: Wiley.

Masuoka, N. (2006). Together they become one: Examining the predictors of panethnic group consciousness among Asian Americans and Latinos. *Social Science Quarterly, 87*(5), 993–1011. doi:10.1111/j.1540-6237.2006.00412.x

Matheson, D. (2000). The Birth of News Discourse: Changes in News Language in British Newspapers, 1880-1930. *Media Culture & Society, 20*(5), 557–573. doi:10.1177/016344300022005002

Matsunaga, M. (2011). Underlying circuits of social support for bullied victims: An appraisal-based perspective on supportive communication and postbullying adjustment. *Human Communication Research, 37*(2), 174–206. doi:10.1111/j.1468-2958.2010.01398.x

Mayer-Schonberger, V. (2009). *Delete: The virtue of forgetting in the digital age*. Princeton, NJ: Princeton University Press.

Maza, C. (2015, August 18). NBC Universal invests $200 million in BuzzFeed: Can it win over Millennials? *Christian Science Monitor*. Retrieved from http://www.csmonitor.com/Business/2015/0818/NBC-Universal-invests-200-million-in-BuzzFeed-Can-it-win-over-Millennials

McCabe, D. (2015, August 17). Welcome to social media election. *The Hill*.

McCaughey, B. (2013). *Beating Obamacare: Your handbook for the new healthcare law*. Washington, DC: Regnery Publishing.

McChesney, R. W. (2013). *Digital disconnect: How capitalism is turning the internet against democracy*. New York, NY: New Press.

McCombs, M. E., & Shaw, D. L. (1972). The Agenda-Setting Function of Mass Media. *Public Opinion Quarterly*, *36*(2), 176–187. doi:10.1086/267990

McCombs, M. E., & Shaw, D. L. (1993). The Evolution of Agenda-Setting Research: Twenty-Five Years in the Marketplace of Ideas. *Journal of Communication*, *43*(2), 58–67. doi:10.1111/j.1460-2466.1993.tb01262.x

McEwan, B., & Sobre-Denton, M. (2011). Virtual cosmopolitanism: Constructing third cultures and transmitting social and cultural capital through social media. *Journal of International and Intercultural Communication*, *4*(4), 252–258. doi:10.1080/17513057.2011.598044

McManus, A. M. (2017). What's in a Name Revisited. *Reference and User Services Quarterly*, *56*(3), 156–157. doi:10.5860/rusq.56n3.156

McPherson, M., Smith-Lovin, L., & Cook, J. M. (2001). Birds of a feather: Homophily in social networks. *Annual Review of Sociology*, *27*(1), 415–444. doi:10.1146/annurev.soc.27.1.415

McQuail, D., & Windahl, S. (1993). *Communication Models* (2nd ed.). New York: Routledge.

Mead, G. H. (1934). *Mind, self and society* (Vol. 111). Chicago: University of Chicago Press.

Meeks, L. (2012). Is she "man enough"? Women candidates, executive political offices, and news coverage. *Journal of Communication*, *62*(1), 175–193. doi:10.1111/j.1460-2466.2011.01621.x

Meis, M. (2017). When is a conflict a crisis? On the aesthetics of the Syrian civil war in a social media context. *Media, War & Conflict*, *10*(1), 69–86. doi:10.1177/1750635216653903

Melody, W. (2006). Markets and policies in new knowledge economies. *LIRNE.NET.* Retrieved from: https://idl-bnc-idrc.dspacedirect.org/bitstream/handle/10625/41875/129520.pdf?sequence=1

Menard, S. (1995). *Applied logistic regression analysis*. Thousand Oaks, CA: Sage Publications.

Meng, J., Martinez, L., Holmstrom, A., Chung, M., & Cox, J. (2017). Research on social networking sites and social support from 2004 to 2015: A narrative review and directions for future research. *Cyberpsychology, Behavior, and Social Networking*, *20*(1), 44–51. doi:10.1089/cyber.2016.0325 PMID:28002686

Merchant, G. (2016). Together and apart: Social and technical networks. In A. Kurylo & T. Dumova (Eds.), *Redefining communication in the era of social networking: Cultural, social, and political perspectives*. Madison, NJ: Fairleigh Dickinson University Press.

Metzger, M. J., Flanagin, A. J., Eyal, K., Lemus, D. R., & Mccann, R. M. (2003). Credibility for the 21st century: Integrating perspectives on source, message, and media credibility in the contemporary media environment. *Communication Yearbook*, *27*(1), 293–335. doi:10.1207/s15567419cy2701_10

Metzger, M. J., Flanagin, A. J., & Medders, R. B. (2010). Social and Heuristic Approaches to Credibility Evaluation Online. *Journal of Communication*, *60*(3), 413–439. doi:10.1111/j.1460-2466.2010.01488.x

Middaugh, E., & Kahne, J. (2013). New media as a tool for civic learning. *Comunicar*, *20*(40), 99–107. doi:10.3916/C40-2013-02-10

Miller, D., & Madianou, M. (2012). *Migration and new media: Transnational families and polymedia*. London: Routledge.

Miller, M. J. (2007). A bilinear multidimensional measurement model of Asian American acculturation and enculturation: Implications for counseling interventions. *Journal of Counseling Psychology*, *54*(2), 118–131. doi:10.1037/0022-0167.54.2.118

Mishra, N., & Silakari, S. (2012). Image mining in the context of content based image retrieval: A perspective. *International Journal of Computer Science Issues*, *9*(4), 69–76. Retrieved from http://ijcsi.org/papers/IJCSI-9-4-3-69-76.pdf

Mitchell, A. (2015, April 29). State of the News Media 2015. *Pew Research Center.* Retrieved from http://www.journalism.org/files/2015/04/FINAL-STATE-OF-THE-NEWS-MEDIA1.pdf

Mitchell, A., & Holcomb, J. (2016, June 15). State of the News Media 2016. *Pew Research Center*. Retrieved from http://www.journalism.org/2016/06/15/state-of-the-news-media-2016/

Mitchell, A., Gottfried, J., Barthel, M., & Shearer, E. (2016, July 7). The Modern News Consumer: News attitudes and practices in the digital era. *Pew Research Center.* Retrieved from http://www.journalism.org/2016/07/07/the-modern-news-consumer/

Moghaddam, F. M. (2005). The staircase to terrorism: A psychological exploration. *The American Psychologist*, *60*(2), 161–169. doi:10.1037/0003-066X.60.2.161 PMID:15740448

Mohdin, A. (2016, Nov. 9). American women voted overwhelmingly for Clinton, except the White ones. *Quartz*.

Mokros, H. B. (2003). *Identity matters: Communication based explorations and explanations*. Cresskill, NJ: Hampton Press.

Mollering, G. (2001). The Nature of Trust: From Georg Simmel to a Theory of Expectation, Interpretation and Suspension. *Sociology*, *35*(2), 403–420. doi:10.1177/S0038038501000190

Moon, S. J., & Park, C. Y. (2007). Media effects on acculturation and biculturalism: A case study of Korean immigrants in Los Angeles' Koreatown. *Mass Communication & Society*, *10*(3), 319–343. doi:10.1080/15205430701407330

Moqbel, M., Nevo, S., & Kock, N. (2013). Organizational members' use of social networking sites and job performance. *Information Technology & People*, *26*(3), 240–264. doi:10.1108/ITP-10-2012-0110

Moraru, V., & Rusu, L. (2017). New media – The reforming factor of political communication. *International Journal of Communication Research*, *7*(1), 50–57.

Morley, D. (2006). Globalisation and cultural imperialism reconsidered: old questions in new guises. In J. Curran & D. Morley (Eds.), *Media and cultural theory* (pp. 30–43). New York, NY: Routledge.

Morozov, E. (2009, May 19). Foreign policy: Brave new world of slacktiv-ism. *NPR*. Retrieved from http://www.npr.org/templates/story/ story.php?storyId=104302141

Mouttapa, M., Valente, T., Gallaher, P., Rohrbach, L. A., & Unger, J. B. (2004). Social network predictors of bullying and victimization. *Adolescence*, *39*(154), 315–335. PMID:15563041

Mussell, J. (2012). Social media. *Journal of Victorian Culture*, 1.

Myrick, J., Holton, A., Himelboim, I., & Love, B. (2016). #Stupidcancer: Exploring a typology of social support and the role of emotional expression in a social media community. *Health Communication*, *31*(5), 596–605. doi:10.1080/10410236.2014.981664 PMID:26453480

Naffziger, D. W., Bott, J. P., & Mueller, C. B. (2008). Factors influencing study abroad decisions among college of business students. *International Business: Research Teaching and Practice*, *2*(1), 39–52.

Nagel, J. (1994). Constructing ethnicity: Creating and recreating ethnic identity and culture. *Social Problems*, *41*(1), 152–176. doi:10.2307/3096847

Natsios, A. (1996). *Illusions of Influence: The CNN Effect in Complex Emergencies. In From Massacres to Genocide: The Media, Public Policy, and Humanitarian Crises* (pp. 149–168). Brookings Institution.

Ndhlovu, F. (2007). The Role of Discourse in Identity Formation and the Manufacture of Ethnic Minorities in Zimbabwe. *Journal of Multicultural Discourses*, *2*(2), 131–147. doi:10.2167/md073.0

Neagu, A. a., Pavaloiu, B. k., & Mateescu, L. M. (2017). Social media and virtual platforms facilitators for intercultural dialogue. *E-learning & Software for Education, 2,* 502-508. doi:10.12753/2066-026X-17-156

Nedelcu, M. (2012). Migrants' new transnational habitus: Rethinking migration through a cosmopolitan lens in the digital age. *Journal of Ethnic and Migration Studies*, *38*(9), 1339–1356. doi:10.1080/1369183X.2012.698203

Negroponte, N. (1996). *Being digital*. New York, NY: Vintage Books.

Nerlich, B., & Richard, J. (2009). "The post-antibiotic apocalypse" and the "war on superbugs": Catastrophe discourse in microbiology, its rhetorical form and political function. *Public Understanding of Science (Bristol, England)*, *18*(5), 574–590. doi:10.1177/0963662507087974 PMID:20027773

Netzley, S., & Hemmer, M. (2012). Citizen journalism just as credible as stories by pros, students say. *Newspaper Research Journal*, *33*(3), 49–61. doi:10.1177/073953291203300304

Neuman, W. R. (1991). *The future of the mass audience*. Cambridge, UK: Cambridge University Press.

Newland, K. (2010). *Voice after exit: Diaspora advocacy*. Migration Policy Institute.

Ng, K. (2014). Asian American new media communication as cultural engagement: E-mail, vlog/blogs, mobile applications, social networks, and YouTube. In P. Cheong, J. Martin, & L. Macfadyen (Eds.), *New media and intercultural communication* (pp. 255–274). New York, NY: Peter Lang.

Nielsen, F. (1985). Toward a theory of ethnic solidarity in modern societies. *American Sociological Review*, *50*(2), 133–149. doi:10.2307/2095405

Nie, N. E., & Erbring, L. (2000). *Internet and society: A preliminary report*. Los Altos, CA: Stanford Institute for the Quantitative Study of Society.

Noelle-Neumann, E. (1974). The spiral of silence: A theory of public opinion. *Journal of Communication*, *24*(2), 43–51. doi:10.1111/j.1460-2466.1974.tb00367.x

Noelle-Neumann, E. (1984). *The spiral of silence: Public opinion – Our social skin*. Chicago, IL: University of Chicago Press.

Noels, K., Yashima, T., & Zhang, R. (2012). Language, identity and intercultural pragmatics. In J. Jackson (Ed.), *The Routledge handbook of language and intercultural communication* (pp. 52–66). New York, NY: Routledge.

Norris, P. (2000). *A virtuous circle: Political communications in postindustrial societies*. Cambridge, UK: Cambridge University Press. doi:10.1017/CBO9780511609343

O'Dowd, R. (2003). Understanding the "other side": Intercultural learning in a Spanish-English email exchange. *Language Learning & Technology*, *7*(2), 118–144.

O'Hara, K., & Stevens, D. (2015). Echo chambers and online radicalism: Assessing the Internet's complicity in violent extremism. *Policy and Internet*, *7*(4), 401–422. doi:10.1002/poi3.88

O'Leary, M. (2014). BuzzFeed and the New Virality. *Information Today*, *31*(3), 20–21.

Obar, J., & Wildman, S. (2015). Social media definition and the governance challenge: An introduction to the special issue. *Telecommunications Policy*, *39*(9), 745–750. doi:10.1016/j.telpol.2015.07.014

Odabaşı, H. F. I., Kabakçı, I., & Çoklar, A. N. (2007). *İnternet, aile ve çocuk* [The internet, family and children]. Ankara, Turkey: Nobel Yayıncılık.

Odejobi, R., & Adegbola, T. (2010). Computational and engineering issues in human computer interaction systems for supporting communication in African languages. In R. Taiwo (Ed.), *The handbook of research on discourse behavior digital communication: Language structures and social interaction* (Vol. 2, pp. 876–881). New York, NY: Information Science Reference. doi:10.4018/978-1-61520-773-2.ch056

Ogilvy. (2010). *Infographic: China's social media evolution.* Retrieved from http://www.thomascrampton.com/china/china-social-evolution

Oh, D. C. (2015). *Second-generation Korean Americans and transnational media: Diasporic identifications*. Lanham, MD: Lexington Books.

Okamoto, D. G. (2003). Toward a theory of panethnicity: Explaining Asian American collective action. *American Sociological Review*, *68*(6), 811–842. doi:10.2307/1519747

Okrent, A. (2014). The listicle as literary form. *The University of Chicago Magazine*. Retrieved from http://mag.uchicago.edu/arts-humanities/listicle-literary-form

Olzak, S. (1994). *The dynamics of ethnic competition and conflict*. Redwood City, CA: Stanford University Press.

Omero, M., & McGuinness, T. (2012). *How women changed the outcome of the election.* Center for American Progress.

Orbe, M. P., & Warren, K. T. (2000). Different standpoints, different realities: Race, gender, and perceptions of intercultural conflict. *Qualitative Research Reports*, *1*, 51–57.

Orbe, M., & Harris, T. M. (2001). *Interracial communication: Theory into practice*. Belmont, CA: Wadsworth.

Ota, H., Giles, H., & Gallois, C. (2002). Perceptions of Younger, Middle-aged, and Older Adults in Australia and Japan: Stereotypes and age group vitality. *Journal of Intercultural Studies (Melbourne, Vic.)*, *23*(3), 253–266. doi:10.1080/07256860216390

Oxford English Dictionary. (2017a). *Identity*. Retrieved from https://en.oxforddictionaries.com/definition/identity

Oxford English Dictionary. (2017b). *Image*. Retrieved from https://en.oxforddictionaries.com/definition/image

Oxford English Dictionary. (2017c). *Brand*. Retrieved from https://en.oxforddictionaries.com/definition/brand

Oxford English Dictionary. (2017d). *Reputation*. Retrieved from https://en.oxforddictionaries.com/definition/reputation

Oxford English Dictionary. (2017e). *Presence*. Retrieved from https://en.oxforddictionaries.com/definition/presence

Oyserman, D., Coon, H., & Kemmelmeier, M. (2002). Rethinking individualism and collectivism: Evaluation of theoretical assumptions and meta-analyses. *Psychological Bulletin*, *128*(1), 3–72. doi:10.1037/0033-2909.128.1.3 PMID:11843547

Oyserman, D., & Lee, S. (2008). "Does culture influence what and how we think?" Effects of priming individualism and collectivism. *Psychological Bulletin*, *134*(2), 311–342. doi:10.1037/0033-2909.134.2.311 PMID:18298274

Oyserman, D., & Sakamoto, I. (1997). Being Asian American: Identity, cultural constructs, and stereotype perception. *The Journal of Applied Behavioral Science*, *33*(4), 435–453. doi:10.1177/0021886397334002

Padilla, F. M. (1985). *Latino ethnic consciousness: The case of Mexican Americans and Puerto Ricans in Chicago*. Notre Dame, IN: University of Notre Dame Press.

Paluck, E., Shepherd, H., & Aronow, P. (2016). Changing climates of conflict: A social network experiment in 56 schools. *Proceedings of the National Academy of Sciences of the United States of America*, *113*(3), 566–571. doi:10.1073/pnas.1514483113 PMID:26729884

Paluck, E., Shepherd, H., & Smith, E. R. (2012). The salience of social referents: A field experiment on collective norms and harassment behavior in a school social network. *Journal of Personality and Social Psychology*, *103*(6), 899–915. doi:10.1037/a0030015 PMID:22984831

Panayırcı, U. (2016). Are communication theories affected by new communication technologies? A look at spiral of silence theory. *Online Academic Journal of Information Technology*, *7*(22), 51–66. doi:10.5824/1309-1581.2016.1.004.x

Paolini, S., Harwood, J., & Rubin, M. (2010). Negative intergroup contact makes group memberships salient: Explaining why intergroup conflict endures. *Personality and Social Psychology Bulletin*, *36*(12), 1723–1738. doi:10.1177/0146167210388667 PMID:21051766

Paolini, S., Harwood, J., Rubin, M., Husnu, S., Joyce, N., & Hewstone, M. (2014). Positive and extensive intergroup contact in the past buffers against the disproportionate impact of negative contact in the present. *European Journal of Social Psychology*, *44*(6), 548–562. doi:10.1002/ejsp.2029

Papacharissi, Z. (2004, May). *The blogger revolution? Audience as media producers*. Paper presented, International Communication Association, New Orleans, LA.

Pariser, E. (2012). *The filter bubble: How the new personalized web is changing what we read and how we think (reprint edition)*. New York, NY: Penguin Books. doi:10.3139/9783446431164

Park, D. (2009). *Conglomerate rock: The music industry's quest to divide music and conquer wallets*. Lanham, MD: Lexington Books.

Park, D. (2016). The battle over SNS privacy for United States employees and job applicants: An analysis of 2012-2013 state legislation. *Information Communication and Society*. doi:10.1080/1369118X.2016.1202303

Parker, D., & Song, M. (2006). Ethnicity, social capital and the Internet: British Chinese websites. *Ethnicities*, *6*(2), 178–202. doi:10.1177/1468796806063751

Pasek, J., Sood, G., & Krosnick, J. A. (2015). Misinformed about the Affordable Care Act? Leveraging certainty to assess the prevalence of misperceptions. *Journal of Communication*, *65*(4), 660–673. doi:10.1111/jcom.12165

Peeters, A. L., & d'Haenens, L. (2005). Bridging or bonding? Relationships between integration and media use among ethnic minorities in the Netherlands. *Communications*, *30*(2), 201–231. doi:10.1515/comm.2005.30.2.201

Peters, B., & Lubken, D. (2011). New Media in Crises: Discursive instability and emergency communication. In D. W. Park, N. W. Jankowski, & S. Jones (Eds.), *The long history of new media: technology, historiography, and contextualizing newness* (pp. 193–209). New York: Peter Lang.

Peters, E., & Slovic, P. (1996). The role of affect and worldviews as orienting dispositions in the perception and acceptance of nuclear power. *Journal of Applied Social Psychology*, *26*(16), 1427–1453. doi:10.1111/j.1559-1816.1996.tb00079.x

Petrocchi, N., Asnaani, A., Martinez, A., Nadkarni, A., & Hofmann, S. (2015). Differences between people who use only Facebook and those who use Facebook plus Twitter. *International Journal of Human-Computer Interaction*, *31*(2), 157–165. doi:10.1080/10447318.2014.986640 PMID:26997849

Pettigrew, T. F., & Tropp, L. R. (2006). A meta-analytic test of intergroup contact theory. *Journal of Personality and Social Psychology*, *90*(5), 751–783. doi:10.1037/0022-3514.90.5.751 PMID:16737372

Pettigrew, T. F., & Tropp, L. R. (2008). How does intergroup contact reduce prejudice? Meta-analytic tests of three mediators. *European Journal of Social Psychology*, *28*(6), 922–934. doi:10.1002/ejsp.504

Petty, R. E., & Cacciopo, J. (1986). The elaboration likelihood model of persuasion. *Advances in Experimental Social Psychology*, *19*, 123–205. doi:10.1016/S0065-2601(08)60214-2

Pew Internet and American Life Project. (2017). *Internet and Technology: Fact Sheets*. Retrieved from http://www.pewinternet.org

Pew Research Center. (2009). *Iran and the "Twitter Revolution": PEJ New Media Index*. Retrieved from http://www.journalism.org/2009/06/25/iran-and-twitter-revolution/#

Pew Research Center. (2012). *The Rise of Asian Americans*. Retrieved from: http://www.pewsocialtrends.org/2012/06/19/the-rise-of-asian-americans/

Pfister, D. S. (2011). Networked Expertise in the Era of Many-to-Many Communication: On Wikipedia and Invention. *Social Epistemology*, *25*(3), 217–231.

Pflug, J. (2011). Contextuality and computer-mediated communication: A cross cultural comparison. *Computers in Human Behavior*, *27*(1), 131–137. doi:10.1016/j.chb.2009.10.008

Phillips, W. (2012). What an Academic Who Wrote Her Dissertation on Trolls Thinks of Violentacrez. *The Atlantic*. Retrieved from https://www.theatlantic.com/technology/archive/2012/10/what-an-academic-who-wrote-her-dissertation-on-trolls-thinks-of-violentacrez/263631/

Phinney, J. S., & Chavira, V. (1992). Ethnic identity and self-esteem: An exploratory longitudinal study. *Journal of Adolescence*, *15*(3), 271–281. doi:10.1016/0140-1971(92)90030-9 PMID:1447413

Phinney, J. S., & Ong, A. D. (2007). Conceptualization and measurement of ethnic identity: Current status and future directions. *Journal of Counseling Psychology*, *54*(3), 271–281. doi:10.1037/0022-0167.54.3.271

Picciano, A. G. (2002). Beyond student perceptions: Issues of interaction, presence, and performance in an online course. *Journal of Asynchronous Learning Networks*, *6*(1).

Poindexter, P. (2012). *Millennials, news, and social media: Is news engagement a thing of the past?* New York: Peter Lang.

Political Parity. (2017). *Women of color in American politics*. Retrieved from https://www.politicalparity.org/wp-content/uploads/2015/08/Parity-Research-Women-Of-Color.pdf

Polletta, F. (2015). Public deliberation and political contention. In C. W. Lee, M. McQuarrie, & E. T. Walker (Eds.), *Democratizing inequalities: Dilemmas of the new public participation* (pp. 222–246). New York: New York University Press. doi:10.18574/nyu/9781479847273.003.0012

Pornsakulvanich, V. (2007). Television portrayals of ethnic minorities in the United States: The analysis of individual differences, media use, and group identity and vitality. *ABAC Journal*, *27*, 22–28.

Portillo, S. (2010). How race, sex, and age frame the use of authority by local government officials. *Law & Social Inquiry*, *35*(3), 603–623. doi:10.1111/j.1747-4469.2010.01197.x

Postmes, T., Spears, R., & Lea, M. (2002). Inter-group differentiation in computer-mediated communication: Effects of depersonalization. *Group Dynamics*, *6*(1), 3–16. doi:10.1037/1089-2699.6.1.3

Potts, L. (2013). *Social media in disaster response: How experience architects can build for participation*. Routledge.

Putnam, R. (1995). Bowling Alone: America's Declining Social Capital. *Journal of Democracy*, *6*(1), 65–78. doi:10.1353/jod.1995.0002

Putnam, R. D. (2001). *Bowling alone: The collapse and revival of American community*. New York: Simon and Schuster.

Qui, J. (2010). Mobile communication research in Asia: Changing technological and intellectual geopolitics. *Asian Journal of Communication*, *20*(2), 213–229. doi:10.1080/01292981003693393

Raes, J. (2017). Microbiology: Crowdsourcing Earth's microbes. *Nature*. Retrieved on Nov 12, 2017 from https://www.nature.com/articles/nature24756

Rahim, A. (1983). A measure of styles of handling interpersonal conflict. *Academy of Management Journal*, *26*(2), 368–376. doi:10.2307/255985 PMID:10263067

Rahman, O., & Rollock, D. (2004). Acculturation, competence, and mental health among South Asian students in the United States. *Journal of Multicultural Counseling and Development*, *32*(3), 130–142. doi:10.1002/j.2161-1912.2004.tb00366.x

Rakou, L. F., & Wakwitz, L. A. (2004). *Feminist Communication Theory*. Thousand Oaks, CA: Sage Publication.

Rakow, L. (2013). Worldviews and mediatization: In search of a metatheory. *Journal of Multicultural Discourses*, *8*(3), 190–194. doi:10.1080/17447143.2013.849712

Rantanen, R. (2005). Giddens and the 'G-word': An interview with Anthony Giddens. *Global Media and Communication*, *1*(1), 63–77. doi:10.1177/1742766505050173

Rauschnabel, P., Kammerlander, N., & Ivens, B. (2016). Collaborative brand attacks in social media: Exploring the antecedents, characteristics, and consequences of a new form of brand crises. *Journal of Marketing Theory and Practice*, *24*(4), 381–410. doi:10.1080/10696679.2016.1205452

Reich, R. (2015, Sept 30). Bernie Sanders tells the truth: Former Clinton Labor Secretary Robert Reich on his surging campaign. *Democracynow!* Retrieved from: http://www.democracynow.org/2015/9/30/bernie_sanders_tells_the_truth_former?autostart=true&get_clicky_key=suggested_next_story

Reicher, S., Spears, R., & Postmes, T. (1995). A social identity model of deindividuation phenomena. *European Review of Social Psychology*, *6*(1), 161–198. doi:10.1080/14792779443000049

Renn, K. A. (2000). Patterns of situational identity among biracial and multiracial college students. *The Review of Higher Education*, *23*(4), 399–420. doi:10.1353/rhe.2000.0019

Reppler.com. (2011). Job Screening with Social Networks. *Reppler.com*. Retrieved from http://blog.reppler.com/2011/09/27/managing-your-online-image-across-social-networks/

Rettie, R. (2009). Mobile phone communication: Extending Goffman to mediated interaction. *Sociology*, *43*(3), 421–438. doi:10.1177/0038038509103197

Reyes, A. (2007). *Language, identity, and stereotype among Southeast Asian American youth: The other Asian*. Mahwah, NJ: Erlbaum.

Rezabakhsh, B., Bornemann, D., Hansen, U., & Schrader, U. (2006). Consumer power: A comparison of the old economy and the internet. *Journal of Consumer Policy*, *29*(1), 3–36. doi:10.1007/s10603-005-3307-7

Rheingold, H. (1994). *The virtual community*. Retrieved from http://www.rheingold.com/vc/book/3.html

Rieder, R. (2015, June 16). Rieder: BuzzFeed a burgeoning journalistic force. *USA Today*. Retrieved from http://www.usatoday.com/story/money/columnist/rieder/2015/06/15/buzzfeed-expands-as-journalism-force/71250444/

Rim, H., Ha, J. H., & Kiousis, S. (2014). The evidence of compelling arguments in agenda building: Relationships among public information subsidies, media coverage, and risk perceptions during a pandemic outbreak. *Journal of Communication Management*, *18*(1), 101–116. doi:10.1108/JCOM-05-2012-0044

Roberts, L. M., & Ely, R. J. (2016, November 23). Why Did So Many White Women Vote for Donald Trump? *Fortune*.

Robinson, P. (1999). The CNN effect: Can the news media drive foreign policy? *Review of International Studies*, *25*(2), 301–330. doi:10.1017/S0260210599003010

Robischon, N. (2016, February 22). BuzzFeed's Quest for Impact in the Viral News Era. *Fast Company*. Retrieved from https://www.fastcompany.com/3056365/buzzfeeds-quest-for-impact-in-the-viral-news-era

Roccas, S., & Brewer, M. B. (2002). Social identity complexity. *Personality and Social Psychology Review*, *6*(2), 88–106. doi:10.1207/S15327957PSPR0602_01

Rocha, M. E. M., Gutiérrez, E. O., & Cortés, G. U. (2017). Youth and political participation: #Yosoy132 and the struggle for freedom of expression in Mexico. *Communicatio Socialis*, *30*(1), 87–105.

Rogers, E. M. (2003). *Diffusion of Innovations* (5th ed.). New York: Free Press.

Rogers, E. M., Hart, W. B., & Miike, Y. (2002). Edward T. Hall and the history of intercultural communication: The United States and Japan. *Keio Communication Review*, *24*, 3–26. Retrieved from http://www.mediacom.keio.ac.jp/publication/pdf2002/review24/2.pdf

Rogers, J. (2013). *The Death & Life of the Music Industry in the Digital Age*. New York: Bloomsbury Academic.

Rogers, P., & Lea, M. (2004). Cohesion in online groups. In K. Morgan, C. A. Brebbia, J. Sanchez, & A. Voiskounsky (Eds.), *Human perspectives in the Internet society: Culture, psychology and gender* (pp. 115–124). Southampton, UK: WIT Press.

Rohrmann, B. (1992). The evaluation of risk communication effectiveness. *Acta Psychologica*, *81*(2), 169–192. doi:10.1016/0001-6918(92)90004-W

Roldan, Z., & Gracia, M. D. (2015). Locating civic engagement through social media during calamities: The Philippine experience. *International Journal of Interdisciplinary Studies in Communication*, *10*(2), 1–7. doi:10.18848/2324-7320/CGP/v10i02/53611

Rollins, M., & Lewis, S. (2012). Communication practices of certified public accountants. *Journal of Organizational Culture, Communications and Conflict*, *16*(1), 107-112. Retrieved from https://search.proquest.com/docview/1037693138

Romanucci-Ross, L. (2006). Matrices of an Italian identity: Past as prologue. In L. Romanucci-Ross, G. A. De Vos, & T. Tsuda (Eds.), *Ethnic identity*. Oxford, UK: AltaMira.

Romero, A. J., & Roberts, R. E. (1998). Perception of discrimination and ethnocultural variables in a diverse group of adolescents. *Journal of Adolescence*, *21*(6), 641–656. doi:10.1006/jado.1998.0185 PMID:9971722

Romo, R., & Brocchetto, M. (2017, April 20). *Venezuela protests: What you need to know*. Retrieved April 20, 2017, from http://edition.cnn.com/2017/04/18/americas/venezuela-protest-explainer/

Rosen, J. (2011). The Deciders: Facebook, Google, and the Future of Privacy and Free Speech. In Constitution 3.0: Freedom and Technological Change. Washington, DC: Brookings Institution Press.

Rosenbaum, L. (2014). "Misfearing"—culture, identity, and our perceptions of health risks. *The New England Journal of Medicine*, *370*(7), 595–597. doi:10.1056/NEJMp1314638 PMID:24521105

Ross, K., Fountaine, S., & Comrie, M. (2015). Facing up to Facebook: Politicians, publics and the social media(ted) turn in New Zealand. *Media Culture & Society*, *37*(2), 251–269. doi:10.1177/0163443714557983

Rourke, L., Anderson, T., Garrison, D. R., & Archer, W. (2000). Assessing social presence in asynchronous text-based computer conferencing. *International Journal of E-Learning and Distance Education*, *14*(2), 50–71. Retrieved from http://www.ijede.ca/index.php/jde/article/view/153/341

Ruelle, O., & Peverelli, P. (2016). The discursive construction of identity through interaction on social media in a Chinese NGO. *Chinese Journal of Communication*, *8*, 1–26.

Ruggiero, T. E. (2000). Uses and gratifications theory in the 21st century. *Mass Communication & Society*, *3*(1), 3–37. doi:10.1207/S15327825MCS0301_02

Ruth, W., Monica, L., & Forbes, G. (2003). The WEB Book experiments in electronic textbook design. *The Journal of Documentation*, *59*(4), 454–477. doi:10.1108/00220410310485721

Ryan, K. (2013). The media's war on women: Gendered coverage on women candidates. *Xavier Journal of Politics*, *4*(1), 13–25.

Rybas, N. (2014). Producing the self at the digital interface. In P. Cheong, J. Martin, & L. Macfayden (Eds.), *New media and intercultural communication: Identity, community and politics* (pp. 93–108). New York, NY: Peter Lang.

Ryder, A. G., Alden, L. E., & Paulhus, D. L. (2000). Is acculturation unidimensional or bidimensional? A head-to-head comparison in the prediction of personality, self-identity, and adjustment. *Journal of Personality and Social Psychology*, *79*(1), 49–65. doi:10.1037/0022-3514.79.1.49 PMID:10909877

Ryle, R. (2018). *Questioning gender* (4th ed.). Thousand Oaks, CA: Sage Publication.

Salazar, A. J. (2009). Groupthink. In S. W. Littlejohn & K. A. Foss (Eds.), *Encyclopedia of Communication Theory* (Vol. 2, pp. 461–462). Thousand Oaks, CA: SAGE Publications. doi:10.4135/9781412959384.n169

Salmon, C. T., & Kline, F. G. (1985). The spiral of silence ten years later: An examination and evaluation. In K. R. Sanders, L. L. Kaid, & D. Nimmo (Eds.), *Political Communication Yearbook 1984* (pp. 3–30). Carbondale, IL: Southern Illinois University Press.

Samovar, L. A., Porter, R. E., & McDaniel, E. R. (2007). *Communication between cultures*. Belmont, CA: Thomson.

Sancer, G. A. (2013). Political public relations 2.0 and the use of Twitter of political leaders in Turkey. *Online Journal of Communication and Media Technologies*, *3*(1), 181–194.

Sanders, S. (2016, Nov. 8). Did Social Media Ruin Election 2016? *National Public Radio.*

Sangwan, S. (2005). Virtual community success: A uses and gratifications perspective. *Proceedings of the 38yh Hawaii International Conference on System Sciences,* 1-10. doi:10.1109/HICSS.2005.673

Sarbaugh, L. E. (1988). A taxonomic approach to intercultural communication. In Y. Y. Kim & W. B. Gudykunst (Eds.), *Theories in intercultural communication* (pp. 22–40). Newbury Park, CA: Sage.

Sar, R., & Al-Saggaf, K. (2014). Contextual integrity's decision heuristic and the tracking by social network sites. *Ethics and Information Technology*, *16*(1), 15–26. doi:10.1007/s10676-013-9329-y

Scardamalia, M., & Bereiter, C. (2003). Knowledge building. In J. W. Guthrie (Ed.), *Encyclopedia of education* (pp. 1370–1373). New York: McMillan.

Scardamalia, M., & Bereiter, C. (2010). A brief history of knowledge building. *Canadian Journal of Learning and Technology*, *36*(1), 1–16. doi:10.21432/T2859M

Schiller, D. (2014). Digital depression: Information technology and economic crisis. Urbana, IL: University of Illinois Press.

Schiller, D. (1996). *Theorizing communication: A history*. New York: Oxford University Press.

Schmidt, A. (2013). Groupthink. In *Britannica Online Academic Edition*. Encyclopædia Britannica, Inc. Retrieved from https://www.britannica.com/contributor/Anna-Schmidt/9345859

Schroeder, R. (2010). Mobile phones and the inexorable advance of multimodal connectedness. *New Media & Society*, *12*(1), 75–90. doi:10.1177/1461444809355114

Schwartz, S. J., Montgomery, M. J., & Briones, E. (2006). The Role of Identity in Acculturation among Immigrant People: Theoretical Propositions, Empirical Questions, and Applied Recommendations. *Human Development*, *49*(1), 1–30. doi:10.1159/000090300

Schwartz, S. J., Unger, J. B., Zamboanga, B. L., & Szapocznik, J. (2010). Rethinking the concept of acculturation: Implications for theory and research. *The American Psychologist*, *65*(4), 237–251. doi:10.1037/a0019330 PMID:20455618

Schwartz, S., & Bardi, A. (2001). Value hierarchies across cultures: Taking a similarities perspective. *Journal of Cross-Cultural Psychology*, *32*(3), 268–290. doi:10.1177/0022022101032003002

Scott, J. (2013). *Social network analysis* (3rd ed.). London: Sage.

Seelye, H. N. (1997). *Experiential activities for intercultural learning*. Boston, MA: Intercultural Press.

Seifert, J. L. (2015). A Culture of Survivors: SlutWalk, Third Culture, and New Media Communication. *International Journal of Interactive Communication Systems and Technologies*, *5*(1), 1–13. doi:10.4018/IJICST.2015010101

Sentse, M., Kiuru, N., Veenstra, R., & Salmivalli, C. (2014). A social network approach to the interplay between adolescents' bullying and likeability over time. *Journal of Youth and Adolescence*, *43*(9), 1409–1420. doi:10.1007/s10964-014-0129-4 PMID:24752280

Serazio, M. (2013). *Your Ad Here: The Cool Sell of Guerrilla Marketing*. New York: New York University Press.

Serazio, M. (2015). Selling (Digital) Millennials. *Television & New Media*, *16*(7), 599–615. doi:10.1177/1527476413491015

Shade, D. D., Kornfield, S., & Oliver, M. B. (2015). The Uses and Gratifications of Media Migration: Investigating the Activities, Motivations, and Predictors of Migration Behaviors Originating in Entertainment Television. *Journal of Broadcasting & Electronic Media*, *59*(2), 318–341. doi:10.1080/08838151.2015.1029121

Shah, R., Chauhan, N., Gupta, A. K., & Sen, M. S. (2016). Adolescent-parent conflict in the age of social media: Case reports from India. *Asian Journal of Psychiatry*, *23*, 24–26. doi:10.1016/j.ajp.2016.07.002 PMID:27969073

Shao, G. (2009). Understanding the appeal of user-generated media: A uses and gratification perspective. *Internet Research*, *19*(1), 7–25. doi:10.1108/10662240910927795

Shao, G., Lu, J., & Wu, J. (2012). New media and civic engagement in China: The case of the Xiamen PX event. *China Media Research*, *8*(2), 76–82.

Shapiro, A. (1999). *The control revolution: How the internet is putting individuals in charge and changing the world we know*. New York, NY: Public Affairs.

Sharma, M., Yadav, K., Yadav, N., & Ferdinand, K. C. (2017). Zika virus pandemic—analysis of Facebook as a social media health information platform. *American Journal of Infection Control*, *45*(3), 301–302. doi:10.1016/j.ajic.2016.08.022 PMID:27776823

Shelton, J. N., & Sellers, R. M. (2000). Situational stability and variability in African American racial identity. *The Journal of Black Psychology*, *26*(1), 27–50. doi:10.1177/0095798400026001002

Shirts, R. G. (1977). *BaFa BaFa: A cross cultural simulation*. Delmar, CA: Smile II.

Shi, X., & Babrow, S. A. (2007). Challenges of adolescent and young adult Chinese American identity construction: An application of problematic integration theory. *Western Journal of Communication*, *71*(4), 316–335. doi:10.1080/10570310701672935

Shi, Y. (2005). Identity construction of the Chinese diaspora, ethnic media use, community formation, and the possibility of social activism. *Continuum*, *19*(1), 55–72. doi:10.1080/1030431052000336298

Shontell, A. (2013). *Actually, Snapchat Doesn't Delete Your Private Pictures And Someone Found A Way To Resurface Them*. Retrieved from http://www.businessinsider.com/snapchat-doesnt-delete-your-private-pictures-2013-5

Shuter, R. (2011). Introduction: New media across cultures—prospect and promise. *Journal of International and Intercultural Communication*, *4*(4), 241–245. doi:10.1080/17513057.2011.598041

Shuter, R. (2012a). When Indian women text message: Culture, identity, and emerging interpersonal norms of new media. In P. H. Cheong, J. N. Martin, & L. Macfadyen (Eds.), *New media and intercultural communication: Identity, community and politics* (pp. 209–222). New York, NY: Peter Lang.

Shuter, R. (2012b). Intercultural New Media Studies: The Next Frontier in Intercultural Communication. *Journal of Intercultural Communication Research*, *41*(3), 219–237. doi:10.1080/17475759.2012.728761

Shuter, R., Cheong, P., & Chen, Y. (2016). The influence of cultural values on U.S. and Danish students' digital behavior: Exploring culture, new media, and social context. *Journal of International and Intercultural Communication*, *9*(2), 161–178. doi:10.1080/17513057.2016.1154183

Shutter, R. (2012). Research and pedagogy in intercultural new media studies. *China Media Research*, *8*(4), 1–5.

Sijtsema, J. J., Rambaran, J. A., Caravita, S. C. S., & Gini, G. (2014). Friendship selection and influence in bullying and defending: Effects of moral disengagement. *Developmental Psychology*, *50*(8), 2093–2104. doi:10.1037/a0037145 PMID:24911569

Simon, B. (2004). *Identity in modern society: A social psychological perspective.* Oxford, UK: Blackwell. doi:10.1002/9780470773437

Singh, C. (2010). New media and cultural identity. *China Media Research, 6*(1), 86–90.

Skågeby, J. (2012). The irony of serendipity: Disruptions in social information behavior. *Library Hi Tech, 30*(2), 321–334. doi:10.1108/07378831211239988

Sloam, J. (2014). "The outraged young": Young Europeans, civic engagement and the new media in a time of crisis. *Information Communication and Society, 17*(2), 127–231. doi:10.1080/1369118X.2013.868019

Slobogin, C. (2011). Is the Fourth Amendment Relevant in a Technological Age? In Constitution 3.0: Freedom and Technological Change. Washington, DC: Brookings Institution Press. doi:10.2139/ssrn.1734755

Slovic, P. (2016). *The perception of risk.* New York: Routledge.

Smith Pfister, D., & Soliz, J. (2011). (Re)conceptualizing intercultural communication in a networked society. *Journal of International and Intercultural Communication, 4*(4), 246–251. doi:10.1080/17513057.2011.598043

Smith, C. (2016, July 14). By the Numbers: 28 Amazing BuzzFeed Statistics. *DMR*. Retrieved from http://expandedramblings.com/index.php/buzzfeed-statistics/

Smith, D. (2017). *'Extreme vetting' would require visitors to US to share contacts and passwords.* Retrieved from: https://www.theguardian.com/us-news/2017/apr/04/trump-extreme-vetting-visitors-to-us-share-contacts-passwords

Smith, G. A. (2017). *Most Americans oppose churches choosing sides in elections.* Pew Research.

Smith, P. (2011). Cross-cultural perspectives on identity. In V. Vignoles, S. Schwartz, & K. Luyckx (Eds.), *Handbook of identity theory and research* (pp. 249–265). London: Springer. doi:10.1007/978-1-4419-7988-9_11

Smith, R. D. (2006). Responding to global infectious disease outbreaks: Lessons from SARS on the role of risk perception, communication and management. *Social Science & Medicine, 63*(12), 3113–3123. doi:10.1016/j.socscimed.2006.08.004 PMID:16978751

Snow Bailard, C. (2015). Ethnic conflict goes mobile: Mobile technology's effect on the opportunities and motivations for violent collective action. *Journal of Peace Research, 52*(3), 323–337. doi:10.1177/0022343314556334

Snyder, M., Tanke, E. D., & Berscheid, E. (1977). Social perception and interpersonal behavior: On the self-fulfilling nature of social stereotypes. *Journal of Experimental Social Psychology, 35*, 656–666. doi:10.1037/0022-3514.35.9.656

Sobre-Denton, M. (2016). Virtual intercultural bridgework: Social media, virtual cosmospolitanism, and activist community-building. *New Media & Society*, *18*(8), 1715–1731. doi:10.1177/1461444814567988

Sola-Morales, S., & Hernández-Santaolalla, V. (2017). Voter turnout and new forms of political participation of young people: A comparative analysis between Chile and Spain. *Revista Latina de Comunicación Social*, *72*, 629–648.

Somolu, O. (2007). Telling our own stories: African women blogging for social change. *Gender and Development*, *15*(3), 477–489. doi:10.1080/13552070701630640

Sontag, S. (1988). *Illness as Metaphor & AIDS and Its Metaphors*. New York: Farrar, Strauss, and Giroux.

South China Morning Post. (2015). *Chinese tourist invasion transforms remote Palau and not everyone is happy*. Retrieved from http://www.scmp.com/news/china/foreignrelations/article/1738288/chinese-descend-remote-palau-wanderlust-deepens

Spangler, T. (2015, August 18). NBCUniversal Invests $200 Million in BuzzFeed. *Variety*. Retrieved from http://variety.com/2015/digital/news/nbcuniversal-invests-200-million-in-buzzfeed-1201572244/

Spencer-Oatey, H. (2007). Theories of identity and the analysis of face. *Journal of Pragmatics*, *39*(4), 639–656. doi:10.1016/j.pragma.2006.12.004

Splichal, S. (2009). 'New' media, 'old' theories: Does the (national) public melt into the air of global governance? *European Journal of Communication*, *24*(4), 391–405. doi:10.1177/0267323109345522

Spurgeon, C., Ferrier, L., Gunders, L., & Graham, P. (2012). Young citizens, values and new/s media. *Journal of Media & Cultural Studies*, *26*(6), 911–922. doi:10.1080/10304312.2012.734598

Sreberny, A. (2000). Media and diasporic consciousness: An exploration among Iranians in London. In S. Cottle, S. (Ed.), Ethnic Minorities and the Media: Changing Cultural Boundaries (pp. 179-196). Maidenhead, UK: Open University Press.

St. Amant, K. (2014). Culture, context, and cyberspace: Rethinking identity and credibility in international virtual teams. In P. Cheong, J. Martin, & L. Macfadyen (Eds.), *New media and intercultural communication: Identity, community and politics* (pp. 75–92). New York, NY: Peter Lang.

Stacks, D. W. (2016). *Primer of public relations research*. New York: Guilford Publications.

Stafford, T. F., Stafford, M. R., & Schkade, L. L. (2004). Determining uses and gratifications for the internet. *Decision Sciences*, *35*(2), 259–288. doi:10.1111/j.00117315.2004.02524.x

Stanley, J. W., & Weare, C. (2004). The effects of Internet use on political participation: Evidence from an agency online discussion forum. *Administration & Society*, *36*(5), 503–527. doi:10.1177/0095399704268503

Statista. (2017). Annual Revenue of Alibaba Group from 2010-2016. *The Statista Portal*. Retrieved from https://www.statista.com/statistics/225614/net-revenue-of-alibaba/

Steel, E., & Marsh, B. (2015, October 3). Millennials and Cutting the Cord. *The New York Times*. Retrieved from https://www.nytimes.com/interactive/2015/10/03/business/media/changing-media-consumption-millenials-cord-cutters.html?_r=0

Steele, G. A., & Plenty, D. (2015). Supervisor-subordinate communication competence and job and communication satisfaction. *International Journal of Business Communication*, *52*(3), 294–318. doi:10.1177/2329488414525450

Steiger, K. (2010). 99 PROBLEMS. *Bitch Magazine: Feminist Response To Pop Culture*, (49), 15-16.

Steinberg, S. (2001). *The Ethnic Myth: Race, Ethnicity and Class in America*. Boston, MA: Beacon Press.

Sternadori, M. M., & Thorson, E. (2009). Anonymous Sources Harm Credibility of All Stories. *Newspaper Research Journal*, *30*(4), 54–66. doi:10.1177/073953290903000405

Stern, J., & Berger, J. M. (2015). *ISIS: The state of terror*. New York, NY: Harper Collins.

Sterns, P. N. (2009). *Educating global citizens in colleges and universities: challenges and opportunities*. New York, NY: Routledge.

Stoddard, M. C. J. (2007). Ideology, Hegemony, Discourse: A Critical Review of Theories of Knowledge and Power. *Social Thought & Research*, *28*, 191–225.

Strauss, A., & Corbin, J. (1998). *Basics of qualitative research: Techniques and procedures for developing grounded theory*. London: Sage.

Sundararajan, B., Finch, D., & O'Reilly, N. (2016). *Homophily in Authors Team Networks: A Network Analysis of Authors and Authors Teams in Leading Management Journals*. Presented at the *2016 Administrative Sciences Association of Canada (ASAC) Conference*, Edmonton, Canada.

Sundararajan, B., & Macdonald, L. (2016). *Lean, Ethical Business Communication*. Toronto, Canada: Oxford University Press.

Sundararajan, B., & Sundararajan, M. (2012). Like us on Facebook and follow us on Twitter: Corporate identity management across social media platforms. In C. Cunningham (Ed.), *Social Networking and Impression Management* (pp. 129–146). Lexington Books.

Sundar, S. S. (2008). Self as source: Agency and customization in interactive media. In E. Konjin, S. Utz, M. Tanis, & S. Barnes (Eds.), *Mediated interpersonal communication* (pp. 58–74). New York, NY: Routledge.

Sundar, S. S., & Limperos, A. (2013). Uses and grats 2.0: New gratifications for new media. *Journal of Broadcasting & Electronic Media*, *57*(4), 504–525. doi:10.1080/08838151.2013.845827

Sunstein, C. (2001). *Republic.com*. Princeton, NJ: Princeton University Press.

Sunstein, C. (2007). *Republic.com 2.0*. Princeton, NJ: Princeton University Press.

Sunstein, C. R. (2005). Misfearing: A reply. *Harvard Law Review*, *119*, 1110.

Sun, W., & Starosta, W. J. (2006). Perceptions of Minority Invisibility Among Asian American Professionals. *The Howard Journal of Communications*, *17*(2), 119–142. doi:10.1080/10646170600656870

Sutton, J., Gibson, C., Phillips, N., Spiro, E., League, C., Johnson, B., ... Butts, C. (2015). A cross-hazard analysis of terse message retransmission on Twitter. *Proceedings of the National Academy of Sciences of the United States of America*, *112*(48), 14793–14798. doi:10.1073/pnas.1508916112 PMID:26627233

Swanson, D. L. (2000). The homologous evolution of political communication and civic engagement: Good news, bad news, and no news. *Political Communication*, *17*(4), 409–414. doi:10.1080/10584600050179031

Swasy, A., Tandoc, E., Bhandari, M., & Davis, R. (2015). Traditional Reporting More Credible than Citizen News. *Newspaper Research Journal*, *36*(2), 225–236. doi:10.1177/0739532915587298

Tajfel, H., & Turner, J. (1986). The social identity theory of intergroup behavior. In S. Worchel & W. Austin (Eds.), *Psychology of intergroup relations* (2nd ed.; pp. 7–24). Chicago, IL: Nelson-Hall.

Takemura, K., Yuki, M., & Ohtsubo, Y. (2010). Attending inside or outside: A Japan-US comparison of spontaneous memory of group information. *Asian Journal of Social Psychology*, *13*(4), 303–307. doi:10.1111/j.1467-839X.2010.01327.x

Tanis, M., & Postmes, T. (2003). Social cues and impression formation in CMC. *Journal of Communication*, *53*(4), 676–693. doi:10.1111/j.1460-2466.2003.tb02917.x

Taylor, P. (2012). *Young people and political engagement*. Retrieved from http://www.pewresearch.org/2012/07/16/ask-the-expert-young-people-and-political-engagement/

Tesser, A. (1993). The importance of heritability in psychological research: The case of attitudes. *Psychological Review*, *100*(1), 129–142. doi:10.1037/0033-295X.100.1.129 PMID:8426878

The Canadian Press. (2017). Brother: Las Vegas gunman was wealthy real-estate investor. *Yahoo News*. Retrieved from https://ca.news.yahoo.com/gunman-killed-50-las-vegas-151003919.html

The Lancet. (2014). The medium and the message of Ebola [editorial]. *Lancet*, *384*(9955). Retrieved from http://www.thelancet.com/journals/lancet/article/PIIS0140-6736(14)62016-X/fulltext

The Thiagi Group. (2014). *Training Games*. Retrieved from http://www.thiagi.com/games.html

Theiss-Morse, E., & Hibbing, J. R. (2005). Citizenship and civic engagement. *Annual Review of Political Science*, *8*(1), 227–249. doi:10.1146/annurev.polisci.8.082103.104829

Thiagarajan, S., & Steinwachs, B. (1990). *Barnga: A simulation game on cultural clashes. Yarmouth*. Intercultural Press.

Thompson, K. (2002). Border crossings and diasporic identities: Media use and leisure practices of an ethnic minority. *Qualitative Sociology*, *25*(3), 409–418. doi:10.1023/A:1016038114625

Thorne, S. L. (2003). Artifacts and cultures of use in intercultural communication. *Language Learning & Technology*, *7*(2), 38–67. Retrieved from http://llt.msu.edu/vol7num2/thorne/

Thumim, N. (2012). Socializing and self-representation online: Exploring Facebook. *Observatorio Journal*, *6*(1), 087-105. doi: 1646-5954/ERC123483/2012087

Thurlow, C., Lengel, L., & Tomic, A. (2004). *Computer-mediated communication: Social interaction and the Internet*. Thousand Oaks, CA: Sage Publications.

Thussu, D. (2011). Media identities in a "post-American" world. In R. Chopra & R. Gajjala (Eds.), *Global media, cultures and identity* (pp. 235–249). New York, NY: Routledge.

Thussu, D. K. (2006). *Media on the move: global flow and contra-flow*. London, New York: Routledge.

Ting-Toomey, S. (2005). Identity negotiation theory. In W. Gudykunst (Ed.), *Theorizing about intercultural communication* (pp. 211–233). Thousand Oaks, CA: Sage.

Ting-Toomey, S., Yee-Jung, K., Shapiro, R., Wright, T., & Oetzel, J. (2000). Ethnic/cultural identity salience and conflict styles in four US ethnic groups. *International Journal of Intercultural Relations*, *24*(1), 47–81. doi:10.1016/S0147-1767(99)00023-1

Tokuda, Y., Fujii, S., Jimba, M., & Inoguchi, T. (2017). The Relationship Between Trust in Mass Media and the Healthcare System and Individual Health: Evidence from the Asia Barometer Survey. In T. Inoguchi & Y. Tokuda (Eds.), *Trust with Asian Characteristics: Interpersonal and Institutional* (pp. 191–207). Springer Singapore. doi:10.1007/978-981-10-2305-7_12

Tokunga, R. (2009). High-speed internet access to the other: The influence of cultural orientation on self-disclosures in offline and online relationships. *Journal of Intercultural Communication Research*, *38*(3), 133–147. doi:10.1080/17475759.2009.505058

Tomasello, T. K., Lee, Y., & Bear, A. P. (2010). "New media" research publication trends and outlets in communication, 1990-2006. *New Media & Society*, *12*(4), 531–548. doi:10.1177/1461444809342762

Tomes, N. (2000). The making of a germ panic, then and now. *American Journal of Public Health*, *90*(2), 191–198. doi:10.2105/AJPH.90.2.191 PMID:10667179

Tomlinson, J. (1997). A phenomenology of globalization? Giddens on global modernity. In C. Bryant & D. Jary (Eds.), Anthony Giddens: Critical assessments (vol. 4, pp. 116-136). New York: Routledge.

Tora-Joy, P. (2013). Socio-Cultural Tradition. *Communication Theory Blog*. Retrieved from https://torajoypatrick.wordpress.com/2013/10/07/socio-cultural-tradition/comment-page-1/

Torbati, Y. (2017). Donald Trump administration approves social media checks for U.S. visa applicants. *Globalnews.ca*. Retrieved from: https://globalnews.ca/news/3498115/u-s-visa-social-media-checks/

Tour, S., Thomas, K., Walker, D., Leighton, P., Yong, A., & Batchelor, J. (2014). Survey and online discussion groups to develop a patient-rated outcome measure on acceptability of treatment response in vitiligo. *BMC Dermatology*, *14*(1), 10. doi:10.1186/1471-5945-14-10 PMID:24929563

Towner, T. L., & Muñoz, C. L. (2017). The Role of Instagram in Issue Agenda Setting during the 2016 Presidential Primary Campaign. In The Internet and the 2016 Presidential Campaign (pp. 263-284). Academic Press.

Tracy, K. (2002). *Everyday talk: Building and reflecting identities*. New York: Guilford Press.

Treadwell, D. (2017). *Introducing communication research: Paths of inquiry*. Los Angeles, CA: Sage Publications.

Treem, J. W., & Leonardi, P. M. (2012). Social media use in organizations: Exploring the affordances of visibility, editability, persistence, and association. *Communication Yearbook*, *36*, 143–189. doi:10.2139/ssrn.2129853

Treviño, L. K., Webster, J., & Stein, E. W. (2000). Making connections: Complementary influences on communication media choices, attitudes, and use. *Organization Science*, *11*(2), 163–182. doi:10.1287/orsc.11.2.163.12510

Triandis, C. H. (1995). *Individualism and collectivism*. Boulder, CO: Westview Press.

Triandis, H. C. (1995). *Individualism-collectivism*. Boulder, CO: Westview.

Trier, T., & Khanzihn, A. (2007). Introduction. In T. Trier & A. Khanzihn (Eds.), *Meskhetian Turks at a crossroads: Integration, reparation or resettlement?* (pp. 1–42). Berlin, Germany: Lit Verlag.

Tsikerdekis, M. (2012). *Social interaction design for social media: The case of groupthink and aggression* (Unpublished doctoral dissertation). Masaryk University.

Tsikerdekis, M. (2013). The effects of perceived anonymity and anonymity states on conformity and groupthink in online communities: A Wikipedia study. *Journal of the American Society for Information Science and Technology*, *64*(5), 1001–1015. doi:10.1002/asi.22795

Tufekci, Z. (2008). Grooming, gossip, Facebook, and Myspace: What can we learn about those sites from those who don't assimilate? *Information Communication and Society*, *11*(4), 544–564. doi:10.1080/13691180801999050

Tufekci, Z. (2017). *Twitter and tear gas: The power and fragility of networked protest*. New Haven, CT: Yale University Press.

Turel, O., & Serenko, A. (2012). The benefits and dangers of enjoyment with social networking websites. *European Journal of Information Systems*, *21*(5), 512–528. doi:10.1057/ejis.2012.1

Turkle, S. (2011). *Alone together: Why we expect more from technology and less from each other*. New York, NY: Basic Books.

Turow, J. (1997). Breaking up America: Advertisers and the new media world. Chicago: University of Chicago Press. doi:10.7208/chicago/9780226817514.001.0001

Turow, J. (2011). *The daily you: How the new advertising industry is defining your identity and your worth*. New Haven, CT: Yale University Press.

Twitter. (2017). *FAQs about top search results*. Retrieved August 24, 2017, from https://support.twitter.com/articles/131209

UNESCO. (2007). *Statistics on cultural industries: Framework for the Elaboration of National Data Capacity Building Projects*. Bangkok: UNESCO Bangkok. Retrieved from: http://unesdoc.unesco.org/images/0015/001549/154956e.pdf

UNESCO. (2015). Cultural times: The first global map of cultural and creative industries. *UNESCO*. Retrieved from: http://en.unesco.org/creativity/sites/creativity/files/cultural_times._the_first_global_map_of_cultural_and_creative_industries.pdf

UNWTO. (2012). *International tourism hits one billion*. Retrieved from http://media.unwto.org/en/press-release/2012-12-12/international-tourism-hits-one-billion

Utz, S. (2010). Show me your friends and I will tell you the type of person you area; How one's profile, number of friends, and type of friendships influence impression formation. *Journal of Computer-Mediated Communication, 15*(2), 314–335. doi:10.1111/j.1083-6101.2010.01522.x

van dijk, T. (1993). *Elite Discourse and the Reproduction of Racism*. Thousand Oaks, CA: Sage Publication.

Van Niekerk, B., & Maharaj, M. (2013). Social media and information conflict. *International Journal of Communication, 7,* 1162-1184. doi:1932–8036/20130005

Verghese, A. (2004). What Is in a Word? *Clinical Infectious Diseases, 38*(7), 932–933. doi:10.1086/382365 PMID:15034822

Verloo, M. (2013). Intersectional and Cross-Movement Politics and Policies: Reflections on Current Practices and Debates. *Intersectionality: Theorizing Power, Empowering Theory, 38*(4), 893–915.

Vernuccio, M., Pagani, M., Barbarossa, C., & Pastore, A. (2015). Antecedents of brand love in online network-based communities. A social identity perspective. *Journal of Product and Brand Management, 24*(7), 706–719. doi:10.1108/JPBM-12-2014-0772

Vignoles, V., Schwartz, S., & Luyckx, K. (2011). Introduction: Toward an integrative view of identity. In V. Vignoles, S. Schwartz & K. Luyckx (Eds.), Handbook of identity theory and research (pp. 1-19). New York: Springer.

Villar, M. E., & Zamith, R. (2011). Comparing frequency of online news coverage, worldwide mortality and perceived risk of leading diseases and injuries: Challenging paradigms in the new media landscape. *Journal of Health & Mass Communication*, *3*(1-4), 193.

Vincent, J. (2014, August 27). *The 'spiral of silence': How social media encourages self-censorship online*. Retrieved February 27, 2017, from http://www.independent.co.uk/life-style/gadgets-and-tech/the-spiral-of-silence how-social-media-encourages-self-censorship-online-9693044.html

Viswanath, K., & Arora, P. (2000). Ethnic media in the United States: An essay on their role in integration, assimilation, and social control. *Mass Communication & Society*, *3*(1), 39–56. doi:10.1207/S15327825MCS0301_03

Volkan, V. (1999). *Bloodlines: From Ethnic Pride to Ethnic Terrorism*. Boulder, CO: Westview Press.

Volkan, V. (2003). The re-libidinalization of the internal world of a refugee family. *Group Analysis*, *36*(4), 555–570. doi:10.1177/0533316403364012

Vygotsky, L. (1978). *Mind in Society: The Development of Higher Psychological Processes*. Cambridge, MA: Harvard University Press.

Waheed, H., Anjum, M., Rehman, M., & Khawaja, A. (2017). Investigation of user behavior on social networking sites. *PLoS One*, *12*(2), e0169693. doi:10.1371/journal.pone.0169693 PMID:28151963

Waisbord, S. (2013). A metatheory of mediatization and globalization? *Journal of Multicultural Discourses*, *8*(3), 182–189. doi:10.1080/17447143.2013.822504

Wallis, P., & Nerlich, B. (2005). Disease metaphors in new epidemics: The UK media framing of the 2003 SARS epidemic. *Social Science & Medicine*, *60*(11), 2629–2639. doi:10.1016/j.socscimed.2004.11.031 PMID:15814187

Walther, J. (1992). Interpersonal effects in computer-mediated interaction: A relational perspective. *Human Communication Research*, *19*(1), 52–90. doi:10.1177/009365092019001003

Walther, J. B. (1995). Relational aspects of computer-mediated communication: Experimental observations over time. *Organization Science*, *6*(2), 186–203. doi:10.1287/orsc.6.2.186

Walther, J. B. (1996). Computer-mediated communication: Impersonal, interpersonal, and hyperpersonal interaction. *Communication Research*, *23*(1), 3–43. doi:10.1177/009365096023001001

Walther, J. B. (2009). Computer-mediated communication and virtual groups: Applications to interethnic conflict. *Journal of Applied Communication Research*, *37*(3), 225–238. doi:10.1080/00909880903025937

Walther, J. B., & Bazarova, N. (2008). Validation and application of electronic propinquity theory to computer-mediated communication in groups. *Communication Research*, *35*(5), 622–645. doi:10.1177/0093650208321783

Walther, J. B., & Bunz, U. (2005). The rules of virtual groups: Trust, liking, and performance in computer-mediated communication. *Journal of Communication*, *55*(4), 828–846. doi:10.1111/j.1460-2466.2005.tb03025.x

Walther, J. B., Hoter, E., Ganayem, A., & Shonfeld, M. (2015). Computer-mediated communication and the reduction of prejudice: A controlled longitudinal field experiment among Jews and Arabs in Israel. *Computers in Human Behavior*, *52*, 550–558. doi:10.1016/j.chb.2014.08.004

Walther, J. B., Slovacek, C., & Tidwell, L. C. (2001). Is a picture worth a thousand words? Photographic images in long term and short term virtual teams. *Communication Research*, *28*(1), 105–134. doi:10.1177/009365001028001004

Walther, J. B., Van Der Heide, B., Hamel, L., & Shulman, H. (2009). Self-generated versus other-generated statements and impressions in computer-mediated communication: A test of warranting theory using Facebook. *Communication Research*, *36*(2), 229–253. doi:10.1177/0093650208330251

Walther, J. B., Van Der Heide, B., Kim, S., Westerman, D., & Tong, S. T. (2008). The role of friends' appearance and behavior on evaluations of individuals on Facebook: Are we known by the company we keep? *Human Communication Research*, *34*(1), 28–49. doi:10.1111/j.1468-2958.2007.00312.x

Wan, C., Chin, C.-y., & Tam, K. (2007). Perceived cultural importance and actual self-importance of values in cultural identification. *Journal of Personality and Social Psychology*, *92*(2), 337–354. doi:10.1037/0022-3514.92.2.337 PMID:17279853

Wang, K. Y., Atkin, D. J., & Lau, T. Y. (2014). Media versus individual frames and horizontal knowledge gaps: A study of the 2010 health care reform debate online. *Electronic News*, *8*(1), 30–48. doi:10.1177/1931243114524419

Wang, Z., Walther, J., & Hancock, J. (2009). Social identification and interpersonal communication in computer-mediated communication: What you do versus who you are in virtual groups. *Human Communication Research*, *35*(1), 59–85. doi:10.1111/j.1468-2958.2008.01338.x

Ward, O. (2017). Intersectionality and press coverage of political campaigns. *The International Journal of Press/Politics*, *22*(1), 43–66. doi:10.1177/1940161216673195

Warren, T. C. (2015). Explosive connections? Mass media, social media, and the geography of collective violence in African states. *Journal of Peace Research*, *52*(3), 297–311. doi:10.1177/0022343314558102

Wasburn, P. C., & Wasburn, M. H. (2011). Media coverage of women in politics: The curious case of Sarah Palin. *Media Culture & Society*, *33*(7), 1127–1041. doi:10.1177/0163443711415744

Washer, P. (2004). Representations of SARS in the British newspapers. *Social Science & Medicine*, *59*(12), 2561–2571. doi:10.1016/j.socscimed.2004.03.038 PMID:15474209

Washer, P. (2005). Representations of mad cow disease. *Social Science & Medicine*, *62*(2), 457–466. doi:10.1016/j.socscimed.2005.06.001 PMID:16046039

Washer, P., & Joffe, H. (2006). The "hospital superbug": Social representations of MRSA. *Social Science & Medicine*, *63*(8), 2141–2152. doi:10.1016/j.socscimed.2006.05.018 PMID:16782254

Webster, F. (1995). *Theories of the information society*. New York: Routledge.

Wegge, D., Vandebosch, H., & Eggermont, S. (2014). Who bullies whom online: A social network analysis of cyberbullying in a school context. *Communications- European Journal of Communication Research, 39*(4), 415-433. doi: 10.1515/commun-2014-0019

Weidmann, N. B. (2015). Communication networks and the transnational spread of ethnic conflict. *Journal of Peace Research*, *52*(3), 285–296. doi:10.1177/0022343314554670

Wei, H., & Lee, W. (2014). Individual and social network predictors of physical bullying: A longitudinal study of Taiwanese early adolescents. *Violence and Victims*, *29*(4), 701–716. doi:10.1891/0886-6708.VV-D-12-00173 PMID:25199395

Weinreich, P. (2009). "Enculturation", not "acculturation": Conceptualising and assessing identity processes in migrant communities. *International Journal of Intercultural Relations*, *33*(2), 124–139. doi:10.1016/j.ijintrel.2008.12.006

Weisband, S., & Atwater, L. (1999). Evaluating self and others in electronic and face-to-face groups. *The Journal of Applied Psychology*, *84*(4), 632–639. doi:10.1037/0021-9010.84.4.632

Weller, K. (2016). Trying to understand social media users and usage. *Online Information Review*, *40*(2), 256–264. doi:10.1108/OIR-09-2015-0299

Wellman, B., Quan-Haase, A., Boase, J., Chen, W., Hampton, K., Díaz, I., & Miyata, K. (2003). The social affordances of the internet for networked individualism. *Journal of Computer-Mediated Communication, 8*(3).

Wellman, B., Quan-Haase, A., Witt, J., & Hampton, K. N. (2001). Does the Internet increase, decrease, or supplement social capital? Social networks, participation, and community commitment. *The American Behavioral Scientist*, *45*(3), 436–455. doi:10.1177/00027640121957286

Westerman, D., Spence, P. R., & Van Der Heide, B. (2014). Social media as information source: Recency of updates and credibility of information. *Journal of Computer-Mediated Communication*, *19*(2), 171–183. doi:10.1111/jcc4.12041

White, D., & Absher, K. (2013). Red Devils, Royals, and the River Thames. *Sport, Business and Management*, *3*(4), 312–326. doi:10.1108/SBM-05-2013-0011

White, F. A., Harvey, L. J., & Hisham, A.-R. M. (2015). Improving intergroup relations in the Internet age: A critical review. *Review of General Psychology*, *19*(2), 129–139. doi:10.1037/gpr0000036

Wilder-Smith, A. (2006). The severe acute respiratory syndrome: Impact on travel and tourism. *Travel Medicine and Infectious Disease*, *4*(2), 53–60. doi:10.1016/j.tmaid.2005.04.004 PMID:16887725

Wilkinson, S. (2011). Constructing ethnicity statistics in talk-in-interaction: Producing the 'White European.'. *Discourse & Society*, *22*(3), 343–361. doi:10.1177/0957926510395446

Williams, L., & Peguero, A. (2013). The impact of school bullying on racial/ethnic achievement. *Race and Social Problems*, *5*(4), 296–308. doi:10.1007/s12552-013-9105-y

Winseck, D. (2016). Reconstructing the political economy of communication for the digital media age. *The Political Economy of Communication*, *4*(2), 73–114.

Wondwesen, T. (2016). An experiential model of consumer engagement in social media. *Journal of Product and Brand Management*, *25*(5), 424–434. doi:10.1108/JPBM-05-2015-0879

World Health Organization. (2005). *Outbreak Communications Guidelines*. Communicable Disease Cluster, WHO document number WHO/CDS/2005.28. Retrieved from http://www.who.int/infectious-disease-news/IDdocs/whocds200528/whocds200528en.pdf

Wright, K. (2000). The communication of social support within an on-line community for older adults: A qualitative analysis of the senior net community. *Qualitative Research Reports*, *1*, 33–43.

Wright, S. C., Aron, A., McLaughlin-Volpe, T., & Ropp, S. A. (1997). The extended contact effect: Knowledge of cross-group friendships and prejudice. *Journal of Personality and Social Psychology*, *73*(1), 73–90. doi:10.1037/0022-3514.73.1.73

Wu, T. (2011). Is Filtering Censorship? The Second Free Speech Tradition. In Constitution 3.0: Freedom and Technological Change. Washington, DC: Brookings Institution Press.

Wu, D. D., & Li, C. (2016). Sociolinguistic approaches for intercultural new media studies. *Intercultural Communication Studies*, *21*, 14–31.

Wu, J., Chen, L., Yu, Q., Han, P. P., & Wu, Zh. (2015). Trust-aware media recommendation in heterogeneous social networks. *World Wide Web-Internet and Web Information Systems*, *18*(1), 139–157. doi:10.1007/s11280-013- 0243-3

Wunnava, P. V., & Leiter, D. B. (2009). Determinants of Intercountry Internet Diffusion Rates. *American Journal of Economics and Sociology*, *68*(2), 413–426. doi:10.1111/j.1536-7150.2009.00634.x

Wu, S., Shi, Y., & Yan, Y. (2013). Media exposure and Chinese cultural identity. *Studies in Communication Sciences*, *13*(2), 129–132. doi:10.1016/j.scoms.2013.11.007

Wyatt, R. O., Katz, E., & Kim, J. (2000). Bridging the spheres: Political and personal conversation in public and private spaces. *Journal of Communication*, *50*(1), 71–92. doi:10.1111/j.1460-2466.2000.tb02834.x

Xu, Q. (2013). Social Recommendation, Source Credibility, and Recency: Effects of News Cues in a Social Bookmarking Website. *Journalism & Mass Communication Quarterly*, *90*(4), 757–775. doi:10.1177/1077699013503158

Xu, Z., Zhang, H., Hu, C., Mei, L., Xuan, J., Choo, K. K. R., ... Zhu, Y. (2016). Building knowledge base of urban emergency events based on crowdsourcing of social media. *Concurrency and Computation, 28*(15), 4038–4052. doi:10.1002/cpe.3780

Yaeger-Dror, M. (1988). The influence of changing group vitality on convergence toward a dominant linguistic form: An Israeli example. *Language & Communication, 8*(3-4), 285–305. doi:10.1016/0271-5309(88)90023-7

Yamagishi, T., & Yamagishi, M. (1998). Trust and commitment in the United States and Japan. *Motivation and Emotion, 18*(2), 129–166. doi:10.1007/BF02249397

Yang, C., Wu, H., Zhu, M., & Southwell, B. G. (2004). Tuning in to fit in? Acculturation and media use among Chinese students in the United States. *Asian Journal of Communication, 14*(1), 81–94. doi:10.1080/0129298042000195151 2

Yang, D., Olesova, L., & Richardson, J. (2010). Impact of cultural differences on students' participation, communication, and learning in an online environment. *Journal of Educational Computing Research, 43*(2), 165–182. doi:10.2190/EC.43.2.b

Yang, G. (2009). *The power of the Internet in China: Citizen activism online*. New York, NY: Columbia University Press.

Yin, S. (2016, November 9). Exit polls were wrong about how many Asian Americans supported Trump. *Fusion.*

Yin, J. (2017). Rethinking cultural identity in the context of globalization: Comparative insights from the Kemetic and Confucian traditions. In X. Dai & G.-M. Chen (Eds.), *Conflict management and intercultural communication: The art of intercultural harmony* (pp. 155–174). New York, NY: Routledge.

Yoon, M. Y. (2005). Sub-Saharan Africa. In Y. Galligan & M. Tremblay (Eds.), *Sharing power: Women, parliament, democracy* (pp. 79–90). Burlington, VT: Ashgate.

Young, M. E., Norman, G. R., & Humphreys, K. R. (2008). Medicine in the Popular Press: The Influence of the Media on Perceptions of Disease. *PLoS One, 3*(10), e3552. doi:10.1371/journal.pone.0003552 PMID:18958167

Yuan, E. (2013). Recent literature on new media and intercultural communication. *Journal of Multicultural Discourse, 8*(3), 260–265. doi:10.1080/17447143.2013.829480

Yum, Y., & Hara, K. (2006). Computer-mediated relationship development. A cross-cultural comparison. *Journal of Computer-Mediated Communication, 11*(1), 133–152. doi:10.1111/j.1083-6101.2006.tb00307.x

Yusuf, N., Al-Banawi, N., & Rahman Al-Imam, H. (2014). The social media as echo chamber: The digital impact. *Journal of Business & Economics Research (Online), 12*(1). Retrieved from https://search.proquest.com/docview/1477975226

Zeitzoff, T. (2017). How social media is changing conflict. *Journal of Conflict Resolution*, *61*(9), 1970–1991. doi:10.1177/0022002717721392

Zeitzoff, T. (2018). Does social media influence conflict? Evidence from the 1012 Gaza conflict. *The Journal of Conflict Resolution*, *62*(1), 29–63. doi:10.1177/0022002716650925

Zeitzoff, T., Kelly, J., & Lotan, G. (2015). Using social media to measure foreign policy dynamics: An empirical analysis of the Iranian-Israeli confrontation (2012-13). *Journal of Peace Research*, *52*(3), 368–383. doi:10.1177/0022343314558700

Zhang, S., Jiang, H., & Carroll, J. M. (2010). Social Identity in Facebook Community Life. *International Journal of Virtual Communities and Social Networking*, 2(4), 64–76. doi:10.4018/jvcsn.2010100105

Zhang, S., & Moradi, B. (2013). Asian American acculturation and enculturation: Construct clarification and measurement consolidation. *The Counseling Psychologist*, *41*(5), 750–790. doi:10.1177/0011000012456882

Zhang, S., & Prosser, M. (2012). Globalization, Asian modernity, values and Chinese civil society. *Chinese Media Research*, *8*, 18–25.

Zhao, S., Grasmuck, S., & Martin, J. (2008). Identity construction on Facebook: Digital empowerment in anchored relationships. *Computers in Human Behavior*, *24*(5), 1816–1836. doi:10.1016/j.chb.2008.02.012

Zhejiang, R. J., Jia, M., & Shoham, M. (2016). Online social connection: Exploring international students' use of new media in their adaptation process. *China Media Research*, *12*, 76–89.

Žibėnienė, G., & Brasienė, D. (2013). Using the Internet, online social networks and potentially incurred risk: Student opinions. *Social Technologies*, *3*(1), 53-67. Retrieved from https://search.proquest.com/docview/1426562879

About the Contributors

Nurhayat Bilge is an Assistant Professor of Communication at Florida International University. She earned an M.A. in Interpersonal Communication at Central Michigan University and earned her doctorate in Intercultural Communication at Arizona State University. Dr. Bilge's research focus on culture, cultural identity, ethnicity, intercultural conflicts, immigration, refugees, cultural adaptation, and third-party facilitation. She conducts and publishes research exploring culture, identity, and communication in various contexts; such as immigration, healthcare, and intercultural new media.

María Inés Marino is a Senior Instructor of Communication Arts at Florida International University (https://communication.fiu.edu/faculty-directory/). She earned an M.S. in Mass Communication from Florida International University and an M.A. in Educational Technology from Northwestern State University. She received her doctoral degree from University of Florida in Educational Technology. Dr. Marino has been teaching a wide range of face-to-face and online courses in communication. Her interdisciplinary research interests include emerging technologies that unite the fields of technology and communication, specifically online emerging group structures and culture.

* * *

Ioana A. Cionea is an assistant professor in the Department of Communication at the University of Oklahoma. Her research lies at the intersection of interpersonal and intercultural communication, with a specific focus on interpersonal argumentation processes, examined from a quantitative, social-science perspective.

Mariko Eguchi (MA, University of Illinois at Chicago) is a Professor in the Faculty of Policy Studies at the University of Shimane, Japan. She teaches courses such as American and British Cultures, Global Understanding, English Phonetics, and English both at the undergraduate and the graduate level. She is a coordinator of

Global Understanding and a study abroad coordinator of the University of Shimane. Her research interests include effective English language instruction via new media as well as learning cultures through media.

Beth Bonniwell Haslett is professor emerita in the Department of Communication at the University of Delaware. Her research and teaching interests span both organizational and interpersonal communication, and focus on issues of face, cross-cultural communication, and the social impact of information and communication technologies. Dr. Haslett has written four books (Communicating and Organizing in Context: The Theory of Structurational Interaction; Communication: Strategic Action in Context; The Organizational Woman with F.L. Gets and M.R. Carter, and Children Communicating with W. Samter. Dr. Haslett has published more than 35 book chapters and articles.

Amy Janan Johnson (Ph.D., Michigan State University) is a Professor in the Department of Communication at the University of Oklahoma. Her research specialties include interpersonal argument, conflict, friendships, and family communication.

Anastacia Kurylo (Ph.D., Rutgers University) is an assistant professor in the Communication Studies Department at St. Joseph's College. She has taught communication coursework for 15 years, including interpersonal communication, public speaking, organizational communication, and communication theory, at a variety of schools—New York University, Borough of Manhattan Community College, and Marymount Manhattan College. Her research focuses on stereotypes communicated in interpersonal, intercultural, and organizational contexts, with additional interests that include intercultural new media research and pedagogy and mentorship. She has published over 25 publications, including teaching activities, book reviews, encyclopedia entries, blind-peer reviewed research articles, book chapters, and books. She has authored The Communicated Stereotype: From Celebrity Vilification to Everyday Talk, and she edited Inter/Cultural Communication: Representation and Construction of Culture, which featured 40 contributors from around the world.

Sun Kyong (Sunny) Lee, (Ph.D. Rutgers University), is an Assistant Professor in the Department of Communication at the University of Oklahoma. She studies socio-cultural aspects of communication technology uses and immigrant communication networks. Her research in these areas has been published in *Journal of Computer-Mediated Communication*, *Communication Research*, and *International Journal of Intercultural Relations*.

Elizabeth Marsh, MFA, is an Assistant Professor of multimedia for the SCJ. She holds a master of fine arts degree from the University of Miami and an AB in English and American literature (Honors) from Brown University. Her professional experience is in broadcast and video production. Her research and teaching focuses on social media, audience analysis and popular culture.

Zachary B. Massey is a Ph.D. student at the University of Oklahoma studying social influence and risk communication. His research interests include the use of persuasion in extreme or radical messages, crisis communication in health and disaster preparedness campaigns, and intergroup conflict between different ethnic and cultural groups.

Mito Ogawa is an International Exchange Student at Millersville University. She is interested in language, culture, and new media, and has presented at National Communication Association 102nd Annual Convention.

Sean R. Sadri, Ph.D., is an Assistant Professor at Old Dominion University teaching courses in online journalism, broadcast journalism, and media studies. He attended UC Davis and Syracuse University as well as received a Doctorate of Philosophy in Mass Communication from the University of Florida. His research interests include media credibility, digital media spaces, social identity in the modern media ecosystem, and sports communication.

Sachiyo M. Shearman (Ph. D., Michigan State University) is an Associate Professor in the School of Communication at East Carolina University. She teaches courses such as Global Understanding through Intercultural Communication, English and Global Communication, Cross-Cultural Communication, Conflict and Communication, and Research Methods, both at the undergraduate and the graduate level. Her research has been published in journals such as Communication Quarterly, Human Communication Research, Journal of Intercultural Communication Research, Journal of Family Communication, and The International Journal of Human Resources Management.

Godfrey A. Steele, PhD, is Senior Lecturer in Communication Studies at The University of the West Indies (UWI), Trinidad and Tobago where he coordinates the graduate program in human communication studies. His current research and publishing interests lie in communication, culture and conflict; health communication; student engagement, assessment and the development of the human communication discipline in the Caribbean; supervisor-subordinate relationships, and crisis and reputation management in organizational and corporate communications in the Caribbean. Godfrey published Health Communication in the Caribbean and beyond: A reader, is editor of The Journal of Human Communication Studies first published in 2015 and is pleased to work with colleagues in founding and developing this indigenous, internationally peer reviewed journal that contributes to The UWI's mission in the Caribbean region and beyond.

Wei Sun's research interests include intercultural communication, media studies, health communication and minority invisibility. She is a graduate faculty at Department of Communication, Culture and Media Studies, Howard University. She teaches Intercultural Communication, Qualitative Research Methods, Social Media, Communication and Culture, Diversity and Leadership, etc. Her publications have appeared on The Howard Journal of Communications, Intercultural Communication Studies, and World Communication. Her scholarly works have been included in several academic books.

Binod Sundararajan is an Associate Professor of Management and Business Communication in the Rowe School of Business at Dalhousie University, Halifax, NS Canada. He is also currently serving as the Associate Director of the Rowe School of Business. He is also one of the founding Co-Directors of CELNET, Collaboration, e-Learning & Networks Lab, a Faculty of Management initiative. He has an undergraduate degree in Electronics & Communication Engineering, a Masters in Electrical Engineering and a PhD in Communication & Rhetoric. He has over 10 years of industry experience in Business-to-business Sales and Marketing, in India, UAE, Oman and in Microsoft Corporation, USA. He teaches Business Communication, Corporate Communication & Organizational Theory/Behavior. His research interests lie in organizational, professional and business communication; computer-mediated communication; Computer-supported cooperative work, Computer-supportive collaborative learning, social media communication, and social network analysis. He conducts research in business and professional communication practices, adoption and diffusion of mediated technologies, use of CMC in such diverse areas as entrepreneurship, justice, teaching, collaborative work and learning and management education. He has an additional stream of research that involves using social network analysis to study historical events like the Underground Railroad Movement in the USA, Irish immigrants in 19th Century Halifax, and Maritimes multi-generational family businesses.

Elizabeth Tetzlaff is originally from Ottawa, Ontario. She moved to complete both a Bachelor's of Arts Honours and a Master's of Arts in English Literature at Dalhousie University. Her research interests include works by female modernist poets and the intersections of major historical events, like the Great War, and literature.

In addition to her historical interests, Elizabeth has published literary reviews on female Indigenous poetry. Elizabeth is currently working towards pursuing a PhD in Management with a focus in Family Business and Entrepreneurship. Separate of her academic pursuits, she also leads an active lifestyle coaching running and writing creative pieces about the relationship between fitness and academia.

María Elena Villar is associate professor and chair of the Department of Communication at the School of Communication + Journalism at Florida International University and teaches courses in communication theory, research methods, multicultural communication, and advanced seminars in strategic communications. She holds a doctorate in communications and master's in public health from the University of Miami, and a bachelor's degree in economics from Columbia University. Her research focuses on culturally competent communication for social and behavioral change, and on strategic communication for diverse audiences.

Kevin Y. Wang (Ph.D., Mass Communication, University of Minnesota-Twin Cities) is an Associate Professor of Strategic Communication at Butler University. His research examines the influence of digital communication technologies on a variety of political actors and processes. Kevin has authored several journal articles and book chapters on political knowledge, political campaigns on the Web, e-government and smart cities, online public diplomacy, and virtual communities. He also regularly presents his work at national and international conferences.

Ping Yang (Ph.D., Arizona State University) is an Assistant Professor in the Department of Communication & Theatre at Millersville University. She holds M.A. in Communication and Linguistics, a B.A. in English Language and Culture, and her Doctorate in Intercultural Communication. Her scholarship and teaching focus on the intersection of culture, communication, and technology. Her primary research interests include identity negotiation, cultural adaptation, media representation, and intercultural online communication. She has published book chapters and journal articles in most of these and related areas.

Niekitta Zephyrine is a graduate student in the Human Communication Studies Program at The University of the West Indies, Trinidad and Tobago with research interests in #BlackLivesMatter, Twitter and social media.

Index

D

E

F

G

H

I

L

M

www.ingramcontent.com/pod-product-compliance
Lightning Source LLC
LaVergne TN
LVHW080347011026
849161LV00009B/2221